RECORDS of the COURT OF THE STATIONERS' COMPANY

1602 to 1640

RECORDS of the COURT OF THE STATIONERS' COMPANY 1602 to 1640

Edited by

WILLIAM A. JACKSON

LONDON
THE BIBLIOGRAPHICAL SOCIETY
1957

BIBLIOGRAPHICAL SOCIETY
PUBLICATION FOR THE YEARS
1955 and 1956

PRINTED IN GREAT BRITAIN

PREFACE

THE Council of the Bibliographical Society is happy to be able to publish this second instalment of the Records of the Court of the Stationers' Company on the occasion of the fourth centenary of the grant of the Charter of Incorporation to the Company of Stationers in May, 1557.

The Society is grateful to the Court of the Stationers' Company for permission to print these records, which contribute so much to our knowledge of the book trade in this country during the 16th and 17th centuries. The Society is also greatly indebted to Professor W. A. Jackson for his labours, extending over many years, on the work of editing this volume and for the great erudition he has displayed in it.

F. C. F.

March, 1957

CONTENTS

INTRODUCTION

THE first volume of these Records was published by the Society, edited by Dr. W. W. Greg and Miss E. Boswell, in 1930. The present instalment covers the years 1603 to 1640 and includes part of the first separate volume of the records of the Court, *Court-Book C*, as well as the same part of the letter book entitled 'Orders of Parliam^{t}. & L^{d}. Mayor Liber A' and the whole of the 'Book of Entraunce of Fines'. The letter book contains much material of an earlier date which it is to be hoped will some day be published, while *Court-Book C* continues on to 1654/5, and together with the succeeding books and supplementary documents, ought likewise to be published.

Court-Book C has a somewhat bescribbled title reading, 'The booke of orders in the company of staconers made the ffirste daye of Nouember Año 1602 Quadragesimo Quarto R Rĩs Elizabethe Mr Byshope then beinge Master Mr Mann Mr Waterson then beinge Wardens Liber C:'. It was kept by the various clerks in succession not as a book of original entry, for evidently they made hasty and in some cases more extended notes of the proceedings of the Court in 'Waste' books of which several of a later date are preserved. Later these entries were transcribed and compressed in Liber C. By this practice the records of some meetings of the Court were omitted entirely as can be deduced not only from the gaps in dates but also from references in the *Book of Fines* and elsewhere in the muniments of the Company. Other matters of importance or interest were likewise omitted as, for example, any mention of the letters of Sir Thomas Wilson and the Earl of Salisbury, 14 and 15 May 1610, addressed to Simon Waterson, Master, commanding him to prevent anything being printed, without sanction, on the assassination of Henry IV[1] which, from the endorsement of Lord Salisbury's letter, must have been discussed by the Court. The Decree of the Star Chamber, 1637, is not even mentioned except to record a gratuity to the Attorney General in connexion with it (p. 300).

Sometimes the records of two or more Courts were conflated under one date, e.g. the Court of 1 September 1617 which is recorded under that of 19 August (p. 95); the Court of 27 January 1622 which is recorded under 14 January (pp. 140–1); and the Court of 1 October 1638 which is recorded under 27 August (pp. 314 and 319). And, while we are noting some of the omissions and inaccuracies of the clerks, it might be mentioned that despite the fact that to most users of this volume (it is not to be expected that there will be many readers of it) there may be far too many references to the leases of properties belonging to the Company, it is apparent that even in this the records are not complete, for in a 'Schedule of Leases' of 1624,[2] among some sixteen leases listed, five are not recorded in the *Court-Book*.

After fairly elaborate, but still incomplete, tables of the properties belonging to the Company and to the various stocks had been prepared, it was decided that they would have little utility and therefore they have been omitted. For the sake of space, also, no general introduction has been prepared. The reader is referred to the

1 *S.P. Dom. 1603–1610*, p. 609. At least five pamphlets on this subject were printed in 1610, two of which though surviving are not in the STC.

2 Attached to a deed of covenant to purchase Pembrookes Inn. Document No. 230 in the Stationers' Archives.

admirable one prefixed to the first volume of these Records by Dr. W. W. Greg. The minor ways in which the present records would supplement or alter his account of the organization and procedure of the Court need not be here specified. However, as the period from 1603 to 1640 covers the establishment of the joint stocks organized within the Company of Stationers, it has seemed fitting to give a brief account of them.

THE ENGLISH STOCK

The English stock was not only the first of these enterprises but also the only one which was continuously profitable. It is still in existence. There is no adequate record of the organization and ordinances of this stock nor any account books of this early period, but the following notes may be of some use. The shares originally consisted of fifteen assistants' parts valued at £200, thirty livery shares valued at £100, and sixty yeomen's shares valued at £50.[1] When the stock was organized some of the assistants acquired livery and yeomanry shares as well as assistants'; likewise some livery shareholders also bought yeomen's shares, but apparently no one had more than one share of each class, and, later, only one share of any class at one time. The demand for shares was such that yeomen's shares were often divided between two suitors in equal halves.

The £9,000 raised in this manner enabled the stock to obtain a royal patent for 'Prymers Psalters and Psalmes in meter or prose with musycall notes or withoute notes both in greate volumes and small in the Englishe tongue', except for the King's Printer's privilege for the *Book of Common Prayer* and its accompanying *Psalter*. The stock's privilege also included 'all manner of Almanackes and Prognosticacons whatsoever in the Englishe tongue'.[2]

No doubt the passing of such a patent was expensive, but probably it cost the stock much more to buy up the unexpired privileges with which it conflicted. For example, the patent for Primers and Psalters of William Seres, Jr., and the metrical Psalms and ABC's of Richard Day had already been bought up by a syndicate (*C-B.B*, p. 76) which no doubt had to be well paid. Likewise Verney Alley had another patent for Psalms for which £600 was paid (p. 68) although this may have been connected in some way with the Day and Seres privilege. An annuity of £3 was given to Alice Wolf for the ABC's for horn-books (p. 13) and the estate of Richard Watkins was paid at least £160 for his privilege for almanacs (p. 9), though each year the various compilers must have received gratuities similar to the fifty shillings paid to Brecknocke in 1618 (p. 100). When the stock was established no doubt there were plenty of others having claims who, either of necessity or for the sake of peace, were paid varying sums.

The stock also purchased Henry Stringer's patent for schoolbooks which probably involved payments to the estate of Robert Dexter and to Richard Bradock.[3]

[1] These figures differ from those given in T. C. Hansard, *Typographia* (1825), p. 268, but appear to be correct. They are confirmed by the assessments noted on pp. 66 and 347 of the present work.

[2] This patent was granted 29 Oct. 1603, renewed and enlarged 15 Mar. 1616 (p. 83) and, on its expiration, again renewed in 1634, as a note under date 27 Oct. 1634 refers to the inquiry by the High Commission concerning the fidelity of the Company in carrying out the provision of the patent for the licensing of almanacs (p. 260).

[3] Cf. Arber iii. 87, *C–B.B*, p. 84, and *C–B.C.* p. 7.

INTRODUCTION

In 1599 Bonham Norton and Thomas Wight had bought the patent of Charles Yetsweirt, the Queen's Secretary for French, for the printing of books concerning the Common Law. The stock bought this privilege also (p. 13) for a sum which is not specified, but it probably was not cheap. Indeed, an entry concerning Mrs. Bing's share (p. 13) might be interpreted that the law patent cost as much as the royal patent of 1603. However, the law patent was evidently lucrative if one may judge from the fees paid the authors and editors of new titles to be published under it, as, for instance, £300 to James Pagett for STC 841 (p. 82), and more than £33 to Mr. Jones, Common Sergeant of London, for editing a volume of Coke's *Reports*, STC 5488 (p. 71).

The stock was unable to enjoy the law patent undisturbed, for on the expiration of the Wight and Norton privilege, 10 March 1629, a reversion was granted to John Moore who assigned his rights to Miles Flesher, John Haviland, and Robert Young. These partners immediately displayed a good deal of initiative and brought out within a year or two several new works on the common law as well as reprints of works which the English stock had neglected.[1] From then on, well past the period covered by these records, the stock ceased to publish law books.

Once established,[2] the stock continued to pay considerable sums to prevent competition by the universities, or by new patentees such as George Wood or Roger Wood and Thomas Symcock, concerning whom see below. At the same time it appears to have been ready to buy out the patentees of lucrative single works, such as Samuel Daniel (p. 57), John Speed (p. 317), and others noted by Arber iii. 671.

When in 1611 the stock purchased Abergavenny House, on the site of which the present Stationers' Hall stands, the money being presumably obtained by assessment, the value of each share was raised 50 per cent., making the three classes worth £300, £150, and £75 respectively (p. 50). The stock's investment in the Ulster Plantation again increased the value of the shares to £320, £160, and £80 respectively (pp. 63, 130, 185, 186, and 247), &c.;[3] but otherwise, in good years or bad, the declared value of the shares was the price at which they passed from one partner to the other.

The shares in the stock were frequently used as security for loans and there are numerous records of such transactions which could only be registered with the consent of the Table. No shares could be transferred or sold without permission although the Court would in many cases listen favourably to requests that a share be conferred on a candidate named by the owner who surrendered or yielded it up, usually either a relation or a creditor. In one case, where Thomas Purfoot had privately agreed to transfer his livery part to George (?) Bradley, the Court 'vtterly disliked his Contract wth soe young a man' and refused to let Bradley have the livery part but granted him the yeomanry part that had belonged to the candidate on whom they bestowed Purfoot's livery part (p. 288).

[1] The books which the stock included in the law patent are listed in Arber iii. 668–9.

[2] There is an entry of the division of a livery share in two equal parts to Richard Field and Humphrey Lownes in which a half share is valued at £43–8–4 (p. 14). Whether this is because at that date, the middle of 1605, the shares were not all paid up is not made clear. No other division of a livery part is recorded.

[3] The stock invested £520 in the Irish Society Plantation, while the added value of all the shares amounts to £900.

Widows of 'partners' were permitted to keep one share (p. 38) so long as they did not marry out of the Company, and occasionally shares were held in trust for orphans although then the dividends were not paid, only a fixed interest. In one case a share was divided, one-fourth to a son and three-fourths to a widow (p. 248) but the son was a freeman of the Company. If a shareholder resigned or surrendered his share the Court might declare him ineligible to be elected to such a part again, or to attend the regular meetings of the stock or take part in its business (pp. 144, 275, and 291). The competition for shares was sufficient to bring in outside influence, and two letters to this end are recorded (pp. 57 and 261).

The stock was governed by the Master and Wardens and a committee of shareholders called the stock-keepers, two elected annually from each class on the first of March, or if that was a Sunday, on the second.[1] There was also a committee of auditors, chosen annually at the same time, two from each class; and a treasurer elected with them who was bonded and well paid for his labours. If a stock-keeper, being elected, refused to serve, he was fined generally £6, and once, at least, when three stock-keepers evidently declined, a new election was held in July (p. 111). The keys to the warehouse of the stock were kept one each by the stock-keepers of each class. In 1628 William Aspley and John Parker, the two livery stock-keepers, withheld their key, and the business of the stock was disrupted (pp. 204-6).

The Master, Wardens, and stock-keepers at their fortnightly meetings (p. 23) evidently voted on what books should be printed, the size of the editions and who should print them, what should be paid for the printing, and at what price the books should be sold. The stock-keepers kept the accounts, delivered out the paper to those chosen to print for the stock, gave receipts, and paid the bills. Much of this was no doubt delegated to the treasurer and the clerk of the Company.

As many of the books published by the stock were valuable titles, great care had to be taken that extra copies were not printed and retained for private sale. When a printer was selected to print a book, or a part of a book, he was supplied the paper for it from the warehouse and not paid for his work until the number of copies and the waste overrun sheets were added and found to equal the paper he had been issued (p. 200). Furthermore, as it was the custom of the Company that the overrun and waste or 'extra' copies were the property of the workmen who could sell them as their perquisite,[2] it was necessary to forbid the printers engaged to print books for the stock to allow their workmen to sell any copies of such books (p. 481), or for any stationer to buy books published by the stock from a journeyman or an apprentice (p. 468). Adam Islip, who for some years printed the law books published by

[1] When, in 1608, the 'New Ordinances' were adopted, they were amended to provide that the under-warden should 'not always' be a stock-keeper. So far as noted, he never was. According to a late seventeenth-century memorandum on 'The Annual Course of Business' which occurs at the end of a 'Minute Book' in the Archive of the Stationers' Company, '1 March Master Wardens and Assistants and all Partners in English Stock summoned to Hall at ten in the morning to hear Bylaws relating to English Stock and Partners not of Court then withdraw and return to Court four persons for the Livery, six persons for the Yeomanry to be Stock Keepers for ensuing year and the Court chooses two Assistant Stockkeepers and two out of four and two out of six. The Master, Wardens and Assistants and the Partners then present choose a Warehousekeeper [i.e. a treasurer] who then takes oath and gives security.' Something like this must have been the practice at the time of these records.

[2] Cf. *Trans.* xii (1931), p. 379.

the stock, testified that he was accustomed to pay his workmen four pence a week in lieu of a copy, and was allowed that sum in addition to his usual payment (p. 148).

It was likewise apparently an offence for a printer appointed to print a book for the stock to permit another printer to print even a portion of that book (p. 240). The punishment for this was forfeiture of whatsoever share the second printer might own which seems somewhat severe until it is realized that the gravest view was taken of any attempt to pirate or counterfeit the books belonging to the stock, particularly the perennial large-selling ones such as the Psalters, Almanacs, and ABC's. The poor workmanship of the printers appointed by the stock was also the subject of considerable complaint, though it was not very heavily punished.

The stock-keepers were continually harassed by the delinquent debtors who had bought books from the warehouse but had not paid for them. Unless the accounts were cleared, they evidently could not make up the quarterly dividend,[1] and so at one time it was ordered that the share belonging to a delinquent should be forfeited and another partner elected in his place (p. 74). Debtors to the stock were refused credit, their dividends were stayed, and finally it became the practice to take up money and charge the debtors 10 per cent. for their debts overdue (pp. 100, 145, 146, &c.).

Not much is known about the dividends except that they are usually referred to as 'quarterly dividends', although in a late seventeenth-century 'Minute Book' in the Stationers' Company Archives, among some notes on the 'Annual Course of Business' evidently made for the guidance of a clerk, it is stated: 'At the December Court and June Court the Master declares the state of the English Stock and whether a 6-months' divident will be paid and the Court appoints a day for payment and entertainment is made for the Master Wardens and Stockkeepers and such Assistants as the Master invites. Dinner paid for by English Stock.' In 1606 Robert Barker received £20 dividend on an assistant's share of £200 (p. 20), but whether it was a quarterly dividend is not clear. In 1631 the dividends on a yeomanry part were considered sufficient to cover an annual debt of £18 (pp. 187 and 229). However, when the stock held shares in trust for orphans, only 5 per cent. was normally paid as interest (e.g. p. 105). The dividends were often sequestered to pay fines or to punish offenders who defied the Court.

Besides what one would consider normal business, the stock is found in these records buying shares in the Virginia Lottery (pp. 53, 65), giving a 'Gratuitie' to King James of £100 (p. 66), and even giving £4 for the dowry of the daughter of a poor freeman of the Company (p. 268).

THE LATIN STOCK

No connected account of the Latin stock, which was set up 3 January 1616, is to be obtained from these records. Fortunately, however, from a Chancery suit of George Swinhowe to recover the balance of the Martin loan of £600 for which he was surety, and the answers to it, Henry R. Plomer has been able to tell a good deal of

[1] The stock borrowed £30 in 1608 in order to make up the dividend (p. 31) and may often have borrowed various sums later, but, if so, the transactions are not recorded.

the organization and history of this stock.[1] Not much more can be added from the *Court-Book* except to point out that besides importing books from Europe, in which enterprise the Latin partners bought out John Bill's stock (pp. 132, 199, 208, &c.) and evidently for a time had an interest in his Frankfort Fair catalogues, the Latin stock also published a number of books,[2] most of which, if not all, were entered in the Registers and ordered disposed of in 1637 in winding-up the affairs of the stock (p. 301).

Not all Latin books whose imprints state that they were published 'pro Societate Stationarum' were the property of the Latin stock. The English stock had much earlier taken over Henry Stringer's patent for schoolbooks (p. 25), and presumably the books listed by Arber iii. 669–70, editions of most of which can now be traced, belonged to that privilege which, in any case, only lasted for fourteen years. The Latin titles listed as the property of the English stock in 1631 (Arber iv. 255) somehow were related to the old privilege of Thomas Vautrollier, originally granted in 1574.

The Latin stock also became involved with Bonham Norton in the Latin grammars which he controlled by reason of the privilege for Latin, Greek, and Hebrew books which the Nortons had deviously acquired from John Battersby.[3] The patent for the Latin grammars (p. 117) was finally taken back by Norton (p. 164), but he and Bill ended by taking over most of the assets of the stock (p. 208) after they had both been made stock-keepers and Norton joined to a committee to wind up the business (pp. 164–5).

The efforts of the Company and the shareholders to avoid repaying the money borrowed from the orphans of Mrs. Martin (p. 278, &c.) is not a pleasant passage in this record. Eventually, when faced with suits and threats of suits, the Stationers' Court, 29 March 1638, ordered the remainder due should be paid out of the House Account, to be reimbursed by the partners in the stock. It was not, however, until 27 August 1638 that the debt was paid and all bonds cancelled (p. 314).

THE IRISH STOCK

The Irish stock was organized not only to buy out John Frankton's privilege as King's Printer but also to export London-printed books for sale in Dublin. Before long, in order to keep the press in Dublin busy, it was found necessary to set it to print books which were mainly to be sold in London, such as the 1621 edition of Sidney's *Arcadia*. By 1630, the sale of Irish-printed books in London warranted the rental of a small warehouse in the garden of Stationers' Hall. It is not clear, however, whether this latter trade was limited to the books registered by the Partners in the Hall Book[4] or whether it included such others as the 'Twelfth impression' of *A wife, now a widowe of Sir T. Overbury*, 1626; T. C.'s *A short discourse of the New-Found-Land*, 1623; and C. Sutton's *Disce vivere, learn to live*, 1634, which were all

[1] *The Library*, 2nd S. viii (1907), pp. 286–97.

[2] Some, like STC 22167, have imprints reading 'Londini Bibliopolarum Corpori excudebat Guilielmus Stansbeius', or, like STC 1390, 'Londini pro Societate bibliopolarum.'

[3] Bonham Norton somehow managed to use money belonging to the Company for which he paid only 5 per cent., but when he lent the Company money he received at one time 11 per cent. for it.

[4] Cf. Arber iv. 217, 228, and 468.

printed in Dublin for the partners. Most of the other seven score or more books and proclamations which have survived printed in Dublin for the stock before 1640, however, would have had a small sale in England, and, indeed, the business in Ireland itself was apparently disappointing, for as early as 1621 a committee was appointed to advise about the affairs of the stock.

The number of shares and their value cannot be ascertained from these records, but from the time Felix Kingston and the treasurer of the English stock were empowered to treat with Sir George Calvert about obtaining a patent for the office of King's Printer in Ireland (p. 99) we can glean some facts about how the business was conducted.

The patent was granted 9 March 1618[1] and by June Felix Kingston and others were already in Dublin (p. 99, n. 1), by November one of the original shareholders mortgaged his share (p. 104), and by December, presumably after a report from Kingston, a large stock of books was purchased from Edward Blount to be shipped to Dublin (p. 106). The following summer either Thomas Snodham or Richard Higginbottom, or both, went to Dublin to settle Kingston's accounts (pp. 110, 112), and by the next May Kingston was back in London (p. 122), and soon after Thomas Downes was sent to Dublin in his place (p. 123). He may have been accompanied by Richard Redmer. How long Downes stayed in Dublin is not known, but in the spring of 1623, Robert Young was there and had bound, without permission, an apprentice whom he was allowed to keep (p. 157), but who was evidently turned over to Arthur Johnson, who was sent to Dublin the following June (p. 167). Four years later, 1628, Young was sent over to Dublin to check Johnson's accounts (p. 202). The accounts were not satisfactory and to settle them Johnson sold his yeomanry part in the English stock (p. 208).

From these records little more can be learned about the affairs in Dublin. Evidently William Bladen was sent as agent in succession to Johnson. He was admitted to the Franchise of Dublin January 1631, and later rose to be sheriff and a man of wealth. When the patent of 1618 terminated in the spring of 1639, Bladen evidently bought out the partners for a sum said to be £2,600, of which he paid only a part.[2] The terms of purchase evidently compelled Bladen to retain, at least for a time, the imprint of the partners, and forbade his printing without permission any books registered in London.[3] It should be noted, however, that as late as 1 July 1639, Thomas Weaver engaged his 'parts' in the Irish stock for a debt (p. 324).

THE BALLAD PARTNERS

At no time apparently was there a stock-company formed for the publishing of ballads. So far as the Stationers were concerned, the trade in ballads was largely a wholesale one, the purchasers being mainly itinerant chapmen. In 1612, the printing of all ballads was limited, ostensibly in order to control the publication of unlicensed and offensive ballads, to five printers, Edward Allde, George Eld, William White, Simon Stafford, and Ralph Blore (p. 53). In 1614, George Purslowe took the

[1] *Acts of the P.C. Jan. 1618–June 1619*, p. 64.
[2] *The Library*, 2nd S. viii (1907), pp. 295–7.
[3] Arber iv. 36.

place of Simon Stafford (p. 68). In 1620, this order was voided and ballads might be printed by any printer chosen by the publisher (p. 133). During the earlier part of this period (1612–20), the rule seems to have been observed,[1] but for several years before 1620 very few if any ballads were entered in the Register Book.

On 6 November 1624, an order was recorded (p. 171) that a group of partners, Thomas Pavier, John Wright, Cuthbert Wright, Edward Wright, John Grismand, and Henry Gosson, should enter 'the Balletę that are now printed' without prejudice to others who might have rights by entrance or otherwise. These partners on the 14 December following entered 128 ballads of which nine, at least, can now be traced in editions printed for one or other of the partners.[2] From August 1628 to June 1629 the Ballad partners evidently were dormant under the competition of Thomas Symcock and his patent, concerning which see below. Thomas Pavier, who was one of the original partners, had died 17 February 1626, but by the time, 1 June 1629, the partners took over Mrs. Trundle's ballads (p. 210) Francis Coles had taken his place.[3] Thereafter, at intervals of a year or less, one or other of the partners entered ballads that had been licensed in the preceding months.[4] A number of the ballads so entered have been preserved with imprints of one of the partners, not necessarily the one who entered it, e.g. STC 6907, which was entered by Francis Coles and the partners in the ballads but bears the imprint 'f. H. G[osson]'. Sometimes, as in the case of STC 19282, which was entered at the same time, the imprint is that of the enterer.

By 1634, however, the Ballad partners had very strong competition from Francis Grove, Thomas Lambert, Edward Blackmore, and Mrs. Anne Griffin, all of whom, before 1641, entered and published numerous ballads, some of which still exist. The later history of the partnership is well told by Cyprian Blagden, *Studies in Bibliography*, VI (1954), pp. 161–80.

GEORGE WOOD'S PATENT

Two apparently independent patents, both granted in 1619, gave considerable trouble to the Company. One of these, renewed and apparently altered several times, continued to harass them quite legally for more than a decade (see pp. xvi–xxii). The other patent could only injure them if the patentee exceeded the terms of his patent, and such injuries the Company could punish under the Decree of 1586, and did.

This latter patent belonged to a journeyman printer named George Wood, who

[1] Henry Roberts entered a ballad 30 July 1612 (Arber iii. 492) entitled *Londons Lottry*. This was published 'W. W[hite]. f. H. Robardes, 1612' and a copy of it is in the Pepys collection. As time went on, however, the printers generally failed to put their names in the imprints. The voiding of the rule in 1620 probably has some connexion with Wood and Symcock's patent, concerning which see below.

[2] Four bear imprints 'f. H. Gosson', STC 22, 3728, 5559, and 23635; three 'f. E. Wright', STC 1328, 1971, and 17262; and two 'f. J. Wright', STC 6317 and 23436. An edition of 23436 'f. H. Gosson' is in the Pepys collection but it is thought to be earlier, though perhaps not with good reason.

[3] Pavier's widow assigned his copyrights, including 'His parte in any sorte of Ballads', to Edward Brewster and Robert Bird, 4 Aug. 1626, Arber iv. 164–6. Presumably these rights were soon acquired by the Ballad partners, for the ballads are not mentioned when John Wright obtained these rights, with others, from Brewster and Bird, 13 June 1642, Eyre and Rivington i. 43–44.

[4] Arber iv. 216, 236, 254, 260, 268, 278, 299, and 323.

took up his freedom in 1613, and bought an invention for printing linen cloth from a James Jenkinson. This invention, according to a petition,[1] which probably should be dated about 1621, Jenkinson had hawked about for some time and sold to various persons for 'any money that he could get and they sold it to others'. In 1619, presumably having obtained some wealthy or influential backer, Wood obtained a grant for 21 years at an annual rent to the king of £10 for the sole use of this invention of printing upon linen in colours, with power to enter houses to search for printed linen cloth, &c. The first grant was dated 14 June 1619, but for some unexplained reason was surrendered and a second grant, dated 25 October 1619, was issued with a clause that it be withdrawn if six or more of the Privy Council objected.[2] The printers of linen cloth very soon found that Wood intended to force them out of business whether or not they infringed his particular invention, for he broke into their houses, claiming to protect his patent rights, and otherwise acted in a high-handed manner. In July 1620, they petitioned Parliament and brought a *quo warranto* in the Exchequer about the validity of the grant, which Wood refused to answer. A committee of the Commons recommended in August, with the concurrence of the aldermen of London, that the king should be informed of the harm done by this patent.[3] The mayor and aldermen of London ordered that a bill to suppress the patent be preferred to the next Parliament, and Sir Robert Heath, when the king referred the matter to the Privy Council, noted that the real question was whether or not Wood's invention was a new one and therefore patentable, and recommended that the matter be left to the law.[4] On the 10 July 1621 was issued a proclamation[5] which specified that this patent, along with many others, 'cannot be pleaded against any injury to the Subjects' who might take their remedy at common law, which ought at any rate to have protected Wood's competitors.

Meanwhile Wood began—as may have been his intention from the beginning—to employ his linen press for printing books, and particularly the primers and almanacs belonging to the English stock. In December 1621, the Company seized printed almanac sheets at his press at Stepney and preferred charges against him before the High Commission (pp. 142, 375–80). The Stepney press was destroyed, Wood sentenced to twelve months' imprisonment, and the four workmen whom he employed there admonished (pp. 142, 376–7). In May the typefounders of London were bonded not to deliver any fount of type without notifying the Master and Wardens (p. 146). Nevertheless, Wood did obtain some type and a press which he set up at his house in Grubstreet even though he was supposedly then confined in the new prison in Maiden Lane. This second press was seized by the Stationers toward the end of September (p. 377), at which time Wood's workmen opposed them violently with swords and other weapons (p. 378). Wood then evidently decided that he had better humble himself to the Archbishop and to the Stationers if only to retrieve the value of this second press.[6] In November the Company ordered (p. 151) that George

[1] *The particular grievances of those . . . which lye under the oppression of George Woods patent*, a copy of which is in the library of the Society of Antiquaries, Lemon No. 222.

[2] W. Notestein, *Commons Debates 1621*, vii, p. 426. An abstract of this second patent was printed, STC 8614.

[3] *Commons Debates 1621*, viii, p. 426.

[4] Op cit. vii, p. 427.

[5] STC 8667.

[6] According to the order of 23 Sept. 1622 (p. 377) the press was destroyed, but according to Wood's release of 14 Dec. 1622 (p. 379) it was appraised and sold by the intervention of Archbishop Abbot.

Wood was to have nothing to do with Roger Wood and his patent, concerning which see below. The Archbishop, a lenient man by nature, held out the hope to Wood that if he behaved himself he might become a master printer (p. 379).

There appears to be no record of the revocation of his patent, but evidently it was not profitable and Wood presumably for a while contented himself as a journeyman printer, but in July 1624 he was found with a press in the Ward of Bishopsgate Without, which was seized and destroyed (pp. 168–9), and in September with still another press near Holborn Bridge with which he was printing George Wither's *Schollers purgatory*, unlicensed. That press was also seized and destroyed (p. 169). He is said to have acquired the press of Thomas Snodham in the autumn of 1625, but was not permitted to be a master printer. The following May another secret press belonging to him was taken at Borley in Essex and destroyed (p. 187). According to some notes transcribed in Arber iii. 703, Wood had William Lee as a partner in the Snodham press, and they later sold out to Thomas Harper, with whom there was some litigation (Arber iii. 701). No books are known with Wood and Lee's imprint, but quite a few attributed to them exist after 1625 printed with Snodham's materials.[1] The lawsuits, if found, might settle the date of transfer to Harper. In any case, Wood's defiance of the Stationers' Company can hardly have been a profitable venture, for, besides imprisonment and the loss of four of the five presses seized from him, he was excluded from becoming a master printer and the profitable business which conformity with the ordinances of the Company might have brought him. It is not known what happened to him in the end, or when he died.

THE PATENTS OF MARIN DE BOISLORÉ, ROGER WOOD, AND THOMAS SYMCOCK

About the time George Wood purchased from Jenkinson his invention and before he had paid out, as he claimed, £200 for his patent,[2] a squire of King James's bodyguard named Marin de Boisloré[3] requested that he might be granted a patent for things printed on one side only, which it was his intention to assign to some printer or printers, and thus be recompensed for his years of service to the king. This request was apparently the subject of a conference between Sir Julius Caesar and Sir Thomas Wilson, 2 October 1618.[4] The Stationers, when consulted, protested that under their charter nothing might be printed without their sanction but that the printing of briefs and other things printed on one side they usually gave to their poorer members. The Solicitor General and Sir Thomas Wilson appear to have sided with the Stationers but recommended, however, that this grant, if given, should not be made out to Boisloré, who was an alien, but to his assignees.[5] The Stationers were disturbed because among the broadsides specified in Boisloré's

[1] STC 3926 has Wood's initials. See also Sayle ii, p. 1083.

[2] *The particular grievances* . . . &c., Lemon No. 222.

[3] Boisloré apparently came to England soon after James's coronation, or so he claims in a broadside now in the Guildhall (*Commons Debates 1621*, vii, p. 536) and had been for some time an agent of the Huguenots, being sent on various missions into France for the Duc de Rohan and others (cf. *S.P. Venetian 1613–1615*, p. 549, &c.). He was frequently at the English court and was 'imployed by his Maiestie in waighty affairs in divers forraigne Countries'.

[4] *S.P. Dom. 1611–1618*, p. 581.

[5] *S.P. Dom. 1623–1625*, Addenda, p. 554.

patent were many lucrative ones which the leading liverymen had monopolized for many years by entry in the Register Book. For example, playbills were the property of William Jaggard (p. 6), briefs for casualties of Thomas Purfoot (p. 90), indentures and recognizances of John Beale (Arber iii. 544), and apprentices' indentures of Humphrey Lownes (p. 57). It was these four men who apparently controlled much of the business which would pass to Boisloré's assignees if the patent were granted and who are mentioned as leading the protest of the Stationers recorded by Boisloré in his printed answer to the Stationers' petition.[1]

Nearly a year later, after Boisloré had nominated Roger Wood[2] and Thomas Symcock[3] as his assignees, letters patent were granted to them 30 October 1619 'in recompense of the acceptable service of Marin de Boisloré, esquire of the body to his Maiestie'.

As it finally emerged the privilege granted for 31 years to Roger Wood and Thomas Symcock was for the sole printing on one side of paper and parchment of all briefs for collections, all publications concerning letters patent, all indentures, bonds, and recognizances, licences, epitaphs, playbills, indentures for apprentices, &c., and all portraits and pictures and everything printed on one side of the paper, except such things as are to be bound in books, and proclamations, ballads, almanacs, and anything else already granted by letters patent. The rent payable to the king was £10 yearly, and the penalties for infringement were the customary ones.[4]

The Stationers appealed to the king against the patent and he referred the matter to the Archbishop of Canterbury, Mr. Secretary Naunton, and Sir Edward Coke. The Stationers likewise petitioned the Lord Mayor and Court of Aldermen to endorse their grievance to the Archbishop and the others.[5] They finally addressed themselves to Parliament in a printed petition,[6] a copy of which is now preserved in the Guildhall Library. In this document they claim that the privilege included other matters not revealed, viz. that the patentees, who were not freemen, might set up presses and take apprentices, and besides the items noted above, might print bills, articles for visitations of bishops and other officials, passports, charts, tables, and oaths for freemen and others—indeed a large part of the job-printing of that time.[7]

In their answer to the petition to Parliament of the Stationers the patentees declare that it is their intention to place the printing of their work with the 'poore

[1] *Commons Debates 1621*, vii, p. 536.

[2] There were several Roger Woods, one a sergeant of the House of Commons in 1607 (cf. *Great Britain Pell Office, Issues of the Exchequer*, p. 69); another registered at Gray's Inn the same year (*The Register of Admissions to Gray's Inn, 1521–1889* [London 1899], p. 114); and the third, the most likely, a grantee on 12 Mar. 1617 (*S.P. Dom. 1611–1618*, pp. 444, 455), and a farmer of wine licences in July 1628 (*S.P. Dom. 1628–1629*, p. 197, and *1631–1633*, p. 482). He may also have been the Roger Wood appointed a commissioner for leets in 1614 (*Commons Debates 1621*, vii, p. 393). In any case neither he nor his partner was a Stationer.

[3] He was probably the Thomas Symcock who was granted an office under the Great Seal, June 1601 (*The Index Library*, Series iv, p. 107). This office was possibly 'Sergeant of the Bears', for a Thomas Symcock holding that position died 5 Sept. 1635 (*S.P. Dom. 1635*, p. 368).

[4] An abstract was published, STC 8615.

[5] *Analytical Index to Remembrancia of London 1579–1664*, p. 100.

[6] This petition, together with the printed answer of the patentees, is transcribed in *Commons Debates 1621*, vii, pp. 535–9.

[7] Actually all the items specified by the Stationers, except the oaths for freemen, are listed in the abstract, STC 8615.

Masters and Journey-men Printers' of the Company and not with the 'fewe rich Printers'. This they evidently endeavoured to do but met with a good deal of opposition.[1] The abstract of their grant they gave to Edward Allde, a trade printer, but the few others of their broadsides of this period which survive[2] have no name of printer.[3]

The Parliament of 1621 which the Stationers petitioned was one which was much concerned with the abuses of letters patent. The very day that the Stationers' petition arrived, 23 March, the Committee of Grievances, headed by Sir Edward Coke, snapped it up and ordered immediately that Wood and Symcock, the nominal patentees, appear for examination the next week.[4] The result of this examination does not appear but when Wood and Symcock applied to the Privy Council for letters of assistance, the 22 June 1622, they were told that as between the Stationers and the Patentees they might 'be left indifferently to the common law'.[5] However, in August 1622 a letter to the Lord Chief Justice of the King's Bench appears to support the patentees by urging all officers to assist them.[6]

After the 7 March 1623 the Stationers procured a reference to the Archbishop of Canterbury, the Bishop of Lincoln, then Lord Keeper, and the Lord Chief Justice, who heard counsel on both sides in the Star Chamber dining hall. A Lawrence Norcott testified in a later Chancery suit on this matter that he was present at this hearing and that the referees advised the Stationers to make their peace with the patentees and that some of the Stationers then present said that they would give £200, or £30 per annum, to have the patent assigned into their hands. Thomas Mountford, Clerk of the Company, denied that such an offer was ever made.[7]

The same March, the Stationers brought suit against the patent although apparently not very hopefully (p. 156), and in July two Privy Councillors were ready to 'move the King in behalf of Mr Wood's patent for printing'.[8] Presumably in con-

[1] In answer to an examination by the Court of Chancery at a subsequent period in the history of this patent a William Norcott testified (17 June 1630, C. 24–561–118) 'that at the request of the def[t] Simcocke hee this dep[t] did goe to most of the m[r] printers in & about the Cittie of London and told them y[t] it had pleased the late king[e] Ma[tie] to graunt vnto him the def[t] & the sd Wood a patent for the printing of diu'se thinge in the sd patent exp[r]ssed & did desire the said printers that they would print the same this dep[t] then offring to the sd printers on the behalfe of the said def[t] as great or rather greater prices or rates then the said printers did vsually print for to the compl[te] [i.e. the Company of Stationers] But saith y[t] the said printers did refuse to print the same, some of them alledging that they had soe much worke to doe y[t] they could not haue tyme to goe aboute the same, others alledging y[t] they would not doe it for feare of the Compl[te] displeasure & others that they would doe it but they did demaund such excessiue rates and prices as would amount vnto the worth of the thing printed when the same was dd by sd def[t] or his assignees.' Similar testimony was given by John Hamond, 4 Jan. 1629/30, and also by Lawrence Norcott, 24 Nov. 1630, except that they spoke from hearsay.

[2] STC 8616, 8646–8, 8651–4, 8658, and *Letters patent for collecting money for ransom of captives from a vessel of Lyme Regis taken by the Turks* [1621 ?], a copy of which is in the Lyme Regis Museum, are all that appear to have survived with the imprint of Wood and Symcock. They are all 'briefs for collections' and dated, except for STC 8616, 1620 or 1621. No others of a later date, or any broadsides of other kinds published by them, are recorded with their imprint.

[3] Allde may well have been involved in some of these, see pp. 138 and 159; and George Wood, likewise, see p. 151.

[4] *Commons Debates 1621*, iv, p. 189, and vi, p. 462.

[5] *Acts of P.C. July 1621–May 1623*, p. 258. This enforced the proclamation of 10 July 1621, STC 8667, which specifically mentioned this patent.

[6] *S.P. Dom. 1619–1623*, p. 442. A letter of some sort addressed to the patentees this same month is recorded in W. P. W. Phillimore, *An Index of Signet Bills* (The Index Library), p. 182.

[7] Chancery suits, C. 24–561–118, pp. 16 and 25.

[8] *S.P. Dom. 1623–1625*, p. 35. This might, of course, refer to George Wood.

nexion with their defence the patentees reprinted the abstract of their patent.[1] When Parliament opened in 1624 the Stationers again petitioned, this time apparently that the patent had been 'gotten out by a false Suggestion', and the patent was ordered brought in. Later a sergeant at arms was sent for Wood, who had evidently not appeared with the patent.[2] What action, if any, was taken on this petition does not appear, but it was this Parliament which enacted that no letter patent should entail any monopoly unless the patentee were 'the first and true inventor' or a corporation or chartered body like the Stationers themselves.[3] Consequently, if the patentees continued in business it must have been as not the 'sole' publishers of broadsides but merely in competition with the Stationers. In any case, nothing of this date with the imprint of Wood and Symcock has survived,[4] but the patent was not revoked, for some time in 1626 the Stationers again petitioned the Privy Council that the validity of the Boisloré patent might be tried at law.[5] It may be that the rising public resentment against the French, in which Boisloré himself would seem to have been involved,[6] gave the petition a better chance of success.

Roger Wood was apparently by now discouraged, or perhaps had sold out his interest to Thomas Symcock, for in May (?) 1628 there is recorded a petition of Thomas de Vaux and Henry Savage for the transfer of Boisloré's patent,[7] and the 20 August 1628 a new patent was issued to Thomas Symcock alone, an abstract of which was published with his name in the imprint.[8]

This new patent included 'Ballads' and, although during the year or more preceding the passing of this patent no ballads whatsoever were entered to the Ballad

[1] STC 8616. This 1623 abstract is considerably altered. The 1620 edition (STC 8615) had recorded certain exceptions including 'All Proclamations and other thinges now belonging to his Maiesties Printer, by vertue of his Highnes Letters Patents formerly graunted in that behalfe: and all Ballades, prognostications & Almanackes, and other things heretofore granted by any Letters patents from his Maiesty, or any of his progenitors for any tearme not yet expired onely excepted.' No patent for ballad printing to which this might refer is known. The 1623 edition of the abstract, which lists in four columns 'The thinges belonging to this Graunt', includes all those mentioned in 1620, without mentioning any exceptions, and adds 'Ballads . . . Damaske paper, Borders, Printed paper for Silkes, Fustians, and other Wares. . . .', &c. Since both abstracts are of the same letters patent, the exclusion of ballads from the 1620 abstract and their inclusion in 1623 are puzzling. However, no ballads have survived with the imprint of Wood and Symcock. This 1623 edition was also printed by Edward Allde.

[2] *Journals of the House of Commons*, ii (1803), pp. 689, 774, and 704, 789.

[3] J. R. Tanner, *Constitutional Documents of the Reign of James I*, pp. 269–72.

[4] It will be noted that it was at this very moment, 6 Nov. 1624, that the Ballad partners were organized.

[5] *S.P. Dom 1625–1626*, p. 526. The date of this petition is uncertain.

[6] Boisloré, although advanced in rank from esquire of the bodyguard to gentleman of the Privy Chamber to Charles I, sued for a passport for himself and family into France, *S.P. Dom. 1625–1626*, p. 527, and was granted a pass for two servants and possessions, *Acts of P.C. June 1626–Dec. 1628*, p. 316. The following June, Boisloré was placed in the Tower, *S.P. Venetian 1626–1628*, p. 256, *S.P. Dom. 1627–1628*, p. 266. And the eighth October ensuing, together with his wife and children, he was banished, P.C. 2–36 ff., 168 d., 170 and 175 d.

[7] *S.P. Dom. 1628–1629*, p. 144. Their petition is as follows: 'They were farre engaged for Mons Boisloree, and hee beeing banished they had noe meanes to helpe themselves but by taking assignemente from him of a guifte of 100 marks graunted him by his late Maty payable out of the Court of Warde, and of Letters Pattente concerning printing long since transferred vpon one of the Peticoners. They humbly pray that his Maty will be pleased to confirme vnto them the said guifte and Patent towards the repairacon of theire greate losses.'

[8] S.T.C. 8903. This abstract very closely approximates the abstract of 1623 (S.TC 8616) but adds 'Lycenses for Marriages' and omits damask paper, borders, printed paper for silks, fustians, and other wares, 'Letters Patents texed' and 'Indentures texed'. This was printed by William Stansby.

partners or anyone else, Symcock lost no time in entering the ballad market. There are extant at least thirty-nine ballads with his imprint, 'Printed by the Assignes of Thomas Symcocke'.[1] Of these at least ten are known in earlier or later editions published by one or other of the Ballad partners, while still others, which have not been traced in editions published by them, were entered to them. Indeed, most of Symcock's ballads are of a date of composition much earlier than 1628, and since all but one have no name of publisher it might be thought that he construed his patent to give him the right to publish any ballad that he considered saleable whether or not it was registered as someone else's property. However, there is reason to think that Symcock regarded himself as much a 'trade printer' as a publisher and stood ready to print for any copyholder such ballads or broadside documents as were brought to him.[2]

Evidently Symcock when associated with Wood had found it impossible to engage master printers of the Company to print for him and was forced to 'erect a press' of his own. For this he hired a freeman of the Company named John Monger[3] and at least one other workman named Farmer.[4] Since the Company forebade journeymen printers to work for him, it is not unlikely that he found himself forced to deal with disaffected ones. For instance, John Hamon, or Hamond, who from his extended testimony in the later Chancery suit between the Company and Symcock must have been closely associated with Symcock to have had such personal knowledge of the details of the matters concerning which he was examined, is the same Hamond who is recorded at this date as having had at least five presses seized by the Company (p. 201).

[1] Those recorded in STC are 1327, 3729, 5773, 5877, 6102, 6191, 6809, 14544, 14577, 14961, 15186, 16758, 16863, 16865, 17187, 19246, 19271, 21689, 22655, 24369, and 25230. Those not recorded, except for two found only in the Ewing collection, are all, like those listed above, in the Roxburghe collection. The Roxburghe ones are as follows: *A new ballad, intituled, a warning to youth*; [Campion, T.] *A friends advice is an excellent ditty*; D., F. *An excellent new medley*; [Deloney, T.] *A pleasant new ballad of Daphne*; *The lamentable fall of Queen Elinor*; *An inconstant female*; *A lover forsaken*; *A lovers desire*; *The revolted lover*; *A pleasant new ballad of two lovers*; *The deceased maiden-lover*; [Marlowe, C.] *A most excellent ditty of the lovers promises*; [Murray, Sir D.] *The complaint of the shepherd Harpalus*; [Parker, M.] *The countrey lasse*; *Ragged, and torne, and true*; and *An excellent song, wherein you shall finde great consolation.* In the Ewing collection are: A., M. *The tragedy of Phillis*; and [T., W.] *The shepheards delight.* Besides these ballads the only other broadside known with Symcock's imprint, besides the abstract of his patent STC 8903, is a brief of *Letters patent to William Earl of Banbury and William Viscount Say and Seale . . . to raise money on account of a fire at Banbury* [28 June 1628], a copy of which is in the library of the Society of Antiquaries (Grant collection II, No. 11). Since his publications were of the most ephemeral type it is not possible to estimate their number. The considerable run of his ballads in the Roxburghe collection may be due to the enterprise of one contemporary collector, for there are very few duplicates at Manchester and in the Pepys collection, and no others are known.

[2] John Hamond testified 'that the sd deft or some other in his behalf did offer to print for the Staconers and all other his maties subiects wth as good paper & printing and at as reasonable rates & prices as the thinges graunted were printed & sold for by the Company before the sd two Pattentȩ or eyther of them were graunted, and that every Staconer should enioye his owne Coppies, and that all Rowling pressemen should enioye theyre plates & stampes paying as easie rates vnto the sd deft as any other hath taken to print Rowle or stampe the thinges wch were graunted, before such tyme as the sd two Pattentȩ were obtayned'. (Chancery Interrogatories, Symcock vs. Stationers, C. 24–561–118, pp. 2–3.)

[3] He can hardly be the John Monger made free 18 June 1619 (Arber iii. 685) for he testified in 1630 that he was 45 years old, but more likely is the quondam partner of Robert Raworth with whom he bought out Islip's law printing press but was soon 'ousted' by Raworth (Arber iii. 704). He was said by another witness, however, to have been free of the Company.

[4] Probably not the Robert Farmer or Fermor who was made free 2 Oct. 1579 (Arber ii. 93, 679). Monger was interrogated and Farmer mentioned in the Chancery suit of 1631, mentioned above.

Symcock is also said to have paid better wages to his journeymen than the Stationers customarily allowed and, when the Bishop of London threatened him with imprisonment early in May 1629 if he printed under his patent, he stopped the press but continued to pay the wages of both Monger and Farmer, although they did no work for weeks. There is also testimony that Symcock sold both ballads and briefs cheaper than the Company had been accustomed to do.[1]

Francis Grove testified[2] 'that he never bought Ballade that were printed by the Defendant but once att wch time he this depont paid vijs the Reame for the same'. Presumably that is the ballad, STC 19246, which has the imprint 'The Assignes of T. Symcock, and are to be sold by Francis Grove on Snowhill'.

Evidently all of the ballads with Symcock's imprint, and probably many others which have not survived, were printed in the period between August 1628 and 20 October 1631.[3] The 10 February 1629, the Stationers ordered John Beale, Miles Flesher, Robert Young, William Jones, John Wright, and Richard Shorlayker[4] 'to follow the busines in the Parliamt' (p. 208). The petition to the Lords which they presented is still preserved, and another petition which was read in the House of Commons 12 February 1629, and sent to the Committee for Grievances, is recorded.[5]

In May 1629 Humphrey Lownes, Clement Knight, T. Purfoot, and John Beale, again all Stationers who were directly concerned in this matter, petitioned the king as 'poor printers' (although John Hamond testified that they were worth £4,000) to refer the matter once more to a commission, which, to make a long story short, was done and the king appointed the Earl of Holland, Viscount Rochester, and the Bishop of London to examine into the matter. A hearing was held by the two latter, who, with the signature of the Earl of Holland also affixed, recommended that Symcock's patent be cancelled on the grounds that it 'had been surreptitiously procured upon untrue suggestion', that the 'referrance' was not legally carried out &c. Symcock contested this ruling and at last in 1630 it was brought before a Court of Chancery. Months were consumed in taking depositions concerning various interrogatories,[6] and finally a decision was given by the Lord Keeper, Thomas, Lord Coventry, 20 October 1631,[7] which ordered that the Company pay Symcock what 'indifferent' referees should value his press and letters, that he should refrain

[1] Hamond declared that the Ballad partners sold ballads for £0–13–4 the ream whereas Symcock sold them for a noble [i.e. £0–6–8 or 10 shillings] in the pound cheaper and upon better paper. Elsewhere he says that Symcock charged £0–7–6 a ream for ballads whereas the Ballad partners charged a mark [i.e. £0–13–4] a ream; and that Symcock sold briefs of collections for £0–2–0 shillings the hundred, and some for £0–1–6, whereas the Stationers sold them for £0–3–6.

[2] Interrogatories cited above, p. 23.

[3] The controversy dragged on in the courts until the autumn of 1631, and it may be that Symcock continued to print until that time.

[4] These Stationers were all interested parties. Beale, for instance, had made entry for indentures and recognizances (Arber iii. 544) and for bonds (Arber iv. 189); Flesher, among other matters, had the petitions for prisons (pp. 198–9); Young entered a long list of indentures (Arber iv. 192); Jones entered recognizances (Arber iv. 161); Wright was a Ballad partner; and Shorlayker, one of the principal dealers in prints.

[5] The Lords' petition, *Fourth Report of the Royal Commission on Historical Manuscripts* (1874), p. 21; and the Commons' petition, *Journals of the House of Commons*, i, p. 929.

[6] C. 24–561–118. Twenty-one witnesses were examined between 4 Jan. 1630 and 27 Nov. 1630.

[7] C. 78–295–4.

from exercising his rights under his patent, and that—which must have been a bitter pill to the Company—the Bishop of London was desired 'to sett a course for the disposeing the Printinge for the good of the poore sorte of the said Companie and for the appointinge such fitting addicōn of Wages for the said poore Workmen as shalbee fitt . . .'. No reference to this is to be found in the Court-Book, nor since the original order (p. 156) concerning the payment of the legal and other charges in following this suit, is there any account of how this matter was conducted on the Stationers' side.

When affairs momentarily looked brighter in June 1629, the Ballad partners and other publishers had entered several lots of ballads,[1] and, without waiting for the decision of the courts, John Bellamy and George Fairbeard, who evidently had a stock of bills of lading printed by Symcock, were ordered, 5 October 1629 (pp. 212–13), to turn them over at cost to Nicholas Bourne whose copyright they were. Two weeks after the Chancery Court decision, William Jones was fined for printing briefs 'in preiudice of m^r^ Purfoots graunt' (p. 234) and so, after all the struggle, it is probable that matters reverted very quickly to the way they had been before M. Boisloré first obtained his patent.

ACKNOWLEDGEMENTS

When, in 1938, I asked if I might examine the photostat of *Court-Book C*, which the Bibliographical Society had had made with the permission of the Court of the Stationers' Company, I did not realize that for more than a decade and a half I should devote a large part of my holidays, as well as countless weekends and evenings, to it. I found it so fascinating, however, that when Mr. F. C. Francis suggested that I might edit it for the Society I have no doubt that even if I had then known how much of a task it would be I should nevertheless have undertaken it.

Two more or less extended visits to London were devoted to exploring the relevant archives of the Stationers' Company, one as a Guggenheim Fellow and the other as a Sheldon Fellow from Harvard, to both of which most generous patrons I owe thanks. In the old cupboards and in the new vault at Stationers' Hall I spent many busy weeks and enjoyed the kindness of the Beadle and, on occasion, the hospitality of the Stationers' board. Three summers were happily spent at the Huntington Library transcribing and annotating photostats of these texts, and for the many kindnesses shown me at both places I am grateful. To Miss Frederica Oldach and Miss Carolyn Johnson, who typed my handwritten transcripts, and to Miss Anne W. Henry, who caught many an error, I owe much. I have never met the compositors and proof-readers at the University Press at Oxford, who have provided me with such clean proof, but I know that no containable rounds of beer could measure my gratitude to them. Mr. F. C. Francis, who first induced me to undertake this task and who has put up with my impatience patiently, I also wish to thank. Indeed, all who have had anything whatsoever to do with this book have given of their best. Its errors and inadequacies are all mine.

[1] Arber iv. 213 and 216.

INTRODUCTION

MEMORANDA

In transcribing these documents, the limitations of type of necessity had to be kept in mind. The relative placing on the page of the original has only been approximated, with indication of page-endings, but not of line-endings. The position of full-stops in relation to superior letters has not been observed and the position of the straight or curved overline, whether used for abbreviation, suspension, or contraction, and in the original covering more than one letter, has usually been assumed to be over the vowel if in the original the vowel is one of the letters covered. Henry Walley, who was clerk from 1630 to 1640, apparently often used the sign for *es* or *is* when only *s* would be proper, e.g. 'Iȩlip', and, therefore, in that portion of the transcript that sign is used only when it appears in the original at a logical place.

The procedures described in the 'Memoranda' in the preceding volume (pp. lxxvii–lxxxi) have in general been followed here, except that the annotation has been placed at the foot of the page rather than in the side margins. The reader is urged to consult those 'Memoranda'. However, it may be well to repeat here: 'All mutilations in the original—happily rare—are indicated by the use of pointed brackets, and any letters printed within such brackets are more or less conjectural. Words printed in roman type within square brackets are additions in the original, either interlined or written in the margin. Words printed in italic type within square brackets are deleted in the original. (However, no notice has been taken of small alterations and deletions made *currente calamo* and of no apparent significance.) Words printed in italic type within round brackets are editorial comments explanatory of the original but not appearing in it. Italic type, without brackets, is used for ostensibly autograph signatures. Thus: ⟨mutilations⟩ [additions] [*deletions*] (*comments*) *signatures*.'

COURT BOOK

1602 44to Ri'e
29° Octobris/

Fol. 1[a]

Mr Byshope M[r]
Mr Mann
Mr Waterson } wardens

pñte
m[r] Byshop m[r]
m[r] Mann
m[r] waterson } wardens
m[r] Harryson sen[r]
m[r] Coldocke
m[r] Newbery
m[r] Binge
m[r] Barker
m[r] dawson
m[r] Ponsonby
m[r] windet
m[r] whyte
m[r] Seton
m[r] Hoop/

At the sute of Richard Collins and for diuerse consideracõns yt is ordered [& agreed] by A full Courte of Assistantę holden this day. That [from] the tyme that he shałł depte to dwell out of his house in the hałł leavinge his hangingę and pticõns there to thuse of the Companie he shalbe alowed by the Companie yerelie duringe the tyme that he shałł continue their Clerk Teñ poundę by the yere for his stypend viz': L[s] a quarter to be Charged in the renters accoumpt ouer and besydes the vsuałł duties of entries apperteyninge to his office And the first payment to begiñ at the next quarter after his said deptinge from dwellinge in the said house.[1]

The Cooke/ By A fułł Courte of the Mr Wardens and Assistantę holden this day yt is ordered/ That all dinners and feastę to be dressed and made in the hałł of this Companie, shalbe dressed by the Cooke of the said Companie for the tyme beinge/ Whether yt be for the Wardemote inquest, or for Maryages or any other cause or occasion[2]/ And that the hałł shałł not be lett forthe by any Wardens for the tyme beinge to any pson or psons that shałł refuse to pforme the effect and contentę of this order/ Provided alwaies that he shałł doo yt reasonablye by the Judgement of the M[r] and wardens of the Companie for the tyme beinge./

13 decembr' 1602. 45 Rie

m[r] Robertę
w[m] Jagger

Vppon the hearinge of the clayme of wiłłm Jagger to the printinge of the billę for the company of stage players—appteyninge to the right hon'able the Erle of Worcester. W[che] is found to be the right of the said James Robertę in the right of his wyfe.[3] Yt is ordered by assent of the said

[1] Regarding Collins's occupancy of this house see *Reg. B*, 17 Jan. 1599, 469[b].

In 1578 Collins was granted £8 a year because he chose not to live in the 'house w[th]in y[e] hall of this cũpany w[ch] to y[e] clarke thereof for the tyme beinge heretofore hathe ben appointed, [but] hathe puided a dwellinge house for him selfe elswhere'. It was also provided that he might have the house back on six months' warning. Cf. *Letter Book*, 38[a], 29 Oct. 1578.

Collins was granted an office in the Hall, cf. *C–B.C*, 11[a], 20 Oct. 1606.

[2] Cf. the cook's fees as set forth *Reg. B*, 2 July 1577, 427[b]; 16 Jan. 1589, 447[b]; and 4 June 1599, 473[a].

[3] Jaggard's effort to obtain the reversion of the rights to the printing of playbills (*Reg. B*, 23 Apr. 1593, 457[b]) was frustrated by James Roberts, who

pties And the said James Roberte is content And Dothe graunt for him and his wyfe, That the said Willm Jagger shall haue the onely and sole ymprintinge of the said bille for the said company of players nowe appteyninge or hereafter to appteyne to the said Erle of Worcestre/ ffrom this daye forthwarde Duringe the contynuance of the Interest of the said James & his wife or either of them in the same Without any lett ympediment or yntermedlinge in the printinge of any of the same of or by ye said James & his wife or either of them or any other by their meanes. The said Willm yeildinge & payinge therefore to ye said James & his said wife or one of them monethly ffoure shillinge duringe so longe as ye said Erle hathe or shall haue a company of stage players & duringe ye sed Interest of ye said James & his wife or either of them. The said monethly payment to be [made] on the Last day of eu'y moneth at the nowe dwellinge house of the said James at Barbican. And the first paymt to be made on the Last day of this instant moneth of december. And the said Willm Jagger to medle with the printinge of no other bille for players but these onely of the said Erles company of players. And ye said Willm to be bound to the said James in vli to pforme this order for his pte.

James Roberte
Willm Jaggard.

FOL. 1b

·1603· Ao primo R Ris' Jacobi
13 April

present
Mr harrison thelder
Mr Binge.
mr dawson.
mr ponsonby
mr Seton
mr Hooper
Richard Collins.

Whereas vppon the hearinge & examininge of the matters touchinge the printinge and sellinge of the book called Basilicon Doron: yt Appeareth by viewe & perusinge of the orders of the Company. That the entrance of the said booke made in the hall book to mr John Norton and others that therein are Joyned wth hym is a Lawfull And Orderly Entrance,[1] accordinge to the same orders, And that contrary to the order of the companie, whiche lymiteth the pryces of booke[2] they haue sold great nũbers thereof at a greater rate then ys appointed by the same order for the pryce of booke And yt also appereth that Edward Aldee & diu'se others of the Company haue wthout Aucthoritie licence or entrance prynted An Impression[3] of 1500 of the said booke contrary to the Order for lycensinge & entranc' of Copies. And whereas all the said parties of bothe sydes haue submyted them selues & Agred to stand to the order & determinacon of the Assistente here prsent touchinge all the premisses/ Yt is nowe thereuppon, after good deliberacon had of the same, Ordered that the sayd Mayster Norton & his said parteners shall
fol. 2 enioy the sayd booke As their prop copye accordinge to the said entrance, And that for transgressinge the said order lymytinge the prices of booke/ in sellinge the said booke at a greater pryce then the same order appointeth they shall pay ffortie marke to thuse of the Companye to be employed as the fynes sett down in the Company are vsually employed accordinge to the orders of the same The said fforty m'ke to be payd in good Englishe money on the Sixt day of Maie next or before. And also

married John Charlewood's widow. Cf. *C–B.C*, 3a, 2 Apr. 1603. Jaggard printed a playbill for 'his Maiesties seruants' [*c.* 1610], a copy of which is in the B.M. (C.18.e.2 (74)).

[1] Arber iii. 230.
[2] Cf. *Reg. B*, 464a, 19 Jan. 1598.
[3] STC 14354.

yt is ordered that Edward Aldee & his ꝑteners for whome he hathe disorderly printed the said book shall presently bringe into the hall all suche numbers thereof as they haue in their handꝭ & the value of the rest whiche they haue alredy sold. And that he and eu'y of them shall presently paye iij[s] iiij[d] a pece for a fyne[1] for their offence in dealinge therew[th] contrary to the said order for licensinge & Entringe of Copies[2] And that neither he nor they nor any of them̃ shall hereafter deale wth thym-printinge of the same booke or any ꝑte thereof And in further consideracoñ of the case of the said Edward Aldee and those Joyned wth hym, yt is ordered that euery of them̃ vppoñ payment of their said ffines accordinge to this order shall haue agayne suche nũbers of the said bookꝭ as they shall bringe into the hall, and the som̃es that they shall bringe in for the rest whiche they haue alredy sold as aforesed.

John haryson
J Bing
Thomas Dawson
Wiłłm ponsonby
Gregory Seton
Ri: Cołłins.
Humfry hooper/.

1603· A° primo R[is] Jacobi — Fol. 2[a]

30 Maij

Present
Mr Bisshop m[r]
m[r] man }
m[r] waterson } W'dens
m[r] Haryson sen[r]
m[r] newb'ye
m[r] dawson
m[r] ponsonby
m[r] wyndett
m[r] Setoñ
m[r] hoop
m[r] nortoñ
Ric' Collins.

Here were redd the order of the high com̃ission's & A copy of A bond taken before them concerninge m[r] Edw. White and Edw. Aldee. dat' 26 instañ maij

And the contentꝭ of the said order & the cõmaundem[t] therein gyven to the m[r] & wardens considered of.

Yt is thought mete & ordered that ye m[r] & wardens accord-inge to the said order & cõmaundem[t] of ye Cõmission's shall ꝓcede to execute the decree of the hon'able Court of Starchamƀ ag[t] Edw aldee for his presse & letters & to all other ententꝭ and effectꝭ mencoñed in the said decree[3]

fol. 1 — M[r]. Edw. white — fyne

Also yt is found that m[r] Edw. white had V[C]. of the bookꝭ of Basilicõn Doron of the second ympression[4] printed by Edw. Aldee disorderly. yt is therfore ordered that m[r] white havinge Dispsed the said bookꝭ that they cannot be seised by reason of the forfayture of them beinge Disorderly printed Shall pay vj[li] xiij[s] iiij[d] for a fine to thuse of the Company.[5] And his ymprisonment is respited to the further ord[r] of y[e] company

1 Paid 14 Apr. 1603 (Arber ii. 835).
2 Cf. *C–B.C*, 2[a], 30 May 1603.
3 Cf. *C–B.C*, 2[b].
4 No copy of this second edition printed by Allde has been traced, although there are several unrecorded editions by other printers.
5 Cf. Arber ii. 836.

mr. Edw. white
Ro. Triplet.

ffor thendinge of the controu'sie touchinge the pictures belonginge to the Calendar of the writinge tables:[1] Yt is ordered that Rob̃t Triplett shall presently pay to Edw white the xls wche he paid for Jo wolff to mr Robertę for the said pictures. And that mr white shall desist his clayme to the said pictures. And that Rob̃t Triplett shall prynt the said Calenders wth the said pictures and bynd them̃ wth his wrytinge tables[2] And so sell them all together onely to the ffreemeñ of this Company & nõne other. And yf he prynt and make greater nũbers of them̃ then the said freemeñ of the Company will buye That theñ he shall bringe all the rest into the hall and there lay them̃, where he shall receaue contentmt for them at reasonable prices. Alwayes provyded that yf he sell any of his wrytinge tables calenders & pictures or any of them̃ out of this company contrary to the true meaninge of this Order. Then his Right & clayme to the said Calenders & pictures shalbe voyd and the same shall then be disposed by the mr. wardens & Assistentę accordinge to their discrecons̃/[3]

7 Junij

mr. East
mr haryson Jun'
assistentę

This day mr Thomas East and mr Joh̃n Harrison the younger were accordinge to the ordon̄ance in that behalf Elected admytted and placed to be of the Assistentę of this Companye

Febr' 1603. Mr. Binge mr of the Company died
And mr Bysshop was chosen̄ mr in his stede

5to m'cij

Tho. pavier

Yt is ordered that he shalbe com̃itted to ward and pay xls for a fine for printinge certen bookę and balladę wtout licence[4] & keping a p'ntise iij yeres vnp'sented and for receavinge & dealinge wth other mens copies disorderly printed. The sed xls to be pd on monday next after or Lady day next[5] And shall also p'ntly bring into the hall as forfaited accordinge to thordon̄ance so many of the sed bookę & balladę as he hath in his handę wch he ꝑmiseth to doo Neu'theles it is ordered yt if he shall on the next day after this day enter into bond in xlli to ye Kinge [*in gold*] not to print buy or sell any thinge hereafter contrary to the ordon̄ancę or decrees That then his imprisonmt shalbe remitted.//

paid xxxs
& the rest
Remitted.

·17·Junij
1604.

[1] The pictures apparently are the cuts of coins which were used in at least ten editions of F. Adams's *Writing tables*, 1577–1601, and possibly earlier. Of these the editions of 1598 and 1601 were printed by J. Roberts for E. White. From 1581 to 1594 they were printed by R. Watkins and J. Roberts for F. Adams.

[2] S.T.C. 24284.

[3] The editions of 1604, 1607, 1609, 1611, 1615, 1618, and 1628 were printed 'for the Co. of Stationers'.

[4] Among the unentered books published by Pavier in 1603, some of which may be here referred to, are STC 6476, 7594, 10798, 14421, 20868, and 22045; of ballads there are STC 7589 and 22900. STC 14671 is not only not entered but has been shown to be largely plagiarized from 21225 (*St. in Philol.* xxxiv, 1937, 186–90). Pavier was fined for selling 75 copies of Allde's second edition of the *Basilicon doron*, Arber ii. 836.

[5] The partial remission of Pavier's fine is recorded Arber ii. 838.

Edward Aldee. his [*admission*] submission

pñte at the doinge hereof
mr Byshop mr
mr Mann [*mr*]
mr waterson } wardens
mr Harryson sen'
mr Newberie
mr Binge
mr dawson
mr Barker
mr Ponsonby
mr windet
mr Seaton
mr Hoop.
mr Norton
mr Easte
mr Jo: Harryson Jun'
Ric: Collins.

I Edward Aldee havinge ben nowe latelie convented before the moste Reuerend ffather in god the Lord Archbishop of Canterburie and other his highnes Comissioners for Causes Ecclesiasticall for my disorders in pryntinge[1] and by them found to haue offended in the printinge of Basilicoñ Doron Contrarie to the decrees of the moste hon'able Courte of Starrechamber & the ordynancę of my owne Companie./ Wherebie my presse and ltres were iustlie to haue ben defaced & broken in peeces besydes ymprysonment and diu's forfaytures to have beñ inflicted vppon me accordinge to the said Decrees & Ordynaunces./ Doo herebie voluntarylie of my owne free motion wthout any Compulsion fayninge or dissimulacoñ Acknowledge & confesse to my mr wardens & Companie, that I haue Comitted these disorders wherewth I haue beñ socharged & haue offended the said decrees and ordynancę and so iustlie incurred the dangers & penalties aforesaid./ wherebie I should be vtterlie vndone foreu', yf Comisseracoñ contrarie to my deserte should not be shewed vnto me./ But wth full intent & purpose to reforme and keepe myself hereafter from all offences of these kindes and hartilie & vnfainedlye sory for my present offences and all others of the like kinde paste./ I doo hereby in all humblenes & plaine dealinge submyt myself to my mayster wardens & companye desyringe them to shewe [me] the[i]re Comisseracoñ for all that is paste vppon condicoñ that I neu' offend hereafter in the like kinde or in any respecte in printinge contrarie to the said decrees and ordonaunces or any of them promisinge neu' hereafter to be ꝑtie or pryuie or in any sorte consentinge or furthering into or aboute any suche thinge/ Renounsinge herebye all favor and comisseracoñ to be [*be*] prayed or demaunded for the Contrarye/ And I doo herebye ꝑmise neu' hereafter to offend contrarie to the said decrees & ordonaunces or any of them/ Nor to praye or require any favor or Remission at thandę of my mr wardens & Companie or any ꝑsonages of Aucthoritie for the contrarie/ And for that I printed 1500 the second tyme wche were dispersed as followeth/ That is to saye to Edw: whyt 500c and the reste to certeñ ꝑsons expressed in a note delyu'ed to the wardens of my Companie/ That this my request may be graunted I moste humblie Craue yt vppon my knees before my mayster wardens & their Assistentę this Sixt of June Aõ Primo Regni dñ̃ nrĩ Regis Jacobi &cę 1603

Edw: Aldees submission (*in another hand*)

sic sign' Edward Aldee
sic testificat' {Subscr' pnte / Rico Collins No}

[1] Cf. *C–B.C*, 2a, 30 May 1603.

FOL. 3ª

1603. jmo Rę Jacobi

12 m'cij

Mr Bisshop mr
mr Dawson } wardeñs
mr Hoop

mr humfrey Lownes

He havinge maried the wydowe of mr Short informeth the company that mr Short hath gyven xls a yere to thuse of the poore of this Company yssuing out of a rent in mugwell streete that he held of St Barthnẽs hospitall. To contynue for 26 yeres. and to be payd by xs a quarter. The wch Anuytie mr lownes promiseth shalbe pformed for the said terme. Whereof he will pay xxs. for 2 quarters wch shall end at or Lady day next.

The 26 yeres are accoumpted from Christmas 1603

[*The first paymt he broght the first of mar next.*]

27 m'cij. 27 m'cij 1603

Comittees Mr Man. mr Jo Norton Ric' ffield and Adam Islip are chosen & appointed to endevo' and folowe the preferinge of a bill to the plament for thobteyninge of an Act for the good of the Company touchinge certen articles & matters here imparted to the consideracoñ of the Company/.[1]

R Breconñ Yt is ordered in consideracoñ of the weak & distressed estate of Robert Brecon[2] an old workmañ & his labo' nowe past. That the wardens shall pay vnto hym xijd a week henceforward till further order be taken.

Gyven by order of Court to margery Grantham[3] wydowe toward her Relief vs—}vs

2 april

mr. Robertę wm Jagger Vpon ye hearinge of the matter in controu'sie betwene them̃ touchinge the [billę of the] company of stageplayers late pteyning to the Erle of worc' & nowe to ye quenes maiesty & Refered by ye Kingę Highnes to the hearinge & determinacoñ of this Company.[4] yt is ordered that wm Jagger shall enioy the printinge of the seid billę for the seid company of stageplaiers nowe aptening to the Queenes matie that nowe is. payinge iiijs a monethe therafter to James Robertę during his Interest. The first paymt to begyn the ffirst of May next. And that yf ye seid Erle hereafter entertayne any company of stageplaiers agayne Then wm Jagger shall print the billę of that Company onely and leave printinge the billę of her seid matę company of players. paying also iiijs a moneth for the same to ye sed James. Also yt is ordered that Wm Jagger shall pay vnto the sed James Robertę xls wch he owth him in arrerage for the billę of the seid Erles seid late company. In forme folowing Viz̃. xxs the first of may next/ xs at midsom' next and xs at michãs next.

James Robartę
Witłm Jaggard

[1] This may refer to the patent for the privilege of Psalters, Psalms, Primers, Almanacks, &c., the foundation of the English Stock, which was granted 29 Oct. 1603, and recorded *Reg. B*, 19 Dec. 1603, 485b. According to a mutilated marginal note beside that record, Field, at least, was paid, presumably for expenses incurred. The patent is printed in full in Arber iii. 42–44.

[2] Brecon admitted freeman 5 Oct. 1569, Arber i. 419.

[3] Presumably widow of Thomas Grantham, admitted freeman 2 Mar. 1601, Arber ii. 728.

[4] Cf. *C–B.C*, 1a, 13 Dec. 1602.

23 April[1]

mr Stringers p'uilege mr Dexters bookę/ Yt is ordered by a Court holdeñ this day That the bookę Remayninge of the form' ympressions of Robert Dexter belonginge to mr Stringers p'uilege[2] shall not be reprinted wthout the order and Consent of a Court of the mr wardens and assistentę for the tyme beinge/[3]

Dispensations Yt is ordered that these ꝑsons folowinge shall pay these sõmes hereunder expressed for dispensacons for [not] servinge certen placę in the Company as folowth Which the said ꝑsons doo yeild and assent vnto

viz

mr Barker for not servinge his second [upper] [*vnder*] wardenship[4]} xxli. payd. 17. Junj

mr whyndett, mr white, mr Seton, mr waterson, mr Hooꝑ } eu'y of them xli a pece for not servinge the second vnderwardenship[5] } lli

mr John norton for not servinge bothe the vnderwardenships[6]} xxli. pđ 10 Junij

mr newbres accoumpt mr norton mr Burby and Willm Helmes wthin 10 dayes to examine the stock of mr newbre and to cast vp thaccoumpt that yt may appeare what Remaineth due vnto hym[7]

mr East Yt is ordered at mr Easts Request That he shalbe dispensed wth from the bearinge of all offices in this Company payinge to thuse of the Company A pece of plat of 30 ouncę or xli in money. And a sute of Lynneñ. Which he is Content to ꝑforme for his discharge from all the seid offyces/[8]

14 Maij

Edw. Blunt, Tho. Man Jun'} ffor thendinge of the controu'sie betwene them about the booke of the pageantę[9] yt is ordered that Edw Blunt shall delyu' all his Remayno' thereof, (wch he saieth are 400) to Tho mañ. Receavinge of hym vjs for euery Reame thereof. Wch yt is ordered the seid Tho man shall pay vnto hym/

[1] There was evidently a court held 16 Apr. 1604 which is not here recorded but which restored the regular quarter dinners, cf. *Reg. B*, 467a.

[2] Cf. Arber iii. 87, 4 July 1597.

[3] The privilege was for Grammars and this order would appear to be part of the organization of the English Stock.

[4] Cf. Arber ii. 838.

[5] Cf. Arber ii. 838, and *C–B.C*, 7a, 3 July 1605.

[6] Cf. Arber ii. 838.

[7] Possibly in connexion with his work as stock-keeper for the partners in Day's privilege, but more likely this relates to the settling of Ralph Newberry's estate, for, despite McKerrow's *Dictionary*, p. 199, he was evidently dead before 19 June 1604 when a receipt was given for a bequest of £15 to Bridewell Hospital, cf. *Letter Book*, fol. 79a.

[8] Cf. Arber ii. 838–9.

[9] Blount entered STC 14756, 19 Mar. 1604; while Man entered STC 6510 on 2 Apr. 1604. If this controversy concerns these books it is difficult to understand why Man should apparently be favoured by the Court.

mr Edw. white
Tho Clerk

Whereas mr White hath Complayned of Thomas Clerk for printinge of mary magdalens Lamentacoñs for the losse of her mr Jesus.[1] mr white at the entreatie of the mr wardens and assistentẹ is content and thereuppon yt is ordered That Tho Clerk wth his bookẹ shall equall the nũber of mr whits bookẹ viz. to lay so many to mr whites as mr white hath. And the same so layd together. The seid Thomas for hym self and mr white shall sell them together and Answere mr white as they shalbe sold ijd ob[2] a pece for eu'y book of mr whites moytye. And shall from tyme to tyme vntill the seid nũbers so equalled & layd together be sold make mr white a true accoumpt in wryting of the sale of all and eu'y of the same numbers And delyu'[*r*] hym his moytie of all the mõney cõming of the sale thereof alwaies vppon Request made by mr white. And yf the seid Tho Clerk hath any greater nũber of the seid bookẹ then will equall the nũber that mr white shall deliu' vnto hym. Then the seid Thomas shall reserue the seid ou'plus [*in his owne handẹ*] and not sell nor dispse any of theñ till he hath sold all the seid numbers Layd together by mr white and hym And made hym a full accoumpt thereof and Satisfaccõn for his pte at the ratẹ aforesed The whiche ou'plus, yt is ordered that yt shall Remaine in mr whitẹ custody till the nũbers equalled as aforeseid be all sold. And then to be deliu'ed or answered to the sed Tho Clerk.

mr. windet
Felix Kingston

ffor the satisfyinge & ending of mr windettẹ complaint & demaund against Felix Kingston for printinge the billẹ of the sicknes ij weekẹ in wrõng of mr windet whose the copie was. Yt is Ordered that Felix shall pay to mr windet Teñ shillingẹ presently or by Satterday next. wch was pd ..25to..Junij[3]

18 maij

T Sare

Tho Sare accordinge to form' order[4] hath paid to mr hoop for the renters accoumpt ijs for all his arr' of qrterag vntill & at or Lady day last 1604.

mr. Edw. white
wm aspley

ffor thendinge of the controu'sie betwene theñ. whereas mr white hath paid to wm aspley xxs and hath Receaued a quarterne of the bookẹ of thanswere to the popish peticoñs[5] Yt is ordered that in discharge of the same xxs he shall deliu' vnto mr white a quarterne moore of the same bookẹ besidẹ that quarterne wch he hath alredy Receaued

xj. Junij

mr. Leake
mr. feild

By a full Court of assistentẹ holden this [day] Mr. Wiłłm Leake and mr Richard ffeild are chosen to be of the Assistentẹ of this Company froñ henceforth.

[1] John Danter, since dead, entered for this book 24 July 1595 (Arber iii. 45). No Danter edition exists, but it was printed for White in 1601, STC 17569. Clark entered it again 24 Apr. 1604 (Arber iii. 259), and published his edition, STC 17570.

[2] Abrev. for obolus = halfpenny.

[3] Windet entered for the annual bills and for the blank briefs 1 Aug. 1603 (Arber iii. 243); the weekly ones he apparently did not enter but printed in his capacity as printer to the city of London. The bills for the weeks ending 20 Oct. and 3 Nov. 1603 printed by him are in the Guildhall Library. No bills printed by Kingston can be traced.

[4] No such order has been found.

[5] STC 14430-1. The order of these editions should be reversed.

1604. .2. Regis

20 Junij

FOL. 4b

Mr Ironside — Yt is ordered by a full Court of assistentę That Richard Ironside Administrator of the goodę Chattellę Rightę and Creditę of mr Richard Watkins deceased/ for the full Releas and discharge of all the pretendyd Right and Clayme which the said Richard Ironside [*hat*] as administrator aforesed or otherwise Hathe or may haue in and to the preuilege and printinge of the Almanackę and ꝑgnosticacoñs[1] shall haue and Receaue at the handę of the Company. ffourty poundę yerely duringe the terme of ffoure yeres nowe next cõminge. The same to be yerely payd duringe the said terme at the feast of the byrth of our lord god by the handę of the Wardens of the Company for the tyme beinge The first payment to begyñ at the feast of the birth of or lord next

Jo. Hardy — Yt is ordered that fromhenceforth John hardy the bedell[2] shall haue iiijli eu'y quarter viz xvjli a yere for his wagę in Regard of the service which he nowe doth wch is greater then yt was before

25 Junij

Tho. Busshell
Olyuer hindley — Vppon the hearinge of the controu'sie betwene the seid ꝑties yt is ordered that the seid Olyver shall presently pay to the seid Tho xls. And that the seid Tho shall sett ou' Tho hendley his appr'/ to Tho Archer for the Residue of the terme of his Apprentiship[3]

vltiõ July

Mr Man mr.
mr Nortoñ
mr Leake
Wardens — Mr. Burby and mr Adams are this day chosen to be in the lyuery/ Joyned to the mr and wardens/. in the Dealingę of the Accoumptę and affayres of the newe ꝑuilege//[4]
Likewise mr Hooꝑ and mr Feild for the Assistentę.

1604. .2. Ris'

July

6 Augusti

FOL. 5a

Mr. Man. mr.
mr. Jo. Norton } wrdens
mr Leak.

Jo Smythick
Ri Bradock. — Vppon the hearinge of the matter in Controu'sie betwene them about the book of the Erle of Essexes Apologie[5] by them̃ submitted to a court holden this day. yt is Ordered for the endinge of all thingę touching this matter: That Ric Bradock shall pay vnto Jo. Smythick. Vli. the one half at Christmas next And thother half at our Lady day in Lent next And herevnto bothe the seid ꝑties doo agree/.

Richard Bradocke
John Smethick

[1] In the patent 29 Oct. 1603, granting a privilege to the Company for Almanacks and Prognostications, no mention is made of the cancellation of previous privileges in Psalters, Psalms, and Primers. (See text printed Arber iii. 42–44.) This was evidently an expensive omission.

[2] Cf. *Reg. B*, 474a, 8 Oct. 1599.

[3] The transfer was registered the same day, Arber ii. 280.

[4] The patent for the English Stock, cf. Arber iii. 42–44.

[5] STC 6788 was printed by Bradock in quarto. An imperfect copy of an octavo edition, possibly printed by Smethwick, is in the Huntington Library. It differs

3. Septembr

Mr. Linge — Yt is ordered that he shalbe cõmitted to prison and pay xli for a fine[1] for Disobedience & obstinacie in refusinge to serue out the Rentership of the Company beinge orderly chosen Renter and havinge serued one yere in the place.

Tho. Purfoot Jun' — Yt is ordered that he shalbe cõmitted to ward and pay vs for a fine for begynninge to print a booke[2] cõntrary to the warninge & Direccoñ of the wardeñs/

David Ward — He hathe pd to mr Leake for his arr' of quarterage in full paymt } vjs viijd
yt is deliu'ed to Jo. Hardy to deliu' to mr Lownes Renter

.1. oct'

Jo oswald. — Yt is ordered that Jo oswold shall haue his bond frely deliu'ed him to be cancelled wherein he and Ric' Becket are bound to to the Company for xls.[3]
Gyven to hoskins[4] wydowe ....iijs iiijd
Item gyven to Henr' Clerk[5].........vjs viijd

4 oct'

mr. Edw. white
Edw. Chambers — yt is ordered that Edw. chambs[6] shall pay to mr Edw. white xs at or before the next Court day. pvided that if defalt be made of the same paymt Then mr white to be at Libtie to take all advantage of his demaunde against the seid Edw. Chambers./

Fol. 5b

4 oct 1604

Mr. Windet.
Jo Smithick. — ffor thendinge of the con'trou'sie betwene them touching the book of the pagente[7] yt is ordered that mr windet shall pay to John Smithick—xxs oñ Symon & Jude day next and other xxs at Christmas next.

somewhat in content from the Bradock edition. But since C. Burby made a provisional entry for this title, 8 June 1603 (Arber iii. 236) and there is no transfer, it is not possible to know what the controversy was about.

In the catalogue of Humphrey Dyson's Library at All Souls is listed 'An Apologie of the Earle of Essex against those wch Jealously & malitiously taxed him to be the hinderer of the peace of his Country penned by himself, 1598, in 4o.' Possibly this refers merely to an imperfect copy of STC 6788.

1 This fine was paid 1 Oct. 1604, cf. entry Arber ii. 839, 3 Sept. 1604.

2 The book has not been identified. Purfoot paid only half the fine, 8 Apr. 1605, cf. Arber ii. 839, 3 Sept. 1604.

3 Cf. *Reg. B*, 485b (margin) and Arber i. 572.

4 Helen Hoskins, widow of William Hoskins, who died before 23 Jan. 1604, cf. Arber ii. 735.

5 Admitted freeman 11 Dec. 1581 (Arber ii. 685).

6 Presumably the E. C. admitted freeman 3 Sept. 1594 (Arber ii. 714).

7 This may refer to STC 12863 which was printed by Windet and which contains matter taken from STC 6264–5 and 6510. The Daniel piece was not entered, though it is more likely that Waterson controlled it than Smethwick.

16 oct'

Helen Hoskins yt is ordered that helen hoskins[1] shall haue a pencoñ of xx^s p Anñ to be p^d by v^s a quarter

Rafe Blore Item that Raff' blore shall pay vnto her x^s in hand & x^s at xp̄istmas next for an end of all controu'sie she to deliu' him his old bond & a gen'all quitance. And he to make her a bill for the x^s to be p^d at xp̄istmas next

16 octo^r

Rob̄t Dexters Will A note of Rob̄t Dexters Legacy

The last will and testam^t of Robert Dexter[2] late cit' and Stac' of London Deceased, ys dated 24 Octobr 1603 and Approved in the p^rrogatiue Court of Canterbury: 26. Decemb̄r eodm̄ A°.

His legacie in his last will Item I gyve vnto the Company of Stacõners xx^li to be lent forth by y^em vpõn securitye for Three yeres Vnto poore yonge-meñ freeborne of the same Company. gratis And so from tyme to tyme for Three yeres gratis vnto Twoo others of the same Company beinḡe poore yongmen as aforesed

Executo^rs of his will
Myles Colty of holbourne in the county of Mid (*paraph*) Tailor
his brother Nichãs Dexter of Chempton in couñ Suff marchan'
And Mr Stephen Egertoñ p^rcher of gods word.

1604. 2 Ris Fol. 6a

4. dec'

Rowland Foster. The Armorership The Armorership of the Company wch m^r Lodyham deceased late had is graunted to Rowland Foster. wth the yerely fee [*x*] of xxvj^s viij^d for thexercisinge of the same as the said Lodyham[3]/ [and it] is graunted to [the said] Rowland Foster Armorer. To hold during his good behavio^r thereiñ. And he to putt in good security for the pformance thereof

W^m. Reade. Gyven to wiłłm Reade[4] by Consent of a Court holdeñ this day .xx^s. toward his Relief beinge a poore man lyinge in pryson. yt is gyven hym̄ to redeme his tooles (Lying at pawne) to woork w^t them to gett his Lyving.

1 Cf. *C–B.C*, 5a, 1 Oct. 1604.
2 Cf. Plomer, *Wills*, pp. 37–38.
3 Cf. *Reg. B*, 7 July 1600, 476a.
4 Read was admitted a freeman 27 June 1580 (Arber ii. 682).

die et a^{o} p'd

Mr Thomas Dawson
2 decembr 1605
3 Rę

M^{r}. Dawson payd in this moneye Accordinge to this order. And deliu'd m^{r} warden ffield xiij^{s} iiij^{d} to thuse in this order exp'ssed wth an acquitance for the Lij^{s} from the Churchwardens And there upon by A Court holden this day. the said
fol. 8. L^{li}. is lent vnto hym̃ againe
14. 24 till the Company haue occasion to vse yt. Vppon the very same assurance & pawne & vnder the like chargę condicons & agremtę as are conteined in this order.

Teste. R.C.
Thomas Dawson

Whereas the companie haue Receaved a legacie of Lij^{li} from thexec' of Henrie Billage late of the pshe of St Martin in the vinterye Dyer deceased, ffor whiche they are to paye yerelie for eu' to the Church wardens and ouer seers for the poore of the said pishe ffyftie and Twoo shillingę viz: xiij^{s} a q^{ter} the same to be distributed by xij^{d} eu'ye weeke in bread to the poore and nedy of the [said] pishe./ Nowe vppon [the] requeste of Mr Dawson yt is ordered that the said som̃e of ffyftie poundę shalbe layd downe by the Companie for him to make vppe his stocke[1] [C^{li} toward the stocke] for thexecucon̄ of the priviledge whereof he hathe payd L^{li} already before this daye/ And he Agreeth to repay the said som̃e of L^{li} to the Companie at the end of One yere next/ And in the meane space from tyme to tyme to paye and discharge the said yerelie payment to the Churche wardens & ou'seers of the said pishe to thuse of their poore as aforesaid/ And also to give xiij^{s} iiij^{d} to thuse of the poore of this Companie wthin ye said yere And yt is graunted & agreed vnto by the said Thomas Dawson/ That yf he or his exec' doo not repaye the said som̃e of L^{li} to the Companie wthin the said yere next/ And in the meane space doo not satisfie the yerelie paymentę aforesaid/ That then the Companie to their owne vse shall have & enioy for euer, the Moytie and one half of his wholle stocke of C^{li} remayninge in stocke as aforesaid w^{che} is made vppe wth the L^{li} as aforesaid/ And also all encrease pffittę and Com̃odities growen or to growe of the said Moytie or half pte of the said stocke of C^{li}.

Thomas Dawson

20. octobr' 1606.
Fol. 6^{b} 4to Ris Quarter day

Yt is graunted by the full Court holden this day That m^{r} Billagę money shalbe contynued in m^{r} Dawsons handę for another yere after thend of this in this order. Vppon the mortgage & assurance of his pte wth all allowancę & condycons as yt was before/

printers Admitted/

7 april 1605

Humfrey lownes[2] is admitted to be a prynter

29. Jan 1606.

Lyonell Snodam gyveth ou' his place. And Nichas Ockes is admitted to be in his place wth Geo. Snodam in the same sort in all respectę & nōne other as Lyonell was./

George Snodam[3] is admitted to be a printer. And lyonell Snodam̃[4] is to be pten' with him̃ both to be accoumpted but one prynter And to kepe butt one printinge house Betwene them̃/

[1] Cf. *C–B.C*, 8^{b}, 2 Dec. 1605; 11^{a}, 20 Oct. 1606; 14^{a}, 5 Oct. 1607; 19^{a}, 11 Oct. 1608; 21^{a}, 21 Oct. 1609; 24^{a}, 14 Jan. 1611; 29^{b}, 5 Oct. 1612; 33^{a}, 25 Nov. 1613; 36^{b}, 18 Nov. 1614; 49^{a}, 3 Nov. 1617; 52^{a}, 4 Oct. 1618.

[2] H. Lownes had been a bookseller only and, though a liveryman of the Company, was not a printer until this date. He had married the widow of Peter Short in 1604 and succeeded to that business.

[3] G. Snowdon.

[4] L. Snowdon.

6 may 1605

Alice Wolf. Md̄. there is graunted vnto her an Annuyty of iij li by the yere duringe her life to be payd by xv[s] a quarter in Recompence and full discharge for all her clayme to the .A. B. C. for the horne book.[1] The which she wholy yeildeth vp to the Compañy for this anuitie The first payment whereof is to be made at mydsom̃' next

Poore Re[d] of St Gregories ꝑishe for the poore ......xx[s]

m[res] Binge yt is ordered that m[res] Binge shall haue L[li] stocke goinge, in the p'uilege graunted by the Kinge and the like stocke in thother p'uilege purchased of m[r] wight.[2] To hold to her duringe her wydowehead onely and no longer.

Jo. Bateman
Jo. Combes yt is ordered (by election made) that John Batemañ shall haue a yomans ꝑte in all the seid preuilege. And That Johñ Combes shall shall (*sic*) haue a lyke yomans ꝑte

Suters to be Remembred hereafter for ꝑtes[3] Wiłłm Smythe. Thomas pavyer. Henry Tomes Wiłłm Hall Tho. Snodam̃, Ric' Tomes. Roger Jackson [*Likewise Tho Snodam/ Ri Tomes.*] Henr cooke/ Wiłłm̃ Jagger

1605. 3 Re Fol. 7[a]

Die et Anno p'd

Wydowe Butter & Nathanaell her son yt is ordered that wydowe Butter ałs newbery and Nathanaell her soñ shall haue łli stocke in the P'uilege graunted by the Kinge. and the lyke stocke of L[li] in thother p[r]uilege p[r]chased of m[r] wight To hold betwene them. And shee to haue her ꝑte thereof duringe her wydowhead onely as mres Bing hath hers

Jo. Oswold yt is ordered that Johñ Oswold[4] shall haue xiij[s] iiij[d] a quarter duringe the Companyes pleasure./. Attendinge such service as the Company will appoint hym̃ and as his own leasure will serue/

27 maij 1605.

melchisedeck Bradwood He is a suter for a yomans ꝑte in the p'uilege And is to be remembred when any ꝑte falleth void.[5]

[1] John Wolf presumably acquired his right to this as his share, or part of his share, in Day's privilege. Presumably, this was merely the ⅛ sheet intended to be placed under the horn window in a horn-book.

[2] This is the earliest reference to the purchase by stock partners of the patent for law books which Bonham Norton and Thomas Wight had acquired from Charles Yetsweirt, cf. *Reg. B*, 2 Apr. 1599, 471[a]. When Wight bought out Norton's interest has not been discovered.

[3] Cf. *C–B.C*, 15[a], 12 Oct. 1607.

[4] J. Oswall appointed porter 26 June 1592, *Reg. B*, 454[b].

[5] Cf. *C–B.C*, 15[a], 12 Oct. 1607.

mr. Barker mr.
mr. norton } wrdeñs
mr. Feild

3 Julij

mr white
mr. Setoñ
mr waterson
mr hoop

They haue promised in full Court holdeñ this day to pay the rest of their fines sett downe 23 April 1604.[1]

5to. [*Julij*] Junij

Arnalt Hatfeild

He is a suter for a yomans pte. And assoone as any suche pte shall fall voyd/ He shalbe in the Electioñ for the same/[2]
Entred by directioñ froñ mr Wardeñ Norton. in wrytinge vnder his hand.

Primo Julij 1605

mr windet.

yt is ordered that mr windet shall haue his vli agayne wche he paid for a fine the last yere as appereth in the book of fines/.[3]

Ri. Collins
Ri. feild.
humfr lownes

memorand that oñ Satterday last beinge the 29 of June 1605 3 Rę. beinge thelection day of mr & wardens for the yere insuinge. (The mr wardens and assistentę beinge there assembled in full Court.) A lyverie pte in all the preuilegę was alotted by Consent of this Court to Richard Collins. And a lyke lyu'ie pte was there alotted to Ric ffeild and humfrey lownes equally betwene theñ Twoo/

29 oct' 1605.

preseñt the mr. wardens & assistentę.

yt is ordered that mr lownes payinge to mr ffeild 43li 8s 4d wthin viiij. dayes next shall [from henceforth] enioye the moytie of the Lyvery pte aboue alotted to mr ffeild [& hym]/ Together wth all the proffittę henceforward growing of the said moyty/

FOL. 7b

1605. 3. Ris Jacobi

Mr. Barker mr
Mr Norton } wardeñs.
mr Feild

29 Julij/

For printinge of pruileged bookę

A full Court of Assistentę holden this day.

Yt is ordered that no booke appteyninge to the pruilegę of the Company shall hereafter neither in pte nor in all be putt to printinge or taken in hand by any printer or other to be printed Except it shalbe done wth the consent of the Mr. Wardens. & Assistentę or the moore pte of theñ, and the printer & the nũber of the ympressioñ and the pryce for woorkmanship by theñ [first] appointed rated & sett Down/
Agreed vnto by the mr wardens & Assistentę in full Court holdeñ this day

[1] Cf. *C–B.C*, 3b, and Arber ii. 838, 840, and 841. [2] Cf. *C–B.C*, 15a, 12 Oct. 1607. [3] Cf. Arber ii. 838.

6 Augusti

Tho. purfoote the elder — Yt is ordered by a Court holden this day. That Thoms̃ Purfoote thelder Shall haue the woorkmanship of printinge one leafe of the prym̃ers[1] for the company. Vntill the Company shall otherwise Dispose of yt Provyded alwaies that he shall not begyñ at any tyme to woork vpoñ the same wthout the Companies expresse order —

.12. Augusti

For payinge of printers by warrant from̃ the m^{r} & ward̃. — Yt is ordered by a Court holdeñ this daye That the Treasurer shall not pay for the printinge of any thinge wthout warrant from the m^{r} and Wardens or sõme twoo of them̃ vnder their handꝭ And that wheñ any thinge is printed, the printer signifyinge the same to the Thrẽs shall ꝑcure a warrant from̃ the m^{r} & Wardeñs or any twoo of them̃ for his satisfaccõn.

Edw^{r}d Venge/ — yt is ordered by a court holden this day. & that wth his assent That he shall not hereafter bynd or print his book called A weekꝭ woorkꝭ.[2] otherwise theñ yt was here deliu'ed vnto hym̃ by this Court. nor sell yt to haberdashers nor alter yt in any sort vppoñ payne of forfayture of his Right to the copie & to haue the entrance thereof stryken out of the book

yt is deliu'd him in 16. Conteyning onely & nothinge else but The vij speciall consideracõns of

Synne	Of gods benefitꝭ
Deathe	Of the misery of
The Judgm^{t}	our estat
of hell & the	Of gods elect
tormentꝭ	Wthout any other Addicoñs

1605. .3. Ris — Fol. 8^{a}

m^{r} Feild wardeñ — yt is consented that m^{r}. Feild may at this present Prynt one ympression of the psalmes of David in meter in the Scottishe tongue[3] for Andrewe hart or suche as haue Interest in it. payinge Twenty shillingꝭ to the Company in regard of this ympression onely. The w^{che} m^{r} Feild promiseth to pay

The Scottish Psalmes xx^{s}. ꝑmised to ye cõpanie.

A gilt salt. m^{r} Dawson & m^{r} Hooꝑ. — They haue gyveñ this day to the Company. A gilt salt of Silu' wth A cou' weyinge xj ouncꝭ wth these ꝉres. T.D. & H.H. sett oñ the outside

[1] There is at Harvard a copy of *The A.B.C. with the catechisme*, 8°, f. the Company of Stationers, 1605, which has on title an unrecorded printer's device of vase with snails and initials 'TP'. It collates A^{8}B^{4} and it would appear that it was all printed by Purfoot.

[2] This work has not been identified, though it was entered 9 Nov. 1604 (Arber iii. 275), and transferred by Venge's widow, 15 Mar. 1616 (Arber iii. 584). From the reference to the Haberdashers presumably it was a little volume suitable for putting in an embroidered binding.

[3] STC 2704 was not apparently printed by Field. If he printed an edition for Hart, it has not been identified.

nichãs hart iiij[s] viij[d] p[d] for his q[r]terage̜ till & at Mic'. 1605.

he hath clerd all his q[r]terage̜ till & at michãs 1605. And hath nowe payd the same beinge—iiij[s] viij[d]. w[ch] is cõmitted to thande̜ of m[r] Feild Wardeñ to be Deliu'ed to the renter

9 Sept' 1605

Audito[rs] appointed to take thaccoumpt froñ the stockkeps

Of Thassistente̜

m[r]. white
m[r] hoop

of the lyu'ie

m[r] Burby
m[r] holm̃e

of the yomanry

Jo. Bill
Edm. Weaver/

16 Sept' 1605. 3 Ris

Adam Islip for the Lawebooke̜

Here ffelip Kingston gaue ou' to deale w[th] this w[r]kmanship

yt is ordered that Adam Islip shall haue the w[r]kemanship of the printinge of the Lawebooke̜ belonginge to the p[r]uilege[1] thereof Duringe y[e] companies pleasure. And to haue for y[e] w[r]kemanship thereof suche reasonable rate̜ & alowance̜ as shalbe iudged to be sufficient by the order & Judgem[t] fo the m[r]. wardens & assistente̜ from tyme to tyme/ [*And*] Also he is to pay the Company for havinge the printinge stuff to his owne vse w[che] the Company bought of m[r] wight,[2] suche rate̜ as they are appraised at by y[e] appraise[rs] appointed by y[e] company amountinge to 131[li] whereof a third pte to be paid at xxistm̃s next. And the rest in suche sort as the Company are to Pay m[r] wight for the stock they bought of him whereof this printing stuff is pcell/

Fol. 8[b]

1605. 3 Re̜.
7 oct'

m[r] hũfr' lownes

This day he paid xs for a q[r]ters paym[t] of the xls a yere w[ch] comes froñ m[r] Shorte̜ bequest/[3] } x[s].

Edw[rd] Bysshop.

he hath gyveñ to the Company a gilt salt of Silu' w[th] a cou': In regard whereof the playne mans pathway[4] is graunted vnto him for his copy. as appeth in the Register of copies/

[1] Among the law books printed for the Company with the date 1605 or 1606 are STC 5504 (2 edits.), 5505, 5525, 9297, 9547, 9602, 10982, 15156, 15170+ (1605), and 25271. STC 20712 is a ghost. Most of these, if not all, were printed by Islip, and all of them presumably were taken over by the Law Stock partners when they bought out Thomas Wight and Bonham Norton's patent for law books, cf. *C–B.C*, 6[b], 6 May 1605. Cf. also Arber iii. 704.

[2] This transaction does not appear to have been elsewhere recorded in detail, cf. *C–B.C*, 6[b], 6 May 1605. Among the printing materials which Islip obtained from Wight probably were compartments, McKerrow and Ferguson, Nos. 147, and 223.

[3] Cf. *C–B.C*, 3[a], 12 Mar. 1604.

[4] Arber iii. 248 and 303. There is in the University of Illinois Library a copy of the 'eight impression' of Arthur Dent's book, printed by T. C. for Bishop, 1606.

M[res] Holland. Gyven vnto her [*x*]ls in full satisfaccoñ for all her demaundȩ concerning m[r] Grenhams woorkȩ.[1] And she ꝑmiseth to deliu' the company her bond wch her husband had from m[r] Dexter/ } ij[li]. x[s] solut'/

2 decembr

m[r] dawson for m[r] Billagȩ money/ — m[r] dawson paid to m[r] ffeild xiij[s] iiijd to thuse of the poore accordinge to an order sett downe for m[r] Billagȩ moneye[2] 4 dec' 1604. . wth a quitance froñ the churchwardens of S[t] martyñ the vintry for Lij[s] due to theñ this yere for the same matter/

fol. 6

29 Sept' 1605.

Michas 1605 l[li] ꝑcell of the 200[li] Añuity[3] — m[r] feild warden Receaued froñ the accoumpt of the ꝑteners by thandȩ of the Stockekeꝑs } L[li]

20 Deceñb 1605

Christñs 1605 L[li] ꝑcell of the 200[li] Añuity — m[r] feild wardeñ Receaued froñ thaccoumpt of the ꝑten's by thandȩ of the stockekeꝑs } L[li]

20 Jan'

Wiłłm Hall — yt is ordered that wheñ any yomañs ꝑte shall fall voyd./ Wiłłm Hall shalbe one of theñ that shalbe in electioñ for the same/[4]

17 Febr'

m[r] windet m[r]. East — Vpoñ the hearinge of the matter in controu'sie betwene them:[5] ffor thendinge thereof yt (is) ordered, that m[r] windet in recompenc' of the hindrance he hathe doñe m[r] East & for costȩ of sute shall pay to m[r] East fforty shillingȩ viz xx[s] on the Third of Marche next. And xx[s]. oñ the xxv[th] of March next/

[1] STC 12317. Richard Greenham's *Works* were edited by Henry Holland and originally were entered to Robert Dexter and Ralph Jackson (Arber iii. 103, 105, 108). They published two editions in 1599, and in 1601 they published an enlarged edition again edited by Holland (Arber iii. 170). On Jackson's death Cuthbert Burby registered the transfer of Jackson's rights (Arber iii. 205), but on Dexter's death the Company took over his rights (Arber iii. 248) so that in order to print the fourth edition of 1605, Burby had to pay the Company £4 for the right to print 'one Impression' of that part which was formerly Dexter's (Arber iii. 251). This edition was revised and enlarged by Henry Holland, who died before it was printed, so that it was dedicated to King James by his widow Elizabeth Holland. Apparently Dexter had originally agreed to pay Henry Holland for this work and the Company in taking over Dexter's right also assumed this obligation.

[2] Cf. *C–B.C*, 6[a], 4 Dec. 1604, *et loc. cit.*

[3] Although this annuity does not appear to be elsewhere recorded it was probably some such arrangement as that noted in *Reg. B*, 19 Oct. 1601, with regard to Day and Seres's privilege.

[4] Cf. *C–B.C*, 15[a], 12 Oct. 1607.

[5] This presumably refers to STC 20905 which was printed by Windet and entered 15 Jan. 1606 (Arber iii. 309), and cancelled by order of the Court which met this day, together with STC 6514, likewise a work based on STC 18371, which was entered 25 Jan. 1606 (Arber iii. 312). It is not clear what connexion East had with either of these works for the Dekker was printed by R. B[lower] for W. Ferbrand.

FOL. 9a

Tertio Martij 1605 3 Ris Jacobi

Betwene the parteners[1] in the booke called Ryders Dictionarie of thone partie/

And John Legatt Citizen and Stacoñ' of London on thother partie/

At a full Courte holden this daye it is ordered/ That if m^r John Legatt shall at any tyme wth in Three yeeres nexte cominge, ymprinte or cause to be ymprinted the dictionarie comonlie called Thomas Dictionarie[2] in the volume called 4to or in the volume called 8°, Then m^r Legatt shall deliuer all ye same dictionaries to the said partners in Ryders dictionarie, at the pryces followinge viz/ The dictionaries in 4to at ij^s vj^d a peece, And the dictionaries in 8° at [x] viij^d a peece Provided that yf the said parteners, shall before that tyme haue solde those they haue alreadie boughte of Mr Legatt, and that there be want of the same, Then Mr Legat shalbe at libertie to ymprinte the same dictionarie called Thomas dictionary and to dispose of them at his pleasure/ And further yt is also ordered, [*that by*] that the said parteners in Ryders dictionarie shall not reprynt any ympression of the said Ryders Dictionarie, at any tyme wth in the said 3 yeres, as nowe yt is, to the preiudace of Mr Legatt, nor then neyther, wth out gyvinge to Mr Legatt Advertysment thereof one quarter of a yere aforehand, to the end the controu'sie nowe in question betwene the said parties may be resolued vppon whether the said parteners maye laufullie prynt yt wth out preiudice to Mr Legatt or not./.

John Legate

24. m'tij. 1605 .—4 Ris

Humfr' Lownes } ffelix Kingston } Whereas they haue printed disorderly as is proued by good testimonye & their owñ confessions, diu'se great nũbers of the Leaues of the prymer aboue the nũbers appointed by the Wardens or stockeps & wth out any direccoñ from the said wardens or stockeps, w^che is directly ag^t the constitutions sett downe for the orderinge & gou'ninge of the printinge of the p^r uileged Bookes belonginge to the Company And thereby haue forfaited their stockes & ptes by vertue of the said constitutions yf the force thereof should be vsed against them. Notw^t standinge yt is ordered by a full court holdeñ this day That they shall forfayt & lose the pap of the said ou'plus of leaues by them printed disorderly as aforesaid The same to be distributed amongest the poore of the Company And that no further aduantage shalbe taken against them for this matter [*at* for] this tyme

.6. maij .1606. 4 Ris

A scholer Yt is ordered, as was form'ly agreed vpon by voices.[3] That the Company shall gyve xx^t' nobles a yere toward the Exhicoñ (*sic*) of a scholer. And nowe also yt is ordered that m^r Andrewe Adams[4] shall haue the same yerely

[1] The partners are listed in Arber iii. 276, 26 Nov. 1604. Their rights to Rider's *Dictionary* were obtained from C. Burby, who acquired them from J. Barnes, cf. Arber iii. 207, 223, 225, and 276.

[2] STC 24013 was probably already printed and was the edition of which the partners had bought up the remainder.

[3] The date of this agreement is not known. The payments recorded in Greg and Boswell and in Arber were somewhat less, i.e. £5. Twenty nobles at 6*s*. 8*d*. is £6. 13*s*. 4*d*.

[4] A. Adams, B.A. from Christ Church, Oxford, 25 Oct. 1599; M.A. 8 June 1602.

exhibicoñ of xx^t' nobles towards the furtherance of his study during the Companies good wilł, he is a mayster of arte in Christę churche in Oxoñ/ fol. 56. 109

6. maij. 1606. 4. Ris Fol. 9b

Mr. Robertę }
mr. Bankwrth } Wth their assentę yt is ordered that mr Deringę Catechisme[1] shall neuer hereafter be prynted wth the A.B.C. in yt

2 Junij

Jo: Bill }
Edw. Bishop } Are this day by a full Court choseñ to be of the lyu'ye

25 Junij. Ao. suprdicte.

Mr. Easte.
Wm. Barley: Whereas the said ꝑties, Thomas Easte and Wiłłm Barley haue submitted them selues to ꝑforme thorder & determinacoñ of the Mr. Wardens, & Assistentę, of this Company concerninge diu'se settę of songę whereunto the said Thomas Easte hathe right beinge lawfully Entred for his copies, accordinge to the Charter & ordonnancę of the Company: The said Willm̃ makinge a pretence of clayme thereunto by vertue of a łres patentę graunted of Musick bookę by the late Quene Elizabeth to Tho. Morley whose Interest therein the said Wiłłm claymeth to haue. Nowe vppoñ the delib̃ate hearinge & consideracoñ of the said cause yt is by the said Mayster, Wardens, and Assistentę, by thassent of the said ꝑties, ordered as folowth.[2] Videlicit, That the said Tho. East & his wyfe and the longer lyuer of them duringe their lyves and the lyfe of the Longer lyuer of them̃ shall accordinge to the Charter & ordonnancę of the said Company, Aswell Enioye all the settę of songę & musicke bookę whiche were Entred & Registred for the said Thomas Eastę Copies in the said Companye before this present Day of the Date hereof, As also ymprint eu'y of the same in the name or names of the said Wiłłm his ex'. ad'. or ass': and make sale of eury of the same at all tymes hereafter at the will & pleasure of the sayd Thomas & his wyfe and the survivor of them̃ and to their owne benefit & behoof. And that the said wiłłm his ex'. Ad'. or ass' or any other clayminge from̃ or vnder the Tytle of the said Morley shall not Deale or intermeddle with the printinge of any of them in ꝑte or in all wthout the consent of the said Thom̃s East & his wife or one of them. In regard whereof and for the settlinge of a finall ende & agrement of all questions and controu'sies all-ready moued or begũne concerninge any thinge heretofore attempted or Doñe by force of the said łres patentę or pretended to be doñe against any matter or thinge therein conteined,: Yt is ordered that the said Tho. East & his wyfe duringe their said lyves and the lyfe of the longer lyuer of them̃, from̃ tyme to tyme hereafter

[1] STC 6682. Richard Bankworth's part in this book cannot be determined. James Roberts derived his copyright from J. Charlewood (Arber ii. 652, 31 May 1594).

[2] Under this agreement T. East published in 1606, as the 'assigne of W. Barley', STC 18123, which East had entered 6 Dec. 1596; the following year, 1607, he published, again as the assign of Barley, STC 4243, which East had entered subsequent to this agreement 19 Feb. 1607; in 1608 East published two books as the assign of Barley, STC 25204 and 26105. The first East had entered 7 Aug. 1598, while the second was not entered until 25 Sept. 1607. By 7 Nov. 1608 East was dead (*C–B.C*, 19b), but his widow, Lucretia, as the assign of Barley, in 1610 re-published STC 4257 (=4258), which East had entered 6 Dec. 1596.

so often as they or either of them shalbe resolued to prynte any of the said copies Registred as aforesaid, shall thereof gyue notice to the said Willm, and pay vnto hym̃ before the begynnynge of any ympressioñ of any suche sett of songꝭ Twenty shillingꝭ And shall also allwaies delyuer vnto hym̃ w^th^in Seven dayes after the fynishinge of euery suche ympressioñ Sixe settꝭ of the same songe bookꝭ so prynted/ And lastly the said Thom̃s & Willm hereby doo Assent & agree, And wth their consentꝭ yt is ordered, That they and either of them̃ for their seu'all ꝑtes, and all others that may clayme from̃ or vnder them or either of them, for & in all questions that may arise concerninge any matter to be moued or pretended vppoñ or touchinge any of the premisses or any other thinge heretofore doñe concerninge any matter supposed to ꝑteyne to the graunt conteined in the said letters patent shall alwayes ꝑforme suche order & Determinacõn as in that behalf shalbe made by the M^r^. Wardens, & Assistentꝭ, of the said Company for the tyme beinge or the moore ꝑte of them̃ W^th^out further strife quarrell or Controu'sie in any Wise

By mee Thomas Este:
William Barley

FOL. 10^a^

.1606. 4 R.

4. Julij

M^r^. Barker. m^r^
M^r^. White
m^r^. Leake } Wardens

M^r^. Barker
m^r^. Dawson.

m^r^ Dawson yeildeth vp. the testam^t^ in .8. to m^r^ Baker.

M^r^. Barker vndertaketh the paym^t^ of .400^li^ to the ꝑten's in the p'uilegꝭ to their own vse/

He nowe payeth the first 100^li^ thereof/

M^d^. that m^r^. Barker in consideracõn that m^r^ Dawson: Hathe Remitted and yeilded vp vnto hym̃, all the full Right Interest & Clayme to the printinge of the book of holy Scripture called the newe Testament in the volume called .Octauo. of m^r^ Cheakꝭ translation/[1] hathe Vndertakeñ and Agreed to pay vnto the ꝑten's in the preuileges to their owñ ꝓp vse, ffowre hundred poundꝭ either [out] of his diuid^te^ of his ꝑte in the said p'uilegꝭ, as they shall growe due, vntyll they Amount to so muche Or els in some spedyer sorte as he shall thinke conuenient: Be yt remembred that oñ this present day m^r^ Barker hathe payd vnto the said ꝑten's, Aswell Twenty poundꝭ whiche he Receaued for the Diuid^t^ of his ꝑte Vppoñ the Diuid^t^ made this day. As also ffowre score poundꝭ moore in present money. Whiche maketh vp one Hundred poundꝭ. And is the first hundred poundꝭ ꝑcell of the said. ffowre hundred poundꝭ/

[1] Originally the privilege for printing *New Testaments* in 8° had belonged to Richard Jugge and was later, apparently, exercised by his son-in-law Richard Watkins. T. Dawson was the apprentice of Jugge and partner of Thomas Gardiner, who had been partner with Watkins. When Christopher Barker obtained his patent for Bibles Dawson was generally the 'Deputy' who printed the Bishops' version of the *N.T.* in 8° (e.g. STC 2893, 2897, and 2904). On 12 Apr. 1591 (*Reg. B*, 452^a^) Dawson agreed to pay to the use of the poor £5. 5*s*. 'for suche Impressions as he is behind for of the Testam^te^ in 8 and .16. and for one Impression nowe in hand of that in, 8/.' So far as can be seen Dawson's rights were based merely on the fact that he had for several decades printed the 8° *N.T.* as deputy of Barker.

The attribution of the Bishops' *N.T.* to Cheke is apparently an error.

.11. Julij 1606. 4 Rs FOL. 10b

Edmond More Porter. Vppon his peticõn and vppoñ Condycoñ that he Contynue of good behavyor to the Companye The Company by A Court holdeñ this day haue Increased his wage And made yt nowe from hensforth

xxvjs viijd a yere. viz. vjs viijd a quarter for servinge the portership of the Companye

.11. Julij. 1606. 4to Ris

Mr. Burby Memorand that where Cuthbert Burbie did heretofore receaue at and by the hande of Mr Thomas [*Easte*] Dawson and Mr Humfrey [*Lownes*] Hooper in the tyme of their wardenships. of Mr John Norton & mr William Leake in the tyme also of their wardenships of Nathaniell Butter Threasorer and of the Stock keepers then beinge at sundrie tymes seu'all somes of money beinge the moneys of this Companie, amountinge in the wholle to the some of One Thowsand One hundred & ffortie pounde, To be ymployed aboute the busines and affayres of the Companie/ It is found and evidentlie appeareth by the Accoumptes of the said Cuthbert Burbie that the wholle some of [the said] One Thousand one hundred and ffortie pounde, hathe by him the same Cuthbert from tyme to tyme bene dewlie & truelie disbursed and laid out in and about the busines and affayres of the said Companie/ And that noñe of the said [*Company*] some of 1140li nowe remaineth in the hande of the said Cuthbte and therefore he is not to be accoumptable for the same or any pte thereof./

Mr Barker Mr

Mr Ed. White, mr Leake } Wrdens

14 Julij

Lent by Mr Barker to the Company to be Repayd vnto him at Michãs next } Lli

14 Julij 1606

Mr Askewe[1] Whereas mr Askewe is a suter to the Companie to be dispensed wth from servinge any of the wardens places, or the Maysters place or any other office in the Companie whensoeu' he shalbe elected to any of the same, and from all other charges services and dueties whatsoeu' to the Companie (Excepte suche quarterage as others of his callinge in the said Companie paye, and all Loanes to the Kinge Matie) And dothe offer xxxli to the Companie for the same Thone half to be paid within iij monethes nexte, and thother half wthin Sixe monethes nowe nexte/ The wch the Companie in good will toward him and vppon his earneste intreatie doo accepte and yeilde to receaue the said xxxli of him in forme aforesaid, wch he promiseth to paye accordinglie to free him as aforesaid/

The first paymt was paid accordingly Teste *Ric' Collins*/

The second paymt was paid accordingly to mr white Warden Teste *Ri: Collins*/

1606. 4 Ris FOL. 11a

20 Julij

Wilłm Cotton is chosen Thrẽr in stede of Na Butter, to the pten's in the pruilege

[1] Admitted freeman 15 July 1591 (Arber i. 545). He was a merchant in Spain, Portugal, and Barbary and apparently not a practising Stationer.

.20. oct' 1606. 4 . Ris

Quarter day

Mr. Dawson — yt is graunted that mr Billage money shalbe Contynued in his hande for another yere vppoñ thassurance of his pte as yt was befor[1]

A viewe for the stocke keps and the clerk — Mr. Norton and mr Hooper are appointed by this Court to Viewe Whiche Rowme will serue the stockekeps and Whiche the Clerk.

A Rowme alowed to the Clerk for the Companyes Busynes — They made their viewe presently, and made their Report to the Court, that the Rowme oñ the southe syd of the yarde next the great warehouse toward the streete ys fytt to be alowed to the clerk—Whereuppoñ yt is graunted to hym̃ accordingly

Wydowe venge 13s. 4d — Gyven this day to wydowe Venge[2] toward her relief } xiijs iiijd.

Wydowe dawson 10s — Gyven Lykewise to wydowe Dawsoñ[3]—xs

mr Dawson. — Payd by mr Dawson to mr [*Leak*] warden Leake. 13s 4d. for the poore in respect he hath in his hande mr Billage money.[4]

10. Novembr

The old hall in Paules Churchyard. — yt is ordered that Edward Kynnaston Vinten'. for xlli Incom̃e. Whereof xli to be payd at Christyde next And the rest by xli eu'y quarter feast day then consequently folowinge shall haue a leas of the old hall wth thapp'tennce in Paules Churcheyard belonginge to the Company for the terme of xxjty yeres from Christmas next for the yerely rent of xlli to be payd at iiij termes of the yere. And he to be at the charg of all repacõns. And to buy thimpedme or els the Company to dispose of them̃ at their pleasure/[5]

adam Islip. for the .Eirenarche. — yt is ordered that Adam Islip shall have ffyve shillinge a reame for printinge this Impression of 1200½. of mr Lamberde Eirenarche.[6] And iijli for the gente that corrected the copie/

Wydowe Oswold — Graunted to wydowe Oswald[7] that pencõn of mr Lambes whiche is nowe voyd/

[1] Cf. *C–B.C*, 6a, 4 Dec. 1604, *et loc. cit.*

[2] Edward Venge must then have died between 2 Dec. 1605, the date of his latest entry in the Registers, and this day.

[3] This must be the widow of Thomas Dawson, Jun., who may then have lived for some years after the latest date hitherto known.

[4] Cf. *C–B.C*, 11a, 20 Oct. 1606.

[5] Cf. *C–B.C*, 18b, 6 Dec. 1608.

[6] STC 15171. From the ornaments this was printed by Islip. The 'gente' has not been identified. His work was apparently limited to adding to the various lists of statutes those of King James.

[7] John Oswald apparently must have died sometime between 1 Oct. 1604 and this date. William Lamb's bequest is described in Arber v. xlvi, and more fully in *Letter Book*, 11a–12a. This pension is a misuse of it, but not the first, cf. *Reg. B*, 6 Dec. 1602, 485a.

Mr. Hyde — The Company haue graunted to mr Hyde their celler in mylkstrete for which he is a suter. To hold from Christmas next for one yere only & no longer yeildinge & payinge therfore vli at ffoure quarterly paymtę by euen porcons. provyded that he is to lay nothing in yt but wynes only wthout the Companyes consent And at thend of this yere he is to yeild it vp vnles he will then gyve asmuch for yt as any other will/

Na Butter wm. Cotton — Yt is ordered that Na buttr shall haue the iiijli and wm. Cotton the vjli for the qrter from mydsom' to michās Last/[1]

29. Januar'.

Ad Islip. Termes of the Lawe. — Yt is ordered that Adam Islip shall print an Impression of xijC.Dd. of the book of the termes of the Lawe.[2] And to haue for his woorkmanship. xvs a heape whiche Amounteth to vjs a reame/

This is respited till another tyme/ — And to print an Impression of viijc of mr Kytchens book of Courtleete & Courtbaron And to haue for the woorkmanship xijs the heap// — vide infer9 3 ffebr'.

3 ffebr'

mr Kytchens book to goo forward — Yt is agred that Adam Islip shall prynt the said 800 of mr Kytchens book[3] and to haue for the printinge xiijs iiijd the heape

A Court eu'y ffortnight for the busynes of the stock/ — Yt is ordered that ones eu'y fortnight there shalbe a Court holden at the hall to take orders for thaffayres of the cōmon stock of the pten's and that no bookę pteyning to the said stock be putt to print wthout consent of the said Court. And the nūber of eu'y ympression and the price of woorkmanship to be appointed and Rated by the said Court/

This order to be duly executed from henceforth/

23 febr' — 2 m'cij

Rafe Blore/ — mr Dawson and mr ffeild to heare & determine the cause betwene Raffe Blore & his woorkmañ. — it is ordered that Raffe blore shall pay to the scottishman that was his Journeman 30s The same to be paid p'sently

And Raffe Blore to haue his forme & heape[4] agayne

[1] Cf. *C–B.C*, 11a, 20 July 1606.

[2] STC 20713. A heap = $2\frac{1}{2}$ reams. The term evidently arose from the practice of limiting an edition to 1,250 copies, each sheet of which would equal a heap.

[3] STC 15023.

[4] R. Blower signed at least four books as printer in 1607, STC 5876, 10159, 11232, and 23607.

Willm Hall/ — Willm Hall ys admitted to be a prynter in the place of Valentine Symmes[1]

Fol. 12ª

1606. 5to .Ris
2 marcij

1607 26. m'cij

Mr. Newton[2]
mr. Bankw'th — Are chosen renters of the Companye and mr newton to be in thelder place this yere

13 april

mres holland. — Gyven to her as a benevolence by a full Court holden this day as a benevolence for her full satisfaccõn for mr Grenhams woorke[3] } xxxs.

Wydowe Day. — Gyven to Richard dayes[4] wydowe for her relief } vijs.

Ad. Islip. — He is to print an Impression of 800.½. of a book of Cannon & civil Lawe.[5] To be prynted at .xs. a heape.
The book is thought to be called reptoriũ canonicũ.

Nic Oake — George Snodan by consent & order of a court holden this day. Resigneth and gyveth ou' to Nic oakes his right & place of printinge which was graunted to Lyonell Snodam and the said Geor in april 1605.[6] Lyonell havinge also heretofore assigned ou' his place therein to the said nic Oake 29 Jan 1606.

mr windett — Mr Windet by a court holden this day is dismissed from thassistentship and from the Lyu'ye. And to take his ease/

Fol. 12b

Chambers appointed and Rente sett down
by order of the Company.

The rente paiable from the feast of the birth of our lord. 1606. 4 Ris To be quarterly paid by equall porcõns. The first paymt begynninge at the feast of Thann'c' of or Lady. 1607 S.R.

Mr Geo. Bysshop. — Alowed to be occupied by hym. the great Chamber next the streete, of the Southside beinge the Churcheside with a studie in it. And he to pay yerely for yt . . . . ijli

[1] It is not known for what offence Simmes was struck off the roll of master printers, but he is not known to have printed any book between 1607 and 1610. Some of his printing materials were acquired by Henry Ballard and Felix Kingston. Cf. *C–B.C*, 13b, 1 June 1607.

[2] Made free 31 Oct. 1583 (Arber ii. 690).

[3] Cf. *C–B.C*, 8b, 7 Oct. 1605.

[4] The date of R.D.'s death has not been established.

[5] Probably an edition of STC 11415, no copy of which has been traced.

[6] Cf. *C–B.C*, 6b, 7 Apr. 1605.

The Parten's of the grãmers accidencę & Dictionaries	Alowed to be occupied by them. the next great chamber toward the streete of the Northside And they to Pay yerely for yt.. ijłi

Mr. Jo. Norton.— Alowed to be occupied by hym, the Chamber next behynd that great Chamber which is for the grãmers Accidencę and Dictionaries. And he to pay yerely for yt........................ jłi.vjs.viijd

Mr. leake nowe yong' warden	Alowed to be occupied by hym. the Chamber and garrett betwene Mr Bysshops Chamber and the grãmer Warehouse. And he to pay yerely for them .... jłivjs. viijd

Mr. Si: Waterson Alowed to be occupied by hym. the Matted Chamber betwene Mr Nortons Chamber and Witłm Aspleyes. And he to paye yerely for yt .... jłi. vjs viijd

Mr Cuth. Burbye. Alowed to be occupied by hym the Chamber next to mr Watersons Chamber And he to pay yerely for yt ...... jłi. vjs. viijd

Wm. Aspley. Alowed to be occupied by hym, the Matted Chamber next behinde Mr Bysshops Chamber And he to pay yerely for yt....
jłi. vjs. viijd

Sm̃ Reddituũ istoꝝ p Annũ } xłi. xiijs iiijd

These alowãncę were made by order of Court.
.10 Novembr 1606. 4 Ris/

1607. 5to. Ris
primo Junij

FOL. 13a

Mr. Stringers preuilege. By a Court holden this day for diu'se good respectę and consideracõns here moued, Yt is ordered and agreed wth gen'all consent of all Whom̃e the case may concerne, that fromhensforthe [there] [*yt*] shall not be prouyded or brought hither from the ꝑties of beyond the seas, Any of the bookę comprised in mr Stringers priuilege and łres patentę[1] Whiche he hathe Assigned to the Company, or by any other right belonginge to the Companie (Except onely a verye fewe, that is to say, not aboue xxvtie of a sorte, in sõme small and extraordinary Volumes, and neither in Octauo. nor Decimo Sexto, nor any in Englishe Whatsoeu': vppoñ payne of forfayture of all Bookę that shalbe brought in contrary to this order and vppon payene of suche fine & further penaltye

[1] Cf. *C–B.C*, 3b, 23 Apr. 1604.

as shalbe adiudged by the Mr. Wardens & assistentℯ for the tyme beinge or the moore pte of them/

Robt Barker
Edward whit
Gre: Seton
John harsyon
William Leake
Thomas Man.
Simon Waterson.
Humfry Hooper
Richard Field
Thomas Este.

FOL. 13b

die et Anno vltim' infrascripte.

R. Raworthe.
wm hall.

Mr. ffeild and mr. Kingston to be surveyors of the printinge house betwene Willm hall and Robert Raworth and to Judge of the pryces and charge thereof that Willm Hall may contribute for his pte to the same as they shall thinke reasonable.[1]

xs. to a pursuy[u]ant

Gyven by consent to a pursuyuant—xs. Whiche was payd by mr white to mr Barker who had deliue'd yt to the pursuyuant

Mr Keylle.

The reu'con of the Clerkship[2] is graunted to mr Keyle when it shall fall voyd

15. Junij

Mr Man thelder
Jo. hardy.[3]

Mr. Tho man thelder vppon the motion and intreaty of the company in Court holden this day is contented And wth his assent yt is ordered that he shall receaue the debt which John Hardye owth him, by xxs. a quarter whiche he shall haue out of John Hardyes wages at the renters handℯ The first payment to begyn at this feast of the Natie. of St John baptist 1607 And the certenty and truthe of the debt to be examined and Determined by mr Leake nowe Warden/

FOL. 14a

.1607. 5to. Ris
.3. Augusti

Mr. Norton. Mr

Mr. Seaton }
Mr. Standishe } Wardeñs.

This day. Mr. White and mr Leake wardens of the Last yere made their accoumpt/
And haue gyven to the house.
viz. mr white. a bole all gilt wth letters for his name.
Item mr Leake a bole all gilt wth [*his*] letters for his name/

[1] It is not clear just whose printing materials are referred to. Among the possible owners are V. Simmes, cf. *C–B.C*, 11b, 23 Feb. 1607; A. Islip, cf. Arber iii. 703–4; and R. Raworth, whose printing office was suppressed about this time for printing *Venus and Adonis*, which was W. Leake's copy, cf. Arber iii. 703–4.

[2] Cf. *Reg. B*, 6 Sept. 1602, 484b. He was made free 13 Jan. 1578 (Arber ii. 675).

[3] Made free 5 Aug. 1594 (Arber ii. 714).

17. Augusti.

Payd to the Collectors in mylkestrete for Two ffiftenes. xxiiij^{s}. for the hall [*in*] there./ Assessed in the Kinge name.

solute p man^{9} mri Standish custodis./

7. Septembr

Katharine Dawson. sueth for the rowme that is nowe voyd of one [of] the Almesfolk of m^{r} Lambes foundacõn.[1] And yt is graunted vnto her/

Jo Hodgette. To haue the vj^{li} w^{che} is nowe to be putt forth vppon sureties accordinge to m^{r} Nortons Will[2] And his sureties were here nominated & accepted. viz. Ni: parke payntersteyn' & henry marshe leatherseller. both of St Gregories pish by Paules

5to. oct

M^{r}. dawson fol. 6. M^{r}. Dawson hath paid to thwardens .xiij^{s} iiij^{d} for m^{r} billage money.[3] And will deliu' an acq[i]tance from the pish for this last yere/ And yt is ordered that he shall haue thoccupyinge of m^{r} Billage L^{li} for another yere after yt shalbe due by thorder of the Last yere/ Vppon the same Assurance of his pte and stocke in the preuilege: as he gave before/ Whereuppon he hath hereby accordingly assigned and sett ou' to the Company his said pte and stocke. vppon condicoñ that this assignemt shalbe voyd yf he pay the said L^{li} at thend of the said yere now graunted. And discharge the Company of the Lij^{s} for this yere to the pish of S^{t} martyn in the Vintry and pay xiij^{s} iiij^{d} to thuse of the poore of the company this yere/

Adam Islip to haues (*sic*) .v^{s}. a reame for the dc'or & student[4]

5to Octobris 1607 5to R^{is} Fol. 14^{b}

Jone Cooke and Sam: Macham It is ordered that shee shall haue [half] of the booke wch Sam: Macham hathe prynted,[5] shee payinge halfe the Charge of the ympression, And likewyse that shee shall haue halfe of the Booke wch he is in hand to prynte shee bearinge halfe the Charge of the ympression./ And like[wise] for all the reste of the Copies that were entred to him and her husband that shee shall haue the halfe of euerye ympression [hereafter] bearinge

[1] Cf. *C–B.C*, 11^{a}, 10 Nov. 1606.

[2] Cf. Greg and Boswell, p. xlix. The bond is entered *Liber C2*, 8^{b}, and cancelled without date.

[3] Cf. *C–B.C*, 6^{a}, 4 Dec. 1604, *et loc. cit.*

[4] STC 21578.

[5] Matthew Cooke and Samuel Macham entered 8 books, STC 3775, 5101, 12642, 12666, 15561, 21461, 24567, and Joseph Hall's *A briefe some* which has not been identified. The two books referred to here might be STC 12643 and 12668. However, since there is a 'Third edition' of STC 3775 dated 1607, that might be one of the books here referred to.

It is of possible relevance to note that Major J. R. Abbey has recently presented to the Stationers' Company a copy of STC 12680 bound with 12643, 12668, and 12671 in a plaque stamped binding with the arms of the Company.

Joan Cooke married Laurence Lisle, a stationer.

halfe the Charge thereof/ And yf she Marrye in the Companye then her intereste to contynue still accordinge to like proporcoñ in all the said bookę, But yf shee Marrye out of the Companye then her said intereste to Cease./ And he from thenceforth to enioy all the said Copies to his owne vse/

.12. Octobr'

A. Islip. yt is ordered that for printinge this ympression of 1500 of my Lo Cokę newe book[1] he shall haue as he had for his Lo. form' booke.

M^r^ warden Tythes — Payd by m^r^ warden Standishe to m^r^ Seton by order of Court—Liij^s^ iiij^d^ for m^r^ Spaght parson in milkstrete for his tithes for a yere endinge at this Michas 1607 } Liij^s^ iiij^d^

Fiftene — paid by m^r^ Standishe to thandę of Ri: Collins to delyuer to the Collectors of the ffiftene in mylkstrete for his ma^te^ ffiftene nowe due } xij^s^.

yt was paid ou' to the Collectors accordingly the same day

Mr Feild — By election and order of Court holden this day m^r^ Feild is dispensed wth for the second yonger Wardenship. And for his discharge from the same by thorder of this Court, hath paid } xx^li^

Debt paid by m^r^ Warden to m^r^ Feild — Payd by m^r^ Warden Standish to Mr Feild as folow^th^ viz ffor a Remayno' of debt owinge to m^r^ Feild Vppon his accoumpt of Wardenship xv^li^ vij^s^. iij^d^. wch makes full satisfaccoñ of the debt owinge to hym vpon the same accoumpt } xv^li^. vij^s^. iij^d^

Item paid vnto him vij^s^ vj^d^ moore for a debt owinge to him by m^r^ Rogers and ꝑteyninge to the same accoumpt } vij^s^. vj^d^

FOL. 15^a^

.1607. 5. Ris.

12. octobr

M^r^. Bowker. Wiłłm Bowker one of my Lo. maio^rs^ offycers[2] is chosen to serue the Companye in y^t^ place whiche m^r^ Dodde deceased Late serued them. And m^r^ Bowker to attend eu'y quarter day vppon the Company and otherwise as he shalbe called to serue. And in respect of his good seruice to be done therein. there is graunted to hym̄ an yerely stipend of xxvj^s^ viij^d^ by the yere Whiche is moore by xiij^s^ iiij^d^ then m^r^ dod had.

[1] STC 5509. The amount he was paid for the 'form' booke' is not recorded.
[2] Cf. *Reg. B*, 3 Dec. 1593, 458^a^.

The names of the suters for the lyu'ie pte wch is voyd. and Lykewise for the yomans pte.[1]

For the lyu'y pte.	For the yomanry pte.	
M[r]. Grene.	Ric. Boyle.	
m[r] Windet.	Willm Hall	
M[r]. Braddock.	Jo. ward.	
M[r]. Newtoñ	Jo. Busby	Brethrẽ dn'n als clothin'
W[m]. Smith.	Leon'd Kempe. who offereth yf he have it to gyve his profitt thereof to the Company for the first yere. And yf he die [vnmarried][*within that yere*] then to gyue them the whole stock	Tho. Watsons
M[r] W[m]. Jones.		ma Selman
M[r]. Knight		Walt' burr
M[r]. Pavyer/		Jo. Rodwell
Jo. Herbert/		Jo beale
Edw. Romeney		phip harison
Jo. Tape/		Sa. Macham
Raffe Blore 1594/	Tho. Snodam̃ Alias East } sueth for half this yomans pte having alredy half a like pte wth m[r] knight.	Jonas man
Tho. Downe[s]/		Jo. Bas.[2]
Jo Budge.		Geo. Eld
Jo Hardy/		Edw Aggas
Ri. Bonyon.		Jo Combe
Robert Jackson	Ri. Tom̃es.	
W[m]. James	[*W[m]. Smythe*]	
W[m] Barley.	Hen: Tom̃es.	
Jo. Bache.	Willm Jaggerd	
Rob. Triplet.	Roger Jackson.	
Na. ffosbrook	Henr' Cooke/	
Lau' Lyle.	W[m]. Welby.	
T. archer	Melchisedeck Bradwood	
w[m]. Haulton	Arnalt Hatfeild	
	ar'. Johnson	
	Jo. Bathoe	
	Michaell Baker.	
	Willm Blackwall	
	Tho. Vautrollyer.	
	Edm yate	
	ar'. Collins/	
	Fr'. Burton	
	andr' Hill	
	Tho. Drap[3]	
	Ri. Hudson	

[1] These lists were not all written at one time. The list of liverymen, arranged in the order of their clothing, originally ended with Pavier. The other names in that column, with one or two exceptions, were apparently applicants for the yeomanry part. The original list of yeomen, likewise arranged in the order of their freedom, ends with Welby. Several of the names do not occur in the dictionaries of English printers, but all except Thomas Watson are to be found in Arber. It is likely that Watson was not a stationer and that that is the meaning of the heading immediately above his name, but the stationers whose names follow were all freemen. Beale and Man, however, did not become members until after the date of this entry.

[2] Barnes.

[3] Cf. Arber ii. 738.

.1607. 5to. Ris
26: Octobr

Mr. Edwrd white Sen'. Whereas. mr Edwrd white sen' hathe caused an Impression to be prynted for hym by Edwrd aldee of the .A.B.C. for Children[1] contrary to thorders of the Company. Yt is ordered that mr white shall forfayt all the booke of the said ympression whiche he hathe nowe left and not sold away. And that he shall presently brynge them into the hall to be disposed as forfayted accordinge to thorders of the Company.

Mr white And also that he shall paye xxs for a fine for transgressinge thorders in that behalf

Edw. Aldee And that Edw. Aldee shall pay xs for a fine for printinge the said booke wthout order.

The said fines to be paid on Monday the 2. of Nouemb next. Wch is the next Court Day.

2 nov.

Edw. aldee Red of him for his fine as is aboue sett downe[2].....xs.

Chosen into the Lyu'ie this day. Edm. Weaver, ffelix Kingston, Adam Islap, Wm. Cotton, Henr. Cook — They are to be sett according to their Anncienty when they be sett downe in the Booke of the Lyuerye

1607 :16. Nov.

Ma lawe solut yt is ordered that he shall pay xiijs iiijd for a Fine[3] for disobedience to the Mr & Wardens & other offence done in the Companye and beside to be comitted to prison

1606 17. nov.

Mr norton Whereas henry holland[4] is thapprent' of mr Jo. Norton for the terme of Nyne yeres wch shall expire at the feast of St Michaell tharchangell next. Yt is agreed And the said Jo Norton is content [*this*] That from this day till the said feast of St Michaell next the said Henry may employ him self wth any freeman of the company of Stac' in servyce, Or Remayne wth his parente wthout any advantage therfore to be taken of any bond made either by him self or any of his friende and wthout barringe him of his freedome for the same cause.

1 No copy traced.

2 Cf. *Book of Fines*, 2a, 2 Nov. and 7 Nov. 1607, when White paid his fine.

3 Cf. ibid., 1b, 26 Mar. 1608.

4 Bound 26 June 1599 (Arber ii. 237), free 5 Dec. 1608 (Arber iii. 683).

1607. 5 Ris
7 Decembr' — Fol. 16a

Entrance of copie to none but Resiantę in & about London.

Yt is thought meete and so ordered by a full Cour (*sic*) of the Maister, Wardens and assistentę holden this day. That the wardens of this Company shall not hereafter assigne appoint or suffer to be entered or Registred in this Companye, Any Copye or booke whatsoeu', for any ꝑson or ꝑsons but suche onely (& none other) as shalbe Resiant and dwellinge here amongst the Companye in and about the citie of London and be contributors to all charges of the companie. And that no prynter nor any other ꝑson or ꝑsons of this Company Shall by any vnderhand or overt dealinge, assiste, further, Ayde, or Helpe any ꝑson or ꝑsons to Haue gett or prynte any Copie or booke in ꝑte or in all contrary to the true meaninge of this order, or that shalbe to be prynted or Authorised here or els where beinge not first entred and registred in this Companie. Vppoñ payne to be punished for doinge to the contrary of this Last clause or Article, Accordinge to the qualitie of thoffence by Fine, Forfaiture, ymprisonment or otherwise accordinge to the discretioñ of the Maister, Wardens, and Assistentę, for the tyme beinge or the moore ꝑte of them.[1]

16. April' 1608. .6. Ris
divident day

Lent by mr Standishe Warden, by consent of or Mr & the Rest. out of the [Hall] stocke, to the stocekeꝑs .xxxli. for this tyme to be vsed toward the dyvident. and to be Repayd from the ꝑtible stock/

Whereof xli was deliu'ed back agayne So resteth due from the stock—xxli wch. xxli. was paid by mr Leake to mr Standish .21. July. 1608.6.Ris from thaccoumpt of the stockekeꝑs.

1607. .5. Ris
Primis Martij. — Fol. 16b

This day the ꝑten's in the p'uilegę were assembled in the hall, and called by their names as they were sett downe in a book made for that purpose/

Willm Cotton is chosen Treasorer agayne for the next yere/

Stockeꝑs chosen for the next yere/
viz

of thassistentę	mr Leake mr Feild
Of the lyu'ie	mr [*Ockold*] Pavier/ mr Kingston
Of the yomanry	Rob. Bolton Jo. Harrison the yongest.

[1] Another attempt to control this practice was made by the Company 19 Jan. 1598, cf. *Reg. B*, 464b.

Auditors Chosen for the pfectinge & fynishinge of this yeres accoumpt.

Of thassistente } Mr. Waterson. Mr. Hoop.

Of the lyu'ye } Mr. Dight Mr. Weaver.

Of the yomanry } Edw. Aldee Jo. Tap.

Here the newe Ordonnance were redd vnto all the pteners. But after yt was concluded by most Voyces. that the yonger Warden should not alwaies be a stockep

FOL. 17a .1608. .6. Ris.

A note of mr. Burbyes will/ for xxli by hym bequethed to be lent from 3 yeres to 3 yeres. to 2. poore yongemen bookesellers free of the Comp. of Stac'/

Mr. Burbies Will[1] I will that my Executrix shall pay and delyuer into the hande of the Mr. & wardens of the Company of Stacõners for the tyme beinge, within Sixe monethes next after my deceas, the sõme of Twentye pounde to be lent vnto .2. poore yonge men bookesellers free of the same Companye, Either of the said yonge men to haue xli a pece in vse & occupyinge for the terme & space of 3 yeres without payinge any interest or any other consideracon for the same And to becõme bound with .2. sufficient suerties wth either of them vnto the Mayster and Wardens of the same Companie for the tyme beinge to repay the said seu'all xli to either of them Lent at the ende of 3 yeres next after the lendinge thereof And after the first 3 yeres expired the same xli to be lent to .2. other poore yonge meñ bookesellers for other .3. yeres And so from 3 yeres to 3 yeres to be employed for euer.

This will is dated . 24 Augusti 1605.[2] 5 Ris

2 maij. 1608. 6 regis.

Mystres Elizabeth Burbye executrice to Cuthbert Burby her late husband paid the same xxli. into thande of the mr and Wardens of the Company. And had an acquitance from them vnder their hande and seales for the same. Mr. Jo. Norton then beinge mr. Mr Seton and Mr. Standish then wardens.

Also shee paid vnto them at the same tyme .xls. whiche her husband, hathe by his will bequeathed to be distributed amongst the poorest and most nediest psons in this Companye.///

Augmentacon of Alowance tow'd the quarter dynn's. .6. Junij

Vppon good delibacoñ & consideracoñ it is ordered, yt ye form' alowance[3] of vli a yere alowed to ye wardens toward the foure quarter dynn's for ye company shall from henceforthe be made xli a yere. And ye first xli to be alowed to the nowe wardeñs at mydsom' next

[1] Cf. Plomer, *Wills*, p. 41. Other similar funds which the Company could lend without interest had been bequeathed by W. Norton, 14 Dec. 1593, T. Stuckey, 2 May 1597, and R. Dexter, 16 Oct. 1604. The bonds of money lent under Burby's bequest are recorded in *Liber C2*, 184–5.

[2] Actually it is dated 1607.

[3] There appears to be no record of this former allowance, although cf. *Reg. B*, 4 Oct. 1585, 438a.

Augmentacoñ of yᵉ Cooke̜ fee/ Also yt is ordered [yᵗ yᵉ cooke̜ fee][1] shall from hensforth be made ffowre m'ke̜ a yere And he in respect thereof to satisfie all servante̜ & wʳkmen that he shall employe vnder him in his & yᵉ companies s'uice And the ffirst Mark to be paid at mydsom' next/

.1608. .6. Ris/ Fol. 17ᵇ

.6. Junij

Mystres Bysshop wyfe of Mʳ Geo. Bysshop. Mystres Bysshop hathe of her owne motion & voluntary good will freely gyven to the Company. A table cloathe, A towell, and Twoo Dozen of napkyns, wrought with white Layde woorke/ The whiche were Delyuered to mʳ Seton and mʳ Standish Wardens, at a court holden this daye/

Mʳ· Hooper Mʳ
Mʳ. Bysshop }
Mʳ. H. lownes } Wardeñs

1608. Ris Fol. 18ᵃ

2 Augusti

The copie of a Warrant for the booke of Rates.

fforasmuch as the Kinge̜ most excellent Maᵗⁱᵉ. in the Second yeare of his Raigne of great Brittayne caused a newe Booke of Rates for the Custome & Subsidye of poundage[2] to be made, and that in respect of yᵉ gen'all vse thereof the same was p'sently to be printed, And in regard of yᵉ great Corrupcoñ yᵗ aforetyme grewe in the printinge of the former Booke of Rates, yt pleased the LL. of his Maᵗᵉ. most Ho'ᵇˡᵉ. privye Counsell by Warrant vnder their hande̜ to Co͞mitt the printinge thereof vnto *Richard Lever* and *William Elmhurst* twoo Clerke̜ of the Custome-house of London forbiddinge all others to intermeddle therewith as by the same warrant appeareth. And nowe that his maᵗⁱᵉ. is pleased to sett newe Imposicõns vpon diverse Co͞modityes, and by his Highnes lrẽs patente̜ thereof hath Co͞maunded yᵗ neyther the Rates of Imposicõns nor the sayd Rates of Custome and Subsidy be printed by any but only by suche as shalbe nomynated and appoynted thereto by the L. Trẽr of Englande for the tyme beeinge. And forasmuch as yt is thought meetest yᵗ the Rates of the same Imposicõns should bee printed in one booke together wᵗʰ the Rates of Subsidy, I haue hereby nominated & appoynted the sayd *Richard Lever* and *William Elmhurst* as fittest men to vndertake the Charge and Care of printinge aswell of the sayd Rates of Imposicõns as of the Custome and Subsidye/ These are therefore by vertue of his Maᵗᵉ. sayd lrẽs patente̜, and accordinge to their LLᵖˢ. sayd warrante to will and co͞maunde yoᵘ and eu'y of yoᵘ. whome yt may any way concerne, that p'sently vpon the sight hereof yoᵘ take suche notice of this his Maᵗᵉ. pleasure yᵗ noe Impression neyther of the sayd Rates of Imposicõns, nor of the sayd Rates of Custome and Subsidy be hereafter made, but att the appoyntmᵗᵉ. direccõn, disposinge, and ou'sight of

[1] Cf. *C–B.C*, 1ᵃ, 29 Oct. 1602. The cook was paid 26*s*. 8*d*. in 1577 and the butler 13*s*. 4*d*. at the same time. As the cook now was expected to pay all his assistants, an increase of 1 mark to £2. 12*s*. 16*d*. is not unreasonable. The fees paid to Reginald Foord in 1589 (cf. *Reg. B*, 16 Jan. 1589, fol. 447ᵇ, and comment, p. xxxviii) are unintelligible.

[2] A copy of this edition, a quarto, with colophon reading 'At London Printed by G. E. the Assigne of Richard Lever and William Elmhirst, and are by them to be sould at the Customehouse in London. 1604', is in the Folger Library. This revision was made after Chief Baron Fleming's famous decision in the case of John Bate.

the sayd *Richard Lever* and *William Elmhurste* vpon payne not only of Confiscacõn of all suche bookẹ as shalbe otherwyse printed, but also suche further punishm^te. as shalbe fitt to be inflicted for suche a Contempte/. And Whereas a newe Impression of the sayd Book of Rates of Subsedye[1] is nowe in hand by the direccõn of the sayd *Richard Lever* and *William Elmhurste,* but stayed att the procurem^te. of one *Alde.* These are also to require yo^u. to permitt the same Impression to proceede by the direccõn of the sayd *Richard Lever* and *William Elmhurst* notw^th standinge anye staye or restraynt whatsoeu'/. And hereof fayle you not as you Will answere the Contrary att yor. ꝑills/. Att White hall this xxx^th of Julye 1608

R. Salisburye/.
Jul. Cæsar./.

To the m^r and wardens of the Companye of Stacõn's in London, and to all others his Ma^tẹ. Officers and louinge Subiectẹ whome yt may concerne & eu'y of them/.

Fol. 18^b

1608. .6. Ris

3 Octobr

Quarterne bookẹ	Itt is ordered that noe q^rtayne[2] bookẹ shalbe allowed henceforth of any sort of Bookẹ from the stocke of the ꝑtn's, to any ꝑson except he buy a quarterne together of one sorte of bookẹ/.

11 oct'

m^r Billagẹ money. fol. 6.	Mr Dawson this day paid to m^r Lownes Warden. xiij^s iiij^d due for a quarter at michãs Last for m^r Billagẹ money[3] And his money Remayning in m^r Dawsons handẹ to be renewed vnto him for another yere vppon the form' assurance/	
Tho man Jun' Jo Tappe	Rẹ^d of Tho man in respect of copies graunted to him wth the half ꝑte of thart of navigation[4]	vj^s viij^d
	And of Jo Tap in respect thother half of the art of navigation is entred to him/	iij^s iiij^d
Rob. Lawe	Giuen to Robert Lawe[5] vpon his peticõn for his releife his house beeinge visitted	xx^s
A poore boye	Giuen to a poore boy that discou'ed c'tayne prim̃ers—xiij^s iiij^d	

[1] STC 7691. Edward Allde may have claimed rights in this book under the original entry of his father John Allde, 1561–2 (Arber i. 177), and the fact that both he and his father had printed editions in 1567 (copy SAL.), 1582 (STC 7689), 1587 (copy SAL.), and 1590 (STC 7690).

[2] Quartern = 25 copies. Presumably in this instance the word also refers to an extra copy given to a purchaser of two dozen copies on the principle of a 'baker's dozen'.

[3] Cf. *C–B.C,* 6^a, 4 Dec. 1604, *et loc. cit.*

[4] Cf. Arber iii. 412, 16 June 1609, where Man's copies are entered, and iii. 393, 7 Nov. 1608, where STC 5804 is entered to Tapp and Man.

[5] Neither Law nor his house can be identified.

6. Decembr

Mr. Kynnaston 20li.

The Company at this Court haue consented to accept of mr. Kynnaston for their ymplemtes[1] whiche were left in thold hall in paules churchyard the sõme of xxli
To be paid in this man'. viz

In hand betwene this & Christmas next	vli
On the 25th day of m'ch next	xli
And on the 24th day of June next	vli

1608. 6to Regis/. Fol. 19a

16to Decembris

Geo. Shawe/. John Heaz/.

Itt is ordered & agreed wth thassent of the ptyes that John Heaz[2] ffounder shall haue vs a qrter out of George Shawes pencõn in the hall duringe their Twoo liues toward suche debte & dam̃ages as the sayd Heaz hath payd & is to pay for the sayd Shawe/.

mr Lownes warden

Rd of mr Lownes xxs due att Michãs last & this Christmas 1608. 6to Regis from mr Shortę bequest[3] for twoo qrters } xxs/.

mr Ashe/.

Whereas mr Tho. Ashe esqr hath deliu'ed into thandę of the Compnie. of Stacõn's the Copye of a booke intituled *Epychaia*[4] or a table for thexposicõn of Statutę by an equitye, The wche they haue by his assent caused nowe to be printed, And for the same haue giuen him a c'tayne sũme of money in hand. Neu'theles ytt is nowe ordered by a full Courte holden this day, That the sayd mr Ashe att suche tyme as the sayd booke shalbe agayne ymprinted (yf hee be then liuinge) shall haue Tenne poundę more in money, Provided that yf there bee any impfeccõns in the sayd booke, That then in consideracõn of the same 10li soe to be payd to him he shall correcte the sayd impfeccõns att the same second ymp'ssion/.

:7. octobr'

mr Lownes Losse by corne

The stocke att the nexte diuident to pay mr Lownes the losse and charge of the Corne;[5] The wche the house accompte to allowe agayne to the stocke as yt shalbe hable/./

.11. oct'.

mr Dawson for mr Billagę money/. fol. 6.

mr Dawson this day payd to mr Lownes warden xiijs iiijd due att michaelmas for mr Billagę money[6] } xiijs iiijd

And it is graunted that mr Billagę money remayninge in mr Dawsons handę shall continue in his handę for another yeare vpon the former assurance and in all respectę as before payinge as he vseth to pay/.

11 oct'/.

[1] Cf. *C–B.C*, 11a, 10 Nov. 1606.

[2] There appears to be no record of Heaz (Hayes or Haas?) as a type-founder. Shaw may have been the one apprenticed to R. Warde, 25 Nov. 1577 (Arber ii. 82).

[3] Cf. *C–B.C*, 3a, 12 Mar. 1604.

[4] STC 840, cf. *C–B.C*, 35b, 14 Oct. 1614.

[5] No other reference to Lownes's financing of this year's Corn Money has been found.

[6] Cf. *C–B.C*, 6a, 4 Dec. 1604, *et loc. cit.*

FOL. 19b

1608. 6 Ris
.27. Septembr'

Audito's chosen for thaccoumpt of the preuileges this day

Of thassistents

Mr. Hooper. elder warden
Mr. Standyshe/

Of the lyu'ye

Mr. Adams.
Mr. Bill.

Of the yomanry/

Ma. Selman.
Na. Butter.

.19. Octobr'

Wm Hall
Tho. Havilond

This day vpon the sute of William Hall and Thomas Havylond/ They haue the Consent of the Company in full Courte holden this day to Contracte wth Richard Braddocke for his printinge stuffe & to vse the same themselues in their arte of printinge as pteners in one printinge house/.[1]

7 Nouembris

Tho Snodham a mr prynter

The mr, wardens, & Assistants in full Courte haue ordered & graunted this day, That Thomas Snodham shalbe from henceforth a mr printer in stead of mr Easte printer deceased[2] whose printinge stuffe, presses, lrẽs, & printinge stuffe he hath bought of mystres Easte executrice to her husband/.

FOL. 20a

1608. 6to. Ris
Primo Martij

This day the pteners in the p'uileges were assembled in the hall. and called by their names as they are sett downe in ye booke for that prpose

And here the ordonnances concerning the Kings graunt[3] were Redd vnto them.

Andrwe hill beinge deceased. Melchisedeck Bradwood hath his half pte.

Also Andrewe hill[4] a pten' for [half] a yomans pte beinge Lately deceased: An election of another of the yomanry in his stede was made by scrutinie accordinge to the said ordonnances. And thelection fell vppon Melchisedeck Bradwood. Who here took his oathe for the same accordinge to the sayde ordonnãnces

[1] Cf. *C–B.C*, 11b, 23 Feb. 1607, Hall admitted to be a printer. This transaction was apparently carried out, for McKerrow Device No. 207 was used by Hall in STC 18620, No. 280 in STC 22375, and No. 346 passed from these partners to J. Beale.

[2] The date of Thomas East's death has not been established.

[3] Cf. text as printed, Arber iii. 42–44.

[4] Admitted a freeman 7 Aug. 1592 (Arber ii. 711).

Stockekeps chosen for the next yere and havinge taken their oathes accordinge to the said ordonnãnce

viz

Of thassistente	mr white Sen' mr waterson
Of the lyu'ie	mr. Ockold mr. Smythe.[1]
Of the yomañry	Roger Jackson Phillip Harrison [*Roger Jackson*]/

Auditors chosen for the pfectinge of the yeres Accoumpt.

Of thassistente	mr man Sen' mr Standishe
Of the lyu'ie	mr Bankworth mr. Gilman
Of the yomanry	Josias parnell wm Jaggrd
Treasorer	Willm Cotton chosen agayne for the next yere & havinge taken his oathe accordinge to the said ordonnance/[2]

1609. 7 Ris **Fol. 20b**

27 m'cij

Mr. orrian[3]	yt is ordered that he shall pay. xxli for his dispensation from not servinge the rentership	xxli	paid in the wardens accoumpt
Mr. Gilman	he is chosen renter and hath taken it vpon him/		

2do. Maij

Henry Ballerd beinge deceased, William Jaggerd hath his halfe pte/.	Henry Ballerd a pten' for half a yeomans [pte] beinge deceased & his wyfe nowe marryed ;[4] An eleccõn of another of the yeomanry in his steed was made by scruteny accordinge to thordinãnce, And theleccõn fell vpon William Jaggerd who here tooke his oathe for the same accordinge to the ordinãnce/.

[1] Presumably John Smythe.

[2] Cf. *C–B.C*, 16b, 1 Mar. 1608.

[3] Allan Orrian, cf. Arber ii. 132. This was paid 6 May 1609, see *Book of Fines*, 3b.

[4] As Ballard printed several books in 1608, and possibly one in 1609, his widow apparently lost little time.

2. Junij

Edm. Yate deceased Symon Woodcocke hath his half ꝑte.
21.

Edmond Yate[1] a ꝑten' for half a yeomans ꝑte, beinge deceased vnmaried. Thelection of another of the yomanry in his stede was made this day by scrutenye accordinge to thordonãncɇ And thelection fell vppon Symeon Woodcocke who here took his oathe for the same accordinglye

Fol. 21^{a} Mr Dawson mr.
Mr Waterson }
Mr Standishe } wardens/.

1609. 7mo. Regis/.
Die lunae 24to. Julij Court day/.

Wydowe Vautroliers half ꝑte
20

M^{d} that Symoñ Woodcocke. Johñ Hothe & John Rodwell were suters for wydowe Vautrolyers[2] half of a yomans ꝑte. And the same beinge putt to scrutynie this day. Thelection fallɇ vppon Symon woodcocke who by vertue thereof is to eñioye the same/

16. Octobr'

one of mistres Burbies ꝑtes.

One of mystres Burbies[3] ꝑtes whiche was moore then she should haue was putt to election by scrutinie And m^{r} Lawe, m^{r} Serger, m^{r} Bateman,[4] m^{r} Bradwood, m^{r} Bolton and m^{r} Vincent, beinge in nomination for yt. the election by most voyces fell vppon m^{r} Lawe and m^{r}. Bolton.//

21 octobr'

Thother of m^{res} Burbies ꝑtes.

Thother of mystres Burbies ꝑtes (She beinge nowe married[5]) was putt to eleccon by scrutinie. And m^{r} Serger. m^{r} Bateman, m^{r} Bradwood and m^{r} Vincent beinge in nõiacon for yt, theleccon by most Voyces fell vppon m^{r} Bateman & m^{r} Bradwood./

Poore

Paid this 23 of oct' by m^{r} warden Standish to the coll'tors of mylkestrete[6] for the poore for 2 quarters ending at this michãs 1609. after 18^{d} ꝑ weeke........................39^{s}.

2 arrestɇ.

Paid to m^{r} Sharpe thofficer for 2 arrestɇ.......2^{s}.

M^{r}. Dawson m^{r}.: for m^{r} billagɇ 13^{s}.4^{d}
fol. 6

M^{d} that on the 3 of this october m^{r} Dawson paid to Thwardens for m^{r} Billagɇ moneye[7] dewe at this michãs 1609......13^{s}.4^{d}

[1] Yate only took up his freedom in 1605.

[2] The widow of Thomas Vautrollier, Jun., cf. Arber ii. 737. Why Woodcock, who did not take up his freedom until 7 Dec. 1607 (Arber iii. 683), should have been preferred at this and the preceding court over J. Hoth, who was admitted 24 Apr. 1598 (Arber ii. 720), and J. Rothwell, who was admitted 7 Apr. 1600 (Arber ii. 725), is not apparent.

[3] Burby had been a leader in the organization of this stock, cf. *C–B.C*, 4^{b}, 31 July 1604.

[4] John Bateman, admitted freeman 14 Jan. 1580, Arber ii. 681.

[5] She married Humphrey Turner, cf. *C–B.C*, 37^{a}, 13 Feb. 1615.

[6] This contribution was for the Old Hall property in Milk Street.

[7] Cf. *C–B.C*, 6^{a}, 4 Dec. 1604, *et loc. cit.*

mr Burbies Will

A note of mr Burbies Will[1]

The surplusage or ou'plus of myne owne third pte to my self reserued as is aforesaid wch shall [then] remaine after my fun'all chargę and legacies before bequeathed be paid and discharged I fully and wholy gyve & bequeathe to my sõne Edw'd Burbye to be paid to him at his full age of 21. yeres And if he happen to die before he cõme to full age then the same to be paid to & amongest all other my children pte & ptelike at their seu'all ages or dayes of mariage first happeninge.

The companye The wche said surplusage or ou'plus of myne owne third pte I will that my executrix shall wthin 2 yeres next after my deceas pay & delyuer into the handę and Custodye of the mr. Wardens & Assistantę of the Company of Stacõners to be by them either lent vnto yonge men of the same Companie vppon securitie or otherwise emploied duringe my sõnes minoritie as they shall thinke meete So as they doo gyve alowãnce for vli for eu'y Cli thereof vnto my wyfe for & toward my Childrens education and maynetenãce/

1609. 7 Ris
30. Octobr' FOL. 21b

mr Adams. Wm Barley. Whereas the saide pties Thomas Adams and Wylliam Barley have submytted themselves to pforme the order of the mr Wardens & Assistentę of this Company Concerninge all suche settę of songes wherevnto the said Thomas Adams hathe right beinge lawfully entred for his Copies accordinge to the Charter and Ordinances of the Company the said wylliam makinge a pretence of Clayme thereto by vertue of a lrẽs patentę graunted of musique bookes by the late Quene Elisabeth to Thomas Morley[2] whose interest therein the said Wylliam Claymeth to have./ Nowe vpon the deliberate heringe and Consideracon of the said Cause, yt is by the said Mr Wardens & Assistentę with thassent of the said pties ordered as foloweth. Viz. That the said Thomas Adams duringe his lyfe shall according to the Charter and ordinãncę of the said Company aswell enioye all the settę of songę & musicke bookę which were entred and registred for the said Thomas Adams Copies in the said Company before this pñte daie of the date hereof As alsoe ymprinte euery of the same in the name or names of the said Wylliam his executors admĩstr' or assignes & make sale of euery of them at all tymes hereafter at the will & pleasure of the said Thomas Adams & to his owne benefit & behouf And that the said Wylliam his executors admĩstr' or assigns or any other Clayminge from or vnder the title of the said Morley shall not deale or entermeddle with the printinge of any of them in pte or in all withoute the Consente of the said Thomas Adams./ In regard whereof & for the settinge of a finall ende & agrement of all questions & Controuersies already moved or begunne Concerninge any thinge heretofore attempted or done by force of the said

[1] Cf. *C–B.C*, 17a, 2 May 1608, and references there made.

[2] Morley's patent was similarly enforced against T. East, cf. *C–B.C*, 9b, 25 June 1606. The terms here set forth, however, can have profited Barley very little, for Adams apparently did not republish any of his new music publications (e.g. STC 7099, 7100, 18853, 20756, 20757, and 20758 do not refer to Barley in their imprints).

lres patentꝭ or pretended to be done against any matter or thinge therein Conteined. Yt is ordred that the said Thomas Adams during his life from tyme to tyme hereafter soe often as he shalbe resolved to printe any of the said Copies registred as aforesaid shall thereof give notice to the said Wylliam & paie vnto him before the begynninge of anye ympression of any suche sette of songes Twenty shillingꝭ And shall alsoe alwaies deliver vnto him within Seven daies after the finishinge of euery such ympression Sixe settꝭ of the same songe bookes soe printed./ And yt is further ordered that the said Thomas shall paie vnto the said Wylliam fforty shillingꝭ in hande on the laste daie of this instant October./ And lastly the said Thomas & wylliam doe assente & agree, & with their Consentꝭ it is ordered. That they & either of them for their seueralle ptes & all others that maie Claime from or vnder them or either of them for & in all questions that maie arise Concerninge any matter to be moved or pretended vpon or touchinge any of the premisses or any other thinge heretofore done Concerninge any matter supposed to pteyne to the graunte Conteined in the said lres patentꝭ shall alwaies pforme suche order as in that behalf shalbe made by the m^r^ Wardens & Assistantꝭ of the said Company for the tyme beinge or the more pte of them without further strife or Controuersie in any wise./

Fol. 22a

1609. 7mo. Regis

6to. Nouembris/.

mr H. Lownes. ffor his booke of Martyrs[1] vsed in this ympression for the Copy booke, It is ordered that he shall haue Twoo bookꝭ of Martyrs vpon the finishinge of this ympression/.

Die Lunas 6to. Nouemƀ Court day/.

Geffry Charlton } ffrauncis Archer } Whereas ffrauncis Archer Citizen & Stacõner of London hath lent vnto Geffrye Charlton of the same Citty Stacõner the sũme of ffyfty poundꝭ of lawll: money of England to be payd to the sayd ffrauncis his executors. or assignes when the yeomans pte of the sayd Geffrye shalbe disposed by scrutinye & eleccõn in the Compnie: of Staconers accordinge to thordinañcꝭ in that behalfe/. It is therevpon, att the instance & request of the sayd ptyes, ordered by the mr, wardens, & assistantꝭ of the sayd Compnie: That there shalbe no eleccon made in the sayd Compnie: to dispose or passe the sayd pte from the sayd Geffrye or his executors. vntill the sayd ffrauncis Archer his executors. or assignes shall haue notice thereof/: And also that the sayd ffrauncis his executors: or assignes shall att the disposinge of the sayd pte be made privy thereunto, to thende he the sayd ffrauncis his executors. or assignes may then receiue the sayd 50li. from the sayd Geffrye or his assignes/.

Jeffrey Chorlton./

Signũ *A C* Anne Charlton
vxor dc̃i Galfridi Charlton

[1] STC 11227. Lownes was the printer of this edition.

27mo. Nouembris

Auditors. chosen for the half yeares accompte att Michaelmas last/.

mr ffeilde
mr Harrison Jun' } of the Assistante./

mr Dight
mr Pavyer } of the Livery/.

Richard Boyle
William Barrett } of the Yeomanrye/.

Die Martis 16to. Januarij: Courte daye/.

mr Waterson/. warden/. Whereas there is lxli remayninge in the house belonginge to the orphans of william Holme[1] deceased/. It is ordered that mr waterson warden shall haue his choyse to haue the sayd sume, payinge after viijli p Cent'. for the same to the vse of the sayd orphans, so longe as he shall thinke good to vse the same att that Rate/.

1609. 7 Ris

29. Jan'. Court day

FOL. 22b

John Bathoe. mr. Dawson mr. of the Compnie. Whereas Mr Thomas ⟨Da⟩wson mr of the Compnie is bound as suretie for John Bathoe[2] to Robert Jason of Enfield in the countie of midd gent' in Cxxli for the payment of Lxiiijlixs on the xxijth day of October next. Nowe at the instance & request of the said pties and for the securitie of the said Thomas dawson & his executors touchinge his & their indemnitie of the said bond yt is ordered that there shalbe no eleccon made in the said compnie to dispose or passe the yomans pte of the said [*Geffrey*] John Bathoe from the said John or his exec' vntill the sayd Thomas Dawson his exec' & adm' shall haue notice thereof & be discharged & saved harmeles of the said suertyship & bond. And that the said Thomas his ex' & adm shall by the said pte be discharged & saved harmles of the same sureteship & bond And to that ende shall at the disposinge of the said pte be made pryvie thereunto/

John bathou

the m'ke of m Elizabeth Bathoe/.

29no. Januarij/.1609.

mres. Bloomes pte/. George Edwarde havinge marryed mres. Bloome the late wyfe of Manasses Bloome[3] who hath a yeomans pte/. The same pte was putt to eleccon by scruteny this day, And the sayd George Edwarde & John

[1] This is probably the W. Holme who was made free 22 July 1580, Arber ii. 683. The date of his death is not known, but in 1603 he published from the 'Peahenne over against Serjeants Inn in Fleetstreet', *A plaine and perfect method for the vnderstanding of the whole Bible*, by Edward Vaughan, of which a copy is in the University of Chicago Library, entered Arber ii. 553, iii. 481. There is another W. Holmes who was made free 4 Apr. 1614 (Arber iii. 684), who published STC 3541 and 18590 from 'Popes Head Pallace' and who has been confused by Arber and McKerrow with the Chester stationer, W. Holme.

[2] J. Bathoe admitted freeman 17 Oct. 1588 (Arber ii. 703).

[3] Manasses Blond, bookbinder.

Dawson & willm Tyme beinge in nomynacon for itt, Thelection by most voyces fell vpon the sayd George Edwardę/.

22do. Februarij Courte day/.

William Barrett/ — William Barrett elected to mres. Cottons[1] ꝑte whome he hath married Richard Serger & George Vincent weie in eleccõn with him/.

Raffe Mabbe/. — Raffe Mabbe elected to that yeomans ꝑte wche was william Barrettę/ William Hall & John Dawson were in eleccõn wth him/.

FOL. 23a

1609. 7mo. Regis/.

Die Jouis Primo Martij/.

Officers Chosen for the stocke of the ꝑteners for the yeare ynsuinge from Thannũciacon nexte 1610.

Of Thassistentę	mr Seton mr Harrison Jun'
Of the Lyvery	mr Bill mr Cooke
Of the yeomanry	Richard Boyle Willm Welbye

Auditors. for the whole yeares accompte/.

Of Thassistentę	mr Leake mr Lownes
Of the Lyvery	mr Dighte mr Pavyer
Of the yeomanry	Edward Blunte Arthur Johnson
Thresorer	Mr Weaver/.

12mo. Junij 1610. 8uo. Regis/.

xli. of mr Dexters/. — Rd from mr Kingstone xli. ꝑcell of the xxli. gyuen by Robt Dexter[2] whiche xli. is pñtly accordinge to his will lent out by order to Lawrence Lysle for Three yeares/.

18uo. Junij 1610. 8uo. Regis/.

Stationers/.

Mr. Bradwoodę .6. prentises./

The Companie of Stationers beinge assembled in a full Courte holden in their hall this day, to consider of the matter concerninge the .6. prentises whiche Melchisedecke Bradwood requireth to retayne for the printinge of Chrisostoms workę in Greeke,[3] Hauinge deliberatly consulted thereof, Are therevpon contented, That he may retayne the sayd .6. prentizes, to be ymployed in the

[1] Mrs. William Cotton. [2] Cf. *C–B.C*, 5b, 16 Oct. 1604. [3] STC 14629.

sayd workę, duringe the tyme of the printinge thereof; And from thend of the same ympression That he may retayne the same .6. prentises to thend of their termes of appñtishipps, and then make them free, accordinge to thorders of the Companie & Citty/. Provided that after the sayd ympression is finished he shalbe allowed to haue noe moe prentises, but onely the sayd .6. vntill their sayd termes of pñtishipps be expired and ended/.

1610. 8uo. Regis/. FOL. 23b

23°. Julij. Courte day

mr. Mann mr./
mr. Leake & mr.
Adames. wardens./.

The Companie &
mr Weaver/.

Yt is concluded, ordered, & agreede that the Mayster, Wardens, & Cōmunaltye shall pay to mr Weaver, for all his righte & interest to the booke of testamentę & last wills,[1] wth all addicōns made or to be made therevnto, the sume of Twenty poundę, from thaccompte of the pteners by Twenty nobles a qter, the first at Michās nexte/ And that the sayd Mayster, Wardens, & Cōmunaltye & their successors. shall for ever haue & enioy the same Copye, as their proper Copye, to thuse & accompte of the sayd pteners, in the priuileges graunted by his Matie. to the Companie/.

Lawrence Lisle
Mr. Bill

Agreed by this Courte that mr Bills matter touchinge Lawrence Lisles pte shalbe renewed for one yeare from Ste. John Baptist day last accordingly as it was before/ Provided that yt shalbee neuer renewed agayne vpon any cullor or pretence whatsoever/.

4to Decembr 1610. 8uo. Regis.

Courte day

My lord Maiors
and the Shrieues
Dynners/

It is thought convenient for the good of the Companie, and ordered, That yearely from henceforth Sixe meete men of the Companie, shall att fitt tymes resorte to the Lord Maior & to eyther of the Shreiues, to dyne wth them,[2] as the order of the Citty, is for Companies vsually to doo/. Of the whiche Sixe, The mayster & wardens of the Companie, for the tyme beinge, shalbe Three/ And thother Three shalbe yearely elected & chosen by the mayster & wardens/. And yf any of those Three so elected & chosen shall refuse to repayre to the same places or to any of them, when he shalbe chosen & appoynted so to doo, That then & in eu'y suche case eueryone so elected & refusinge to doo accordingly shall for eu'y suche refusall pay Twenty shillingę for a fyne, to bee disposed accordinge to the order of the Companye/ And also yt is further ordered, That toward the chargę of the sayd Sixe ptyes repayringe to the sayd places accordinge to this order, There shalbe allowed from the cōmon accompte of the Companies, the sume of xviijli That is to say, for eu'y place vjli. And the residue of the whole charge to be borne by the ptyes resortinge to the sayd places/

[1] STC 23548 and Arber ii. 562, iii. 288 and 342.

[2] For a list of those attending the Lord Mayor's dinners, 1601–29, see Arber iii. 695–6, 691.

Accordinge to whiche order the ffirst that were to goe were these

ffor the Maior

The mayster & wardens, m[r] Harrison senio[r]. m[r] Barker, m[r] John Norton/.

ffor one of the Shreiues

The mayster & wardens, m[r] Barker, m[r] John Norton and m[r] Dawson/

ffor thother shreiue/.

The mayster & wardens, m[r] Barker, m[r] John Norton, & m[r] Waterson

FOL. 24[a] 1610. 8[uo]. Regis.

Die Lunæ. 14[to]. Januarij/. Quarter day & full courte

M[r] Billages money/ m[r] Dawson hath payd vnto thwardens xiij[s]iiij[d] for the vse of m[r] Billages money[1] for a yeare endinge at this Christmas 1610 And hath delyuered to them an acquittance for the vse money due from the fol. 6. Companie to the pishe att this Christmas 1610. 8[uo]. Regis. And at his request yt is ordered that he shall vse the 50[li]. gyuen by m[r] Billage, for another yeare from henceforth, And that his pte in the stocke shall stand & bee the Companies securitye & assurance for the same as it was before/.

Fryday 18[uo]. Januarij 1610. Court day & a full Courte holden/.

The Copy of a certificate touchinge the plantation in Ireland/.[2]

Stationers/. To the right wo[r]shipfull the Gou'no[r]. and assistent*e* of the Companie for the Plantation in Ireland/.

Copia/. May it please yo[r]. wo[r]shipps to be aduertised, that wee haue considered of the Twoo offers expressed iñ my Lorde Maiors precepte of the xiiij[th] of this January to vs directed, touchinge a proportionable share of land*e* in the Provynce of Ulster in Ireland, And wee haue resolued for our pte, to accepte of the latter offer, namely to referre the lettinge of the same land*e* & the managinge of the busines thereof, att this present, to yo[r]. wo[r]shipps, And so leaue yo[u]. to God, this 19[th] of January 1610

By the m[r] & wardens of the Companie of Stationers/.

Copia Thomas Mann
William Leake
Thomas Adames

Munday 4[to]. Februarij 1610 8[uo]. Regis.

Stationers/. To the right wo[r]shipfull the Gou'no[r]. & Assistant*e* of the Companie for the Plantacõn in Ireland/.

Copia/. May it please yo[r]. wo[rps]: to be adu'tised, That accordinge to my Lo: Maiors precepte of the last of this January 1610: to vs directed, wee haue agayne considered of the Two Offers touchinge a pporcõnable pte allotted to

[1] Cf. *C-B.C.*, 6[a], 4 Dec. 1604, *et loc. cit.*

[2] The City of London was a large undertaker in the Plantation of Ulster, cf. G. Hill, *An historical account of the Plantation in Ulster.*

or. Compnie: in the landę & plantacõn in Ireland, as wee hadd afore doñe vpon his Lops. form' precepte of the 14th of this January 1610 to vs directed to the same effecte/. To wche former precepte wee caused our resolucõn to be delyu'ed to yor. worps. in writinge oñ Satturday nexte after ye sayd form' precept; wche was to theffecte, That wee accepted of ye latter offer, namely to referre ye lettinge of or. Compnies. pte of ye sayd landę, & ye managinge of ye busines thereof to yor. worships/ And nowe agayne vpon this or. second assembly & consideracõn touchinge the same cause wee are of ye same mynd wee were before, and doo accordingly resolue to referre ye lettinge & disposinge thereof, to yor. worps. as wee did before And so leaue you. to god, this 5th of ffebruary 1610

By the mayster & wardens of ye Compnie: of Stationers/.

Copia/.

Thomas Mann/.
William Leake/
Thomas Adames/

1610. 8uo. Regis/. Fol. 24b

Mr Bishoppes will

In the last will & Testament of mr George Bysshopp[1] late Citizen & Stationer of Londoñ deceased, bearinge date the ffyue and Twentyeth day of ffebruary 1607. and in the ffyfte yeare of the raigne of our soueraigne Lord Kinge James, beinge prooued in the Prerogatyue Courte of Canterbury the Eighte & Twentyeth day of January in the yeare of or. Lord, accordinge to the Computacõn of the Churche of England 1610. yt is contayned and expressed, as followeth; After an excepcõn first in the former pte of the same will, made of those Twoo Ten'tę called Newton, wth the landę, hereidtamtę. & apprtennçę thereto belonginge, scituate in the pishe of Mylbornestoke in the County of Salop, beinge excepted out of the devises of his freehold landę and Ten'tę made to his daughter Martha & the heyres of her body, wth Remaynders ouer, As by the same will appeareth/.

Videlicet/.

And furthermore whereas by my Indenture of lease bearinge date the Twentyeth day last past of this instant moneth of ffebruary aboue written, I haue demysed vnto the mayster & wardens of the sayd Companie of Stationers in Londoñ, All those the sayd Twoo Ten'tę called Newton, wth the landę, hereditamentę, & apprtennçę, thereto belonginge/. To holde to them & their successors. ffrom the feast day of Ste. Michaell Tharchangell, whiche shall nexte happen after the decease of mee the sayd George Bysshopp & Mary my wyfe, for & duringe the terme of ffyue Hundred yeares from thence nexte ynsuinge & fully to be Compleate and ended/. Yeildinge & payinge vnto my heyres or assignes one Pepper corne yearely (yf yt be demaunded) On Condicõn neuertheles, That yf the sayd mayster & wardens of the sayde Company of Stationers of the Citty of Londoñ, for the tyme beinge, or their assignes, shall not from tyme to tyme, yearely duringe the sayd terme, by & out of the rentę, yssues, and pfittę to be hadd or raysed, by or vpon the sayd Twoo Ten'tę called Newtoñ wth thapprtennçę, well & truly pay vnto the Maior, Cominalty, and Citizens Gouernors. of the house of the poore called Christę

[1] Cf. Plomer, *Wills*, pp. 43–44.

Hospitall aforesayd & to their Successors. for to the reliefe and maynteñance of
the poore theire harbored, the suṁe of Sixe poundę of lawfull money of England,
Att Twoo feastę or termes in the yeare, That is to say, Att the feastę of Ste. Michaell
Tharchangell, & Thannũciacõn of our Lady the Virgin, or wthin Twoo monethes
nexte after euery of the same feastę by euen porcõns, Att or in the Countynghouse
in Christę Hospitall aforesayd/ And putt forth and Delyuer vnto suche yonge men
free of the sayd Companie of Stationers, as the Mayster & wardens wth the Assistantę
of the same Companie for the tyme beinge or the more ꝑte of them shall thinke
good, Sixe poundę yearely of the same rentę, yssues, and ꝓfittes, by suche yonge
men to be held and occupyed from Three yeares to Three yeares, wthout yeeldinge
any Consideracõn or allowance therefore but gyuinge sufficient security for the
same as aforesayd; And that also yf the sayd Mayster & wardens of the sayd
Fol. 25a Companie of Stationers for the tyme beinge shall not from tyme to tyme | yearely,
duringe the sayd terme of ffyue Hundred yeares, well and truly pay & distribute
vnto & amongst suche preachers as shall happen to coṁe and Preache at Paules
Cross [*at*] in Londoñ from tyme to tyme, and are not sufficiently provided for, in
maynteñance, in the Judgmte. and discrecõn of the Maior, Cominalty, & Citizens
aforesayd, for the tyme beinge, the suṁe of Tenne poundę of lawfull money of
England, That then & from thence forthe the sayd demyse & lease shalbe vtterly
voyd, As by the same more at large may appeare/. Item I gyue & bequeathe vnto
the sayd Maior, Cominalty & Citizens of the City of Londoñ Gouernors. of the
house of the poore coṁonly called Christę Hospitall in Londoñ & to their Successors.
for euer, the sayd Twoo Ten'tę called Newton wth the landę, Ten'tę, and hereditamtę.
therevnto belonginge, lyinge & beinge in the sayd ꝑishe of Milbornestoke in the
sayd County of Salop/. To haue & to holde the same Twoo Ten'tę wth thappr.teṅncę,
from & after the deathes of mee the sayd George Bysshopp & Mary my wyfe &
the longest lyuer of vs, vnto the sayd Maior, Cominalty & Citizens of the City of
Londoñ, Gouernors. of the sayd house of the poore called Christę Hospitall in
Londoñ, and to their successors. for eu', payinge & ꝓforminge, from & after the
determinacõn of the sayd lease, by what meanes soeuer, yearely for euer, out of
the rentę, yssues, & ꝓfittę of the same Twoo Ten'tę wth thappr.teṅncę, the sayde
seuerall suṁes of Sixe poundę and Tenne poundę before limited & intended to the
sayd Hospitall, & to the sayd Companie of Stationers, & to the sayd Preachers,
preachinge at Paules Crosse in forme as aforesayd, Accordinge to my intente &
true meaninge therein/. In witnes whereof to euery one of these Thurteene sheetę
of paper contayninge my sayd will I haue sett to my hand, & to the toppe of them
fixed my seale, the day & yeare first aboue written/ George Bysshopp/. Sealed,
delyuered, & published by the sayd George Bysshopp, for & as his last will &
Testamente, in the ꝑñce of vs, Edwarde White Scr'. William Aspley, William
Harsnett servte. vnto the sayd Scr'. Josephe Browne/.

Exr ꝑ Ri: Collins

Fol. 25b 1610. 8uo. Regis/.

Certayne other clauses of mr Bysshopps last will & Testamte/

Item I gyue & bequeathe all & singuler my sayd ffreehold landę, Ten'tę, & hereditamentę whatsoeuer, vnto the sayd Mary my wyfe, for & duringe her naturall

lyfe, And after the decease of the sayd Mary my wyfe, I gyue & bequeathe all & singuler the same my freehold landꝭ, Ten'tꝭ & hereditamᵗᵉ. whatsoeu' (Excepte those Twoo Ten'tꝭ called Newtoñ, wᵗʰ the landꝭ, hereditamᵗᵉ. & apprtennceꝭ thereto belonginge, scituate in the pishe of Milbornestoke in the County of Salop) vnto the sayd Martha my daughter & to the heyres of her body lawfully begotten or to be begotten for euer/ And for default of suche yssue then I gyue and bequeath all & singuler my sayd freehold landꝭ, Ten'tꝭ, & hereditamᵗᵉ. whatsoeu' (Excepte before excepted) vnto the Maior, Cominalty, & Citizens of the Citty of Londoñ Gou'noʳˢ. of the house of the poore coṁonly called Christꝭ hospitall in Londoñ & to their Successoʳs for euer, ffor & to the intente that all the rentꝭ & pfittꝭ thereby & therevpon to be hadd & raysed, shalbe from tyme to tyme from thence forthe yearely, for euer ymployed & bestowed in forme followinge, vizt Threescore poundꝭ thereof yearely for euer equally vnto & amongest Three suche schollers studentꝭ in Divinity & wanting sufficient meanes to be mayntayned at learninge by their freindꝭ, shalbe from tyme to tyme for euer, wᵗʰout affeccõn or ptiality elected named, & chosen, Vizt The first Three thereof alwayes by the sayd Maior, Cominalty & Citizens of the Citty of Londoñ, for the tyme beinge, And the nexte Three alwayes by the Mayster, wardens, & Cominalty of the Arte or Mystery of Stationers of the Citty of Londoñ, for the tyme beinge or the more pte of them/ And suche eleccõn & choyse for the sayd schollers to be alwayes held & obserued consequently & respectiuely for euer, so often as those roomes or schollershipps shall fortune to becõme voyd from tyme to tyme for euer, in the Vniuersity of Oxford in Christchurch rather then in any other Colledge or Hall there, for the affeccõn I the sayd George Bysshopp, bear thereto, in that John Bysshopp my late sonne & heyre deceased was of that house, & lyeth there buryed/. And that in suche eleccõn & choyce of the sayd schollers from tyme to tyme suche kindred of me the sayd George Bysshopp & Mary my wyfe or eyther of vs beinge fitt for learninge, & wantinge sufficient meanes to be mayntayned att learninge by their freindꝭ, vpon request, shalbe preferred to the sayd mayntenance for schollershipps before any other/. And that suche of the sayd schollers as shalbe so elected as aforesayd, shall not haue the sayd mayntenance or yearely allowance of Twentye poundꝭ a peece or any pte thereof after suche hee or they of them shall be benificed, or shall happen to doo or cõmitt any Acte or offence worthy of dismission or deprivacõn out of the house suche of them shall be of/. And the one moity or half pte of the rest & residue of the sayd rentꝭ & profittꝭ yearely of all the sayd landꝭ, Ten'ꝭ, & hereditamᵗᵉ. shalbee yearely for euer, for & toward the mayntenance & Releife of the poore children & others harbored in Christꝭ Hospitall aforesayd; And the other moity thereof shalbe yearly for euer, payd & delyuered by the sayd Maior, Cominalty & Citizens Gou'noʳˢ. of the sayd house of the poore called Christꝭ Hospitall in Londoñ & their successoʳˢ. vnto the mayster & wardens of the sayd Companie of Stationers in Londoñ for the tyme beinge for euer, Att their mancõn house for the tyme beinge called the Stationers hall in Londoñ, Att Twoo feastꝭ or termes in the yeare, That is to say, Att the feastꝭ of Sᵗᵉ. Michaell Tharchangell & Thannũciacõn of oʳ. Lady the virgin, or wᵗʰin Three | Three (*sic*) monethes nexte after the same FOL. 26ᵃ feastꝭ, by euen & equall porcõns for the vse of the sayd Companie of Stationers for euer, By them from tyme to tyme for eu' to be putt forthe & delyuered vnto suche yonge men free of the sayd Companie of Stationers, as the Mayster and wardens wth the Assistantę of the same Companie for the tyme beinge or the more ꝑte of them shall thinke good/. By them the same yonge men to be occupyed from Three yeares to Three yeares wthout yeeldinge any Consideracõn or allowance therefore, but gyuinge sufficient security vnto the sayd Mayster & wardens of the sayd Companie of Stationers for the tyme beinge, suche as they shall like of, for repayment vnto them & their successors. [of] suche money as so shalbe putt forth & delyu'ed from tyme to tyme accordingly/. Provyded alwayes, That yf the sayd Maior, Cominalty & Citizens for the tyme beinge, shall by the Judgmte. & opinion of the sayd Mayster, wardens & Assistentę of the sayd Companie of Stationers of Londoñ for the tyme beinge or the more ꝑte of them signifyed by writinge vnder their Coñon seale, be held or found altogether remysse & negligent in ꝑformance of the ymployinge & bestowinge of the sayd rentę & profittę as aforesayd, contrary to my true yntent & meaninge herein as afore is mencõned & declared/. That then & from thenceforth the sayd gyfte & bequest of my sayd landę, Teñ'tę, & hereditamtę. to the sayd maior, Comiñalty, & Citizens of Londoñ & their successors. shalbee vtterly voyde & of none effecte/.

Exr. ꝑ Ri: Collins

Primo Marcij 1610.

William Hall for mres. Clerks half parte.

Maystresse Clerke[1] beinge marryed out of the Companie, The election for her half ꝑte was made this day, And Arnold Hatfeild, William Hall, & John Dawson were in eleccõn, And yt fell vpon William Hall; Who presently tooke the oathe in that case ordayned/.

Officers chosen for the stocke of the ꝑteners for the yeare ynsuinge from thannũciacõn nexte 1611.

	Stockekeepers/.	Auditors. for the whole yeares accompte	
Of thassistantę	mr Standishe mr Humfry Lownes/	mr Hooper mr ffeild	of thassistentę/
Of the Lyu'y	mr Vincent mr Barrett	mr Bankworth mr Knighte	of the Liuery/.
Of the yeomanry	Edward Aldee Arthur Johnson	John Smithicke Henry ffetherstoñ	of the yeomanry

Threasorer} Mr Weaver/.

Fol. 26b

1610. 8uo. Regis/.

14to. Marcij

Receiued from Oxoñ by the delyuery of mr Dor. Kinge Deane of Christ church & vicechauncellor of Oxoñ the Counterꝑte, vnder the vniu'sities seale, of one Indenture before sealed at mr Leakę house in Paules churchyard, vnder the coñon

[1] Widow of Thomas Clarke.

seale, [15to. ffebr'. vlt'] for one booke of eu'y newe Copy to be gyuen to the publique library at Oxoñ, And they appoynt S^r. Thomas Bodley to receiue them/.[1]

It is ordered that m^r Pinfold[2] shalbe satisfyed his demaund for dressinge the dynner att m^r Bysshopps funerall, And the puidinge of a Cooke thenceforth, for the service of the Companie, is left to the discrecõn of the mayster, wardens, & assistante/.

1611. 9no. Regis.
8^uo. Aprilis

Mr White
M^res. Gosson

Yt is ordered wth m^r Whites consente, that duringe m^r Smithes life he shall gyue to m^res. Gosson vpon eu'y ympression of Granadas meditacõns,[3] xxv^tie. of those booke/ And also that he shall presently gyue her xxv^tie. booke of that ympression thereof w^che he hath nowe lately printed, And to all this m^r white dothe gyue his consente in this full courte beinge qter day/.

Plantation in
Irelande

Yt is agreed the 16th day of October last That the 4 paym^te. for the plantation of Ireland shalbe borne out of the stocke of the pteners, And all benefitt that shall come thereof shall belonge to the same stocke/ Provyded that the Mayster & wardens may assesse & cause to be collected from those of the Company that are not ynteressed in the stocke, toward the sayd Plantation, suche sumes of money, as they thinke fitt, And those sumes to be repayd to the disbursers, when pfit cõmeth of the disbursm^te. toward the sayd Plantation/.

The 2 first paym^te. were l^li. a peece
And the 2 last paym^te. were lxx^li. a peece[4]

Garners in
Bridewell/.

R^d on Munday the 4th of December 1610 by m^r Adames warden of m^r Dighte & m^r Jones collecto^rs in the Company for the garners in Bridewell[5] } xxiiij^li ix^s x^d

[1] The 'Confirmation' of the Stationers' gift to the University by the High Commission, 22 Jan. 1611, is Bodleian MS. 8489 n. 10.

[2] Nicholas Pinfold was elected cook 4 June 1599, *Reg. B*, 473^a.

[3] There is a copy of this edition of Luis de Granada's *Of prayer and meditation*, 12°, W. I[aggard]. f. E. White, 1611, at Stanbrook Abbey, Worcs., and another at Peterhouse, Cambridge. Another edition, [J. Roberts] f. T. Gosson a. R. Smith, 1596, is at Teignmouth Abbey, Devon, and at Harvard. This Protestant translation may have been made by a son of Dr. John Banister who dedicates the second part to his father. It was originally entered to T. Gosson and J. Perrin, 7 July 1592 (Arber ii. 616), and published in that year, STC 16909. William Wood entered this book, with mention that Gosson had claims, with six others which had been the property of Richard Smith (Abel Jeffes and Richard Jones may have had shares) on 6 Nov. 1598 (Arber iii. 131). He published only two of the seven books, STC 16910 (as well as an edition of 1601 printed for him by J. Harrison of which a copy of both parts is in the London Oratory [Pt. I = STC 16900]) and STC 17349 (concerning which see *Reg. B*, 26 Mar. 1599, 470^b). On 2 Aug. 1602 Edward White was granted this and Gervase Markham's *Horsemanship* (STC 17349), although the same day (*Reg. B*, 484^b) he was prohibited from selling any copies of the *Meditations* for six months in order that George Potter might sell his copies. There seems no way of ascertaining who Mr. Smith may be unless he is Richard Smith, the publisher from whom Wood apparently derived his rights.

[4] According to G. Hill, *An Historical account of the Plantation in Ulster* (1877), p. 433, the Stationers' Company subscribed £520.

[5] For the Corn Levy.

FOL. 27^{a}

1611. 9no. Regis.

The 4th. paym^{te}. for the Plantation in Irelande.

R^{d} the xjth day of Aprill 1611. of the m^{r} and wardens of the Companie of Stationers Londoñ the sũme of Threescore & Tenne poundꝭ of lawfull money of England, due by the sayd Companye for the 4th payment for the Plantatioñ in Ireland, I say R^{d} } lxx^{li}.

ꝑ me Arthurum Panther Clic' (*sic*)
Cornelij ffyshe Camerarij Ciui^{t}ꝭ. Londoñ

Note that this sũme was payd from the stocke of the ꝑteners as the Three former paym^{t}ꝭ. for the sayd plantation were/.

8^{uo}. Aprilis 1611: 9no. Regis.

Bergauenny house.

Yt is ordered that the purchase of Bergavenny house[1] shalbee payd for, from the stocke of the ꝑteners in the Privilegꝭ, And the sayd purchase to bee to the vse of the same ꝑteners & their heyres, accordinge to the rates of their ꝑtꝭ in the sayd stocke And as any ꝑtener dyeth or goeth from his or her ꝑte, his stocke to [bee] receiued out, shalbee made one Thirde ꝑte more then is limited by former ordinañces, vĩz euery 200^{li}. to be made 300^{li}. & eu'y 100^{li}. to be made 150^{li}. & euery 50^{li}. to be made 75^{li}.

26to. Maij Courte day/.

Ouerseers for the works att Bergauenny house.

Yt is ordered that m^{r} Hooper & m^{r} ffeilde, m^{r} Swynhowe and m^{r} Kingstoñ shalbee ou'seers for the Companie, and directers of the buyldingꝭ, alteracõns & reꝑacõns of Bergavenny house/.

The sale of the house in Milkstreete.

Also that o^{r}. m^{r}. the Twoo wardens & m^{r} Nortoñ shall contracte & bergayne for the sale of the lease of the hall in Milkestreet,[2] as they shall thinke most fitt for the good of the Companie/.

Allowance toward the Quarter dynners.

Also it is ordered & agreed that the wardens shalbe allowed xx^{li}. euery yeare henceforward toward the ꝗter dinners/[3] The first xx^{li}. to be allowed att this Midsom̃er nexte/.

3°. Junij Court day/

John Dawson for Eleaz: Edgars parte./.

Eleazar Edgar hauinge yeilded vpp his yeomans ꝑte to the Companie, The election for itt was made this day And John Dawson, Richard Tom̃es, & John Busby Juñ were in eleccõn, And it fell vpon John Dawson, who presently tooke the oathe in that case ordayned/.

[1] This is the first mention of Abergavenny House, the present Stationers' Hall. According to a schedule of leases, 1625, preserved in almost illegible condition in the archives of the Company of Stationers, No. 230, Abergavenny House was leased 20 Jan. 45 Eliz. during the life of George Betty, Robert Betty, and James Walmersley, for an annual rental of £4. 9*s*. 8*d*.

[2] The Old Hall.

[3] This is double the allowance made 6 June 1608, *C–B.C*, 17^{a}.

1611. 9no. Regis/. FOL. 27b

6to. Julij/. beinge Election day/.

mr John Nortoñ/. Whereas mr Jo: Nortoñ dyd lend vnto the Company,[1] on the ffirst day of May last the sũme of Nyne Hundred poundꝭ/. It is ordered that the same debte of .900li. shalbe payd vnto him by the Companye, att the ende of Sixe Monethes to be accompted from the sayd ffirst day of Maye; Together wth allowañce after Tenne ꝑ Cent', for the same, for so longe tyme as itt hath bene [and] shalbee vnpayd/.

paid accordingly

mr Humfry Lownes/ Whereas mr Humfry Lownes dyd lend vnto the Company on the ffirst day of Maye last the sum̃e of Twoo Hundred poundꝭ/. It is ordered that the same debte of 200li. shalbee payd vnto him by the Companie, att the ende of Sixe Monethes to bee accompted from the sayd ffirst day of Maye; Together wth allowance after Tenne ꝑ Cent' for the same for so longe tyme as itt hath bene [and][*or*] shall bee vnpayd/.

paid accordinglye

9no. Julij publicacõn day of the eleccõn/.

mr Pynfold the Cooke./. It is ordered that mr Pynfolds fee[2] shalbee made iiijli ꝑ Annũ, from henceforward/ The first paymte. of xxs. to beginne at Michãs nexte/.

And the wardens to consider him for this ꝗter att midsom̃er as they thinke good/.

[8uo. *Octobris*]

1611. 9no. R. FOL. 28a

8uo. Octobris

Mr Nortoñ mr
Mr ffeild } wardens
Mr Lownes }

Almanacks & Prognostications/. ffor thaugmentinge of the printers wagꝭ henceforth for the woorkemanshipp of printinge the Almanackꝭ & ꝓgnosticacõns, as thoccasion & necessity of the tyme requireth, that they may be reasonably payd for their woorke & the woorke the better doñe/ And for ꝓvision of good papꝑ for the printinge of the same, to thende they may be well printed bothe wth good woorkmanshipp & good papꝑ/ It is ordered by a full Courte holden this day That the sayd Almanackꝭ & ꝓgnosticacõns [*shold*] shall henceforward be sold att ijs vjd the ꝗrterne, whiche was the price here agreed vnto by most voyces/.

14to. Octobr.

Richard Moore }
Nicholas Oaks } It is ordered, That the Concordancy of yeares[3] lately printed by Ni: Oakes for Ri: Moore shalbe taken into the stocke & there pyled vpp & kepte & not be sold till further order be

[1] Presumably this and the following loans were used in the purchase of Abergavenny House.

[2] Cf. *C–B.C*, 17a, 6 June 1608.

[3] STC 13778. This book was entered by N. Okes 18 July 1611 (Arber iii. 462). The cause of this action was that Adams claimed that the book was a mere *réchauffé* of his copy, Grafton's *Table*, STC 12166, which he had printed just the year before but which he had obtained from R. Walley, 12 Oct. 1591 (Arber ii. 596). Adams was not allowed the peaceful possession of his copy, cf. *C–B.C*, 42b, 6 Mar. 1616, and *Letter Book*, 86a.

taken for itt/. Also that Ni: Oakę & Ri: Moore, as ꝑfitt & sale shalbe made of the sayd booke, when it shalbe ordered to be sold, shalbe satisfyed suche sum̃es of money, as they shall iustly prooue themselues to haue layd out for the sayd booke, bona fide/.

Mr Leake &
Mr Adames

Item that it shall neu' be printed agayne wthout consent of mr Leake & mr Adam̃es/.

18uo. Nouembr.

Arn. Hatfeild
Ri: Tomes

Nathanaell Butter hauinge forfeyted his yeomañ ꝑte,[1] & it Judged by the Companie to be forfeyted, accordinge to the constitucõn in that behalf, The election was made for it And theleccõn by most voyces fell to Arnold Hatfeild for thone half & to Richard Tomẽs for thother half, And so eyther of them wth the half yeomans ꝑte they hadd before haue nowe eache of them a whole yeomans ꝑte/.

9no. Decembr.

mr Billags
matter

fol. 6.

Mr Dawson hath payd vnto thwardens xiijs iiijd for the vse of mr Byllagę money for a yeare endinge at this Christmas 1611.[2] And hath delyu'ed to them an acquittañce for the vse money due from the Compnie. to the ꝑishe at Michas last/. And at his request it is ordered That he shall vse the 50li. gyuen by Mr Byllage for another yeare from henceforth vnder the condicõn as he had it before viž. That his ꝑte in the stocke shall stand & be the Compnies. security & assurañce for the same as it was before/

10mo. ffebr'.

William Bladon/.
for Wm yongę ꝑte

William Yonge hathe resigned & yeilded vpp his yeomans ꝑte into the handę of the Companie And it is this day by eleccõn orderly graunted to William Bladoñ/.

Fol. 28b

1612: 10mo. Regis.

6to. Aprilis

Mr Norton mr.

It is agreed by full consente of the Company that mr Nortoñ shall haue a lease from the companie of the farme and towneshipp of Newtoñ demised by mr Bysshopp to the Company,[3] To holde to mr Nortoñ from mres. Bysshopps decease for 499 yeares, at the yearely rente of 22li. And out of that rente the Company to satisfye the Legacyes gyuen by mr Bysshop, to Pauls Crosse Christę Hospitall & this Company from mres. Bysshopps decease forward/.

[1] Butter had procured an edition of the Primer to be printed for him at Dort by George Waters and imported into England; cf. *Letter Book*, 82a, 26 Oct. 1611.

[2] Cf. *C–B.C*, 6a, 4 Dec. 1604, *et loc. cit.*

[3] Cf. *C–B.C*, 24b–26a, and 43a, 8 Apr. 1616.

19no. Maij

Lottery. 20^{li}. to be Ventred therein by the hall./.

It is ordered that xx^{li}. shall be ventured in the Lottery[1] out of the hall stocke, And the hall stocke to haue all the benefitt that shall comẽ thereof, And the Poesie to be in the name of the mayster and wardens/.

Geffrey Charlton his parte. gr^{ted}. to Geo: Elde and John Rodwell./.

Geffrye Charltoñ his yeomans ꝑte is graunted by eleccõn vnto George Elde and John Rodwell equally betweene them whiche makes their seu'all half yomens ꝑtę w^{che} they hadd before to be full yeomans ꝑtę/.

The order for Ballads.

Whereas diu'se greate abuses haue bene and dayly are practised aswell in printinge of many leude balladę, offensiue bothe to god, the Churche and the state, and to the corruptinge of youthe & euill disposed people that delighte moore in suche scurrile & euill thingę then in exercisinge themselues to reade better matters, As also in the printinge of all other sortę of balladę wthout lawfull aucthoritye, and contrary bothe to the decrees of the Courte of Starrechamber, and also thordonnañcę of the Comp^{nie}. of Stacõners/ ffor reformacõn whereof yt is ordayned by the mayster, wardens, & Assistentę of the sayd Companie, That ffyue printers onely, free of the sayd Comp^{nie}. beinge suche as the sayd m^{r}, wardens, and Assistentę or the moore ꝑte of them shall nomynate and thinke fitt (and nõne other) shall alwayes, from henceforthe haue the sole and onely printinge, Aswell of all balladę whatsoeuer already extant in printe & not entred and registred in the sayd Companye, As also of all newe balladę hereafter to be made and sett forthe/ And that they shall ꝓcure all manner of balladę hereafter to be first, before the printinge thereof, lawfully aucthorised & entred & registred in the sayd Companie for their or sõme one of their Copyes, And that the sayd ffyue printers onely & nõne other shall haue the woorkmanshipp of the printinge of all other balladę that are or shall be entred & registred in the sayd Comp^{nie}. for other freemens Copyes/ And that it shall not be lawfull for any that hathe or shall [haue] any suche ballad to putt the same to printinge, to any other printer then onely to one of the sayd ffyue printers/ And that any freeman of ye sayd Comp^{nie}. may ꝓcure a lawfull ballad to be aucthorised and then to be entred & registred for him in the sayd Company for his Copye/ And that he shall putt the same to sõme or one of the sayd ffyue printers onely (and nõne other) to be printed for him, vpon payne to forfeite & loose the same Copye and all the balladę that he shall putt to any other to be printed, The same forfeyture to goe to the vse of the poore of the Companye/ And it is also ordayned, That alwayes when & as often as any of the sayd ffyue printers shall decease, another printer shall be chosen and appoynted in his place by the sayd Mayster, wardens, and Assistentę or the moore ꝑte of them, accordinge to their discrecõns for the printinge of the sayd balladę
wth the survivo^{rs}. of the sayd ffyue || Printers/ And that yf any of the sayd ffyue Fol. 29^{a}
printers shall mysdemeane himself in any of the premisses, and by the Judgm^{te}.

[1] The Virginia Company by Royal Patent, 12 Mar. 1612, was granted the right to hold a lottery. Cf. also *C–B.C*, 34^{a}, 17 May 1614; and *Three proclamations concerning the lottery for Virginia*, Providence, R.I., 1907. Among the Pepys ballads is one entitled 'Londons lotterie: with an encouragement to the furtherance thereof, for the good of Virginia'. 2 pts. s. sh. fol. W. W[hite]. *f. H. Robards*, 1612.

of the sayd mayster, wardens, and Assistentę shall deserue to be putt from the printinge of the sayd balladę, That in eu'y suche case euery suche offender shall by their order be putt therefrom/ And that any of the sayd ffyue printers shall be at liberty to haue any lawfull balladd aucthorised & entred & registred for him in the sayd Comp^{nie}./ And also it is ordayned, That Edward Aldee, George Elde, William White, Symon Stafford, and Raffe Blore shall be the ffirst ffyue printers of the sayd balladę, accordinge to these ordonnãncę/ And it is further ordered, That none shall hereafter printe any balladę whatsoeu' vpon any paper of lesse price then ij^{s} viij^{d} the reame/. And that nõne that nowe vse or hereafter shall vse to sell balladę, shall sell, vtter, or putt away any manner of leude, lasciuious, scurrilous, or popishe balladę w^{che} heretofore haue bene ꝑhibited to be printed or solde, contrary to any order or ordonnan̄cę heretofore made for the good gou'm^{te}. of the sayd Companie/.

ffor bynders & others.

Apprentises

this order was made voyd by an order. 6°. Martij. 1619. fol. 61./

fforasmuche as it hathe bene [*founde*] and is founde by dayly experience, That the Decree of the Hono^{r}able Courte of Starre-chamber in the poynte concerninge [the] takinge of appr'tices,[1] is greately [*hindered*] to the hindrãnce of the poore bookebynders and others free of the comp^{nie}. by reason they may not by the sayd decree take any appr'tice to trayne him to their Artę and occupacõns, till their former appr'tice hathe serued out his appr'tishipp, whereby they are destitute for a longe tyme after of any helpe to ꝑforme their woorkę, to the vtter vndooinge of them their wyues, children, and familyes, whiche hathe caused many greate abuses to be practised by the euill disposed to defraude the true meaninge of the sayd decree/. Therefore (vpon often complayntę thereof and vpon the often shewinge of the greiuañcę of the sayde bookebynders and others of the Company in the premisses, and for ye releeuinge and helpinge them therein asmuche as conveniently may bee, wthout any preiudice or ympeachment to the true meaninge of the sayd decree, whiche was intended to bee for the good and not hurte of the Companie) Yt is ordayned, That nõne of the sayd bookebynders or others of the sayd Company shall at any one tyme hereafter haue or keepe any moo appr'tices then suche onely as they may by the sayd decree (Excepte it be in the cases and accordinge to these orders followinge, That is to say) It is ordayned, That alwayes when the appr'tice of any bookebynder free of the Companye hathe serued ffowre yeares of his appr'tishipp wth his mayster, and that then his mayster after thende of those ffowre yeares shall sue vnto the mayster and wardens of the Companye to haue another appr'tice allowed vnto him to trayne & bringe vpp to his occupacõn agaynst the tyme that his former appr'tice shall haue serued out his appr'tishipp In euery suche case the sayd mayster and wardens by their good discrecõn shall well consider of the case, And yf they shall fynde it fytt then they shall and may allowe vnto him another appr'tice accordingly as they shall fynd his sute to be iust and reasonable/. And that the like order and course shall be vsed wth the booke sellers & other tradesmen free of the Companye alwayes when their appr'tices shall haue serued their appr'tishipps wthin one yere of the terme of their appr'tishoodę/.

[1] Cf. Arber ii. 812, section 8.

July

Mr. Jo. Norton Mr.
Mr. Hoop }
Mr. Harison Jun'} Wardens/

.3. Augusti

Edw. Gosson[1] ys elected to that yomãns pte whiche was Jo. Surbutte,[2] the same Surbut beinge deceased and his wydowe maryed to the said Gosson

21. Sept'

Mr Harisoñ the yonger, nowe yonger wardeñ is elected to that Assistante pte whiche was mr Setons, the said mr Setoñ beinge deceased and his wydowe maried againe in August last or thereaboute.[3] And mr. Harisoñ hathe takeñ his oathe accordingly for it.

Mr. Edw. Blunt is thereuppoñ elected to that lyuerye pte Whiche before was mr Harisoñ the yongers pte. before his electioñ to mr Setons pte/ And he hath takeñ his oathe accordinglye/

Nichãs Bourne is thereuppoñ elected to that yomans pte whiche was mr Blunte before his electioñ to the said lyu'ie pte/ And he hathe taken his oathe accordinglye

ffrauncis Burton is elected to that half yomans pte whiche was Johñ Herberte. The said Herbert havinge here first resigned his said pte and yeilded it to the free electioñ of the compnie And thelection falleth vppoñ ffr' Burtoñ, which wth the half yomans pte wch the said ffraunce had before maketh hym̃ nowe a whole yomans pte. And he hath takeñ his oathe accordinglye/

5to oct'

Mr Dawson— for mr Billage matt' — hathe deliu'ed to the wardens an acquitance from̃ the pish of St m'tin in the Vintry for Lijs due to their poore for one yere ending at the feast of St michael last[4]

Mr Dawsoñ — And hath also deliu'ed to the Wardens xiijs iiijd due at the same tyme for A yere for the same matter, to thuse of the Compnie &c'

[1] Edward Gosson apprenticed 3 Aug. 1601 (Arber ii. 256).

[2] John Surbut apprenticed 6 Nov. 1581 (Arber ii. 108), admitted 8 Oct. 1589 (Arber ii. 706).

[3] Mrs. Mary Seton married the Rev. Edward Topsell, 12 Aug. 1612, cf. *D.N.B. sub* Topsell.

[4] Cf. *C–B.C*, 6a, 4 Dec. 1604, *et loc. cit.*

FOL. 30[a] 1612. 10. Ris Jacobi

Ambr' Garbrand
Jo. Pyndley.

The sanctuary of the soule.
Learne to dye/
2 bookꝭ

Yt is ordered wth thassent of the said ꝑties that of eu'y ympression from tyme to tyme & at all tymes hereafter to be prynted by ambr' Garbrand or his ass' free of this Compnie, of either of the said bookꝭ, he shall not prynt aboue xvc. of any ympression.[1] Also he or his ass' shall not begyñ any ymprssion thereof wthout first gyving the said Jo. Pyndley or his ass' free of the Compnie knolege thereof Also that at the begynninge of eu'ye ympression of either of the said bookes the said Ambr' or his ass' shall pay to the said John Pyndley or his ass' free of this Compnie. ffyftie shillingꝭ And that yf the said Ambr' or his ass' prynte any greater nũber of any ympressioñ of either of the said bookꝭ then is afore lymited or otherwise Defrawd the said Jo. Pyndley or his ass' in any of the prmisses or make default in payment of any of the said sõmes of ffyftie shillingꝭ or any ꝑte thereof. That theñ the said bookꝭ shalbe absolutely the copies of the said Jo. Pyndley & his ass' free of the Compnie. And the said Ambr' or his ass' nor any other clayminge froñ him to haue no further to deale therewth

Ambrose Garbrand
John Pindley

.9. Nov.

Auditors chosen for the last half yeres accoumpt

Mr. Dawson, mr. waterson. } of Thassistantꝭ
mr. knight., mr. kingston } of the lyu'ye/
Tho Snodañ, Jonas Man } of the yomanry

FOL. 30[b] 1612. 10 Ris

22. decembr'

Mr. Bonham Norton Mr
mr hoop, mr harison } wrdens

Court Daye

Mystres Tryp.[2]

Yt is ordered that mystres Tryp shall haue xxs a quarter. during her wydowehood onely & no longer. The first payment to begyñ this day beinge the Day of Distributioñ to the poore

[1] Both of these books, Sir J. Hayward's *The sanctuarie of a troubled soule* and C. Sutton's *Disce mori*, were originally entered to J. Wolf, 13 Nov. 1600 (Arber iii. 176), and 21 Aug. 1600 (Arber iii. 170). On 19 Jan. 1601 they were re-entered to Wolf and C. Burby (Arber iii. 179). Burby's interest was transferred by his widow to W. Welby, 16 Oct. 1609 (Arber iii. 420), and by him to Garbrand, 15 June 1610 (Arber iii. 437). Wolf's part was transferred by his widow to Pindley, 27 Apr. 1612 (Arber iii. 483), and his widow transferred her rights to G. Purslowe, 2 Nov. 1613 (Arber iii. 535). Later, 22 Mar. 1616 (Arber iii. 585), N. Bourne acquired Garbrand's rights in the Sutton and possibly Purslowe's rights also, for according to Arber the transfer, 2 Nov. 1613, of that book, though paid for, is 'run through', and the editions of 1616 and 1618 were printed by Purslowe for Bourne. There is in the Folger a copy of 'The eight impression' of the Hayward, with imprint 'f. E. Edgar and A. Garbrand, 1610'. For the later history of the copyright of the Hayward book, cf. *C–B.C*, 36[b], 22 Dec. 1614, and *C–B.C*, 40[b], 4 Dec. 1615.

[2] Presumably widow of Henry Tripp.

Jo. Harison the yongest. yt is ordered that he shall paye. Ten shillingꝭ a yere for the lyttle Celler or warehouse that he hathe next the gardeñ/ The same to be paid during the tyme that he shall hold it. wherein no tyme is graunted him otherwise theñ as tenn'ᵗ at will

2 Januar'.

mʳ. Samuel Dañiell yt is agreed that he shall deliu' into the hall 200 ꝑfect bookꝭ.[1] whereof 40 be in thandꝭ of wydowe Crosley of Oxoñ whiche the Compⁿⁱᵉ shall receaue of her as ꝑcell of the said 200 bookꝭ. And also that he shalbe presently paid for the said 200 bookꝭ .xxˡⁱ. Also he promiseth that yf he mend or add any thing to the book hereafter. That theñ yt shalbe prynted according to thorders of the Compⁿⁱᵉ.

Mʳ. Humfrey Lownes. Wᵐ. Jaggerd Vppoñ the hearinge of the matter betwene them yt is ordered that wiłłm Jaggard shall pay to mʳ Lownes .xˢ. for his damagꝭ in printinge prentises Indentures contrary to order and iijˢ iiijᵈ for a fine to the House.[2]

/28 Januar'

Butlers. yt is ordered that Ric' Moretoñ & wiłłm Tym̃ shalbe butlers to the Compⁿⁱᵉ. fromhenceforth[3] And that either of them̃ henceforward shall haue xxˢ a pece. vīz. xlˢ a yere betwene them̃ equally for the well doinge of their service thereiñ And all other ꝑffitꝭ of the place to be equally shared betwene them̃

23 Febr' 1612 10 Regis

Buyinge of impʳssions Yt is ordered by a full court of the Mʳ Wardens & assistants holden this day that alwaies hereafter when any Prynter or owner of a copy, shall sell a whole impression of a booke or copy to any freeman or brother of the companie, That in eu'y or any such [case]. The prynter or owner of the booke printed vppon any such impression shall not new prynt the same booke or copie againe, vnlesse hee doo first agree in that behalfe wᵗʰ the ꝑtie or ꝑties that bought thympression, or first acquainte the Mʳ wardens & assistantꝭ or the more ꝑte of them therewᵗʰ & stand to their order therein.

The copie of my Lo. Cookꝭ letter to the Compⁿⁱᵉ. in the behalf of Edw. Letherland[4] FOL. 31ᵃ

My very lovinge good frendes. I am gyven to vnderstand by the bearer hereof Edward Letherland, my houshold servᵗ. that he synce the yere 1577. hathe bēn a freemañ of yoʳ Compⁿⁱᵉ. Notwithstandinge his so longe discontynuance, ys nowe

[1] STC 6246, which Daniel had privately printed in a 'few copies only' for distribution to friends. From this sale it would appear that at least 200 were printed. The only edition which the Company published was that of 1613, for Daniel obtained a patent for the book in 1618.

[2] H. Lownes had entered blanks for apprentices 14 Nov. 1604 (Arber iii. 276). Cf. *Fine Book*, 8ᵇ, 28 Jan. 1613.

[3] Apparently since 6 June 1608, *C–B.C*, 17ᵃ, the cook of the Company had hired and paid the butlers.

[4] Leatherland was apprenticed to T. Marsh, 25 July 1568 (Arber i. 376).

agayne Wyllinge to reencorporate and Retourne to y^t societie in whiche he was first planted. and therein to ende & spend the fruitꝭ of his latter age. I am therefore in his behalf to pray you^u. and the rather at my request, to entreate yo^u, for his admittance agayne into yor fraternitie, and wth all to graunt vnto hiṁ, the next Roome that shalbe voyd by deathe or otherwise for puttinge in suche a sõme of money as vnto one of his rancke or place shalbe convenient & agreable to the orders of yor hall. In doinge of whiche I shall take it as a great favo^r. at yor handes. & be ready to requite yor kyndnes in any thinge lyinge in my power. Of whiche I hope yo^u will not fayle me. And so with my hartie cõmendacõns I cōmitt yo^u to god. Remayning alwaies

Yo^r very lovinge frend
Edw. Coke/

ffrom my house in Holbourne the
27 of ffebruary 1612.

To my very lovinge frendꝭ. the m^r. wardens & other their assistantꝭ of the comp^nie of Stacõners gyve these./

primo die m'cij 1612. 10 R^is

Officers chosen for the stocke for the yere from the feast of thanuñc' next 1613. .xj^s. R^is.

vĩz

Stockeps chosen as folow^th.

Of thassistantꝭ.....m^r. ffeild. m^r Adams

Of the lyu'ie........m^r. purfoot Jun' m^r Lawe

Of the yomanry.....josias parnell. Tho. downes

Treasorer. m^r weaver.

All haue taken their oathes.

Auditors chosen for the last yeres account ending at o^r Lady day next.

of thassistantꝭ— m^r Dawson. m^r Waterson

of the lyvery.— m^r. Bankworth. m^r Swynhoe

of the yomanry—Tho. Snodam. ffr'. Burton.

18 m'cij. 1612. 10 Ris

Assistantꝭ — M^r. Bankworth. Mr Swynhoe. Mr Math. Lownes. and m^r John Jaggard/ Are choseñ and takeñ into the Assistantꝭ. accordinge to the constitutioñ.

ffossbrooke Yt is ordered that Nathaniell ffossbrooke shall p'ntely haue xiij[s] iiij[d] a quarter till a pencōn of xx[s] a quarter fall void And then to haue the xx[s] a quarter theis añuities to bee payable solong as hee dwelleth in the Country wth his freinds & cometh not to the Citty to trouble either the city or the companie And his kinsmã the skinner to giue his bill that hee shall [*giue his*] dwell in the country & not cōme againe to the citty[1]

Primo Martij 1612

John Pindley, John Beale It ys consented by a court holden this day That John Bealle & John Pindley shalbe allowed for one printer. in the house & printing house that was William Halls.[2] Vppon condicon that they vse the same peaceablie & lyue quietly together as ptn's in such sort that the Companie may like well of their pceedings & doings. And yf default bee made therein by them then it is ordered wth their assent that the said house & prynteing house & the prynteinge stuffe wth all things thereto belonging [*as*] shall bee dysposed by the M[r] wardens & assistants accordingely as the said M[r] wardens & assistants shall thinke fit.

8 Martij 1612

M[res]. Hatfeild & her daughter Martha./ Mystres Hatfeilds[3] C[li] is by a Court holden this day accepted & payd to the hall account And shee is to haue [*x[li] a yere*] xij[li] a yere duringe her owne lyfe. And after her death her daughter is to haue duringe her life x[li] a yere The same to be paid by ffoure quarterly paym[ts] eu'y yere from o[r] Lady Day next And the C[li] is by her gyven to the hall for euer.

18 m'cij Courte daye/.

Prentises. ffor thavoydinge of thexcessiue nūbers of prentises w[che] the prynters nowe haue aboue the nūbers alowed to them by the constitutions & decree. Vppoñ complaynt thereof made,[4] yt is ordered, that henceforth no prynter shalbe alowed by the M[r]. & wardens to receaue and take any other or newe prentise vntill the said excessiue nūbers of apprentises be abated diminished & brought downe to suche nūbers onely (& no moo) as eu'y prynter in his callinge & Degree in the Comp[nie] is qualified & limited to haue accordinge to the said constitutions & decree/

[1] The Company paid him 13*s*. 4*d*. the 23 Mar. and 23 June 1613, but only 5*s*. the 27 Sept., 22 Dec. 1613, and 13 Mar. 1614, while after his name in the *Liber pro pauperibus* 22 June 1614 occurs the entry 'nil'. What Fosbrook did to make such a nuisance of himself is not apparent, but he continued to publish at different addresses in London until 1629.

[2] Regarding Hall's printing materials cf. *C–B.C*, 13[b], 1 June 1607. Pindley died before 2 Nov. 1613.

[3] Arnold Hatfield's widow, Winifred Howles Hatfield. This is the first such annuity recorded in the *Court Book*.

[4] On the last two leaves of the *Liber pro pauperibus* is a copy of the 'Journemens petition to y[e] Right Ho[ble] the Lord Elsmere Lord Chauncellor of England' dated 16 May 1613, signed by 54 journeymen, in which they allege that they have 'Laid open o[r] intollerable greifies by way of Peticon to the gou'n's of o[r] companie but they will not herken to o[r] complaints'.

5 July .1613. 11mo Ris

Mr Watersoñ — ffor Diu'se vrgent causes yt is ordered that mr. Watersoñ/ henceforward shalbe in electioñ for mr of the Compnie wthout beinge any moore putt into electioñ for the elder wardenship.[1]

mr. Watersoñ 20. nobles — And that in respect hereof he shall paie Twenty nobles for his dispensatioñ for the place of Vpp Wardeñ any moore hereafter — paid this 20 nobles to mr harisoñ warden as appeth in his accounts of wardenship. July 1613

Fol. 32a

1613. .11. Ris Jacobi

3 Augusti

Mres Marye Bysshop. — This day in full court mrs Bysshop her Last will & testamt was deliu'ed into the hall to be there kept And yt was receaued Accordingly and there Layd in safe keping/[2]

6to Septembris Court day

Mr Mathew Lownes/ — Electoñ beinge made for Mrs Bysshopps pte/ And Mr Adams, Mr Banckwoorth, & Mr Mathew Lownes beinge in electione Thelection falleth Vppon Mr Mathewe Lownes/

Mr Vinson — Mr Mathew Lownes his Lyu'ye pte falle by election vpon George Vinson/ Mr Purfoot Jun' & Mr Harrison Ju' were in election with him/.

Humfrey Lownes Jun' — Thelection for Mr Vinsons yomans pte And yt falleth thereby vpon Humfrey Lownes Jun'/ John Wright & Richard Taylor were in election with him.

And they haue all taken their oathes accordinglye/.

27mo. Septemb. Courte daye

George Elde. — It is ordered that George Elde shall be comitted to prison & to pay xxxs. for a fyne[3] for beinge disobedient to the mayster of this Company & vseinge vndecent & vnfittinge speeches to the wardens/ contrary to the orders

William Hall — It is ordered that William Hall shall haue no dyuident out of his pte before he come and appeare before the mayster wardens & Assistente Att a Courte[4]

[1] He was not elected until 1617, cf. *C–B.C*, 47b, 8 Jul. 1617.

[2] The 'two tenements called Newton' by the will of George Bishop now become the property of the Company, cf. *C–B.C*, 24b.

[3] This fine was apparently not paid.

[4] Hall paid 10*s*. fine 15 July 1614, 'for vnfitting wordes vsed to or Master and wardens', cf. *Book of Fines*, 10a, which may be the offence here noted, cf. *C–B.C*, 35a, 15 July 1614.

2° die Octobris 1613 et Rę Jacobi 11° &c'.

Tho. Mountforte Clarke./

p̃nte mr Norton mr
mr ffeild } wardens
mr Ockeld }
mr Harison senior
mr Samson
mr Hooper
mr Lownes senior
mr Adames
mr Harison Junior
mr Swynhowe
mr Lownes Junior
mr Jaggard

It is ordered by a full Court holden this day that Thomas Mountforte, (havinge satisfied John Keile for the reversion of the Clarkeshipp of the Companye)[1] shalbe Clarke and solicitor of the said Company in the roome and place of Richard Collyns late deceased[2] and to haue all wages fees pencõns and other Comodities belonginge to the said offices of Clarkeshippe and solicitorshippe in as lardg and beneficiall manner as the said Ric' Collins enioyed the same, And the said Thomas Mountforte was sworne and admitted accordinglye/.

Quarter day

FOL. 32b

4to die Octobris 1613 et Rę Jacob. 11mo

Mr Ditton./ It is ordered that mr Ditton shall haue in his bond wherein he standę bound together wth Randall wolley in the some of 150li to the mr and keepers or wardens and Cominaltie of the Mistery or art of Stacionrs Concerning the enioyeing by Marye Bishoppe during her Naturall life two tenemtę called Newton in the parrish of Milbornestocke in the Countie of Salope.[3]

The Coppie of my Lo. Cheife Justices ler to the Company in the behalfe of Thomas Sam̃on.

Tho. Sam̃on. Whereas this bearer my servant Thomas Samõn is a sutor to you for the Clarkeshippe of yor Hall in reversion, which whether he shall enioye is in godę handę I could not but Com̃end his suite to you for that I knowe he is an honest and sufficient man for that place, and one that hath taken paynes bout my reportę allreadie published and shall take the like about others wch god willing ere it be long shall come to the presse, And so I Com̃end my self to you and Comitt you to the blessed protection of the almightie. .3. octobris 1613

yor verye loving freind
Ed: Coke/.

To the right worll and my very loving freindę The mr the wardens and the rest of the worll Companye and societie of the Stacioners this be dd.

[1] Cf. *C–B.C*, 13a, 1 June 1607.
[2] Regarding his appointment 30 May 1575, Arber ii. 35.
[3] Cf. *C–B.C*, 24b.

11° Octobris 1613:

mr. welbey & mr. Jackson. It is ordered by a full Court of Assistantę that mr welbey (having printed among Grenhamę workes a part of a coppie heretofore entred to mr Jackson contrary to order) shall giue vnto the said mr Jackeson in recompence 2 of the said Grenhamę workes whole [for] everye Impression that the said wm welbey shall print[1]

Th. Mo

Fol. 33a

A clause of a Codicill annexed to the last will and Testament of Mary Bishoppe widowe./[2]

Mres Bishoppe 24 Item she did give and bequeath to the Company of Stacõners in London being at her funerall, ten poundę foure arras wrought cushens a cubberd cloth and two long flaxen table-clothes of her owne spinning. The said ten poundę foure arras wrought cushens the Cubberd Cloth and two long flaxen table clothes were paid and deliu'ed to the wardens by willm Aspley her executr the 11 day of october 1613.

The scavenger of St Martins. It is ordered that the scavenger of St Martins next Ludgate shall haue vs p annũ for Burgeny house nowe Stacioners hall and xvjd for an other house that was Austens.

Mr Norton M- This day Mr Norton gave to the wardens to make a feast for the Companye—vl in respect of a bankett he shoud haue made, when he was [*sen*] master, the seconde time/

25 Novemb 1613

Mr Dawson........hath deliu'ed to the wardens an acquittance from the prish of Mr Billagę matter 6. St Martins in the vintry for lijs due to there poore for one yeare ended at the feast of St Michẽll the archangell last past.[3]

And hath also deliu'ed to the wardens xiijs iiijd due at the same time for a yeare for the same matter to the vse of the Company

mr Norton mr This day mr Norton or master paid to the wardens for one half yeares rent of Newton demised by mr Geo. Bishoppe late alderman and stacioner of London to Paules Crosse, Christę hospitall, and this Companye......xjl./[4]

Sexto Decemb: 1613

Mr Browne John Keele[5] having surrendred his Lyuery parte into the handes of the Companye there stoode in election for it mr Harrison the yonger, mr Boyle, mr Browne. Th'election falleth vpon mr Browne.

[1] STC 12318. Cf. *C–B.C*, 8b, 7 Oct. 1605.
[2] Cf. *C–B.C*, 32a, 3 Aug. 1613.
[3] Cf. *C–B.C*, 6a, 4 Dec. 1604, *et loc. cit.*
[4] Cf. *C–B.C*, 28b 6 Apr. 1612.
[5] J. Keyle admitted freeman 13 Jan. 1578 (Arber ii. 675). Having sold the reversion of the clerkship, he now evidently desired to sell out of the Company entirely.

John wright Tho. downes. mr Brownes yeomandry pte fell vppon John wright and Thomas downes to make there half yeomans pte whole yeomans pte there stood in election wth them Ephram Dawson./ they tooke there oathes according to the ordinance in that behalf

Nono Decemb: 1613.

My Lo: Maiors dinner 23 According to an order heretofore made by a full Court, there was appointed to goe to my Lord Mayors to dinner this yeare: Mr Man and the wardens mr Dawson mr Leake and mr H: Lownes.

To mr Shreiue [*Bannette*] [Bennette].

Mr Man and the wardens mr Adames mr Harrison Junior, and mr Swynnoe./.

To mr Shreive Gayes.

mr Man and the wardens mr waterson mr Math: Lownes and mr Jaggard.

17° Januarij 1613.

Ireland 27 It is ordered that Lxxl be payde in to the Chamber of London for Ireland the first of ffebruary next according to a warrant directed to [*a warrant directed*] to the Company from the Lo. Mayor/[1]

This was paid in accordingly

7° ffebr 1613 Re Jacob. 11°./ FOL. 33b

Ireland:/ It is ordered by consent of a ffull Court holden this day That when and as often as any of the Partners in the Priveledge shall depart this Life or otherwise giue ou' there parte he or they that shall be elected to [the] said pte, shall pay to him or his executors, ouer and aboue his full part so giuen ou' so much rateably as the said Partener hath heretofore disbursed towarde the Plantacion in Ireland.

Auditors. Chosen Auditors for the half yeares account

mr dawson, mr waterson } of the Assistante

mr knight, mr welby } of the lyverye.

walter Burr, ffrances Archer } of the yeomandry.

Thomas Bushell. It is ordered by a Court holden this day that Thomas Bushell the beadle[2] shall haue the xli for 3 yeares that mr kingston payd in of mr Dexters bequest[3] his suerties were likd of by the wardens, the bond sealed accordingly and delivered to mr warden Ockeld 22° Januarij 1613.

[1] This precept has not been found, but cf. *C–B.C*, 27a, 11 Apr. 1611.

[2] Just when Bushell was appointed Beadle is not clear. John Hardy, his predecessor, entered books as late as 1609.

[3] Cf. *C-B.C*, 5b, 16 Oct. 1604. His bond is registered in *Liber C2*, 14b.

Die Marties primo Martij 1613 Re Jac. 11°/.

Officers for the stocke/ Officers Chosen for the stocke for the yeare from the feast of the Aoũ next 1614 12° Re.

Mr Hum: Lownes } of the Assistante
mr Jaggard.....

mr Selman } of the Liverye
mr Tomes

ffrances Burton } of the yeomandrye.
Joh: Dawson..

All haue taken there oathes accordingly.

Auditors chosen for this last yeares account

Mr Man } of the assistante
Mr Leake

Mr Gilman } of the [*assistante*] liuery
mr Dight.

Raffe Mabb. } of the [*assistante*] yeomanry
Joh. Wright.

FOL. 34a

Primo Die Martij 1613.

Mr Bradwood./ It is ordered that Mr Bradwood shall pay for a fyne for refusing to be stoc keep being there vnto Chosen } iiijli

paid accordingly[1]

8° die Martij 1613.

Mr ffayrebrother Whereas Willm ffairebrother and Lott Sivedale are sutors to this Company, to renewe the lease of a tenement nere Ave Marye Lane part of that wch was Lanes lease nowe in the Occupacõn of the sd ffairebrother and Sive[dale] or there Assignes It is ordered by Consent of a full Court holden this day That mr warden ffeild mr waterson mr Leake mr H. Lownes calling vnto them Thomas Montforte there Clarke shall consider whether it be fitt to devid the said tenement or no, and what is necessary for either of them and also to sett and Compound for the fyne according to the number of yeares that shalbe agreed vpon and to determyne and make such end thereof as may tend to make peace betwen the said ptie and be convenient and beneficiall to the Companye./

Saint Martines It is ordered that the Churchwardens of Saint Martines next Ludgate shall haue xxs p Annũ for there pson toward the stipend for reading of a Lecture. on sundayes—the afternoone./

26 Martij 1614

ffelix Kingston./ This day ffelix Kingston Chosen Renter Warden/

[1] There is a note following the entry for this in the *Book of Fines*, 9a, which reads '11° Maij 1615, this iiijli was paid by Mr Griffin when he receiued his divident, to mr Adames warden. / pñte Tho: Moñtforte'.

Duodecimo Aprilis 1614 R℮ Jac'. duodecimo

Mr Faire-brother This day mr ffairebrothers lease was sealed according to the agremt by them made to whom it was Comitted vt supra, that is to say for 31 yeares to begin at the feast of the Aõn of the blessed virgin Mary wch shalbe in Anno Dñi 1616. he is to pay 110l viz at Midsomer next 36l—13s—4d at Christmas next 36l—13s—4d and at or Ladie day 1615 next 36l—13s—4d./

17° Maij 1614.

Lotterye./ Vpon Certayne lres written from the Counsell as also from the Lord Maior to this Company (as they are [regestred] in the booke of Precept℮)[1] to venter [*to*] in the Lottery. it is ordered that 45l be sent to Sr Thomas Smith to venter in the sd Lottery, and that the prises if any happen; shalbe to the partenrs in the stocke, because the said 45l is ventred out of there money.

17° Maj Anno 1614: 12 R℮ Jac. Court day FOL. 34b

John Garrett
Richard Redmere Vppon Complaynt made at this Court by one John Garrett against [*one*] Richard Redmere for misvsing Wm Garrett[2] his apprentice, the sonne of the said John Garrett, wherevpon the said Richard Redmere [was warned to] [*should*] vse his apprentice well hereafter, and that he should make tryall [*wth*] for one yeare more. And if the said Wm Garret be vsed well the said John Garrett is Content to pay this time twelue moneth to the said Richard Redmere iijl vjs viijd. And it is ordered that if the said Richarde Redmere shall misvse his apprentice, his father shall have him home againe and also receive backe againe the some of xl that the said Richard Redmere hath hereto-fore received wth his said apprentice. and here after be vncapable of any apprentice/

22° Junij. 1614.

Wm Cogram. It is ordered that wm Cogram[3] a pore scholler, (at the request of the Lo: B: of London signified to this Companye by his lr̃es dated Junij 16 1614) shall have iiijl p annũ for 5 yeares out of the poores account, paid to him in hand 20s

30° Junij 1614

Mr Bill./ It is ordered by Consent of a full Court that me John Bill shall receiue from the stocke for Certayne schoole bookes taken of him 45l—13s—6d the one half at Michãs next and the other half at Christmas next.

[1] Cf. *Letter Book*, 83a and b. There are two broadsides in the library of the Society of Antiquaries of London which refer to this Virginia Company Lottery, cf. Lemon, Nos. 135 and 151, and *Three proclamations concerning the lottery for Virginia*, Providence, R.I., 1907. Another broadside of still earlier date is in the John Carter Brown Library, cf. Sabin 99859.

[2] Made free 5 Mar. 1621 (Arber iii. 685).

[3] No doubt the St. Paul's School scholar who matriculated at New College, Oxford, 27 Oct. 1615, and died in Aug. 1621.

eodem die.

The Gratuitie to the Ks Matie/ This day an officer came to the Company from my Lord Mayor wth a mess[*u*]ag that 2 of the assistantę should come presently to the Court of Aldermen, mr warden ffeild and mr Leake were sent, they before or Court rise brought word to the table that the Kingę matie was to be supplied wth 100000li by way of Contribucōn and gratuitie out of the Cittie and that the Stationrs must provide 200li for there ptę; Consideracōn beinge had hereof it was thought fitt and agreed by gen'all consent as well of livery and yeomandry, as by the table that 100li should be levied from the partenrs in the priviledge, that is to say every Assistant 40s every livery man 20s and the yeomandry 10s a peece wch comes to 90li. Mr Norton or Master and mr Barker did offer to give 5li a peece more to make it vp 100li wch said 100li was afterward paid to the Chamber of London and accepted of./

Fol. 35a 2 die Julij 1614. Rę Jacob: 12o

Mr Thomas Man the elder, Mr.
mr Wm Leake }
mr Tho Adams } Wardens./

The same day they tooke there oathes according to the ordinance in that behalf/

15 Julij 1614

John Beale ffine/ This day it is ordered by Consent of a full Court that John Beale shalbe Cōmitted to prison and pay a fyne of 6li—13s—4d. for bynding a prentice at a scrivenors against the order of this house./[1]

Wm Hall ffine/ Item it is ordered that wm hall shall pay 30s for a fyne for being disobedient to the Master of this Company and vsing disobedient speeches to the wardens,[2] he payd xs and vpon his submission it was accepted of by the table in full paymt, and it is further ordered that he shall receiue all his divident that is behind in mr weavers handę.

Tho. Bushell. Item it is ordered that Thomas Bushell[3] shall haue 5li out of the stocke account for his paynes in diu'se Jorneyes in the Companyes busines./ paid vnto [him] accordingly.

Primo Die Augusti 1614. Court day.

John Snowdon ffine It is ordered by Consent of a full Court holden this day that John Snowdan[4] for vnfitting wordę vsed to Raffe blower shall pay to the vse of this Company xxs. And it is further ordered that the said John Snowdam for vnfitting speeches vsed of or Master and mr Adames shalbe Cōmitted to the Counter vpon my Lo: Mayors Cōmand./

1 Cf. *C–B.C*, 40a, 21 Nov. 1615.
2 Cf. *C–B.C*, 32a, 27 Sept. 1613.
3 The Beadle.
4 There are two possible John Snowdons: one was apprenticed 25 Mar. 1584 (Arber ii. 124), the other made free 26 July 1613 (Arber iii. 684).

Rich: Braddocke ffine — It is ordered that Richarde Braddocke for bynding of a prentice at a scrivenors Contrary to order shall pay a fyne of 6^{li}—13^{s}—4^{d}

Raffe Blower & John Hanson. ffine — Item it is ordered that John Hanson[1] for vsing vnfitting speeches to Raffe Blower shall pay for a fyne 5^{s} to the vse of the Company And the said Raffe Blower for the same matter shall pay iij^{s} $iiij^{d}$.

eodem die.

Edward White John Budge — fforasmuch as Edward white stationr hath borrowed of John Budg Stationer the some of 50^{li} and doth engage his part in Stationrs hall being 75^{li} for the payment of the said 50^{li} vpon Condicōn that if the said Edward white doe not pay to the said John Budg the said some of 50^{li} wthin one yeare that is to say vpon the first day of August which shalbe in the yeare of or Lord god 1615. Then the said Edward White doth resigne his said part into the hande of the Master Wardens and assistante of the Company that they may goe to election of || another partenor according to the order in that behalf. Wherevpon It is ordered by Consent of a full Court holden this day that if the said Edward white shall faile in the said payment, the said John Budg shalbe in election [*of*] for the said part, And if the said John Budg shalbe chosen therevnto he shall pay to Edward white 25^{li} more to make the said 50^{li} allreadie Lent 75^{li} in full payment of his whole pte And if the said John Budg be not Chosen then he that shalbe Chosen shall pay vnto the Stockeeps to the vse of John Budg 50^{li} and to the vse of Edward white or his executrs 25^{li} at the time and termes sett downe in the ordinances made and provided for the good gou'ment of the ptenors in the said Company./ (FOL. 35^{b} 1 Aug. 1614. (*Marginal heading on this page.*))

The sd John Budge was Chosen to the sd pte.
Test. T.M.

27 Septemb 1614

Robert Dodge & Robert woodenott. — This day Robert dodg[2] engaged his part being 37^{li}—10^{s} to Robert woodnott for 18^{li}—15^{s} of him borrowed, and it is ordered by Consent of Robert Dodg that [*if*] [when] the said Robert dodg shall depart out of this life, the Master and wardens having elected an other ptenor the one half of the divident to be paid to Robert woodnot vizt 18^{li}—15^{s} and the other haue (*sic*) to the executers of the said Robert dodge./ In the meane time it is agreed betwixt the pties that Robert woodnot shall receiue half the [*profitt*] divident./

14 die Octobris A° 1614

Mr Ash. — This day mr Ash had leaue of the Company to print his tables to the booke of Entryes and his owne booke for one Impression onely. he promised to giue to the Company either one quartern of the said bookes or ten shillinge in money[3]

1 There are likewise two John Hansons: one was apprenticed 29 Sept. 1598 (Arber ii. 230), the other made free 8 Oct. 1611 (Arber iii. 683).

2 Made free 8 Apr. 1584 (Arber ii. 691).

3 R. Blower and Leonard Snodham on the 20 Oct. 1614 (Arber iii. 554), 'Entred (by the license of the

M[r] Aldee. ffine	It is ordered that m[r] Aldee for printing the warres in Germanie[1] shall pay a fine to the Companye of v[s] because the said [*boke*] booke was never entred. paid accordingly
Joh: Snowdam. ffine	Item it is ordered that John Snowdon shall pay for printing of a part of the same booke, v[s].[2] paid accordingly
Joh. Trundle. ffine.	Item it is ordered that John Trundle shall pay for the same booke also—5[s] for a fine.[3] paid accordingly

19 Octob. 1614

M[r] ffeild & M[r] Ockold.	Item it is ordered that M[r] ffeild and m[r] Ockold wardens the last yeare for there election dinner w[ch] was omitted shall pay the some of xij[l] to the Company, paid ut patet in prox:[4]

M[r] Johnson & Lau: Lile — Item it is ordered, that m[r] Johnson shall deliuer and giue vnto Laurence Lile 20 halles workes whole[5] for the said Laurence Liles part that he hath in some [*part*] Copies of m[r] do[r] Halles bookes w[ch] the said Johnson hath printed w[th]out the consent of the said Lile

Fol. 36[a]

14° Novemb: 1614.

George Purslowe. It is ordered by consent of a full Court holden this day that Georg Pursloe shalbe a Master printer in the rome and place of Symon Stafford that hath given over the same. And it is further ordered that the said Georg Pursloe shalbe one of the fiue printers of the ballette[6]:.

15° Novembris 1614.

M[r] Tho. Sanforde. This day m[ris]. Twist and m[r] Gibbons and m[r] Sanford receiued of the Company the 300[l] pound that was left vnpaid for Verney Alleis Pattent of the psalms, so that they haue receiued 600[l] for the same. M[r] Tho. Sanford sealed an assignment thereof to m[r] Man o[r] Master m[r] Leake and m[r] Adames wardens to the vse of the Company.[7]

Company to print one impression of 1500 for master Ash paying to the Company at the finishing thereof either x[s], or one quartern of bookes,) *An appendix to his former booke called "the promptuarie or repertorie generall of the common Lawe of England"* vj[d]'. This was printed as the 'Postscript' to STC 841 (cf. J. D. Cowley, *Bibliography of abridgments*, No. 114). Presumably some arrangement concerning the publication of STC 841 had been made between J. Beale and the Company, for all copies traced except the B.M. and Bodleian have the imprint to both volumes 'Imprinted at London by I. Beale, 1614' (cf. Cowley, *op. laud.*). Regarding the sale by James Pagett of a number of copies to the Company for £300, cf. *C–B.C*, 42[a], 4 Mar. 1616.

[1] STC 11796. From the ornaments, sheets A and B of this book were printed by E. Allde.

[2] Sheets C and D were apparently printed by Snodham. In the *Book of Fines* his name is correctly given as Thomas.

[3] Trundle evidently sold the book, and not Butter whose name it bears.

[4] Cf. *C–B.C*, 36[b], 22 Dec. 1614. In *Letter Book*, 84[a], 24 June 1614, is a precept from the Mayor forbidding election dinners for six months.

[5] The only item to which this may refer appears to be STC 12706[a], in which, however, both Johnson and Lisle appear to have had parts. STC 12706 is a ghost.

[6] Cf. *C–B.C*, 28[b], 19 May 1612.

[7] This purchase presumably was for the English Stock. Cf. *C–B.C*, 36[b], 18 Nov. 1614. It is not certain just whose patent this was, but presumably it was derived from John Day's.

The Coppie of Mr Bonham Norton his bill of Chardges concerning Newton[1]

Disbursed by [my] Cosen John Norton and myself Bonham Norton Concerning the farme of Newton

		ł s—d
28.	Paid the 4th of May 1612 to mrs Bishoppe for one yeares rent due to her at or Ladie day 1612 the some of	22—0—0
	Paid to mrs Bishoppe the 21th of October 1612 and due to her at Michĩs last the some of	11—0—0
	Paid the 11th of Decemb. 1612 to mr George Holland for Chardges in the Chancery against mr Tho. hopton and mr ffowler as appeareth by his bill...........	1—6—0
	Paid to mr Collins the fourth of May 1612 for the passing over the recognisance Statute and mrs Bishoppes estate to the Company.........................	2—0—0
	Paid to mr Holland ut patet by his bill dated triũ 20 (*sic, ? 10*) Jacob:	1—8—6
	Paid for a search in the Statute office.............	0—7—0
	Paid the 27th of ffebru: 1612 to mr Georg holland for chardges in Hillary terme	0—5—4
	Paid the 22th of June 1613 to mrs Bishoppe for half a yeares rent due at or Ladie day last	11—0—0
	Paid the 15th of Novemb. 1613 to mr Ockold warden for half a yeares rent due at Michĩs last	11—0—0
	Paid the twentith of Aprill 1614 to mr Ockold for half a yeares rent due at or Ladie day last	11—0—0
	Paid the 2d of ffebru: 1613 to mr Coventry for a fee	0-11—0
	Paid the 18th of Octob: to mr Adames for one half yeares rent due at Michĩs last past	11—0—0
	Sum tolis..........	82-17-10

22° Novemb: A° 1614 Fol. 36b

Mr Norton The foresaid some of 82ł—17s—10d was paid to mr Bonham Norton for rent and Chardges that he laid out about Newton, and he promised in the presence of mr waterson, mr ffeild mr H: Lownes mr Weaver and me Thomas Montforte at the payment of the sđ some to deliver to the Company all the Conveyances and writtings that he hath concerning the same wch are as he saith at his house in Shropshire

Tho: Montforte

[1] Cf. *C–B.C*, 28b, 6 Apr. 1612.

plus de Newton — The lease of Newton was afterwardꝭ granted by the Company to m^{r} Bonham Norton for 480 yeares to Com̃ence from o^{r} Ladie day 1618 for the Rent of 22^{l} together wth an assignemt (*sic*) of the statutꝭ and the sd̄ m^{r} Norton paid the money backe againe.

T.M.

18 Novemb. 1614

Mr Dawson — Mr Dawson hath deliu'ed to the wardens an acquittance from the ꝑrish of Saint Martins in the vintry for lij^{s} due to the poore

6 for one yeare ended at the feast of Saint Michaell the arke-angell last past[1]

And hath also deliu'ed to the wardens xiij^{s} iiij^{d} due at the same time for a yeare for the same matter to the vse of the Company

Mr Sanford. vt ante/ — This day m^{rs} Twist m^{r} Gibbons and m^{r} Sanford receiued of the Company the 300^{l} that was left vnpayd for Verney [*es pattent*] Allies pattent of the psalmes &c. And m^{r} Sanford sealed an assignem^{t} thereof to m^{r} man m^{r} Leake and m^{r} Dauies to the vse of the Company.[2] extra./

22 decemb. 1614

M^{r} ffeild, Mr Ockold — This day m^{r} warden Adames receiued of m^{r} ffeild and m^{r} Ockold wardens the last yeare the som̃e of xij^{l} wch was there gift to the Company because they made no dinner vpon the election day.[3]

Ambrose Garbrand & w^{m} Stansbey. — Vpon Complaynt made to this table [*that*] by m^{r} do^{r} Haward against w^{m} Stansbey and Ambrose Garbrand for printing the Sanctuarie of a troubled soule wth[out] his priuitie. It is ordered that the said w^{m} Stansbye shall bring the Coppie and sheetꝭ that he hath printed to the Master and wardens to be delivered to m^{r} do^{r} Haward the author and that Ambrose Garbrand whose Coppie it is shall print it in that volume m^{r} do^{r} Haward shall thinke fitt and in no other[4]

Ambrose Garbrande ffine/ — It is further ordered that the said Ambrose Garbrand shall pay for vsing vnfitting speeches to w^{m} Stansbey for a fine to the vse of the Company......iij^{s} iiij^{d}

Mr Smethicke. — Mrs Bankworth being maried the election for her livery part[5] was made this day it fell vpon Mr Smethicke there stood wth him m^{r} Serger and m^{r} ffetherstone in election

Nath. Butter. Rich. Bagger. — Mr Smethickꝭ yeomans part fell vpon Nathaniell Butter and Richard Bagger,[6] half partꝭ a peece: they all tooke there oathes accordingly

[1] Cf. *C–B.C*, 6^{a}, 4 Dec. 1604, *et loc. cit.*

[2] Cf. *C–B.C*, 36^{a}, 15 Nov. 1614. Mr. 'Davies' is possibly an error for a representative of John Day's family.

[3] Cf. *C–B.C*, 35^{b}, 19 Oct. 1614.

[4] For the earlier history of this copyright cf. *C–B.C*, 30^{a}, 5 Oct. 1612. Nothing is known of Stansby's edition and no Garbrand edition of this date is known. For the later history of this book cf. *C–B.C*, 39^{b}, 21 Aug. 1615, and 40^{b}, 4 Dec. 1615.

[5] Regarding Elizabeth Bankworth cf. *T.L.S.* 7 June 1923. As she married Edward Blount, her livery part evidently was sold because he already had one.

[6] Richard Badger.

1614, 12 Reℯ Jac; 16° Januarij

pn̄tibus
mʳ Man, master
mʳ Leake } wardens
mʳ Adames }
mʳ Barker
mʳ dawson
mʳ waterson
mʳ ffeild
mʳ Lowneѕ sen'.
mʳ Harrison Jun'
mʳ Ockold.
mʳ Swynhowe.
mʳ Lowneѕ Jun.
mʳ Jaggard.

Whereas mʳ Humphery Lownes did lend vnto the Company on the 24 day of december last the some of one hundred poundℯ It is ordered that the same debt of 100ˡ shalbe paid vnto him by the Company at the end of sixe Monethes to be accounted from the 24ᵗʰ of december last, together wᵗʰ allowance after ten p centũ for the same so long as it hath ben and shalbe vnpaid:

30 Januarij 1615 Paid vnto Mʳ Lownes the some of one hundred[1]

Lord Maior — There is appointed to goe to the Lord Maioʳˢ and the Shreues this yeare to Dinner, according to an order heretofore made.
Mʳ Man master mʳ Leake & mʳ Adames wardens, mʳ Barker mʳ Dawson mʳ waterson mʳ Hum: Lownes mʳ Swynhowe.

To mʳ Shreife Probey.
Mʳ Man Master mʳ Leake & mʳ Adames wardens mʳ Hum: Lownes mʳ Harison mʳ Math. Lownes

To mʳ Shreife Lumley.
Mʳ Man oʳ Master Mʳ Leake mʳ Adames wardens mʳ Dawson mʳ Ockold mʳ Jaggard./

Mʳ Jones. pntib3 vt supra/ — It is ordered by consent of a full [Court] holden this day that mʳ Jones Com̄on sergant of London for his great paines that he hath taken about the booke of Entries[2] shall haue paid him the some of 33ˡ—13ˢ—4ᵈ more then he hath allreadie had wᶜʰ said some was afterward paid vnto him by the Thresurer/

13 ffebru: 1614

Edward Burbey Legacie [*to his sonne*] [to be] kept by the Companye. — Md That by vertue of a decree in the h[*oᵇˡᵉ*]igh Court of Chancery, [*this*] Mʳ Turnoʳ who married the widowe of Cutbert Burbey Citizen and stacionʳ of London paid to mʳ Leake and mʳ [*ward*] Adames wardens the some of 604ˡ—17ˢ—4ᵈ, Item for Chardges susteyned in the suit 6ˡ—13ˢ—4ᵈ more for damages 40ˡ The said some of 604—17—4 is to be paid to Edward Burby orphan to the said Cutbert, when he comes to age, and in the meane time 5ˡ p Centũ to the executrix of the said Cutbert Burbey towardℯ the bringinge vp of all his Children

[1] Cf. *C–B.C.*, 41ᵇ, 20 Jan. 1616.

[2] STC 5488. Sir Edward Coke gives him no credit for his labours. It is possible that Jones is one of the three whose names are concealed in the monogram 'Aenigma' on the last page of the fourth part of STC 841, the others being Thomas Ashe and James Pagett.

as by the [*said*] will of the said Cutbert appeareth, Mr Man, m^r^ Leake, m^r^ Adames m^r^ waterson m^r^ Hum: Lownes are bound to the Chamber of London for the pformeance hereof.

Mr Leake and Mr Adames Wardens at the receit of the said money sealed and deliu'ed an acquittance to m^r^ Turno^r^, the Copie where of followeth on the other side.

FOL. 37^b^ Copia/
Edw: Burbey,

Md that according to an order or decree made in the high Court of Chancery the fourth day of November nowe last past betwene the Master wardens and Cominaltie of Station^rs^ plantifs and humfery Turno^r^ and Elizabeth his wife and Alban James Defend^te^ wee Willm Leake and Thomas Adames the nowe wardens of the said Company haue receiued and had of the sd humfery Turno^r^ and Elizabeth his wife in the hall of the said Company comonly called station^rs^ hall the full some of 604^l^—17^s^—4^d^ of lawfull mony of England for the legacie part or porcõn of Edward Burbey sonne of Cutberd Burbey late one of the said Company deceased, wch he the said Cutbert did appoint by his last will to be brought and Deliu'ed into the Master and wardens hande of the same Company, And also according to the same Decree wee the said wardens haue nowe receiued of the said humfery Turno^r^ and Elizabeth his wife twentie nobles[1] wch the said high Court of Chancery did order to be paid to the said wardens and Cominaltie for there chardges susteyned in the same suite, And moreover we the said wardens vizt w^m^ Leake and Thomas Adames doe hereby acknowledg to haue receiued of the said Defendante Mr Turno^r^ and Elizabeth his wife at the day and place aforesaid the some of fortie pounde for damages wch the Lord Maio^r^ and Court of Aldermen by and vnder the authoritie of the aforesaid Decree did adiudg the said Defendante to pay vnto the said wardens and Cominaltie for detayneing the said legacie of 604^l^—17^s^—4^d^ Contrary to the said last will of the said Cutbert Burbey In wittnes whereof wee the said wardens haue herevnto sett o^r^ hande and seales the seauenth day of february 1614 stilo anglie and in the yeares of the raigne of o^r^ sou'aigne Lord King James of England ffrance and Ireland the twelueth and of Scotland the xlv^th^.

Sealed and deliu'ed in the pñce of

Wm Leake.
Tho. Adames.

Tho: Dawson. Symo. Waterson
Edw. Swinhowe[2] Edw. Weaver.
Tho. Montforte. Joh. Warren.[3]

pñtibus
m^r^ dawson
m^r^ waterson
m^r^ Lownes sen'
m^r^ Swinhowe

The said some of 604^l^—17^s^—4^d^ aboue specified was afterward deliuered to the stockeps and There to be by them repaid to the aboue said Edward Burby when he comes to age and in the meane time [*to giue*] 5^l^ p Centũ to the xecutrix of the said Cutbert Burbey towarde the bringing vp of all his Children according to his will, so that the said wardens m^r^ Leake and m^r^ Adames [*are*] hereby are quite dischardged of the said some of 604^l^—17^s^— 4^d^ for ever./

[1] Twenty nobles equals £6. 13*s*. 4*d*. [2] Error for George. [3] Presumably a representative of H. Turner.

20 ffeb. 1614 Rẹ. 13°/

Pntib3: mr Man mr leake mr Adams mr Norton mr dawson
mr waterson mr ffeild mr Lowndẹ mr Harrison
mr Ockeld mr Swinhow mr Jaggarde

Mr Pavier — It is ordered by Consent of this Court that mr Pavier shall haue theis 3 Copies turned ou' to him from the Company payeing therefore 3l—6s—8d

The first part of the pensiue mans practise
The godley gardeñ
The xpeñs prayers.[1]

Primo Die Martij 1614 Rẹ Jacobi 13° — Fol. 38a

Present
Mr Man Mr
Mr Leake } Wardens
Mr Adams }
Mr Norton
Mr Dawson
Mr Waterson
Mr Feild
Mr Lownes
Mr Harison
Mr Ockold
Mr Swinhowe
Mr Lownes
Mr Jaggard

Officers Chosen for the stocke for the ensuing (*sic*) begining at th'anunciacōn 1615 Rẹ 13°/ vizt/

Stockepes.

Mr Waterson } Assistantẹ — Mr Rodwell } of the
Mr Swinhowe } — Mr Fetherston } Livery
Joh: Hodgettẹ } of the
Joh Wright. } yeomandry

Auditors Chosen for the last yeares account

Mr Feild } — Mr Bishoppe } — Josias Parnell
Mr Lownes Jun' } — Mr Pavier } — Walter Burre/

It is ordered this day by Consent of a full Court that hereafter Mr Weavers wages shalbe 50l p annũ./

Raff Mab et alij ffine/ — It is also ordered that Raffe Mabb, wm Bladon, Geo: Gibbes and Fran. Constable shall pay for printing of a booke called (Abuses stript & whipt) being the Copie of Fran. Burton wch is Contrary to the order of this house .iijl that is to say 15s a peece[2]
paid accordingly vt patet in lib̄. de ffinib3

Wm Stansbye. — It is ordered that wm Stansby for bynding a prentice at a scrivenors shall pay for a fine to the Company 6l—13s—4d[3]

[1] Pavier evidently paid well for these three little books, for besides the fee here recorded there is registered a bill of sale from R. Bradock; cf. Arber iii. 564, 3 Mar. 1615. Of the three, only one which Pavier printed in 1615 now survives, STC 18621 (Pt. I only). He published editions of the second, STC 11560, in 1619 and 1621 (copy at Huntington), and probably also earlier. Of the third, there is an addition of 1612 printed for Bradock (STC 4032+). The history of the copyright in these books is complicated but can be traced in Arber and Greg and Boswell. Cf. also *C–B.C*, 55b, 3 May 1619.

[2] In the Palmer Collection at Wellesley College is a copy of an edition of STC 25896 with imprint 'Printed by T. Snodham for G. Norton . . . 1615' which may be the edition referred to. For an earlier pirated edition, STC 25893, which was not detected, cf. *Trans.* xv. (1934–5), pp. 365–7.

[3] Cf. *C–B.C*, 40b, 4 Dec. 1615, and 44b, 21 June 1616.

Present

22° Martij 1614.

Mr Man Mr Mr Leake } Wardens Mr Adams }	Mr Norton Mr Barker Mr Wateson	Mr Feild Mr Lownes Mr Ockold.	Mr Swinhow Mr Lownes Mr Jaggard

Wheate. Where by vertue of a precept from the Lo: Mayor[1] the Company is p̄ntly to provide 140 quartrs of wheate for the seruice and provision of this Cittie, It is thought fitt that one Laurence Roe be agreed wthall to dischardg the Company of the said provision who this day for the so m̄e of 13l—6s—8d hath taken vpon him the performance hereof

Mr Weaver chosen Renter

Mr Norton
Mr Leake
Mr Adams
Mr Dawson
Mr Swinhowe
Mr Bischopp.
Parteners in the Gramer stocke/

This day it is agreed vpon by all parties that they wch haue partę in the Grammer shall pay to Companyes stocke the some of 60l towardę the Chardges that hath ben xpended about searching for Gramrs and accedences and maynetayneing the priveledg thereof and all the Gramrs and accedences which haue ben taken in the search are to be deliu'ed to the said ꝑtenrs in the Gramr stocke[2]

Samuell Macham

[Agreed vnto by the Master and wardens 28 Martij 1615. teste Tho: Mon̄tforte/]

[This day Samuell Macham engaged his part in the hall being 37l 10s to Mr Hump: Lownes, vpon Condicon that if the said Sam. Macham do [a] not pay to Mr Lownes the said some of 37l 10s before the anuncicōn of the blessed virgin Mary 1616. then the said Macham doth resigne his said part into the handę of the Master and wardens for the time being to Chose another ꝑtener and the money that shall come thereon to be payd to Mr Lownes.]

3° August 1615.

this said some of 37l xs was paid vnto Mr Lownes by the widowe of Mr Macham and Crost out of the booke by the Consent of the said Mr Lownes.

Tho Mon̄tforte

Fol. 38b

9° Maij 1615 Rę Jac' 13°/

Present

Mr Man Mr Mr Leake } wrd̄s Mr Adams }	Mr Norton Mr Waterson Mr Feild	Mr Lownes Mr Harison Mr Ockold	Mr Swinhow Mr Lownes Mr Jaggard.

Order for payeinge of money to the stocke

Whereas diuers of the partners in his Maties. Priveledge haue not this quarter payd to the stocke such som̄es of money as they owe for bookes deliuered vnto them by the Th'er. for wch cause the quarterly Dividentę cannot be made in such Convenient times

[1] Cf. *Letter Book*, 85a, 31 Jan. 1615.

[2] In the *Letter Book*, 85a, 8 Feb. 1614, is a copy of a letter from the Archbishop of Canterbury protesting to the Lord Mayor that the seizure from William Nethersall and Richard Pierce of certain books was lawfully done by the Commissioners for Ecclesiastical Causes. It is probably in connexion with this seizure that some, at least, of these charges were incurred.

as is [*Convenient*] [fitt.] It is this day ordered for avoyding such Inconveniences hereafter that if any partener shall not pay to the Th'er so much as he oweth vnto the said stocke at or before every quarter day that then the Master and wardens and more part of Assistentę will goe to election of an other ꝑtener in the Rome of him that is so behind hand in his paymte.

Printers.[1]
76. Vpon Complaint made to this Court (by the Master printers) of the multitude of Presses that are erected among them It is ordered by consent of a full court and agreement of the said Master printers that none shall haue more presses then are here sett downe vizt

1 Mr Dawson........2 presses
2 Mr Feild..........2
3 Mr Lownes........2
4 Mr Islipp..........2
5 Mr Kingston.......2
6 Mr Allde..........2
7 Mr Purfoote.......2
8 Mr Jaggard........2
9 Mr Eld............2
10 Mr Stansby........2
11 Mr Snodam........2
12 Mr Beale..........2
13 Mr Griffin.........2
14 Mr Legatt.........2
15 Mr White.........one
16 Mr Creede.........one
17 Mr Okes..........one
18. Mr Blower.........one
19. Mr Pursloe........one.

9° Maij 1615 Fol. 39a

A Copie of an note from Skinners Hall for Armor for Ireland

To the Company of Stationrs
Yor Company is forthwth vpon Receit hereof by virtue of a precept from the Governors and Court of Comittees for the Irish plantacõn london to send downe to Skinnrs hall one Corslett and one Muskett furnished wch are appointed for yor Company for to lent for the better defence of the Citties land in Ireland and are to be Conveyed thither among other the Companyes by the shippes nowe readie to be sett furth dated at Skinnrs hall 4° Maij 1615

Vpon the receit of wch note a Corslett and Muskett furnished by direction of both the wardens was taken downe out of the provision in the armory of the Company and sent to Skinners hall accordingly

[1] This list, apparently from another copy in *State Papers Dom.*, vol. lxxx, no. 98, is printed in Arber iii. 699. Probably this was an answer to the petition of the Freemen and Journeymen Printers who had the preceding year sent a printed petition to Parliament, copies of which are in the Society of Antiquaries and Bagford collections, reprinted Arber iv. 525–6.

Joh: Budge.
mirror of martirs

It is ordered that John Budge shall pay 40[s] to the Company for printing a booke Called the mirro[r] of Martirs[1] being taken out of the great booke of Martirs w[ch] belonge to (*the*) Company.

[paid accordingly] And it is further ordered that vpon euery Impression of 1500 he shall pay to the Company 40[s] more

5° Junij 1615

Rich: Neile It is this day ordered that Richard Neile[2] a Jorney man Printer shalbe comitted to the Counter in Woodstreet for departing from Mr Aldee not giuinge him a fortnighte warneing according to an ordinance in that behalfe.

7 Julij 1615 Re Jac. 13°.

pñtibȝ.

Mr Dawson M[r]		Mr Man	M[r] ffeild	Mr Ockold
Mr Lownes sen'	wardens	Mr Waterson	Mr Adams	Mr Lownes
Mr Swinhowe		Mr Leake	Mr Harison	Mr Jaggard

Mr Lownes iue' Mr Lownes Jun' chosen stockekeper in the rome of Mr Swinhowe warden and sworne accordingly

Mr Gilmym
Mr Cole

M[r] Gilmyn, M[r] Cole chosen in to the Assistante.

John Tapp
Nath. Butter

This day also election was made for Mrs Newburyes[3] yeomanry parte. it fell upon John Tapp and Nathaniell Butter to make there half parte whole parte a peece. Richard Taylor and ffrances Constable stoode in electon wth them.

Fol. 39[b]

7° Augusti 1615 Re Jac'. 13°.

pñtibz

M[r] Dawson Master		M[r] Man	M[r] Adams.	M[r] Gilmyn
M[r] Lownes sen'	wardens	M[r] Waterson	M[r] Lownes.	M[r] Cole.
M[r] Swinhowe		M[r] ffeild	M[r] Jaggard.	

Nath. Newbery It is this day ordered that Nathaniell Newbery paying for a fine fortie shillinge, and the fees of the house. shall be admitted to the freedome of this Company by translacõn from the haberdashers. paid accordingly[4]

[1] STC 5849. This was paid the same day, cf. *Book of Fines*, 10[b]. Cf. *C–B.C*, 143[a], 7 Nov. 1636.

[2] No such person is recorded as affiliated with the Company.

[3] Widow of Ralph Newbery?

[4] This was not paid until 21 Nov. 1615, cf. *Fine Book*, 11[a].

21° August 1615.

pñtibȝ vt supra

John Budge — Edwarde White haueing resigned his yeomans part into the handes of the Mr and wardens and Assistantꝭ, they went to election of an other partner, and it fell vpon John Budge, there stoode in election wth him ffra. Conotable and Rich. Taylor.

Ambrose Garbrand / Walter Bure / Wm Stansby — Ambrose Garbrand hath leaue this day to take his course by Lawe against Wm Stansbye.[1]

Walter Bur hath license also to take course by lawe against the said Stansbye.[2]

3° die Octob: 1615 et Rꝭ Jacob. 13°

pntibȝ

Mr Dawson Master	Mr Man	Mr ffeild.	Mr Lowns Jun'
Mr Lownes sen' } wardens	Mr Waterson	Mr Adams.	Mr Jaggard.
Mr Swinhowe } wardens	Mr Leake.	Mr Ockold.	Mr Gilmin.

Mr Leake. — Whereas this pñte day Mr Leake hath lent to the Company the so͞me of one hundred poundes of lawfull money of England It is ordered by Consent of a full Court that the said debt shalbe paide vnto him at the ende of sixe monethes to be accounted from this pñte day, together wth allowance after ten p Centũ for the same so longe as it shalbe vnpaide[3]

This said some of an hundred poundꝭ, was paid accordingly

The Apocripha. — This day also was publique notice given by the table to many of the Company that were pñte, according to my Lorde of Canterbury his Graces direction that no more bibles be bounde vp and sold wthout the Apocripha in them vpon paine of one whole yeares Imprisonment.[4]

Mr Wm Nortons bequest — It is ordered that the money giuen to the Company by Mr Wm Nortons bequest[5] shalbe all putt out to young men of the Company according to the will. whereof

John Gwillim is to haue	12l
Sam. Joslinge to haue..	12l
Rich. Higgenbotham...	12l
Tho: Gubbin..........	12l
John Ashton	12l
Wm Bayard...........	6l
Parr Bettye	6l

It is also ordered that Wm Butler shall haue—10l of Mr Burbeyes bequest[6] Abrah. Ripley to haue—10l of Mr Dexters bequest[7] Rob: Lewis to haue—5l of Mr Stukies bequest[8]

1 Presumably in connexion with STC 13006, cf. *C–B.C*, 36^{b}, 22 Dec. 1614.

2 Possibly in connexion with STC 20637, concerning which see *Letter Book*, 89^{b}, 22 Dec. 1614.

3 Repaid 22 Mar. 1616, cf. *C–B.C*, 42^{b}.

4 Regarding the omission of the Apocrypha in English Bibles of this period, cf. *C. H. Pforzheimer Cat.* i. 69–71, &c. The editions referred to here are probably some of STC $2174–80^{a}$. Cf. also *C–B.C*, 50^{a}, 2 Mar. 1618.

5 Cf. Greg, *Reg. B*, 458^{a}, 13 Dec. 1593. The bonds for these are registered *Liber C2*, $14^{b}–15^{b}$.

6 Cf. *C–B.C*, 17^{a}, 1 Mar. 1608. He was actually lent it from Dexter's bequest, *Liber C2*, 177^{a}.

7 Cf. *C–B.C*, 5^{b}, 16 Oct. 1604. He was lent it from Burby's bequest, *Liber C2*, 184.

8 Cf. Greg, *Reg. B*, 463^{b}, 2 May 1597. The bonds were registered in *Liber C2*, 157^{a}.

FOL. 40a

21 Nouembris 1615 Reg 13°.

Present

Mr Dawson Mr	Mr Norton	Mr Leake	Mr Lownes Jun'.
Mr Lownes } wdēs	Mr Man.	Mr Feild.	
Mr Swinhowe }	Mr Waterson.	Mr Adams.	

Mr Speeds Geneologies — Mr Norton, Mr Man, Mr Waterson Mr Leake Mr ffeild and Mr Adames were appointed by this Court to conferre wth mr John Speed about his pattent of the Geneologies[1] and to report vnto the table, what they thinke fitt to be done theirein.

According to the which reference the said Cōmittees haue meet (*sic*) wth the said John Speed and doe Certifie as foloweth viz. That whereas the Master and keepers or wardens & Cōminaltie of the mistery or art of Stationrs of the Cittie of London, by theire Indenture vnder their Comōn seale beareinge date the 25th of March in the tenth yeare of the raigne of or sou'aigne Lord the Kinge Matie that nowe is, haue Couenanted granted promised & agreed to and wth the said John Speed his executors administrators and assignes to pay the said John Speed for eu'ye booke Intituled (The Geneologies of the Holye scriptures and mappe of Canaan) in the volume called Quarto, the sōme of ten pence as in the said Indenture among other thinge therein contayned more at lardge appeareth, Nowe the said John Speed because the Master wardens and assistante shall vse and Imploy their best meanes and indeavors that no bibles of what volumes or translacōn soeu' shall dureing the said terme of the said Indenture be bound up or vttered vnles one of the said Geneologies and Mappes be inserted and bounde in the said bibles, is content and hath agreed that the sd master and keepers or wardens and Cominaltie shall pay to the said John Speed for euery Geneologie and Mapp in quarton onely eight pence any thinge to the said Indenture to the Contrary in any wise not wthstanding. And the said Cōmittees thinke fitt that it myght be ordered by Consent of a full Court that hereafter whensoeu' and as often as any booke of psalmes in meeter shalbe deliu'ed out of the ware-house there shall likewise then be deliu'ed therewth so many of the said Geneologies and Mappes as of the said psalmes in meeter according to the true intent and meaneinge of the said Indenture afore mencōned. The which report and agreemt of theirs being afterward reade was well liked and approued of by a full Court and ordered to be entred into the hall booke and to be performed accordingly.

Joh. Beales fine. — Whereas John Beale was heretofore fyned by the table[10] in 6l—13s—4d for bindeinge Edward Winchloe his apprentice at a Scrivenors contrary to order. This day the said John Beale paid the company vl thereof and it was accepted by the Table in full payemt. And it is ordered that he shall keepe his said appr' to serue out his yeares

[1] STC 23039. Speed obtained a grant for ten years, *State Papers Dom. 1603–10*, p. 639, 30 Oct. 1610, and a special licence for seven years longer, *State Papers Dom. 1611–18*, p. 431, 4 Feb. 1617. It was obviously extended but just when has not appeared.

[10] Cf. *C–B.C*, 35a, 15 July 1614, and *Fine Book*, 11a, 27 Oct. 1615.

4° Decemb. 1615

Present

Mr Dawson Mr.	Mr Mann	Mr Feild	Mr Lownes
Mr Lownes	Mr Waterson	Mr Adams.	Mr Gilmyn
Mr Swinhowe	Mr Leake	Mr Ockold	

Ambrose Garbrand Geo. Purslowe — Whereas Ambrose Garbrand doth owe vnto the Stocke the some of xxli and is content to assigne to the Companye his Copie Called (The sanctuarye of a troubled soule)[1] for the said 20li Now it is ordered by consent of a full court that if George Pursloe pay to the Company the said some of 20li in forme following that is to say at the finishing of the first Impression 10li, and 6 monethes after 5li and 6 monethes after that the other 5li. That then he the said George Pursloe shall haue the said Copie entred vnto him as his Copie for euer

Mr Corden: — Also it is ordered this day That Mr Corden keeper of the english house at Middleborough shall haue 15li for 55 realme (*sic*) of Primers there printed and to be deliu'ed at Stationrs hall and Mr Weaver is to writt to him to that purpose

Wm Stansbye. — This day Wm Stansbye promised to paie to the Companye 6li—13s—4 in the first weeke of Hillary terme next for a fine sett vpon him in Court for byndeing apprentice at a Scrivenors contary to order.[2]

My Lord Maiors Dinnrs. — Appointed to goe to my lo. Maiors to dinnr this yeare.
The Master and wardens mr waterson mr ffeild & Mr Adams
Appointed to goe to the vpper Shreiues.
The Master and wardens mr Ockold mr Lownes mr Gilman
Appointed to goe to the other Shreiues.
The Master and wardens mr leake mr Jaggard Mr Blount

20 Decemb. 1615

Present — Mr Dawson. Mr Lownes. Mr Swinhoe Mr Norton Mr Man Mr Waterson mr leake mr Feild mr Adams mr Harison mr Ockold mr Jaggard Mr Gilmyn mr Cole

mr Adame. — This day election was made for mr White assistante parte. and it fell vpon mr Adame mr Swinhowe and mr Jaggard were in electõn wth him.

mr Aspleye — mr Adame yeomandry part fell vpon mr Aspley mr Aldee and mr Purfoote stood in election wth him.

Ephram. Dawson. — Mr Aspleyes yeomandry part fell vpon Ephram Dawson Tho: montforte and Fran. Constable stood in election wth him.

[1] STC 13006, cf. *C–B.C*, 30a, 5 Oct. 1612.
[2] Cf. *C–B.C*, 38a, 1 Mar. 1615, and 44b, 21 June 1616, although entered in the *Book of Fines* under 6 July 1616.

Fol. 41a A Clause in Mrs Whites Last will

In the last will and Testament of Mrs [*Edward*] White late wife to mr Edward White late Citizen and Stationr of london deceased beareing date the 7 of Decemb. 1615 Rę Jac' 13°. and proued in the Prerogatiue court 17° Decemb. eodem anno is contayned and expressed as followeth. viz.

Mrs. Whites will

Imprimis I giue and bequeath vnto Sara white daughter to my sonne Edward white (ouer and aboue the some of three score poundes formerly bequeathed vnto her by the last will and testament of my late husband Edward White) the some of twentie poundes of lawfull money of England Also I giue and bequeath vnto Lodge white and Robert white the sonnes of my said sonne Edward White to each of them fouretye poundes a peece of lawfull money of England. And I giue to Cutbert Hutchins ou' and aboue the some of thirtie poundes by my said late husbandes will bequeathed vnto him and ouer and aboue the soīe of ten poundes by the said will limited and apointed to such person as he should become apprentize vnto allreadie paid and disbursed the some of ten poundes of lawfull money of England to make vp his legacie fortie poundes Which said seu'all legacies to my said Grandchildren amountinge to the some of 160l my will and desire is should be and remaine in the handes and Chardg of the Master wardens and assistantę of the Company of Stationrs of the Cittie of London vntill the said Children should haue seu'ally atteined vnto their full ages of 21tie yeares they the said Master wardens and assistantę alloweing and answereing to my executor and ou'seers hereafter named for and towardes the mayntenance and bringing vp of the said Children or such of them as shall happen to surviue after the rate of fiue poundes yearely for eu'ye hundred poundes. And if it shall happen any of the said Children do depart this life before he she or they shall haue attened vnto the full age of 21tie yeares. Then my will and meaneinge is that the said soīe of 160l shall be equally devided betwixt such of the Children of my said sonne before named as shall survive. And if it shall happen two of them to dye before their said full age then the said some to descend to the surviueing Child. And if it shall happen all the said Children to depart this life before they haue attened vnto there full ages of 21tie yeares. Then my will is that the aforesaid soīe of 160l shall descend come and bee due and payable vnto my executor hereafter named to the vse of him his heires and assignes for euer. And which said legacie of 40tie poundes so as aforesaid willed and bequeathed to the said Cutbert Hutchins my will and like meaneing and desire is shall be remaine and abide in the like handes and chardge of the said master wardens and Assistantę of the said Company of Stationers to be by them Imployed vntill he shall haue accomplished the full experacōn of his terme of Apprenticehood to which he is bound by Indenture if he so longe shall liue they the said Master wardens and assistantę alloweinge vnto him when he shall haue finished his said apprenticeshipe after the said rate of fiue poundes in the hundred. And if it shall fortune that the said Companye of Stationrs shall not be willinge and Contented to answere and allowe for and towardes the
Fol. 41b educacōn of the said Children || after the rate of fiue poundes in the hundred for the said soīe of one hundred and thre score poundes, Then my will and meaneing is that out of the said money as is nowe remaineing in the handes of the said Company of my said husbandes stocke the said soīe of 160l shall be taken and

deducted out of the said Stationers hall and shalbe placed out by order and direction of my ou'seers herefter (*sic*) named for the best behoofe and advantage of my said Grand=children wth this proviso and Condicõn that such good and sufficient securitie be putt in for the said soñe to the master wardens and Assistantę of the said Company of Stationers for the time beinge for ther answereinge of the said Children of there said seu'all Legacies at there said full ages as they my said ou'seers shall thinke meete or Convenient for the same.

20° Januarij 1615 Rę. 13°

Presente. Mr Dawson, m[r] Lownes, sen' m[r] Swinhowe, m[r] man m[r] waterson, m[r] Feild, m[r] Adams, m[r] Harrison m[r] Ockold, m[r] Lownes Jun', m[r] Jaggard m[r] Gylmyn

m[r] Feilde 50[ti] Whereas m[r] Feild this pñte day hath lent vnto the Company the soñe of fi[*ue*]ftie poundes. It is ordered that the said debt shalbe paid vnto him at the ende of sixe monethes together wth alloweance after ten p centũ for the same so longe as it shalbe vnpaide.[1]

m[r] Gilmyn 50[ti] Whereas also m[r] Gilmyn this pñte day hath lent vnto the Company the some of fi[*ue*]ftie poundes. It is ordered that he shall haue the said Debt paide vnto him at the ende of three monethes together wth alloweance of ten p Centũ for the same so longe as it shalbe vnpaide/[2]

m[r] Lownes, warden And it is further ordered that wth this said 100[l] borrowed of m[r] Feild and m[r] Gilmyn, m[r] warden Lownes shalbe paid his 100[l] heretofore borrowed of him by the Companye.[3]

m[r] Allde m[r] Kempe Mđđ this day m[r] Alldee had leaue of the Table to engage his parte in the stocke to m[r] Kempe for the paiement of 63[l]—10[s]. vpon the 21th day of August next.

3° ffeb. 1615

m[r] Jackson and Edw. Wright It is ordered that m[r] Jackson shall haue the 700 bookę called Dents sermon, being his Copie, which said bookę Edward Wright causd to be disorderly printed,[4] and [therefore] by the [*orders*] ordinances are forfeited to the Company, and the said m[r] Jackson is to paye for the same......x[s]. paid accordingly.

It is also ordered that the said Edward wright shall pay to the Company for printinge the said booke disorderly. ......xl[s].

[1] Repaid 22 Mar. 1616, cf. *C–B.C*, 42[b].

[2] Repaid 22 Mar. 1616, cf. *C–B.C*, 42[b].

[3] Cf. *C–B.C*, 37[a], 16 Jan. 1615.

[4] There are editions of STC 6662 dated 1615 and 1616 (copy at Folger) which bear imprints 'T. Snodham f. R. Jackson'. One of them may be the edition 'disorderly printed' for E. Wright. For some reason Wright has been omitted from the *Dictionaries*. He received his freedom 12 Aug. 1611 (Arber iii. 30), and flourished until 1640, at Christ Church Gate, cf. STC 18753. Cf. also *Fine Book*, 11[a], 5 Feb. 1616.

FOL. 42[a] ## j[mo] martij 1615

Present mr Dawson mr Lownes sen' mr Swinhowe mr Man, mr Waterson mr Feild mr Adams mr Harrison, mr Lownes mr Jaggard mr Gilmyn, mr Cole.

Stockekeepers chosen to begin at or ladie day next.

mr Feild / mr Gilmyn } of the Assistants

Mr Bishoppe / mr Kempe } of the Liverye

Tho. Snowden / Nich. Borne } of the yeomandrye

Auditors mr Adams mr Jaggard mr Blount, mr Barrett Fran. Archer and Lawrence Lisle.

4° Martij 1615.

mr Pagett Whereas Jeames Pagett of the middle Temple London esq3 hath solde vnto the Company a certaine number of booke Called A promptuarye or Repertorye generall of the yeare booke of the Comon Lawe of Englande.[1] It is ordered by a full Courte holden this day that the Company shall shall (*sic*) pay vnto him for the same duringe the space of sixe yeares nowe next ensueinge the date hereof the some of 50l p annũ quarterly the first payment to begin at the 30th of June next till the some of 300l be paide. And the said Jeames Pagett is Content to enter into Couenant to saue the Company harmeles from Tho. Ashe and his assignes. and therevpon this day a paire of Indentures were sealed betwen the said James Pagett and the master and wardens &c for the payment of the said 300l and performance of other Conenante therein specified.

5° Die Martij 1615.

pñte. Mr Dawson mr Lownes sen' mr Swinhowe mr Man mr waterson mr ffeild mr Adams mr Lownes Jun' Mr Gylmyn Mr Cole/

The Psalter. This daye a writteinge was sealed wth the Comon seale to Mr Barker and his sonne and others,[2] the effect whereof was that the Company should take no aduantage by a certaine Clause that is enserted in [*a*] the newe pattent to the Company the Copie whereof is entrede in the Red booke in the hall.

Raffe Mabb. / Wm Barrenger Item Raffe Mabb had license of the Table to engage his parte in the hall to Wm Barrenger for the payement of 52l 10s. vpon the seauenth day of September next.

[1] STC 841. According to the monogram 'Aenigma' on the last page of the fourth part, Pagett was one of the three authors, with Thomas Ashe and (?) Serjeant Jones.

[2] See *Letter Book*, 89[a]. The patent is printed in Arber iii. 679–82.

6° Die Martij 1615. Re. 13°.

Pñte — Mr Dawson. Mr Lownes, mr Swinhowe. mr Man mr waterson mr ffeilde mr Adams mr Harrison mr Lownes Mr. Gilmyn mr Cole.

Mr Adams. — It is this day ordered that for the some of 55l to be paid to the Company by mr Adams the one half on midsomer day next and the other half on Michĩs day next the said mr Adams shall haue the whole impression of a booke called Hoptons Concordancye beinge in number 3000 or thereaboute and also that the Copie shalbe entred vnto him in the hall booke for the said mr Adams Copie for euer.[1]

15° Martij 1615.

lr̃e pattente. — This day the newe pattent for psalters almanacke &c[2] was publiquely reade in the hall in the pñce of a full Court most of the partenors and many others beinge also pñte

22° Martij 1615

pñte. — Mr Man loco mr mr Lownes sen' mr Swinhowe mr waterson mr ffeild mr Adams mr Harrison Jun' mr Lownes mr Jaggard mr Gilmyn.

Mr Swinhowe. — Whereas mr Swinhowe hath lent to the Company the some of 100l. It is ordered that the said Debt shalbe paid vnto him at the end of sixe monethes accountinge from the eighteenth of March 1615 together wth allowance after eight per Centũ for the same so longe as it shalbe vnpaid.

paid 3° August. 1616:

Mr Apsley. — Whereas also mr Aspley hath this pnte day lent to the Company the some of 100l. It is also ordered that the said debt shalbe paid vnto him at the ende of sixe monethes together wth allowance of 8l p centũ so longe as it shalbe vnpaide—.

paid in 3° August 1616

mr Leake. — Md paid to mr Leake, 100l he lent heretofore to the Company[3]
mr Feilde — Item paid to mr Feilde 50l } lent to the Company before/[4]
mr Gilmyn — Item paid to mr Gilmyn 50l }

Mrs Fairebrother — The ffeoffees, mr Man, mr Waterson, mr Leake, mr Feilde, mr Adams sealed a newe lease to mrs Fairebrother wth the same Couenante in the other lease lett to her husbande deceased onely some wordes

[1] Cf. *C–B.C*, 28a, 14 Oct. 1611. There are three letters from the Bishop of London regarding STC 13779 in the *Letter Book*, 86a, 14 and 29 Sept. 1615 and 14 Oct. 1615. This last is an order to stop N. Okes from printing it. Adams's claim to this book came from its resemblance to his copy, R. Grafton's *Table of yeares*, STC 12166. Actually, however, it is a very much enlarged version. A close comparison of STC 13779 and 13780 indicates that except for the first sheet, which is at least in part reset, they are made up of the same sheets. The fact that the later one has the imprint of the Stationers' Company is hard to explain. The day after this entry, i.e. 7 Mar. 1615, O.S. Adams entered for this book (Arber iii. 584).

[2] Printed in full in Arber iii. 679–82, apparently from the *Grant Book*, p. 177, 8 Mar. 1616.

[3] Cf. *C–B.C*, 39b, 3 Oct. 1615.

[4] Cf. *C–B.C*, 41b, 20 Jan. 1616.

were altered in the demise better to expresse the Companyes meaneinge Concerninge a roome Claymed by Lott Sivedale.[1]

26° Martij 1616. Reᶒ 14°.

pñte vt supra.

Mr Weauer. ffine — It is ordered that he shall paie xxl for his dispensacõn for not seruinge the Rentershippe, he paide 6l 12s thereof and by reason of his other Imploymt in the Company, the rest was remitted.[2]

Mr Searger ffine. — It is ordered that he shall pay xxl for his dispensacõn from seruing the Rentershippe.

Mr Lawe. — he is Chosen renter and hath taken it pon (*sic*) him.

FOL. 43a

4° April 1616. Reᶒ. 14°.

pñte. — Mr Dawson. mr Lownes. mr Swinhowe mr Norton, mr Waterson, mr Feild, mr Adams mr Harrison mr Ockold mr Lownes iun', mr Jaggard. mr Gilmyn mr Cole.

mr Norton for the 1000l giuen by mr Jo. Norton to the Companye. — It is agreed and Concluded betwen the Company and mr Norton That the said mr Norton, wthin a moneth after the Company haue agreed for Land to the value of 1000l and gaue notice thereof in writtinge at his house in Paules church yard then the said mr Norton shall paye the saide 1000l to the hands of the mr and wardens and in the meane time as well for the time that he hath had it, as for so longe as he shall keepe it to pay 50l p annũ to the said Company for the forbeareance thereof.[3]

8° Aprill 1616.

pñtibȝ vt supra.

Mr Norton for Newton. — It is ordered that if mr Norton shall paie to the Companye all the arrerages of Rent [*of*][for] the farme or Towneshippe of Newton giuen to the Company by mr Geo. Bishoppe deceased for so longe time as the Company haue had it in their handᶒ. That then the said mr Norton shall haue a lease thereof accordinge to a former order made to mr Joh. Norton[4]

Mrs Smith — Mrs Smith gaue to the Company[5] for attendinge at her husbandᶒ funerall vl

[1] Cf. *C–B.C*, 34a, 12 Apr. 1614.

[2] Cf. *Book of Fines*, 11b, 26 Mar. 1616.

[3] Bonham Norton was the executor of his cousin John Norton's will, see below, 8 Apr. 1616. Cf. Plomer, *Wills*, pp. 45–47. In 1895 the Royal Charity Commission permitted the Stationers' Company to redeem by purchase an annual charge of £8. 6*s*. *od*. payable to St. Faith, under St. Paul's, due under the will of John Norton.

[4] Cf. *C–B.C*, 28b, 6 Apr. 1612, and 36b, 22 Nov. 1614.

[5] Ten freemen were fined a shilling apiece for not attending, cf. *Book of Fines*, 11b, 8 Apr. 1616.

mr Norton
mr Bill

mr Norton and mr Bill sealed a bonde for the 1000l given to the Company by mr Jo. Norton. mr Norton sealed an other bond for the 50l yearely.

eodem die

Wm Blackwall — Wm Blackwall had license to engage his parte to Thomas Montforte for 44l the 17th of Aprill 1617.

Tho: Bushell — Item it is ordered that Thomas Bushell shall haue the 50l receiued of mr Norton for the forbearance of the 1000l giuen by mr Joh. Norton, due at all Sainte day 1616. and that the said Tho. Bushell shall putt in good securitye for the paymt of the same by 5l a quarter the first payment to begin at Christmas 1616.[1]

quartr dinnrs — Also it is agreed and ordered that the wardens shalbe allowed xxxl eu'ye yeare henceforwarde toward the quarter dinnrs.

6o Maij 1616. Re. 14o. — Fol. 43b

Barth. Downes. — This day election was made for Hugh Jacksons yeomãn part, it fell vpon Barth. Downes to make his half part a whole parte

Fr. Constable. — The other half part fell vpon ffran. Constable.

23o Maij 1616.

Mr Serger — This day election was made for mrs Bynge livery parte and it fell vpon mr Serger mr Allde and mr Purfoote were in Electõn wth him.

Geo. Miller. — Mr Sergere yeomandry parte fell vpon Geo. Miller.

mr Legatt. — It is ordered that mr Legatt shall pay to the Company for byndinge Tho. Jackson an app' at a scriuenors Contrary to order—xs. and for eu'ye moneth that he shall keepe him after midsomer next xxs.

7o Junij 1616.

Pñte. — Mr Dawson, mr Lownes, sen', mr Swynhowe, mr waterson, mr Feild mr Adams, mr Ockold mr Lownes. Jun' mr. Jaggarde mr Gilmyn mr Cole/

The Companye and his Maties printer. — Whereas there are Differences dependinge betwen his Maties printer and the Company touchinge the printinge of the psalter and psalmes of Dauide[2] which Differences haue ben referred to the Lo. B of london and others of his Maties high Comissionrs to be determined. The table beinge nowe [*not*] moued to knowe whether they would referr all other matters pretended by the Kinge printer to be in question betwene them

[1] The bonds are recorded in *Liber C2*, 108a. [2] Cf. *Letter Book*, 88b, 1 May 1616, and 91a, 3 Sept. 1616.

yea or no and to deliu' their opinions therein, they answered they would referre the differences betwene them concerninge the psalter and no other matters whatsoeuer, And in case the Comittees could not ende the Controuerses touchinge the psalter & psalmes. That then it was agreed by generall Consent That the m^r and wardens should be peticõnrs to the said Comittees that they would be pleased to giue leaue to the Company to take such Course [*as*] herein as by Counsell learned they should be aduised.[1]

FOL. 44^a

10 Junij 1616. Re 14°.

Present. Mr Dawson m^r Lownes sen' mr Swinhowe m^r Waterson m^r ffeild. m^r Adames m^r Ockold m^r Lownes Jun' m^r Jaggard m^r Gilmyn m^r Cole.

Joh. Basse. This day John Basse[2] by Consent of a Court engaged his part in the Stocke to mr Weaver for the paym^t of 10^l.

Mr Jackson. Tho. Langley Where Tho. Langley hath lately printed a booke Called Markhams Method which is supposed to be taken out of a Copie of m^r Jacksons, both of them referringe themselues to the Table It is ordered, that Tho. Langley shall assigne the Copie to m^r Jackson, and that m^r Jackson shall pay vnto him therefore the some of xlv^s. to which order they both assented.[3]

Rich. Meyhen. It is ordered that Richard Meighen shall haue a booke called The Couenant betwext god and man, prouided that none of the Company haue any right therevnto:[4]

Tho. Havilonde Joh. Havilonde This day Tho. Havilonde resigned by Consent of the Table one half part of his part in the hall to John Havilonde.

M^r. Bill. Whereas mr Bill hath this (*sic*) entred a booke called Doctrina et politia ecclia Anglicanæ, wherein are Certayn Copies belonging to the Company and others. It is this day ordered That the said mr Bill when the booke is printed being allowed for paper and printing for so much as belongeth to others, that mr Bill shall deliu' so many bookes sheet for sheet to them to whom the Copies belonge as there on any of there part shall amount or Come to according to the Custom of the Company in y^t behalf.[5]

M^rs: Bynge Mr Swinhowe receiued of [*the*] ffrances Burton, 40^s giuen by m^rs Binge to be distributed among poore workemen of the Company: and it was distributed accordingly

[1] The Bishop of London's decision in this controversy is recorded in the *Letter Book*, 91^a, 3 Sept. 1616.

[2] Apprenticed 26 Mar. 1581 (Arber ii. 107).

[3] STC 17381, which should be dated [1616?] and placed before 17380. Jackson presumably claimed this as an infringement of his rights in STC 17336 and 17342. Cf. Arber iii. 590.

[4] STC 10639. An edition of this book which has been attributed to J. Fotherby was published in 1596, 8°, R. Robinson f. R. Jackson. A copy of that edition is in the Folger.

[5] STC 17991. Besides the Prayer Book, Mocket had included a translation of Jewell's *Apology* and Nowell's *Catechism*. The Jewell was the property of T. Chard, but the Nowell belonged to the English Stock. This book was ordered burnt, cf. W. H. Hart, *Index expurgatorius Anglicanus*, p. 57.

Mr Wm Nortons. bequest — Re from Christe hospitall mr Wm Nortons bequest—6l—13s—4d whereof paid to the master wardens [*Beadle*] [Clark] & Beade.—13—4d[1]

Mr Bishops — paid to Christe hospitall for Newton giuen by mr Geo. Bishope deceased .... 6l.[2]

21 Junij 1616. FOL. 44b

pñte. — Mr Dawson, mr Lownes mr Swinhowe mr Waterson Mr Leake mr Feild, mr Adams mr Harrison mr Ockold mr Lownes.

Wm. Stansby. Joh. Barnes. — Where there are Certayn differences between wm Stansby and Jo. Barnes, about printing Sr Dudly Digge his booke, nowe all matters in question are referred by order of a Court and Consent of both partyes, to mr Jaggarde and mr Gylmyn, and in the meane time all suite to stay[3]

Newe Liverye — Phillip Harrison, Nath. Butter Tho. Yardley Joh. Busby Eman. Exoll Walter Burr. Joh. Edwards, wm Pickering wm. Parnell Tho. Snodham Fra. Burton Joh. Combes, Joh. Budge Tho. Downe Rich. Moore Wm. Barrenger Nicho. Bourne Rob. Meade Joh. Beale Edward Griffin Tho. Montforte. elected into the Livery and sworne accordingly[4]

Fra. Burton — Item it is ordered that Frances Burton shall pay his fine at or Ladie Day next if he be then lyvinge.[5]

Mr Harrison — Item it is ordered that mr Joh. Harrison the elder shall pay a fine of 6l—13s—4d for his dispensacoñ for his seconde vnderwardenshippe, and thereby is made Capable, to be in election for vpper-warden.

Wm. Stansby. — This day wm Stansby paide to the Company for a fine heretofore sett in Court for bynding of Randall Booth an appntice at a scriuenors and keepinge him Contrary to order—6l—13s.[6]

paid accordingly

12o Julij 1616 Re. 14o. FOL. 45a

Mr Man master
mr Adams } Wardens
mr Lownes Jun'

eodem die

Mr Jackson — Whereas by the death of Hugh Jackson there are Certayn Copies falne to the Company It is ordered that mr Roger Jackson shall

[1] Cf. Plomer, *Wills*, pp. 30–33.
[2] Cf. *C–B.C*, 24b.
[3] STC 6845. What the dispute was about is not clear.
[4] T. Yardley, J. Edwards, W. Pickering, and W. Parnell are not recorded in the *Dictionaries*, but are all listed by Arber as having been admitted to the freedom of the Company.
[5] This apparently was not paid, cf. *C–B.C*, 47a, 3 Mar. 1617.
[6] Cf. *C–B.C*, 40b, 4 Dec. 1615. According to the *Book of Fines*, 11b, this was paid 6 July 1616.

haue the said Copies entred vnto him paying to the vse of the said Company forty shillingę.[1]

Ann Snodham/ A pencõn of iij[l] a yeare is this day granted by a full Court vnto Anne Snodham widowe.[2]

mr Fetherston It is ordered that mr Fetherstone shall paie for his warehouse in the old hall 20[s] a yeare for so longe as he hath had it—that is 2 yeares and a half—toto L[s].

3° Augusti 1616.

mr Dawson Given by mr Dawson toward making vp the staires in the Garden vp to the Cittye wall—xx[s].

2° Septemb. 1616

p̃nte mr Man mr mr Adams mr Lownes Jun' wardens mr dawson mr waterson mr Lownes sen' mr Ockold mr Swinhowe mr Jaggarde mr Gilman

mr Harison
Tho: Montforte This day mr John Harison the elder by Consent of a full Court did engage his assistantę part vnto Thomas Montforte for the paiem[t] of 250[l] at Mich̃s 1617

mr Waterson mr Swinhowe mr Jaggarde mr Gilman are by this Courte apointed to viewe the olde hall. They are also appointed to agree wth the workemen for the buildinge of a newe shoppe and warehouses for the latten stocke.

vltimo Septemb. 1616.

Joh. Harrison Rę by mr warden Lownes of mr Joh. Harison the yonger the 12[l] of mr Jo. Nortons bequest, hereto for lent vnto him by the Company.

Tho. Bushell Tho. Bushell also paid this day 50[l] to mr warden Lownes[3] who deliu'ed to the said Tho. Bushell a bonde of 100[l] the other 50[l] was paid at midsomer last [*by*] to mr Swinhowe then Warden.

mr Boyle It is ordered that mr Boyle shall haue the 12[l] of mr Nortons bequest lately paide in by mr Harisoñ[4]

mr Needham It is agreed betwene mr Nedham and the Company that the Company shall build mr Nedham a house and make him a lease thereof for the som̃e of 200[l], and 10[l] a year,[5]

[1] These were entered 22 July 1616 (Arber iii. 593), cf. *Book of Fines*, 12[a], 22 July 1616.

[2] Presumably the widow of George or Lionel Snowdon, as the name is spelled indifferently, cf. *C–B.C*, 6[b], 7 Apr. 1605.

[3] This may refer to the transaction of 8 Apr. 1616, *C–B.C*, 43[a].

[4] His bonds are registered in *Liber C2*, 16[a].

[5] Cf. *C–B.C*, 46[b], 8 July 1617.

pñte — Mr Man, mr Adams mr Math. Lownes mr Dawson mr Waterson mr Leake mr Feilde mr Lownes mr Ockolde mr Swinhowe mr Jaggarde mr Gilmyn/

mr. Allde / mr Aspley — This day license was given to mr Allde to assigne his parte vnto mr Aspley for the paiemt of 64l vpon the eleauenth of July next.

20 Decemb. 1616

mr Johnson — It is ordered that mr Johnson shall haue the 50l of mr Joh. Norton bequest for 3 yeares accordinge to the Tenor of his last will and Testament[1]

Wm. Bladon — It is also ordered that wm Bladon shall haue his bonde renewed for 3 yeares more and the same security to be Continued.[2]

my Lo. Mayorę and the shreiues Dinnerę — ffor my lo. Mayor. sr Jo. Lemãn

The mr and wardens mr Dawson mr Leake mr h. Lownes. mr Swinhowe mr Knight

ffor mr shreuie Cotton.

The mr and wardens mr Feilde mr Gilman mr. Dight mr Bill mr Cooke mr Aspley

ffor mr shreiue Hackett

The mr and wardens mr Dawson mr Waterson mr Leake mr Jaggard mr Blunt

Mr Edwards. / Mrs. Harrison. — Whereas vpon good and sufficient reasons shewed by Roger Edwardę gent executor of the last will and Testament of mr Joh. Harrison the elder[3] deceased the mr wardens and assistantes of this Company caused the Last divident that did arise of the soñe or stocke of 300l remayninge and left in the handę and Custodie of the said Company, to be staide and kepte in their handę and possession vntill some matters in Controu'sie betwen the said Roger Edwardę and Julian Harrison wid late wife of the said Joh. Harrison deceased about the same stocke or some of money might be decyded and determyned. This the said Roger Edwardę signiefyeinge vnto the Table That Composicõn and agreemt betwen him and the said Julian that said soñe of 300l is agreed to be allotted to the said Julian and all the profittę and Comodityes therof. It is therefore ordered accordingly by a full Court that as the dividendę that remayneth in the handę of the Company as also all that which shall hereafter growe due or arise out of the said stocke of 300l shalbe paid to the said Julyan at the vsuall times, and according to the Customes & order of the Company.

[1] Cf. *C–B.C*, 43a, 4 Apr. 1616. His bonds are registered in *Liber C2*, 108a.

[2] Bladon borrowed £12 to be repaid 30 Aug. 1616. His bonds and the renewal are recorded *Liber C2*, 14a.

[3] Cf. Plomer, *Wills*, pp. 48–49.

FOL. 46a

16° Januarij 1616.

Present mr Dawson Loco mr. mr Adams mr Math Lownes mr waterson mr Leake mr Feilde mr Lownes sen' mr Ockolde mr Swinhowe Mr Jaggarde mr Gilmyn mr Cole/

mr Purfoote It is ordered this day that mr Purfoote shall enter eu'y newe Breife that he printeth and pay the fees of the house for the same and also deliu' one of a sorte to the Clarke for the vse of the Company[1]

Rich Haukins Wid. Oliffe It is ordered that Rich. Hawkins shall haue the booke called Nosce teipsum and Hymes of Astrea turned ou' vnto him by the Consent of mrs Standish which was signified to this Court by her lres and Testimony of Wm peere her brother, and it is further ordered that the said Rich. Hawkins shall pay to the wid' Oliffe 6s. 8d in hand and 6s 8d when the booke shalbe ymprinted by the said Rich. Haukins because Rich. Oliffe her husband had some right or Interest to the said booke/[2]

22° Januarij 1616.

Mr Man. mr Adames mr Ma. Lownes mr dawson mr waterson mr Leake mr ffeilde mr Lownes mr Swinhowe mr Jaggard mr Gilman.

Richard Graves. After divers meetingę and Conferences betwen the Company and mr Graves about the Letting the olde hall It is this day Concluded and agreed by Consent of a full Cort and the said mr Graves, That he the said mr Graues shall haue a Lease of the said olde hall and yardes wth the appurtenances accordinge to a plott drawne by workemen on both sides for the Terme of 40ty yeares to begin at Midsom' next for 100li fine and 15li rent a yeare, wth such Covenantę as are in other leases Lately lett by the said Company. of the which fine he hath paide in hand 55li And more ou' the said mr Graues [hath solde] to the said Company a yard or bakeside vpon parte whereof Lott Siuedale hath builded a house the said yard Contayneth in length from East to west 24 foote and from North to South 14 foote for which the saide Company are to pay 20li, and that 20li is allowed for parte of the said 100li so there remayneth vnpaid 25li to be paid to the said Company at the sealinge of the Lease/

mr W: Norton Rę from Christę hospitall of mr Wm. Nortons bequest[3] due 16 Decemb. 1616 .... } 6li—13s—4

mr Geo Bishope Paid to Christę hospitall of mr Bishoppes bequest[4]—6li

[1] This must have been an annoyance to Purfoot, for 28 Jan. 1587 (Arber ii. 463) his father had entered for 'the ymprinting of the Briefes of all letters Patentes . . . for . . . Casualtyes . . .', and 6 Nov. 1615 (Arber iii. 576) he had registered it in his own name. However, he followed the order, cf. Arber iii. 607, 14 Apr. 1617. Only a few of these briefs have survived, e.g. STC 8541 and 8542.

[2] STC 6358 (STC 6352 is part of it, mentioned on title and with continuous signatures). How Oliffe had any part in this is not clear.

[3] Cf. Plomer, *Wills*, pp. 30–33.

[4] Cf. *C–B.C*, 24b.

3° Febr: 1616 Rę. 14°/ FOL. 46b

Present mr man mr Adames mr Lownes mr Dawson mr waterson mr Leake. mr Feilde mr Lownes sen' mr Ockold mr Swinhowe mr Jaggard

Provision Wheate By vertue of a precept from the Lord Mayo^r directed to this Company[1] the said Company is to provid 140 quarters of wheate for the seruice and provision of this Citty. and because the Company cannot haue the Granary in Bridwell which they [*the*] haue payd for the buildinge of they are forced to Compound for the provision thereof wth one

Anthony. warde. Anthony warde dwelling in Newgate markett who beinge pñte this day hath vndertaken to provide the same wheate at his owne Charges, and to answere for the same at all times when it shalbe required In Consideracõn whereof the said Company hath promised to giue vnto him the some of 13^l—6^s—8^d.

1mo. Martij 1616.

Present. mr Man mr Adames. mr m. Lownes, m^r Norton m^r waterson m^r Dawson m^r Feild m^r Lownes mr Swinhowe mr Ockold m^r Jaggard mr Gilmyn mr Cole.

Phillip Harison Tho. Montforte Phillipe Harrison havinge assigned his part into the handę of the m^r wardens and assistantę they went to election of an other parteno^r and the election fell vpon Thomas Montforte there stood in election wth him Geo. pursloe and Nicho. Okes, and the said Thomas montforte tooke his oath accordingly/

Stockeps Chosen to begin at o^r Ladie day next

Stockepers. Mr Hum. Lownes, m^r Swinhowe } Assistantę

m^r Kingstone, m^r Smithicke } Livery

w^m. Bladon, Law. Lisle } yeomandry,

8° Julij 1617.

m^r Lownes and mr Swinhowe being Chosen wardens m^r leake and mr Ockold were chosen stockepers in their Romes/

Auditors. m^r waterson. m^r Ockolde, m^r Browne mr Selman Josias Parnell Joh. Tappe.

Mr Needham Md m^r Needham hath paid to the Company 200^l for a lease of a house that is [*to*] nowe buildinge and is to haue a lease thereof according to a Copie which was deliu'ed vnto him/[2]

m^r Budge It is ordered that if Hen. Buckell[3] nowe dwellinge wth mr Bugde (*sic*) be not putt away before Easter next the said John Budg shall pay such fine as the Company shall thinke fitt, for keeping him aboue his numb^r

[1] Cf. *Letter Book*, 92^a, 29 Nov. 1616.
[2] Cf. *C–B.C*, 45^a, 30 Sept. 1616, and 47^b, 5 July 1617.
[3] Not recorded as apprenticed.

Fol. 47[a]

3° Martij 1616. Re. 14.

Present vt ante.

Rich. woodriffe Barn. Alsope. — It is also this day ordered That Richard woodriffe and Barnard Alsoppe shall pay for Imprintinge of 3 sermons of mr Hernes and puttinge mr Hum. Lownes name therevnto, being the Copie of mrs. Macham, the some of x[s] a peece/[1]

m[r]. Burton/ — The xx[l] oweing to the Company by m[r] Burton for his admittance into the Livery was this day remitted vnto his wife and his bond for the same Deliu'ed vp vnto her to be Cancelled[2]

Joseph Harison — Joseph Harrison had leaue by the m[r] and wardens to morgage his parte to Rich. Brookebanke for the paiement of 26[l] at o[r] ladie day 1620.

27° Marcij 1617 Re. 15°/

Present — m[r] man m[r]. Adames, m[r] Lownes Jun' m[r] dawson m[r] waterson m[r] ffeild m[r] lownes sen' m[r] Ockold m[r] Swinhowe m[r] Jaggard m[r] Cole.

M[r] Bradwoode — m[r] Bradwood being Chosen Rento[r] this day was fined to be dispensed from the service thereof in the some of } xx[l]
pd.

M[r] Bolton — mr Bolton[3] Chosen Rento[r]

mr Dawson — This day also m[r] dawson at a full Court did vndertake and promise that the said m[r] Bolton should performe the sayd office wth Creditt as other men haue done before him and gaue his worde that the said m[r] Bolton should pay vnto the wardens all the Rente and quarteridges [that] should Come to his handes at the vsuall time paieable

M[r] Lawe. Ed. Blakemore — whereas m[r] lawe and his late seruant Ed. Blackmore[4] haue referred the differences betwixt them for wages vnto the Table It is ordered that the said m[r] Lawe shall pay vnto the said Edward the some of 8[l] 4[s] before midsomer next or deliu' him bookes from m[r] Weaver to that value as the said Edw. Blakemore shall like of.

W[m]. Wright Chr. Crowe — vpon the death of mary Lufeman[5] It is ordered that w[m] wright shall haue his pencõn made up xx[s] and Christofer Crowe[6] xv[s]

[1] An imperfect copy (A–B[8] only) at Christ Church, Oxford, of S. Hieron's *Three sermons ful of necessarie advertisment*, has the imprint 'H. Lownes of f. I. Smith, 1615' and is evidently the edition here referred to. Cf. *Fine Book*, 12[b], 1 Mar. 1617.

[2] Cf. *C–B.C*, 44[b], 21 June 1616.

[3] Possibly Robert Bolton who was apprenticed to T. Dawson, Sen.

[4] Made free 3 Apr. 1615 (Arber iii. 684).

[5] Presumably widow of James Luffman, made free 17 Oct. 1588 (Arber ii. 703).

[6] Apprenticed 1567 (Arber i. 325).

13° Apr 1617

Rob. younge
Joh. Havilonde
mr Meade

This day Robert younge and John Havilonde had lycense to engage both there stockes as well in the English as the Lattin vnto Robert Meade for the payment of 105l[1] vpon the first day of Nouemb. 1617.

6° Maij 1617

mr Lawe — This day mr Lawe brought in his Rentors account beinge—41l 19s.

2° Junij 1617 Re. 15°. — Fol. 47b

Mr Charde. — Md mr Charde hath this day Receiued his pencõn for midsomer quarter next and Michis quarter. Item at an other [time] he rec' Christmas quarter Item at an other time he receiued for or ladye quarter 1618 and for midsomer quarter 1618...xls. so that he is to receiue no pencõn till Michis 1618

5° Julij 1617.

Wm Arundle. — It is ordered that wm Arundle by his owne Consent shall paie his debt to the stocke by 50s a quarter the first paiemt to begin at michis next. and this day mr Swinhowe hath giuen his worde for paiemt of all the sd wm Arundle oweth to the said stocke/

Mr Ockolde. — This day also mr Ockolde disiered to be dispensed from serving vnderwardenshippe the seconde time, And putt himself vpon the table for his fine. And it was ordered that he should paye...xxli

mr Needham/ — It is ordered that mr Needhams lease of his new house called the [*wholly*] holy Lambe shall begin at michis next for 41 yeares. he hath payd 200l for building thereof and is to pay 10l a yeare[2]

8° Julij 1617. Re. 15°.

mr Waterson elected mr. mr Humf. Lownes and mr. Geo. Swinhowe wardens, this day the said wardens tooke their oathes accordingly

Stockeeps. — mr Leake and mr Ockold chosen stockep's in the Romes of mr. Lownes. and mr Swinhowe and tooke there oathes accordingly

16° Julij 1617.

Mr Adames. — This day mr Adames lent vnto the Company the somẽ of one hundred and three skore pounde, And it is ordered that the said debt shalbe paid vnto him by the Company at the ende of three monethes together wth allowance after ten p Cent' for the same so longe as it shalbe vnpaid

This was paide to mr Adames by mr weauer the Threr accordingly.

[1] Paid 19 Aug. 1617, *C–B.C*, 48b.

[2] Cf. *C–B.C*, 46b, 1 Mar. 1617.

Raffe Mabb.
Rob. Cotton

This day also. Raffe Mabb had lycense from the Table to engage his parte in the English stocke to Robert Cotton for the paiement of 80ˡ

mʳ Islipe.

It is ordered that mʳ Islippe shall printe 1250 of mʳ Poultons last booke Called a Collection of the Statutes &cs for which he shall haue vˢ viijᵈ a Reame.[1]

Fol. 48ᵃ

21 Julij 1617 Re. 15°.

Mʳ Waterson. Master.
mʳ Hum. Lownes. } wardene
mʳ Swinhowe.

mʳ Dawson, mʳ Cooke. mʳ Butter. mʳ Budge. John white and Tho. Norton chosen stockeeps for the Lattin stocke.

Rob. Willis

It is ordered that Robert Willis shalbe admitted to the freedom of this Company by Translacõn from the Inholders payeing to the vse of the said Company—vˡ.[2]

Tho. woodhouse.
Ellen Pindley.

Md that Tho. woodhouse did at a full Court promise and agree to pay Ellen Pindley before such time as he should be made free of this Companye, the some of vjˡ.[3]

Wm Blackewall
Rob. Meade.

This day wᵐ Blackewall was Lycensed by the Table to engage his pte in the English stocke vnto [*John Beale*] [Robert] Meade. for the paiement of Lijˡ. xˢ vpon the 2ᵈ day of ffebr' next.

2° Augusti 1617

Fra. Constable.
John. Beale.

This day election was made for Mʳˢ Hatfielde pte.[4] The one half thereof fell vpon Frances Constable and the other half parte vpon John Beale There stood in election wᵗʰ them. Ed. Griffin and Rich. Heggenbotham:

4° Augusti 1617 Re. 15°

Pñte.

mr waterson mr Lownes. mr Swinhowe, mr Man, mr Dawson mr Feild mr Adames mr Harison mr Lownes mr Jaggard mr Gilmyn.

mʳˢ Baker

It is ordered that mʳˢ Baker[5] shall haue her divident that at the instance of mʳ Leake was staide in the hande of the stockepers the last quarter/

[1] STC 9328.
[2] Cf. Arber iii. 684, 9 Oct. 1617.
[3] If this is the T. Woodhouse who was apprenticed 15 Sept. 1589 (Arber ii. 164) he apparently never was made free.
[4] Widow of Arnold Hatfield.
[5] Widow of Michael Baker.

Latten Stocke	It is thought fitt by the table that the ptenors in the Latten stocke[1] should allowe the partenors in the English stocke 40l p annũ for the Shoppe.
mr Man mr Adames mr M. Lownes.	Three cuppes of silver were giuen this day to the Companye by mr Man mr Adames and mr Mathewe Lownes, Late mr and wardens, wayghing 26 ounce wantinge 12 g3
mr Man	It is ordered that mr Man[2] shall haue his lease made vp 21 yeares.

19° Augusti 1617 Re. 15°. FOL. 48b

Presente — Mr Waterson. mr Lownes. mr Swinhowe, mr Man mr Dawson mr Feilde mr Adams mr Harrison mr Lownes.

Wm Aspley — Whereas wm Aspley vpon the tenth day of this pñte August lent vnto the Company the some of one hundred pounde It is ordered that the said debt shall be paid vnto him the Tenth day of August next together wth allowance after 8 p cent' for the same so long as it shalbe vnpaide accounting for the said Tenth day of August last past that is to say for one whole yeare, the some of 108l.

Mr Jackson / Joh. Marriott. — The Controversie between Roger Jackson and John Mariot for the printinge of the booke called Markhams farewell to horsemanshipp and husbandry[3] beinge by the pties Referred to the table. It is ordered that the sd John Marriot shall assigne his Copie to the said Roger Jackeson that the sd Roger may printe it in what manner he shall thinke fitt, And that the said Roger Jackeson shall paie vnt' the said John Marriott the some of vl vjs for the said Copie and also deliu' vnto him 25 bookes wthin ten dayes after the sd Roger Jackson shall first Imprinte the same proportionably to the Number of sheete as the same new Copie printed shall fall out.

Mr Martin — It is ordered that mr Martin shall haue a lease of the pine aple for 31 yeares from michĩs next for Cl fine to be paid 50l at thensealinge and 50l at or ladye day[4]

mr Ockold/ — This day mr Ockold paid in the xxl that he was fined at for his dispensacoñ for not seruing the second time vnderwarden[5]

[1] The Latin Stock was organized in Jan. 1616.

[2] Jonas Man, cf. *C–B.C*, 96b, 30 June 1627. This was part, evidently, of Abergavenny House, and in a schedule of leases, 1625, now in the archives of the Stationers' Company, No. 230, the lease is said to have been dated 22 Dec. 1617, for twenty-five years, and to be for a house in Amen Corner.

[3] STC 17372. The delay in publication may have been because Markham had to re-edit it. A comparison with STC 17355, the copyright of which Marriott later owned, shows that there is little duplication. However, in this connexion see the promise Markham made, transcribed in Arber iii. 679.

[4] According to a schedule of leases, 1625, now in the archives of the Stationers' Company, No. 230, Ambrose Martyn's rent is given as £10.

[5] Cf. *C–B.C*, 47b, 5 July 1617, and *Book of Fines*, 13a, 1 Sept. 1617, which is probably the proper date for this entry.

1mo septemb. 1617

Phillip Harrison. It is ordered that Phillippe Harrison shall haue a pencõn out of the poores account of 4li p annũ to Continue three yeares and no longer the first paiemt at michĩs 1617

mr Martin. Vpon the peticõn of Ambrose Martin It was thought fitt by this Courte to mitigate the fine for the lease of his house and therevpon ordered that he shall pay but 70li for 31 yeares to be all paid at the ensealinge

mr Graues, It is ordered that mr Graues shall haue 50 yeares in his lease in regard of his great chardg in building.[1]

Fol. 49a

4o Septemb. 1617 Rc 15o.

Presente/ mr waterson, mr Lownes, mr Swinhowe. mr Dawson mr Feild mr Adames, mr Harrison mr Lownes Jun' mr Jaggard mr Gilmyn

Mr Jones. Counsellor. It is ordered by Consent of a full Courte holden this day That mr Thomas Jones[2] shalbe Intertayned to be of Counsell for this Company and shall haue for his fee, xliiijs p annũ to be paide vnto him quarterly that is to say xis eu'ye terme/

Wm Bladon mr Swinhowe. This day wm Bladon had lycense to engage his pte in the English stocke to mr Swinhowe for the paiemt of 80li to be paid by xxli a quarter the first paiemẽt at Christmas next/

Barnard Alsope Item lycense was giuen to Barnarde Alsope to printe The Dyall of princes[3] paieinge to the vse of the poore vjd in a li

7o Octob. 1617

wm. Hobson It is ordered that wm Hobson shall haue a lease of his house for 41 yeares from michĩs last for 12li a yeare rent and 40li fine.

mr Sivedale. This day mr Sivedale beinge a sutor to the Company to enlardge his seller The Court answered him That if it might not be preiudicall to the Company nor their tenantc they see no reason for the pñte but it might be granted vnto him.

3o Nouemb. 1617

mr. Dawson mr dawson this day deliu'ed an acquitt' for mr Billagc money and paid to the wardens xiijs iiijd according to the order[4]

[1] According to a schedule of leases, 1625, preserved in the archives of the Stationers' Company, No. 230, the rent of 'The Old Hall' here leased was £15.

[2] This is probably the Mr. Jones, Common Serjeant of London, regarding whom see *C–B.C*, 37a, 16 Jan. 1615.

[3] STC 12430. This edition was 'lately reperused, and corrected from many grosse imperfections', and dedicated to Sir Henry Mountague by A[nthony]. M[unday].

[4] Cf. *C–B.C*, 6a, 4 Dec. 1604, *et loc. cit.*

Tho. Havilonde
John. Havilonde
mr Meade

Tho. Havilond and Joh. Hauilonde had leaue to assigne their pte to m^r Meade for the paiem^t of 105^l vpon the 3^d of maye 1618.

m^r Norton

It is agreed that m^r Norton shall haue the lease of Newton accordinge to former orders in this behalf[1]

m^r Norton

This day also the sđ m^r Norton paid 50^l for the forbeareance of the 1000^l giuen to the Company by m^r John Norton deceased.[2]

Fran. Constable.

It was pñte[ly] granted to Frances Constable puttinge in good securitye accordinge to the will[3]

1mo Decemb. 1617. Re. xv^o. Fol. 49^b

Present

m^r Waterson. m^r Lownes m^r Swinhowe, m^r Man Mr Dawson m^r Leake m^r Feild m^r Adames m^r Ockold mr Gilmyn

mr Leake,

It is ordered this day by m^r Leakes owne Consent that m^rs Baker shall haue 40^s a quarter out of the divident and that the rest of the divident shalbe paid to Mr Leake for his debt till it be all paide and that the sđ m^r Leake shall shewe his demande to the Company that they may Consider howe much is due vnto him.[4]

Christof. Drydon

vpon the peticōn of Christofer Drydon It is ordered that the said Christofer shall haue the next pencōners place that shall fall voide[5]

This day the lease of Tho. Montforte house was sealed at a full Courte

Wm Arundle.

It is ordered that w^m Arundle shall be trusted wth 5^l worth of Bookes out of the stocke vntill o^r Ladie day next[6]

8° decemb. [*1618*] 1617

My lo. Mayo^rs and Shreiues Dinners.

The Names of thos that are appointed to goe to the lo: mayo^rs and Shreiues to dinner this yeare

To my lo. Maiors.

The m^r and wardens m^r dawson m^r Harison m^r Adames m^r Kingstone m^r Aspely

To mr Shreiue Holyday.

mr. dawson m^r Leake m^r Ockold m^r Jaggard m^r dight, m^r Islippe

To mr Shreiue Johnsons,

The wardens m^r leake m^r ffeilde m^r Math: lownes. m^r Blount/

[1] Cf. *C–B.C*, 43^a, 8 Apr. 1616.
[2] Cf. *C–B.C*, 43^a, 8 Apr. 1616.
[3] Cf. Plomer, *Wills*, pp. 45–47. His bonds are registered in *Liber C2*, 108^b.
[4] Cf. *C–B.C*, 48^a, 4 Aug. 1617.
[5] He was placed on the rolls for 15*s*., 23 Mar. 1618, *Liber pro Pauperibus*.
[6] Cf. *C–B.C*, 47^b, 5 July 1617.

B 1435

o

Geo. Elde miles Flesher.	George Elde and miles fflesher are sutors to the table to be ioyn'd in Coptenorshippe in mr Eldes printing house which is granted vnto them so far forth as the Company may doe by their orders.

8° Januarij 1617 Rę. xv°.

Latton stocke — whereas mr welby mr Jones mr Smithicke Joh. Roystone Raffe mabb Ric' woodriffe and Joh. Hamon haue this day Resigned their ptę in the Lattin stocke into the handę of the mr wardens and assistantę. This day election beinge made according to order

mr Swinhow mr leake mr Cole Hen Shorte Ric' Hawkins John Branch mr leake	was elected to	mr welbyes pte mr Jones pte mr Smithickes pte John Roystones pte Raffe mabbes pte Ric woodriffes pte John Hamon pte

Fol. 50a 29° Januarij 1617 Rę. xv°.

Present — mr waterson. mr Hum. Lownes mr Swinhowe mr Norton mr Man mr Dawson mr Leake mr Feilde mr Adames, mr Ockold mr Lownes Jun' mr Jaggard mr Gilman mr Cole.

Rich Badger — Vpon the death of Thomas Bushell late Beadle[1] election was made of Rich. Badger to succed in the place of the said Tho. Bushell There stood in election wth him Ric' Taylor and Samuell Wallpoole And the said Richard Badger tooke his oath as Beadle accordinge to order

John. Hoth. — mr welby hauing resigned his pte in the English stocke. John Hoth[2] was elected therevnto by Consent of a full Court

Christę Hospitall — Md paid to Christę hospitall mr Bishopp's annuitye—vjl [3]
Rę of Christę hospitall mr Wm Norton's Annuity—vjl xiijs iiijd
paid to the mr wardens Clarke and Beadle—xiijs iiijd [4]

Mr Jones. — Item paid to mr Jones for Michis terme and Hillary Terme 1617—22s.[5]

2° Martij 1617 Rę xv°.

Stockekeepers,	Mr Lownes, Junior mr Cole—	mr Aspley. mr Combes.	Fran. Constable Jonas. Man.
Auditors	mr Feild mr Gylmyn	mr Pavier mr Blount.	John Hodgettę. Joh. Dawson.

[1] The date of Bushell's election as Beadle is not known. Cf. *C–B.C*, 33b, 7 Feb. 1614.
[2] Made free 24 Apr. 1598 (Arber ii. 720).
[3] Cf. *C–B.C*, 24b.
[4] Cf. Plomer, *Wills*, pp. 30–33.
[5] Cf. *C–B.C*, 49a, 4 Sept. 1617.

Printer for Irelande. It is ordered that m[r] Kingstone and m[r] weaver shall Confer wth S[r] Geo. Calvert about the patent for the kinge printer in Ireland And make Report to the table what they thinke fitt to be done therein.[1]

Raffe Kircombe Ric Garnett Anne Reade It is ordered that Raffe kircombe[2] shall haue a pencon of 40[s] p annũ. The like to Ric' Garnett[3] And Alice (*sic*) Reade[4]—5 nobles p annũ.

Apocripha. Att this Court mr Adames did declare to the Court that it is my lo. Bishoppe of london's pleasure that all the Bibles w[th]out Apocripha be deliu'ed to mr Phillip Kinge.[5]

9° Martij 1617

M[r] Islippe It is ordered that mr Islippe put away his seruant Math. Williamson[6] which he keepeth in his house vnbound Contrary to order

26° Martij 1618 Re xvj°.

Fol. 50[b]

M[r]. Leake. Rob. younge This day Robert younge had license of the Table to engage his parte in the english stocke and that in the latten vnto m[r] Leake for the paiement of Lij[l] x[s] vpon the first of October next.

M[r] Kempe Chosen Rentor warden

Mr Needham. Whereas m[r] Needham is a suto[r] to renewe his lease It is ordered that for a lease of 21 yeares in Reu'sion after that which is nowe in beinge he shall paie 100[l] fine and v[l] a yeare.[7]

6° Maij 1618

M[ris]. Vincent John Banridge This day John Banridge made complaint to the table that he gaue with his sonne John Banridge the some of xx[l] to M[r] Vincent[8] to teach him as an appr', and that nowe M[r] Vincent being dead M[ris]. Vincent hath turned him away and the said John Banridge and M[ris]. Vincent referring themselues to the Table, It was ordered that the said M[rs]. Vincent should pay the said John Banridge the some of 4[l]. that is to saie xl[s] vpon the next divident daie, [and] the other xl[s] at Michĩs next the which order the said parties haue giuen their Consent to pforme accordinglie.

1 Cf. letter from Privy Council, 9 Mar. 1618, in *Letter Book*, 92[a]. James Usher, afterwards Archbishop of Armagh, wrote to William Camden from Dublin, 8 June 1618: 'The Company of Stationers in London are now erecting a Factory for Books and a Press among us here: Mr. Felix Kingston, and some others are sent over for that Purpose. They begin with the printing of the Statutes of the Realm; afterwards they purpose to fall in Hand with my Collections *De Christianarum Ecclesiarum Successione & Statu.*', R. Parr, *The Life of James Usher*, 1686, pt. II, p. 64.

2 Ralph Kirkham, made free 7 Dec. 1607 (Arber iii. 683).

3 Made free 5 Oct. 1592 (Arber ii. 711).

4 Apparently not the widow of Richard Read.

5 Cf. *C–B.C*, 39[b], 3 Oct. 1615.

6 Made free 6 Oct. 1623 (Arber iii. 685).

7 Cf. *C–B.C*, 47[b], 5 July 1617.

8 This must be G. Vincent, Senr. His son was made free 4 Oct. 1624. It does not appear that the younger Banridge was presented.

Arthur Johnson. Nicholas Bourne. Edw: Blounte. Wm. Barrett. Lau: Lisle.— Whereas there are some of the ꝑtenors in the English stocke, that are endebted to the said stocke soe that the dividentę Cannot be made in due time It is ordered by the Consent of those that are soe behind hand. that money be taken vp where it Can be borrowed, and that if the ꝑties soe behind doe not pay the somes of money they owe to the said stocke within three monethes, the mr wardens and assistantę shall goe to eleccõn of newe ꝑtnors in their places and in the meane time the said ꝑties are Content to allowe for the said money soe to be taken vp as afore said after x ꝑ Centum.

18° Maij 1618 Rę xvj°/

Anthony Warde Wheate. This day Anthonie Ward did vndertake to serue the Markett wth wheate for the Companie, according to a p'cept from the Lord Maior dated vltimo Aprilis 1618. for which the Companie are to giue him xs/ pđ.[1]

Mr. Brecknocke. It is ordered that Mr Brecknocke shall haue ffitie shillingę this yeare for his Almanacke of England and Ireland and 100 Almanackę.[2]

The Clarke of this Company It is ordered that the Clarke shall haue hereafter—xvjd a paire for makeing the Indentures for appr'tizes

Fol. 51a

18° Maij 1618 Rę xvj°.

Edward French. Daniell Speede. This day vpon hearing the Contrau'sie betweene Edward ffrench and daniell Speede. It appeared to this Courte that the said Daniell Speede had much misvsed his app' William ffrench sonne to the said Edward ffrench & hath giuen him many blowes and some woundes wherby the said app' hath beene vnder the Surgions handes and Chargeable to his ffather for curinge the hurtes the said daniell Speed vndulie and vnseasonablie gaue vnto him, And therefore the said Edward ffrench desired that the said appr' might be taken from his master And the said daniell Speed was also vnwilling to keepe the said app' anie longer alledging he did greatlie suspect that he had taken some money out of his box, but did not directlie make proofe thereof, And the said daniell did Confesse that he receiued aboue Ten poundes with the said appr', and it appeared also that he had ben with him but six monethes or thereaboutes of the Terme of .8. yeares. The matter by Consent of all ꝑties was referred to the consideracõn of this Court to sett downe what some of money the said daniell should repay to the said Edward of that which he receiued with his said app', And John Speed ffather of the said daniell Speed did promise and giue his word that his sonne should repay soe much vnto the said Edward ffrench as this Court should thinke meete and order to be paid. It was therfore ordered by the Court (due Consideracõn

[1] This precept is transcribed in the *Letter Book*, 92b.

[2] Neither Brecknocke nor his almanack has been identified. It is presumably not a copy of STC 420 (1618), for that would have been printed in 1617 and is, in any case, calculated for London and the south of England.

being taken of all the premises) that the said daniell Speed should repay or Cause to be repaide vnto the said Edward ffrench the some of Ten poundes of lawfull money of England vpon the sixt day of August next ensewing the date And that the said app' (being not inrolled) shall be free from his said master soe that the said Edward ffrench might dispose of him as he should thinke fitt.[1]

1mo Julij 1618 Re xvj°.

Present. Mr. Waterson, Mr Hum: Lownes, Mr. Swinhowe mr. Dawson, Mr Leake. Mr Feild, Mr. Adames, Mr. Math: Lownes Mr Jaggard.

Mr. Norton. Mr. Aspley. Whereas William Aspley Citizen and Stationer of London As well at and vpon the speciall request of the Master wardens and assistantes of the Companie of Stationers and according to their nominacōn in this behalfe As also in performance or accomplishing of a grant or assignement made by Mary Bishop widdowe deceased vnto the Master wardens and Comaltie of the mistery or Art of Stationers of the Citie of London, Hath as much as in him is assigned and settouer vnto mr Bonham Norton, one Recognizance of 700^li^ and one statute[2] of 400^li^ acknowledged by one Thomas Hopton to George Bishop deceased, and all profitte and advantages to be taken therby as by an Indenture thereof made may appeare. It is therefore ordered by consent of a full Court holden this day That the Master wardens and assistante for the time being shall at all times hereafter sufficientlie saue and keepe harmles the said Wm. Aspley his executors and administrators and euery of them of and from all Coste charges expences and damage which shall or may happen by reason of the said Recognizance or of any suite that may be brought for or Concerning his passing of the said Recognizances ouer to the said mr Norton in any wise howsoeuer.[3]

8° Julij 1618 Re. Jac' 16°. Fol. 51^b^

Mr Leake master
mr Adams } Wardens.
mr Gilmyn }

Tertio Augusti 1618.

Mr. Bill. This day a letter[4] from the kinge Ma^tye^ was brought to the Table in the behalf of John Bill about the printinge and bringinge ouer of the Bishoppe of Spalatoes[5] and Causabones[6] workes.

Vltimo Augusti 1618

Present. Mr Man Loco. Mri. Mr Adams mr Gilmyn mr dawson mr ffeild mr Hum. Lownes mr Jaggard.

Mr Wilkinson It is ordered and agreed betwen the Company and mr John wilkinson that the sd mr wilkinson shall haue for the Copie of

[1] Evidently he was not apprenticed to any other stationer.

[2] A bond or recognizance by which the creditor had the power of holding the debtor's lands in case of default.

[3] This transaction presumably is connected with Bonham Norton's lease of Newton.

[4] Transcribed in *Letter Book*, 94^a^.

[5] Marco Antonio de Dominis, STC 6994, &c.

[6] Isaac Casaubon, STC 4744–5.

the Booke Called The office of a Coroner and a shreiffe and the manner of keepinge Courtꝭ the som̄e of 13[l]—6[s]—8[d] and fiftye of the sđ Bookes w[th]in sixe dayes after they be finished—[1]

25° Septem. 1618

Present. m[r] Leake mr Adams, m[r] Gilmyn, mr man mr Dawson mr waterson mr Feild mr Lownes mr Ockold mr Swinhowe mr Jaggard

Cutbird Wright It is ordered that Cutberd Wright shall paie to the Company for a fine for keepinge Henry Chamberleine an apprentize Contrary to order being himself but a iorneyman and also for byndinge him at a Scrivenors the som̄e of —[v[li]]— fiue poundꝭ.

Ric: More This day also w[m] Blackwall hauinge surrendered his yeomandry ꝑte in the English stocke. The Table went to election of an other ꝑteno[r] accordinge to order. There stood in election Rich. More Robert Meade and Edw. Griffin, the election fell vpon Richard More and he tooke his oath accordingly.

Fol. 52[a] quarto Octob. 1618 Reꝭ. 16.

Present M[r] Leake mr Adams mr Gilmyn mr Dawson mr waterson mr Feilde mr Lownes. sen' mr Ockeld mr Swinhowe mr Jaggard mr Lownes. Jun'.

mr Dawson This day mr Dawson brought in 13[s] 4[d] for mr Billages money and an acquittance for Lij[s] paid to the Churchwardens of Saint Martins in the Vintry.[2]

M[r] Bill This day being quarter day the leȓ from his Ma[tye] Concerninge the printinge of the Bishoppe of Spalatoes workes and Causabones prohibiting the bringinge them from beyond the Seas, was openly reade in the Hall.[3]

2° Nouemb 1618

Barn. Alsope. Tho. Jones Whereas Tho: Jones oweth vnto Barnard Alsope the some of fiue poundꝭ they hauing putt themselues to the Table it was ordered that the sđ Tho. Jones shall paie the one half the last day of this terme and the other half the last day of Hillary terme.

M[r] Norton This day mr Norton paid to mr warden Gilmyn for one half yeares Rent of Newton due at michĩs 1618—eleauen poundꝭ.[4]

[1] STC 25648.

[2] Cf. *C–B.C*, 6[a], 4 Dec. 1604. This is the last entry regarding that loan. Apparently it is not recorded as having been repaid.

[3] Cf. *C–B.C*, 51[b], 3 Aug. 1618.

[4] Cf. *C–B.C*, 49[a], 3 Nov. 1617.

11° Nouemb. 1618

Present Mr Leake mr Adames mr Gilmyn mr Norton mr Dawson mr waterson mr Feild mr lownes sen' mr Ockold mr Swinhowe mr Lownes Jun' mr Jaggarde.

Math. Walbanke. It is ordered that Mathewe walbanke shall paye for a fine for keepinge Rob. Walbanke[1] app' vnto Tho: Jones Costermonger Contrary to order xx[s] and to putt him away forthwith.

Mr Norton This day mr Norton paid to mr warden Gilmyn for Rent and Charges for Newton—103[l].[2] more for the forbearance of the 1000[l]. 50[l].[3]

Rob. Meade This day vpon the death of the wife of Tomas Man the younger election was made of her pte in the English stocke, There stoode in election Rober. Meade Edw. Griffin and Rich. Heggenbotham the election fell vpon Rob. meade and he tooke his oath accordingly.

23 Novemb. 1618 Re 16° Fol. 52[b]

Present. mr Leake, mr Adams mr Gilmyn mr Man mr Dawson mr waterson mr Feild mr Lownes, sen. mr Ockold mr Swinhowe mr Lownes. Jun' mr Jaggard.

Order for the Weavers This day Came certaine of the Company of Weauers to this Court. viz. John Rowden wm Smith and John Browne, And [*declared*] [Complayned] to the Table, against one Tho: Ha-warde[4] and others that beinge free of the stationers they vsed nevertheles the trade of Weavinge which by Charter they Could not doe, And vpon shewing forth their Charter to this Court and a Decree of the Court of Aldermen It was the opinion of the Court that this Company Could not retaine them any longer, And It was ordered and agreed that the sd Thomas Haward and the rest that vse Weavinge hereafter should bynde their appn'tizes at Weauers hall but that the said Tho Hawarde and the rest as longe as they liue if they will shall remaine still in this Company wthout molestacon [*vnto*] which order the weavers aforesd did like well of and gaue Consent therevnto.

27 Nouemb: 1618

Present as before

Mr Beale. This day election was made for m[rs] vincente Livery parte in the englishe stocke, There stood in election mr Jackson mr Beale mr Heggenbotham. Yt fell vpon mr Beale, and he tooke his oath accordingly

[1] R. Walbancke was made free 14 Jan. 1628 (Arber iii. 686).
[2] Cf. *C–B.C*, 36[b], 22 Nov. 1614.
[3] Cf. *C–B.C*, 43[a], 4 Apr. 1616.
[4] T. Haward's connexion with the Weavers was not new, cf. Arber ii. 267.

Mr Griffin — Then election was made for mr Beales halfe yeomandry pte There stood in election mr Barrenger mr Griffin mr Heggenbotham and it fell vpon mr Griffin and he tooke his oath accordingly

Mr Parnell. mr Cooke. — Also this day license was giuen to mr Parnell to assigne his pte in the lattin and Irish stockes vnto mr Cooke for the paiement of 80l on the 2d day of febr 1619

1mo Decemb: 1618

My Lord mayors, and the shreifes Dinners. — To the Lord maiors. Sr Sebastian Harvy.
The mr and wardens, mr Dawson mr Norton mr Hum. Lownes. mr Ockold mr Bill.

To mr Shrefe Hernes.
The mr and wardens mr Dawson mr Feilde and mr Swinhowe.

To mr Shreife Hamersley.
The mr and wardens mr Dawson mr Lownes Jun' and mr Bill.

Fol. 53a A Copie of the Releaſe made from Joseph Barnes and John Barnes his sonne concerninge Riders Dictionary[1] vnto.—

Mr Leake mr Adameſ mr Norton mr Man mr Waterson mr Blount — Be it knowne vnto all men by theis pñtes That wee Joseph Barnes of the Citie of Oxford Stationer, and John Barnes Citizen and Stationer of London as well for and in Consideracõn of the some of Threescore poundeſ of lawfull money of England to them in hand before the sealing and deliu'ie hereof, by Willm Leake, Thomas Adams, Bonham Norton, Thomas Man, Symon Waterson & Edward Blount trewlie paid whereof they confesse the receipt by theis pñtes, As for diuers other good Causes and Consideracõns them there vnto moving, doe by theis pñtes grant, Remise, Release, and for euer quite Clayme vnto the said Willm Leake, Thomas Adames, Bonham Norton, Thomas Man, Symon Waterson, and Edward Blount their exrs and asseſ. All and eu'ie the estate Right, title, Interest propertie Clayme and demand whatsoeuer which the said Joseph Barnes and John Barnes or either of them heretofore had nowe haue or of right ought to haue or may Clayme or demand of or vnto the Printing of all or anie of that Copie or booke Called Riders Dictionary. Soe that neither the said Joseph Barnes, and John Barnes nor either of them, nor the executors or adm'trators of them or either of them nor anie other person or persons whatsouer for them or either of them shall may or can at anie time or times hereafter aske, Claime, Challenge sue for anie manner of Estate, right, title interest of in or to the premisses or anie part thereof but of and from all accõn suite, right,

1 STC 21034. Cf. *C–B.C*, 9a, 3 Mar. 1606. E. Blount is the only new partner not included in the original list of 26 Nov. 1604 (Arber iii. 276). His rights were apparently derived from R. Bankworth, whose widow he had married. What became of the rights of E. White and C. Burby is not apparent. Copies of this 1617 edition are known, printed for Man, Adams, and Leake. It is not unlikely that the others had copies with their names in the imprint.

title Interest or demand, to be by them or anie of them asked, Claymed, Challenged sued for or demanded of in or to the premisses or anie part thereof, they and euerie of them are & bee vtterlie excluded and debarred for euer by theis p̃ntes, In witnes whereof the said Joseph Barnes, & John Barnes haue herevnto sett their hande and seales, Geouen the Eleauenth day of Nouember in the sixteenth yeare of the raigne of our sou'aigne Lord James by the grace of god King of England ffrance and Ireland defendo[r] of the faith &c, and of Scotland the twoo and ffifteeth. 1618

Joseph Barnes.
p moy. *Jean Barnes.*

7° Decemb 1618 Re 16°.

Present. mr Leake m[r] Adams mr Gilmyn mr Dawson mr waterson mr Feild mr Ockold mr Swinhowe mr Ma: Lownes mr Jaggard

Mr Blount } mr Serger. } This day mr Blount had lycense from the Table to assigne his pte in the English stocke vnto m[r] Serger for the paym[t] of 105[li] vpõ the Ninth day of June next /

John Hodgette Tho. Jones. Also the Court did order that Thomas Jones should not ymprint or Cause to be ymprinted in the booke Called the fathers blessinge[1] any thinge that is in the booke called the Practice of Pietye[2] which belongeth to John Hodgette.

eodem die P̃ntib3 vt ante Fol. 53[b]

Geo. Vincent. Whereas Katherin Vincent deceased Late wife of Geo: vincent deceased did giue vnto Geo. Vincent[3] the sonne by her last will and Testament beareing date the 17th of Septemb. 1618, All that her stocke of money in the stationers hall London to remayn in the Custody of the m[r] and wardens of the said Company vntill the said George shall Come to the age of 21 yeares and then the stocke wth such profitt as the M[r] and wardens shall thinke fitt to be deliu'ed & paid vnto him. It is therefore ordered by Consent of a full Court that the sd stocke shalbe retayned in the hande of the said Company accordinge to the sd will and that the Company shall allowe for the same after the rate of fiue pounde p Cent' from the time that the said stocke by the order of the said Company is to be payd out [*to the ex's of the said Katherin if the said will had not ben made*]

M[r] Fetherstone It is ordered that mr Fetherston shall avoid Robert Martin (which he keepeth disorderly in his house) w[th]in 8 dayes vpon paine of the penaltye Contayned in the ordinance for forreno[rs] that is to say if he keepes him after 8 dayes to pay 40[s] for a fine and for eu'ye [*day*] [weeke] that he shall keepe him after that 20[s].[4]

[1] STC 14359.
[2] STC 1603.
[3] There has been some confusion about the George Vincents, father and son. The son was made free 4 Oct. 1624 (Arber iii. 686).
[4] According to the *Book of Fines*, 14[a], 7 Dec. 1618, Featherstone paid the 40*s*. fine, but evidently he did not put Martin away, cf. *C–B.C*, 66[b], 4 and 13 Dec. 1620, and 16 Jan. 1621. Finally Martin was translated to the Stationers' Company, 19 Dec. 1622, *Book of Fines*, 18[a].

Rent out of Ireland.	Paid to mr weaver which I receiued from Skinners hall for the land in Ireland the soṁe of 18li—4s—2d due at All sainteȼ day 1617.

21° Decemb. 1618 Reȼ 16°.

Mr Blounte — whereas the ꝑtenors in the Irish stocke haue bought of mr Blount a Certaine ꝑcell of bookes for the some of 900li to be payd at 3–8 monethes accounting from the 28 of October last It is this day ordered that the said 900li shalbe paid vnto mr Leake mr Adams mr Swinhowe to dischardge three Recognizances of 300li a peece for which they stand bound in Guildhall for the sđ mr Blounteȼ debt.

Mr Serger	This day Samuell Joslin did surrender his ꝑte in the Latten stocke to mr Serger by Consent of a Court
John Wright	This day also mr Leake did assigne a yeomandry ꝑte in the Latten stocke by the Consent of a Court vnto John wright

Fol. 54a

19° January 1618 Reȼ Jac. 16° /

Pnte'	mr Leake mr Adams mr Dawson mr Waterson mr Feild mr Lownes sen' mr Ockold mr Swinhowe mr Lownes Jun' mr Cole mr Knight mr Cooke /
Mr Weaver	It is ordered that mr Weaver shall haue 10li a yeare to keepe the Irish stocke.

Mr Kingston — It is ordered that mr Kingston shall assigne ou' to Raffe Mabb the 3 Copies called Elton on the Collossians[1] Downham's 5 treatizes,[2] Downham on Hosea.[3] which the said Raffe Mabb did heretofore assigne vnto him. And that the sđ mr Kingston shall haue the printing of Elton on the Collossians doeing the same as another will doe.

7° Feb. 1618 Reȼ Jac. 16°.

Present.	mr Leake mr Adams mr Gilmyn mr Man mr Dawson mr Waterson mr Feild mr Lownes sen' mr Ockold mr Swinhowe.
Rob. Ventris.	It is ordered that Robert Ventris that had his house burnt in Cornehill shall haue 5li giuen him by the Company toward the reedifyeing thereof.

John Piper — whereas John Piper hath kept disorderly in his house Richard Reston,[4] which was bound to Josias Harrison and not turned ou' to him, and for [that] the father of the said Richard Reston did desire to haue

[1] STC 7613.

[2] STC 7142. Although called 'Foure treatises', this book should have bound at the end an edition of STC 7150 dated 1613 and mentioned on the title of STC 7142. There is such a copy at York Minster. Cf. likewise Sayle No. 7901–2. These Treatises were also known as 'Of the five sinnes' (cf. Arber iii. 444).

[3] STC 7145.

[4] Made free 6 Aug. 1627 (Arber iii. 686).

him away and the said John Piper was willing likewise to parte wth the said appr', the matter was referred to the Table, and it is ordered that the said John Piper shall pay vnto the sđ mr Reston xvijli of the xxli that he had wth him.

Christs hospitall — Received from Christę hospitall one yeares annuity of mr wm Nortonę bequest[1] .... } 6li—13s—4d

Paid to Christę hospitall one yeares Annuity of mr Geo. Bishopę bequest[2] .... } 6li /

To the mr wardens Clarke & beadle. xiijs iiijd.[3]

Mr Fetherston. — This day mr Fetherston paid to the Company for a fine for keepinge Robert Martin disorderly } xls.

Primo Martij 1618 Rę 16°. — Fol. 54b

Stockekeepers for the English stocke	Mr Swinhowe. mr Jaggard.	mr Cooke mr Budge	John Tappe Eph. Dawson.

Reynold Smith — This day Lycense was giuen by the table to Reynold Smith to ymprint his table & Computacõn[4] that he hath made and to sell them wthout interruption of the Company.

Auditors for the English stocke.	mr Norton mr Ockold	mr Bill mr Pavier.	Josias Parnell Hen. Peniehay

3° Martij 1618 Rę Jac. 16°.

Pñte. — mr Leake mr Adams mr Dawson mr Feild mr Hum. Lownes mr Ockold mr Swinhowe mr M: Lownes mr Cole

Bartho. Downes. — Whereas by the helpe and furtherance of the right hoble. Sr George Caluert knight principall secretary to the state The Company of stationr̃s in London haue obtayned lr̃s pattente from his Matye vnder the great seale of Ireland for the office of his Matyes printers for the said realme[5] And therefore in regard of the Loue and goodwill the said Sr Geo. Calvert beareth vnto the Company they haue agreed to graunt an Anuitye of xxli p annũ to whomsoeu' the said Sr Geo. Calvert should nominate & appoint. It is therefore ordered by Consent of a full Court holden this day That the Company shall make a sufficient grant or dede vnder the seale of the hall of the said Annuitye of xxli p annũ for 21

[1] Cf. Plomer, *Wills*, pp. 30–33.

[2] Cf. *C–B.C*, 24b.

[3] Cf. Plomer, *Wills*, pp. 30–33.

[4] A broadside, of which copies are in the libraries of the Society of Antiquaries and of Harvard College entitled 'A table, containing an almanacke for LXXII yeeres . . . by Reinold Smith, Servant to the Right Hon. Francis Lord Verulam. by J. Bill, 4 Oct. 1620'. Later almanacks by the same author are at Lambeth.

[5] Under date 23 Mar. 1618 some of the negotiations regarding this may be traced in the *Acts of the Privy Council 1617–19*, pp. 64–66. The first note, 9 March 1618, is transcribed in the *Letter Book*, 92a. Cf. also *The Library*, N.S. viii (1907), 295–7. By this time F. Kingston had already gone to Ireland and had there printed a 'Notice of warrant appointing deputies to seize any books imported into Ireland contrary to patent', as well as several proclamations (STC 14169, 14170, and 14172).

yeares from the feast of Saint John Baptist Last past and deliu' the same on this side the [*feast*] [first] day of [*saint Barthelomewe the apte*] [Aprill] next vnto Bartholomewe downes[1] vpon whom the said Sr Geo. Calverte as the Company is enformed entendeth to Confer the said Annuitye.

This Grant was sealed accordingly, and the said Añuitye is to be payd out of the Irish stocke

Stockeeps for the Irish Stocke	mr Dawson m^r^ Ockeld	assist	mr Islippe mr Heggenbotham	liv.	Edw. Bruster John. wright	yeom.

FOL. 55^a^ 9° Marcij 1618 Re̜ Jac. 16° /

Pñte / Mr Leake mr Adams mr Gilmyn mr Dawson mr waterson mr Feild mr Lownes sen' mr Swinhowe mr Lownes Jun' mr Cole

Rob. Cotton This day Thomas Havilonde having surrendred his half yeomandry pte in the English stocke election was made therefore and it fell vpon Rober. Cotton there stood in election wth him Edw. Griffin and Rich. Heggenbotham The said Robert Cotton tooke his oath accordingly

Edw. More
Rob. Wilson It is ordered that Edw. moore[2] shalbe dischardged from his master Rob. wilson[3] for that the said Rob. Wilson is not able to teach him his Trade.

Symon Stafford. It is ordered that Symon Stafforde shall haue a pencõn of 4^l^ p anum to begin this quarter so that he doe make a gen'all releas vnto mr Dawson

26° martij 1619 Re̜ Jac. 17° /

Pntibȝ ut supra.

mr Kempe It is ordered that mr Kempe for being dispensed w^th^all for serving the Rento^r^shippe being there vnto elected shall pay for a fine —xxij^li^.

mr Barnett It is likewise ordered that mr Barnett for beinge dispensed w^th^all for serving the Rentorshippe being therevnto elected, shall pay for a ffine—xx^li^.

mr Blount It is likewise ordered that mr Blount for being dispensed w^th^all for serving the Rento^r^ship being therevnto elected shall pay for a fyne xx^li^.

[1] Downes was, with F. Kingston and M. Lownes, one of the patentees for the Irish Privilege. Why Sir George should have given him this annuity is not apparent.

[2] This is probably not the E. Moore who was made free 2 Oct. 1637 (Arber iii. 688).

[3] What was the cause of his inability is not known. In 1617 he published STC 5528 and 18788, and later several others.

Mr Allde. It is ordered that mr Allde for being dispensed wthall for not serving the rentorshippe shall pay for a fyne—xxli.

Mr Purfoote } Rentors for this yeare
mr Harison }

John Pemberton It is ordered that Joh. Pemberton shall haue his Rolling presse when he hath entred into bond not to ymprint any vnlawfull thinge[1]

John: Barnes It is ordered that John Barnes shall assigne his fathers Copies to whom he will, his said father being lately deceased and haueing giuen his [*said*] Copies to his said sonne.[2]

5° Apr. 1619.

mr Fetherstone. By Consent of Leonard Greene, & order of a Court the said mr ffetherston is to haue Leonard Greenes Interest in Perkins 3d Tome[3] & Taylor on the Temptacions.[4]

3° Maij 1619 Re. Jac' 17°. Fol. 55b

Pnte. mr Leake mr Adams mr Gilmyn mr Dawson mr Feild mr Hum Lownes mr Jaggard

mr Pavier This day mr Pavier paid vnto the Company for 3 Copies he heretofore bought of the Company viz the first part of the pensiue mans practise, the godly garden and the xiãn prayers—3l—6s—8d[5]

Mr Beale It is agreed vpon betwen mr Eldred mr Anguish and mr Beale, That the said mr Beale shall print for them of Recognizances for alehouses[6] 1000 for 40s vizt 500 in paper and 500 in parchmt, and for mr Millyson half so manye of each and for mr Rowley 200 of each at the same rate and it is ordered that if they cannot hereafter agree then by their owne consente they shall referr themselues to the Table, and stand to their order Concerning the [*prise*] price of printing any more

[1] Pemberton was not enrolled in the Company, but neither were many, if not most, of the printers of engravings.

[2] By 20 Jan. 1620 Barnes had transferred eighteen titles to ten different publishers.

[3] STC 19651. C. Legge published the third volume with his name in the imprint in 1609, 1613, and 1618. His widow transferred to Boler, 1 June 1629 (Arber iv. 212), her rights to the Tables in the third volume. Greene's rights appear to have been transferred by Featherstone to W. Stansby, and by him to J. Haviland, cf. Arber iv. 238 and 431.

[4] STC 23822. The B.M. and Lincoln Cathedral have copies with L. Greene's name in imprint. C. Legge retained a third interest, cf. Arber iv. 212 and 435. (In the first of these entries Taylor's name is given as Cooke.)

[5] Cf. *C–B.C*, 37b, 20 Feb. 1615.

[6] Cf. STC 8588, which contains the form for the recognizances to be printed, the parchment ones to be kept, and the paper ones to be given to the alehouse keepers. Eldred and the others were presumably the patentees mentioned in the proclamation or their agents. No copies of these recognizances are recorded, but they may be in the Public Record Office, as there are there over a thousand of Sir W. Raleigh's licences, cf. *Devon Assoc. Rep. and Trans.* xli (1909), 106.

Mr Jackson mr Elde — It is ordered that mr Eld and mr Flesher shall pay to mr Jackson vjs viijd for ymprinting the booke called Madmen of Gotam[1] which was formerly entred to the said mr Jackson

Hen. Hem̃ings.[2] — vppon a lr̃ from the right hoble the Lo. Chamberleyne[3] It is thought fitt & so ordered That no playes that his Matyes players do play shalbe printed wthout consent of som̃e of them

7° Junij 1619 Rę Jac 17°.

Mr Needham. — It is ordered that mr Needham shall haue a leas of his house called the white horse for 40 yeares to begin at Midsomer next for the rent of 4li ꝑ annũ, paying 100li fine at thensealing thereof[4]

Mr Alldee — whereas mr Alde is fyned in the some of xxli for his dispensacõn for serving the Rentorshippe[5] This day he did alledg he could not pay it till after michĩs next, and the Company did giue him the feast of saint Symon and Judes day vpon which day he promised faithfully to pay in the same wthout further delay

mr Jones. — paid to mr Cenion Sergeant for a whole yeares fee[6]...... }44s

Fol. 56a

14° Junij 1619 Rę Jac. 17°.

mr Leake mr Adams mr Gilmyn mr Dawson mr Waterson mr Feild mr Lownes sen' mr Swinhowe mr Cole

Rob. Cotton 55. — This day mr Boyle did surrender into the handę of the Company the one half of his yeomandry parte in the english stocke election being made thereof It fell vpon Robert Cotton to make his half parte a whole yeomandry parte

Mr Snodham — Whereas mr Snodham at the request of the Company is Contented to goe into Ireland to take the account[7] It is ordered by this Court that the said mr Snodham shall haue worke for 2 presses vntill his returne & that the Company shall pay to his wife eu'ye saterday 4li if the worke amount to so much.

Assistantę — This day election was made for 3 newe assistantę out of the Livery, and it fell vpon mr Knight mr Pavier & mr Cooke.

Pñte — Mr Leake mr Adams mr Gilmyn mr Dawson mr waterson mr Feild mr Lownes sen' mr Swinhowe mr Lownes iun' mr Jaggard mr Cole mr Knight mr Pavier mr Cooke

[1] Cf. STC 1021. Roger Jackson entered this book, which had been Hugh Jackson's, 22 July 1616 (Arber iii. 593); and his widow transferred her rights to Francis Williams 16 Jan. 1626 (Arber iv. 149). There is a cancelled note, 26 Aug. 1617 (Arber iii. 613), that M. Flesher obtained rights in it. No copy of the edition here referred to is known.

[2] Perhaps a relation of John Heming, principal proprietor of the King's Players.

[3] William Herbert, 3rd Earl of Pembroke.

[4] Cf. *C–B.C*, 50b, 26 Mar. 1618. By waiting Needham obtained much better terms.

[5] Cf. *C–B.C*, 55a, 26 Mar. 1619.

[6] Cf. *C–B.C*, 49a, 4 Sept. 1617.

[7] For the Irish Stock.

3° Julij 1619 Re Jac. 17

Joh. Robins wm Agborough Joh. White. — John Robbins wm Agborough[1] & John White are this day taken into the Liverye of the Company

Joh. Hoth. — It is ordered that mr Hoth[2] shall pay for a fine for refusing to Come on to the Livery of the Company being therevnto elected—xls.

Jeames Randall/ — At a full Court holden this day Jeames Randall[3] was elected and Called to be of the Liverye of this Company and hath made request to the table to be exempted & free from taking vpon him the same, It is ordered by Consent of a full Court That the said Jeames Randall in Consideracõn of the some of 6li—13s—4d paid by him to the hande of the wardens shalbe for eu' hereafter exempted and freed from taking vpon him the said place of Livery or clothing and neu' hereafter be elected or Called therevnto.

Mr Lawes. fol. 9 — It is ordered that mr Lawes sonne[4] shall haue allowed vnto him 4li. a yeare for 2 yeares & a half for his mayntenance in the vniu'sitie.

Sexto Julij 1619. Re Jac. 17°. Fol. 56b

Mr Feild master
Mr Swinhowe, mr Jaggarde. } wardens

Stockekepers for the English stocke[5]	mr Hum. Lownes.	mr Budge	John Tapp
	mr Cooke	mr Meade.	Eph. Dawson.

20 Julij 1619.

Mr Bladon. — It is ordered that wm Bladon shall haue 50li of mr John Nortons bequest putting in good security.[6]

Stockeepers for the Latten Stocke.	mr Leake	mr Browne	wm Bladon
	mr Gilmyn	mr Barrenger	Tho. Langley.

Nich. Okes. — It is ordered that Nich Okes shall pay for a fine for printing a booke Called a Preparaton to the Psalter[7] wthout the Consent of the wardens. xxs.

2° August 1619.

Geo. Faireberd Mic. Sparkes. — It is ordered that Geo. Faireberd shall pay vnto Michell Sparkes a debt that he oweth vnto him by xs eu'ye fortnight the debt is confest to amount vnto 4li 16s.

1 Made free 6 May 1612 (Arber iii. 683).

2 Made free 24 Apr. 1598 (Arber ii. 720).

3 Made free 6 Feb. 1604 (Arber ii. 736).

4 Matthew Lawe, B.A. Cantab. 1617–18, M.A. 1621. Rector of Allerton, Somerset, 1636. Cf. *C–B.C*, 9a, 6 May 1606.

5 Three of the stockkeepers chosen this year had evidently declined to serve.

6 Cf. *C–B.C*, 43a, 4 Apr. 1616. His bonds are registered in *Liber C2*, 108b.

7 STC 25914. Okes entered it 13 Aug. 1619 (Arber iii. 654). Cf. *Book of Fines*, 14b, 26 July 1619.

vltimo August 1619.

Present mr[r] Feild mr Swinhowe m[r] Jaggard mr Dawson mr waterson mr Hum. Lownes mr Adams mr Math Lownes. mr Gilmyn mr Knight mr Pavier mr Cooke.

Tho. Archer. It is ordered that Tho. Archer shall pay a fine for Bynding Fran. Williams [*on*] at a scriveno[rs] and for keeping him Contrary to order—xl[s].

Woodstrett Md mr Feild mr Swinhowe mr Jaggard m[r] Waterson mr Math. Lownes mr Knight mr Cole mr Cooke are appointed by this Court to be ffeoffees for the purchase in Woodstrett, of mr Langhorne for mr John Nortons money.[1]

M[r] Harrison
mr Heggenbothm̃ This day election was made for m[rs] Jones Livery part and it fell vpon mr Harrison, Then election was made for mr Harrisons Yeomandry ꝑte and it fell vpon m[r] Heggenbothm̃.

And it is ordered that m[r] Heggenbothm̃ in respect of his paynes taken for the Companye in his Jorney to Ireland shall haue the next liu'ye ꝑte that falles in the English stocke/

Fol. 57[a]

6° Septemb. 1619.

Present. mr Feild mr Swinhowe mr Jaggard mr Dawson m[r] Waterson mr Leake mr Lownes sen. M[r] Adams mr Gilmyn. mr Cole mr Knight mr Pavier mr Cooke

Tym: Barlowe It is ordered that Tymothie Barlowe having a yeomandry ꝑte in the Latine stocke shalbe trusted with ware for twentie poundes worth of bookes, and his stocke to be engaged for the payment thereof.

Tho: Archer &
Nich: Okes. This daie license was giuen by the Table to Thomas Archer to engage his halfe yeomandry parte in the Englishe stocke for the payment of ffortie poundes [to Nycholas Okes] provided that all hee oweth to the said stocke shalbe first paid in and ffortie shillingę of his next Divident to be staid for a fyne which the said Thomas Archer oweth to the Companie.[2]

1[mo] Septemb. 1619.

An agreement made betweene Thomas Pavier and John Wright on the one partie, and Edward White on the other partie.

Tho Pavier.
Joh. Wright
Ed. white / ffor the Consideracōns herein expressed I haue sold vnto Thomas Pavier and John Wright for seauen yeares theis Copies vnder written which I desire maie be entred for their Copies, for that time soe the Condicōns on their partes be performed.[3]

[1] Cf. *C–B.C*, 43[a], 4 Apr. 1616.

[2] Cf. *C–B.C*, 56[b], 31 Aug. 1619.

[3] This agreement was evidently altered, for according to the entry 13 Dec. 1620 (Arber iv. 44), Greene's *Quippe* was omitted from the list of books here given and three others (STC. 16960, 15534, and *The vine-*

Imprimis that they pay me 18[d] p̱ Reame, for euerie seuerall Reame that they shall ymprinte or Cause to be ymprinted on euerie seu'all ympression of anie of the said bookę within 14 daies after the same booke or bookes shalbe finished.

Secondlie that it shalbe Lawfull for me or my assignes to require to see howe manie of the same bookes they shall haue left in their handę vnsold and if they shall not haue aboue the nomber of 150 bookes of anie sorte that then they shall within one moneth after notice giuen or left [*in*] in writeinge with them or either of them, reimprinte the said copies, which if they shall not doe or Cause to be done that then it shalbe Lawfull for me to dispose of them as I thinke fitt.

Thirdlie that they shalbe printed by whome I thinke fitt of the company prouided the same Printer shall doe them as well, and for as reasonable a price as another will (bona fide) print them for, and if the said printer shalbe found to print anie more then the said Thomas and John shall agree for, and shall not doe them well and as reasonable for price as another will, that then it shalbe Lawfull for them to put them to print for the terme limitted, and vnder the Condicõns expressed to whome they thinke fitt, soe that I maie both knowe the printer, & haue libtie to come into the printing house to see what nomber shalbe done from time to time vpon anie ympression of the said seuerall bookę.

ffourthlie that they shall ymprinte anie other copies that belonge vnto me vpon the same Condicõns that are formerlie expressed.

M[rs]. Katharine Stubs.[1]
Schoole of Vertue.[2]
Dreame of Diues.[3]
D[r]. Faustus.[4]
Quippe for a Courtier.[5]
Long Meg of West[r].[6]
Paradice of dainty deuices.[7]
Handfull of pleasant delights.[8]
Hospitall for diseased.[9]
the Widdowes treasure.[10]

Ed. White.

I thinke it fitt to enter this according to their desire for this terme if White or his wife liue soe longe, or the Copies be not otherwise disposed of.

Geo: Swinhow

yard of devotion) were substituted. G. Purslowe had evidently objected that he had entered the *Quippe* 7 Jan. 1620 (Arber iii. 662), and White was unable to produce an assignment from Wolfe. With the exception of the Seager and the *Long Meg*, White appears to have had regular entries for all the others. Pavier's rights were transferred by his widow, 4 Aug. 1626 (Arber iv. 165–6), to E. Brewster and R. Bird who, 29 Apr. 1634 (Arber iv. 318), divided the copies between them. Editions of several of these titles are known published under those entries. *The vineyard*, however, is not known in any edition though listed by Maunsell, p. 87, as printed by E. White in 16°.

[1] STC 23387.

[2] STC 22137+[Anr. ed.] 8°, G. E[ld]. f. T. P[avier]. a. I. W[right]., 1621. Copy at Harvard. The title of an edition, E. All-de f. E. White, 1620, is in Bagford Collection (Harl. 5910, II, 29).

[3] Cf. STC 16948.

[4] Cf. STC 10713.

[5] Cf. STC 12303, see note above.

[6] Cf. STC 17782. The edition dated 1582 is a forgery, being a *c.* 1650 edition with a faked title taken from STC 6749, but there is an edition, now at Yale, 4° E. Allde f. E. White, 1620.

[7] Cf. STC 7524.

[8] Cf. STC 21105. In the Huntington is a fragment, a paginary reprint of the 1584 edition, presumably of a late sixteenth-century date. The leaf in the Bagford Collection has been shown by H. E. Rollins (in his edition of this book published in 1924 by the Harvard University Press) to be of an edition earlier than 1584.

[9] Cf. STC 4308.

[10] Cf. STC 19437.

FOL. 57b 8° Octob. 1619 Re Jac' 17°

Present Mr Feild mr Swinhowe Mr Jaggard Mr Lownes seni', Mr Lownes Juni' Mr Knight, and Mr Pavier.

Mr Barrett. This daie Willm̃ Barrett Citizen and Stationer of London did acknowledge himselfe to be endebted vnto Walter Graie of Cuddicott in the Countie of Hartf' gent the some of 150li of lawfull money of England to be paid vnto the said Walter Gray his Executors or Assignes vpon the Tenth daie of October which shalbe in the yeare of our lord god 1620 And for the securitie and better payment thereof at the said daie, the said William Barrett did surrender and assigne his whole liuerie pte in the English stocke which he hath remayninge with the Companie of Stationers London, vnto the handes of the Master wardens and Assistantes of the said Companie for the time beinge. And it was therevpon ordered by the said Mr wardens and Assistante that were then present, and Consent of the said Willm̃ Barrett, That if Default be made in payment of the said some of 150li. vpon the said tenth Daie of October in the said yeare of our lord god 1620 as aforesaid, That then the Master wardens and assistantes shall goe to election of an other partnor in the stead and place of him the said Willm̃ Barrett And the stocke or some of money that shalbe then Due shalbe paid vnto the said Walter Gray his Executors or assignes, within such time as by the orders of the Companie in that behalfe is limitted and appointed.

Nic. Smith It is ordered that Mr Smith shall haue a new lease of his house in Woodstreete for One and twentie yeares to begin at Midsomer next for 23li a yeare and 40li fyne together with a Celler that is in Lease to Mr Ayres [the lease of the Celler] to begin when Mr Ayres Lease is expired. [except mr Smith can compounde wth mr Ayres in the meane time/]

Mr. Lawe. Geo. Purslowe It is ordered that mr Lawe shall pay vnto Geo. Purslowe xxs for a debt he Confesseth to owe vnto him, and hath retayned in his hande for that as he saith Geo. Purslowe hath printed a Booke of his in his Survey of London.[1] The matter in Contreversye betwixt them is referred to mr warden Swinhowe and mr Hum. Lownes who made an ende of the matter betwixt them.

But it is further ordered that the said mr Lawe shall pay for a fine for vsing vnfitting worde to Geo. pursloe in the pñce of the wardens—xs.

Mr Hoth. This day mr Hoth admitted into the Livery of this Company and tooke his oath accordingly he hath paid xls in hand & is to pay 18li more the 23th of June next, by bond—paid accordingly.[2]

[1] There seems to be no doubt that M. Lawe was correct, for after p. 624 of STC 23344 Purslowe has included a large part of the text of STC 13583, with very slight alterations.

[2] Cf. *Book of Fines*, 14a, 26 Mar. 1619.

15 Nouemb 1619 Re Jac' 17°.

Present — mr Feild mr Swinhowe mr Jaggard mr Man mr Leake mr Lownes sen' mr Adams mr Knight mr Cooke

Lord maiors to Dinner.

To the Lord Mayo[rs]

The Master and wardens M[r] Leake, M[r] Adams, M[r] Knight M[r] Bill, and M[r] Islippe.

To M[r] Sheriffe Deane.

The Master and M[r] Swinhowe M[r] Waterson, M[r] Leake, M[r] Hum: Lownes and M[r] Adams.

To M[r] Sheriffe Cambells.

The Master and wardens, M[r] Math. Lownes, M[r] Cole, and M[r] Cooke.

24° Nouemb. 1619

m[r] Griffin
Joh. Norton,

This Daie election was made for Thomas Waterhouse[1] his yeomandry parte, who is latelie Deceased, the election fell vpon M[r] Griffen, to make vp his halfe yeomandry part a whole pte. And John Norton was elected to M[r] Griffens halfe yeomandrie pte, And the said M[r] Griffen, and John Norton tooke their oathes accordinglie. There stood in election with them Mr Edwardes and Mr Barrenger.

Wm Jones

It is ordered that Willm̃ Jones shall haue eight poundes in booke from Mr Weauer and that Mr Weauer shall take it againe by 20[s] a quarter out of the poores money as a pencõn granted to his sonne[2] for his maintenance at the vniu'sitie.

6° Decemb. 1619

Alice Wright

It is ordered that Alice Wright[3] shall haue a pencõn of Ten shillinges a quarter.

Rose Feild

Item it is ordered that Rose ffeild[4] shall haue 5[s] a quarter more then shee hath to make her pencõn ffifteene shillinge a quarter.

Geo. Elde
mr Chambers
Joh. Dawson

Theis pñtes witnes that whereas I Geo: Eld stac' am endebted vnto Geo: Chambers ffishmonger the some of 123[li]—15[s]—6[d] and vnto Robte Bolton the some of 15[li] more which amounteth to the some of 138[li]. 15[s]. vj[d] in toto, Nowe for that John Dawson Stac' is Contented to vndertake to paie the said some for me as it ariseth out of the profitt & encrease of my stocke in the Stacõers hall, The said George Eld doth agree that the said John Dawson shall receiue my Divident vntill such time as 138[l]. 15—6[d] be paid to the pties abouenamed, And if it please god that I the

[1] Presumably Amer Waterhouse, apprenticed 25 Dec. 1561 (Arber i. 171).

[2] Presumably Jones's son.

[3] Widow of William Wright.

[4] Possibly the widow of Jasper Field, made free 3 Aug. 1601 (Arber ii. 730).

said Geo: Eld & ffrancis my nowe wife both shall die, before the sđ some be satisfied & paid That then after the Master wardens & assistantę for the time being haue accordinge to their Constitucōns elected some other fitt pson to haue the said pte, All the money or Comoditie then Cominge by Disposinge thereof shalbe Deliu'ed to the said John Dawson for the payment of the said Debte, & soe much thereof as shalbe then vnsatisfied according to the true meaninge hereof, In witnes whereof y[e] said Geo: Eld & ffrancis his said wife haue herevnto sett their handę & seales y[e] 23 daie of Nouem: In the seauenteenth yeare of the raigne of our soueraigne Lord king James, of of (*sic*) England ffrance & Ireland, and of Scotland the Liij[th]. 1619

6° Dec. 1619

This was made at a full Court and ordered to be Entered accordingly.

Geo. Eld *Fran. Eld.*

Fol. 58[b]

20 Dec. 1619

Present. mr Field mr Swinhowe mr Jaggard mr waterson mr Lownes sen' mr Adams mr Lownes Jun' mr Gilmyn mr Cole mr Knight

M[r] Aldee

Whereas M[r] Alldee is to paie the some of xx[li] for his dispensacōn for not seruinge the rentorshippe being therevnto elected, It is nowe ordered by a full Court vpon the humble request of the said M[r] Alldee that he shall paie but fiue poundes vnto the Companie, and it shalbe accepted of in full satisfaction of his said fine. And the said M[r] Alldee hath Consented and is Content that the Companie shall haue his next Christmas Divident being v[li] for the same.[1]

Arcadia

It is agreed vpon that the Booke called the Arcadia that is begun to be ymprinted in Ireland shalbe forth w[th] [*fis*] finished and that so many shalbe kept there as shalbe thought fitt to serue that kingdome & the Residue to be brought ou', & mr waterson and mr math Lownes to haue them at that Rate that they paid for those they last printed herein England.[2]

A copie of a note vnder the hand of the Minister and Churchwardens and Clarke of Plymouth

No. 10. 1619.

John Batersbey Grañer

John Batersbye[3] Late of Plymouth was buried in Plymouth Church the 24 of Dec. 1618 as appeareth by the Register Booke there the same to be true wee witness vnder o[r] hand

Hen. Wallis pastor.

W[m] Byrch.
Tho. Crampponer } Churchwardens.

Nic. Knight Clarke.

[1] Cf. *C–B.C*, 55[a], 26 Mar. 1619, and 55[b], 7 June 1619.

[2] STC 22545.

[3] The death of Battersby was of considerable interest to the Company, for 6 Apr. 1597 he was appointed Royal Printer in Latin, Greek, and Hebrew for life, cf. Arber ii. 16.

m^{r} Wm Norten — Received from Christę hospitall of mr w^{m} Nortons bequest[1] .... } 6^{li} 13—4.

mr Geo. Bishope. — Item paid to Christę hospitall of mr Geo. Bishoppes bequest[2] .... } 6^{li}

Paid to the master wardens clark & beadle of mr wm. Norton's bequest[3] .... } 13^{s} 4^{d}

mr Norton the Grammer. — This day the draught of m^{r} Norton's assignment of the gram^{r} which was drawne by mr Jones was reade and ordered to be engrossed.[4]

At a meeting the 23° Decemb. 1619 Rę Jac' 17° — Fol. 59^{a}

Present — Mr Feild, Mr Swinhowe, Mr Jaggard, Mr Norton, Mr Waterson, Mr Lownes seni', Mr Lownes Jui' Mr Gilmyn, Mr Cole Mr Knight. Mr Blounte, M^{r}. Weauer, Mr Montforte, John Dawson.

Gram̃er — Mđ the Daie and yeare aboue written, It is agreed vpon betweene the Companie, And Mr Swinhowe, Mr Waterson, Mr Blounte and John Dawson, in stead of the rest of the late p̱tno^{rs} in the Gramer stocke, That all Books Deliu'ed out to them, and the rest of the sđ p̱tno^{rs}, vizt. Mr Waterson 115^{l}. Mr Blounte 115^{li}. Mr Dawson 57^{l}. 10^{s}. Mr Leake 57^{l}. 10^{s}. Mr Adams 57^{l}. 10^{s}. Mr Swinhowe 57^{l} 10^{s} M^{ris}. Bishop 57^{l} 10^{s}. shalbe all forthwith brought backe againe to the warehouse. And that Mr Nortons eight p̱te beinge taken out of the generall stocke the residue amounting vnto 1115^{l} besides those sold to M^{r} ffetherstone abating 4^{s} in the pound Doth amount vnto 892^{l}. And moreouer in Consideracõn of the Counterfeitę there is to be added 70^{l}. to the foresaid some of 892^{l} in toto 962^{l} which is to be paid to the seauen p̱tno^{rs} by 50^{l} a quarter, the first payment to begin at the Nativitie of St John Baptist which shalbe in the yeare of our lord god 1621.

Mđ the Companie are to paie also to the same late p̱tno^{rs} the some of three hundred poundes in forme followinge that is to saie at our Ladie Day next 100^{l}. at Midsomer next 100^{l} and [*and*] at Michaellmas next the other 100^{l} for the bookes they receiued from M^{r} ffetherstone as he should haue paid it.

Mr Norton and the company about the Gram̃er. & about Newton — Mđ the Companie are to paie Mr Norton for the Gram̃er patentę 300^{l} fine and 300^{l} p̱ annũ Duringe the life of Joice Norton Widđ howbeit in respect the Companie haue [*sold*] [assigned] vnto him the farme Called Newton, there is to be abated 22^{l} a yeare soe that hee is to receiue but 278^{l} p̱ anũ, that is to saie 69^{l} 10^{s} a quarter the first payment at our ladie daie 1620, And after the death of Joice Norton the Companie are to paie but 200^{l} a yeare for the residue of the Terme, [The said] Mr Norton hath also sold to the Companie his eight part of the Gramers of the value of 200^{li} wherewith the Companie are to purchase 22^{l} a yeare in liewe of the farme Called Newton, and the rent is to be put out & ymploy'd according to Mr Bishop's intent in his guift of the sđ Newton to the Companie That is to saie

[1] Cf. Plomer, *Wills*, pp. 30–33. [2] Cf. *C–B.C*, 24^{b}. [3] Cf. Plomer, *Wills*, pp. 30–33. [4] See below.

6[l] to Christes hospitall, 10[l] to Paules Crosse, and vj[l] to be lent out to poore men of this Companie from three yeares to three yeares.[1]

Ric. Mansell. It is orēd That Richard Mansell scholemaster that had his house sadly burnt shall haue v[li] giuen him by the Company. toward the building of his house.

19 Jan' 1619.

Latten stocke mr Tiffins lease This day the lease of the house for the latten stocke[2] was sealed by m[r] Tiffin for 21 yeares from Michã 1619 Rent 90[li] p a'ffyne—110[li].

FOL. 59[b] 20 Januarij 1619 Re Jac' 17°

Nich: Reeve This Daie the Companie borrowed of Nicholas Reeve a scriueno[r] in Corne[*wall*][hill] three hundred pounde[3] the money belonge to Willm' & Nicholas Children of Ellen Martin Widd Deceased, and is to be paid againe when they Come to age together with six poundes p Centũ for the interest which is to be paid euerie six monethes viz[t] on the 20th of Julie and the twentieth of Januarie 9[li] at a time.

M[r] Feild, M[r] Swinhowe, M[r] Jaggard, M[r] Waterson, M[r] Hum: Lownes, & M[r] Math: Lownes haue entred into a Recognisance in the lord Mayo[rs] Court for the payment hereof: and it is ordered that the seale of the house shalbe giuen to the said Nicholas Reeve being executo[r] to the said Ellen for the pformance of the said Recognizance, which at the payment of the money must be againe Called for from Nicholas Reeue or his Executo[rs] and Cancelled.

The Copie of the Condicon of the foresaid obligacõn

Wm Martin Nich. Martin.

This Condicõn is cancelled by consent and an newe made and sealed for 600[li] as appeareth after.

62

[*The Condicõn of this obligacõn is such That whereas the aboue named Nycholas Reeue hath before thensealinge and Deliuerie hereof paid to the aboue bound the Master and keeps or wardens and Comynaltie of the Misterie or Arte of Stationers of the Citie of London, the some of three hundred pounde of lawfull money of England being pte of a legacie remayning in the handes of the said Nich. Reeve to the vse of Willm̃ & Nicholas Children of Ellen Martin late of London widd Deceased to them giuen by their said Mother by her last will and Testament whereof the said Nicholas* [*Reeve*] *was and is sole executo[r] which some of 300[l] is to be repaid to the said Children when the same shall fall Due vnto them by the teno[r] of the said recited last will and testament of the said Ellen or to such other pson or psons to whome the same*

[1] This complicated arrangement was found unprofitable to the partners and the Company, though no doubt, as usual, Bonham Norton did not suffer, cf. *C–B.C*, 73[a], 25 June 1622, and 80[b], 25 Mar. 1624. The grammar patent here referred to is that granted to Bonham Norton, 6 Jan. 1613, for grammars in Greek and Latin, cf. *Letter Book*, 98[a], 24 July 1621.

[2] Cf. *C–B.C*, 48[a], 4 Aug. 1617, and 97[b], 19 Nov. 1627, where evidently this property was leased to Mathew Billing, though parts of it were leased earlier to Barrett and Bladen, cf. *C–B.C*, 72[a] 26 Mar. 1622, &c.

[3] This money, later increased to £600, was borrowed for the Latin Stock, cf. *The Library*, 2nd Ser., viii (1907), pp. 287–95.

shalbelonge & be due & payable by the teno^r and true meaninge of the said recited last will, And for securitie of repayment thereof accordinglie Richard ffeild George Swinhowe, John Jaggard Symon Waterson, Humphrey Lownes, and Mathew Lownes brethern of the said Companie haue entred into Recognizance in the Court of Lo: Mayo^r and Aldermen of the Citie of London holden in the Chamber of the guildhall of the same Citie before the said Lord Mayo^r and Aldermen, to Cornelius ffish Chamberlane of the Citie of London and his Successo^rs of the penaltie of five hundred pound℮ of lawfull money of England. And for payment of interest for the same for soe longe time as it shall remaine in the hand℮ of the said Companie after the rate of 6^t ꝑ centũ pro Anno and for performance of other thing℮ meñconed in the Condicõn of the same Recognizance as thereby more at large may appeare. Nowe if the said some of 300^t shalbe repaid accordinge to the tenor & true meaninge of the Condicõn of the said recited obligacõn & of the said last will & testament of the said Ellen Martin Deceased as in ꝑte for & conc'ning the legacy money giuen by the sđ Ellen to ye sđ children by the same her last will. Together with the sđ some of vj^t. pro cento ꝑ anũ, That theñd &c.]

Fishstreet—pish — W^m. Martin Christned on Sondaie the xth of Septem: 1615. / dead. / Nicholas Martin Christened on Sondaie the 30th of March 1617.

7° Feb. 1619. R℮ Ja. 17°. Fol. 60^a

Present. — m^r Feild mr swinhowe mr Jaggard mr Dawson mr waterson mr Hum. Lownes. mr Gilmyn m^r Knight

m^r Piper. — This day mr Piper was admitted into the Livery of this Company and gaue his bond for the paym^t of 20^li on the 27 of June next and to be exempted from attendance till then.

pđ accordingly

M^rs. Siluester. — whereas Thomas Jones and Lawrence Chapman haue printed a booke Called the woodmans beare[1] wth out the Consent of m^rs. Silvester being of her husband m^r. Jos. Siluesters doeing & Compiling. It is ordered that the said Jones & Chapman shall giue m^rs Siluester 20^s for a recompence

Lott Sivedale — It is ordered that Lott Sivedale shall haue a new lease of both his houses & the yard[2] for 51 yeares from o^r Lady day next at the old rent & 120^li fine/

Thomasin Fairebrother — It is ordered that m^rs. ffairebrother shall haue a lease of her house[3] for 51 yeares from o^r Lady day next at the old Rent & 15^li fine.

[1] STC 23583.

[2] Cf. *C–B.C*, 49^a, 7 Oct. 1617, and 46^a, 22 Jan. 1617. This was the Old Hall, or part of it, in Milkstreet. According to a schedule of leases preserved in an almost illegible state in the archives of the Company (No. 230) one of the houses was called 'The Three Mermaids'.

[3] Cf. *C–B.C*, 42^b, 22 Mar. 1616. This was part of the Hall on Ave Maria Lane. According to the above schedule the rent was £10.

mr Alldee
mr Kempe.

It is ordered that mr Alldee shall haue lycense to Continue his securitye for 6 monethes longer to mr Kempe for 60li to be paid on the 7th of July. 1620.

Mr Norton.
The Gramer.

This day mr Nortons assignemt of the Gramer was sealed by mr Norton & the Counterpte [thereof] wth the Comon seale.[1]

Newton

And likewise the Company did seale wth the Comon seale the assignemt of Newton lease vnto mr Norton.

mr Blount.
Latten stocke

It is ordered, That whereas the Irish stocke doth owe vnto mr Blount 300li (pcell of 900li) due the 28 of June last That the sd 300li shall be paid in to the vse of the Latten stocke which stocke from this day is to be answerable both for the said 300li and for the Interest at 5li p Cent'

Grammer:

Whereas the Company are to pay 1262 to the late ptenors in the gramer stocke for wares bought of them It is ordered that it shalbe paid in forme following that is to say 100li at or Lady day next 100li at midsomr next & 100li at Michis next 50li at Christmas next and so forward 50li a quarter vntill the some of 1262 be fully paid.[2]

Fol. 60b

17° ffebruarij 1619 Re Jacobi 17°

Ric. Morris
Tho: Milner

This daie it appeared vnto the Court, That Richard Morris[3] is endebted vnto vnto (*sic*) Thomas Milner[4] the some of three pounde & sixteene shillinge long since due vnto him, And it is therevpon ordered by the said court and by consent of both parties, that the said Rich. Morris shall paie the said debt by two shillinge a weeke, the first payment to begin on saterday next, and for euery saterday ijs till the said some be paid. And it is further Consented vnto by all pties, that the Master printer that the said Richard Morris worketh withall, or shall worke withall, shall deduct ijs a weeke out of his wages euery weeke, and deliuer it vnto the said Tho. Milner vntill the said some of 3l—16s be paid, except the said Rich. Morris do take order before hand for the payment thereof according to this agreement.

22° ffebr. 1619

mr Ockold.
mr M. Lownes.

Whereas Mr Ockold doth acknowledge himselfe to be endebted vnto Mathew Lownes the some of one hundred poundes, It is ordered at a full Court held on the seauenth of ffebruary last & by consent of both pties, that the said Mr Ockold shall paie mr Lownes 25l thereof in hand, and for the residue vizt. 75l. the said Mr Ockold hath promised to paie it by 12l 10s a yeare euery Michis or within 21 daies after till it be fullie paid the first payment to begin at Michis next: for the securitie and payment thereof the said Mr Ockold hath engaged his [*stock*] [part] in the English stocke, that if default

[1] Cf. *C–B.C*, 59a, 23 Dec. 1619.
[2] Ibid.
[3] Made free 2 Sept. 1616 (Arber iii. 684).
[4] Made free 20 Apr. 1618 (Arber iii. 684).

of payment be made in anie of the said paym^te, the Master and wardens are to goe to election of an other ptno^r in m^r Ockolde place according to their orders, and the whole debt to be paid to Mr Lownes at one entire payment out of Mr Ockolde stocke.

1mo Martij 1619

mr Johnson. w^m Jones.	The matter in Controuersie betwixt Willm̃ Jones. and Arthur Johnson is referred to m^r Knight, and m^r Aspley, by consent of both parties.

To the right wo^ll. the master wardens & assistante of the Companie of Stationers

According to y^r wor: order, wee haue had Consideracõn of the differences between m^r Johnson, and Willm̃ Jones by y^u referred vnto vs, and accordinglie to Certifie your wor: that wee thinke it fitt the said Wm Jones shall paie to m^r Johnson the some of L^s in bookes called the Christian watchfullnes[1] nowe in printing at 9^s. 6^d the reame, the bookes to be deliuered to m^r Johnson within one weeke after it is first put to sale, in consideracoñ of the wronge done by W^m. Jones in dispersing of m^r Grangers divine logicke[2] contrary to his agreement, And whereas m^r Johnson hath paid more money then W^m. Jones hath deliuered bookes of Grang^rs logicke wee doe order that Wm Jones shall pñtelie deliuer him soe many more of Grangers logicke as the ouerplus money Cometh vnto at 7^s 6^d all which wee leaue it to y^r wor. Confirmacõn. In witness whereof we haue sett to our hande this 23 of ffebr: 1619

6° Martij 1619 — Fol. 61^a

Present	m^r Feild, m^r Swinhowe, m^r Jaggard, m^r Waterson m^r Lownes senior m^r Lownes Junio^r, m^r Gylmyn, m^r Cole, m^r Knight m^r Pauier & m^r Cooke.
Binders fol. 29.	This day it is ordered that a former order[3] concerning binde^rs made the xix^th of May 1612 shalbe reversed and Crossed out of the booke as void being made Contrary to the decrees in the starchamber.
M^r. Sivedall—	This day the draught of m^r Sivedales leases were read agreed vpon at a full Court, and ordered to be ingrossed.[4]
M^rs. Fairbrother	This day likewise the draught of m^rs. ffairbrothers lease was read & agreed vpon and ordered to be ingrossed.[4]

27° Martij 1620 Re Jac' 18°.

M^r. Boyle—	This day m^r Boyle is chosen Rento^r, and he is to paie for a fyne for his dispensacõn for not serving the same. xx^l.

[1] STC 21185.

[2] STC 12184.

[3] Cf. *C–B.C*, 29^a, 19 May 1612. In the Society of Antiquaries there is a broadside 'A generall note of the prises for binding of all sorts of bookes. Imprinted at London, 1619', which may have something to do with this.

[4] Cf. *C–B.C*, 60^a, 7 Feb. 1620.

Mr. Jaggard Junr. is Chosen Rentor to Joyne with mr Harrison for the yeare followinge.

3o Aprilis 1620.

Present, as aboue/

Dinners— It is ordered by consent of a full Court holden this day that the wardens shall make but two Dinners in a yeare, that is to saie vpon the sixt of may, and the election dinner, and that the said wardens shall hereafter be allowed but 5l a yeare from the house towardes the said two Diñers,[1] and whereas the Cooke hath been allowed 4l a yeare for his fee, it is nowe ordered that he shall haue onlie xxs for euery Dinner he shall dresse.[2]

3o Maij 1620

Mr. Bourne. It is ordered that mr Bourne shall haue the last 50l that is brought in by Mr Johnson, being of Mr John Nortons bequest,[3] & this court is content to accept of Thomas Harper, and John Powle to be his sureties, soe that also he does assigne ouer his pte in the English stocke to the Company for further securitie.

Mr. Johnson
Mr. Kingston &
Mr. Searger.
43: 53.

It is ordered that mr Johnsons pte in the Irish stocke (accordinge to a note vnder his hand) shalbe assigned to Mr Kingston, And Mr Kingston being present at this Court did likewise assigne the same to Richard Searger.

Fol. 61b

6o Maij 1620 Re Jac' 18o

Present Mr Feild Mr. Swinhowe, Mr Jaggard, Mr Dawson, Mr Waterson, Mr Leake, Mr Lownes senir, mr Lownes Junir, Mr Knight, Mr Pauier, Mr Cooke/

Wm. Stansby This day mr Stansby at a full Court had Warning to avoid two forraynors that he keepeth in his house, vizt. Peter Smith,[4] and Phillip Jinkes his sonne, and if he avoid them not within 8 dayes he is to paie for a fine 40s and 40s a weeke [a peece] for soe long as he shall keepe them in his house, contrary to the orders of the Company.[5]

Joseph Harrison
Jacob Bloome.

This day Joseph Harrison hath license from this table to engage his pte in the English stocke vnto Jacob Bloome for the paymt of 80li vpon the 25 of June 1621.

[1] Cf. *C–B.C*, 27a, 26 May 1611, when the allowance was raised to £20 a year.

[2] Cf. *C–B.C*, 27b, 6 July 1611.

[3] Cf. *C–B.C*, 43a, 4 Apr. 1616. His bonds are registered in *Liber C2*, 109a.

[4] P. Smith and C. Jenks are known only by the notice of them, as publishers of popish books, in J. Gee's *Foot out of the snare*, 1624; cf. also *C–B.C*, 79a, 6 Oct. 1623.

[5] Cf. *C–B.C*, 66b, 4 Dec. 1620, and 69b, 3 Sept. 1621.

2° Junij 1620

Present Mr Feild, Mr. Swinhowe, Mr. Jaggard, Mr. Dawson, Mr Waterson, Mr Lownes seni', Mr Lownes Juni', Mr Gilmyn, Mr. Cole, Mr Knight, Mr. Pauier, Mr Cooke/

Wm. Barrenger This day election was made for the Wid Bathoes[1] yeomandry part, the said Wid being married yesterday vnto Mr Dawson. There stood in election for the same, William Barrenger, John Piper, and Nathaniell Newbury, the election fell vpon William Barrenger, and the said William Barrenger tooke his oath accordinglie.

15° Junij 1620

Tho: Downe. It is concluded vpon, at a generall meeting of the ptnors in the Irish stocke, that Thomas Downe shall goe in to Ireland, and be the Companies factor in [*the said*] [that] stocke, and he is to haue 100l p Anum for himselfe, and ten pounds a yeare for an appr', and besides to bee allowed as much, as will hire a Jorney man vntill he hath brought vp a prentice fitting for the busines and then to be allowed 20l for two prentizes, and one hundred pounds p annu for himselfe as aforesaid[2]

Mr Islippe— It is ordered that mr Islip shall pay for binding of Mathew Williamson[3] his appr' at a scrivenors Contrary to order, the some of three poundes, besides the fees of the house.

Mr. Legate. It is ordered that Mr Legate shall pay the some of [*three*] fifty shillings, (besides the fees of the house) for binding Thomas Jackson[4] his appr' at a scrivenors Contrary to order.

27° Junij 1620.

Chri: Hunlocke. It is ordered that Christopher Hunlocke shalbe Cooke to the hall next in reuersion after Mr Pinfold nowe Cooke to the said hall.

eod die et anno pred. Fol. 62a

Mris. Bishoppe
Mr Constable. This day Mris. Bishop[5] having surrendred vp her liuery pte in the English stocke The Table went to election of an other ptenor and the election fell vpon ffrancis Constable, there stood in election wth him Mr Jaggard and Mr Higgenbotham.

[1] John Bathoe had been given security by T. Dawson, the uncle of J. Dawson, Sen., to the latter of whom presumably Elizabeth Bathoe was married, cf. *C–B.C*, 22b, 29 Jan. 1610.

[2] Downes appears to have proceeded to Ireland and commenced printing. Among his first publications were broadsides, 'Notice of appointment of deputies' and 'Bookes as they are sold bound', with English and Irish prices; cf. Dix, *Early Dublin printed books*, p. 327.

[3] Made free 6 Oct. 1623 (Arber iii. 685).

[4] Made free 9 June 1623 (Arber iii. 685).

[5] Presumably widow of Edward Bishop.

Geo: Latham. Then election was made for m[r] Constables yeomandry ꝑte and it fell vpon George Latham, there stood in election with him Nath. Newbury and Rich. Badger, and the said George Latham tooke his oath accordinglie.

1[mo] Julij 1620.

M[r] Feild M[r] Swinhoe M[r] Jaggard, M[r] Dawson, M[r] Waterson, M[r] Leake, M[r] Lownes seni' M[r] Lownes Juni', M[r] Gilmyn, M[r] Cole, M[r] Knight, M[r] Pauier, M[r] Cooke, and M[r] Harrison, and M[r] Jaggard Junio[r] Rento[rs].

M[r]. Math. Lownes M[r] Gilmyn. This day the M[r] Wardens and Assistantę according to the custome of the Companie, are to elect newe M[r] and wardens for the yeare ensewing, and it soe fell out that there were none of the Assistantę that had ben twice vnder Warden to stand in election with m[r] Swinhowe for vpper Warden, And it was therefore ordered that M[r] Math. Lownes and M[r] Gilmyn shalbe dispensed withall from the seruice of the second time vnder Warden and they yeilded to give vnto the Companie for the same five poundę a peece, and soe were made Capable to stand in election for vpper warden according to the Custome of this Companie.

Nich. Reeue. Whereas the Companie haue heretofore borrowed[1] of Nicholas Reeue scrueno[r] the some of three hundred poundę, and as appeareth by a former order, M[r] ffeild, M[r] of the Companie, M[r] Swinhowe [&] M[r] Jaggard wardens, and M[r] Waterson, M[r] Lownes seni', and m[r] Lownes Juni' 3 of the Assistantę of the said Companie haue entred into a Recognizance in Guildhall London for repayment thereof to Willm̃ and Nicholas Martin Children to Ellen Martin deceased when they come to their seuerall ages of 21 yeares, And whereas also the said Company haue sealed an obligacõn with the Comon seale vnto the said Nicholas Reeue, with a Condicõn vnder written for ꝑformance of Certaine Couenantę and agreem[tę] ther in mencõned. Nowe the said Company haue borrowed of the said Nicholas Reeue the some of 300[l] more, and the said M[r] ffeild, Mr Swinhowe Mr Jaggard, Mr Waterson m[r] Lownes seni', and Mr Lownes Juno[r] haue likewise entred into Recognizance in Guildhall for repayment thereof vnto the said W[m] and Nicholas Martin when they come to age as aforesaid. And it is ordered by a full Court holden this day. That the former obligacõn (being first Cancelled) a newe obligacõn shalbe made and sealed with the Comon seale, and deliu'ed vnto the said Nicholas Reeue, Condicoñed for repayment [*thereof*] of the said seuerall
Fol. 62[b] somes of 300[li]. at such times and when as is || mencõed in the said Condicõn and with further Clause that the Companie shall not pay in the said money to the Chamber of London vntill it fall due by the last will and testament of the said Ellen and then to pay it to such persons as in the said will is limitted, & in the meane time to pay to the said Chamber of London for the Interest of the first 300[l] after 6[l] ꝑ Centum pro anno, at two seuerall dayes, that is to saie vpon the 20th of Julie, and the 20th of January by euen porcõns, And also to paie to the said Nicholas Reeue for interest of the other 300[l]. after 6[l] ꝑ Cent' pro Anno, at two other seuerall

[1] Cf. *C–B.C*, 59[b], 20 Jan. 1620.

Dayes in the yeare, that is to saie the 24th of December, and the 24th of June also by euen porcõns, with other Articles and Clauses in the Condicõn of the said obligacõn mencõed and expressed, which said obligacon was read agreed vpon and sealed by consent of a full Court of Assistantꝭ at Stationers hall as aforesaid.

Bonde to mr Nich. Reeue, Nou'int vni'si per pñ'tes nos Magistrũ et Custođ siue Gardian' et Com'tat misterij siue Artis Stationar' Civitatis London' teneri et firmiter obligari Nicholao Reeve Civi et Scriptor' London' in Octingentis libris bone et ległis monete Anglie, Soluenđ eidem Nicholao Reeve aut suo Certo Atturnat' executor vel admi'strator' suis, Ad quam quiđ. solucoem' bene et fideliter facienđ, Obligamus nos et successor' nrõs firmiter per pñ'tes, Sigillo nr̃o Comuñi, Sigillat' dat' Tertio die Julij, Anno regni Dni' nri' Jacobi dei gra' Anglie ffrancie et Hiƀnie regis fidei defensor &c decimo octavo, et Scotie Quinquagesimo tertio. 1620

The Condicoñ of this obligacoñ is such, That whereas Ellen Martin late of london Widowe deceased did in her life time make & declare her last will and testament in writing bearing date the 13 day of July Anno 1608 And in the 16th yeare of the raigne of our soueraigne lord king James &c And in and by the same amongst other thingꝭ did giue and bequeath vnto her sonne William Martin soe much as would make vp the legacy which her husband Richard Martin deceased by his last will and testament had given to him the said William the full some of 600l. To be paid him at his full age of 21 yeares, And in like manner did giue and bequeath vnto her sonne Nicholas Martin soe much as would make vp the legacy her said Husband Richard Martin deceased by his said [*Last*] will had given to him the said Nicholas Martin the like full soñe of 600l, To be paid him at his full age of 21 years And if it should happen her said Children Willm̃ & Nicholas to dye or departe this mortall life before they should accomplish || their full ages of 21 yeares; Then she gaue willed Fol 63a
and demised the legacies guiftes and bequestes before to them by the said Hellen given vnto and amongst her sisters, Elizabeth Baell, Mary Wily, and Martha Sutton equally to be devided, or to that effect, as by the same her last will and testament may appeare. Of which her last will and Testament she made and ordayned the aboue named Nichãs Reeve her full and whole Executor and after deꝑted this life, after whose death the said Nicholas Reeve did prooue the said will according to the Ecclesiasticall lawes of this Realme and tooke vpon him the Execucõn thereof. And whereas the seuerall legacies given by the said Hellen to her said Children by her said last will as it appeareth to the said Nicholas Reeve; and as he Conceiveth doth amount to 300l a peece and vpwardꝭ, and he the said Nicholas Reeve having a purpose and desire to prouide for the safe Custody of the said Legacies given to the said Children by the said Hellen with some reasonable proffitt to the said Children hath in the moneth of January last past paid to the abouenamed Mr and keepers or wardens and Com'altie the some of 300l of lawfull money of England being ꝑte of the said legacies given by the said Hellen to her said Children to th'end and purpose that the same should remaine in the handꝭ and vse of the said Master & keeꝑs or wardens and Com'altie and their successors vntill the same legacyes shall fall and become due and be payable by the tenor of the said last recited last will of the said Hellen, And then the same to be repaid

according to the tenour & true meaninge of the said last recited last will and
Testament of the said Ellen to such ꝑson and ꝑsons to whome the same shall fall
due and bee payable and not before to be paid to the Chamberlaine of the citie
of London for the time being And that the said Mr and Keepers or Wardens and
Com'altie their successors and assignes shall in the meane time vntill the same
shalbe soe repaid satisfie and paie vse for the same after the rate of 6l. ꝑ Centũ pro
Anno, And for better securitie of repayment thereof accordinglie Richard ffeild,
George Swinhowe, John Jaggard Symon Waterson, Humphrey Lownes and Mathew
Lownes brethren of the said Company haue entred into recognizance in the Kingꝭ
Mate. Court holden before the Mayor and Aldermen of the Citie of London in the
Chamber of the Guildhall to Cornelius ffish Chamblaine of the Cittie of London
and his Successors of the penaltie of 500l of Lawfull money of England, And for
paiment of vse or Interest for the same after the rate of 6l ꝑ Centũ pro Anno, And
for ꝑformance of other thingꝭ mencõed in the Condicoñ of the said Recognizance
Fol. 63b as thereby more at Large may appeare: And the said Nicholas || Reeve hath nowe
also before the date hereof paid to the said Master and keepers or wardens and
Com̃altie another some of 300l of lawfull money of England being also part of the
said legacies given by the said Hellen to her said Children to the like end and
purpose that the same should remaine in the handꝭ and vse of the said Mr, and
keepers or wardens and Com'altie and their successors vntill the same lagacyes
shall fall due and be payable by the tenor of the said last recyted [*last*] will of the
said Hellen. And then the same to be repaid according to the tenor and true meaninge of the said last recyted last will and Testament of the said Hellen to such
ꝑson and ꝑsons to whome the same shall fall due and bee payable and not before
to be paid to the Chamberlayne of the Cittie of London for the time being his
Successors or assignes. And that the said Mr and keepers or wardens and Com̃altie
their successors and assignes shall in the meane time vntill the same shalbe soe
repaid satisfie and paye to the said Nicholas Reeve his Executors and assignes vse
money for the same after the rate of 6l. ꝑ Cent' pro Anno, And for better securitie
of repayment of the said last mencõed some of 300l accordinglie the said Richard
ffeild, George Swinhowe, John Jaggard, Symon Waterson, Humphrey Lownes and
Mathew Lownes haue entred into Recognizances in the kingꝭ Mate Court aforesaid
holden before the Mayor and Aldermen of the Citie of London in the Chamber of
the Guildhall to the Chamberlayne of the Citie of London for the time beinge and
his Successors Chamberlaines of the said Citie of the penalty of 500l of lawfull
money of England And whereas it is fully and absolutelie Concluded and agreed
vpon by and betweene the said Mr and keepers or wardens and Com̃altie, and
Richard ffeild, George Swinhowe, John Jaggard, Symon Waterson, Humph. Lownes,
and Mathew Lownes in th'one ꝑty, And the said Nicholas Reeve on th'other ꝑtie,
That the said Master and keepers or wardens and Com'altie their Successors and
assignes shall not at anytime hereafter pay to the said Chamberlaine of the Cittie
of London his Successors or assignes the said seuerall somes of 300l or either of
them, or any ꝑte of them or either of them, vntill the said Legacies given by the
said Hellen to her said Children by her said recited last will shall fall due and be
payable according to the Tenor and true meaninge of the said last will and testament of the said Hellen. Nowe if therefore the said Master and keeps or wardens
and Com'altie their Successors and assignes shall well and truelie paie the said

seuerall somes of 300^{l} & 300^{l} in p̱te of the said recited seuerall legacies devised by the said || Hellen to the said Children W^{m}. and Nicholas by her said last will & Fol. 64^{a}
Testament, and that in such manner and forme and at such time and times, and when and to such person and persons as the same shall fall or become due and is limitted meant and purposed to be paid by the teno^{r} and true meaninge of the same her said last recyted last will and that in all thingꝭ according to the tenour and true meaninge of the same her last will and testament, And if the said Master & keepers or wardens and Com'altie their Successo^{rs} or assignes doe not in the meane time vntill the said legacyes shall soe fall or become due and be payable satisfie paie or discharge the said seuerall somes of 300^{l} or anie p̱te of them or either of them to the Chamberlaine of the Citie of London for the time beinge his successo^{rs} or assignes, And also if the said Master & keepers or wardens and Com'altie their successo^{rs} or assignes shall in the meane time vntill the said last mencõed some of 300^{l} now last paid shall so fall or become due and be payable, and be dulie & truelie paid according to the tenour and true meaninge before mencõned well and truelie paie to the said Nichãs Reeve his Executo^{rs} Adm'strato^{rs} or Assignes yearlie after the rate of 6^{l} p̱ Cent' pro anno for the said last mencõed some of 300^{l} at two daies in the yeare (that is to saie) the 24th of December and the 24th of June in euery yeare by equall porcõns, And in case the said seuerall somes of 300^{l} or either of them or any part of them or either of them shalbe paid vnto the Chamberlaine of the Citie of London for the time being his successo^{rs} or Assignes by occasion of breach of the Condicõns of the said Recognizances or either of them or otherwise of the owne will and disposicõn of the said M^{r} and keepers or wardens and Com̃altie their successo^{rs} or assignes or of the said Richard ffeild, George Swinhow John Jaggard, Symon Waterson, Humphrey Lownes and Mathewe Lownes or anie of them their or anie of their executo^{rs} [or] adm^{rs}. or in any otherwise vnlesse it be with the good will liking and Consent of the said Nicholas Reeve his Executo^{rs} Adm'strato^{rs} or assignes yet notwithstanding if the said M^{r} and keepers or wardens and Com'altie their successo^{rs} or Assignes doe continue payment of the said vse money of 6^{l} p̱ Cent' pro Anno aswell for the said first mencõned 300^{l} as also for the said other mencõned 300^{l} vntill the said Legacies given by the said Hellen to her said Children by her said [*Children*] will shall fall due and be payable by the teno^{r} and true meaning of her said last will and Testament, and that in all thingꝭ as the same vse money ought to haue ben paid or should be paid if the said seuerall somes had Continued and remayned in the Custody or Vse of the said Master and keepers or wardens and Com'altie their successo^{rs} or assignes, or of the said Richard ffeild, George Swinhowe, John Jaggard, Symon Waterson Humphrey Lownes and Math. Lownes or any of them, their or anie of their Executo^{rs} Adm'strato^{rs} or ass' || And Fol. 64^{b}
also if the said M^{r} and keepers or wardens & Com'altie their Successo^{rs} and assignes doe vpon euery reasonable request well & sufficientlie acquitte discharge saue and keepe harmlesse the said Nicholas Reeve his Executo^{rs} Adm'strato^{rs}, landꝭ ten'tes, hereditamentꝭ and goodꝭ and euery of them of and from all such accõns, suitꝭ extentꝭ, bills of Complaint, orders decrees & Costes, Charges Damages and expences as shall or may arise or growe for or by reason of the non payment of the said seu'al somes of 300^{l} and 300^{l} at such times and when as the said Legacies given by the said Ellen to her said Children by her said recyted last will and Testament shall fall or become due or ought to be paid to the said Children or other person or persons,

according to the tenor and true meaninge of the said last will & Testament of the said Hellen, That then this &c

Order for paymt of Nicho. Reeues. 600li & Interest. This sayd some of 600li was putt into the Latten stocke to be imployed therein and out of that stocke as well the sayd 600li as allso the Interest from time to time is to be answered and paid accordinge to the forme and meaninge of the precedent condicon; And it was so ordered at a full Court holden the j of July. 1620 p̃ñtibȝ vt ante.

Teste *Tho. Montforte* Norie

In the last will & testament of Thomas Adams Stationer deceased is contayned among other thinge as followeth. Dat: Secundo Martij 1619.

Mr. Adams his guift to the Company Item I give and bequeath to the Master & keeps or wardens and Cominaltie of the mistery or Art of Stationrs of the Cittye of London, the some of one hundred pounde to be paid wthin a yeare after my decease and my will is that the benifitt & increase here of shalbe expended and layd out towarde the defraying of publique Chardges in the said Company at the discretion of the Master wardens & assistante of the said Company for the time being or the greater part of them.

This 100li was paid in accordingly, and by order of a Court putt into the latyne stocke[1]/

Fol. 65a Mr Humphrey Lownes. mr.
mr. Mathewe Lownes }
mr Geo. Cole .... } wardens.

7° Augusti 1620. Re Jacob. 18°.

Present. Mr Lownes. mr. mr Lownes and mr Cole wardens mr Waterson. mr Feild mr Swinhowe mr Gilmyn mr Jaggard mr Knight. mr Pavier

Stockeepers for the Latten stocke[2] mr Leake, mr Jaggard } assist. mr Blount, mr Piper } Liver. Edw. Aggas., Ric Whitacres } yeom.

The Purchas in Woodstreet. Whereas, mr John Norton deceased by his last will and testament[3] did giue vnto the Master wardens and assistante of the Company of Stationrs the some of 1000li to be paid wthin two yeares after his decease, which he willed should be laid out by them for the purchase of Lande or tenente The yearely rente whereof he did deuise should be by the said mr wardens and assistante or their successors in their best discretions from time to time for eu' disposed in Loane answerable and agreable proportionably to a perpetuall devise or legacye contayned or menconed in the Last will & testamt of his vncle Wm. Norton deceased[4]

[1] Cf. *C–B.C*, 75b, 21 Jan. 1623.

[2] The original stockkeepers chosen in 1616 had refused to permit a new state to be elected; cf. *The Library*, 2nd Ser., viii (1907), pp. 293–4.

[3] Cf. Plomer, *Wills*, pp. 45–47, and *C–B.C*, 43a, 4 Apr. 1616.

[4] Cf. Plomer, *Wills*, pp. 30–33.

The master therefore & the wardens & assistantę of this company having found out a convenient purchase of certaine messuagę & tenem[te] in Woodstreet, London, for which they were to pay 1200[li] that is 200[li] more then m[r] Norton gaue vnto them they tooke 150[li] which the said mr Norton gaue vnto the parrish of saint ffaithes,[1] and 50[li] more which one master Billage gaue likewise vnto this Company[2] which together wth the 1000[li] doe make vp the said some of 1200[li] wherewith the Company did purchase the said messuagę or tenem[te] in woodstreet accordingly as by the euidences and assurances doth appeare

And concerning the disposicõn of the Rentę & profittę there of. It is this day ordered by a full Court That 50[li] be yearely lent out to some one man or other of this Company putting in securitye according to the said will, and that there shalbe allowed to the mr wardens Clarke & beadle out of the said Rentę for their paines 4[li] yearely. viz[t]. to the mr & wardens xxs. a peece and to the Clark & beadle xxs betwixt them.

And further in respect of the said 150[li] giuen to saint ffaithes there shall be paid to 12 poore people at saint ffaithes church aforesaid iiijs. weekely eu'ye wednesday vizt ij[d] a peece in money and one penny loafe. And there shall [be] paid to the preacher on Ashwednesday xi[s]. besidę wine Cakes & ale to the Company on that day according to the said will.

And there is to be paid in respect of the 50[li] aforesđ to the parish of saint martins in the vintrye the some of Lij[s] yearely. by xiij[s] a quarter to be distributed in bread weekely to xij poore people of that ꝑish at the discretion of the Church wardens Fol. 65[b]

And it is ordered that Thomas Montforte Clark of this Company shall collect the Rentę in Woodstreet aforesđ & pay the ꝑish of saint ffaithes weekely and that for his paines he shalbe allowed 26[s] 8[d] by the yeare out of the said Rentę & profittę.

mr Purfoote — It is ordered that mr Purfoote shall printe Ouidę metamorphosis in English according to his Request, paying vj[d] in the pound to the vse of the poor.[3]

12° August. 1620.

Presente. — m[r] Lownes. sen'. m[r] Lownes Jun'. m[r] waterson m[r] Feild. m[r] Swinhowe m[r] Gilmyn m[r] Jaggard m[r] Knight m[r] Pavier m[r] Cooke.

m[r] Swinhowe. — It is ordered that according to m[r] Barkers desire and his assignem[t4] m[r] Swinhowe shall haue m[r] Barkers assistantę ꝑte in the english stocke.

m[r] Jackson — Then the table went to election for m[r] Swinhowes Liverye ꝑte and it fell vpon Roger Jackson.

[1] According to Norton's will the £150 was to be used to purchase lands, the income from which was to be divided between the poor of the Stationers' Company and of St. Faith's parish. Evidently the parson and churchwardens had left the money with the Company.

[2] Cf. *C–B.C*, 6[a], 4 Dec. 1604.

[3] Cf. STC 18962. This was one of the 'yielded' copies, cf. Arber ii. 789. Presumably Purfoot did not print the edition here proposed.

[4] Printed below.

m^r^ Sam. Man:	Then they went to election for m[r] Jacksons yeomandry pte and it fell vpon Sam. Man.

Mr Barkers assignem[t].

mr Barker
m[r] Swinhowe

Be it knowne vnto all men by theis p̃nt͡e That I Robert Barker of London esq͡ for certaine good consideracõns me therevnto moving haue assigned surrendred and sett ou' and by theis p̃nt͡e doe assigne surrender & sett ou' vnto George Swinhowe Citizen & station̄r of London, All that my assistant͡e pte in the English stocke amounting to the some of 320[li] or thereabout͡e. which I nowe haue remayning running & being in the hand͡e & custody of the Master wardens & assistant͡e of the Company of Station̄rs in London, And I doe desire the said mr wardens & assistant͡e to elect & Choose the said Geo. Swinhowe into my said stocke & pte according to the ordinances & Constitucõns of the said Company in that behalf In witnes hereof I haue herevnto sett my hand and seale this xi[th] day of August in the 18 yeare of the Raigne of o[r] sou'aigne Lord King James &c.

Signatur *Rob. Barker.*

Sealed & deliu'ed in the p̃nce
of *Tho: Montforte.*
Rob. Constable

Fol. 66[a]

4° Septemb. 1620 R͡e Jac. 18

Present. m[r] Lownes. sen'. mr Lownes Jun'. mr Cole mr Waterson mr Feild mr Swinhowe mr Gilmyn mr Knight

mr Alldee.
mr Kempe.

This day m[r] Alldee had license from the table to engage his pte in the english stocke vnto m[r] Kempe for 60[li] to be paid at 6 monethes.[1]

John Legate Jun'.

It is ordered that Joh. Legate the yonger shall haue all his fathers Copies entred vnto him paying the fees due to the house viz[t] x[d] a Copie.[2]

John Sharpe
m[r] Man

Be it knowne that I John Sharpe[3] for a certaine some of money to me in hand at the ensealeing hereof by Thomas Man truly payd haue bargained sold & released and hereby doe fully and Clearely bargaine sell & release vnto the said Thomas Man his ex[rs] & ass͡e all & singuler Copies heretofore deliu'ed for the presse to be printed & all my right purporte estate & interest therein or in any of them in any wise. And also I doe release vnto him all erro[r] & erro[rs] and writ͡e of error accõns suit͡e trespasses debt͡e duties somes of money account͡e reckoning͡e claimes & demand͡e whatsoeu' they be from

[1] Cf. *C-B.C*, 60[a], 7 Feb. 1620.

[2] These books were entered 2 Jan. 1621 (Arber iv. 45–46), where it is said that this order was made at a court held 21 Aug. 1621.

[3] This would appear to be an error, for it is Henry Sharpe whose name is appended and whose joint entries with T. Man are several times later recorded as passing from one member of the Man family to another.

the beginning of the worlde vntill the day of the date hereof Sealed wth my seale the 28 day of August 1620 and in the 18th yeare of the raigne of o^r^ sou'aigne Lord King James of England &c

Hen. Sharpe.

25. Septemb. 1620

Aug. Mathewes. This day Augustine Mathewes had warning at a full Court to avoyd ffrances Gastonie a forreno^r^ which he keepeth disorderly.

Bar: Alsoppe. Likewise Barnard Alsop had warning to avoid on Malkin a forreno^r^.

2 Oct'. 1620

Mr Bill. This day mr Bill was elected into the assistantę of this Company.

Mr Halwood. Rob. Lownes. It is ordered that the Company shall accept of 400^li^ offered by m^r^ Halwood[1] to pay vnto him 40^li^ p̨ annu' during his life & 32^li^ afterwardę a yeare during the life of Robert Lownes. This 400^li^ is ymployed in the englishe stocke /

4° Decemb. 1620 Rę Jac. 18°. Fol. 66^b^

Present. mr Lownes. sen' mr lownes Jun' mr Waterson mr. Swinhowe. mr. Field mr Gilmyn. mr Jaggard mr Knight mr Pavier mr Cooke.

Lord Mayor^s^ dinners It is ordered that in regard the house is vpon extraordinary occasions & suitę growne behind hand that the Company shall not goe this yeare to the Lord Mayo^rs^ & shreues to there dinn^rs^ as of late time they haue vsually done

m^r^. Fethersten It is ordered by Consent of a full court holden this day. that mr Fetherstone according to a former order shall pay to the vse of this Company xx^s^ a weeke for so many weekę as he hath kept one Rob. Martin a forreno^r^ in his house or shoppe contrary to a confirmed ordinance of this house being warned to put the said Robert away vpon the 7 of decemb. 1618 at a full Court then holden as by the sd̄ order appeareth.[2]

w^m^. Stansby It is ordered that w^m^ Stansby shall bring in his fine of 40^s^ vpon the 2^d^ monday in the next moneth[3]

[1] Not recorded as connected with the Company.

[2] Cf. *C–B.C*, 53^b^, 7 Dec. 1618, and below.

[3] In the *Book of Fines*, 15^b^, 7 Aug. 1620, 'It is ordered that Wm Stansby for printing a booke of m^r^ Lidiatę [STC 17046] wth out entrance & obstinately refusing to come to the wardens & for vsing vnfitting speaches shalbe comitted to prison & pay a fine of xl*s*'. This was commuted 6 Sept. 1624 to a fine of 3*s*. 4*d*. and Stansby pardoned.

13 decemb. 1620

mr Fethersten — This day mr Fetherston was warned to bring in his ffine on wednesday next

18. Januarij 1620

Present. — mr Lownes sen' mr Lownes. Jun'. m^r Cole, mr Waterson mr Feild mr Swinhowe mr Knight mr Pavier mr Bill.

mr Fetherston — This day mr Fetherston being required by the table to pay his fine for keeping Rob. Martin a forreno^r Contrary to order did vtterly Refuse the paym^t thereof. Wherevpon it is ordered by this Court that the said mr Fetherston shall haue no more booke from the English stocke wth out ready money vntill the said fine be payd And it was further ordered that the divident & profitt of mr Fetherstons stocke shalbe staid from time to time for the paym^t of the said ffine.

Christs Hospitall — Rec' from Christe hospitall of m^r w^m Nortons bequest[1]........... } .vj^li xiij^s iiij^d.

Item paid to Christe hospitall of.... m^r Bishoppes bequest[2]............ } vj^li

To the m^r wardens clarke & beadle[2]......xiij^s iiij^d

FOL. 67^a

23 Januarij 1620 Re Jac. 18°.

Present — mr Lownes sen' mr Lownes. Jun'. mr Cole mr Waterson mr Feild mr Swinhowe mr Jaggard mr Knight mr Pavier mr Cooke m^r Bill

mr Bill and the Company — Wheras [divers of] the Company [of Stac'] haue [an entent to] deale wth m^r Bill for all his forren booke and leases of his houses & [*that*] to that purpose Certaine articles are agreed vpon by consent of all ptíes. It is this day ordered by this court That the said m^r Bill shall haue the seale of the house [*and a b*] to the said articles and a bond to pforme covenante for his securitye. which was this [day sealed and] done accordingly. And the said mr Bill sealed the other pte of the said articles & a bond [likewise] to pforme the same [*articles*][3]

John Dawson — Vpon a peticoñ[4] exhibited to my lorde grace of Canterbury by Joh. Dawson Desiring thereby to be a Master printer in his vncles place and vpon my lo. graces consent therevnto signified vnder his hand It is ordered that the said John Dawson shall be a master printer & haue his vncles copies.

[1] Cf. Plomer, *Wills*, pp. 30–33.

[2] Cf. *C–B.C*, 24^b.

[3] Bill may have been raising money in connexion with the lawsuits regarding the King's Printing Office, cf. *The Library*, N.S. ii (1901), 353–75.

[4] Arber iii. 689; *State Papers Dom. James I, 1619–1623*, p. 215, vol. cxix, n. 39, 23 Jan. 1621.

Balladꝭ. Whereas it was ordered 19 Maij 1612[1] among other thingꝭ that 5 printers onely should haue the printing of all balladꝭ It is nowe ordered by this Court that for some Inconveniencꝭ that haue Risen by reason thereof that the said order in that point shall be void. And that the sellers of balladꝭ may print their owne copies where they thinke good

5° Martij 1620

Mr. Parker. John Parker is this day elected into the livery of this Company. and it orded (*sic*) at the request of a freind of his that he shall pay his fine of xxli by 5li a quarter the first paymt midsomer next.

mr Alldee. mr Bourne. The difference betwen mr Bourne & mr Alldee being put to the table. It was ordered that mr Alledee shall not print the Trumpett of the soule &c.[2] any more in any volume wthout consent of mr Bourne, And that mr Bourne & his ass' when he or they haue occasion to print this booke shall lett mr Alldee or his assigne doe the same & also some other of mr Smithes sermons

26. Martij 1621 Rꝭ. Jac. 19°. Fol. 67b

Present mr Lownes. sen'. mr Lownes Jun'. mr Cole mr Norton mr Waterson mr Feild mr Swinhowe mr Gilmyn mr Jaggard mr Knight mr Pavier mr Cooke. mr Bill.

mr Tomes. This day mr Tomes is chosen Rentr for the next yeare.

mr. Purfoote This day election was made for mrs Dightꝭ[3] livery pte. & it fell vpon mr Purfoote.

mr Edwardꝭ. Election also was made for mr Purfootꝭ yeomandry pt & it fell vpon mr Edwardꝭ.

And they tooke their oathes accordingly

Raffe Wedgwood It is this day ordered that Raffe Wedgwoode shall haue [*so*] the kitchin, a little buttrye adioyning therevnto and one rome ou' them which he nowe hath in his possession during his life & his wiues paying to the Company vs. a yeare vizt ijs vjd at michĩs & ijs vjd at or Ladye Day[4]

mr Bakers parte. It is ordered that mr Bakers[5] yeomandry pte in the English stocke shall not be made ou' or taken out wthout consent of mr Nicholls.

1 Cf. *C–B.C*, 28b.

2 STC 22710. When originally entered by C. Burby, 17 Feb. 1595 (Arber ii. 671), Allde was to have the workmanship of it and of one other of Smith's sermons. No mention of this was made when Mrs. Burby assigned her rights to N. Bourne, 16 Oct. 1609 (Arber iii. 421).

3 Widow of Walter Dight.

4 Presumably at Abergavenny House.

5 Possibly Thomas Baker, made free 17 Feb. 1620 (Arber iii. 685).

7 maij 1621.

The foote of the Rento[rs] account......50[li]. 10[s]. j[d].

Mr Alldee. It is ordered that mr Allde shall pay for a fine for bynding Tho. ffawcett[1] his appr' at a scriveno[rs] Contrary to order the some of....................xl[s].

Tho. Gubbin. Item it is ordered that Thomas Gubbin[2] shall haue xxij[d] a reame for so many Reames of Accedences as the Company had of him being wast pap.

John Legate. Item that John Legate the younger shall pay for 4 Reames of paper which was taken of a marchant to finish Josephus.[3]

FOL. 68a

16° May 1621 Re Jac. 19°.

Present mr Lownes sen' mr Lownes Jun' mr Norton mr Waterson mr Knight mr Pavier mr Cooke.

Mr Burr. mr Stansby. mr Pollard. Whereas there is a Controversye betwen mr Burre and Mr Stansby & mr Pollard about the printing of sir walter Raw-leighes booke.[4] The matter being put to the Table by all ptyes. It is ordered that mr Stansbye shall deliu' all the paper that he hath received for the printing thereof, as well that which is printed as that which is vnprinted and also all tables & other thinge[5] which the said Stansby hath concerning this booke of Sr walter Rawleighes, And that the said mr Pollard shall pay to mr Stansby the some of 10[li] for damage in regard that the said Stansby hath made provision of lẽr & other thinge for the printing thereof and that all the said pties shall make releases one to an other. The mony to be paid vpon the deliu'ye of the paper & other thinge before the 27 of this pñte May.

vltimo Maj 1621.

Mr Jo. Jaggard This day election was made for mrs Harrisons[6] assistante part and it fell vpon mr John Jaggard[7] there stood in election wth him mr Gilmyn and mr Cole.

[1] This seems unlikely to be the one who was made free 7 May 1621 (Arber iii. 685), but it is less likely to be the one made free 5 Mar. 1639 (Arber iii. 688). Cf. *Book of Fines*, 16a, 7 May and 9 July 1621.

[2] Gubbin was a bookseller and bookbinder (his receipt for payment for binding a manuscript armorial, 1624, is still preserved at the College of Arms), so that these Accedences must have been disorderly printed by someone else.

[3] STC 14811 and 14811a. Although the colophon states that this was printed by H. Lownes, he only printed quires Pp–Llll. The preceding portion was printed by Legatt and has his initials and device (McKerrow, No. 329) on title. Why the printer should have to pay for part of the paper is not clear.

[4] STC 20639. According to the colophon W. Jaggard printed this book, but from the ornaments and initials Stansby printed quires B–K, while N. Okes printed the Preface.

[5] The woodcut genealogical tables and the copperplate maps.

[6] Agnes Harrison, widow of J. Harrison II.

[7] Cf. *Letter Book*, 93a and b, for letters regarding Jaggard's petition to be permitted a share.

mr Wm. Jaggard — Then election was made for mr Jaggardę livery pte and it fell vpon mr. wm. Jaggard, ther stoode in elction wth him mr Tomes & mr Heggenbotham.

Mihill Sparkes. — Then election was made for mr wm Jaggardę yeomandry pte & it fell vpon Michall Sparkę there stood in election wth him Rich. Hawkins & Badger.

And they tooke their oathes accordingly.

Mrs Chard. — Md giuen to mrs Chard[1] this day xxs whereof 15s is her quarterage at midsomer next, the other 5s is giuen vnto her

4° Junij 1621 Rę Jac. 19°. — Fol. 68b

Mr Waterson Loco magistri mr Lownes Jun' mr Cole mr Feild mr Swinhowe mr Jaggard mr Knight mr Pavier mr Coke.

John Marriott — It is ordered that John marriot shall pay for a fine for printing Withers Motto.[2] wthout lycense or enterance and also for printing a second Impression of 1500 in Contempt of the orders of this company 5li.

John Grismond — It is likewise ordered that John Grismond for ioyning with him and dispersing the said bookę shall pay for a fine........20s.

Augustine Mathewes — It is likewise ordered that Augustine mathewes for printing of the said booke shall pay.............iiijli.[3]

Nich. Okes. — It is likewise ordered that Nicholas Okes for printing the same booke wthout license or entrance shall pay..........iiijli.

Withers Motto. — And it is further ordered that this booke shalbe printed no more vntill it be allowed and entred according to order.[4]

22 June 1621

Geo. Edwardę. — This day Geo. Edwardę is elected to be of the Clothing of this Company.

Ireland. — Paid to mr Weauer from skinners hall for Rent out of Ireland. 40li. 18s. 5d. for Rent due at All Saintę 1620[5]

[1] Mrs. Thomas Chard, whose husband must therefore have been dead at this date.

[2] STC 25924. For account of the printers of the several editions, and of the inquisition into the publication of this work, cf. *C.H. Pforzheimer Cat.* iii, 1124–6.

[3] Cf. *Book of Fines*, 16a. He paid only 30*s.* and was pardoned the rest.

[4] Entered 16 June 1621 (Arber iv. 56); cf. also 14 May 1621 (Arber iv. 53).

[5] From the Ulster Plantation.

30 Junij 1621

Paule Man. It is ordered that Paule Man shall pay for his translacõn to this Company from the haberdashers[1]}4[li].

John Phillips. It is ordered that John Phillips for vsing vnfitting worde to Badger as saying he is an arrant knaue shall pay for a fine. xxs.

FOL. 69[a] Anno Dm'. 1621. Re Jacobi. 19°.

M[r]. Waterson. M[r].		m[r] Lownes sen'	mr Pavier
m[r]. Swinhowe	wardens.	m[r] Lownes. Jun'	m[r] Cooke
m[r]. Knight		m[r] Jaggard.	m[r] Islip.

9°. Julij. 1621

Latine Stocke. The busines Concerning the Latine stocke is this Daie referred to M[r]. Waterson, M[r]. Knight and M[r]. Pavier, and it is ordered that for taking vp of money for the benefitt and advancement of that stocke, the partno[rs]. therein shalbe lyable to the repayment thereof as well as those that are or shalbe bounden perticulerlie for the same[2]

M[r]. Islippe Assistante. This daie M[r]. Islipp is elected to be of the Assistante of this Companie.

Stockeepers in the English stock	M[r]. ffeild.	M[r]. Bolton.	John Hodges[3]
	M[r]. Islipp.	M[r]. Beale.	John Dawson.

20°. Julij. 1621

Present M[r]. Waterson, M[r]. Swinhowe, M[r]. Knight, M[r]. Lownes Senio[r]. M[r]. Lownes Ju[r] M[r]. Jaggard, M[r]. Pauier, M[r]. Cooke, M[r]. Islip.

Gramer. It is ordered that the Wardens, and M[r]. Jaggard, and M[r]. Islip doe attend M[r]. Jones, for his Councell, about the printing the gram̃er by Cantrell Legg, and doe certifie the table, what they thinke [is] fitting to be done therein.[4]

Robte Rider. It is ordered that Robte Ryder[5] shall either not sett his maid serv[t]. on worke, to binding or sowing of bookes, contrarie to the order of this Companie, or that he shall put her awaie within .8. daies.

31°. Julij. 1621

The Latine house It is this Daie ordered that the house at the Corner in Ave Mary lane shalbe let at 300[l]. [fine] and 10[l]. a yeare rent, for 31 yeares.[6]

[1] Took up his freedom 30 June 1621 (Arber iii. 685), and paid 23 Aug. 1621 (*Book of Fines*, 16[b]).

[2] See *The Library*, 2nd Ser., viii (1907), 289.

[3] John Hodges no doubt is John Hodgett.

[4] The several petitions and reports on this matter are included in the *Letter Book*, 98[a] and [b]. Cf. also S. C. Roberts, *The Cambridge University Press*, pp. 34–40.

[5] Made free 3 Feb. 1601 (Arber ii. 728).

[6] This must have been a house forming part of the Abergavenny property, cf. *C–B.C*, 69[b], 25 Sept. 1621.

It is likewise ordered that Mr. Tiffins house in Paules Churchyard, where the Latine shop is, shalbe assigned, or sold outright for 150li.[1]

6o. Augusti. 1621

Present Mr. Waterson, Mr. Swinhowe, Mr. Knight, Mr. ffeild, Mr. Lownes senr. Mr. Pauier. Mr. Islippe.

Mr. Alldees. fine — Md Mr. Alldee, hath this daie consented that the fine of 40s. heretofore sett on him, for binding an appr' contrarie to order shalbe paid by Mr. Weaver, out of Mr. Alldees worke.[2]

Fran: Constable. — Md receiued of ffrancis Constable ffiftie poundes, heretofore lent to him of the bequest of Mr. John Norton.[3]

John Dawson. — This .50l. was lent vnto John Dawson, by consent of the Table.[4]

13o. Augusti. 1621 — Fol. 69b

Present. — Mr. Waterson, Mr. Swinhowe, Mr. Knight, Mr. Norton, Mr. ffeild, Mr. Lownes senior. Mr. Lownes Junior. Mr. Pauier.

Mr. Alldee & Tho: Archer — It is ordered, that Mr. Alldee, and Thomas Archer, shalbe comitted to prison, vpon Mr. Secretaries Calverte Comands for printing a booke called, A breife discription of the reasons, that make the declaracon of Ban made against the King of Bohemia, as being Elector Palatine Dated .22. Januarij last of noe value or worth, and therefore not to be respected.[5] It is alsoe ordered, that the barres of his presses shalbe taken downe.

3o. Septembris. 1621 Re Jacobi. 19o.

Present — Mr. Waterson, Mr. Swinhowe, Mr. Knight, Mr. Feild, Mr. Lownes, senior. Mr. Lownes Junior, Mr. Gilmyn, Mr. Jaggard, Mr. Pauier, Mr. Cooke. Mr. Islippe.

Mr Constable Mr. Waterson. — This Daie Mr. Constable assigned ouer his parte in the Latine stocke to Mr. Waterson, by Consent of this Courte. And alsoe the said Mr. Constable assigned his partes in the Irish & Gramer stockes vnto John Waterson, and the said John was elected thervnto.

Wm. Stansby. — It is ordered that Wm. Stansby shall avoid Jeremy Maynstone and Peter Smith two forreinors[6] within .8. daies according to the order in that behalfe, otherwise to paie xs for euerie moneth that he shall keep them

1 Cf. *C–B.C*, 59a, 19 Jan. 1620.
2 Cf. *C–B.C*, 67b, 7 May 1621.
3 Cf. *C–B.C*, 49a, 3 Nov. 1617.
4 His bonds are recorded in *Liber C2*, 109a.
5 STC 11353. Archer was fined £2 for printing 'certaine bookes vnlicensed' 9 July 1621, *Book of Fines*, 16a.
6 Cf. *C–B.C*, 61b, 6 May 1620. Neither foreigner is in the records.

Irish Busines. Mr. ffeild, Mr. Humphrey Lownes, Mr. Islipp, and Mr. Kingston are appointed to take Consideracoñ of the Irish stocke, and report to the table, what they thinke fitting to be done therein.

25o. Septembris. 1621

Mr. Locke the Corner house. It is ordered that Mr. Locke shall haue a lease, of the Corner house for 31 yeares, to begin at Michis 1621 paying 250l fine and Ten pound a yeare rent,[1] And the Companie are Content, that he shall haue a back doore in to the yard during his owne life and his wiues they themselues dwelling in the said house. And there is a Couenant to be drawne vp, that if it shall happen that there come a Comandemt. that the said house shalbe Cut, and the Jetties[2] taken downe, and be builded with Bricke, then the said Mr. Locke, is to doe it at his owne proper Costes and Charges, and vpon payment of ffiftie poundes more, he is to haue twentie yeares added to the time that he shall haue in the said Lease, at the Cutting of the said Jetties.

Appointed to take Mr. Downes accounte of the Irish wares/ Mr. Lownes Jun'r. } Mr. Cooke— } Mr. Edwarde Mr. Moore— Mr. Wright } Mr. Brewster. }

1mo. Octobris. 1621

Mr. Waterson, Mr. Swinhowe, Mr. Knight Mr. Leake, Mr. Lownes sen' Mr. Jaggard, Mr. Cooke, Mr. Islippe.

Mr. Locke— It is this daie ordered that Mr. Lockes lease shal begin at Christmas 1621.[3]

Fol. 70a

8o Octobris. 1621 Re Jacobi. 19o

Present Mr. Waterson, Mr. Swinhowe, Mr. Knight, Mr. Leake, Mr. ffeild, Mr. Lownes senior. Mr. Lownes Junior Mr. Gilmyn, Mr. Cole Mr. Cooke, Mr. Islippe.

Mr. Alldee— Whereas Mr. Alldee, hath latelie Imprinted diuerse bookes without lycense or entrance,[4] and being called into question for the same, hath vsed verie vnfitting wordes and scandalous speeches of the Master and wardens, and table of Assistante. It is therefore this daie ordered that he shall not be warned to attend anie more as a liuerie man vntill he shall submitt himselfe to this table.

John Walker. It is ordered that John Walker shall put awaie a prentice that was bounde to one Beckett within eight daies.

[1] Cf. *C–B.C*, 69a, 31 July 1621.

[2] According to the proclamation of 17 July 1620, STC 8639. 'Jetties' are overhanging upper stories.

[3] Cf. above.

[4] Possibly STC 17895 is one of these books.

12°. Nouembris. 1621

Present. Mr. Waterson, Mr. Swinhowe, Mr. Knight, Mr. Norton, Mr. Lownes Junior, Mr. Jaggarde Mr. [*Jaggard*] Cooke, Mr. Pauier, and Mr. Islippe.

Rich: Redmer. It is ordered that Richard Redmer shall haue in his bond, wherein he standeth bound to the Companie for his truth in his seruice, in his Imployment in the Irish stocke.

Edw: Brewster It is ordered that Edward Brewster shall not keep his appr' William Lluellin, having another allowed vnto him.

Mris. Chard. It is ordered that Mris. Chard shall haue paid vnto her 2 quartrs pencõn before hand, vizt. Christmas 1621 and our Ladie day 1622 to furnish her necessitie in her Jorney to the Contrie, as in her peticõn she desireth.[1]

Mr. Butter ffine. It is ordered that Nathaniell Butter for printing two letters from the Pope to the ffrench king[2] without entrance, shall paie for a fine to the Companie—xs

Mr. Warde It is ordered that Mr. Ward this yeare shall haue six poundes thirteene shillings, and fower pence to furnish the Markett with wheate according to a precept, from the Lord Mayor.[3]

Rich: Badger. It is ordered that Richard Badger, shall haue the roome ouer the Inward Councell Chamber for xxs a yeare soe long as the Companie shall haue noe occasion to vse it themselues.

3°. Decemb. 1621

Present. Mr. Waterson, Mr. Swinhowe, Mr. Knight, Mr. Norton, Mr. ffeild, Mr. Lownes senor. Mr. Jaggard, Mr. Cooke, Mr. Islippe

Rich: Badger. This daie Richard Badger paid in the ten poundes, he heretofore borrowed of the Companie.[4]

Rich: Woodrose. It is ordered that Richard Woodroose[5] shall haue the 10l. that Badger brought bringing such securitie as the table shall like of. His security was enquired of by Mr. warden knight, and afterwards allowed of, & ordered to passe, And Richard Woodrose promised this daie, to paie his debt to the English stocke by 20s. a quarter, the first payment at our Lady daie next.

[1] Cf. *C–B.C*, 68a, 31 May 1621.

[2] STC 12356. This contains both the English and French letters.

[3] In the *Letter Book*, 97b, there is a precept dated 17 July 1621 regarding corn, which is referred to as having not been attended to in another precept of 10 Jan. 1622 (98a, repeated).

[4] This was borrowed of Dexter's bequest 28 Nov. 1618 and his bonds are registered *Liber C2*, 177a.

[5] R. Woodroffe or Woodriffe, whose bonds are registered *Liber C2*, 177a.

10°. Decembris. 1621

Present M^r. Waterson, M^r. Swinhowe, M^r. Knight, M^r. Norton, M^r. ffeild M^r. Lownes senio^r. M^r. Lownes Junio^r. M^r. Gilmyn, M^r. Jaggard M^r. Pauier, M^r. Cooke, M^r. Bill, M^r. Islippe.

M^r. Gilmyn. This Daie election was made for M^ris. Hooper assistantę parte M^r. Gilmyn, M^r. Cole, and M^r. Knight stood in election, and it fell vpon M^r. Gilmyn.

M^r. Higgenbotham Then election was made for M^r. Gilmyns liverie parte, M^r. Tomes, M^r. Selman, and M^r. Higgenbotham stood in election, and it fell vpon M^r. Higgenbotham.

Rich: Taylor. Then election was made for M^r. Heggenbothams yeomãry parte Richard Taylor, Richard Haukins, and ffrancis ffalkner stood for it, and it fell vpon Richard Taylor.

Rich: Haukins. Then Election was made for Richard Taylo^rs halfe parte, Richard Haukins, ffrancis [*Constable*] [ffaulkner] and John Waterson stood for it, and it fell vpon Richard Haukins. M^r. Gilmyn and Richard Higgenbotham tooke their oathes accordinglie.

Amb: Garbrand. It is agreed vpon, by M^r. Waterson, M^r. Knight, M^r. Norton, and M^r. Bill, in the pn'ce of M^r. Weauer, and Thomas Montforte in the matter betweene M^r. Bill, and Ambrose Garbrand — That M^r. Bill shall accept of .15^l. for his whole debte, whereof he hath receiued 5^l. in hand, and the other .10^l. to be paid by 20^s. a quarter, the first payment at our lady next; which is desired maie be paid out of the poore money, the said Ambrose being verie poore, and having manie children and hath lyen long in prison.

14°. Januarij. 1621

M^r. Waterson, M^r. Swinhowe, M^r. Knight, M^r. Hum. Lownes, M^r. M: Lownes M^r. Gilmyn, M^r. Cole, M^r. Jaggard, M^r. Pauier, M^r. Cooke, M^r. Bill.

Rich: Whittakers. It is ordered that Richard Whittakers shall haue the 50^l. that George Edwardę brought latelie in, of M^r. John Nortons bequest.[1]

M^r. Montagues Booke It is ordered that M^r. ffeild, and M^r. Lownes senio^r, shall set downe what M^r. Islippe, and John Haviland shall haue a Rea[*l*]me for printing M^r. Montagues booke.[2]

[1] His bonds are registered in *Liber C2*, 109b.

[2] STC 18029. The preliminaries and the first part of the text, through quire K, as well as quires Mm–Ddd were printed by Haviland. The rest by Islip.

Arcadia.
Ireland.

It is ordered that Mr. ffeild and Mr. Islippe by Consent of Mr. Waterson, and Mr. Lownes Junior shall order and sett downe what the said Mr. Waterson, and Mr. Lownes Junior shall pay for the Arcadias that are brought out of Ireland.[1]

Nicho: Okes &
Edw: Gosson.

In the matter betwixt Nicholas Okes, and Edward Gosson, It is ordered that the said Nicholas Okes shall paie vnto Edw: Gosson 3l. by 20s. a weeke, the first payment on Saterday next.

To goe to my Lord
Mayors. to Dinner.

The Mr. and wardens Mr. Lownes Junior, Mr. Islippe, Mr. Purfoote. Mr. Beale, Mr. Parker.

eodē die et Anno. predē — Fol. 71a

Latine stocke &
Irish stocke.

Whereas the Latine stocke, receiued from the Irish stocke, the soṁe of Three hundred poundes, in ffebruarij. 1619.[2] Nowe it is ordered that because the Irish stocke is endebted to the said Latine stocke, that the soṁe of Three hundred poundes shalbe set of from the Latine and the Irish vndertake the payment thereof for parcell of the debte which the Irish oweth vnto the said Latine.

4o. ffebruarij. 1621

Present.

Mr. Waterson, Mr. Swinhowe, Mr. Knight, Mr. Norton, Mr. Lownes senior, Mr. Lownes Junior, Mr. Gilmin, Mr. Jaggard, Mr. Pauier, Mr. Cooke, Mr. Bill, Mr. Islippe.

Mr. Feild &
Mr. Islippes price
for the Arcadia.

Whereas at a Courte holden the 27 of January 1621[3] there was Coṁitted vnto vs whose names are vnderwritten the Care to sett a Convenient price vpon certan bookes of Arcadia brought out of Ireland for Mr. Waterson, and Mr. Math Lownes, vpon due Consideracōn whereof wee haue thought viijs vjd the Reame a Convenient price. They paying the Charges of the Carriage from Diuelin to London.

Rich: ffeild
Adam Islippe.

The nomber of Arcadia's brought from Ireland,
and sold to Mr. Waterson and Mr. Lownes.

Mr. Waterson,
Mr. M. Lownes
Arcadia.

577. Arcadia's. 143 sheetes, is 165 [Rea:]—0—11sh. at 8s. vjd
p̱. Rea: comes to the some of, 70l. 2s—6d.
Charges from Ireland is valued at two Tuns, at 3—10—0.
In toto..........73—12—6.

The said some of 73l. 12s—6d. is (by consent of Mr. Waterson, and Mr. Lownes) to be paid to the Companie, at the feast of the Nativitie of St. John Baptist Next.

[1] STC 22545. Cf. *C–B.C*, 58b, 20 Dec. 1619. [2] Cf. *C–B.C*, 60a, 7 Feb. 1619. [3] Cf. *C–B.C*, 70b, 14 Jan. 1622.

Order for a proclamation. It is ordered that a proclamacōn shalbe presentlie drawne vp, and Counsell taken therevpon and to be followed by Mr. Knight, Mr. Bill, Mr. Weaver, and Thomas Montforte. And further it is ordered by Consent of Mr. Norton and Mr. Bill, that they the said Mr. Norton, and Mr. Bill, shall paie halfe the Charge, for obtayning thereof.[1]

Rich: Pitham. This daie Richard Pitham[2] brought in xijl that he heretofore borrowed of this Companie, of Mr. William Nortons bequest.[3]
This was afterwards lent to John Cleaver.[4]

Ireland. Mr. ffeild. Mr. Kingston. Mr. Dawson. Mr. Islipp. Mr. Moore. Mr. Hawkins. Are to Consider what is fitt to be done concerning the printer for Ireland.

15° ffebruarij. 1621

Present. Mr. Waterson, Mr. Swinhowe, Mr. Knight, Mr. Norton, Mr. Lownes senior. Mr. Lownes Junior Mr. Pauier. Mr. Islippe.

Geo: Wood. fforasmuch as George Wood, and his Complices, erected and vsed a printing presse at Stepney in the Countie of Midd and with the same printed primers and Almanackes, Contrarie to his Maties. grante and the decrees in Starchamber. Which press with Certen [*other*] letters, and other
Fol. 71b Instrumentes for printing, and Certen leaues of || Almanacks. were found there, and seized and brought to the Staconers Hall (according to the said decree,) on the 20th. Daie of December last past. It is therefore ordered at a full Courte holden this daie That (according to the said decree) the said presse and letters, and Instrument of printing, shalbe sawed in peeces, melted, & defaced and made vnseruiceable for printing.
The Copie of the order of the Comission Courte, concerning George Wood, is in the booke of preceptes:[5]

Christes hospitall. Paid to Christes hospitall of Mr. Bishops bequest[6]—vjl.
Received from Christes hospitall of Mr. Wm. Nortons bequest[7]—6l—13s—4d.

[1] This proclamation has not been identified, but it does not relate to a broadside now in the Harvard College Library which is headed 'A brotherly meeting of the masters and workmen-printers: begun the fifth of Nouember 1621, and continued by these stewards whose names follow in this catalogue', for it is evidently of a much later date. It is much more likely to be 'A briefe of the bill concerning printers, booksellers and bookbinders', n.d., *s.sh.fol.*, in civilité type, a copy of which is in the British Museum (Ames Collection, 1.58). The purpose of that bill is to prevent the importation of Latin books first printed in England. There is in the Guildhall Library a petition of the Stationers Company, 'To the right honourable the house of Commons', *s.sh.fol.* [1621], against R. Wood and T. Symcock which may be the item in question.

[2] R. Pyttam, made free 6 May 1611 (Arber iii. 683). He borrowed the money 23 Jan. 1618 and his bonds were registered in *Liber C2*, 16b.

[3] See Plomer, *Wills*, pp. 30–33.

[4] His bonds were registered in *Liber C2*, 17b.

[5] George Wood obtained a patent for the 'sole printing of lynnen-cloath', 25 Oct. 1619, STC 8614. Not content with that, he began to print books and particularly privileged books. The story is more fully told in the *Letter Book*, 98b (repeated)–101b. The case of George Wood should not be confused with that of Roger Wood and Thomas Symcock, although it is possible that George Wood later was employed by the other patentees.

[6] Cf. *C–B.C*, 24b.

[7] Cf. Plomer, *Wills*, pp. 30–33.

Mr. Hobson. — It is ordered that if Mr. Hobson doe enter into Bond, to take away his water course, when the Companie shall think fitt, he shall haue leave to make a watercourse, thoroughe the Courteyard.[1]

1mo. Martij. 1621

Present. — Mr. Waterson, Mr. Knight, Mr. Norton, Mr. Lownes senior, Mr. Lownes iuor. Mr. Gilmyn, Mr. Jaggard, Mr. Pauier, Mr. Cooke, Mr. Islippe.

Stockeepers for the English stocke	Mr. Lownes Junior Mr. Gilmyn	Mr. Purfoote. Mr. Hoth.	Hum: Lownes George Latham.
	Mr. Weauer Threasuror.		

Fine ...... — Mr. Higgenbotham and Mr. Constable .... ijs for being in the bowling Alley, when they should haue been hearing of the ordinances Read.

4o. Martij. 1621

Present — Mr. Waterson, Mr. Swinhowe, Mr. Knight, Mr. ffeild, Mr. Lownes senor. Mr. Lownes Junior, Mr. Gilmyn, Mr. Pauier, Mr. Islipp.

Mr. Ayres. — It is ordered that Mr. Gilmyn, and Mr. Islip, shall veiwe Mr. Ayres house in woodstreete.[2]

Geo: Latham. — It is ordered that George Latham shall haue 50l of Mr. John Nortons bequest,[3] putting in such securitie, as the Companie shall like of. This 50l. is parte of the rente of woodstreet, collected this yeare.

Mr. (*sic*) Chard. — This daie Mris. Chard receiued xxs for Midsomer quarter. 1622.[4]

Bondes deliuered to Mr. Warden Knight. — Md Deliuered to Mr. Knight, 3 bonds vizt John Edgars bond for 12l Rich. Woodrofs bond, for 10l, and Rich: Whittakers bond for 50l.[5]

22o. Martij 1621

Mr. Waterson, Mr. Swinhowe, Mr. Knight, Mr. Norton, Mr. ffeild, Mr. Lownes Mr. Lownes Junior, Mr. Cole, Mr. Pauier, Mr. Islippe.

Mr. Gilmyn & Mr. Cole — This Daie Mr. Gilmyn, by his letter requested the Table to elect Mr. Cole to his Assistante parte in the English stocke, which the said Mr. Gilmyn doth resigne [*doth resigne*] vp into their handes to || that purpose, and therevpon the whole Table by one full consent, FOL. 72a

[1] Of Abergavenny House.

[2] Cf. *C–B.C*, 72a, 1 Apr. 1622.

[3] Cf. Plomer, *Wills*, pp. 45–47. His bonds are registered in *Liber C2*, 109b.

[4] Cf. *C–B.C*, 70a, 12 Nov. 1621.

[5] These bonds are for loans made without interest under the terms of bequests to the Company for that purpose. Edgar's bonds were registered in *Liber C2*, 17b; regarding Woodroffe, see *C–B.C*, 70a; and regarding Whittaker, see *C–B.C*, 70b.

did elect the said Mr. Cole therevnto, And the said Mr. Gilmyn by his owne Consent and agreement is not to be elected to an Assistantes parte anie more, but to content himselfe with his liverie part only.

The Copie of Mr. Gilmyns Letter — Sr I heartilie Cōmend me vnto you, and all the rest of the Assistantę and the cause of this my writing vnto you at this time, is to entreat a kindnes at yor handes, that you wilbe pleased to elect Mr. Cole into that parte which you did latelie Conferre vpon me, which was Mris. Hoopers soe that he maie haue a full Assistantę parte, and I will content myselfe with that which I had before which was a liverie parte promising neuer to seeke for anie more, then onlie a liverie parte, and if it please you to enter an order in your booke to that purpose I will subscribe vnto it when you shall please. Noe more to you at this time but entreating yor fauors. herein, I bid you heartilie farewell. this 22th. of March. 1621 & Rest

Yor very loving friend
Anthonie Gilmyn.

26°. Martij. 1622. Rę Jacobi. 20°.

Present. — Mr. Waterson, Mr. Swinhowe, Mr. Knight, Mr. Norton, Mr. ffeild, Mr. Lownes senior. Mr. Lownes Junior, Mr. Gilmyn. Mr. Jaggard, Mr. Cole, Mr. Pauier, Mr. Cooke, Mr. Islip.

Mr. Browne Rentor. — This Daie Mr. Browne is Chosen Rentor to ioyne with Mr. Tombes for the yeare following.

Mr. Barrett. — It is [*likewise*] ordered that Mr. Barrett, shall haue a lease of pcell of Mr. Tiffins lease for 15l a yeare, from Midsomer 1622 for 15. yeares.[1]

Mr. Bladen. — It is likewise ordered that Mr. Bladen shall haue a lease of an other parte of the said house for .15l. a yeare from the same time.

Tho: Dewe — It is ordered that Thomas Dewe for printing the little Catechisme[2] which belongę to the Companie shall pay for a fine— vjs viijd.

1°. Aprilis. 1622.

Present. — Mr. Waterson, Mr. Swinhowe, Mr. Knight, Mr. Norton, Mr. ffeild, Mr. Lownes senior, Mr. Lownes Junior, Mr. Gilmyn, Mr. Jaggard, Mr. Cole, Mr. Pauier Mr. Bill, Mr. Islip.

Mr. Ayres. — This Daie Mr. Ayres did offer xl. to renewe his lease, and the Company did aske him 25l. for a lease for 21 yeares to begin at Midsomer next, he surrendring his old lease.[3]

[1] Cf. *C–B.C*, 69a, 31 July 1621. What signs Barrett and Bladen used at this house in St. Paul's Churchyard have not been discovered.

[2] No copy is now known, but it was probably an edition of *The A.B.C. with the catechisme*.

[3] Cf. *C–B.C*, 71b, 4 Mar. 1622.

Mr. Harrison
Mr. Hale.

Mr. Harrison had license at this Courte to engage his [*stocke*] parte in the English stocke, to Mr. Hale, for the payment of 150l. a yeare hence.

26o. Aprilis. 1622

Mr. Waterson, Mr. Swinhowe, Mr. Norton, Mr. Knight, Mr. ffeild, Mr. Lownes senior. Mr. Lownes Junior, Mr. Gilmyn, Mr. Cole, Mr. Pauier, Mr. Cooke, Mr. Bill, Mr. Islippe.

Mris Dawson,
Mr. Knight.

This Daie Election was made, for Mris. Dawsons[1] assistantę parte, shee being latelie married out of the Companie. And the said election fell vpon Mr. Knight, there stood in election with him, Mr. Pavier, & Mr. Cooke.

eodē Die pn̄tibus vt ante — Fol. 72b

Mr. Tombes.

Then election was made for Mr. Knightę liverie parte, and it fell vpon Mr. Tombes, there stood in election with him, Mr. Selman and Mr. Rodwell.

Mr. White.

Then election was made for Mr. Tombes yeomandry parte, and it fell vpon Mr. White, there stood in election with him, Mr. Piper and Mr. Parker. And they all tooke their oathes accordinglie.

6o. Maij. 1622

Present.

Mr. Waterson, Mr. Swinhowe, Mr. Knight, Mr. Norton, Mr. ffeild, Mr. Lownes senior Mr. Lownes Junior, Mr. Gilmyn, Mr. Cole, Mr. Pauier, Mr. Cooke, Mr. Islippe.

Raffe Mabbe.

This Daie Raffe Mabbe had license of the Board to Morgage his parte, in the English stocke, for the payment of 50l on the sixt of Maie. 1623. vnto Thomas Montforte, according to a certen writing made betwixt the said parties.

Tho: Salisburie
Mr. Norton.

It is ordered by Thomas Salisburies owne Consent, that he shall paie out of his pention xs. a quarter, till iijl—vjs—viijd be paid for Perkins Catechisme in Welsh[2] to Mr. Norton.

11o. Maij. 1622.

Mr. Butter.

This daie Mr. Butter did promise to paie his debt to the English stocke, on Tewsdaie next, or to allowe xl p Centum till it be paid

[1] Widow of Thomas Dawson, Sen.
[2] No edition earlier than 1649 has survived; cf. *Journal Welsh Bibl. Soc.* iv (1932), 262–5.

Tho: Archer

This Daie Thomas Archer promised to paie 40s. that heretofore he was fined to paie, for printing bookes contrarie to order.[1]

Edw: Wright.

This Daie Edward Wright did agree to paie xl ꝑ Cent'. for his debte to the English stocke, vntill he shall discharge the said debte.

John Grismand

John Grismand did this daie promise to paie his debte on Tewsday next to the English stocke.

The founders:

The founders are to be bound to the Companie, not to Deliuer anie founte of newe letters, vntill they make the Mr. and wardens acquainted therewithall, and they were bound accordinglie.[2]

John Grismand.

John Grismand is to be bound to the Companie, not to buy or sell anie Bookes printed against anie letters patentę, or orders of the Companie.[3]

English Stocke
73.

It is ordered that all the Debtors to the English stocke shall Cleare the Booke before the first of June, and if they doe not, then Mr. Weaver is not to Deliuer them anie more bookes, [*then*] vpon anie newe accounte to anie of them.

20°. Maij. 1622

Present.

Mr. Waterson, Mr. Knight, Mr. Norton, Mr. ffeild, Mr. Lownes senior, Mr. Jaggard, Mr. Pauier, Mr. Cooke, Mr. Islippe.

Mr. Blounte —

Mr. Blount being endebted to the English stocke 120l, is contented that the money shalbe taken vp at Interest at xl. ꝑ Cent'. and hath engaged his parte in the said stocke for the payment thereof.

John Wright —

John Wright likewise engageth his parte for 30l. to be taken vp till he paies it.

Fol. 73a

24°. Maij. 1622. Rę Jacobi. 20°.

Present.

Mr. Waterson, Mr. Swinhowe, Mr. Knight, Mr. ffeild, Mr. Lownes senior, Mr. Lownes Junior Mr. Gilmyn, Mr. Cooke, Mr. Islippe.

Wm. Turnor. ffine.

It is ordered that Mr. Turner shall paie to the Companie for his Admission therevnto. ffortie shillinges.[4]

[1] Cf. *C–B.C*, 69b, 13 Aug. 1621.
[2] The bond was presumably £40; cf. Arber v. liii.
[3] Cf. *C–B.C*, 95a, 2 Apr. 1627.
[4] Cf. Arber iii. 685.

Par Bettie, & John Dutton — It is ordered that Par. Bettie[1] shall allowe vnto the ffather of John Dutton 40s. to apparrell him if he be bound to anie other Trade then a Stationer, but if he be bound to a Stacõner then he is to allow him but Twentie shillinges.

3°. Junij. 1622

Geor: Edwards ffine — It is ordered that George Edwardes[2] shalbe translated to this Company paying for a fyne, twentie shillingę.

13°. Junij. 1622

Wm. Jones. — It is ordered that William Jones shall haue eight poundes of Mr. Weaver to be paid out of the poores money by 20s. a quarter.

Edw: Blackmore Elinor Norton. — This Daie Elenor Norton[3] resigned her parte in the English stocke into the handes of the Mr. wardens, and Assistantę of this Company, and desired them to elect Edward Blackmore therevnto. which they did at the request of Mr. Speed. And the said Edward Blackmore tooke his oath accordinglie.

25°. Junij. 1622.

Present — Mr. Waterson, Mr. Swinhowe, Mr. Knight, Mr. ffeild, Mr. Lownes senior. Mr. Lownes Junior. Mr. Pauier.

Proposicõns sent to Mr. Norton, about the Gramer by Mr. Pavier.[4]

Mr Norton. about the grammer

1. If Mr. Norton will take his patent of the Gramer againe [into] his handes, the Companie will be accomptable vnto him, and be contented to take their owne money againe, which hath been laid out of their purses. 2 yeares and a halfe agoe without anie proffitt for the forbearance or Consideracõn for their paines.
2. Whether he will take the bookes that are nowe begun to be printed to finish and disperse them, that the Cōmon wealth maie not be vnserued, or suffer the Companie to goe forward therewith, and they wilbe accomptable for the same. for without his Consent they will not meddle anie further.
3. If he will doe neither of theis thinges, then the Companie doe desire to knowe what he will propound to bring this matter to a quiet end without further suit of lawe.

[1] Parr Betty, made free 18 Jan. 1602 (Arber ii. 731). Dutton is not recorded.

[2] Doubtless G. Edwards, Jun.

[3] She has not been identified.

[4] Cf. *C–B.C*, 59a, 23 Dec. 1619.

1mo. Julij. 1622

Mr. Waterson, Mr. Swinhowe, Mr. Knight, Mr. ffeild, Mr. Lownes senior, Mr. Lownes Junior, Mr. Gilmyn, Mr. Pauier, Mr. Cooke, Mr. Islippe.

Rich: Brookbank Tho: Wright. — Whereas Richard Brookbank[1] hath taken a Prentice, and bound him at a scriuenors contrarie to order, It is ordered that he shall put him awaie, within .8. daies, and paie for a fine to the Companie. xs.

Fol. 73b

6o. Julij. 1622

Present. — Mr. Waterson, Mr. Swinhowe, Mr. Knight, Mr. ffeild, Mr. Lownes senior. Mr. Lownes Junior. Mr. Cole, Mr. Pauier, Mr. Cooke, Mr. Islippe.

Mr. Jaggard, & Mr. Cole. — It is ordered that Mr. Jaggard, and Mr. Cole, shall paie. 5l. a peece for their dispensacõns for not serving the second time vnderwardens And if Mr. Jaggard, (being this daie absent) will not accept thereof then Mr. Cole is to haue precedence, and Mr. Jaggard to be elegible the next yeare, for vnderwarden.

9o Julij. 1622

Mr Feild mr
mr Gilmyn } Wardens
mr Pavier }

22o. Julij. 1622

Mr. Islippe — It is ordered that whereas Mr. Islipp alleadgeth that he vsually doth paie to euery workman that worketh vpon anie Booke iiijd a weeke in liewe of a Copie due to them by the Custome of the Companie, That he shalbe allowed that iiijd from the stocke [*and*][2]

Mr. Bowler — It is ordered that James Bowler shall paie the xxl he was fined at for Coming on the liuerie, in forme following vizt. xl. at Michis and xl at Christmas next, and he is not to be warned or giue anie attendance till Midsomer vnlesse he be willing.

Mr Parker. — Mr. Parker promised this daie to paie the residue of his fyne, for his admission to the liuerie at Michis next.

[1] Made free 3 June 1600 (Arber ii. 725).
[2] Regarding these extra copies, cf. *Trans.* xii (1931), 379.

20°. Augusti. 1622

Present. Mr. ffeild, Mr. Gilmyn, Mr. Pauier Mr. Waterson Mr. Lownes senior, Mr. Lownes Junior, Mr. Knight, Mr. Cole, Mr. Cooke, Mr. Islippe

English stocke 72 It is this daie ordered That if all the debtors to the English stocke doe not cleare the booke before the first of September next, That then Mr. Weauer is not to deliuer anie more bookes vpon anie newe Accompt vnto them, or anie of them.

eod̃ die p̃ntibus vt ante Fol. 74a

Mr. M. Lownes Whereas the price of Henry the seauenth is Complayned of to be [*presentlie*] vnreasonable, It is ordered by the Boord & Mr. Mathewe Lownes his owne Consent, that he shall sell the [said] Booke called, The Historye of Henry the seauenth for fower shillings in quiers/[1]

Present Mr. ffeild, Mr. Gilmyn, Mr. Pauier, Mr. Lownes senior, Mr. Lownes Junior Mr. Knight.

Mr. Knight. [*This daie Mr. Knight did surrender his Assistantę parte in the English stocke to the handes of the Master wardens and Assistantę for the securitie of Mr. Humphrey Lownes Mr. Swinhowe & John Budge from diuerse recognizances in which they stand bound in Guildhall for him the said Mr. Knight for the payment of Certen som̃es of money to the Children and Orphantę of William Taylor of London draper deceased when the said Orphantę Come to their seuerall Ages, and if the said Children be paid and the said Recognitors discharged then* [then] *Mr. Knight and his executors to enioy his said parte, but if the said porcõns be not paid then the Mr. and wardens to Choose another ꝑtnor according to their orders, and the money that shalbe made thereof by anie new partnor to be paid to the said Humphrey Lownes, Geo: Swinhowe and John Budge towardę the discharging of the said porcõns.*]

20. Maij 1629 The said Recognizances are acknowledged to be dischardged, and by consent of the ꝑties this order to be crossed out, and mr Knightę. part cleared /

27°. Septembr. 1622

Present Mr. ffeild, Mr. Gilmyn, Mr. Pauier, Mr. Waterson, Mr. Lownes senior, Mr. Lownes Junior Mr. Jaggard, Mr. Cooke, Mr. Islippe.

Mr. Jo: Jaggard (*sic*) It is this daie ordered that noe Printer shall print anie booke except the Clarke of the Companies name be to it to signifie that it is entred in the hall Booke according to order.

Mr. John [*Griffin*] Jaggard — It is ordered that Mr. John Jaggard shall haue the 50l of Mr. John Nortons bequest latelie receiued of Mr. Bladen.[2]

[1] STC 1159. At least two editions of this date are known, as well as large paper copies of the second.

[2] Cf. *C–B.C*, 56b, 20 July 1619. His bonds were recorded in *Liber C2*, 110a.

John Griffin — It is ordered that John Griffin[1] shall haue x[l] lent him by the Company.

Geo: Potter. This daie Geo: Potter paid to M[r]. Pauier .10[l]. of the 12[l] he borrowed heretofore of the Companie, and the other 40[s]. is to be paid out of his diuident. pd.[2]

7°. Octobris. 1622

Present. M[r]. ffeild M[r]. Gilmyn M[r]. Pauier, M[r]. Waterson, M[r]. Lownes senio[r] M[r]. Swinhowe, M[r]. Lownes Junio[r], M[r]. Jaggard, M[r]. Knight, M[r]. Cooke M[r]. Islippe.

If any of the Assistantę come late to pay xij[d] a peece. This daie it is ordered that if anie of the Assistantę Come after the boord is sett they shall pay xij[d] a peece.[3]

150. M[r]. Pavier, M[r]. Knight, M[r]. Islip, and M[r]. Weauer are to Confer with Geo: Wood, and reporte to the Table what they think fitting to be done therein.[4]

FOL. 74[b]

19°. Octobris. 1622

Present. M[r]. ffeild, M[r]. Gilmyn M[r]. Pauier, M[r]. Lownes senio[r] M[r]. Swinhowe, M[r]. Lownes Junio[r], M[r]. Jaggard, M[r]. Knight, M[r]. Pauier, M[r]. Cooke, M[r]. Islip.

James Bowler Robte Woodnett. This daie eleccõn was made for M[ris]. Burtons yeomandry part, and it was ordered that it should be diuided between 2 of the yeomandry, and the election fell vpon James Bowler, and Robte Woodnett. and they tooke their oathes accordinglie.

M[r]. Jaggard & John Griffin bondę. Deliuered to M[r]. Pavier .2 bondę vizt. M[r]. Jaggardę for 50[l]. and John Griffins for 10[l].[5]

Henry Rider Robte Ryder. Henry Ryder is to haue 40[s] a yeare and Robert Ryder to haue 20[s]. a yeare by order of this Courte. viz[t]. 3[l]. betwixt them.[6]

24°. Octobr'. 1622

William Lee. William Lee is this day warned to avoid his apprentice which hee keepeth Contrary to order.

[1] If this is the John Griffen who was apprenticed 24 June 1566, he would at this time be at least 69 years old. The money was lent from Burby's bequest and his bonds were recorded in *Liber C2*, 184[b].

[2] This was borrowed from William Norton's bequest, 10 Apr. 1619, and his bonds were recorded in *Liber C2*, 16[b].

[3] Cf. *C–B.C*, 150[a], 28 Sept. 1637.

[4] According to a letter to the Archbishop from the Company, *Letter Book*, 101[a], it is stated that the Company advised with Wood at this time 'how to further him in any good or lawfull course he would devise'.

[5] Cf. *C–B.C*, 74[b], 27 Sept. 1622.

[6] Henry Rider does not appear to be connected with the Company. Robert was made free 3 Feb. 1601 (Arber ii. 728).

eod̄ die.

Present. Mr. ffeild, Mr. Gilmyn, Mr. Pauier, Mr. Waterson, Mr. Lownes senior. Mr. Swinhowe, Mr. Lownes Junior Mr. Cole, Mr. Knight, Mr. Islippe.

Latine stocke. It was this daie ordered That all those of the Companie which doe owe anie money to the Latine stocke shall within .14. daies next after the date hereof (or before the Mart) make vp their Accompte and see all the bookes Crost, and what shalbe found due by anie one, he is to giue his bond to the Stockeepers (then being) for payment of the same, and that in this manner (vizt.) whatsoeuer is due twelue monethes he is to pay the same presentlie, or at least to Cleare the same before the last of Nouember next ensewing, and the rest the next Mart followinge being the first of Aprill 1623, And whosoeuer shall not accordinglie performe theis Condicōns, It is likewise (*ordered*) that Mr. Weauer shall not deliuer them anie wares out of the English stocke vpon Creditt nor Mr. Barrett out of the latine stocke Which Course is thought fitt to Continue from Marte to Mart. And that Mr. Weauer maie the better knowe to whom he shall deny Creditt Mr. Barrett is to giue him a note of the names of such as doe not p̱forme all thinge accordinglie.

21°. Nouembr. 1622

Present. Mr. ffeild. Mr. Gilmyn, Mr. Pauier, Mr. Waterson, Mr. Lownes senior Mr. Swinhowe, Mr. Jaggard, Mr. Knight, Mr. Cooke, Mr. Islippe.

Geo: Wood
Roger Wood. It is ordered that noe waie or leaue be giuen to Geo: Wood to deale with Roger Woode patent for thinge on one side,[1] The said Patent being very preiudiciall to the Companie.

Augustine Mathewes. Augustine Mathewes is warned to put awaie his appr' that he keepeth Contrary to order.

Mr. Kingston. Mr. Kingston is this daie elected to be one of the Assistante of this Companie.

2°. Decembr. 1622 Fol. 75a

Present. Mr. ffeild, Mr. Gilmyn, Mr. Pauier, Mr. Waterson, Mr. Lownes senior Mr. Swinhowe, Mr. Lownes Junior, Mr. Jaggard, Mr. Knight, Mr. Cooke Mr. Islip, Mr. Kingston.

ffran: Lownes.
80. It is ordered that Mr. ffrancis Lownes shall haue a newe lease of Mr. Smithes house in Woodstreet for one & twenty yeares to begin at [*Miso*] Midsomer 1622 for 3^l fine and the same rent it went before. He is to giue the Companie a Bucke at Midsomer.

[1] Roger Wood and Thomas Symcock as the nominees of Marin de Boisloré were granted, 30 Oct. 1619, a patent for 31 years of printing all briefs to be printed on one side only of paper or parchment, concerning letters patent, recognizances for victuallers, playbills, indentures for apprentices, &c., and all portraits and pictures and anything printed on one side, with certain exceptions, mainly things otherwise patented. STC 8615 is an abstract of this patent. For a discussion of this affair see Introduction. Regarding George Wood and his patent, cf. *C–B.C*, 71a, 15 Feb. 1622.

Henry Seile. Henry Seale is to haue the booke of the Arte of Stenography[1] [*to be*] entred vnto him.

Mr. Blounte
Mr. Lawe.

Whereas Mr. Lownes and Mr. Weauer are bound to Mr. Halwood for 200l. which was taken vp to the vse of Mr. Blounte & Mr. Lawe to paie their debts to the english stocke,[2] who were Contented to pay the money at .6. monethes with the vse thereof the time ending about the 24 of Nouember 1622. They hauing neither paid debtę nor vse. It is ordered that they shall haue noe benefitt of anie stocke in the Companie till the debtę and vse be discharged.

Mr. Blounte 166l.
Mr. Lawe.....34l.

Jorneymen Printers. It is ordered that Mr. Warden Pavier Mr. Swinhowe Mr. Knight Mr. Islip and Mr. Kingston doe Conferr with the Jorneymen Printers. about their complaint for want of worke

13° Decembr'. 1622

Present. Mr. ffeild, Mr. Gilmyn, Mr. Pauier Mr. Waterson, Mr. Hum: Lownes Mr. Swinhowe, Mr. M. Lownes, Mr. Cole, Mr. Knight, Mr. Cooke, Mr. Kingston.

Val: Symmes — Whereas Valentine Simmes hath been lately a sutor to the Lo: Archbp. of Canterburie his Grace to be a master Printer and to haue his copies It pleased his Grace to referre the Consideracõn thereof to Sr. Wm. Bird and Sr. Hen: Martin, who at the hearing of the matter[3] did not think it fitting that he should be restored to be a Mr. Printer. Neuerthelesse the said Sr. Wm. Bird and Sr. Hen: Martin did desire the Companie for their sakes and at their request because he is a very poore man and a member of the Companie to giue him ten poundę. Wherevpon the Companie at a Court holden this daie did think fitt at their requestę, either to giue him. 10l. and his pencoñ of 4l. a yeare to cease [*to*] or to ouerease his pencõn to 6l. a yeare for .5. yeares. and Concerning his Copies such as are not in Patent or entred to anie other maie be assigned ouer to anie of the Companie whom the said Sym̃es shall agree withall for the same

Mr. M. Lownes
Geo: Latham.
Mris. Burre.

This Daie Mris. Burre is Content to assigne all her right in the history of the World written by Sr. Walter Rawleighe to Mr. Mathewe Lownes and Geo: Latham to be entred to them.[4]

1 Copies of the eighth edition of John Willis, *The art of stenographie*, 8°, f. H. Seile, 1623, are in the W. J. Carlton Collection and the New York Public Library. When entered 2 Dec. 1622 (Arber iv. 87), it is stated that it 'formerlie was the Copie of Robert Willis, latelie deceased', but it was entered to C. Burby, 19 Apr. 1602 (Arber iii. 204), and transferred by his widow to W. Welby, 16 Oct. 1609 (Arber iii. 420). There is no record of Welby's transferring it, but it evidently did not go to Snodham.

2 It is not clear whether this is part of Mr. Halwood's annuity, cf. *C–B.C*, 66a, 2 Oct. 1620.

3 Their report is printed in the *Letter Book*, 102a, 6 Feb. 1623.

4 STC 20639. Entered 13 Dec. 1622 (Arber iv. 87).

19°. Decembr. 1622

Jos: Harrison
Jacob Bloome.

This daie Joseph Harrison assigned his yeomandry part in the English stocke to Jacob Bloome, and by Consent of the Boord the said Jacob Bloome was elected therevnto. and the said Jacob [*Bloom*] tooke his oath accordinglie[1]

eod̄ die vt ante. **Fol. 75b**

Steph: Gest.

Stephan Gest[2] is admitted to haue a pencõn of vj^s^ a quarter vpon his good behauio^r^ and if anie Complant be made of him and proued before our ladie daie next his pencõn is to cease.

Rafe Mabbe
Rich: Badger.

Rafe Mabbe this daie paid in 12^l^ that was lent him heretofore of M^r^. W^m^. Nortons bequest and presentlie after it was lent to Rich. Badger.[3]

21°. January. 1622

Writings concerning the Latine stocke.

All writinge Concerning the latine warehouses were this daie deliuered to M^r^. Warden Pauier, and M^r^. Knight to be carried thither vizt.

Articles to stand to the award of Symon Waterson, Tho: Pauier
M^r^. Bills Bond.
The Arbitrament of Symon Waterson &c.
Assignement of a lease of W^m^. Aspley
Assignement of a lease from the Bridghouse.
Acquittancee of M^r^. Bille.
The Lease from W^m^. Aspley
The Originall Lease from the Bridghouse.

Receiued this daie from Christe hospitall of m^r^. Nortons bequest[4] .... } vj^l^ xiij^s^ iiij^d^
Item paid to Christe hospitall of Mr Bishops Bequest[5] .... } vj^l^
To the Master, Wardens, Clarke & Beadle xiij^s^ iiij^d^ [6]

3°. ffebruarij. 1622

Present.

M^r^. ffeild, M^r^. Gilmyn, M^r^. Pauier, M^r^. Waterson, M^r^. Lownes senio^r^ M^r^. Swinhowe, M^r^. Jaggard, M^r^. Cooke, M^r^. Islip, M^r^. Kingston.

M^r^. Bolton
M^r^. Mead.

This daie M^r^. Bolton assigned his Liuerie parte by consent of the Companie to M^r^. Mead Soe that M^r^. Bolton hath his yeomanry part, and M^r^. Mead the Liuery.

[1] Cf. *C–B.C*, 61^b^, 6 May 1620.

[2] Made free 25 June 1601 (Arber ii. 729). No complaint was apparently made and after one payment of 6*s*. his quarterly pension was raised to 10*s*. according to the *Liber pro pauperibus*.

[3] Mabb borrowed this money 6 Sept. 1619 when his bonds were recorded in *Liber C2*, 17^a^. Badger's bonds were registered *Liber C2*, 17^b^.

[4] Cf. Plomer, *Wills*, pp. 30–33.

[5] Cf. *C–B.C*, 24^b^. [6] Cf. Plomer, *Wills*, pp. 30–33.

Wm. Bladen. It is ordered that Wm. Bladen shall haue the 50l that Mr. Bolton brought in this daie of Mr. John Nortons bequest.[1]

Tho: Baker. Tho: Baker[2] is to haue vjl of Wm. Nortons bequest.

Mris. Adams. It is ordered that the 100l. giuen to the Companie by Mr Adams deceased[3] shal be put into the latine stocke to Remayne there as a stocke for the house and the benefit thereof to goe towardȩ publique Charge according to the will.

Mr. Butter & othrs. Nath: Newbury. It is ordered that Mr. Butter Mr. Bourne, Mr. Downes Wm. Sheffard Tho: Archer shall paie to Nathaniell Newburie xls. for printing his Copie vizt. The King of ffrance his Edict &c[4]

Mr. Bucanus. This daie was giuen by the Companie to Mr. Bucanus[5] at the request of Mr. Dor. Hill. xxs.

FOL. 76a

eod̄ die vt ante

Geo. Edwardȩ fine. This daie Mr. Pavier receiued of Geo: Edwardȩ xxs for a fyne to be translated from the Haberdashers to this Companie.

Order for Presses. 38. The order of the .9th. of May. 1615.[6] Concerning the multitude of presses and that none should haue more then are there sett downe was this daie againe openlie read, approued of, and ordered to be forthwith put into execucōn.

8o. ffebruarij 1622

Present. Mr. ffeild, Mr. Gilmyn, Mr. Pauier, Mr. Waterson, Mr. Lownes senior Mr. Swinhowe, Mr. Lownes Junior, Mr. Jaggard, Mr. Cole, Mr. Cooke Mr. Knight, Mr. Islippe /

Mr. Pauier. This daie election was made for Mris. Standishes Assistantȩ parte and it fell vpon Mr. Pavier, there stood in election with him, Mr. Cooke & Mr. Islippe.

Mr. Selman. Then election was made for Mr. Paviers liuery parte, and it fell vpon Mr. Selman, there stood in election with him, Mr. Budge & Mr. Rodway.[7]

1 Bolton's bonds were recorded in *Liber C2*, 109a, 3 Feb. 1619, and Bladen's, 110b, 14 Mar. 1622.

2 Made free 17 Feb. 1620 (Arber iii. 685).

3 Cf. *C–B.C*, 64b, 1 July 1620.

4 STC 16841. The Edict of Nantes. These partners pirated Newberry's book in their newsbook, 'Nov. 5. No. 5. A continuation of the newes of this present weeke. . .' (Dahl No. 85). Cf. also *Trans.*, 4th Ser., xviii. 368. In the *Book of Fines*, 18a, 30 Feb. 1622, 'It is ordered that mr Butter shall pay for a fine for printing the King of ffrance his Edict being the Copie of mr newbery—vs And it is further ordered that he shall pay to mr Newbery for the Iniury done to him xls.'

5 Dr. Robert Hill translated and published in 1606 Gulielmus Bucanus' *Institutiones theologicae*.

6 Cf. *C–B.C*, 38b.

7 This is almost certainly John Rodwell who stood unsuccessfully for a livery part several times, see pp. 145, 156, 166, and 177. So far as here recorded he had only a half yeomanry part, see p. 53. For a similar confusion, see pp. 177 and 221, footnote 5.

Mr. Parker
Wm. Stansby.

Then election was made for Mr. Selmans yeomandry parte, and it was ordered to be diuided betweene two of the yeomandry, and the election fell vpon Mr. Parker, and Wm. Stansby.

And they all tooke their oathes accordinglie.

1mo. Martij. 1622

Present.

Mr. ffeild, Mr. Gilmyn, Mr. Pauier, Mr. Waterson, Mr. Lownes senior, Mr. Swinhowe Mr. Lownes Junior, Mr. Cooke, Mr. Jaggard, Mr. Knight, Mr. Cooke, Mr. Islippe Mr. Kingston.

Rich. Taylor.
Nicho: Okes.

Nicholas Okes by order of this Courte is to haue the 12l that Richard Taylor paid in this daie, of Mr. Wm. Nortons bequest.[1]

Stockeepers for the English stocke.

Mr. Waterson, Mr Kingston } Mr. John Edward, Mr. Budge . . . . . . } Mich. Sparkes. Rich. Hawkins.
Mr Weauer Threasuror.

Auditors.

Mr. Swinhowe, Mr. Knight } Mr. Snodham, Mr. Barrenger } Willm̃ Bladen, Jacob Bloome. }

3o. Martij. 1622

Present /

Mr. ffeild, Mr. Gilmyn, Mr. Pauier, Mr. Waterson, Mr. Lownes senior Mr. Swinhowe, Mr. Jaggard, Mr. Cole, Mr. Knight, Mr. Cooke, Mr. Kingston.

Mr. Ayres.
74

It is ordered that Mr. Ayres shall haue a newe lease of his house in woodstreet for .21. yeares to begin at Midsomer next, for 20l fine and the old rent.[2]

Playes.

This daie a letter from my lord Chamberlayne was openly read to all the Master Printers concerning the lycensing of Playes. &c. by Sr. John Ashley. The Copie whereof is in the booke of letters.[3]

eod̄ die. Fol. 76b

Leases sealed this day.

This daie were sealed the leases, To ffrances Lownes of a house in Woodstreet, for 21 yeares from Midsomer, 1623. rent 23l. p Annũ.[4]

To William Barrett of a [*lease*] house in Paules Churchyard from Midsomer. 1622 for .15. yeares rent. 15l.[5]

To William Bladen a house there, from Midsomer 1622 for 15 yeares. rent 15l[5]

To George Allestre a shop in Paules Churchyard for 10 yeares from Midsomer 1622.

[1] Taylor borrowed this money 3 July 1619 and his bonds were recorded in *Liber C2*, 17a: N. Okes's bonds were recorded in *Liber C2*, 18a.

[2] Cf. *C–B.C* 72a, 1 Apr. 1622.

[3] Unfortunately it is not.

[4] Cf. *C–B.C*, 75a, 2 Dec. 1622.

[5] Cf. *C–B.C*, 72a, 26 Mar. 1622.

10°. Martij. 1622

Mr. Wither. Mr. Pavier, Mr. Knight, Mr. Islip Mr. Kingston and Mr. Weauer appointed to talke with Mr. Withers about his Patent, of the hymnes of the Church.[1]

12°. Martij. 1622

Present. Mr. ffeild, Mr. Pauier, Mr. Waterson, Mr. Lownes senior, Mr. Swinhowe, Mr. Lownes Junior, Mr. Knight, Mr. Cooke, Mr. Islip, Mr. Kingston.

Roger Wood. Concerning the Charge of following the suit against Roger Woods patent It is this day ordered that it shalbe borne by the house, but if the Companie shall preuaile in it, then the parties that Clayme Interest in printing the things mencõned in the said Patent shall repaie the said Charge or els their [*in*] interest in the things to be disposed of as the boord shall thinke fitt.[2]

28°. Martij. 1623 Rs Jacobi. 21°.

Mr. Cooke. This Daie election was made for Mris. Harrisons Assistants parte and it fell vpon Mr. Cooke, Mr. Bill & Mr. Islip stood in election.

Mr. Combes. Then election was made for Mr. Cookes liuery part and it fell vpon Mr. Combes, vpon a lr̃ from my lo: Keeper. Mr. Rodwell & Mr. Johnson stood in election with him

Hen: Walley. Then election was made for Mr. Combes yeomandry parte and it fell vpon Henry Walley vpon a lrẽ from my lord of Canterbury there stood in election with him John Parker and Robte Young, And the said Henry Walley tooke his oath according to the order in that behalfe.

Edward Hulett. Item I giue to the Companie of Stacõnrs in London the sum̃e of five poundes for a drinking amongst them. And a Boule of siluer all guilte in fashion of an owle waighing 60. ounces with myne name grauen on it with these words, The guift of Edward Hulet gentleman. And my minde and will is that all the som̃e & somes of money & legacies in this my will giuen and bequeathed except &c shalbe paid and deliuered by my said executor within one yeare next after my decease or sooner, if the debts owing vnto me can be gotten in.[3]

Wills Child exr.

[1] STC 25908. For brief of Withers's patent, cf. Crawford No. 1351. A good statement of the objections of the binders, which reflects the attitude of the stationers, can be seen in the petition of the binders to the House of Commons, Lemon No. 225.

[2] Cf. *C–B.C*, 74b, 21 Nov. 1622.

[3] Why this gentleman left this legacy to the Company is not known, but his cup was the only piece retained when in 1643 the Royal loans were repaid.

2°. April. 1623

Mr. ffeild Mr. Waterson Mr. Lownes senior Mr. Lownes Junor. Mr. Knight Mr. Kingston, Mr. Weauer.

Robte younge
James Bennett[1]
his appr'

Althoughe Robte Young hath taken a prentice in Ireland without the Companies Consent, yet to incourage him the more it is thought fitt, that || he shall keep him still out his yeares, **Fol. 77a** but for hereafter it is ordered at this meeting and Consent of Robte young here present, That he shall not take anie more, without Consent of the partnors.

Mris. Adams.

Concerning the 100l giuen to the Companie by Mr. Adames deceased The Companie are Contented to accept of seauenty pounde of Mr. Adams money in the latine stocke, and 30l. more in Mr. Weauers hande which he hath taken in bookes and money, and is to answer the same to the said latine stocke, soe that the whole 100l is in the said latine stocke, imployed to the vse of the house till it can be otherwise disposed of, And Mr. ffeild, Mr. Gilmyn and Mr. Pavier gaue their acquittance to Mris. Adams for her discharge of the said legacy.[2]

28°. April. 1623

Mr. Lee

Mr. Mathewe Lownes, Mr. Cooke, Mr. Kingston to veiwe a windowe that Mr. Lee would haue enlarged.[3]

22°. Maij 1623

Mr. Newton
Mr. Moore
Rd. Hawkins
John Waterson.

This daie Mr. Newton[4] Surrendred his parte in the English stocke. Mr. Moore was elected therevnto.
Mr. Hawkins had his yeomandry parte
John Waterson his halfe yeomandry parte.
John Waterson tooke his oath accordingly.

Mr. Newton

Mr. Newton is to haue his money pñtely, and Midsomer divident or if there be none, a proportionable ꝑte of the next divident after.

27° Maij. 1623

Mr. Ayres.
76

This daie Mr. Ayres lease of his house in woodstreet was sealed at a full Court, for 21. yeares to begin at Midsomer next, rent 22l ꝑ Annu'.

Idem

The said Mr. Ayres paid to Mr. Warden Pavier xxl. for a fyne according to a former Agreement.[5]

[1] Made free 26 Mar. 1628 (Arber iii. 686).
[2] Cf. *C–B.C*, 75b, 3 Feb. 1623.
[3] This lease has not been identified, but cf. *C–B.C*, 95a, 29 Mar. 1627.
[4] Possibly William Newton, made free 31 Oct. 1583 (Arber ii. 690).
[5] Cf. *C–B.C*, 76a, 3 Mar. 1623.

August: Mathewes. It is this daie ordered that Augustine Mathewes his presse lately set vp shalbe taken downe hauing been erected Contrary to the decree.[1]

20°. Junij. 1623

Mr. ffeild Mr. Gilmyn, Mr. Pauier, Mr. Waterson, Mr. Lownes senior, Mr. Swinhowe, Mr. Knight, Mr. Cooke, Mr. Islippe, Mr. Kingston.

Ambrose Garbrand. It is Consented vnto this daie that Garbrandę debt to Mr. Bill being five poundes shalbe paid out of the poores Accompt.[2]

Gram̃er. Mr. Pauier, Mr. Lownes senior, Mr. Knight & Mr. Weauer, are appointed to Conferre with Mr. Norton about the Gramer busines.[3]

Fol. 77b

quinto Julij 1623.

Present. Mr Feild, mr Gilmyn mr Pavier mr Waterson mr Lownes sen' mr Lownes. Junior mr Swinhowe mr Cole mr Knight mr Coke, mr Islip mr Kingston/

Number of Presses/ 38 83. Whereas the mr printers of this Company, according to a former order haue reformed themselues for the number of presses that euery one is to haue and accordingly haue brought in their barres to shewe their Conformitie therevnto. It is this day ordered That the said printers or any of them shall not erect any more presses hereafter but keepe themselues to the number that nowe they haue and are here sett downe & allotted vnto them vizt

mr Feild to haue.	Two.	mr Stansby	Two.
mr Lownes. sen'.	Two.	mrs Griffin and John Havilond	Two
mr Islip	Two.	John Legatt.	Two
mr Kingston	Two.	John Dawson.	Two
mr Alldee	Two.	Nich. Okes	one
mr Purfoote	Two.	wm Jones	one
mr Jaggard.	Two.	Geo Purslowe	one
mr Eld and [*John*] [Myles] fflesher	Two[4]	Barnard Alsop.	one
mr Snodham	Two	Augustine Mathewes.	one.[5]
mr Beale	Two		

[1] Cf. *C–B.C*, 77b, 5 July 1623.
[2] Cf. *C–B.C*, 70b, 10 Dec. 1621.
[3] Cf. *C–B.C*, 73a, 25 June 1622.
[4] Cf. *C–B.C*, 49b, 8 Dec. 1617.
[5] The only changes from the list of 9 May 1615 (*C–B.C*, 38b) are that Flesher is now a partner of Eld, and Haviland a partner of Mrs. Griffin, while Jones has taken over the press of Blower, Alsop that of Creed, and Mathewes that of White. The total number of presses is the same.

The Copie of a submission made by Edward Alldee.[1]

Present at the doeinge hereof — Mr Feild mr Gilmyn mr Pavier. mr Waterson mr Lownes sen' mr Swinhowe mr Lownes Jun' mr Knight mr Coke mr Islip.

Mr Alldee. I Edward Alldee doe hereby and of myne owne free mocõn wthout any Compulsion fayning or dissimulacõn acknowledge and Confesse to my mr and wardens and Company that I haue diuerse times of late giuen occasion of much offence to the Company ffirst in printing certaine Currantę and other bookes, wthout lycense or Entrance Contrary to the decrees & ordinancę of the said Company, Secondly in printing some thingę carelesly that haue ben comitted vnto me by the said Company whereby much losse and damge haue Come vnto them, Thirdly in behaueing my self turbulently and disorderly towardę them and vsing vnseemely and vnfitting wordę tending to the disgrace of the said Company especially the assistantę as in saying there was not an honest man that satt at the Table, ffourthly in taking ꝑte and Joyninge my self wth strangers against the well-fare of the said Company which hath putt them to much trouble and Chardg.[2] But wth full intent and purpose to reforme and keepe my self hereafter || from all offences of theise kindę and hartely sorry for the same. I doe in all humblenes and plaine dealing submitt my self to my said master wardens and assistantę desiring them to shewe me their Comisseracõn for all that is past vpon condicon that I neu' offend hereafter in the like kinde, And I doe hereby promise eu' to carry my self honestly and orderly in my Calling and respectiuely and obediently towardę the Master wardens and assistantę of my said Company renowncinge all favor and Comisseracõn to be prayed or demanded of them for the Contrary. That this my request may be granted I most Humbly Craue it before my master wardens & assistantę this thirtith day of June in the one & twentith yeare of the raigne of or sou'aigne lord king Jeames &c 1623. **Fol. 78a**

Actum p̃nte *Tho: Montforte* Notaris publico. *Ed. Alldee/*

Quinto Julij 1623.

August: Mathewes It is ordered that Augustine Mathewes shall take downe one of his presses and bring it into the hall and then the table will Consider further of his peticõn to be a Master printer/

8o Julij 1623 Rę Jac. 21o.

Mr. Swinhowe. Mr.
mr Cole } wardens/
mr Bill }

[1] Cf. *C–B.C*, 70a, 8 Oct. 1621.
[2] Possibly by printing for R. Wood and T. Symcock.

17° Julij 1623.

Present/ mr Swinhow, mr Cole mr Bill mr Norton mr Waterson mr Feild mr Lownes sen'. mr. Lownes. Jun' mr Gilmyn mr Knight mr Pavier mr Coke. mr Kingston.

John Jaggard. It is ordered that John Jaggard[1] shall haue the 50li for 3 yeares from the day that his father had it vpon the same securitie and she is (vizt his mother) to assigne her assistantę pte in the english stocke for further securitie.

mr Weaver . mr Weaver is this day taken in to be of the assistance of the Company.

Fol. 78b

Eodem die pñtib9. vt ante.

Wiłłm Holme
Adam Islip.

md mr Islip hath payd to one John Browne that marryed the eldest of mr Holmes daughters xxli. & the interest thereof, And at another time vizt the 29 of March 1627 mr Islip paid to the said Joh. Browne 10li more, and 56s for Interest thereof, which is the moytye of the parte that belongę to Tho. Holmes, deceased at the East Indies, so there is 30li behind in mr Islips hand which is due to the younger daughter of Wm Holmes

Whereas mr Waterson one of the Assistantę of this Company hath had the vse of three skore poundę belonging to the Orphanes of wiłłm Holme deceased since 26° January 1609 at the Rate of 8li p Cent' nowe the said mr Waterson is desirous to pay the same into the hall.[2] Wherevpon mr Islip moved the Company that he might have it at the same rate, And this day vpon his mocõn it is ordered that the said mr Islipp shall haue the said 60li at the same Rate, And he is to engage his parte in the English stocke for the repaymt thereof which he hath at this Court consented vnto/

Memorandu' Mr. Islip hath paid in 30ł. [more] being the remainder of 60li [*he had*] [& 4li. 16s in full for all interest for the legacie] as by the note in the Margent appeareth. 14°. Junij 1634.

Bookes one of a sort to be brought into the hall

It is this day ordered that euery printer shall deliu' a Copie of euerie booke he printeth to the Clarke of the Companie for the time being to the vse of the same Company according to a confirmed ordinance of this house,[3] And that there be a Chamber or Roome made ready to dispose the said bookes in/

mr Baker
John Havilond
Rob. Woodnett.

This day mr Baker[4] by Consent of the Company assigned his yeomanry part in the English stocke to John Havilond and Robert woodnett and they were admitted accordinglie

Wm Miller wiłłm miller by Consent of a full Court is to haue a lease of a house where wm Fulkes lately dwelt in wood street, for 21 yeares for 8li a yeare rent and 10li fine:

[1] This John is not known to have carried on his father's business. Cf. *C–B.C*, 74a.

[2] Cf. *C–B.C*, 22a, where the date is given as 16 Jan. 1610.

[3] Not found.

[4] Presumably Thomas Baker, made free 17 Feb. 1620 (Arber iii. 685).

20 Augusti 1623.

mr Speed. mr Beale. — The matter betwen mr Speed and mr Beale being referred to mr ffeild mr Islip mr Kingston and mr weaver, They have ordered that mr Beale shall deliu' vnto m' Speed all that belonge to the formes [*that belonge to*] [of] the Geneologies[1] in 12° except the quadrates nomparrell lers together wth one Vinnett and a border:[2] likewise it is ordered that he shall deliu' all other lers and thinge that belong to any other geneologies of mr Speedes, Also it is ordered by the said pties. That the said mr Beale shall printe the half sheete againe in mr Speede Cronicle[3] which are false printed vizt pag. 183. 188. 195. 219. 237. 281. 367. 883. which are to be finished betwen this and the 20th of September next or sooner if he can. And for the false Titles to sett them downe in an Errata together wth other faulte. of lessor Consequence. The thinge concerning the Geneologies in 12° to be deliu'ed betwen this and the 24 of September next/

Ric. Feild. Adam Islip
Felix Kingston Edm: Weaver

1mo Augusti 1623 Re Jac. 21°. — Fol. 79a

mr Swinhow mr Gilmyn loco mri Cole mr. Bill mr Norton mr Wateson mr Feild mr Lownes sen' mr Lownes Jun' mr Knight mr Pavier mr Coke mr Weaver/

John Basse Tho: Lutman/ — This day at the humble request of John Basse[4] lycense is giuen vnto him by Consent of a full Court holden this day to assigne ouer his part in the English stocke to mr Weaver for the paymt of 30li wth interest for the forebearance thereof vnto one Thomas Lutman or his assignes, so mr weaver from henceforth is to receive the dividente as they shall arise and pay it ou' to mr Lutman or his assignes towarde the said debt/

pntibꝰ vt ante 6° Octo. 1623

A presse at Bunhill — This day the presse lately taken nere Bunhill which was printing the Remish Testamt[5] and a booke of the late Conference betwixt mr Fisher and Dor Featly[6] was battered and defaced at Stationrs hall [*lykewise*] [for that] it was erected in a private Corner contrary to the decree in Starrchamber

Peter Smith
Ric: Morris
Chr: Jenkes[7] } workemen at that presse.

Ben: Fisher. — It is ordered that Beniamin Fisher for vsing of vnfitting speeches of the whole Boord shall pay for a fine xxs and make a submission

Present — mr Swinhow mr Cole mr Bill mr Waterson mr Gilmyn mr Knight mr Pavier mr Coke mr Islip mr wever/

[1] STC 23039. These woodcut tables were used with standing type from edition to edition.
[2] Probably McKerrow and Ferguson No. 34.
[3] STC 23047.
[4] Made free 28 June 1591 (Arber ii. 709).
[5] Cf. STC 2923. No copy of this edition is known.
[6] Cf. STC 23530. According to Gillow, *Biog. dict. of Eng. Catholics*, this was probably issued in manuscript.
[7] Cf. *C–B.C*, 61b, 6 May 1620. None of these men is recorded in Arber.

The submission of Ben: Fisher/

Ben: Fisher — I Beniamin Fisher doe hereby and of myne owne [*accord*] [free] Mocõn w^th^out any faineing or dissimulacõn acknowledg and Confesse to my m^r^ wardens & Company That I have of late giuen much occasion of offence to the said Company in vsing vnseemely and vnfitting wordę tending to the disgrace of the whole boord of Assistantę. But wth full entent & purpose to reforme and keepe my self heareafte^r^ from all offences in theise kindę and being hartily sorry for the same I doe in all humblenes submitt my self to my said m^r^ wardens & assistantę desireing them to shewe me their Comiseracõn for all that is past. Vpon Condicon that I neu' offend hereafter in the like kinde & doe hereby promise eu' hereafter to carry my self honestly & orderly in my calling and respectiuely and obediently towardę the m^r^ wardens & assistantę of my company. That this my request may be granted I humbly Craue it before my m^r^ wardens and assistantę this 28 of october, in the 21th yeare of the raigne of o^r^ soueraigne lord king James. 1623.

FOL. 79^b^ — 3° Novemb: 1623. Rę Jacobis/

Present — m^r^ Swinhowe mr Bill mr Norton mr Waterson mr Feild mr Lownes Jun' mr Knight mr Pavier mr Islip mr Kingston mr weaver/

Mr Aires. — This day m^r^ Aires being a suto^r^ to increase his time in his house in wood street. It is ordered that paying 10^li^ fine the old rent of 23^l^ and bestowing 20^l^ vpon digging sell^rs^ he shall surrendring his lease in being have a newe lease for 31 yeares to begin at Michas last/[1]

mr Withers — It is ordered that mr withers shall haue a Copie of the peticõn exhibited by the Company to his ma^tie^.[2]

2° decemb 1623

mr Elton
m^rs^. Byneman.

This day m^r^ Edw. Elton preacher brought in the some of 20^li^ and desired it might be kept by the Company to the vse of the Children of Christofer Bynneman[3] deceased vizt Alice: Charles: Eliz: and Marye, And this 20^li^ is to be paid vnto them pte and pte like as they come to the age of 21 yeares or day of marriage which shall first happen and if any of them die the survivo^r^ or suruivo^rs^ to haue that pte devided amongst them, wherevnto the Company condiscended And ordered that there should be payd for the same thirtie shillingę yearely by quarterly paym^tę^ so long as it remaines in their handę to Jane Bynneman the mother, And when any is paid of the principall they are to pay rateably for that which shall be left: This was the guift of Judeth Rider of Barmonsye in the Countye of Surrey deceased who made the said mr Edward Elton sole execut^r^ of her last will

21th Decemb. 1627. of this 20^l^. there is paid to Alice Bynneman the some of 6^l^. 13^s^. 4^d^

23 Junij 1630 paid more to Charles Bynneman, 6. 13. 4.

[*md* 6^l^. 13^s^ 4^d^ *paid to the Third Child and the ffourth is deade*]

7mo die Decembris 1631 paid more to mary Byneman 6^l^ 13^s^—4^d^, soe the whole 20 —0— is pd & a relese giuen

[1] Cf. *C–B.C*, 77^a^, 27 May 1623.

[2] This petition has not been found, but is referred to as having procured a 'reference' from the King in a memorandum *Acts of P.C. 1623–1625*, p. 274.

[3] Son of Henry Bynneman.

Latten stocke — Md this 20l is to be paid into the latten and yt stocke is to paie it againe and the interest according to this order.

mrs Boyle / Hum. Woodhall. — This day mrs Boyle assigned her half yeomanry pte in the English stocke, and by the Consent of the Boord it was conferred vpon Humfery woodhall[1] & he tooke his oath according to order

Rich. Taylor. — It is ordered that Rich: Taylor shall have the next 50l of this yeares rent[2]

To my lo: Mayors to dinner this yeare: — The mr and wardens mr waterson mr Feild mr Lownes Jun' mr Islip mr Snowdham mr Triplett/

12° Januarij 1623. Re Jac. 21°. — Fol. 80a

Present/ — Mr Swinhowe mr Cole mr Bill mr Waterson mr Lownes sen' mr Lownes Jun' mr Gilmyn mr Knight mr Coke mr Islip. mr Weaver mr Kingston/

Hen: Gosson / Edw. Gosson — This day Hen: Gosson had license from the boord to assigne his part in the English stocke to his brother Edw. Gosson [for security of paiement of 40li] which the said Henry Confesseth he oweth vnto the said Edward. And the said Edward Gosson is [Contented] to take the dividente as they arise vntill the said [debt of] 40li be paid.

4° feb. 1623

Nic: Bourne/ — It is ordered that Nicholas Bourne shall vpon good securitie haue 50li for 3 yeares of mr Joh. Nortons bequest and he is to assigne his latten stocke for further securitie[3]

This day Rich: Rauens[4] bond was deliu'ed to hym at a full Court by or Master/

John Dawson / Eph: Dawson. — This day John Dawson had lycense to assigne all his parte in the English latten and Irish stockes for securitie of paiemt of 100l. the Tenth of feb. 1624. to Ephram Dawson or his executrs.

mr Recorder — It is ordered that Sr Henage Finch Knight Recordor of London shall have an annuall fee of 44s p annu' to be of Counsell for the Companye

Mrs Kempe / Fra: Faulkenor / Nath. Newbery — This day election was made for mrs Kempes yeomanrye parte in the English stocke, she being latelie married out of the Company there stood in election mr Parker mr Stansby ffran:

[1] Made free 20 May 1617 (Arber iii. 684).

[2] He was lent the money 1 Mar. 1624, and his bonds were recorded in *Liber C2*, 110b.

[3] His bonds are recorded 7 Feb. 1624, in *Liber C2*, 110b.

[4] Made free 25 Jan. 1619 (Arber iii. 685).

ffaulkenor Nath. Newberye. and it fell on ffran: ffaulkeno^{r} and Nathanill Newberye to each of them half a part and they tooke there oathes according to order/

1mo. Martij 1623

Stockeepars for the Eng: stocke	m^{r} Lownes sen' } m^{r} Knight—	m^{r} Snodham } m^{r} Barrenger	Edward Blackmore Jacob Bloome/
Audito^{rs}	m^{r} pavier— } m^{r} Islip—	m^{r} purfoote } m^{r} Harrison	w^{m} Bladon Joh. wright/
Stockeeper for ye Latt: stocke	mr Norton } mr Bill	m^{r} Blount— } m^{r} weaver—	m^{r} Edwardę m^{r} Hodgettę.

Tho. Davis — It is ordered that Tho. Davis shalbe the plasterer for the hall

Ric Hudson John Busby. — This day Rich. Hudson by Consent of the boord assigned his parte in the English stocke to John Busby and he tooke his oath accordinglie

Fol. 80^{b}

15 Martij 1623.

Mr Swinhow m^{r} Cole mr Bill m^{r} Waterson mr Feild m^{r} Lownes sen' m^{r} Lownes Jun' m^{r} Knight m^{r} Coke mr Knight mr weaver.

Bridghouse/ — This day the Counterparte of the lease from the bridghouse of the houses in the old Chang belonging to the Latten stocke was sealed wth the Comoñ seale for 23 yeares and one quarter of a yeare from michĩs 1621 rent 5^{l}.

Wm Miller.
75. — Likewise a lease of a house in woodstreet to w^{m} Miller and Dorcas his wife was sealed by the ffeofees, Rent 8^{l} p annu' & ten poundę fine for 21 yeare at Michĩs last

Mr Harvest — It is ordered that m^{r} Harvest shalbe the officer of the Company in m^{r} Bokers[1] place who is lately dead and have the same fee that he had

25° martij 1624. Rę Jac. 22°/

m^{r} Norton and the Company about the grañer. — It is agreed that m^{r} Norton shall take the grañer patent backe againe from the Companye[2] and to allowe [*the*] bookes to paye the old ꝑteno^{rs} and some other for Newton, and besidę m^{r} Norton is to paie the Company 22^{l} ꝑ annu' during the life of mrs Joyce Norton widdow afterward the Company must provide for it

[1] Cf. *C–B.C*, 15^{a}, 12 Oct. 1607.   [2] Cf. *C–B.C*, 73^{a}, 25 June 1622.

Bookes to pay the old ptenors

	l	s	d
1625—Cambdens[1]	65—	0—	0
693—Stockwoods[2]....	41	12—	6
4000—gramers[3]	128	0—	0
3000—Lillies[4].........	60—	0—	0
3000—Accedences[5]	33 .	0—	0
866—Grangers[6]	24 .	5 .	4
1054—Cawdries[7]	10—	10—	10
961—Stockewoods fig:[8]	7	13—	10
313—Barnards[9]	2	10—	2
	372:	12 .	7.

Bookes for Newton[10]

2578 . Cleonarde[11]....	206 .	5—	0
2000 . Cambdens[1]	80 .	0—	0
Debts.......	114—	6—	11
	400l.	11s.	11d

Md at the agremt betwen the Company and mr Norten were pnte mr Cole mr Norton mr Waterson mr ffeild mr lownes sen' mr Lownes Jun' mr Knight mr Pavier mr Islip mr Kingston mr weaver one mr Tho. Hungate & Tho: Montforte.

5° April 1624. Fol. 81a

Present/ Mr Swinhow mr Gilmyn loco mri Cole mr Pavier loco mr Bill mr waterson mr Feild mr Knight mr Cooke mr Kingston mr weaver

Paule Man/ It is ordered by Consent of Mr Tho. Man signified to this Court by a lẽr from him That his Copies shall be entred to his [*sonne*] sonnes Paule man & Jomas man/[12]

Latten stocke. By Consent of this Court mr Norton is ioyned wth mr waterson mr Knight & mr Pavier in the busines of the latten stocke

John Havilond Joh. Haviland is to bring in 40s for minshewes Dictionary to be paid to the poore of the Company[13]

[1] Cf. STC 4514. Copies of editions published by Norton in 1626, 1627, and 1629 are known.
[2] Cf. STC 23279. The Huntington has the 'editio quinta', 12°, per assig. B. Norton, 1634.
[3] Unidentified.
[4] STC 15627. Copies of editions published by Norton or his assigns in 1627, 1629, and 1630 are known.
[5] Unidentified.
[6] Cf. STC 12183.
[7] Cf. STC 4886.
[8] Unidentified.
[9] Possibly an edition of STC 23890.
[10] Cf. *C–B.C*, 59a, 23 Dec. 1619.
[11] Cf. STC 5404.
[12] Cf. Arber iv. 117.
[13] Cf. Arber iv. 97. STC 17945.

John Williams — Joh. williams to bring in 10[l] for John Griffinɇ debt at all Saints day next/[1]

This day order was given to the m[r] printers by direction of the lordɇ Comittees of the vpper house of parliam[t] not to printe any peticōn or breifes to the ꝑliam[t] w[th]out order of the house.

1[mo] Junij 1624.

Irish stock — The busines of the Irish stocke is refferred to mr Norton m[r] Lownes sen' m[r] Kingstone, mr Edwardɇ m[r] Snodham John Hodgettɇ Joh Dawson

mr Weaver — It is ordered that m[r] weaver for his paines in that stocke shall have but—13[l]—6[s]—8[d] ꝑ anum/

mr Aires. — It is agreed that m[r] Aires shall have ten yeares added to his old lease payeing for a fine—5[l].[2]

7° Junij. 1624.

M[rs] Browne
m[r] Downes
mr Younge
mr Jo. Waterson

This Court being certified that m[rs] Browne[3] is latelie married out of the Company The boord went to election of an other ꝑteno[r] and it fell vpon Thomas Downes, there stood in election wth him m[r] Rodwell[4] & m[r] Snodham/

Then election was made for m[r] Downes yeomanrye ꝑte and it fell vpon Robert young & Joh waterson to mak vp there half partɇ whole yeomanrye ꝑtɇ/

Fol. 81[b] Countesse of Nottingham. 2000[li]

Md̄. that on the 14th day of may 1624 the 10 ꝑties herevnder menconed were bound to the Lady Margarett Countesse of Nottinghm̄ for the paym[t] of 2000[li] in grayes Inne hall vpon the 20 of may 1626. viz[t] Geo: Swinhowe Bonham Norton Geo. Cole. Symon Waterson Ric: Feild Hum: Lownes Math. Lownes Clement Knight Tho. Pavier and Adam Islip. And in an other bond vnto her for paiem[t] of 60[li] 20 No: 1624.
60[li] 20 May. 1625.
60[li] 20 No: 1625
60[li] 20 May 1626.[5]

[1] In *Liber C2*, 184[b], it is recorded 'november 1624 md̄ m[r] Cooke rec' of this debt of Joh williams 8l. 20 Martij 1625. Md̄ m[r] Ashe rec' of John williams the other 40[s].'

[2] Cf. *C–B.C*, 79[b], 3 Nov. 1623.

[3] Mrs. John Browne, Sen.

[4] Made free 7 Apr. 1600 (Arber ii. 725).

[5] This money was borrowed for the Latin Stock, cf. *The Library*, 2nd Ser., viii (1907), p. 289.

17. Junij 1624.

mr Elde
Miles Flesher

This day mr Eld assigned ou' his yeomanry ꝑte in the English stocke to miles ffflesher who by Consent was elected there vnto and tooke his oath accordinglie. Provided that m^{r} ffflesher doe giue securitie to John Dawson for the paym^{t} of the residue of a debt to the vse of mrs Chambers to whom m^{r} Eldę parte was morgaged

m^{r}. Johnson

This day also the Articles between the ꝑteno^{rs} in the Irish stocke & m^{r} Johnson[1] were sealed by Ten of the ꝑteno^{rs}.

Rob: younge.

It is ordered that Rob: younge shall have 6^{l}. 13^{s}. 4^{d} for his prentice Jeames Bennett to serve the Company in Ireland.[2]

mrs. White
mr Aldee/

M^{rs} whites Copies are to be assigned to m^{r} Alldee by Consent of this Court salve Jure cuiuscunq;.[3]

1mo. Julij 1624:

Present

Mr Swinhowe m^{r} Cole mr Waterson mr Feild. m^{r} Lownes sen' mr Lownes Jun' mr Gilmyn mr Knight m^{r} Cooke m^{r} Islip m^{r} Weaver

Mr Norton
m^{r}. Bill/

Whereas m^{r} Bonham Norton vpon the first day of Aprill last past did in the pñce of the master of the Company of Stationr̃s and diuers others in a most violent manner most malitiouslye strike m^{r} John Bill warden of the said Company in breach of a Confirmed ordinance of the said Company and in Contempt thereof. The said m^{r} Norton by Consent of a full Court holden this day is fined for this his misdemeano^{r} to the vse of the said Company at the some of twentye poundę.[4]

mr Bolton
Hum: Woodhall

This day m^{r} Bolton[5] assigned half his yeomandry ꝑte in the English stocke to Hum Woodhall[6] to make him the said woodhall a whole yeomanry ꝑte And so m^{r} Bolton hath but half a share left

3° Julij 1624. FOL. 82^{a}

Present

Mr Swinhowe mr Cole mr waterson mr Feild. mr Lownes sen' mr Lownes Jun' mr Gilmyn mr Knight mr Cooke mr Islip mr Kingston mr weaver/

John Dawson

This day John Dawson is admitted into the liverye of this Company .... } xx^{li}/

Md̄ m^{r} weaver hath given his word that this xx^{li} shall be paid by v^{li} a quarter.

[1] Arthur Johnson was sent to Dublin as agent, presumably in succession to Robert Young.
[2] Cf. *C–B.C*, 76^{b}, 2 Apr. 1623.
[3] Cf. Arber iv. 120.
[4] Cf. *The Library*, 2nd Ser., ii (1901), 353–75.
[5] John Bolton, made free 30 Oct. 1598 (Arber ii. 722).
[6] Made free 20 May 1617 (Arber iii. 684).

Rich: Garford	Rich Garford[1] admitted to the liverye of this Company paying..............................	xxli
Ric: Whitacres	Rich: whiteacres admitted to the liverye of this Company	xxli
Geo Latham	Geo: Latham admitted to the Liverye of this Company	xxli
Tho. Dewe	Tho. Dewe admitted to the livery of this Company paying..............................	xxl
Jonas Wellinge Eph: Dawson.	It is ordered that Jonas welling[2] and Ephram Dawson for refusing the Clothing being Called therevnto shall pay for a fine to the Company 40s a peece and be elegible eu'ye yeare according to the order in this behalf...........	iiijli

FOL. 82b

25 Julij 1624 Re Jac: 22°/

Present/ mr. Humf: Lownes mr. mr Math. Lownes mr Cooke wardens/ mr waterson mr Feild mr Swinhow mr Gilmyn mr Knight mr Pavier mr weaver

Geo. Wood. It is ordered that such parte of the presse and lr̃ as were lately taken nere the Spittle from Geo: Wood shalbe battered and melted and deliu'ed to the owner according to the Decree

2° August 1624.

Rob. Bird. This day Robert Bird had warning to avoid Adam Atkins[3] a forrenor.

mrs Griffin. mrs Griffin likewise is to avoid hir man Chr. Jenke[4] wthin 8 dayes.

mr Kingston. This day mr Kingston hath lycense from the boord to morgage his pte in the English stocke to mr math. Lownes for 160li for a yeare

This some of 160li wth interest according to agremt was paid in to Mr Latham executor to mris lownes the 14th day of Aprill 1626: In pñcia mei *Tho: Montforte*/

9° August. 1624.

John Parker
Jeames Bowler. This day election was made for Symeon Woodcocke[5] yeomandry part in the English stocke and it fell vpon John Parker and Jeames Bowler to make them vp whole parte.

[1] Made free 26 Mar. 1616 (Arber iii. 684).
[2] Made free 20 Mar. 1602 (Arber ii. 731).
[3] Unrecorded.
[4] Cf. *C–B.C*, 79a, 6 Oct. 1623.
[5] Made free 7 Dec. 1607 (Arber iii. 683).

18° August 1624.

miles Flesher. miles fflesher is to be allowed a mr Printer if my lo: of Canterb: signifie his Consent which was done accordinglie[1]

mr Piper. Ed: Aggas. mr Piper by his owne Consent is to pay mr Aggas 50s to day 50s saterday come fortnight, and 5li at michĩs next otherwise mr Aggas hath leave to take his Course by lawe/

Wm Jones wm Jones had this day warning to put away a Jorneyman not free, that he keepes disorderly vpon paine of the penaltye in that case provided

Aug. Mathewes. Augustine mathewes is warned to put away a prentice which he keepeth disorderly:

Wm. Stansby. wm Stansby is warned to putt away peter Smith and Jeremy maidstone 2 forrenors wthin 8 dayes.[2]

6° Septem. 1624 Rę Jac. 22°/ Fol. 83a

Present. mr Lownes sen' mr Lownes Jun' mr Cooke mr Waterson mr Feild mr Swinhow mr Knight mr Pavier mr Kingston and mr weaver

Geo. Wood. It is ordered That the lr̃ and peece of presse That was taken from Geo: Wood nere Bedlam[3] being defaced shalbe deliu'ed backe to him or his wife.

Printers
76 whereas sundry orders have ben made against therectinge and setting vp of presses which have not ben duly putt in Execucon: It is nowe ordered by Consent of a full Court holden this day That mr Lownes Jun' and mr Cooke being wardens, mr knight mr Kingston and mr weaver assistantę and mr Stansby shall forthwith repaire to the printers houses and take downe such presses, as they haue, more then the number allotted to them by the order of the fift of July 1623.[4]

9° Septemb. 1624.

Geo Wood Geo: Withers. This day a search was made by the mr & wardens and others by their appointmt, and in this search a presse was found nere Holborne bridge sett vp Contrarye to order, and was ymployed in printing an vnlicensed booke, Therefore the said wardens by vertue of the [*said*] Decree and proclamacon sett forth against disorderly printing &c have

[1] His petition, with order granting it, is recorded in *State Papers Dom. 1623–1625*, p. 379, and reprinted Arber iii. 689.

[2] Cf. *C–B.C*, 69b, 3 Sept. 1621, and 79a, 6 Oct. 1623. The Court might well have been annoyed.

[3] Cf. *C–B.C*, 82b, 25 July 1624. The Spital Bar and Old Bethlehem Hospital were both in the ward of Bishopsgate Without.

[4] Cf. *C–B.C*, 77b.

taken downe the said presse and Caused the same together wth the lers̃ and other Instrum^{ts} for printing therevnto belonging to be brought to Stationrs hall to be defaced and made vnseruiceable,

which the next day being the Tenth of September was executed and pformed accordingly/

This presse was said to be Geo. woodꝭ. And the booke that was printing Called The schollers purgatory or the Stationr̃s com̃on welth by Geo: Withers.[1]

27° Septemb. 1624.

mr. Aires.

This day m^{r}. Aires lease of his house in woodstreet was sealed by the ffeoffees for 31 yeares from midsomer last rent 22^{li} p annu’: ffine. 5^{li}.[2]

Writeings d̃d̃ to Mr Knight by order from m^{r} waterson m^{r} Knight and m^{r} Pavier/

The lease from the Bridghouse dated 16 December 1623 from michĩs before for 23 yeares and a quarter.[3] Rent 5^{li} m^{r} Pigeons lease dated 6° martij 1619 for 20 yeares from xmãs before rent 32^{li}[4]

latyne stocke/

mr Tiffins lease to the Company date 6 dec. 1619 from michĩs before for 21 yeares rent 80^{li}[5]
m^{r} Barrettꝭ lease.[6]
m^{r} Bladons lease.[6]

Fol. 83^{b}

22° Octob. 1624

mr Waterson mr Lownes.

m^{r} waterson and m^{r} Lownes Jun’ have this day agreed to pay for the Arcadias brought out of Ireland eleaven shillingꝭ a Reame and they are to be delivered to the latyne stocke[7]

Caleopeia/

m^{r} weaver is to send for the Caliopeias which are printed in Ireland.[8]

Abergeveny
27. 161. 84

It is ordered that Counsell be taken for Coueying of Abergaveny house to other or some more Feoffees by reason most of the old are deade: There is also to be made a Declaracõn of Trust that it is purchased to the vse of the parteno^{rs} in the English stocke.[9]

[1] STC 25919. Wither answered the Commissioners for Causes Ecclesiastic (*State Papers Dom. 1623–1625*, p. 143) that this book, though partly printed without licence by George Wood, was not intended to be published without licence, and that he thought the press was erected at Wood's own expense. He also stated that 3,000 copies were to be printed, but only a few copies were struck off. An examination of the book indicates that sheets (:) A–B were printed at one press, presumably Wood's, and C–I at another.

[2] Cf. *C–B.C*, 81^{a}, 1 June 1624.

[3] Cf. *C–B.C*, 80^{b}, 15 Mar. 1623.

[4] These leases apparently were for property which was part of Abergavenny House, from the reference *C–B.C*, 98^{b}, 3 Mar. 1628.

[5] Cf. *C–B.C*, 59^{a}, 19 Jan. 1620. Evidently the £10 paid by Barrett and Bladon is here deducted from the £90 rent there noted.

[6] Cf. *C–B.C*, 76^{b}, 3 Mar. 1623.

[7] Cf. *C–B.C*, 71^{a}, 4 Feb. 1622.

[8] STC 7179 + Draxe, T. Calliepeia, Dublin, [1624?] Copy Library of Congress (imprint cut).

[9] Cf. *C–B.C*, 27^{a}, 8 Apr. 1611.

6° Novemb. 1624:

Ballettę. Whereas divers Ballettę have ben heretofore disorderly printed without entrance or allowance. It is nowe ordered that an Entrance be made ꝑticularly of the Ballettę that are now printed vnto m[r] Pavier and his ꝑteno[rs] he paying xx[s] to the house and [*the*] Contenting the Clarke: Provided that if any others have any title to any of the said ballettę by Entrance or other wise this order or the Entrance shall not preiudice them.[1]

m[rs] Browne
mr Dewe
The matter betwixt m[r] Dewe and m[rs] Browne being put to the Table by Consent of both ꝑties. It is ordered that m[rs] Browne shall pay m[r] Dewe for apparrell[2] for Joh. Stempe. xxx[s]

mr Butter
fine.
It is ordered that m[r] Butter shall paie for a fine for printing a Currant w[th]out Entrance Contrary to order—vj[s] viij[d] [3]

John Norton
Luke Norton
It is ordered that John Norton shall pay Luke Norton[4] for not giving him warning but turning him being a Jorneyman printer of on a sudden—xvj[s],

Nic: Okes. It is ordered that Nicho: Okes shall paie for a fine for printing a booke called Good newes from Breda.[5] w[th]out license or Entrance:—xl[s]. and he is warned not to print any booke hereafter w[th]out license vpon payne to have his presse taken downe.

mr Piper
Amb. Retherden
mđđ mr Piper before he turned ou' his man Ambrose Retherden[6] did give him a yeare so howsoeu' his Indenture is, he is to serue but 7 yeares from the date/

20 Decemb 1624 Fol. 84[a]

John Basse
m[r] Stansby.
This day John Basse[7] surrendred his half yeomdry part in the English stocke into the handes of the m[r] & wardens and the m[r] wardens and assistantę did elect w[m] Stansby therevnto to make vp his former half part a whole yeomandrye part.

24 Decemb. 1624.

Present/ mr lownes sen' m[r] Lownes Jun' m[r] Cooke m[r] Swinhow mr Cole m[r] Knight m[r] Islip mr weaver m[r] Kingston.

m[r] Boulton
m[r] Dewe.
This day m[r] Boulton[8] surrendred his half yeomandry part in the English stocke by Consent of the boord to Tho: Dewe, and he tooke his oath accordingly.

[1] This was the beginning of the Ballad Stock. From the entry, Arber iv. 131–2, Pavier's partners were John, Cuthbert, and Edward Wright, John Grismond, and Henry Gosson. Cf. also Arber iv. 144.

[2] Presumably as an apprentice.

[3] In the *Book of Fines*, 19[b], 6 Nov. 1624, this fine is recorded for 'printing Currantes'. These probably are Nos. 34 and 35 of STC 25201, see *Trans.* xviii (1937), 369–71, for which no entry was made.

[4] Made free 2 Mar. 1612 (Arber iii. 683).

[5] This book has not been identified. The fine was paid 6 Oct. 1624, *Book of Fines*, 19[b], and T. Archer was fined £3 for the same offence.

[6] A. Ritherdon.

[7] Made free 28 June 1591 (Arber ii. 709).

[8] Cf. *C–B.C*, 81[b], 1 July 1624.

mr Hurley — This day mr Hurley[1] made request to the boord to be releived vpon a debt of xxli which he stande bound for Wm Barrett deceased which xxli was taken vp to buy Arthur Johnsons part in the latyne stocke. Now for that wm. Barrett is deceased and that the stocke remaynes in the hande of the partenors in that stocke, his request was to be releived out of that stocke. wherevpon it was referred to mr Waterson mr Knight and mr Pavier to take such order herein wth the Consent also of mrs Barrett as they shall thinke fittinge/

17° Januarij 1624 Re Jac: 22°/

Present/ — mr Waterson loco mri. mr Lownes Jun' mr Cooke mr Swinhow mr Cole mr Knight mr Pavier mr Islip mr Kingston mr weaver

wm Barrenger — It is ordered that wm Barenger shall have allowances by the wardens for the losse of his hatt and Cloake that he lost in the Companies busines/[2]

Mr Gilmyn
Tho: Montforte — This day mr Gilmyn did assigne over his livery parte[3] in the English stocke by the Consent of a full Court holden this day [*so it is ordered*] vnto Thomas Montfort so it is ordered that he shall have it absolutilye according to mr Gilmyns request reserving to himself his yeomandry part onely:

Mr Gilmyns lr̃e to the worll. the mr Wardens and assistante of the Company of Stationrs deliu' this/ — I would entreat you yor wardens and the rest of thAssistante that you will be pleasd to make ou' my livry pte in ye English stocke vnto mr Montforte by reason of some money I doe owne vnto him and other mony which I shall have of him to serve my wante at this time and in so doeing I shall rest my self beholding vnto you all & this shall be a sufficient dischardg for you and so for this time I take my leave the 17 January 1624 & rest

yors in what I may to my power
Antho: Gilmyn

postscrip/ — I would entreat you absolutely to assigne my livery pte vnto mr Montfort reserving my yeomanrye to my self
Antho. Gilmyn/

FOL. 84a (bis)

eod die pñtib9 vt ante

Latyne stocke/ — It is ordered that an exact Catalogue be made of the Latyn warehouse before the first of march next and that mr waterson mr Knight & mr Pavier shall take order for the doeing thereof as they shall thinke fitting

[1] Possibly the John Hurley whose apprenticeship is recorded 15 Nov. 1597 (Arber ii. 222).

[2] It would be interesting to know how they were lost.

[3] Cf. *C–B.C*, 71b, 22 Mar. 1622.

mr Kingston

It is ordered that the house shall paye mr Kingston for printing Do^{r} Crakenthorpes booke[1]

Rich. Badger not to come into the Court except he be called.

It is ordered that Rich. Badger shall attend wthout the doore of the Counsell Roome as other Beadles his predecessors have done and not Come in except he be called by the bell or other wise as the Company shall have occasion to vse him.

7° Feb. 1624 Re Jac: 22°/

Present.

mr lownes sen' m^{r} Lownes Jun' m^{r} Cooke mr Waterson mr Swinhow m^{r} Gilmyn mr Knight mr Pavier mr Kingston mr weaver.

Mr Parnell mr Kingston

It is this day ordered that m^{r} Parnell shall receive from the wardens the Tenth of May next as a debt due to mr Kingston for printing Do^{r} Crakenthorps booke. 40^{li}.[2]

ffeoffees for the English stocke

27

mr Lownes Jun' mr Cooke m^{r} Swinhow m^{r} Cole mr Gilmyn mr Knight mr Pavier m^{r} Islip mr Kingston mr weaver are appointed to be ffeoffees for the English stocke. and to have the purchase of Abergaveny house conveyed vnto them in trust from mr Man mr ffeild mr waterson and mr leake to the vse of the said stocke.[3]

mr Butter

It is ordered that mr Butter for vsing vnfitting Speaches to mr (*sic*) Barrett[4] as in calling her durtye slutt shall pay for a fine to the house—vj^{s} viij^{d}.

Printere.

It is ordered that if the m^{r} Printers doe not Conforme them selues to the number of presses as hath ben agreed of by former orders and bring in their barres before o^{r} ladye day next, Then those that are already brought in to be deliu'ed backe againe[5]

Rich Whitacres.

It is ordered that Rich. Whiteacres shall bring in 50^{li} of mr John Nortons bequest and to have it againe p̃ntely for 3 yeares more vpon the same securitye[6]

Ric: Badger.

Vpon the peticon of Ric: Badger leave is given vnto him to ioyne wth some m^{r} Printer so the Companyes busines be not thereby neglected.

[1] STC 5975.

[2] See above.

[3] Cf. *C–B.C*, 83^{b}, 22 Oct. 1624; and 161^{b}, 3 Dec. 1638. This deed of covenant is still preserved, though in very poor condition, in the archive of the Stationers' Company, No. 230. Abergavenny House is there referred to as 'Pembrookes Inn'.

[4] Hannah Barrett.

[5] Cf. *C–B.C*, 83^{a}, 6 Sept. 1624.

[6] Cf. *C–B.C*, 70^{b}, 14 Jan. 1622. His new bonds were recorded in *Liber C2*, 111^{a}.

Primo Martij 1624. Rę Jac. 22°/

Present	m^r Lownes sen' mr Lownes Jun' m^r Cooke m^r waterson mr Swinhow mr Gilmyn mr Cole mr Knight m^r Pavier mr Islip mr Kingston mr weaver.		

Jonah Man. Paule Man. — This day Jonah man signified to the bord by a note vnder his hand That he is endebted to Paule Man his brother the some of fortie poundę, and desired that half his part in the English stocke might be engaged to his brother for the paym^t thereof which This Court assented vnto—

Stockeeperę English stock.	mr Swinhow mr [*Pavier*] [Islip]	mr Downes mr Heggenbotham	Hen Walley John Havilond.
Threasurer	mr Weaver		
Auditorę.	mr Gilmyn mr Pavier	mr Edward mr Stansby	John Tap. John Bellamye.

Wheate. — This day the Company Conferred wth mr warde about provision Corne, and he hath agreed to make provision for the Company according to the precept from the lo: Mayo^r [1] and he is to have 6^l. 13^s. 4^d.

Geo. Miller — George Miller having dealt wth m^rs ffeild for her printing Instrum^tę is this day ordered to attend my lo. Grace to have his Consent to be admitted a master printer, which was done accordingly

Received from Christę hospitall of m^r Nortons bequest[2]	6. 13. 4.
Item paid of m^r Bishops bequest[3]	6^li
Item paid to the m^r & wardens Clarke and beadle according to m^r Nortons bequest[2]	13^s 4^d

John Edgar — John Edgar[4] is to have 12^l vpon good securitye for 3 yeares longer

John Hamon — The presse lately taken downe in Southwarke sett vp by John Hamon Rich. Jackson[5] & others contrary to the decree was this day battered & made vnseruiceable by consent of a full Court

[1] Cf. *Letter Book*, 105^a, 7 Apr. 1625.
[2] Cf. Plomer, *Wills*, pp. 30–33.
[3] Cf. *C–B.C*, 24^b.
[4] Made free 25 June 1606 (Arber iii. 683). His bonds were recorded in *Liber C2*, 19^a.
[5] Made free 6 May 1613 (Arber iii. 684).

26° martij 1625 Rẹ Jac. 23: et vltimo die euis vitæ/

Present — Mr Lownes sen' mr Lownes Jun' mr Cooke mr Waterson mr Swinhow mr Knight mr Islip mr Kingston mr Weaver.

Riders dictionary
mr Waterson
mr Leake
mr Bill
mr Islip
mr Kingston

John Legat

Whereas It pleased the lo. Archb: of Canterburye and lord Keeper, (in the matter where John Legat Complayneth against Adam Islip and others for the printing of Riders dictionary) to direct the said Legat to repaire to the Company and to ende the difference among them selues if they Could. This day the said ꝑtenors in the said booke did referr them selues to the Table of assistantẹ who are no ꝑtenors in this booke but the said Legat would not referr it vnto them, So the Controversye remayneth vndecyded[1]

mr Jackson. — This day mr Jackson is appointed Rentor warden to Joyne wth mr Aspley

mortuus est about the 18 of June 1625[2]

Aug: Mathewes. — Augustine mathewes ffine of 30s for some services done to the Company is this day be Consent of a Court remitted[3]

Nich. Okes. — md received of mr Okes of a fine of iiijli but xs. et ꝑdonatr residuũ.[4]

4° April 1625

mrs Agas.
mr Whitacres

mrs Agas being marryed out of the Company election was made for her half yeomandry parte and it fell vpon mr whiteacres. there stood in election wth him ffra: ffaulkner & Nath. Newbery and the said mr whiteacres tooke his oath accordinglye.

mr Swinhow mr Pavier mr Islip and mr Kingston are appointed to veiwe the hall and Counsell chamber and take some order to repaire the said Counsell chamber as by Conference wth workemen they shall thinke it safe

mr Langhorne/ — mr Langhornes lease[5] to be deliu'ed vp by Consent which was afterwardẹ done by aduise of mr Comon sergeant and in the p̃nce of mr Cooke & mr weaver

[1] STC 21035. This edition leans heavily on STC 24017, which was Legatt's property, cf. *P.M.L.A.* lii (1937), 1014, and for which he had a patent for twenty-one years, 13 Feb. 1621; cf. T. Rymer, *Foedera*, xvii (1727), 283.

There were originally eight partners (Arber iii. 276), but the parts of White and Burby evidently had lapsed. Of the five present partners, Islip owned two shares, which he acquired from Adams and Blount, the latter having married Bankworth's widow (Arber iv. 127). Kingston had acquired Man's sixth part (Arber iv. 97), and Bill presumably had Norton's part.

[2] Roger Jackson.

[3] According to a note in the *Book of Fines*, 19a, the service he had done was in discovering a press. Nevertheless, he is there recorded as having paid 10*s*. Mathewes was fined 4 June 1621 (*C–B.C*, 68b) £4 for printing STC 25924. On 9 July 1621 he paid £1 (*Book of Fines*, 16a), and again before 23 Aug. 1621 he paid another 10*s*., 'so there remayneth vnpaid ls. This ls was afterward pdoned for some seruice don to the Company' (*Book of Fines*, 16a). There is no record of the other 10*s*.

[4] This was Okes's fine for printing an edition of STC 25924, cf. *C–B.C*, 68b, 4 June 1621.

[5] The Woodstreet property, cf. *C–B.C*, 56b, 31 Aug. 1619.

Mr Dickens. Mr Dickins mocõn to renew his lease at Bellingsgate is to be considered of by mr Cooke mr Gilmyn mr Pavier mr Islip and mr Kingston.

Mr Piper/ The Chardg of Pipers Judgmt is to be borne by order of this Court by the English stocke and the latyne stocke part pte like[1]

Fol. 86a

6o Maij 1625 Re Car' primo/

Present/ mr Lownes sen' mr Lownes Jun' mr Cooke mr Norton mr Waterson mr Swinhow mr Gilmyn mr Cole mr Knight mr Islip mr Kingston mr Weaver.

mr Smithicke It is this day ordered that mr Smithicke in regard of his extraordinary paines and Chardg in Collecting the Rente and arrerages, having brought in 63l 6s. 2d/ shall have allowed him out of owne Collection. 3l. 4s.

Wm Garret/ Fine/ Whereas wm Garret in great Contempt of the gou'mt of the Company hath vsed vnfitting wordes to mr Gylmyn an auncient of this societye who was desired by the wardens to search for bookes bound in sheepes leather contrary to order.[2] It is ordered that he shall pay for a ffyne for his misdeameanor—xxs.

Tertio Maij 1625.

The Copie of a note concerning Dor Crakenthorps booke.

Dor Crakenthorps booke/ Memorand that wee the ouerseers of the lattyn Stocke doe hereby acknowledge to have received into the sayd stocke 665 of the bookes Called Defensio Ecclesiæ Anglicanæ[3] sett forth by Dor. Crakenthorpe in 4to Contayning 84 sheets as appeareth by Mr Kingstons account and Whereas mr Cooke nowe warden of the Companye of Stationers out of the house money resting in his hands hath defrayed all Charges for paper and printing the whole ympression thereof we doe alsoe hereby Consent and Condicõn to be accountable to the said warden and to the Successors of the said wardens of the Companye of Stacõners for the tyme being (accountting them as percell of the stocke of the [house]) at iiijs p booke allowing iiijd the booke to the lattyne stocke for as many as shalbe sold according to agreemt. In witnes whereof we the aforesaid ou'seers have herevnto sett or handes the day and yeare above written

Symon Waterson
Clement Knight
John Hodgetts
Godferye Edmondson

1 Presumably this has no connexion with the threatened lawsuit, 18 Aug. 1624, *C–B.C*, 82b.

2 Cf. Arber i. 100, where R. Harvey was fined 'for byndynge of greate bokes in shepes lether'.

3 STC 5975. Cf. *C–B.C*, 84a, 17 Jan. and 7 Feb. 1625. There are actually 83¼ sheets.

Vltimo Maij 1625

Present — mr Lownes sen' mr Lownes Jun' mr Cooke mr Norton mr Waterson mr Coke mr Knight mr Pavier mr Bill mr Islip mr Kingston mr Weaver.

mr Bill
mr. Downes.
Robte Younge
John Waterson

This day election was made for mr Manns[1] Assistants part, and it fell vpon mr Bill their stoode in election mr Islip and mr Kingston. Then election was made for mr Bills livery pte, and it fell vpon mr Downes, mr Alldee and mr Rodway[2] stood in election with him. Then election was made for mr Downes yeomandrye part and it fell vpon John Waterson & Robte younge.

Mr Knight — Md The Counterpte of an assignement of Clement Knight Humfrey Lownes Geo: Swinhowe John Budge John Rodway[3] and Willm Barenger to Roger Jeston. of houses in Paules Churchyard with a proviso to save them harmeles from certaine recognizance in Guildhall for the Children of Edward Taylor was deliu'd by order to the Stockeeps to be safely kept. 19o Maij 1625.

12 Jũij 1625.

Present — mr Lownes sen' mr Lownes Jun' mr Cooke mr Norton mr Waterson mr Knight mr Pavier mr Weaver

Geo: Edwards
Geo: Hodges

This matter betwixt Geo. Edwards and Geo: Hodges being referred by the lo: Mayor to the mr & wardens of this Company. It is ordered by Consent of both pties That forasmuch as it appeareth that Geo: Hodges is endebted to Geo: Edwards the some of 10li That the said debt shalbe paid in forme following vizt 5li thereof to be paid in money by 20s a quarter the ffirst paymt. on michis day next and mr Hodges the father to give his bill for payment of the said 5li. for the other 5li the said Geo: Edwards is to have it in such bookes as mr Pavier and mr weauer shall thinke fitting and appoint

eodem die vt ante

Present

Eph. Dawson — This day Ephrim Dawson is elected into the livery of this Company for a fine of xxli whereof he hath paid xls and is to paye viijli more on saterday come seavennight and xli more on all saints day next which [*I doe hereby*] [he doth] promise to performe accordingly.

witnes [*my*] [his] hand.

Ephraim Dawson

[1] Thomas Man, Sen. [2] Cf. *C–B.C*, 76a, 8 Feb. 1622. [3] Cf. *C–B.C*, 76a, 8 Feb. 1622.

22° Junij 1625.

Mrs Jaggard
Mrs Barret

Vpon hearing of the matter betwixt mrs Jaggard & mrs Barret Concerning the printing of the lo: Verulams Essayes.[1] It plainely appeared that the booke lately printed by mrs Barret is mrs Jaggardę proper Copie wth some alteracōns and addicōns therevnto. And therefore (the matter being put to the table by Consent of both pties) It is thought fitt and so ordered That mrs Barret shall give vnto her the said mrs Jaggard ffiftye of the same bookes in quires. And mrs Barret is not to printe yt any more wthout her Consent, onely so much as is not mrs Jaggards she may printe at her pleasure.

Rich: Meighen

Whereas Rich: Meighen hath kept 2 boyes in his shoppes Contrary to order aboue halfe a yeare vnpresented. It is ordered that he shall pay for a ffine xxs.

Rich: Kynasten
Rich: Trirett.[2]

And it is further ordered that he shall put away one of them with in 8 dayes vpon paine of xls and xxs for eu'ie weeke that he shall keepe after.
And for the other boy he is likewise to put him away or present him here vpon the like penaltye

John de Luna

It is ordered that John De Luna a Converted Spanyard and a preacher shall have given him in bookes 5li for his Incouragement.[3]

27° Junij 1625. Rę Car' primo

Present

Mr Lownes sen' mr Lownes Jun' mr Cooke mr Waterson mr Cole mr Knight mr Pauier mr Islip mr Weauer.

Wm Sheffard
Joh: Bellamy
Ben: ffisher

Vpon the report of mr Knight & mr Pavier in the matter betwixt Ralfe Rounthwaite John Bellamy & Willm Sheffard Concerning a booke called The signes or an Essay Concerning the assurance of gods love & mans salvation with the Touchstone of a Christian or the signes of a godly man by Nichīs Byfeild[4] which was bought of [*Ben. ffisher 2 thirdę*] Jonas Man and by the said Ben: ffisher 2 thirdę thereof sold to Wm Sheffard and John Bellamy. It appeared to the said refferres to be the same booke formerly entred to mr Tho: Man & Jonas Man and so bought & sold as aforesold (*sic*) And therefore it is nowe ordered by a full Court. That it shalbe entred for the Copie of Wm Sheffard John Bellamy and Ben: ffisher.[5]

1 STC 1147. Regarding the ownership of these copyrights, cf. *C.H. Pforzheimer Cat.* i, 33–38.

2 Neither of these men is registered as having been made free.

3 Juan de Luna published several books, cf. STC 16925–8.

4 There is an edition of STC 4236, 12°, with imprint 'I.D. f. W. Sheffard, I. Bellamie, a. B. Fisher, 1624', at the Folger.

5 Entered the same day (Arber iv. 143).

Jonas Wellins. Jonas Welling[1] is elected into the livery of this Company and hath paid in seaven poundę in part of his ffine of xx li and doth promise to pay thirteene poundes more on all saintę day next ensueing

Jonas Wellines.

Mr Swinhow Master Fol. 87b

Mr Gilmyn, Mr Islip wardens.

13°. Septemb. 1625.

Ellen Rockett mr Harper. This day Ellen Rockett[2] resigned her parte being halfe a yeomanry part to Tho. Harper who by Consent of this Court was admitted therevnto and tooke his oath accordingly.

17° Septemb. 1625 Rę Car' primo/

John Edwardę mr Swinhowe. Vpon the request of Mr Joh. Edwardę made to this Court he hath lycense to assigne his yeomanry share in the English stocke to mr Swinhow to secure vnto him an Certaine some of money which the said mr Swinhowe hath lent unto him which appeareth by a bill vnder his hand/

mrs Collins mr Harper Ric Badger. The same day election was made for Mrs Collins[3] lyvery pte she being lately dead, and it fell vpon Mr Alldee his yeomanry part fell vpon mr Harper, & mr Harpers halfe part vpon Rich. Badger.

Josias Parnell. Edw. Bruster The same day also election was made for Josias Parnells yeomanrye parte in the said English stocke and it fell vpon Edw. Bruster[4]

ffine mr Aldee. On the same day mr Aldee brought in x li being parte of his ffine for not serving Rentor warden And it is ordered that the residue of the said ffine shalbe abated out of his worke

Octob. 28 1625.

Humferye lownes. Tho. lownes. This day election was made for humfrye Lownes the younger his yeomanrye parte,[5] and it fell vpon Tho. lownes.

Mrs. lownes This day mrs Lownes late wife of Mathew Lownes deceased sent in x li for a remembrance for her husband, & it was received by mr Islip warden/

[1] Jonas Wellings was made free 20 Mar. 1602 (Arber ii. 731).

[2] Presumably the widow of William Rocket, made free 7 Apr. 1595 (Arber ii. 203).

[3] Mrs. Richard Collins.

[4] Made free 28 Apr. 1615 (Arber iii. 684).

[5] He was evidently deceased, for the entry of a later date cited in McKerrow's *Dictionary* was his father's.

Mr Blount
mr Purfoote. Mr Blount & Mr Purfoote are this day taken in to the Assistantę.

Mr weaver is to ioyne wth mr. waterson & mr Knight in the busines of the latyne stocke/

Fol. 88a 27° Novemb. 1625 Rę Car' primo

Present/ mr waterson loco mr̃i mr Gilmyn mr Islip mr lownes mr Knight. mr Cooke mr Kingston mr Weaver/

mr Rothwell This day election was made for mrs Jaggardę[1] livery pte in the English stocke. it fell vpon mr Rothwell. mr Rothwells yeomandry pte fell vpon Isaake Jaggard/

Fr. Faulkner. Mrs Bonyon[2] this day assigned her half yeomanry pte by Consent of the table to ffran. ffaulkener/

5° Decemb. 1625.

Present/ mr Swinhow mr Gilmyn mr Islip mr Waterson mr Lownes mr Cole mr Knight mr Cooke mr Kingston mr Weaver mr Blount mr Purfoote.

Mr Swinhow
mr Blount

pd the 1st of August 1631 againe engaged to mr Rob: Bankworth

[Whereas mr Blount is endebted to mr Swinhow the some of 160li this day the said mr Blount did assigne ou' his livery part in the English stocke for the paymt thereof at Sixe monethes and the said mr Swinhow is to have the benifitt of the same stocke till such time as the said debt be payd]

Nic: Okes This day one mr Morgan Complayned, that mr Okes hath had a booke called Speculum animæ[3] five yeares to printe and hath done onely sixe sheetę It is ordered that the said Nich. Okes shall bring them pñtely to the hall and goe forward in printing before Candlemas next & finnish the booke before Easter terme next otherwise he is to loose the said Copie and so much of it as shalbe then printed: Nich. Okes.

John Cleaver[4] is chosen porter in Edm: Mose his place.

Eph: Dawson. Mrs Browne[5] assigned her livery pte to Eph: Dawson in the English stocke, so mr dawson hath the livery pte and mrs Browne the yeomanry.

mr Ward. Md mr warden Islip agreed wth mr ward to serue the markettę till or lady day according to a precept from the lo. Mayor[6] for xli. which was pformed by the said mr ward, and paid by mr Islip accordingly

[1] Elizabeth Jaggard, widow of John Jaggard. Her will was proved 22 Nov. 1625.
[2] Widow of Richard Bonion.
[3] Apparently this book was never published.
[4] Made free 5 Mar. 1604 (Arber ii. 736).
[5] Possibly widow of Joseph Browne.
[6] Transcribed in *Letter Book*, 105a, 23 Nov. 1625.

6° Decemb. 1625 Rℯ Car' primo **Fol. 88b**

Pntib⁹ vt ante/

John Norton. This day John Norton is admitted to the livery of this Companye for xx^{li} where of he hath paid in hand x^{li} and is to pay x^{li} more at o^{r} lady day next

mr Lawe: This day Mr Law by Consent of the boord did assigne his livery part in the English stocke to his sonne in law. Joh: Norton[1]

Edw. Medlicote And the said John Norton did assigne his half yeomanrye parte to Edw. Medlicot[2]

Jonah Man Paule Man The matter betwixt Jonah man & Paule man being referred to the boord, It is ordered that where m^{r} Pavier deceased & Joh. Bellamy were to have the printing of some of mr Tho: Mans Copies for a certaine time and to allowe him 16^{d} vpon a reame,[3] That Jonah shall have x^{d} therof and Paule: vj^{d}/

Md̄ Jonah man hath license to morgage his English stocke to Paule man for 65^{l} for a yeare.

5° January 1625.

Pn̄te mr Swinhow mr Islip mr Waterson mr Cole mr Knight mr Bill mr Weaver mr Purfoote.

Na: Newbery Hen. Holland. Election was made for m^{r} Budg his yeomandry p̱te and it fell vpon Nathaniell Newbury and Hen: Holland

mr Cooke Chr. Meredeth In the matter where m^{r} Cooke[4] Complayned against Christofer Meredeth, the said Christofer absolutely refused to referr the matter betwixt them to the Consideracon of this Court neu'theles it is ordered that the said Christofer shall have no other appn'tice bound vnto him till such time as he hath given satisfaction to m^{r} Cooke or submitted him self to such order as the m^{r} & wardens shall sett downe.

And: Bilton. Andrew Bilton[5] is ordered to pay for a fine for refusing to take the Clothing being elected therevnto:—xls.

18° Feb 1625 **Fol. 89a**

Pn̄te m^{r} Swinhow m^{r} Gilmyn mr Islip mr Waterson mr Cooke mr Kingston mr Weaver mr Blount m^{r} Purfoote/

m^{r} Parker. m^{rs} Barret/ This day m^{rs} Barret by Consent of her father did assigne her livery part to mr Parker who is admitted by this Court/ mrs Barret hath a yeomanrye p̱te still/[6]

[1] This clears up the confusion in McKerrow's *Dictionary*, p. 170, for Law's daughter Alice was the wife of J. Norton, Jun.

[2] Made free 14 Jan. 1622 (Arber iii. 685).

[3] No other record of this arrangement is known, but it is similar to that of Edward White, 1 Sept. 1619, *C–B.C*, 57^{a}.

[4] Unidentified, but possibly father of one of the George Cookes.

[5] Made free 6 May 1606 (Arber iii. 683).

[6] Why Mrs. Barrett's father's consent was necessary, unless he had lent money on the security of the part, is not clear.

Mr Isip (*sic*) mr Fetherstone Joh. Patrich/	Election was made for mrs Lownes[1] assistants parte it fell vpon mr Islip. his livery part vpon mr ffetherstone, & his yeomanry part vpon Joh. Patrich[2]
Wm Crawley Wm Garrett	Edward Gossons yeomanry parte fell vpon wm Crawley[3] and willm Garret and they were admitted & sworne/

23 Feb. 1625: Pñtibus, vt supra/

Hen. Seile/	mrs. Snodhams[4] yeomanry parte in the English stocke fell vpon Hen: Seile/

mr Marke House — whereas mr waterson mr Knight and mr Mathew Lownes deceased did become bound to mr Marke House for the paymt of 312li. It is now this day acknowledged that the same money was borrowed and taken vp of the said mr House for the gen'all vse of the ptenors in the latyne stocke And the said ptenors doe agree to stand debtors for the same and doe promise to make paymt thereof to the said mr House his exrs or assignes wth Interest in the meane time as it shall growe due.

mr Stansby	Mr Snodhams Copies are to be entred to mr Stansbye by order of this Court.[5]

Primo martij 1625

Stockeepers for ye English stocke	mr Blount mr Purfoote	mr Mead. mr Stansby	John Bellamy. Ed. Bruster.
	Threasurer mr Weaver.		
	mr Knight mr Kingston	mr Harrison mr Jo. Dawson	Joh: Wright Nat. Newberye.

Hen: Walley	It is ordered that Hen: Walley shall have the next 50li of mr John Norton bequest putting in good securitye[6]
Ric: Badger	That Rich: Badger shall have the second 50li[7]
Rob. younge	That Robert young shall have the third 50li[8]
Tho. Symonds.	That Thomas Symonds shall have 12li.[9]

[1] Mrs. Matthew Lownes.

[2] John Partrich, made free 24 Oct. 1622 (Arber iii. 685).

[3] Made free 16 Jan. 1610 (Arber iii. 683).

[4] Mrs. Thomas Snodham.

[5] Cf. Arber iv. 152–4.

[6] His bonds were recorded 20 Apr. 1626, in *Liber C2*, 111b.

[7] His bonds were recorded 17 May 1626, in *Liber C2*, 111b.

[8] His bonds were recorded 12 June 1626, in *Liber C2*, 112a.

[9] Made free 30 June 1618 (Arber iii. 684). His bonds were recorded 6 Apr. 1626, in *Liber C2*, 19a.

6° Martij 1625 Rє Car' primo — Fol. 89b

Present. mr Swinhow mr Norton mr Gilmyn mr Islip mr waterson mr lownes mr Cole mr Knight mr Bill mr Cooke mr Kingston mr weaver mr Blount mr Purfoote.

Mr Islip. Mr Kingston — This day mr Islip did assigne by Consent of this Court his Assistantє part in the English stocke to mr Kingstone

mr Cooke. — It is ordered that mr Cooke[1] shall pay for his dinner that he should have made on the election day which was not done by reason of the late sicknes, vjli. and vli more he hath in his handє of mr mathew Lownes deceased In toto.—xjli

Item he is to pay for mr Recordrs ffee[2] omitted the last yeare. 2li. 4s.

Brian Greenehill — This day by Consent of the bord Bryan Greenhill[3] had his bond deliu'ed in for 12li but the money remayneth in the latyne stocke.

Mr Aspeley. — It is ordered that Mr Aspley for omitting his rentor dinner shall pay for a fine to the vse of the house—xiijli vjs viijd.

mr Lyon — It is ordered that mr Lyon shall have a lease of a house in Amen Corner[4] for 25 yeares to Comence at Christmas last rent 12li
This lease was sealed afterwardє by the ffeoffees

28 Martij 1626 Rє Car' secundo/

mr Fetherstone/ — This day mr ffetherstone is Chosen rentor to ioyne wth mr Rothwell.

3° April 1626.

mrs Barrett mr Parker — This day mrs Barrett assigned ou' her Copies to mr parker and by order of this Court they are to be entred vnto him salvo Jure cuiuscunqȝ[5]

13° April 1626. Rє Car' Secundo/ — Fol 90a

Present. mr Swinhow mr Islip mr Waterson mr leake mr Lownes mr Knight mr Bill mr Cooke mr Kingston mr Weaver mr Blount mr Purfoote.

mrs Barret. Rob. Allott. — This day election was made for mrs Barrettє yeomanry part in the English stocke she being lately married out of the Company and it fell vpon Robert Allott, there stood in election with him Tho. Bourne and Wm Lee and the said Robert Allott tooke his oath accordingly.

[1] Presumably Henry Cooke.
[2] Cf. *C–B.C*, 80a, 4 Feb. 1622.
[3] Made free 4 Apr. 1608 (Arber iii. 683).
[4] Part of Abergavenny House.
[5] Cf. Arber iv. 157, 3 Apr. 1626.

mr Wellins
Jos: Hurlocke.

This day by Consent of Jonah wellins[1] and Joseph Hurlocke[2] his late appr' The matter being referred to the Master wardens and assistantę of this Company. It is ordered that the said Jonah wellins shall make him the said Joseph Hurlocke free of this Company at midsomer next the said Joseph serving him till then as an apprentice.

Mr Gilmyn

This day mr Gilmyn by his lẽr requested the Company to have a new warden Chosen in his place and in respect of great losses he hath had this yeare to be exempted from further Chardg, The boord taking Consideracon thereof thought fitt and so ordered that he should be exempted from further chardg

mr Cole.

Then it was propounded to mr Cole that if he would supplie the place for the residue of this yeare it should be in stead of his second time vpper warden, but the said mr Cole desired to be spared from further service and offers rather to paie some reasonable fine, but in regard the said mr Cole hath done some good offices for the Company It is ordered that he shall be exempted from further seruice as he desireth and it is referred vnto his owne self what he will give the Company for a fine for his [*his*] dispensacõn/

mr. Knight
mr. Bill
mr Cooke/

whereas there are not any of th'Assistantę that have ben twise vnderwarden whereby there can be no election made for an vpperwarden at the next choyce which will be made in July next, It is thought fitting to putt some to their ffine, And mr Knight mr Bill & mr Cooke having ben once vnder wardens did consent to paie for the second time such fine as should be thought reasonable So it is ordered by this Court that they shall paie fiue poundę a peece for the second time vnderwardens and be eligible for vpperwardens at the next election/

Fol. 90b

18o Aprilis 1626 Rę Car' Secundo.

Present

mr Swinhow. mr Gilmyn mr Islip, mr Norton mr Waterson mr Lownes mr Cole mr Knight mr Bill mr Cooke mr Kingston mr Weaver mr Purfoote

Mr. Kingston.

This day mr Kingston had lycense at a full Court to engage his assistantę pte in the English stocke for Securitie of paymt of 200li which he is to borrowe at Guildhall, And it is ordered that this stocke shalbe lyable to saue harmeles such of the Company as shalbe bound wth him for the said some, wherevpon mr. weaver mr Stansby and mr Montforte became bound wth him for the said 200li and the said mr Kingstone made his deed to them as followeth

mr Kingstones
Covenant/

Bee it knowne vnto all men by theise pn'ts That whereas Edmund Weaver William Stansby and Thomas Montforte Citizens and Stacõners of London at the request and for the onely debt of me ffelix Kingston also Citizen and Stacõner of London Together with

[1] Made free 20 Mar. 1602 (Arber ii. 731). [2] Made free 3 July 1626 (Arber iii. 686).

me the said ffelix Kingston, in and by one Recognizance taken and acknowledged the day of the date of these pn'tẹ in his Maties. Court holden before. Sr Allen Cotton Knight lord Mayo[r] of the Cittie of London and the Aldrẽn of the same Cittie in the Chamber of the Guildhall of the same Cittye are and stand ioyntly and seu'ally bound to Cornelius ffish Chamberlaine of the same Cittye in the some of Two hundred and Three score poundẹ with Condicõn for payment of Two hundred poundẹ to the said Chamberleine or his successors to the vse of Thomas John ffrances and Anne Children and orphantẹ of Thomas Woodcocke marchantaylor being legacye money of Isaacke woodcocke gold smith their Vncle, and for doing and pforming of sundry other matters and things in the Condicõn of the said Recognizance mencõned as thereby more plainely may appeare: Nowe I the said ffelix Kingston for the better Indempnitie and saveing harmeles of all and ey'ue the aforesaid Recognitors their heires executors and Adm̃strators of and Concerning the some and somes of money in the Condicõn of the said Recognizance mencõned Due and belonging to the said Orphantẹ, doe hereby by Consent of the M[r] wardens and Assistantẹ of the Company of Stacõners London grant Assigne and sett ou' vnto the said Edmund Weaver William Stansby and Thomas Montforte all that my Assistantẹ parte in the English stocke, Nowe being in the handẹ and Custodye of the said M[r] wardens stockekeeps and Threasurer of the said Company of Stacõners wch said stocke amounteth at this pn'te or is by me to be made vpp the full sõme of Three hundred and Twentie poundẹ. And I doe Couenante and Agree that if default be made in payment of the said some of Two hundred poundes or in pformance of anie other matters or thingẹ in the Condicõn of the said Recognizance menconed Contrary to the forme and true meaning thereof. Then the M[r] wardens and Assistantẹ of the said Company or the more pte of them for the time being shall goe and proceed to election of an other ptenor in the steed and place of me the said ffelix Kingston, according to their orders in that behalfe. And that all the said stocke and some of money and pfitt that shall then arise or be due vnto me the said ffelix Kingston or to my said pte shall be paid and deliu'ed to the said Edmund Weaver William Stansby and Thomas Montforte their executors or Assignes for the payment of the debt and to acquitte exonerate and discharge them the said Recognitors their heires executors and administrators out of and from the said Recognizance, and of and from all Accõns suites and demaundes whatsoeu' to be had for or by reason of the same, In witnes whereof the said ffelix Kingston hath herevnto sett his hand and Seale the Eight day of June in the Second yeare of the Raigne of our sou'aigne lord King Charles &c. 1626

Felix Kingston/

Sealed & deliu'ed in the pn'ce
of *John Woodcocke*
Wm Longforde/

Eodem die vizt 18° Apr. 1626. pñtib[9] vt ante/ — Fol. 91[a]

mrs. Combes. / Rob. Bird / Tho: Bourne.

Election was made for mrs Combes[1] her livery part and it fell vpon Geo. Latham. his yeomandry parte vpon Robert Bird and Tho. Bourne, the said Robert Bird tooke his oath accordingly:[2]

[1] Mrs. John Combes.

[2] Presumably Bourne took it also.

Wm Peircehay — It is ordered that w^m Piercehay shall have 3^li of the money that the Company have of his.

Parrish Clarkes. — This day m^r Kingston is Chosen printer for the parrish Clarkes and is to enter into 500^li bond to printe nothing on that presse but onely weekely billes &c. according to my lo. of Canterburyes order[1]

2° Maij 1626.

m^r Aspley Rentor. — This day m^r Aspely brought in 7^li 6^s 8^d for the rento^rs dinner he should have vpon the lord mayors day being in the late sicknes time, and it was accepted of in leiwe thereof.

m^r. Purfoote. m^r Triplett. — This day m^r Purfoote and m^r Triplett are entreated to stand bound wth others in a recognizance in Guildhall for money taken vp for the vse of the latyne Stocke. and it is ordered that they shalbe saved harmeles by the parteno^rs in that stocke as they that are bound for the sam̄e heretofore/

20 maij 1626.

Rich: Badger: Policarpus Dawkins John Welles. — Whereas Policarpus Dawkins and John Welles are to be bound together wth Rich. Badger in the some of 100^li for the paiem^t of 50^li vpon the 17th of may[2] which shalbe in the yeare of o^r lord god 1629. vnto the m^r & keeps or wardens and Commaltye of the Stationr̄s which is the onely debt of the said Rich: Badger And whereas the said Rich: Badger hath a stocke in the Stationrs hall of foure score pounde or there aboute. It is this day ordered at the request of him the said Rich. Badger, that the same stocke shall not be taken out till such time as the said debt be paid without Consent of the said Policarpus Dawkins and John welles: And if the said debt be not paid at the aforesaid day by the said Rich. Badger then the stocke to be made ou' to some other pteno^r for the paiem^t of the aforesaid debt of 50^li and the residue to be paid to the said Rich Badger or his executo^rs.

Christe hospitall — Rec' from Christe hospitall of m^r w^m Nortons bequest[3] 6. 13. 4.
Paid to Christe hospitall of m^r Bishops bequest[4]—6. 0. 0.
To the m^r wardens Clarke & Beadle[2]—xiij^s iiij^d

Fol. 91^b

22° maij 1626

Present/ — Mr Norton loco m^ri. m^r Islip m^r waterson m^r lownes mr Knight mr Cooke mr weaver mr Purfoote.

m^rs Est. — At the request of m^rs [*Newbery*] [Est][5] it is this day ordered that in respect she is an auncient woman and that her husband bore all offices in the Company that she shall have a prentice bound vnto her, but this is to be made no president for any other

[1] Cf. James Christie, *Some account of parish clerks*, 1893, pp. 187–8. Kingston agreed 'under the penalty of £100 for divulging or allowing copies to be dispersed before the 7th January next ensuing'.

[2] The money was lent under John Norton's bequest and the bonds recorded in *Liber C2*, 111^b.

[3] Cf. Plomer, *Wills*, pp. 30–33.

[4] Cf. *C–B.C*, 24^b.

[5] Widow of Thomas East.

Geo. Wood — This day by order the presse & lẽrs lately taken at Borley in Essex from Geo. Wood was battered to peeces and the lẽr molten according to the decree in Starchamber

24° Maij 1626

Present. — m[r] Swinhow mr Islip mr Norton mr Waterson m[r] lownes mr Cole mr Knight mr Cooke mr Kingston mr weaver mr Blount mr Purfoote.

M[rs]. Feild — Whereas the some of 150[li] was heretofore borrowed of mr Ric. Feild deceased to the vse of the latyne stocke It is this day ordered that the Parteno[rs] in that Stocke shall be lyable to the said debt and make paiem[t] thereof to m[rs] Mary ffeild her ex[rs] or assignes, wth Interest in the meane time as it shall growe due

An. Euersdon
Ric. Meighen — The matter betwext Anne Everston[1] and Ric. Meighen is this day referred to m[r] Aspley and m[r] Brewster by Consent of both ꝑties and order of this Court who are to make an ende betwixt them if they can or to certifie their opinions before the 8 of July next/

m[r] Knight
m[r] Bill
m[r] Cooke. — Md m[r] Knight mr Cooke & m[r] Bill paid the 5[li] a peece they were fined at for the second time vnder wardens.[2] paid to m[r] Islip warden

John Norton. — John norton paid x[li] residue of xx[li] for coming on to the Clothing paid to mr Islip warden.

22° Junij 1626. Rẹ Car' 2[d]/ — Fol. 92[a]

Present/ — m[r] Swinhow mr Gilmyn mr Islip mr Norton mr Waterson mr Knight mr Cole mr Bill mr Cooke mr Kingston mr weaver mr Blount mr Purfoote.

W[m] Bladon — This day w[m] Bladon here pn'te in Court did agree to engage his yeomanrye ꝑte in the English stocke for the paiem[t] of a debt which he oweth to the latyne Stocke: but his mother in law mrs young is to have the Divident during her life, and after her decease the said Dividentẹ to goe to the paym[t] of the said debt to the latyne stocke

m[rs] Bradwood
m[r] Hoth.
w[m] Lee. — Election was made this day for m[rs] Bradwoodẹ[3] livery ꝑte and it fell vpon m[r] Hoth[4] his yeomandry ꝑte fell vpon w[m] Lee senio[r] and the said w[m] Lee tooke his oath according to the orders in that behalf

[1] No record of Mrs. Everston's complaint or the settlement is known.

[2] Cf. *C–B.C*, 90[a], 13 Apr. 1626.

[3] Mrs. Melchisidec Bradwood.

[4] John Hothe, made free 24 Apr. 1598 (Arber ii. 720).

Livery men Chosen this day.

Miles fflesher paies x^{li} in hand, & x^{li} the first of August next
Paid accordingly to m^r Islip/

John Haviland x^{li} in hand, & x^{li} All saintℯ day next by bond
Rich: meighen x^{li} in hand & x^{li} All saintℯ day by bond
Wm Sheffard x^{li} in hand & x^{l} All saintℯ day by bond.
ffrancis williams xx^{li} pd.
Rob. Allott x^{li} in hand, x^{li} more All saintℯ day next by bonde
All this money was paid to m^r Islip
accordinglie, and accounted for
as appeareth in his account/

Fol. 92^b

m^r Bonham Norton	master
m^r Clement Knight m^r Felix Kingston	wardens/

primo Augusti 1626 Secundo Car' Regis.

m^r Do^r Web. — This day m^r do^r webbes patent was distinctly reade for the teaching of Languages after a new method wth out Rules.[1]

Paule Man. Sara Symmes. — It is ordered that 55^{li} part of that which m^r Thomas Man his executo^r is to have for his part in the English stocke shalbe paid vnto Sara Symmes by Consent of Paule Man executor

Wm Bladon Edw. Bruster. — willm Bladons Copies by order of this Court are to be entred to Edw: Bruster.[2] Saluo Jure cuiuscunq.

m^rs Pavier Edw. Bruster Rob. Bird — Also m^rs paviers Copies by her Consent are to be Entred to Edward Bruster and Rob: Bird[3] Saluo &c.

mr Parker mr Budge. — Whereas by the death of m^r Budge all his Copies by the Custome of the Company are at the disposicōn of the boord, This Court for Consideracōns them therevnto moving doe order that they shall be entred to mr Parker:[4]

4° Septemb. 1626.

mr waterson loco m^ri. m^r Knight m^r Kingston mr lownes mr Cooke mr weaver m^r Purfoote.

Tho: Archer John Harrigate — This day Thomas Archer resigned his half yeomanry part in the English stocke to John Harrigate[5] and the said John Harrigate was admitted and tooke his oathe accordingly

[1] This was Dr. Joseph Webbe, who explained his system in STC 25169, petitioned Parliament for a grant of a patent for it in STC 25170, and, having received the patent, issued under it *Lessons and exercises out of Cicero ad Atticum*, 4°, by F. K[ingston], 1627, copies of which are in the Folger and British Museum; and *Pueriles confabulatiunculae, or children talke*, 4°, by F. K[ingston], 1627, a copy of which is in the Huntington. Both of these books are printed on one side of the leaves only. Besides these, he published under his patent, which was for thirty-one years, STC 23896 and 23898.

[2] Entered 4 Aug. 1626 (Arber iv. 164).

[3] Entered 4 Aug. 1626 (Arber iv. 164).

[4] See below.

[5] Made free 7 Oct. 1622 (Arber iii. 685).

mr Allott — mr Parker [*having*] having resigned his estat in m^{r} Budges Copies they are to be entred to mr Allott[1]

28 Septemb. 1626

Ric: Adams — Election was made for m^{rs} Dewes half yeomandry ꝑte and it fell vpon Rich. Adams and he tooke his oath accordingly

4° Octob. 1626.

Rob. Constable — This day Robert Constable[2] is elected to be of the Clothing and refused to accept thereof wherefore he is to pay according to the order xls which he promiseth to doe before Christmas next.

19° Octob. 1626 Rɇ Car' 2do. — Fol. 93^{a}

Present/ — Mr Norton, mr Knight mr Kingston mr Waterson m^{r} Lownes mr Cole mr Cooke mr Islip mr weaver mr Purfoote.

mr Stansby.
Geo. Woode. — In the matter where Geo. Wood complayneth against m^{r} Stansby for Copies that were Tho. Snodhams deceased It is thought fitt that 4 of the Assistantɇ be chosen by the said ꝑties to heare & ende the matter if they Can or to report their opinions.[3]

It is ordered that there be a portall made to the Counsell Chamber doore wthall Convenient speed

Hen: Bell — Henry Bell is to have 12^{li} of m^{r} w^{m} Nortons bequest[4]

Joh. Brockett — John Brockett[5] likewise to have the next xij^{li}.

m^{r} Segard — The consideracon of m^{rs} Segardɇ[6] peticõn is referred by her owne Consent to m^{r} Blount & mr Fetherstone.

mrs Fairebrother — It is ordered that m^{rs} ffairebrother shall have her rent made viij^{li} ꝑ annu' & have her lease renewed for the same terme for a fine of 40^{s}.[7]

mr Hawkins.
Ric Adams.
Tho. Bourne — mr Hawkins is this day Chosen to m^{rs} Jacksons[8] livery ꝑte mr Adams[9] to have the one half of m^{r} Hawkins yeomandry ꝑte and Tho: Bourne the other halfe.

[1] Entered 4 Sept. 1626 (Arber iv. 167–8).

[2] Made free 12 Dec. 1614 (Arber iii. 684).

[3] Stansby entered over a hundred of Snodham's copies, 23 Feb. 1626 (Arber iv. 152–4), but none of these appear to be the ones which Wood later printed. The basis of Wood's claim was that he had bought Snodham's press.

[4] Cf. Plomer, *Wills*, pp. 30–33. His bonds were recorded 6 Nov. 1626, in *Liber C2*, 19^{b}.

[5] Made free 12 Oct. 1618 (Arber iii. 684). His bonds were recorded 4 Dec. 1626, in *Liber C2*, 20^{a}.

[6] Presumably the widow of Benjamin Segar, alias Nycholas or Nicholson, last recorded 6 Oct. 1595 (Arber ii. 207). Cf. *C–B.C*, 95^{b}, 4 June 1627.

[7] Cf. *C–B.C*, 61^{a}, 6 Mar. 1620.

[8] Mrs. Roger Jackson.

[9] Made free 22 Oct. 1618 (Arber iii. 684).

5° Decemb. 1626

Present — m^r Norton m^r Knight m^r Kingston, m^r waterson m^r Lownes mr Swinhow m^r Cooke m^r Islip m^r weaver m^r Purfoote.

mr Lightfoote. — It is ordered that m^r John Lightfoote shall be of Counsell wth the Company and have a standing ffee of xls p annu' to be payd vnto him by the wardens of the Company for the time being

John Phillips And. Neile Presse. — This day the presse and lr̃s taken at old fford the nynth of this moneth from Joh Phillips and Andrew Neile for that it was erected contrary to the decree in Starchamber was melted & battered according to order

Mr Gough Mr Beale — The matter that Mr Gough Complayneth of against Mr Beale is referred to Mr Norton Mr Knight Mr Kingston Mr Islip and M^r weaver and Mr Beale is to be warned not to deliu' the bookes called Domesticall Dutyes till the matter be decyded and to attend on wednesday at one of the Clocke at our Masters house.[1]

Fol. 93^b

15° Decemb: 1626.

Present — Mr Norton Mr Knight Mr Kingston Mr Gylmyn mr Cole mr Bill mr Islip mr weaver Mr Purfoote.

Hugh Perrye — This day Hugh Perye desired to be made free of this Company by redemption wherevnto the table did Consent to admitt him for a fyne of 3^l. to be paid at Candlemas next.[2]

Wm Percehay — This day Mr Norton Mr Knight M^r weaver sealed a bond of 200^li for payment of 108^l to wil̃m Percehay vpon the ffifteenth of December 1627 for the English stocke.

Mr Burby — M^r weaver likewise and m^r Blount and m^r Sta[n]sbye sealed abond for 200^li to Mr Burbye for the same stocke.

And: Neile John Phillipps — This day a peticõn was brought in the behalfe of Andrew Neile and John Phillipps exhibited to my lord℮ grace, vnto wch the M^r and wardens made answeare that if they put in good bond not to transgresse againe the Company are Content they shalbe released.[3]

M^rs ffairebrother. — This day M^rs ffairebrothers Lease was sealed for 8^li. rent p annũm 44 yeares and a halfe from Michĩs last.[4]

M^d paid to mr weaver for affyne for the same lease according to a former order xls.

[1] STC 12120. This is part of STC 12109. The copyright in it was assigned by Bladen to E. Brewster, 4 Aug. 1626 (Arber iv. 164).

[2] Made free this day (Arber iii. 686).

[3] Cf. *C–B.C*, 93^a, 5 Dec. 1626.

[4] Cf. *C–B.C*, 93^a, 19 Oct. 1626.

18° Decemb: 1626.

Mr Whiteacres. Mr Whiteacers had leave by Mr Knight warden to engage his parte in the Englishe to Rich: Thraile for 20li.

6th Decemb: 1626. Fol. 94a

Mr ffarnabye. It was ordered by Mr Bonham Norton Clement Knight ffelix Kingston Adam Islip and Edmund weaver that the Copies entred to Raffe Rounthaite and printed for Philemon Stephens and Christo: Meredith shalbe Crost out of the booke of Entrancę for Copies and be wholly left to Mr ffarnaby to dispose of to some other of the Company to whom he will, and that Philemon Stephens and Chr: meredith shall give to Mr ffarnaby for 750. wch was last printed to recompence him for the printing of it against his will 45s. to be paid the last day of Candlemas terme.[1]

14° January 1626

Present Mr Waterson loco mr̃i mr Knight mr Kingston mr Swinhowe mr Gilmyn mr Bill mr weaver mr Purfoote.

Mr Cooke
Mr Allott The matters in Controu'sye betwixt mr Cooke and mr Allott Concerning Hen: Cooke[2] the younger the said mr Allottę appn' are referred to mr Islip mr weaver mr Blount and mr Aspley and the said mr Cooke and mr Allott entred into an assumpsit[3] of one hundred poundę by the deliu'ye of 6d. to each other to stand to the arbitrament of the 4. ꝑsons aforenam[ed] soe as they make and deliver their award before the ffirst munday in ffebruary next, provided that the said Allott be not compelled by their Award to receive the said Henry the younger into his service anymore.

6°. ffebru: 1626.

Mr Norton mr Knight mr Kingston mr waterson mr Cooke mr Islip mr weaver mr Blount mr Purfoote.

Wm Jones. Willm Jones confesseth that he keepes in his house desorderlye the appn' wch he had warning to put away: so by the said order he is in miserecordia viijs and he is to be fined besides at the discreacon of the Boord for binding him at a Scrivenors.

Mrs Griffin It is ordered that Mrs Griffin[4] shall have the next 50li that Comes in[5] but it is to be lent in the name of Mr Harp wth 2. other suretyes, mrs Griffin hath promised to engage her stocke in the Hall for his endempnity

[1] Rounthwaite entered, 16 Sept. 1624 (Arber iv. 123), Farnaby's *Phrases oratoriae elegantiores et poeticae*, 'the right being reserved of any perticuler man of the Company'. In the Folger is a fragment of an edition earlier than STC 10707, which may be the edition here referred to. Evidently F. Kingston was the stationer to whom Farnaby gave the right to print, and several unrecorded editions of Farnaby's works printed by him are known. Rounthwaite's entry was not crossed out, but 9 Nov. 1627 (Arber iv. 188) Kingston re-entered the *Phrases*.

[2] Made free 15 June 1627 (Arber iii. 686).

[3] An oral contract founded upon a consideration.

[4] Mrs. Edward Griffin.

[5] Of John Norton's bequest. The money was lent 13 Oct. 1627 and the bonds recorded in *Liber C2*, 112b.

Mr Stansby — This day mr Stansby had order to put away Smithicke[1] that he keepes disorderlye vpon paine of the penaltye in the order for fforrenors

21 ffebru: 1626.

Present — Mr Norton mr Knight mr Kingston mr waterson mr Swinhowe mr Cole mr Bill mr Cooke mr Islip mr weaver.

Mr Withers — It is ordered that if mr withers will deliu' to mr weaver acertaine number of his hymmes of every volume,[2] That mr weaver shall deliu' them out to the bookesellers who are to binde them wth the Psalmes and preferr them to Costomers and he is euery quarter to account wth mr withers and allowe him for soe many of the same as shalbe sold as shalbe agreed vpon betwixt him and the Company

Fol. 94b

eodem die vt ante.

Mr whiteacres, mr Sheffard — This day election was made for George Potters yeomandrye pte in the Englishe stocke and it fell vpon mr Whiteacres and mr Whiteacres halfe parte fell vpon mr Sheaffard and the said mr Shefford tooke his oath accordingly.

primo Martij 1626.

Mr Waterson loco mri mr Knight mr Kingston mr Cole mr Cooke mr Islip mr weaver mr Blount mr Purfoote.

Stockeeps for the english stocke	Mr Cooke Mr Islip	mr Bowler mr Parker	[*ffra: ffa*] [John Patrich] Chr: Meredeth

Mr Weaver Threasurer.

Auditors	Mr Waterson Mr. Swinhowe	Mr Smithicke mr Rodway	ffra: ffaulkner Hen: Holland

Robte Younge, Tho: Lownes. — This day at the humble suite and request of Thomas Lownes made to the Table, It is ordered that all the Copies wch belonged to Mr Mathew Lownes his father should first by the favour of the Companye be entred vnto him, And whereas Robert Younge Claymed all the Copies wch the said Thomas Lownes had anye right vnto vpon an agreemt heretofore made betwixt them, and that it appeared to this Court that the said Robert Younge had not given him a valuable Consideracon for the same, it is therefore thought fitt by this Court and soe ordered that the said Robert younge shall

[1] Presumably either George Smethwicke, made free 1 Aug. 1631 (Arber iii. 686), or Francis Smethwicke, made free 6 May 1633.

[2] STC 25908, &c. Cf. *C–B.C*, 76b, 10 Mar. 1623. No doubt this compliance was in response to an order of the Privy Council, cf. *Acts of P.C., January 1627–August 1627*, pp. 29–30.

give him such further Consideracõn as mr Cooke Mr Weaver Mr Islip and Mr Downes arbitrators indiferentlye chosen by the said ꝑtyes should award, And for the better effecting thereof the said Robert Younge and Thomas Lownes did by assumpsit binde themselues the one to the other in the some of 100li to stand to the arbitrament of the aforesaid 4. ꝑsons for the valuacõn of the said Copies soe as they make and deliu' their award in writeing before the 25 of this Instant March, And if the said 4. arbitrators doe not agree and deliu' vp their award before that tyme, Then the said Robert Younge & Thomas Lownes are to abyde the vmperage and order Concerniing the [*order*] premisses that the Mr wardens and assistantę or more parte of them shall make at the next sitting at Staconers Hall.[1]

5° Martij 1626. FOL. 95a

Robte House
Edw: Hailsby

This day there appeared at a Court Robert House[2] and his appn' Edward Hailseby[3] and vppon hearing of the matter that was alleadged on either side, the mr wardens and assistantę of this Company were of opinion that the said Edward Hailseby (having suffred imprisonment both in little ease and in the Counter[4]) had ben sufficientlye humbled for his lewed Courses, the ꝑtyes referred themselues to this table. It is ordered that the said Robert House vpon the submission of his servant should wth drawe his suite and sett his sayd appn' at libertye, and receive him into his house, and Concerning the Chardgs he hath ben at and the losse of his time It is further ordered that the said Edw: Hailseby shall not be made free of this Companye till such time as he hath given satisfaction to his sayd mr either by service or otherwise as they shall agree.

Newes.

A lr̃e from Mr Secretary Conway Concerning newes[5] wch was brought to the Company the 18th. of March last was this day reade in the pn'ce of Mr Butter and most of the printers in London.

Mr Southwood

It is ordered that mr Geo: Southwood a poore minister vpon his lr̃e shall have given him xs.

29° Martij 1627.

Rentors.

This day mr ffeatherstone and mr Butter are chosen rentors for the yeare following.

Hen: Gossen

The 12li recę of Mr Lee for Tarzey[6] lent to Henry Gossen.

[1] Entered 10 Apr. 1627 (Arber iv. 176); cf. *C–B.C*, 95b, 7 May 1627.

[2] R. Howes.

[3] Unrecorded.

[4] Little Ease and the Counter were prisons.

[5] Nothing appears to be known of this order, although later, 2 Aug. 1627, Butter was sent to the Gatehouse, cf. *Acts of P.C. 1627*, p. 470, and a newsletter of 14 Sept. remarks on the restraint put upon the printers, cf. *Trans.* xviii (1937), p. 374.

[6] Thomas Tarzey, made free 14 May 1612 (Arber iii. 683). The money was lent under W. Norton's will 13 May 1623, and the bonds recorded in *Liber C2*, 18a, where it is stated that the money was later lent to J. Brockett. Brockett was lent £12, 4 Dec. 1626 (*Liber C2*, 20a), and Gossen the same, 14 Mar. 1627 (*Liber C2*, 20a).

2° Aprilis 1627.

mr Waterson loco mr̃i mr Knight mr Kingstone mr Lownes mr Cole mr Bill mr Islip mr Cooke mr Weaver mr Blount mr Purfoote.

Mr Grismond — This day mr Grismond requested the Company not to proceed against him in starchamber[1] and submitted himselfe to the Companye, he Confessed to have .500. psalters and 10. reames of A. b. Cees wch he promised to bring in: he is by order to pay Chardges of suite and be bound not to transgresse any more and to bring in the said bookes.

Fol. 95b

eod̃ die pn'bus vt ante.

Augustine Mathewes — This day Augustine Mathewes had warning to put away 3. boyes that he Keepes disorderlye in his house wthin Eight dayes vpon the penaltye of 40s. for eu'ye eight [dayes] he keepes them or any of them Contrary to the order.

7°. Maij 1627.

Mr Norton mr Knight mr Kingston mr waterson mr Leake mr lownes mr Swinhowe mr Cooke mr Islip mr Weaver mr Blount mr Purfoote.

Mr Lownes / Robte Younge — It is ordered that mr Lownes his Copies and the Copies assigned from Thomas Lownes to Robert Younge shall be entred to mr Lownes and Robert Younge Joynetlye.[2]

4° Junij 1627

Mr Norton Mr Knight Mr Kingston mr waterson mr Lownes mr Islip mr weaver mr Blounte mr Purfoote

Tho: Cotes / Dor: Jaggard — The Copies belonging to Isaacke Jaggard deceased are to be entred to Thomas Cotes and Rich: Cotes by consent of Dorathie Jaggard widowe.[3]

Mr Islip / And: Hebb — It is this day ordered that the ffourth parte of the Copie called the Turkishe Historye[4] shalbe entred to Andrew Hebb by assignemt of Mre Adams and Consent of this Courte, but mr Islip is allwayes to have the workemanshipp of the printinge the whole booke according [to the entent of] the ffirst entrance[5] and to have for printing of it as he hath had heretofore.

1 Cf. *C–B.C*, 72b, 11 May 1622.

2 Entered 30 May 1627 (Arber iv. 180). Cf. *C–B.C*, 94b, 1 Mar. 1627.

3 Entered 19 June 1627 (Arber iv. 182).

4 STC 15054.

5 Cf. Arber iii. 223. T. Adams entered for G. Bishop's fourth part, 14 Mar. 1611 (Arber iii. 454). Cf. *C–B.C*, 149b, 7 Aug. 1637.

Mr Bill }
Mr Harrison } The matter in Controu'sye betwixt Mr Bill and mr Harrison by order of this Court and Consent of the said ꝑtyes is referred to mr Aspley and mr Butter to see the reckonings betwixt them and end all matters if they can, or to Certifye their opynions the next Court.

Eliz. Segar It is ordered that Eliz: Segar[1] shall have a pencõn of 3li a yeare the next quarter she is to have but a iis because the rest was paid for the buriall of the widd Crowe.[2]

16° Junij 1627. **Fol. 96a**

Present/ Mr Norton mr Knight mr Kingston mr waterson mr Lownes mr Swinhowe mr Gilmyn mr Cole mr Bill mr Islip mr weaver mr Blount mr Purfoote

Mr Weaver Election was made this day for mrꝭ ffeildꝭ assistantꝭ parte and it fell vpon Mr weaver there stood wth him mr Blounte mr Purfoote.

Mr Waterson mr weavers livyrye parte fell vpon mr John waterson mr Butter and mr Barrenger were in election.

wm Garrett }
John Grismond } mr John watersons yeomandrye parte fell vpon wm Garrett and John Grismond.

Mr Montforte. It is ordered that mr Thomas Montforte shall have newe leases both of the house where he dwells and that wch was demised to Jonas man for 31. yeares to Comence at Michĩs next paying for both lxli ffyne and for the same Leases 6li ꝑ annu' to be made wth the same Covenantꝭ.[3]

John Cleaver This day a bond of 12li was deliu'ed out to John Cleaver[4] but the money is to be paid by the latyne stocke wch oweth the same to the sayd John Cleaver for worke, it is one of the 12li of mr William Nortons bequest[5] to be lent out from 3. yeares to 3. yeares according to his will.

Eliz: Cotton }
Hugh Brewer } This day Eliz: Cotton[6] surrendered over halfe her yeomandrye in the Englishe stocke to Hugh Brewer who tooke his oath accordinglye.

Mrs Jaggard
Math: Coserdine }
Tho: weaver } This day mrꝭ Jaggard[7] assigned over her yeomandry parte in the Englishe stocke to Math: Coserdine[8] and Thomas weaver and by Consent they were admitted and tooke their oathes accordingly.

[1] Cf. *C–B.C*, 93a, 19 Oct. 1626.
[2] Possibly the widow of Christopher Crow, apprenticed 1567 (Arber i. 325).
[3] Cf. *C–B.C*, 49a, 1 Dec. 1617, and 48a, 14 Aug. 1617.
[4] Made free 5 Mar. 1604 (Arber ii. 736).
[5] Cf. Plomer, *Wills*, pp. 30–33. The money was lent 29 Mar. 1622 (*Liber C2*, 17b).
[6] Presumably widow of Robert Cotton.
[7] Elizabeth, widow of John Jaggard.
[8] Matthew Costerdine, made free 20 Aug. 1599 (Arber ii. 724).

FOL. 96b vltimo die Jnij 1627. pn'tib9 vt ante

Election was made this day for Mr and wardens
Mr Norton mr Lownes mr Cole were in election for Mr
mr Knight mr Bill mr Islip for vpper warden.

Mr Islipe — Mdd that mr Islip hath ben but once vnder warden soe he is not Capable [to] stand for vpper warden vntill he paies a ffine for his dispensacõn wch is respited till some other time.

mr Kingston mr weaver mr Blount in election for vnder warden.

Mr Stansbye. — It is ordered that mr Stansbye for some iniurious and reproachfull wordę vsed against our mr openly in the hall shall forbeare Comyng to the Hall amoung the liverye and shalbe sequestred from the benifitt of his parte in the Englishe stocke till such time as he doth Confesse his fault and give our mr satisfaction by publique acknowledging thereof.[1]

Mr Montforte — This day were sealed two leases made to Tho: Montforte the one of the house where in he dwelleth for 31. yeares to Comence at our lady day last 1627 rent 4li p ann', the other of the house wch was Jonah Mans for 31. yeares to Comence at our lady day last 1627 rent 2li p ann', and whereas affyne of 60li. was sett for him to paye nowe it is ordered vpon further

ffyne 50l. — Consideracõn that he havinge paid 50li. it should be accepted in full and the other 10li. remitted which said some of fifty poundę was acknowledged to be paid to mr weaver to the vse of the partenors in the English stocke.[2]

FOL. 97a Mr Cole Master
Mr Knight } wardens
Mr Weaver }

10 Julij 1627.

Present — Mr Cole mr Knight mr Weaver mr Norton mr Waterson mr Lownes mr Bill mr Islip mr Kingston mr Purfoote mr Harrison.

John Norton — } August: Mathewes } — This day John Norton and Augustine Mathewes bound themselues the one to the other in the so͞me of 500li to abide the awarde of Thomas Harper and marmaduke Persons in all matters in difference soe as they make their Awarde on or before the first of August next and in defect thereof then to abide the order of the Master wardens and Assistantę or more parte of them soe as they make their order before the 7th. of August next.[3]

[1] Cf. *C–B.C*, 97b, 3 Oct. 1627 and 19 Nov. 1627.
[2] Cf. *C–B.C*, 96a, 16 June 1627. Evidently these houses were part of the Abergavenny property.
[3] Cf. below, 6 Aug. 1627.

12° Julij 1627.

Present — mr Cole mr Weaver mr Norton mr Waterson mr Bill m[r] Islip mr Harrison.

Mr Blount. — It is ordered that m[r] Blount shall have 50[li] wch Thomas Montforte hath in his hande of this yeares Colleccõn of the rente in woodstreete to be Lent vnto him for three monthes.

Frances Lownes. — It is ordered That ffrancis Lownes shall have his Lease made vp 31 yeares from Michis next and he to bestowe good Cost on the house according to anote deliu'ed to the Companye and toward the repayring thereof he is to have by Consent of this Court allowed vnto him 10[li].[1]

6°. August 1627.

Present — Mr Cole Mr Knight Mr Weaver mr Waterson mr Lownes mr Swinhowe mr Islip mr Kingston mr Blount mr Purfoote mr Alldee mr Harrison.

John Norton / August: Mathewes — The matter betwixt John Norton and Augustine Mathewes is referred to Mr Islip Mr Purfoote Mr Harper and Marmaduke Persons and M[r] Kingstone to be vmpire who are to ende the matter betwixt this and the ffirst munday in the next moneth or to report to the board howe they finde the matter.[2]

26. Sept: 1627

Present — mr Cole mr Knight mr weaver mr waterson mr Lownes mr Bill mr Islip mr Blount mr Purfoote.

Mrs Griffin / Tho: Harper — It is ordered That mrs Griffin shall have the next 50[li] but the bond is to be made from Thomas Harper and others, because there is no president that money hath ben Lent to anie woman in this kinde, Mrs Griffin hath lycense to engage her pte in the English stocke to save the sureties harmeles.[3]

3° Octob: 1627. — Fol. 97[b]

Present — Mr Cole Mr Knight mr Weaver mr Waterson mr Lownes mr Swinhowe mr Islip mr Purfoote mr Blount.

W[m] Stansby / ffine — Whereas it was latelye ordered That Willm Stansby for some vnfitting worde vsed to our late master mr Norton, should not be warned to the hall amonge the Liverye, and that his parte in the English stocke should be sequestred till such time as he should submitt himselfe &c. Nowe it is ordered That he shall paye a fine

[1] Cf. *C–B.C*, 76[b], 3 Mar. 1623.   [2] See above, 10 July 1627.   [3] Cf. *C–B.C*, 94[a], 6 Feb. 1627.

of xx[t] [s] to the Companye and vpon his humble submission (if mr Norton shalbe soe contented) he shalbe restored in statu quo &c.[1]

John Walker. John Walker had warninge this daye to avoyde a boye Called James Messenger[2] wthin Eight dayes vpon payne of forfeitinge 40^{s}. and 20^{s}. for eu'ye weeke that he keepes him after that.

19° Novem: 1627.

Present Mr Cole mr Knight mr weaver mr Waterson mr Lownes mr Swinhowe mr Islip mr Kingston mr Blount mr Purfoot mr Harrison mr Bateman.

Mrs Lownes
Math Costerdine
Nicho: ffussell. The relicte of Thomas Lownes[3] being married eleccõn was made for her yeomandrye parte in the English stocke and it fell vpon Mathew Costerdine[4] for one halfe yeomandrye parte to make him vp a whole yeomandry parte and the other halfe yeomandrye parte fell vpon Nicholas ffussell and they tooke their oathes accordingly

Mr Swinhowe Memorand mr Swinhowe hath the Counterpt of the Assignement of the Lease of Tiffins house in Paules Churchyard[5] wch himselfe and mr Knight sealed to Math: Billing. Mr Swinhowe hath this Lease in his keepeing.

Jacob Bloome It is ordered That Jacob Bloome shall have the next 50^{li} That Comes in to be Lent out.[6]

Wm Stansby This day mr Stansby paid in xx^{s} for a fine heretofore sett vpon him for vnfitting words. And the board gave him backe againe x^{s} ex gra'.[7]

mr Trussell
98 It is ordered That mr Trussell shall have a newe Lease of the hand and dagger[8] for 31 yeares from Christmas next, x^{li} rent & 55^{li} fine if he buildes he hath leave to bring the foundacõn euen wth Needham and the other house.[9]

5° Decemb: 1627.

Wm Jones. Md That I Wm Jones doe by theise pn'ts disclaime all my estate right Title & intereste in the printing of all peticõns for prisons, as also That of the ffleete, And doe assigne ou' the same to Miles fflesher

[1] Cf. *C–B.C*, 96^{b}, 30 June 1627.

[2] Unrecorded.

[3] Probably of T. Lownes IV.

[4] Made free 20 Aug. 1599 (Arber ii. 724).

[5] Cf. *C–B.C*, 59^{a}, 19 Jan. 1620.

[6] In *Liber C2*, 112^{b}, it is recorded 'md that fifty pounds of the Rents in woodstreet was by order of a Court lent to Mr Bloome and Mr Weaver is to receive it of him out of the Chamber of london who are to pay him quarterly for maytenance of certaine orphans of Richard Bankworthes.'

[7] See above, 3 Oct. 1627.

[8] According to a schedule of leases, 1625, in the archives of the Stationers' Company, No. 230, it would appear that this house was leased to John Jaggard 9 Mar. 1612 for £13. 6*s*. 8*d*. rent.

[9] Cf. *C–B.C*, 98^{a}, 8 Dec. 1627.

to be entred vnto him for his Copies absolutely and for eu'. That nether I nor anie other by my Title shall clayme anie interest in anye of them. In witnes whereof I have herevnto sett my hand the day and yeare above written.[1]

Wm Jones.

8°. Decemb: 1627. FOL. 98a

Present — mr Cole mr Knight mr Weaver mr Norton mr Lownes mr Swinhowe mr Bill mr Islip mr Purfoote mr Harrison.

Mr Trussell.
97
It is agreed That whereas it was ordered That mr Trussell should pay 55^li^. That because it is conceaved to be a little to much in regarde of the Cost he is to bestowe on the house That he shall paye but 50^li^: 10^li^ rent p annu' and to have [it] for 31 yeares to begine at Christmas next.[2]

Mr Bill — At a meeteing this day about the Latine stocke the accounte and reckonings betwixt the partenors in that stocke and Mr Bill were pvsed and Cast vp and his debt by his account came to 920^li^ or thereaboute beside interest wch as he sayd came to 300^li^ more. The assistante That were present insisted vpon a farre lese some and for interest they sawe noe reason to allowe anie at all: In Conclusion after much debate and talke about the reckonings. Mr. Bill was Contented for peace and quietnes sake to accept of 800^li^ for his whole debt to be paid in forme following vizt 461^li^. 6^s^. 8^d^. vpon the 20th day of May next, and the residue vizt 338^li^. 13^s^ 4^d^ in money or bookes vpon the 20th of November following. And the Assistante then pn'te yeilded and Consented to the payment Thereof in manner and forme aforesaid.

George Miller. — George Miller hath Consent of this Court to assigne to willm Hobson and Nathaniell Seborne[3] his parte in the English stocke, that if he make default in payment of 50^li^ he borrowes of the Companye his parte to be sold to dischardge this debt.

4° ffeb 1627.

Present — mr Waterson loco mri mr Knight mr Weaver mr Swinhowe mr Bill mr Islip mr Kingston mr Purfoote mr Harrison mr Bateman.

Rich: Taylor — It is ordered that Richard Taylor shall have a pencon of 4^li^ a yeare for 5 yeares for the payment of 20^li^ wch he sayth he oweth to his landlord.

Mr Lisle
Ni: ffussell — This day mr Lisle assigned ou' his halfe yeomandrye parte in the English stocke to nicholas ffussell, who was admitted therevnto by consent of this Court.

[1] Entered 14 Apr. 1617 (Arber iii. 607), transferred 5 Dec. 1627 (Arber iv. 190).

[2] Cf. *C–B.C*, 97^b^, 19 Nov. 1627.

[3] The assignees were not stationers but had signed bonds for the loan of £50 under J. Norton's bequest recorded 8 Jan. 1628, *Liber C2*, 113^a^.

Robt Bostocke. It is ordered That Robert Bostocke shall have the 50[li] for 3 yeares That mr. Whiteacres is to pay in.[1]

John White
Robt Doleman
This day John White assigned ou' his yeomandrye parte in the English stocke by the Consent of the Companye to Robt Doleman,[2] And the said Robt Doleman tooke his oath accordinglye.

Fol. 98[b]

1°. Martij 1627.

Present mr Cole mr Knight mr weaver [*mr waterson*] mr Bill mr Islip m[r] Kingstone mr Blount mr Purfoote mr Harison mr Bateman

M[rs] Bounst als ffeild. It is ordered That mrs Bounst[3] shall have interest for her money That the latyne stocke owe vnto her late husband mr ffeild deducting the Chardge she hath put the Companye to in arrestinge mr Waterson and mr knight and her nowe husband mr Bounst and she are to wthdrawe the suite otherwise no money at all to be paid vnto them.

3° Martij 1627 pn'tib[9] vt supra

Mr Beale ffine It is ordered That mr Beale for vnfitting worde vsed to the Master of the Companye sitting in Court shall pay for a fine 40[s]. And it was ordered the 5th of May 1628. That this fine should be stayed out of his next Divident. vt patet postea[4]

Printers. Whereas divers Complainte have ben made against some of the printers that printe bookes for the English stocke That albeit they are very well paid for their worke yet the said stocke worke nowe of late for the most pte is done exceeding negligentlye and deceitefully to the preiudice and scandall of the whole Company besides the said printers are complayned of this day by the Stockeepers and the whole ptenors for not bringing in the overplus bookes nor the waste wch they are allwayes to doe vpon the finishinge of eu'ye Impression: for reformacõn hereof, it is ordered That noe printer hereafter shall appropriate anye of the worke, that belongs vnto the stocke, as to belong vnto himselfe but that the mr wardens and stockeeps shall dispose thereof to those that shall pforme the same in the best and most substantiall manner for the Creditt and Benefitt of the Stocke: and Concerning ou'plus bookes and waste the Thrẽr shall not pay the said printers [all] their money for their worke but allwayes keepe some parte thereof in his hande till such time as they have brought in the whole number that they were agreed withall to ymprint together wth the ou'plus bookes and the waste soe that all things being made euen and pfect and eu'ye Impression the Master and wardens and stockeeps may afterwarde dispose of the printing of the same Booke or bookes as they shall thinke fittinge.

1 Cf. *C–B.C*, 84[b], 7 Feb. 1625. His bonds are recorded 19 Feb. 1628, *Liber C2*, 113[a].

2 Made free 15 Dec. 1626 (Arber iii. 686).

3 Mrs. Richard Field.

4 Cf. *C–B.C*, 99[b], 5 May and 9 June 1628.

Evidences & Writeings 83. 89 — It is ordered That the Evidencę and writeings of the purchase of Abergavenny house nowe vsed for the Hall and of the Leases of the Tenemtę or houses that belong therevnto wch are kept by the wardens for the time being shalbe shewed to the stockeeps of the English stock if they desire to see them, and that a note or Inventory thereof be dd to the said stockeeps to be kept by them and to enter it into there bookes of acount if they thinke fitting eu'ye yeare.

eod die et anno vt ante. Fol. 99[a]

John Hamon — This day the presse that was yesterday taken at Lambeth hill,[1] for that it was sett vp contrary to the decree in Starchamber was battered and broken and the lres molten according to the said decree.

Presse. — It was the Presse of one John Hamon and it was at worke vpon the Primer. This is the fift presse that hath ben seized and taken from him.[2]

26° Martij 1628.

Present — mr Cole mr Knight mr Weaver mr Waterson mr Bill mr Blount mr Purfoote mr Harrison.

Hen: Holland — Henry Holland is Chosen Stockeep in John Patrich[3] Place because John Patrich by his peticon doth desire to be spared haveing served this last yeare, he is to be sworne the next Court day: he was sworne accordingly.

8° Apr 1628

Geo: Sandes. — This day mr Sandę Patent[4] for the sole printing of the 15. bookes of Ovidę Metamorphosis by him translated into English verse, was openlye reade in the hall this quarter day. And it is ordered that th'entrance to mr. Barrett and mr Lownes deceased of the first five bookes and the assignmt to Robt Younge, And the entrance of the whole 15. bookes to mr Stansby shalbe all Crost out of the Regester Booke of the Company, soe that noe man shall laye anie claime to the printinge of the same or any pte thereof.[5]

Capt: Rob: Le Grise / Barkley his Argenis — The verses of mr Thomas May in the former Booke of Barkleyes Argenis[6] are to be put to a newe translacon of Capt: Rob: Le Grise:[7] and the Booke is to be entred to mr Meighen and to Henrye Seile.[8]

[1] In Baynard's Castle Ward.

[2] The only earlier one recorded here is that found in Southwark, 1 Mar. 1625, *C–B.C*, 85[a].

[3] A very Bostonian pronunciation.

[4] Cf. T. Rymer, *Foedera*, xviii (1726), 676, granted for twenty-one years, 24 Apr. 1626.

[5] The first five books were entered to Lownes and Barrett 27 Apr. 1621 (Arber iv. 53). A copy of a second edition in 12°, printed for W. B[arrett]., 1621, is now in the Folger and another at Harvard. A third edition, 1623, is at Winchester College. Mrs. Barrett assigned her husband's share to J. Parker, 3 Apr. 1626 (Arber iv. 158), and T. Lownes registered his father's share 10 Apr. 1627 (Arber iv. 176). Stansby entered for the fifteen books 7 May 1626 (Arber iv. 160). Young's rights apparently were not registered, but cf. *C–B.C*, 95[b], 7 May 1627.

[6] STC 1392.

[7] STC 1393.

[8] Cf. Arber iv. 133, 144, and 196. Cf. letter of Le Grys to Philip, Earl of Montgomery, 26 Feb. 1628, *State Papers Dom. 1627–1628*, p. 585, and warrant issued in accordance with it, 28 Feb. 1628, *op. cit.*, p. 589.

5° Maij 1628/

Hugh Perrye This day Hugh Perrye had warninge to avoyde a boy That he keepes in his house disorderly wthin eight dayes according to the order for forrenors.

ffeoffees for Abergavenny house 98 A declaracōn by the ffeoffees of Abergavenny house (That it belongs to the English stocke) was this day reade and ordred to be registred in the booke of Precepts.[1]

Mr Lownes. It is ordered That mr Humphrey Lownes shall Continue to have the printing of the Psalter in octavo doeing of it well and workman like for the Creditt of the Companie.[2]

Robt Younge It is ordered That Robert Younge shall prepare himselfe to goe into Ireland to take accounts of Arthur Johnson,[3] and it is thoughte fittinge and ordered that one of his presses shall be kept at worke in his absence by some booke or bookes from the English stockeeps.

Fol. 99b

eodem die vt ante.

John Beale Whereas the Third of March last it was ordered That mr Beale for vnfitting words vsed to the master of this Companie sitting in Court and Contemptable behaviour should paie for a ffine 40s. It is nowe further ordered That forasmuch as he hath not brought it in and refuseth to paye it according to the same order, that it shall be staide out of his next divident.[4]

9° Junij 1628.

Present mr Norton loco mři mr waterson mr knight mr Weaver mr Lownes mr Swinhowe mr Bill mr Islip mr Kingston mr Purfoote mr Harrison mr Bateman.

Mr Beale It is ordered That mr Beale shall have his Last divident wholly paide vnto him, not wthstanding a former order to staye 40s for a fine and the Table will advise of some other Course to force him to paie th'aforesaid ffine for his Contempt.[5]

mrs Gilmyn It is ordered That mrs Gilmyn[6] shall have a pencōn of 4li a yeare during her widdowhoode.

Robt Young Tho: Weaver It is ordered That the lře of Atturney made to Robte Young and Thomas Weaver to examine Arthur Johnsons Accounts in Ireland, wch was reade this day shalbe sealed with the Coīnon seale.[7]

1 Cf. *C–B.C*, 98b, 3 Mar. 1628.
2 STC 2605.
3 Cf. *C–B.C*, 81b, 17 June 1624.
4 Cf. *C–B.C*, 98b, 3 Mar. 1628, and below, 9 June 1628.
5 Cf. above.
6 Mrs. Anthony Gilman.
7 See below, and *C–B.C*, 99a, 5 May 1628.

16° Junij 1628.

Idem — According to an order of the 13th of this Instant June the lr̃e of Atturney made to Robert Young and Thomas Weaver was sealed wth the Com̃on seale to examine Arthur Johnsons Accountę.[1]

mr Cole
mr Swinhowe
mr Bill/ — And at the same time also were sealed wth the Com̃on seale .3. billes of sale of plate, one to mr Do^r Eden for 100^li. an other to Walter Terrill for an other 100^li. the Third to James Burrage for 100^li more.[2]

23° Junij 1628.

Rich: Taylor
mr Tan.— — It is ordered That Richard Taylor shall have 50^li of mr John Norton bequest[3] for three yeares gratis and that his yeomandrye parte in the English stocke shall not be alienated or taken out till this debt be paid. but remayne in the Companies handę to secure and save harmeles mr Tan and the other suretye from this debt.

Christę hospitall — Rę of mr Rich: Harper thrẽr of Christę Hospitall for mr William Nortons bequest due 14 December 1627.[4] 6^li. 13^s. 4^d.

Item paid to the same hospitall for mr George Bishopps bequest.[5] 6^li.

mr Islip
mr Kingston — It is ordered That mr Islip and mr Kingston shall paye for their dispensacõn for not serving the second time vnder wardens the some of v^li a peece.[6]

Mr Cole master
Mr Islip
Mr Weaver — wardens

Fol. 100^a

17° Julij 1628.

Present — mr Cole mr Islip mr Weaver mr Waterson mr Lownes mr Swinhowe mr Knight mr Kingston mr Blount mr Bateman

Loanes — Whereas, 280^li. is by precept from my Lord to be paid in to the Chamber for parte of the Loane to his Matie. It is ordered That if the Companye be prest to paye it in: That it be taken vpp vpon the securitye

[1] See above.

[2] A precept of 18 Dec. 1627, from the Lord Mayor, demanding the loan to the King of £840 from the Company, part of a loan of £120,000 to be secured by royal lands to be sold by the City, is transcribed in the *Letter Book*, 107^a. After a second precept of 29 Dec. 1627, this was paid 11 Jan. 1628, the money having been raised by the Company in the manner detailed in the memorandum of 9 Jan. 1627, *Letter Book*, 107^b–109^a. This sale of £300 of the plate of the Company was arranged by Knight, Weaver, and Swinhowe, and included only the plate not pawned to members of the Company and later redeemed.

[3] Cf. Plomer, *Wills*, pp. 45–47. This was an old loan, here renewed, which was originally made 1 Mar. 1624, and Edmund Tan was one of his sureties recorded *Liber C2*, 110^b.

[4] Cf. Plomer, *Wills*, pp. 30–33.

[5] Cf. *C–B.C*, 24^b.

[6] Cf. *C–B.C*, 96^b, 30 June 1627.

of Mr Islip Mr Waterson Mr Kingston and Mr Harrison: and That the feathers be morgaged for their Indempnitye and alsoe to secure them that are bound for 300li more taken vp for this busines.[1]

Tho: Montfort — It is ordered That whereas Thomas Montforte hath ben allowed[2] 26s. 8d p annu' for Collectinge the rentę in woodstreete and distributing to the poore of St ffaithes 3s. a weeke, and for other paines Continually taken about the getting the rentę there. In regard of his paines taken therein. It is ordered That hereafter he shall have 2li 13s 4d p annu' out of his owne Collection allowed vnto him duringe his being collecter of those rentę.

4 August 1628.

Present — mr Cole, mr Islip, mr Weaver, mr Norton, mr waterson mr Lownes, mr Swinhowe, mr Knight. mr Bill mr Kingston. mr Blount mr Purfoote mr Harrison mr Bateman.

Mr Smithwick / Mr Havilond — The matter betwixt mr Smithwicke and mr Havilond about the Lord Verulams Essayes is referred to the wardens to heare and determine the Controuersye as they shall thinke fitting.[3]

Wm Aspley / John Parker — [*Md*] An order drawne vp by the mr of the Companye for putting mr Aspley and mr Parker from being stockeeps [*is entred in the reportarye booke*] as followeth made the ffift day of August 1628.

[*Primo Aug:*]

Quinto Augusti 1628 Rę Car' quarto/

Present — mr Cole master mr Adam Islip mr Edmund Weaver wardens mr Humphey Lownes mr George Swinhowe mr Clement Knight mr John Bill mr ffelix Kingston mr Thomas Purfoote mr John Harrison and mr John Bateman Assistantę.

Mr Aspley / Mr Parker — Whereas by the ordinances made and Confirmed vnder the great Seale of England for the managing of the English [stocke] it is ordained that the giueing of all receiptę and paymentę: and the executing managing and directing of all affaires, and the ymploying gou'ning and keepeing of all accountę and reckonings touching or Concerning the same, the master and wardens of this Corporacõn for the time being and 2. of the Assistantę, wth 2. of the liverye and 2. of the yeomandrye to be Chosen by the master wardens

[1] The precept is transcribed in the *Letter Book*, 109b. The Feathers was apparently a tavern property in St. Paul's Churchyard belonging to the Company. After three precepts (*Letter Book*, 110a) the £280 was paid on 1 Aug. 1628, and the money raised as detailed in *Letter Book*, 110b in a memorandum of that date. Cf. also *C–B.C*, 105a, 2 Nov. 1629.

[2] Cf. *C–B.C*, 65b, 7 Aug. 1620.

[3] STC 1149. Cf. *C.H. Pforzheimer Cat.* i. 38, regarding rights of Smethwick and Haviland in this book.

and assistantę or the more parte of them ioyned wth the said mr and wardens for the time || for the time [*sic*] being shall have the execucõn doeing and manageing thereof: Fol. 100[b] as by the said ordinances amongst other things therein Contayned may appeare: And whereas vpon Complaint made to the master wardens and Assistantę that william Aspley and John Parker .2 of the liu'ye of this Companye elected Stockeeps for the liu'ye the first day of March last past; have since the day of their eleccõn wthout the notice and privitye of the mr and wardens put out divers bookes appertayning to the said stocke to printers who have neglected and delayed the printing thereof, and also haue denied to deliu' out paper for the printing of the psalter being an other booke belonging to the said stocke, vnto mr Humphrey Lownes an auncient of this Companye who hath printed the same for many yeares in former times,[1] by reason of wch disorders and of other inconveniencę feared to ensue the said stocke is likely to be much hindred and preiudiced If good Care be not taken for the speedye prevencõn of theise and the like mischeifes vpon due consideracõn whereof the Master wardens and Assistantę calling the said Aspley and Parker as alsoe Henry Holland and Henry Seile two of the yeomandry of this corporacõn elected stockeeps for that rancke before them, the maister after divers Treaties and speeches had wth them in freindlye and peaceable manner about the foresaid complaintę, and their turbulent carriage and demeanor in their places perswaded and moved them often times to ioyne with him, the wardens and other stockeeps in the peaceable and quiett orderinge of the affaires Concerning the stocke; accordinge to the ordinances made for the good gou'mt thereof, and to open the dores of the warehouses, or to deliu' their keyes that the master and wardens wth the other stockeepers might goe in to deliu' out paper for the printing of the psalter, and to put out and dispose of such other worke, as was fitt to be done for the good of the said stocke, and the said Aspley and Parker in a ieereing and scornfull manner, not onelye refused and denied to ioyne wth them, or to open the lower warehouse doore or to deliu' their key, but disobedientlye puersly and frowardly demeaned themselves towardę the master wardens and Assistantę in the sight and hearinge of divers then and there pn'te; and caused diu's others ptenors in the Stocke of their owne faccõn to be called together to the Hall in whose pn'ce they gaue forth very disgracefull and scandalous speeches to and against the maister and wardens then || and there pn'te, wth a purpose to make a tumult or Combustion amongst the whole Fol. 101[a] Corporacõn: Wherevpon for avoyding of a Confusion wch in all likelyhoode is feared may happen vnto the foresaid Stocke by such disorders, the maister wardens and Assistantę this pn'te day being the fift of August at a full Court wth one Consent thought it very fitt and Covenient, and ordered that the forenamed William Aspley and John Parker be removed and put out of the offices and places of Stockeepers for the residue of this yeare ensueing: and soe they were removed, and in their places John Rodway[2] and James Boler two others of the liu'ye and partenors who in former times have borne this office were by the mutuall Consent of the master wardens and Assistantę, Chosen to be Stockeeps for the liu'ye, for the residue of the said yeare, and they tooke their Corporall oathes for the due execucõn of their places accordingly, And lastly for and in respect that the forenamed wiHm Aspley and John Parker have demeaned and behaved themselues disobediently pversly and frowardlye towardes the master wardens and Assistantę as aforesaid: It is

[1] Cf. *C–B.C*, 99[a], 5 May 1628.

[2] Cf. *C–B.C*, 76[a], 8 Feb. 1622.

ordered That the said Aspley and Parker during the time of their disobedience be suspended and removed from all such proffitt*e* as shall or may arise to him and them, by reason of his and their part*e* or porcõns in the said English stocke, and for the said limitted time be sequestred from the benefitt of their said part*e*, and that the benifitt thereof during such time shall goe to the vse of the poore of this Companye according to the ordinances sett downe in this behalfe.[1]

27 Septemb. 1628

Paule Man. Jonah Man. — It is this day ordered by Consent of Paule Man and Jonah Man that the Copies entred vnto them in the hall booke shall continue the one moitie to the said Paule and the other to Jonah as they are now entred and the said Copies not to be assigned or alienated w[th]out Consent of both parties[2]

p me *Paule Man*
Jonah Man/

Fol. 101[b]

6° Octob: 1628 Car' R*e* quarto/

m[rs] Browne W[m] Lee/ — This day m[rs] Browne[3] by Consent of the Boord assigned ou' her yeomandry part in the English stocke vnto w[m] Lee and the said w[m] Lee was admitted and tooke his oath accordingly

29. Octo. 1628

M[r] Gilmyn John Chappell — This day mrs Gilmyn[4] by Consent of the Boord assigned her yeomanry part in the English stocke vnto John Chappell[5] and he was admitted and sworne according to the order

1[mo] decemb. 1628.

Bible. — This day by warrant from the lo. B. of London the m[r] and wardens gave warning to the Bynders not to bynde the Bible wth the doctrine of Bible[6] the history of the Bible[7] or any other booke other then the Comon prayer the Psalmes, the geneologies[8] as are allowed wth authoritye to be bound therewith[9]

1 Under date 7 July 1641, *C–B.C*, 177[a], is an entry referring to this matter. 'Whereas about the yeare 1628. vpon a difference betweene M[r] Parker & M[r] Cole, diuers orders were entered vp in a very harsh manner against the said M[r] Parker (the said M[r] Cole being then Master of this Company) w[ch] remaine vpon record to his disparagem[t]. the said M[r] Parker now moued that the same might be razed out in regard the equity of his Cause then in question was ouerruled by the power of the said M[r] Cole & others of his friend*e* then Assistant*e* of this Company w[ch] the Co[rt]. for the most p[te] (though not then Assistant*e*) knowing the iustnes of the said M[r] Parkers Cause. Haue Now thought fitt & so ordered That all orders submissions & other Acts entred vpon Record in this booke of orders Concerning the said M[r] Parker in y[t] difference shall accordingly be defaced & razed out of the said booke of orders.'

2 Cf. Arber iv. 117, 3 May 1624.

3 It is not certain which Mrs. Browne this is, cf. *C–B.C*, 81[a], 7 June 1624.

4 Mrs. Anthony Gilman.

5 Made free 12 Jan. 1624 (Arber iii. 685).

6 STC 3029.

7 STC 19109.

8 STC 23039.

9 This was evidently an attempt to hinder the spread of puritan annotation, as was the prohibition against binding Bibles without the Apocrypha. Cf. also *State Papers Dom. 1630–1631*, p. 208 (53–54), the petitions of Clement Cotton to permit his Concordance, STC 7126, to be bound with the Bible.

8° decemb. 1628.

Mr Butter
Hen. Holland
Rob. Birde

This day election was made for mrs Sergers livery parte in the English stocke and it fell vpon Mr Butter, and his yeomanry ꝑte fell vpon Hen: Holland and Rob. Birde and they tooke their oathes according to order

Mr Smithicke
Rog: Michell

In the matter betwixt Mr Smithicke and Roger michell which heretofore was referred to mr Islip and mr Blount/ the said Refferees reported that they have examined the matter and finde that Roger Michell hath printed some of Owins Epigrams[1] (which is the proper Copie of mr Smithicke) in a booke which is called Hanmers Quodlibtę,[2] and therefore they thought fittinge that the said Roger Michell should give the said Joh Smithicke 50 of the aforesaid Quodlibtę and that the booke shall not be printed any more wthout Consent of both the said ꝑties which report this court approved of and ordered that it should be observed accordingly

20 Dec. 1628

Mr Cole. mr Islip mr weaver mr waterson mr Swinhowe Mr Knight mr Bill mr Kingston mr Blount mr Purfoote mr Harison Mr Bateman.

Mr Aspley.
Mr Parker.

It is this day ordered that forasmuch as Mr Aspley and Mr Parker have not submitted themselues but continue in their pervernes and Disobedience, That they shalbe still suspended from such profittę as doe arise to them by reason of their partę in the English stocke.[3]

xiiij° Januarij 1628 — Fol. 102a

Present

mr Cole, mr Islip mr weaver mr waterson mr Knight mr Bill mr Kingston mr Blount mr Purfoot mr Harison mr Bateman/

Mr Parker.

Whereas by virtue of a precept from the lord Maior dated 26 Junij 1628[4] This Company were required to levye a great some of money for his Maties vse John Parker of the livery of this Company being sessed as a livery man to paie a proporconable parte thereof and being knowne to be of sufficient abilitie did not onely refuse to disburse any some himselfe but Combyned wth others and diswaded them also from parting wth any money toward the raysing of the said some/ And in the moneth of August last the said John parker wth great violence and force ran against the mg̃r of the Company in such furious manner as if he had not ben assisted by some that stood by the said Parker had borne him downe backwardę and done him some mischeife. And since that time he hath Carryed himself towardę the master and wardens insolently and scornefullie and hath said that he wilbe hanged at the hall gate before he will submitt himselfe

[1] STC 18993.
[2] STC 12974 and 18994.
[3] Cf. *C–B.C*, 101a, 5 Aug. 1628.
[4] Cf. *Letter Book*, 109b.

Now the said mr wardens and Assistantę seeing the said Parker to ꝑsist in his obstinacie and Contempt to the ill example of others at a full Court holden this day Called him before them and told him of his stubbornnes and disobedience and demanded of [him] what he could say for himself why he should not be putt out of the liverye for his ill behaviour and disobedience against the gou'mt of the Company, wherevnto he answered openly and ꝑemptorily you may doe it if you have any such power wherevpon the Master told him that from this day forward (till he should submitt himself) he should not stande or be accounted as a liverye man: which by the said Courte was ordered accordinglie/

iij ffeb. 1628

Present — mr Cole mr Islip mr weaver mr waterson mr Knight mr Bill mr Kingston mr Blount mr Purfoote mr Harison mr Bateman

Arthur Johnson
Hugh Brewer
Tho. Alcorne — This day an assignemt was reade [made] by Arthur Johnson of his yeomanry parte in the English stocke for a debt he oweth to the Irish stocke/ And therevpon the table wente to election of an other ꝑtenor in the said English stocke and the one halfe fell vpon Hugh Brewer to make his former halfe parte a whole yeomanry parte and the other half fell vpon Tho: Alcorne and they tooke their oathes accordinglie

John Browne. — It is ordered that John Browne shall have 50li of mr John Nortonę bequest which Math. Newburyę is to paie in.[1]

Fol. 102b

10 ffeb. 1628

Present — Mr Cole mr Islip, mr weaver mr waterson mr Bill. mr Knight mr Kingston mr Blount mr Purfoote mr Haryson mr Bateman.

Mr Aspley. — This day mr Aspley referringe himselfe to the Table/ for his former Contempt was restored to the Profittę of his parte in the English stocke payeinge for a fine to the poore of the Companie—xxs.[2]

Leases in Paules Churchyard and The Old Chandge/ — It is ordered that Assignemtę of the leases held of mr Aspley and of the bridghouse be engrossed and to be sealed, to passe from the Company to Mr Norton and mr Bill according to agreemte/[3]

Tho. Symcocke — mr Beale mr fflesher mr younge mr Jones mr Joh. Wright mr Sharlakers taking wth them The Clarke of the Company are appointed to follow the busines in the Parliamt against the Patent of Tho: Symcocke for printinge all thingę one one side &c/[4]

[1] His bonds are recorded 12 Apr. 1629, *Liber C2*, 113b. Newbury repaid his loan 12 Mar. 1629, *Liber C2*, 111b.

[2] Cf. *C–B.C*, 101a, 5 Aug. 1628.

[3] Cf. *C–B.C*, 69a, 31 July 1621; 80b, 15 Mar. 1623; and 103a, 12 June 1629.

[4] Regarding this matter, cf. Introduction.

1mo Martij 1628

Stockeeps for the English	Mr Waterson, mr Knight	mr Allot, mr Harper	Fra. Falkner, Rob: Birde
Auditors	mr Blount, mr Harison	mr Butter, mr Busby	Hen: Walley, Raffe mabb

26. martij 1629:

Mr Exoll. This day mr Exoll is Chosen Rentor to assist Mr Busby for the yeere ensueinge, and he accepted of it

Ric. Badger It is ordered that Richard Badger shall have the 50li Continued vnto him,[1] putting in securitie

His suerties Robert Quincey, Policarpus Dawkins } vide in libro obligationũ

Received from Christe hospitall of mr willm Nortons bequest[2] the some of .... vjli xiijs iiijd

Item paid to Christ hospitall of mr Geo. Bishops bequest[3] .... vjli

Item paid to the mr wardens Clarke and Beadle according to mr Wm Nortons bequest[2]......... xiijs iiijd

4° Maij 1629. Re Car' Quinto. Fol. 103a

Present Mr Cole, mr Islip mr Weaver mr Waterson mr Swinhow. mr Knyght mr Bill mr Blount mr Purfoot mr Harison mr Bateman:

Mr Heggenbotham This day mr Heggenbotham assigned his livery part in the English stocke to mr Swinhow for securitie of paymt of 100li which he oweth vnto him by bond to be paid on the sixt of November next, and if default be made in paiement thereof The mr wardens and assistante are to Choose a new partenor in his place and the said mr Swinhow to have his debt out of the said stocke.

Jorney Men It is ordered by the boord and Consent of the mr Printers and the Jorney men that were this day pn'te that the said Jorney men shall be allowed for the hollydayes as heretofore. and that if they loose any worke they the said Jorneymen shall not onely paie for the losse of their owne worke but for their fellowes also that loose their worke thorough their default

[1] Cf. *C–B.C*, 89a, 1 Mar. 1626, and 91a, 20 May 1626. His new bonds were registered 20 Apr. 1629, *Liber C2*, 113b.

[2] Cf. Plomer, *Wills*, pp. 30–33.

[3] Cf. *C–B.C*, 24b.

Ballad stocke — It is ordered that the partenors in the Ballad stocke shall have Margerie Trundles Copies paying such debt to the English stocke as she ought thereunto at her death.[1]

xijº die Junij 1629.

Presente. — Mr Cole mr Islip mr weaver mr Norton mr Waterson mr Bill. mr Knight mr Kingston mr Blount, mr Purfoote mr Harison mr Bateman

Mr Norton
Mr. Bill/ — This day were sealed wth the Comoñ seale Two assignemts of the leases of the houses in Paules Churchyard and th'old Change to Mr Norton and mr Bill by reason of a Bargaine heretofore made betwixt them and the Company for the latyn stocke which they were to have, for English wares [*which*] [that] the Company had of them[2]

Rich: Badger — This day the Peticon of Rich. Badger [*was*] to his Matie was read to the Board to be a master printer wth his Maties refference vnder the hand of the lord viscount dorchester and according to the said refference to the lo: B. of London he is allowed to be a Master Printer giving sufficient Caution to be in all things Conformable to the order of the Starchamber: And by the said Lo: Bishops order and his owne Consent he is not at anytime to assigne his Interest to any other nor take any Partenor to him.[3]

Fol. 103b

primo Julij 1629.

Present — Mr Cole mr Islip mr Weaver Mr Waterson Mr Lownes mr Swinhow mr Knight mr Kingston mr Purfoote mr Harison

English parte
Mrs East
mr Busby
Joh. Grismond
Rob: Milborne/ — This day election was made for mrs Easts livery parte: and it fell vpon mr Busby: and half mr Busbyes yeomanry part fell vpon Joh. Grismond to make his halfe yeomanry part [*fell vpon*] a whole parte and the other halfe fell vpon Robert Milborne:

quarto die Julij [*eod die*] pn'tibus vt supra.

Tho. Montforte
Clarke of the
Company. — It is this day ordered That Thomas Montford Clarke of the Company: for his extraordinary paines taken this yeare in the Companyes busines shall receive as a gratuitie the some of Ten pounds: And his allowance to be encreased for his further encouragemt to have the 26s 8d which is allowed for writeing the Divident Booke [*made*] made vjli p annu' to be paid quarterly for solliciting the Causes of the Company and the English stocke. so he is to have:

from the wardnes account .... xxli p annu'
from the rentor wardens .... xli p a'
The poores account .... iiijli p annu'
The English stocke .... vjli p annu'
by quarterly paymts ....

[1] Cf. *C–B.C*, 83b, 6 Nov. 1624. These rights were transferred to the Ballad Stock, 1 June 1629 (Arber iv. 213).

[2] Cf. *C–B.C*, 102b, 10 Feb. 1629, and 98a, 8 Dec. 1627.

[3] Cf. *C–B.C*, 84a, 7 Feb. 1625.

6° Julij pn'tib^{9}. vt supra.

Mr Islip
Mr Walley
Tho. Weaver

Election was made for mrs Cookes[1] Assistantę parte and it fell vpon mr Islip: his livery parte fell vpon mr Walley and mr Walleyes yeomanry parte vpon Thomas Weaver, and they tooke theire oathes accordinglie.

Sam. Macham
Mr Beale/

The matter betwixt mr Havilond mrs Griffin and Sam: Macham on the one parte and mr Beale on the other is referred to Mr Islip and Mr Kingston and mr weaver and mr Harison to ende the matter if they Can or otherwise to reporte their opinions.

3° August 1629.

Mr Tombes
Mr Smethwicke } taken into the Assistantę this day

Mr Bonham Norton Master

Fol. 104a

Mr John Bill
Mr Tho: Purfoote } wardens.

vij° Septemb: 1629.

Present

mr Norton mr Bill mr Purfoote mr Waterson mr Lownes mr Knight mr Islip mr Weaver mr Blount mr Harison mr Tombes mr Smethwicke/

Mr Lownes.

This day the table demanded of mr Lownes, a legacie of xls p Annu' given to the poore of the Companye by mr Short deceased out of a house in Mugwell street for 26 yeares as appeareth in this booke by an order in anno 1603. fol. 3°:[2] the said mr Lownes is [to] give answere the next Court day whether he will pay it and the Arerages, due to the Company for diverse yeares, and if he shall refuse as heretofore he hath done, Then it is ordered that a Course be taken against him for recou'ye thereof either to the Comission for Charitable vses or otherwise as shalbe further advised/

Ric Badger

It is ordered that Richard Badger shall have the presse and lr̃ which are in the hall[3] and were lately praised by mr Dawson and mr Miller, at 14li 12s, whereof he is to paie 5li 12s in hand and the other 9li to be paid out of his dividentę

And the 74li of mettall the Irish partenors are to have payeing for it as it shalbe valued

Nic Okes.
Fra. Grove/

whereas Nicholas Okes hath morgaged Certaine Copies to ffrancis Grove for money lent to the said Nicholas which is yet vnsatisfied It is ordered that the writeingę made betwixt them be deliu'ed to the said Grove if mr Okes shew not Cause to the Contrary next Court day

[1] Mrs. Henry Cooke.

[2] Cf. *C–B.C*, 3a, 12 Mar. 1604.

[3] According to Sir John Lambe's notes this was the press of Simmes, but from the ornaments that appears to be unlikely, for he seems not to have had ornaments from Simmes's press but from those of H. Lownes and W. Jones.

Primers seized by Mr Bill. Mr Waterson, mr Knight mr Islip, mr Kingston are appointed to Consider of the Primrs which mr Bill seazed to the Companyes vse and either hath in his Custody or hath sold them, and mr Norton and Bill are Contented, to stand to their order what they shall pay the Company for them: And it was agreed that they shall paie the Company 6li. 13s. 4d/ for the said Primers to the vse of the English stocke/

Fol. 104b

eodđ die pn'tib9 vt ante/

Booke of Martirs It is ordered that if Ten of the Company will vndertake to printe the Booke of Marters[1] they shall have leave from the Table paying xijd in the pound to the Company or lesse as shall be agreed vpon when the said ten parties are nomynated and knowne to the Boord.

Apprentizes It is ordered that when the appn'tice of any Staconer hath served his terme wthin two yeares of the expiracõn thereof, the master of such appn'tice may saie to the table to have an other appn'tice which the wardens may allowe vnto him if they thinke it fitting notwthstanding any former order to the Contrary.

Rob: Younge It is ordered that Robert young shall bring in the 50li of mr John Nortons bequest which he oweth the Company:[2] and then the table will Consider whether he shall have it againe for 3 yeares vpon securitie.

John Norton Wm Lee. John Norton hath this day leave to engage his English stocke to wm Lee for the paymt of 120li at sixe monethes.

Wiđ Bynneman widdow Bynnemans pencõn is to be staid till shee submitt to mr Randall and her Landlord[3]

5o Octob. 1629.

Present/ Mr Norton Mr Bill mr Purfoote mr Waterson, mr Swinhow mr Lownes mr Knight mr Islip mr Kingston mr weaver mr Blount mr Harison mr Tombes mr Smithwicke

Mr Bourne Mr Bellamy Bills of lading This day, mr Bourne Complained against mr Bellamye and mr ffairebeard for selling of Bills of Ladinge printed by vertue of a patent, for the sole printing of all thingꝭ vpon one side; fforasmuch as the said Billes is the proper Copie of the said Mr Bourne entred vnto him in the hall Booke.[4] It is ordered that the said Bellamy and ffairebird doe deliu' such Bills as they have to the said mr Bourne And for this time they are to receive so much for them, as (bona fide)

[1] STC 11228.

[2] Cf. *C–B.C*, 89a, 1 Mar. 1626. He was lent the money 22 Feb. 1630, *Liber C2*, 114b.

[3] She appears to have 'submitted', for according to the *Liber pro pauperibus* there was no interruption of her pension.

[4] Cf. Arber iv. 97. Bellamy and Fairbeard presumably were printing under Symcock's patent.

they paid for the same, and they are to take in their Table and sell no more hereafter printed by any other then the said m^r^ Bourne, At the same time the said m^r^ Bellamy desired that an other Bill of lading might be entred vnto him, licensed by Mr Martin, which this Court taking into Consideracõn and examyning both the said Bills found them to be all one in substance varyed onely in wordes, and did Conceive that this new Bill was made on purpose to Circumvent the former & therefore ordered that it should not be entred at all to the said Bellamy but that the said m^r^ Bourne should enioy the the aforesaid Copie as heretofore according to the Custome of the Company/

2° Novembr 1629. FOL. 105ª

Present Mr Norton Mr Bill m^r^ Purfoote Mr Waterson Mr Swinhow Mr Knight Mr Islip Mr Kingston Mr Weaver Mr Blount Mr Harison m^r^ Tombes Mr Smithwicke

Hen. Overton. This day by consent of this Court m^ris^ Sheffard[1] assigned her halfe yeomanry ꝑte in the English Stocke to Hen: Overton, and was sworne accordinglie

Mr Locke/ At this Court Mr Lockes lease was sealed by the ffeoffees. 31 yeares to Comence at Christmas next Rent x^li^ ꝑ a' ffyne xx^li^ as was before agreed vpon/[2]

Plate to be brought in/ Wheras by an order of the 2^d^ of October 1581. 23 Eliz:[3] it was ordered, That euery one that should by election be master of this Company for the first time of his Mastership should freely give at his owne Costę to the vse of this Company w^th^in 28 dayes after the ende of the yeare of his Mastership some ꝑcell of plate waighing 14 ounces at the least, and for euery other time that he should Come to the same degree some other guift according to his owne good will and discretion.

And likewise that euery one that by election should come to either degrees of vpper warden or vnder warden shoulde for euery time as often as he should Come to any of the same degrees freely and of his owne Costę give to the vse of the Company w^th^in 28 daies after the ende of his or their wardenship some ꝑcell of plate of silver waighing three ounces at the least

And if any m^r^ or warden refuse to performe the said ordinancę then eu'ye one so refusing should be by the discretion of the table displaced of the Assistantship and disable for euer being Chosen to any degree or office in the Company or to sett among the Assistantę of the same.

Theise ordinancę and decrees have not ben observed or kept by divers of the Assistantę that have ben Masters and wardens of late times which neglect the table this day (takeing into Consideracõn) have ordered vpon debate about the matter, That the aforesaid ordinancę shall hereafter be strictly observed, according to the

1 Mrs. William Sheffard married Henry Overton.

2 It is not clear whether this is a renewal of the lease made 25 Sept. 1621, cf. *C–B.C*, 69^b^, or another one. It can hardly refer to the lease of The Feathers, for which see *Letter Book*, 110^b^, 12 June 1629.

3 Recorded in *Letter Book*, 43^a^.

true entent and meaneing thereof, And that all such as are now living and have borne the said offices in the Company and have not performed the said order shall bring in their guift before the Sixt of May next, And for those that are deade since they have borne any of the said offices and have (*not*) pformed the said order, The wardens are to talke wth their execut^{rs} about the same and if their widdowes have any stocke in the hall, it is to be staid in the stockeeps handes till the Company be satisfied in the pmisses.

FOL. 105^{b}

13° January 1629.

Present Mr Waterson loco M^{ri}. mr Bill mr Purfoote mr Swinhow mr Cole mr Knight mr Islip mr Kingston mr weaver mr Blount mr Harison mr Bateman mr Tombes mr Smethwicke.

Richard Baldwyn Judeth Taylo^{r}/ This day Mr Stone in behalf of Richard Baldwyn administrato^{r} of the goodes and Chattles of Rich Taylor deceased moved the Company for the ou'plus of so much of the said Rich. Taylo^{rs} Stocke as is not due to the Company which appeareth to be xxj^{li} x^{s} and it is ordered that the said xxj^{li} x^{s} shalbe paid out of of (*sic*) the said Stocke if [*the said*] Judeth Taylo^{r} wife of the said Richard Taylo^{r} take not order otherwise for the paym^{t} thereof/

18 Januarij 1629.

Basill Nicoll This day an assignement and lẽr of Atturney for 840^{li} was sealed to Mr Basill Nicoll wth the Comon Seale[1]

Mr John Wate^{r}son It is ordered that m^{r} John waterson shall have the 50^{li} which Richard Taylo^{r} had of m^{r} John Nortons bequest,[2] the said John Waterson putting in securitye to the likeing of the Table.

Mr Younge. Likewise Robert young is to have his bond renewed for 50^{li} of the same bequest[3]

1mo Martij 1629.

Stockepers for the English Stocke	m^{r} Islip— m^{r} Smethwicke	assistant$_{e}$	m^{r} Man— m^{r} Milborne	lyvry	Joh Harigate Nic ffussell	
Auditors	m^{r} Kingston m^{r} Harison		m^{r} Moore m^{r} Stansby		John Patrich Hen. Holland	

M^{r} weaver Threasurer et Iurat.

Mr Weaver It is this day ordered that m^{r} weaver in respect of his paines taken as Threasurer for the English Stocke and in the affares of the Company shall have xx^{li} a yeare added to his former allowance which is in toto. fourescore poundes p annu'[4]

1 Mr. Nicoll paid the Company the £840 which they had lent the King, cf. *Letter Book*, 114^{a} and ^{b}.

2 Cf. *C–B.C*, 99^{b}, 23 June 1628. His bonds are recorded 2 Feb. 1630, *Liber C2*, 114^{a}.

3 Cf. *C–B.C*, 104^{b}, 7 Sept. 1629.

4 Cf. *C–B.C*, 38^{a}, 1 Mar. 1615.

English Stocke/ 100 Whereas divers of the Company are behinde hand in their paym^te for Bookes taken from the English Stocke whereby marchantꝭ Cannot be paid nor dividentꝭ made in due time. It is therefore this day ordered by a full Court, That no debtor shall have any more bookes deliu'ed out vnto him vntill all former Reckoningꝭ be cleared/

10 Martij 1629. Fol. 106a

Present/ mr waterson loco mři mr Bill mr Purfoote mr Lownes mr Swinhowe mr Cole mr Knight mr Islip mr Kingston mr weaver mr Blount Mr Harison mr Tombes

Warehouses. It is ordered that the sixe warehouses made where the Bowling alley was shalbe lett out for 4li p annu' and fortye shillingꝭ a peece for fines for 21 yeares from or lady day next
The Irish Partenors to have the ffirst mr waterson the second mr Bill the third. Partenors in the musicke Patent the fourth mr Allott the fift & mr Bird the sixt/ They are not to alienate wthout Consent of the Table nor to ymploy them to any other vse then warehouses for Bookes

Ric. Badger It is ordered that Richard Badger shall have the warehouses that mr waterson had ouer the Buttrye[1] and the old Irish warehouse for 50s a yeare for a printing house provided alwaies that if the Company finde any Annoyance or Inconvenience thereby. vpon 6 monethes warning he shall avoid and deliuer them vp into the Companyes handes.

Rob. Lun Robert Lun[2] by order of this Court is to have xli lent vnto him for 3 yeare if he Can putt in good securitie.

Mr Allott Mr Milborne Mr Birde Psalmes & geneologies Item it is this day agreed vpon that Robert Allott Robert Milborne and Robert Birde shall have 800 Psalmes smal fol[3] and 800 geneologies of the same volume,[4] paieing 9d a peece for the Psalmes and 15d the geneologies the Psalmes to be paid for at Midsomr next and the geneologies to be paid for in three yeare at 6 and 6 monethes begining at Michaelmas next

Mr Dor Speed/ Item it is agreed betwixt Mr Dor Speed and the Company that the said Company shall receive from him 800 geneologies small fol[4] which are to be paid for in 3 yeare at 6 and 6 monethes the first paymt at Michaellmas next.

26. Martij 1630 Rꝭ Car' vjo/

Mr Downe. Mr downe is Chosen Rentor this day to ioyne wth mr Exoll for the yeare following.

[1] Is this the 'matted chamber', cf. *C–B.C*, 12b, 10 Nov. 1606, or R. Wedgwood's, *C–B.C*, 67b, 26 Mar. 1621.

[2] Made free 15 June 1627, Arber iii. 686. The money was lent from Burby's bequest 25 Mar. 1630, *Liber C2*, 184b.

[3] STC 2612.

[4] STC 23039.

FOL. 106b

19° April 1630.

Present. Mr Waterson, loco mr̃i, Mr. Purfoote. Mr Swinhow, Mr Knight. Mr Islip. Mr Weaver Mr Blount Mr Harison Mr Tombes, and Mr Smethwecke.

Mr Pettye — It is ordered that Mr Pettye for a lease for 21 yeares after the 2 lives that he hath in being in two tenemte in Ave mary lane shall pay 100li fyne [*for*] the old Rent which is 4l 9s. 8d p annu' and such Couenante as are vsuall in leases lett by the Companye.

John Patrich — It is ordered that if John Patrich doe not sell the booke Called The life and Raigne of Edward the Sixt[1] at xvjd a booke which is according to the order at 2 sheete a penny.[2] That then any of the Company may ymprint it although it be his Copie.

Mr Beale
Tho. Brudnell — This day Thomas Brudnells Peticon to the Lord Keeper and his lops Refference to the Company was reade. mr Beale desired a Copie thereof and a time assigned to answere, And it is ordered That he shall have a Copie thereof and ffriday next to give in his Answere.[3]

6° Maij 1630. pn'te9 vt supra/

mr Busby. — mr Busby Rentor warden his account 56l. 8s.

Mr Warde. — Anthony Warde is this day agreed wthall for xli to serve the markette according to my lord mayors precept,[4] till Christmas next.

7° Junij 1630.

Present — mr waterson loco mri mr Purfoote mr Cole mr Islip mr Kingston mr weaver mr Blount mr Harison mr Tombes mr Smethwick

Mr Lownes — Whereas mr Lownes lately deceased by a Codicill annexed to his last will hath given to three of his grand Children 300li and 20li to the Company which is his English stocke. Which 300li he desired might be kept by the Company till the Childre[*d*][n] Come of age paying for the same 5li p Cent'. It is ordered that it shall be accepted of by the Company and answered when the Children Come of age according to his desire: so as his executrix paid the arrerages of a bequest of 40s p annu' given to the poore of the Company by mr Peter Short which the said mr Lownes promised should be pformed as by an order of the 12 of march 1603. appeareth.[5]

1 STC 12998.

2 Cf. *Reg. B*, 19 Jan. 1598, 464a.

3 Brudenell paid Beale £140 to be taken into partnership on the death of Hall. According to Sir John Lambe, 'Brudenell had much a doe to recover' his investment. Presumably this entry refers to that effort.

4 Cf. *Letter Book*, 115a, 6 Feb. 1630, and 5 May 1630.

5 Cf. *C–B.C*, 3a, 12 Mar. 1604.

Pn'ti9: vt ante/

Mʳ Sparkes
Tho. Paine/ — This day mʳ Sparkes surrendred vp his yeomanry parte in the English stocke and Thomas Paine was elected therevnto and tooke his oath accordingly.

Jonas Man — The matter betwixt Jonas man and the widdow of Paule man Concerning Mʳ Tho: Mans Copies is referred to mr. Kingston and mr Weaver to ende if they can or to Certifie theire opinions.[1]

Rob. Parke/ — It is ordered that Robert Parke[2] putting in good securitye shall have the next 50ˡⁱ of mr John Nortons bequest[3] that Comes into the house/

xvjᵗʰ Junij 1630.

mʳ Lownes
mʳ Purfoote
mʳ Stansby
Joh. Harigate
Wᵐ Smith. — This day election was made for mʳ Lownes[4] Assistantes part and it fell vpon mr Purfoote: his livery part vpon mr Stansby. his yeomary (*sic*) parte vpon John Harigate and Wᵐ Smith.[5]

mʳ Busby — Item it is ordered that mʳ Busby for his extraordinary paines and Chardg in Collecting the Quartrages and arrerages due to the Company bringing in more money then ordinary by reason of great paines taken therein shall have 40ˢ paid him by mr warden Purfoote for a reward[6]

mʳ Blount — It is ordered that mʳ Blount shall have the 50ˡⁱ of this yeares Collection putting in good Securitie[7]

mr Joh. Waterson
Mʳ Adams. — This day licence is given to John Waterson to engage his livery part in the English stocke to mr Adams. for the paiemᵗ of 70ˡⁱ at sixe monethes.

5° Julij 1630 Reg Car' vjᵗᵒ.

Assistantes — mr Aspley, mr Rothwell, mr Fetherstone } taken into the Assistantes.

[1] Cf. *C–B.C*, 101ᵃ, 27 Sept. 1628.

[2] Made free 22 Oct. 1624 (Arber iii. 686).

[3] See Plomer, *Wills*, pp. 45–47. His bonds were registered 18 Aug. 1630, *Liber C2*, 114ᵇ.

[4] H. Lownes, Sen.

[5] There were two William Smiths at this time, one whose name is spelled Smythe was made free 30 Oct. 1609 (Arber iii. 683); the other, W. Smith, was made free 17 Jan. 1614 (Arber iii. 684).

[6] Renter Warden, cf. *C–B.C*, 106ᵇ, 6 May 1630.

[7] Cf. *C–B.C*, 97ᵃ, 12 July 1627. No such loan is recorded in *Liber C2*.

Nath. Mathewes — It is ordered that Nath. Mathewes[1] vpon his peticōn shall have xx^s given vnto him for his releife being a poore member of this Company.

Mr Swinhow. Master
mr. Kingston } wardens
mr. Harison }

Fol. 107^b

2° August 1630 R℮ Car' vj°.

Present — m^r Swinhow m^r Kingston m^r Harison mr Waterson m^r Cole m^r Islip m^r Weaver m^r Purfoote m^r Blount m^r Bateman m^r Tombes m^r Smethwicke m^r Rothwell m^r Aspley.

Judeth Tayler, Edw. Banberye, Tho Crouch. — This day Judeth Taylor widđ by Consent of this Court engaged her part in the English stocke to Edward Banbery[2] and Tho: Crouch[3] for the payment of 80^li which she acknowledgeth to owe vnto them and they are Contented to take the said 80^li from time to time out of the dividentℯ as it shall arise till they be satisfied the aforesaid some/

mr Searle, mr Harison — The matter whereof m^r Searle Complaines about his sonne[4] against mr Harison is referred to mr Kingston and mr Aspley.

6° Septem. 1630. pn'tibus vt supra.

Fran. Nicholls. — It is ordered that ffrancis Nicholls shall have a lease of the house that Brookes had for 5^li a yeare for 21 yeares to Comence from Michaelmas last.

mr Kingston, Geo. Griffin — It is ordered that George Griffins[5] shall paie 41^s to m^r Kingston by ii^s vj^d a weeke, out of his worke

Elmes. — It is ordered That Elmes shall have xiij^s iiij^d a quarter for keeping the Garden during the Companyes pleasure.

4° Octobr. 1630. pn'tib^9 vt ante

Corne to be brought out of Ireland — It is ordered That lrẽs be written to wiłłm Bladon in Ireland to buy 150 quarters of Corne there for the Companyes store.

Mđ the Company pn'tly afterwardℯ Compounded wth the Citty of London for 100 quarters at the rate of 5^s 6^d the Bushell, and paid 100 nobles to m^r Aldrem̃ ffreeman in parte, the rest is to be paid when the Corne Come/ and it is ordered that lrẽs be written to mr Bladon to Contradict the former.[6]

1 Made free 6 Sept. 1602 (Arber ii. 266).
2 Made free 26 Mar. 1607 (Arber iii. 683).
3 Not recorded.
4 Possibly Samuel Searle, made free 3 Apr. 1633 (Arber iii. 687).
5 Made free 5 May 1628 (Arber iii. 686).
6 Several precepts on this matter are transcribed in the *Letter Book*, 116^a.

Mr Younge. The Copies entred in trust by mr Lownes to mr Cole and mr Latham by their Consentę and order of this Court are to be entred to mr Younge.[1]

9° Octob. 1630 Fol. 108a

Present mr Swinhow. mr Kingston mr Harison mr Waterson mr Islip mr Weaver mr Purfoote mr Blount mr Tombes mr Smethwick mr Aspley mr Rothwell

Money lent forth. It is ordered That such moneyes as are or shall be lent out to seu'all ꝑsons for 3 yeares, at the ende of euery thre yeares shall be brought into the house and left to the Borde to dispose of to some other ꝑtye [as] the Table shall thinke fitting/

Mr Hum. Lownes whereas mr Humph: Lownes deceased had an Assistantę share in the English stocke[2] amounting to the some of 320li and by his last will gave vnto 3 of his grand Children 300li thereof and the odd 20li to the Company, and by a Codicill desired that the said 300li should be retayned in the Companies handes at the rate of 5li p Cent' till the said Children Came of age. Now this Court being vnwilling that the Company should be Chardged wth the money thought it not fitting to accept thereof And therefore ordered that the said stocke shall be paid to the Executrix of the said Humph. Lownes or her assignes as it is to be paid by the ordinancę of the Company:

16 Octob. 1630

Welch Psalmes This day at the request of mr Barker the Boord was moved Concerning the printing the Welsh Psalmes. the question was whether the Company would print them or take 5li of mr Barker for their good wills for the printing thereof And it is ordered that mr Barker in Consideracõn of 5li shall have th' Imprinting of this Impression doeing of them in the name of the Company and not otherwise/[3]

Debtę to the Stocke. It is ordered by the Mr wardens and Stockeeps That if all those that doe owe money to the English stocke doe not bring in the debtę before saterday next mr weaver shall sue them all not sparing any.

[1] Entered to Cole and Latham 6 Nov. 1628 (Arber iv. 205), and assigned to Young 6 Dec. 1630 (Arber iv. 245).

[2] Disposed of 16 June 1630, cf. *C–B.C*, 107a.

[3] There is a memorandum among the State Papers which has been dated [May ?] 1630, in which among the books stated to have been printed for the advancement of religion, &c., are included the Bible and Service Books in Welsh (*State Papers Dom. 1630–1631*, p. 271). Evidently Barker wished to be able to bind with the *Book of Common Prayer* (STC 16439) and the Bible (STC 2349), which he was at this time printing, an edition of the 'singing Psalms' in Welsh (STC 2746). He did not follow this direction completely, for the imprint reads 'A'i printio yn Llundain, 1630'.

23° Nouember 1630.

Present — Mr Swinhow Mr. Mr Kingstone Mr Harrison Wardene: Mr Waterson, Mr Cole, Mr Islip, Mr Weaver, Mr Blount, Mr Bateman, Mr Tombes, Mr Smethwicke, Mr Aspley Mr Rothwell, Mr ffetherstone.

These orders following were left vnentred by Mr Mounfort

Mr Harrison
Mr Bourne. — This day Eleccon was made for Mr Knighte Assistante pte & it fell vpon Mr Harrison Warden. Mr Harrisons Liuery pte fell vpon Mr Bourne

They tooke their Oathes according to Order/

Fol. 108b

23°. die Nouembr. 1630

Mr Barker — This day Mr Weauer rcd 5li. from Mr Barker for printing ye Welch Psalmes/[1]

Printers to set their names to bookes they printe.
109 — This day by direccõn from ye Lo: Bp. of London Order was giuen to ye Mr. Printers most of them being pn'te, yt eu'y Printer is to sett to his name to eu'y booke yt he printeth & yt none sett their names to any booke except he be a Mr Printer allowed according to the Decree in Starrechamber/

Ireland.
To yr Clerke Copies of ye grant & ye lease xls. — Mr. Harrison Warden rcd at Skinners hall 60li—01s—04d for Rent for or. Land in Ireland[2] Pd to ye Clerke for acquitt'. 3s—4d to ye Beadle 2s—6d Porter 01s.

6to. Decemb: 1630

Present — Mr Swinhow. Mr Kingston Mr Harrison war, Mr Waterson, Mr Cole, Mr Islip Mr Weaver, Mr Blount, Mr Tombes, Mr Smethwicke Mr Aspley Mr Rothwell Mr ffetherstone/

Mr Halsey. — A Rawleigh Chronicle[3] to be giuen to Mr Halsey by Order of this Court for paines he took in their businesse.

16to. Decemb: 1630.

Lo: Maj'ors Dinner. — Mr Swinhow Mr Kingston Mr Harrison Mr Waterson, Mr Islipp, Mr Weauer Mr Purfoote Mr Blount Mr Smethwicke Mr Rothwell Mr ffetherstone & Mr Downes went to my Lo: Maj: to dinner this day.

Mr Lightfoote. — It is ordered yt Mr Lightfoote shall haue a booke of ye value of xxs giuen him for a New yeares gift.[4]

1 Cf. *C–B.C*, 108a, 16 Oct. 1630.
2 Cf. *C–B.C*, 33b, 7 Feb. 1614.
3 STC 20640.
4 Cf. *C–B.C*, 93a, 5 Dec. 1626.

20. Decem: 1630.

Nathaniel Newbury — It is ordered y^t Mr Newbury shall haue xx^s. p̱ q^rter towardꝭ the maintenance of his son[1] at the Vniu'sity for iiij yeares if he liue so long.

Tho: Archer. — It is ordered y^t Tho: Archer shall haue 10^s p̱ q^rter out of ye poores money/

12° Januarij 1630

Rich: Adams ffine. — ffor keeping his appn'tice contrary to order —02^s—06^d.

Geo: Purslowe Wm. Gaye. — This day Wm. Gay[2] did agree to work with Mr Purslowe one yeare to the 8th. of January next at 8^s. p̱ weeke & to worke xxx^C p̱ day.

18°. Januarij 1630

Present — Mr Swinhow M^r. Mr Kingstone Mr Harrison ward: Mr Waterson, Mr Cole, Mr Islip, Mr Weauer, Mr Purfoote, Mr Tombes Mr Smethwicke, Mr Aspley, Mr Rothwell, M^r ffetherstone.

Printers to sett 2 letters for their names. — It is this day ordered y^t ye Printers y^t vse to printe the Almanackes shall sett their names or 2 letters of it whereby ye Company may knowe by whom they are printed.[3]

Mr Watersons Lease. — This day Mr Watersonꝭ lease of the second warehouse in Stac̄oners garden was sealed by the ffeoffees Mr Swinhow Mr Kingston Mr Cole Mr Islip. Mr Weauer for 21 yeares comencing from o^r Lady day 1630 ffine 2^li. Rent 4^li p̱ Ann.' Date of the lease is 6th. of September 1630.[4]

Jouis [*sic*] Decimo Marcij 1630. — Fol. 109^a

Present — Mr George Swinhow Master. M^r ffelix Kingston & Mr Harrison Wardens Mr Cole Mr Islipp Mr Weauor Mr Purfoot Mr Tomes Mr Rodwell (*sic*),[5] Mr Aspley & M^r ffetherston Ass^t.

Henry Walley. his Reu'c̄on. — Whereas the place of the Clerkeshipp of this Company is become void by the late death of Thomas Mountford The Mr Wardens & Assistantꝭ aboue named mett together this day about th'elec̄on of a new Clerke And forsomuch as they are giuen to vnderstand one Thomas Salmon claimeth a grant or p̱mise of the Clerkes place to be made in Reu'c̄on vnto

[1] Henry Newbery, matriculated Magdalen Hall, Oxford, 1632; B.A., 1635.

[2] There are two William Gays, one made free 2 July 1605 (Arber iii. 683), the other 12 Jan. 1631 (Arber iii. 686). Presumably the latter is here referred to, and the 3,000 which he promised to work was no doubt 3,000 formes.

[3] This order appears to have been fairly regularly followed.

[4] Cf. *C–B.C*, 106^a, 10 Mar. 1630.

[5] Undoubtedly this is a clerk's error for Rothwell. In the next few months the name appears as either Rodwell or Rodway, after which it is again spelled Rothwell.

him long since in the life time of the said Mountford And that vpon diligent search made in the booke of Orders entered vp remayneing in the Hall there cannot yet be found any mencõn of any such Order or grant made vnto the said Salmon;[1] they thought it meet in respect of the many affaires & Imploymte. that the Company continually hath for the prsent vse of a Clarke, & in respect that the said Salmon hath notice that the place is voyd, & yet cometh not vp in pson to prsent himselfe, nor sendeth vpp his graunt or a Copy of any Order of such a grant (if any such bee) to pceed to th'eleccõn of a new Clarke & therevpon the names of diu's psons aswell ffreemen of this Company as others being prsented vnto them, they with one vnanimous consent elected & chose one Henry Walley a Brother of this Company to that place with this limitacõn That in case it shall appeare the said Thomas Salmon hath any lawfull grant in Reu'cõn to the place now void as he prtendeth & do pn'tly come vp & prsent himselfe & be found fitt & sufficient for the discharge of the place & will execute the same in his owne pson, for the vsuall & accustomed yearely ffee & Salary appteyning to the Clarkes place, then th'eleccõn of the said Henry Walley shall stand for the pn'te as Clarke chosen in Reu'cõn & not otherwise And in case the said Salmon shall not forthwith come vp & prsent himselfe in pson & pduce such grant or a Copy thereof if he haue any such, & in case he be found fitt, do not take vpon him th'execucõn of the said place & discharge it in his owne pson for the vsuall & accustomed ffee & Salary. Then th'eleccõn made of the afore-named Henry Walley shall stand as the Clerke elected to that place in pn'te possession Any grant in reu'cõn prtended to be made to the said Thomas Salmon to the Contrary notwithstanding.

15to. Marcij 1630.

Present Mr Swinhow Master. Mr Kingston & Mr Harrison Wardens Mr Waterson Mr Cole Mr Islipp Mr Weauer Mr Purfoote Mr Tomes Mr. Bateman, Mr. Smithicke Mr Aspley Mr Rodwell (*sic*)[2] & Mr ffetherston Asst.

Henry Walley. Clerke. 112. It is ordered by a full Court this day holden That Henry Walley (haueing satisfied Thomas Salmon for the Reu'cõn of the Clerkeshipp of this Company) shalbe Clerke & Sollicitor of the said Companye in the roome & place of Thomas Mountford late deceased. And to haue all wages pencõns ffees & other Cōmodities belonging to the saide Offices of Clerkeshippe & Sollicitorshipp in as large & beneficiall manner as the said Thomas Mountford enjoyed the same. And the said Henry Walley was sworne & admitted accordingly.

FOL. 109b (*The entries from 23 November 1630 through the 18 January 1630/1, with the exception of that for 6 December 1630, which occur on fol. 108b, were copied again by Henry Walley and occupy fol. 109b and the top of fol. 110a. The only difference, other than variations of spelling, is that in the list of Brethren who attended the Lord Mayor's Dinner, 16 December 1630, having confused the list of those present at the Court held 6 December 1630, Walley has omitted Mr Downes and included Mr Cole and Mr Aspley.*)

[1] They might have looked at *C–B.C*, 32b, 4 Oct. 1613. [2] Cf. *C–B.C*, 109a, 10 Mar. 1630 [1631], note 4.

12° Januarij 1630.

FOL. 110ª

Mr Parker Whereas Mr John Parker for his disobedient Cariage towards the Mr. Wardens and Assistants of this Company hath been remoued out of the place of a Stockekeep in the English Stocke, and beeing a Partner in that Stocke sequestred from the profitts thereof & afterwards was suspended from the Liuerie till such time as he should submitt himselfe to the Master Wardens & Assistants[1] And whereas after that haueing brought a Writt of Restitution out of his Maties. Bench it was there ordered that hee should submitt And being indicted for an assault vpon Mr Cole the Master of the said Company standeth Conuicted for the same Now this day vpon his submission made to the Mr & Assistants he was restored againe to all those priueledges & profitts which formerly hee enjoyed in this Company And it is ordered that the profits of his pte wch. were sequestred during his Obstinacie shalbe paid vnto him & all differences ended & reconciled.

The Copie of Mr Parkers submission.

Whereas some differences haue happened betweene my Company & me, & that I stand conuicted of an assault vpon Mr Cole late Mr. of the Company of Stacõners I doe hereby declare that I neuer had thought purpose or intencõn to offer any affront injury or violence to the said Mr Cole or any other And for any offence yt I haue cōmitted I am sorie for the same & do submitt myselfe to the Mr Wardens & assistants in all lawfull mañer & desire this declaracõn & profession of mine may serue for a full Reconciliacõn of all past differences betweene vs & I againe receiued into those priuiledges & pfitts wch. formerly I haue enjoyed And I do hereby pfesse that to the vtmost of my power I shall obserue all lawfull Ordinances of the Company.

John Parker/

7° ffebruarij 1630.

FOL. 110ᵇ

Present Mr Swinhow Master, Mr Kingston Mr Harrison Wardens Mr Waterson Mr Islipp Mr Weauor, Mr. Purfoote, Mr Tombes, Mr Smethwick Mr Aspley Mr Rothwell, Mr ffetherstone.

Decree It is ordered That a Copie of the Decree[2] be sent from the Companie to the Vicechancellor of Oxford/ And it was copied & sent by Mr Kingston Ward:

A. B. C. It is ordered that Affidauit be made against Roger Daniell & Interrogatories putt in the Starrechamber concerning the printing the A. B. C.

Wm. Garritt Md I do resigne my pte in the English stocke into the Companies hands to dispose of as they shall thinke fitting and all the Claime I haue therein this 7th. of ffebruary 1630.

Wm. Garratt.

[1] Cf. *C–B.C*, 100ª, 5 Aug. 1628, 102ª, 14 Jan. 1629.

[2] Presumably the decision in the dispute with Cambridge. Charles I ratified the grant for printing of Henry VIII to the University in 1628, and the Privy Council in 1629 defined what Bibles, liturgies, and grammars might be printed; cf. S. C. Roberts, *The Cambridge University Press*, pp. 45–46. The text of the decree is given in *Letter Book*, 111ª–112ª.

Ambr: Retherden — Ambrose Retherden to haue 50^{li}. of Mr John Nortons bequest putting in good securitie.[1]

Mr Miller 50^{li} — M^{r}. Miller paid to Mr Warden Harrison 50^{li}. borrowed of the Companie of Mr John Nortons bequest.[2]

9° ffebruarij 1630.

August. Mathews ffine. — is to pay for a ffine for printing a booke of Sr Hen: Woottons[3] without entrance .... } v^{s}. pd

Geo: Baker ffine. — ffor putting the same booke to Printing without entrance .... } ij^{s} pd.

Mr Legate W^{m}. Crawley. — Willm Garratt haueing assigned his Yeomanry pte in the English Stock[4] Eleccõn was made this day The one halfe fell vpon W^{m}. Crawley[5] And the other halfe vpon Mr Legate And they tooke their Oathes accordingly.

Almanacks. — M^{r}. Warden Kingston Mr Islip Mr Semthwicke Mr Aspley to take care of the workmanshipp of the Almanacke.

Edw: Blackmore — A ffine for printing a booke called Look back to London[6] without Entrance .... ij^{s}.

Schoole bookes. — Mr Wardens & Mr Weauor to take a course for the renueing of the Patent for Schoole bookes.[7]

Aug: Mathews — It is ordered that August: Mathews shall haue 50^{li} of Mr John Nortone bequest putting in good securitie/[8]

FOL. 111^{a}

20th. ffebruarij 1630

Mr Bostocke. — This day M^{r}. Harrison Warden receiued of Mr Bostock ffifty pounds lent to him of Mr Nortons bequest[9]—50^{li}.

Hen: Gosson. — M^{d}. Receiued the same day in pte of a debte[10] due vpon bond—ix^{li}—x^{s} And more since l^{s} .... } 12^{li}.

[1] This loan is not recorded in *Liber C2*.

[2] Cf. *C–B.C*, 98^{a}, 8 Dec. 1627.

[3] STC 24905. This was reprinted in STC 20645 and in the *Reliquiae*.

[4] See above, 7 Feb. 1630/1.

[5] Made free 16 Jan. 1610 (Arber iii. 683).

[6] STC 16755, attributed by F. P. Wilson to T. Dekker, and included in STC 6175–6 and in a 1636 edition.

[7] The patent was good until 1634, but the Company was apparently aware of the effort of G. W. Weckherlin to obtain the reversion; see petition, *State Papers Dom. 1629–1631*, p. 514 (20 Feb. 1631) and p. 557 (28 Mar. 1631).

[8] His bonds were recorded 8 Mar. 1631, *Liber C2*, 115^{b}.

[9] Cf. *C–B.C*, 98^{a}, 4 Feb. 1628.

[10] Cf. *C–B.C*, 95^{a}, 29 Mar. 1627.

1° Martij 1630.

Present — Mr. Swinhow Master Mr Kingston Mr Harrison Wardens, Mr Waterson, Mr Islipp, Mr Weauor, Mr Purfoote, Mr Bateman, Mr. Smethwicke, Mr Aspley Mr Rothwell Mr ffetherstone/

Mr Beale
Jno. Clarke — It is ordered by this Courte & Consent of Mr Beale That the booke called Justifieing ffaith written by Mr. Dr. Jackson[1] be crost out of the hall Booke & entred to John Clarke In Consideracõn of ls wch. Mr. Clarke paid vnto him this day

Stock-keeps for the English.	Mr Purfoote, Mr Rothwell	Mr Moore, Mr Hawkins	Robert Dolman, Thomas Alcorne
Auditors	Mr Waterson, Mr Cole	Mr Butter, Mr Hoth	Henry Holland, Henry Ouerton

Mr Weauor Treasurer et Jurat'.

Trer̃er — Mr Weauor is to haue but 60li. p Ann'. for executing the Treasurers place.[2]

(*On this page and the top of the next Henry Walley copied out the entries for 10 and 15 March 1631, referring to his election as Clerk, which have already been transcribed from fol. 109a.*) Fol. 111b

Geo: Crockett. — It is ordered That he shall haue a lease of an house in ffryer Alley[3] granted vnto him for 7 yeares from our Lady day next. he giueing bond with a Surety to pforme Couenants and to pay 5li. Rent p Ann' quarterly. It was sealed and deliuered accordingly. Fol. 112a

26to Marcij 1631.

Present — Mr Swinhow Master, Mr Kingston Mr Harrison Wardens. Mr Waterson, Mr Cole, Mr Islip, Mr Weauer, Mr Purfoote, Mr Smethwick, Mr Tomes, Mr Aspley, Mr Rodwell (*sic*),[4] Mr ffetherstone.

Mr Exall.
ffine. — This day Mr Exall Rentor was ffined by the Table at ffiue pounds for being freed from making his Dinner. The Table tooke into Consideracoñ his Losses in Stockes his liueing in the Countrie not haueing gained any thing in the trade did therefore thinke fitt to sett no greater ffine vpon him. But this not to be drawne into Example.

eod̃ 26to. Marcij 1631.

Mr Moore
Rentor — Mr Moore is chosen Rentor this daye to joyne with Mr Downe for the yeare following.

1 STC 14312. Entered to Beale, 2 Dec. 1614, Arber iii. 558, crossed out 1 Mar. 1631, Arber iv. 249.

2 Cf. *C–B.C*, 38a, 1 Mar. 1615; 54a, 19 Jan. 1619; and 81a, 1 June 1624.

3 Part of the Woodstreet property.

4 Cf. *C–B.C*, 109a, 10 Mar. 1630 [1631], note 2.

Mr Allott. Mr Birde.	Two leases were sealed vnto them of their warehouses and they payed their ffines and Rent that was behind vnto Mr Weauor.[1]
Mr Waterson Mr Latham.	The Table ordered That their debt in the Latine Stock book should be croste.

FOL. 112b

30°. Marcij 1631

Present Mr Swinhow Master Mr Kingston Mr Harrison Wardens Mr Waterson Mr Cole Mr Islipp Mr Weauer Mr Purfoote Mr Tombes Mr Smethwicke Mr Aspley Mr Rodway (*sic*)[2]

Tho. Cotes Rich: Cotes. This day vpon a Complaint by Mr Topsell Minister and a Reference from my Lords Grace of Canterburye vnder a Peticõn Deliuered directed to the Mr. Wardens & assiste. After hearing the ꝑties vpon both sides, they thought fitt & so ordered That the Copy called Gesner his third Book in English entred vnto them should be crossed out of the Book & made no Entrance.[3]

Andr: Driuer. It is ordered that Andrewe Driuer[4] shall haue the next 50li of Mr Nortons money that comes in for three yeares, putting in good Security.

23° Aprilis 1631.

Present [*Mr Jo: Waterson*] Mr Swinhow Master, Mr Kingston Mr Harrison Ward: Mr. Waterson [Mr Cole] Mr Islip, Mr Weauor, Mr Purfoote. Mr Smethwicke Mr Rodway (*sic*)[5] Mr ffetherstone.

Mr Jo: Waterson. This day license is giuen vnto him to engage his Liuerie ꝑte in the English stocke for xxli more vnto Mr Adams for 6. Months hee hauing lent lxxli. on it before.[6] And it is Ordered that noe more shalbe lent vpon it vntill his Debt to the English stocke & 50li borrowed of the Hall be paid or further secured.

[1] Cf. *C–B.C*, 106a, 10 Mar. 1630.

[2] Cf. *C–B.C*, 109a, 10 Mar. 1630 [1631], note 5.

[3] Edward Topsell dedicated to Ellesmere an elaborate manuscript entitled 'The Fowles of Heauen or History of Birdes', *c.* 1613–16, which he called 'the third part of liuinge Creatures'. It is now in the Huntington (Ellesmere 1142), and probably resembles closely the work here referred to. T. and R. Cotes entered 16 Nov. 1630, 'A Booke called Gesner his third booke of birds in English' (Arber iv. 242). Topsell had married the widow of G. Seton (cf. *C–B.C*, 29b, 21 Sept. 1612) and doubtless was well known to the Company. On 16 July 1632, T. and R. Cotes and J. Legatt entered 'by vertue of a noate vnder the hand of master Topsell and by order of a Court a booke called Ornithologia or the History of Birdes and foules, one Moiety to remayne to the said master Coates and Richard Coates and th'other moiety to the said master Legatt' (Arber iv. 281). Evidently the cost of printing was too great and the book was never issued.

[4] Made free 7 Nov. 1625, Arber iii. 686. The loan is not recorded in *Liber C2*.

[5] Cf. *C–B.C*, 109a, 10 Mar. 1630 [1631], note 5.

[6] Cf. *C–B.C*, 107a, 16 June 1630.

2do. Maij 1631

Present Mr Swinhow Master, Mr Kingston Warden, Mr Waterson Mr Islipp, Mr Weauor, Mr Purfoote, Mr Bateman, Mr Tombes, Mr Smethwick Mr Aspley, Mr Rodwell (*sic*)[1] & Mr ffetherstone.

Mr. ffarnaby Mr Stansby. This day Mr ffarnaby came to complaine of Mr Stansbye, for the not printing of Martiall & Juuenall & Persius And Mr. Stansby hath promised that they shalbe printed and finished by Allhallontide next.[2]

Wm. Blanchard.[3] Vpon a Peticõn deliuered by his wife that hee is nowe distracted the Table gaue her xs. Mr. Ward: Kingston took it out of the Boxe then.

6to Maij 1631. Fol. 113a

Present Mr Swinhow Master, Mr Kingston Mr Harrison wardens, Mr Waterson, Mr Islipp, Mr Weauor, Mr. Purfoote, Mr Tombes, Mr Smethwick, Mr Aspley, Mr Rodwell (*sic*),[4] Mr ffetherstone.

Mr Exall Rentor This day Mr. Exoll being called accordinge to ancient Custome, [*refused to make the same, requiring*] to make [*vp his Accompts*] vp his Renter wardens accompt for his yeare, refused to doe it, prtending losse in the Latine stocke, where vpon the Table thought fit that he should pay fiue pounds for his Contempt according to the [*Ad*] Ordinances in that behalfe/

Memorandum Mr Exoll came the next day and acknowledged his error, & saying that he was very ill adviced & humbly desired that his accompt might be now taken, wherevpon the Auditors chosen did audite his Accompt & since [*the*] the full was paid in to Mr Warden Harrison. & ye ffyne remitted.

16o. die Maij 1631

Present Mr. Swinhow Master, Mr Kingston Mr Harrison wardens Mr Waterson, Mr Leake, Mr Cole, Mr Islip, Mr. Purfoot, Mr Toomes, Mr Smithwicke Mr Aspley Mr Rothwell, Mr ffetherston.

Mr Leake & his sonn William This day vpon the request of Mr Leake to Conferr his fourth part of his English stocke vpon his sonn, the Table thought fit to grant it & he came & tooke his oath accordingly.

1 Cf. *C–B.C*, 109a, 10 Mar. 1630 [1631], note 5.

2 STC 14892 and 17493. The widow Snodham transferred her rights to Stansby, 23 Feb. 1626 (Arber iv. 153), but there is no record of his transfer of these titles. He did not keep his promise to have them published by 1 Nov. 1631. Numbers of these books were doubtless imported from the Continent, so that Farnaby, not being content with Stansby's action, sought a prohibition of their importation (cf. *State Papers Dom. 1631–1633*, p. 254) and was granted a privilege for their sole printing, 26 Mar. 1632 (*op. cit.*, p. 294).

3 Made free 26 June 1609, Arber iii. 683.

4 Cf. *C–B.C*, 109a, 10 Mar. 1630 [1631], note 5.

Mr Weckerlyn. It is ordered that mr Weckerlyn shall haue a peece of plate giuen him ouer & aboue the money agreed vpon for his extraordinary paynes & the valew is left vnto the Mr. and Wardens discretions.[1]

(*Cambridge Press*) This day some of the Stockeepers & others came vnto the Table wth. an agreemt made by them & mr Bucke Printer to the vniuersity of Cambridge & their was read the Articles. & vpon long debate the matters by them treated were approued of, And it is ordered that they resort vnto Councell for the dispatch & forme of drawnig of it, that this agreement should not be hurtfull vnto the priuiledges granted vnto the Company/[2]

7°. die Junij

Present. Mr. Swinhow Mr. Mr Kingston Mr. Harrison wardens, Mr. Waterson, Mr Cole, Mr Weaver, Mr Toombes, Mr Smithwicke Mr Aspley & Mr Rothwell.

Nicho: Oakes This day four pounds was paid by mr waterson vnto mr warden Harison in part of a debt due vpon bond by Nicholas Oakes/

FOL. 113b eodem die

Mrs: Mountford. It is ordered that mr. Warden Harrison & mr. Weaver and mr Smithwicke or, any one of them wth my selfe[3] shall treat wth. mrs. Mountford about all accompts in generall and to make them euen or certifie the Table how they find it.

English Stocke. It is ordered and thought fitt that the house doe pay vnto the English stocke one hundred pound to be laid out for the Patent for Schoole bookes and the Charges thereof to be in part payment of diuers somes lent vnto the house formerly by the English stocke.[4]

22°. Junij

Present vt antea

Henry Gosson. This day vpon the humble peticõn of Henry Gosson for something towards his sonns[5] Comencement the Table gaue him fiue pound to be paid him by the Treasurer Mr Weaver & the Pention to be Continued vntill the said 5li. be paid

Mr Bateman. Mr Bateman[6] came to the Cort. this day and requested that in regard of his age & many infirmities they would be pleased to spare his attendance & free him from all offices in the Company. The Cort. there

[1] Cf. *C–B.C*, 110b, 9 Feb. 1631, and 113b, 7 June 1631.

[2] The order of the Privy Council ending the dispute with Cambridge was made 16 Apr. 1629, cf. *State Papers Dom. 1628–1629*, p. 520, but, as may be seen in the *Letter Book*, there were some matters unsettled.

[3] Presumably Walley, the clerk.

[4] Cf. *C–B.C*, 110b, 9 Feb. 1631.

[5] Unidentified. The pension was paid at the rate of 10*s*. a quarter.

[6] Made free 14 Jan. 1580, Arber ii. 681.

tooke it into Consideracõn that he should pay fiue pounds & soe to be freed. And the next Co[rt]. being the last of June he paid the said 5[li] to m[r] Warden Harrison

vltimo die Junij

Present vt antea

Wm. Blaiden. It is ordered that his diuidents as they shall arise out of the English stocke, (being by a former order[1] to pay a debt due to the Latin stocke,) shall be receiued by M[r] Weaver towards the payment of Eighteen pound a yeare w[ch]. is the interest for 300[li]. for Orphanage money borrowed by the Partners of the Latin stocke.

2°. Julij

Present vt antea/

M[r]. Humphrey Lownes & M[r]. Grantham. It is thought fitt that [soe much of *the*] the residew of the money, now to pay out of mr Lownes his stocke dec'. vnto m[r] Grantham [*for the payment*] [in regard that some part] of an anuity heretofore bequeathed vnto the Company for the releefe of the Poore of this Company by Peter Short [is behind vnpaid] be detayned [*in the hands of the Treasurer*] till further order be taken and the residew to be paid out vpon demaund.[2]

Richard Badger the Beadle. This day was called into the Liuery [Richard Badger] vpon this Condicõn that during the houlding of his place of Beadle he should goe in the rancke last of all. & if it happen he leaue his place [at any tyme] hereafter, then he is to be rancked according to [*their*] his antiquity [*in th*] as a Liuery man/

[*In*] Goeing home wth. the M[r]. & Ward: on the Election day This day the M[r]. of the Company moued the Table. That whereas there hath byn a Custome on the Election day, that the new Chosen M[r]. & his Wardens were brought home to their houses by the Liuery of the Company & were entertayned there wth. a Banquett by each of them. Now it was ordered & thought fitt vpon Consideracõn thereof that this goeing soe, should be quite left of & noe more to be vsed hereafter.

Schoole bookes. M[r]. Austen & M[r]. Buckner[3] are to haue x[li]. to bestow in Books for a gratuity for Licenceing diuers books for the English stocke/

[1] Cf. *C–B.C*, 92[a], 22 June 1626.

[2] Cf. *C–B.C*, 3[a], 12 Mar. 1604; 106[b], 12 June 1630; 108[a], 9 Oct. 1630.

[3] Presumably officers of the Bishop of London.

FOL. 114a 4° die Julij 1631

Present. Mr Swinhow Mr. Mr. Kingston Mr Harrison Ward: Mr Waterson Mr Islip, Mr Weauer, Mr Purfoot, Mr. Toombs Mr. Rothwell & Mr ffeatherston.

Allowance encreased for the wardens making their dynner — Whereas heretofore there was allowed by order .5li. vnto the wardens towards their Charge for making their dynners. this Cort. taking into Consideracõn the late & now prsent encrease of the Liuery whereby the charge is growne extraordinary. Vpon long debate thereof by full Consent it was ordered & thought fitt that they should haue the 5li. heretofore allowed made vp Twenty marke the first allowance to begin to these prsent wardens.[1]

(*The rest of this page and 114b are blank. A slip of paper is bound in at this point reading as below, with verso blank.*)

Wm [*Busbey*] Tyrrill of Adthrop in ye County of Northamp bound to Richd Woodland in 10l to pay 5l on the 16th of July next.[2]

FOL. 115a 1° Augusti 1631

Mr: Cole.} Master.
Mr: Islip ...... } Wardens
Mr: Smithwicke }

Present. Mr: Cole Mr:, Mr. Islip. Mr. Smithwicke wardens. Mr. Waterson Mr. Swynhow, Mr. Kingston Mr. Harrison, Mr. Weauer, Mr. Aspley mr Rothwell & mr ffetherston.

Mr: Busby gaue vli. — This day Mrs. Busby came & brought vli. left by her husbands will for a meeting for the Company & Mr. Smithwicke Warden recd. it.

Pinfould. — Alsoe Mrs. Busby gaue Pinfould the Cooke xxs [&] by order of the Cort. & he there acknowledged himselfe satisfied.

Booke of Martyrs to goe forwards. — This day an order was read concerning the Booke of Martyrs[3] and being putt to Voyces the maior part consented vnto it & is to be entred in this Booke of entries for an order.

The order for the printing of the booke of Martyrs. — Whereas the Booke of Martirs being out of print and certayne persons of quality desiring that it might be [*newly*] [re-] imprinted for the generall good of the Kingdome, came vnto the Mr. Wardens and assistants and certified that if the Company would not print it for themselues that they would take a Course for the speedy doeing of it elsewhere. Wherevpon the Mr. Wardens & assistants taking Consideracõn of it, and finding that the Coppy did belong vnto the house, vpon a generall

[1] On 6 June 1608 (*C–B.C*, 17a) the allowance was increased from £5 per year to £10. On 26 May 1611 (*C–B.C*, 27a) it was increased to £20. Presumably this increase to £13. 6*s*. 8*d*. is for a single quarter dinner only.

[2] These men are not connected with the Company.

[3] STC 11228. Cf. *C–B.C*, 104b, 7 Sept. 1629.

quarter day in their Comoñ hall gaue order to their officer the Beadle to giue notice to all that were prsent that the said Booke of Martyrs should be taken in hand to be reimprinted. And that what psons of the Company (to a Convenient number that would come in & haue Shares in the doeing of it [might] & further that those of the Company that were willing to lay out money towards it) should repayre vnto the Clarke of the Company and certifie vnder their hands what they would lay out in money & haue books for. Now, they not comeing, Mr. Islip, Mr. Kingston and [*Mr. Hum. Lownes*] Robert Young (by and wth. the Consent of the Table) haue vndertaken to print it, And to that purpose haue bought & agreed for paper wth. the Merchant for the printing & finishing of the said Worke and haue donn a great part of it allready to theire great charges Wherevpon the table haue thought fitt & this day ordered that such as are willinge & haue allready subscribed their names may take this impression vpon such Condicõn & at such rates as they haue or shall agree for And further it is ordered that noe other of the Company shall goe in hand to imprint the said booke. And lastly the said Mr Islip & his Copartners. doe submitt themselues touching the payment of such some of money for the printing of the same to be for the vse of the Poore as the Table shall thinke fitt.

Mr: Blount his part in the English Stocke/

Memorandum Mr. Blunt came to the Table & paid mr. Swinhowe 160li. to Redeeme his part and then & there mortgag'd it agayne to Robert Banckworth for a yeare.[1] FOL. 115b

Eliz: Tapp & Joseph Hurlocke.

The Copies belonginge to John Tapp deceased are to be assigned to Joseph Hurlocke by Consent of this Cort And Elizabeth Tapp Widdow.[2]

18°. die Augusti.

Present. Mr. Cole Mr. Mr. Islip Mr. Smethwicke Wardens, Mr. [*Kin*] Waterson Mr. Kingston, Mr. Purfoot, Mr Harrison, Mr. Aspley & Mr. Rothwell. Mr Weaver came late.

Widdow Tapps part assigned vnto Joseph Hurlocke.

This day the Widdow Tapp assigned ouer her part in the English stocke (by Consent of the Table) vnto Joseph Hurlocke, & he tooke his oath accordingly.[3]

5°. Septembris 1631

Present Mr Waterson loco Mr̃i Mr Islip mr. Smethwicke wardens mr Kingston mr Weaver, mr Purfoot mr Aspley & mr Rothwell.

Mr. Standish his Collection of the Psa: to ffrench tunes

139.

Whereas John Standish gentleman hath Collected the Psalmes of David accorded to the ffrench & Germaine verses and tunes,[4] and became a Sutor to the Mr. Wardens & assistants for leave for to print the same. Wherevpon the Table hath thought fitt & doe giue way That an impression of a 1000 of them shall be printed at the Charge of the Author, and he is to giue onely a quarterne of the said bookes vnto the Company for an acknowledgmt of their Right

[1] Cf. *C–B.C*, 88a, 5 Dec. 1625.

[2] Entered 1 Aug. 1631, Arber iv. 258–9.

[3] It is possible that the widow Tapp married Hurlock; at any rate his widow's name was also Elizabeth.

[4] STC 2734.

& Title vnto all manner of books of that nature & likewise after the said impression sold doth willingly suffer the said Copy and all his interest therein to remaine vnto the sole benifitt and behoofe of the partno[rs]. in the English stocke euer after to be bestowed of according as they shall thinke fitt. And out of the future impressions he wholly referreth himselfe vnto the curteous Consideracõn of this Table Witnes his hand.

John Standish

6°. Septembris.

Present. Mr. Cole Mr., mr Islip, mr. Smethwicke Wardens, mr Waterson, Mr. Swinhow, mr Purfoot, Mr Aspley, mr Rothwell, & mr ffetherston

A doore into the Garden. This day leaue is graunted vnto Henry Walley [*tha*] to make a doore out of a house (wch. he hath taken)[1] into the garden wth this lymitacõn that whensoeuer at any tyme hereafter he shall leave the said house & not dwell in it. Then it is ordered by & wth. his Consent that he shall make vp the wall as it was before wthin Three monthes after his departure.

FOL. 116a A clause in Mrs: Eastes Last Will. In the last Will and Testament of Mrs. Este Widdow deceased [*bearing date*] the 27th. day of June.[2] Anno dñi 1629 Rg̃ę Caroli ye 5°. [*and*] proued [*by*] in the Preragatiue Cort. is contayned and expressed as followeth. (vizt).

Mrs: Esteę Will bearing date the 30th day of January. A°. dñi 1631 Item I giue and bequeath vnto Richard ffeild and Thomas ffeild the Sonns of Richard ffeild late of London Mercer dec.' wch. was the Sonn of my late dec.' Sister[3] the Sum̃e of Thirty pounds a peece to be paid to each of them seuerally at such seuerall tymes as each of them shalbe made free of the City of London or wthin one Month then next following, and my mind and will is that the said Company of Stacõners shall keepe and detaine in their hands the said two seuerall somes of Thirty pounds & Thirty pounds soe by me giuen vnto the said Richard & Thomas ffeild vntill the same accordinge to the true meaning of this my Will shalbe due to be paid and then the said Company to pay the said Legacy respectiuely to the said Richard and Thomas ffeild, as the same according to this my will shalbe due to be paid, wth. such Consideracõn for the same as the said Company shall of their owne good wills and in their owne discretions be pleased to giue and allow for the said Legacies from the tyme of my decease, vntill the same shall be due to be paid [*wth such consideracõn*] as aforesaid. And in respect of the great fauour & kindnes I haue receiued from the said Company of Stacõners my mind & will is that in Case the said Thomas or Richard ffeild or either of them shall depart this life before their [*said*] seuerall Legacies shall according to the limitacõn afore expressed be due to be paid That then the Legacy or Legacies of them or such of them the said Richard & Thomas soe dying before the same shall be due to be

[1] Not, apparently, leased from the Company but adjacent to the garden of Abergavenny House. James Waley, the son of Henry Walley, was ordered 1 March 1664 to wall up this door, *Court-Book 1661–1668*.

[2] According to McKerrow's *Dictionary*, p. 96, this will is dated 1627.

[3] Mrs. Jane Field married a Mr. Bounst, cf. *C–B.C*, 98b, 1 Mar. 1628. She is called Mary Field in error on p. 187.

paid shall goe wholly to the said Company of Stacõners to be by them disposed for the good & benifitt of the said Company or of the [*po*] Poore of the same, as they in their discretions shall thinke most fittinge Item I giue and bequeath vnto the said Company of Stacõners in London for a memoriall and Testimony of my Loue vnto them a fair guilt siluer Salt Seller or any other peeces of Siluer plate to their best likinge of the value of Twenty pounds wth. these words (vizt.) The guift of Lucretia Este Widdowe to be engrauen thereon in fair Roman Letters.

3°. octobris 1631

Present. M^r^. Cole Mr Islip Mr Smethwicke Mr Waterson m^r^ Weaver Mr Purfoot m^r^ Bateman m^r^ Aspley m^r^ Rothwell & m^r^. ffetherston, m^r^ Harrison came late.

This day Mrs East her will was Read in Co^rt^. and order giuen that this Clause aboue inserted (for that it Concerned the Company) should bee entred here Mr Weaver being her executo^r^. brought 60^li^. & paid it to m^r^ Smethwicke warden/

11°. Octobris 1631 Fol. 116^b^

Present. M^r^. Cole, Mr Islip, Mr Smethwicke Mr Waterson M^r^. Kingston M^r^. Weaver, Mr Purfoot Mr Bateman, Mr Harrison Mr Aspley M^r^. Rothwell & M^r^ ffetherston.

M^rs^. Bills assistant part in the English stocke.

This day election was made for M^rs^. Bills assistant part in the English stocke she being late married out of the Company, the Board went to election of another partner & it fell vpon m^r^ Smethwicke, there stood in Election wth. him m^r^ Bateman[1] & m^r^ Aspley. Then election was made for m^r^. Smethwicks Liuery part & it fell vpon m^r^ Samuell Mann there stood in Election wth. him Mr Edwards & m^r^ Allott & then Election was made for m^r^ Manę Yeomandry part & it fell vpon m^r^ Stevens there stood in Election wth. him m^r^ Meredith & m^r^ Alchorne. And they took their oathes accordingly/

7°. Nouembris 1631

Present. M^r^. Cole, M^r^. Islip, m^r^ Smethwicke Mr Waterson, Mr Swinhow, m^r^ Kingston, m^r^ Weaver, m^r^ Purfoot, m^r^ Harrison & mr Rothwell.

Geo: Bradley

This day George Bradley[2] is warned to putt away Robert Bristowe[3] & not suffer him to be in his shopp any longer.

John Norgates debt to the English stocke/

Memorandum John Norgate[4] hath promised the Table to pay xx^s^. when he comes to seale his late apprentices Indentures & ii^s^. a weeke till his debt in the English stocke be paid witnes his hand

John Norgate.

[1] Made free 14 Jan. 1850, Arber ii. 681.
[2] Made free 15 Sept. 1631, Arber iii. 686.
[3] Unrecorded.
[4] Made free 12 Dec. 1614, Arber iii. 684.

William Jones [*W Jones*] fyne. [*fyne*]

This day William Jones for printing a breefe[1] Contrary to order and in preiudice of m^r Purfoots graunt[2] is fyned to pay for euery Rheame xij^d. that he printeth & to bring it to the Table to be disposed of at their discretion.

Present

M^r. Cole, m^r Islip, Mr Smethwicke m^r Waterson, m^r Swinhow, m^r. Weaver m^r Purfoot m^r Harrison m^r. Aspley & m^r Rothwell.

Order to search Binders & all others/

It is this day ordered for the better finding out of Counterfeit books & all other things disorderly printed, that the Wardens shall send whome they shall thinke fitt & meet persons (when and as often as they shall find Cause) to search the Shopps, houses & warehouses of Bookebinders or of any other parsons wch they shall suspect aswell abroad in the Countries as wth in the Citty of London.

Couenant for Bladon. Memorand by the appointment of the Table the Couenants & Bond for William Bladon were deliuered to the Irish Stockeepers to be putt in the Chest wth. the Lrẽs Pattents & there to be kept.[3]

Fol. 117^a

5°. Decembris 1631

Present.

m^r. Cole, M^r. Islip m^r. Smethwicke, m^r Waterson, m^r Swinhow, m^r Kingston m^r. Weaver m^r Purfoot m^r Harrison m^r Rothwell.

M^r. Barrengers Yeomandry part in the English stocke

This day election was made for m^r Barrengers Yeomandry part in the English stocke he being lately dead. There stood in election m^r Mathews, m^r Legatt, m^r Meredith & m^r Alchorne & it fell on m^r Meredith & m^r Alchorne to each of them halfe a part to make them vp full yeomandry parts. & they tooke their oathes accordingly.

11°. Januarij 1631

Present.

M^r. Cole m^r Islip, m^r Smethwicke m^r Waterson m^r. Swinhow, m^r Kingston m^r Harrison m^r Aspley, m^r Rothwell m^r ffetherston m^r Weaver & m^r Purfoot.

Printers.

This day all the Printers that were present (being quarter day) o^r. M^r. gaue order to them that noe bookes (licensed by my Lord B^p: of London) should be printed by any printer whatsoeuer wth out the License printed wth. the booke.

Sam. Matchams Copies

It is ordered that Samuell Matcham shall haue the Copies turned ouer to him that were his fathers.[4]

[1] STC 8981.

[2] Cf. *C–B.C*, 46^a, 16 Jan. 1617.

[3] Cf. *C–B.C*, 113^b, 30 June 1631.

[4] His mother had transferred these copies to J. Grismand, 15 Feb. 1628 (Arber iv. 193). He transferred them to J. Haviland, 8 Apr. 1628 (Arber iv. 196) with the provision that he should pay to S. Macham II 2*s*. per ream on those he printed. As a result of this order they were entered to young Macham 11 Jan. 1632 (Arber iv. 269).

Mr Grantham paid mr. Peter Shorts Legacy.

This day Mr Weaver brought in xxli. (wch. money was paid by mr. Grantham executor of mr Humphrey Lownes dec'.) & was accepted of by the Table for full satisfaction of a Legacy of xls. yearely heretofore bequeathed to the poore of this Company by Peter Short & for some yeares paid by Humphrey Lownes who married his widdow. Wherevpon the Table (for peace and quietnes sake) haue released all further Clayme for that debt.[1]

14°. Januarij. 1631

Present.

Mr Cole mr Islip mr Smethwicke mr Waterson, mr Swinhow mr Kingston mr weaver, mr Purfoot, mr Harrison & mr Rothwell.

ffran: Constabls part in the English stocke assigned to Ro: Constable for 2 yeares.

Whereas [*mr*] ffrancis Constable is indebted vnto Robert Constable[2] his brother the sume of 200li. this day the said ffrancis Constable [had leaue of the Cort to] [*did*] assigne ouer his Liuery part in the English stocke for [security of] the payment thereof at Two yeares & the said Robte Constable is to haue all the benifitt of the same stocke till such tyme as the debt be paid wth. the interest at 8li. p Cent.

mr. Purfoots halfe Assistant part. morgaged to mr. Locke/

This day mr. Purfoot had leave to assigne ouer halfe his assistant pte in the English stocke vnto mr Locke for 104l. for 6 monthes.

26th. of January 1631. Fol. 117b

Present.

Mr. Cole, Mr. Islip, mr Smethwicke, Mr Waterson, mr Swinhow, mr Kingston mr Purfoot Mr Harrison, Mr Aspley, Mr Rothwell & mr. ffetherston.

Mr. Sands.

This day vpon a new Complaint made by mr Sands about the printing of his translacõn of the xv. bookes of (ovids Metamorphosis.)[3] The mr Wardens & Assistants hearing what mr Sands could alleadge. And what mr. Young & mr Haviland could say in Answere. They then for their further satisfaction caused all the Entries heretofore made & an order concerning those Entries to be read wch. order followeth in these words (vide page 99 p Sands) as therein appeareth Wch order being Read this Cort. conceived to be donn vpon very good ground & doe approve of the same in all points And vpon further examinacõn of this Cause doe find that the said Robert Young & John Haviland (at the tyme of their imprinting the said bookes) did know that mr Sands had before obteyned his Mat: Lrẽs Pattents for the Sole printing of his said Translacõn And that they printed the bookes now in question by a copy printed wth. this addicõn (cum priviledgio) wch induceth the Cort. to conceive that they could not be ignorant that the sole printing of the same booke belonged to the said mr Sands. Wherevpon the

[1] Cf. *C–B.C*, 3a, 12 Mar. 1604; 106b, 12 June 1630; 108a, 9 Oct. 1630; and 113b, 2 July 1631.

[2] Made free 12 Dec. 1614, Arber iii. 684.

[3] STC 18965. Cf. *C–B.C*, 99a, 8 Apr. 1628.

Co[rt]. agayne ordered that the printing of the said booke is to remayne soly in the disposicōn of the said m[r] Sands & his assignes/

15° ffebruarij 1631/

Present. M[r]. Waterson loco Magr̃i M[r]. Islip M[r]. Smethwicke, M[r] Swinhow m[r]. Kingston M[r] Weaver M[r] Purfoot M[r] Harrison M[r] Aspley & M[r] Rothwell.

M[rs]: Aldee. This day vpon the humble suite of M[rs]. Aldee to have her sonn[1] Richard Oulton [*made free*] admitted into the fredome of this Company by Redemption, the Co[rt]. hath graunted the same vpon her payment of x. pounds now vnto them & for this their Courtesy she promiseth to pay or leaue them x. pounds more after her decease to be paid or deducted out of her part w[ch] she hath in the English stocke witnes her hand the day above written as appeareth in the wast booke

The m'ke of [*Eli*] ⊕ Eliz: Aldee.

1° Martij 1631

Present vt ante.

[*S[t]. Paul Charch*] [*This day the table haveing taken into Consideracōn a letter sent by my Lo: B[p]: of London concerning a Contribution towards the repayre of S[t]. Paules Church. They have thought fitt & so ordered that 150[li]. shall be paid out of the house by the wardens for the tyme being (viz[t]) xv[li]. at or before o[r] lady day next, & soe xv[li] yearely vntill the said Sum̃e of 150[li]. be paid. provided the worke goe forward otherwise to cease.*][2]

Vide page 119.

Stockeepers for the English stocke.	m[r] Harrison m[r] Aspley	m[r] Bourne m[r] Jo: Dawson	m[r] Miller Henry Overton

m[r]. Weaver Treasurer et Jur'.

Auditors.	m[r] Kingston m[r] Aspley	m[r] Downes m[r] Mead	m[r] Bird Edw: Blackmore

FOL. 118[a]

5° Marcij 1631

Present. M[r]: Cole M[r]. Islip M[r] Smethwicke, M[r]. Waterson, M[r] Swinhow, M[r]. Kingston M[r]. Weaver M[r]. Purfoot M[r]. Harrison & M[r]. Bateman.

Whereas there hath byn in former tymes for the better government of this Company an ordinance sett downe W[ch]. is yet in force, That noe person free of this Company shall print or Cause to be printed any other mans Copy or any Booke wherein any

[1] The statement in McKerrow's *Dictionary*, p. 6, that Oulton was Mrs. Allde's son-in-law is evidently in error, see *Trans.*, 3rd Ser. x (1919), 105.

[2] Among the *State Papers Dom. 1629–1631*, p. 379, 12 Nov. 1631, is a list of the Master Printers with the sums assessed to each one, in the hand of Bishop Laud. Cf. also *C–B.C*, 119[a], 9 Mar. 1632.

other man hath a proper & peculiar interest. And whereas the Booke comonly called the Booke of Martyrs properly apperteyneth to the Hall and Company in generall & noe person free of this Company ought or is by the aforesaid ordinance to imprint the same w^th^out the License of the Master Wardens & assistants of this Company for the tyme being or the more part of them first had & obteyned. And whereas in regard the' foresaid booke of Martyrs hath byn of late tymes out of Print & therevpon it was heretofore by order of this Table[1] proposed to all that were free of this Company in generall that if any of them would vndertake to imprint an impression of the' said Booke at their owne Charge, this [*Boord*] [Co^rt^] would give way to them therein (the Printers who should soe imprint the same allowing such a reasonable sum̄e of money to & for the benifitt of the house as should be vpon the finishing of the said impression sett downe by this Table or the more part of them as by an order made in this behalfe may appeare) And there vpon after a long deliberacōn Mr Adam Islip, m^r^. ffelix Kingston and one Robert Young Printers & Stacōners tooke vpon them by approbacon of this Table to print one impression of 1600. of the same Books at their owne Charge. And afterward they haveing begunn the said impression proposed to the Company in generall to take all the said impression by them printed & to be printed at a certayne rate demaunded by them, and vpon the proposall soe made, onely Sixteene of the said Company Condiscended & agreed to take the whole impression at a rate agreed vpon betweene them, and vpon such agreement the Printers & Takers entred Covenants each to other (vizt.) The Printers vnto the Takers[2] to imprint & deliver to them the said whole impression by a certayne tyme agreed vpon And the Takers to the Printers to pay their moneyes vnto the said Printers at such dayes as were agreed vpon by the said Covenants or Articles of Agreement sett downe vnder their hands & Seales each to other, since wch. tyme the Takers have paid a great part of their moneyes agreed vpon to be paid for the same & are to pay the rest. This day vpon Complaint made by the Takers & Buyers of th'aforesaid Books vnto this Co^rt^. That the aforesaid Robert Young (who is one of the'forenamed Printers & is to have one third part of the money to be made for Paper & Printing of the whole impression of th'aforesaid Books) to hinder the Sale of the said Booke w^ch^. (by reason of the long delay of the finishing thereof) is not yet ready to be published, Combyninge wth. one Miles ffletcher & one John Haviland two other Printers of this Company vnder pretence of a Pattent[3] graunted by o^r^ late soveraigne Lord King James (of famous memory) to one Hellen Mason the late widđ of one Thomas Maison Clarke long since deceased to imprint the Abridgm^t^. of the Booke of Martyrs[4] made & sett forth by th'aforesaid Thomas Maison in his life time & w^th^out any further license or authority have begunn to imprint & are now imprinting (as they pretend) the said Abridgment & out of the Booke of Martyrs now newly printed They have taken a great part of the most speciall & cheefest matters & inserted them into the Abridgment now by them in printing as if the same had byn made & sett forth by th'aforesaid Thomas Maison in his life tyme, Whereas they were neuer made & sett forth by him But the Booke now begunn by them will be enlarged a third part at the least, W^ch^. addicōns are

[1] Cf. *C–B.C*, 104^b^, 7 Sept. 1629, and 115^a^, 1 Aug. 1631.

[2] These covenants have not survived, but the 'Articles agreed vpon' by the sixteen Takers are recorded, *Letter Book*, 182^a^ and ^b^.

[3] See T. Rymer, *Foedera*, xvii (1727), 294.

[4] STC 17622.

FOL. 118[b] noe part of the said || Masons worke. Yet hereby the Takers of the said Booke of Martyrs now newly imprinted will not onely be much hurt in the sale of their books But it tendeth to the vtter destruccõn of the same Booke & Copy for future tymes. And therevpon the said Complaynants desired some Course might be taken by this Co[rt]. for the Suppressing of the said Abridgment now being in the Presse & for stay of further proceeding in the printing thereof for the reasons aforesaid. Herevpon this Co[rt]. taking into their Consideracõn thaforesaid matter & Complaint. And vpon perusall of the Letters Pattents graunted vnto th'aforenamed Ellen Maison as aforesaid conceiveing the said Graunt doth warrant onely the imprinting of that worke wch. was made & sett forth by Thomas Maison in his life tyme & holding it to be a very leud & indirect part of the said Robert Young to ioyne in the impression of the enlarged Abridgment soe soon as he had vented his third part of the impression of the Booke at large thereby to defraud & impoverish those of this Company that bought the same of him. And this Co[rt]. now taking notice that the M[r]. of this Company being enformed of the abusiue printing of the said Booke wth. large addicõns by the forenamed Young, ffesher & Haviland about a month agoe went in person to the printing house of the said fflesher. And there finding the said new Abridgment in the Presse, called for the Copy, some part whereof being delivered vnto him, he found that it was almost all a new written Copy & such as had never formerly byn printed wth the said Abridgment. Wherevpon the said M[r]. Comanded the said fflesher, Young, & Haviland to forebeare in such manner to proceed, till further order should be given in that behalfe. Yet nevertheles the said fflesher, Young, & Haviland Contrary to their oathes & duty in Contempt of the said M[r]., & the Lawes & ordinances established for the government of this Company, doe still proceed, And doe now imprint the said Abridgment w[th]. the said new large Addicõns therevnto. Therefore vpon due Consideracõn had of all the premises, It is this p[r]sent day at & by a full Co[rt]. thought meete & ordered that the wardens of this Company or either of them calling to their assistance such as they or any of them shall thinke meet, shall forthwith take downe the Barrs & Spindles of the Presses of the said Miles fflesher & of such others as doe or shall imprint the said Abridgment or any part thereof soe enlarged. And that they shall bring the said Barrs & Spindles & also soe many sheets of the said Abridgment now or hereafter soe imprinted vnto the Comon hall of this Company, where they shall remayne & be sequestred vntill further direction shall be given by this [*Boord*] [Co[rt].] touching the same.[1]

M[r]. Erswell about his house. Whereas M[r]. Ersewell hath this day by his Letter sollicited the Table for further tyme in his Lease[2] & to give a fyne for abatement of Rent. It is referred to m[r] Kingston m[r] Weaver M[r] Harrison and m[r] Aspley & they to Consider of it & give in their Report of the same by the next Co[rt].

[1] Evidently Young was not content to abide by this ruling, for in *The history of the troubles and tryal of . . . Laud*, 1695, p. 351, the Archbishop wrote, 'Mr. Young the Printer laboured me earnestly and often for an *Abridgment of the Book of Martyrs*. But I still withstood it (as my Secretary here present can Testifie) upon these two Grounds. The one, lest it should bring the large Book it self into disuse. And the other, lest if any Material thing should be left out, that should have been charged as done of purpose by me; as now I see it is in other Books.'

[2] This lease is evidently of the house in Amen Corner, part of the Abergavenny property, which was let to Mr. Lyon, 6 Mar. 1626, *C–B.C*, 89[b], and 120[a], 4 June 1632.

9°. Martij. 1631.

Present. Mr. Cole Mr. Mr. Islip Mr Smethwicke Wardens, Mr Kingston Mr Weaver Mr Purfoot Mr Harrison Mr. Aspley Mr Rothwell & Mr ffetherston.

St. Pauls Church This day the Table having taken into Consideracõn a Letter sent by my Lord Bp: of London concerning a Contribution towards the Repaire of St. Pauls Church they have thought fitt & soe ordered that Cli. shall be paid out of the house by the Wardens for the tyme being in manner & forme following (Vizt.) xvli. at or before or Lady day next & so xvli yearely vntill the [said] Sum̃e be all paid Provided the worke intended goe forwards otherwise the payments to cease.[1]

26°. Martij 1632.

Present Mr. Cole Mr. Islip Mr. Smethwicke Mr Waterson Mr Swinhow Mr Weaver Mr Purfoot Mr Harrison Mr Bateman Mr Aspley Mr Rothwell & Mr ffetherston. Mr Kingston came late.

Genealogies. This day a note was read subscribed with many hande of the Partners in the English Stocke wherein they desire that they may be left at Liberty for taking the Genealogies[2] wth. the Psalmes. It is ordered that it be Considered of by the next Cort. wch. is appointed [*by*] on the next Munday after Low Sunday, in the meane tyme Mr Docter Speed is to be sent vnto and a Copy of the aforesaid Note.[3]

Mr. Moore fyne for Rentor. This day mr Moore made his humble request vnto the Table to be dispensed wthall for serving the second yeare Rentor & the Table admitted him to fyne & they imposed xxiiijli. & so freed him

Mr Bourne fyne for Rentor and Stockeeper 3. yeares Mr. Bourne being called made the like request to be spared for Rentor & further desired that by reason of many occasions he might be freed from Stockeep for 3. yeares. (vnto which he was lately chosen) & he offered to pay for discharge of both places xxxli. wch was accepted of to be paid on the vjth. of May 1632.

Mr. Mead fyne for Rentor. Mr Mead being likewise chosen Rentor humbly craved the Table to be admitted to ffyne which vpon Consideracon was graunted & he then paid xxiiijli & so was freed:

Mr. Ephr: Dawson This day Mr Ephraim Dawson was chosen Stockeep in the place of Mr. Bourne.

[1] Cf. *C–B.C*, 117b, 1 Mar. 1632.

[2] STC 23039.

[3] Obviously this was a bargaining move, as the next month the renewal of Speed's contract was to be signed.

FOL. 119b

eodem die predict'

Mr. Beale and Mr. Higgenbotham chosen Rentors — Mr. Beale & Mr. Higgenbotham are chosen Rentors for the yeare ensewing.

Mr Jo: Waterson — This day John Waterson had License to engage his Livery part in the English Stocke vnto Mrs. Joyce Norton for one hundred & Eight pounds borrowed of her for one whole yeare. The former engagement to mr Adams[1] being paid and discharged. And it is ordered withall that no more money be lent vpon it till his debt which he oweth vnto the English stocke be paid out of his dividents & fifty pounde which he borrowed of the house[2] be paid or further secured.

Memorand the 50li borrowed of Mr. Nortons bequeast was paid the 30th. of March 1638

9° die Aprilis 1632.

Present — Mr. Cole, Mr Islip Mr. Smethwicke, Mr Waterson Mr Swinhow, Mr. Weaver Mr Harrison Mr Aspley Mr Rothwell Mr ffetherston Mr Kingston & Mr Purfoot came late.

Mr. Tho: Harper fyne for printing the Psalmes — This day Mr Harper haveing printed divers sheets of the Psalmes in 8°.[3] wthout any Order & being proved against him by good Testimony and his owne Confession, (he submitting himselfe & desiring favour) the Table have thought fitt to impose a fyne of xxty: Marks vpon him to be paid, halfe on or before the Sixt of May & the other before the Election day & likewise to forfeit all the paper and workemanship so disorderly done by him. And although (for this his offence) he hath by the Ordinance forfeited all his part which he hath in the English Stocke. Notwithstanding this being his first offence the said fyne is accepted of by the Table.

Rich: Cotes fyne — Likewise Richard Cotes was fyned at xxs for consenting that Thomas Harper should print some of the sheets of the Psalmes wch. were (by the Stockeeps) delivered & appointed for him to print

Rich: Badger 50li. continued — This day Richard Badger having paid in 50li. wch. he borrowed of Mr John Nortons[4] bequest vpon his humble suite made hath the same graunted vnto him for 3. yeares more putting in good security.

John Hamons Presse — The Presse that was taken of John Hamon in Petticoate Lane[5] was the 17th. of March last defaced & made vnserviceable in the prsence of ye Mr. Wardens & divers of the Assistants.

[1] Cf. *C–B.C*, 107a, 16 June 1630.

[2] Cf. *C–B.C*, 105b, 18 Jan. 1630.

[3] There are three editions of Sternhold and Hopkins Psalms in octavo printed for the Company without printer's initials in 1631, and one in 1632. None of those seen shows any indication of division of copy. Cf. *C–B.C*, 142b, 28 Sept. 1636, and 152b, 15 Jan. 1638.

[4] Cf. *C–B.C*, 102b, 26 Mar. 1629. His new bonds were registered 23 Apr. 1632, *Liber C2*, 115b.

[5] This press in Whitechapel is the sixth recorded as having been seized from Hamon.

12°. Aprilis 1632.

Mr. Harrison. This day Mr Harrison had License to engage his Assistants part in the English Stocke vnto Mr Thomas Downes for payment of 200li & interest at 8li p Centu' for one whole yeare.

26°. Aprilis 1632.

Geneologies. This day the Covenants between Dr. Speed & the Company (for the Genealogies) were sealed for Three yeares to begin at Midsomer next.[1]

4° Junij 1632.

Present Mr. Cole. Mr Islip Mr Smethwicke Mr Waterson Mr Kingston Mr Weaver Purfoot Mr Harrison Mr Aspley & Mr Rothwell.

Mr Downes Rentor This day Mr Downes for his extraordinary paynes in his Rentorship[2] taken whereby a greater Sum̃e then [euer] [*vsuall*] was brought in, had allowed him by the Table iijli. vjs. viijd.

Mr Bowler 50li renewed This day mr Bowler became a Suiter to the Table that the 50li. formerly by him borrowed might be continued for 3. yeares more, the Table tooke it into Consideracõn & it was granted, provided that he bring in the money first according to order & putt in sufficient Security.[3]

mr Erswill for a new Lease. This day the Matter heretofore moved by Mr Erswell[4] for a new Lease of his now dwelling house & lesse Rent, paying a fyne there after Referred by the Table to mr Kingston & others The Table taking the same into Consideracõn wth a generall Consent graunted him a New Lease for xxxj [yeares.] Eighteene yeares whereof were vnexpired in his old Lease. And for abatement of Rent (being putt to voices) it was by the Maior part agreed & so ordered That whereas he paid before 12li p ann' he should now pay but vjli p ann' In Consideracõn whereof he should pay a fyne of Lxli. vpon the sealing of such now Lease.

28°. Junij 1632.

Anth: Ward to serue the Marketts with Corne This day Anthony Ward Chaundler was agreed wth. to serve the Marketts wth Corne according to my Lord Mayors precept[5] for a yeare from this day, and he is to have Ten pounds for the same

[1] Cf. *C–B.C*, 119a, 26 Mar. 1632. Speed's seventeen-year patent must have been renewed about this time.

[2] Chosen 26 Mar. 1631, *C–B.C*, 112a.

[3] His bonds were registered 29 June 1632, *Liber C2*, 116a.

[4] Cf. *C–B.C*, 118b, 5 Mar. 1632.

[5] In *Letter Book*, 120a, 16 Apr. 1632.

FOL. 120b

vltimo Junij 1632.

Present — Mr Cole Mr Islip Mr Smethwicke Mr Waterson Mr Kingston Mr Weaver Mr Purfoot Mr Harrison Mr Aspley and Mr Rothwell.

Mr. Purfoot & mr Harrison fyne for 2d. tyme wardens — This day Mr Purfoot & Mr Harrison desired to be putt to fyne for their second tyme being vnder warden & they were fyned at ffive pounds a peece.

Mr. Ersewells Lease sealed. — This day Mr Ersewell had a Lease sealed vnto him of his now dwelling house for xxxjty. yeares Comencing from Midsomer day last & [he] paid downe to Mr Weaver [*xlli*] Threescore pounds according to agreement for his fyne.

mr. Ersewell to have a Key of the garden — At a full Cort. this day mr Erswell haveing taken a new Lease of his now dwelling house in Amen Corner became a Suitor to the Court that in Regard his way to the Church was somewhat about & very durty in the Winter tyme they would be pleased to give Leave vnto him to have accesse into & through the Garden[1] for himselfe & his wife to goe to their Church wherevpon the Cort. taking it into their Consideracõn (in a Loving respect towards him & in regard he is their Tenant) graunted his suite & ordered that he have a key & free accesse to & from their Church by & through the garden so long as they shall dwell in the said house themselues & no longer provided they give no way to any Strangers to goe in & out that way.

5o. Julij 1632.

Mr: Cole} Master
Mr. Weauer, Mr Aspley} wardens/

Present — Mr. Cole Mr Weaver Mr Aspley Mr Waterson Mr Swinhow, Mr Islip Mr Harrison Mr Smethwicke & Mr Rothwell.

Auditors chosen to audite ye wardens account — Mr. Waterson & Mr Harrison are appointed to auditt the wardens Account.

19o. Julij

Tho: Jones Copies assigned to mr Mathews. — This day Thomas Jones (vpon his request) had License to assigne ouer all his Copies vnto Mr. Mathews.[2]

[1] Evidently the new garden (cf. *C–B.C*, 107b, 6 Sept. 1630) was an attractive feature, for in *State Papers Dom. 1631–1633*, p. 415, Michael Burton, writing to Secretary Windebank, 14 Sept. 1632, offered him his own house 'which abuts upon the Stationers' garden, to which the Secretary may have a key'.

[2] Entered 24 Oct. 1623 (Arber iv. 307).

6° Augusti 1632.

Present. Mr. Cole Mr Islip (loco gardian') Mr Aspley Mr Waterson Mr Kingston Mr Purfoot Mr Harrison Mr Smethwicke & Mr Rothwell.

Mr. Recorder xli. given him, being Reader of ye. Temple — This day the Cort. taking into Consideracoñ what to prsent Mr. Recorder Littleton wth (he now being Reader of the Temple)[1] It was vnanimously consented & ordered that That Ten pounds should be given [him] for a remembrance of their Love to him. wch accordingly was performed/

Mr Bill & Mr Bon: Nortons Copies to be entred to Mrs. Joyce Norton & Rich: Whitacres — This day vpon the humble request of Mrs. Joyce Norton & Richard Whitaker that all the Copies & parts of Copies belonging vnto Mr. Bill & Mr. Bonham Norton entred in the hall Booke might according to a deed vnder the hand & seale of Mr. Lucas & a note vnder the hand of Mr Bonham Norton by them produced in Cort. Might be entred vnto them for their Copie[2] wch the Cort. granted And whereas diuers Copies belonging vnto them were not entred. they humbly prayed the Cort. that they might be alsoe entred vnto them wch. was then likewise granted but wth this prouisoe Saluo Jure cuiuscunq;.

3°. Septembris 1632. Fol. 121a

Present Mr. Waterson loco Magr̃i. Mr. Weaver Mr Aspley, Mr. Islip Mr. Purfoot Mr. Harrison Mr. Smethwicke & Mr Rothwell.

John Hamon presse — This day a Presse being erected in Shoredich by John Hamon contrary to the Decree in Starchamber was defaced & made vnserviceable the Ninth day of this Month following in ye prsence of the wardens & diuers of the Assistants.

Wm. Harris supposed presse. — Likewise one Presse taken in the Minories supposed to be William Harris[3] being vnlawfully erected was also defaced & made vnserviceable in the prsence as aforesaid.

23° Octobris 1632.

Present Mr. Cole Mr. Weaver Mr. Aspley Mr. Waterson Mr Swinhow Mr. Islip Mr. Purfoot Mr. Harrison Mr. Bateman Mr. Smethwicke & Mr. Rothwell.

Booke of Martyrs money to the Poore — This day there was a Meeting about the booke of Martyrs concerning the payment that should be made by the printers thereof vnto the house according to the Order made in that

[1] On this occasion the aldermen of London presented Edward Littleton with £100, two hogsheads of claret, and a pipe of canary.

[2] Entered 26 Aug. 1632 (Arber iv. 283–5).

[3] Possibly the publisher of STC 10658. According to a note in the Privy Council Papers (P.C. 2/44 (29), 11 June 1634) the Council had given warrant to Miles Flesher and Robert Young to seize some reams of grammars and accidences from Harris. This they had done and delivered them to Stationers' Hall but later made an agreement with Harris whereby he was to turn over the books to Flesher and Young which he was unable to do as the Stationers would not surrender them. They were ordered to do so. Presumably they seized his press in retaliation.

behalfe, It was putt to voyces & seuerall sumes insisted vpon & vpon debate [it] was ordered That Mr Islip M^r^. Kingston & M^r^. Young should pay among then (*sic*) forty-Marks each man to pay an equall share according to the Number of sheets printed by him & no more, wch. was by them assented vnto.[1]

6°. Novembrie 1632.

Present vt ante

The garden of Health — The booke called the garden of health[2] being out of print, m^r^. Harper became a Suiter to the Table (he haveing begun to print it) That he might have leave to finish it wherevpon the Table intring into Consideracõn & finding the booke to be very long out of print & none laying any lawfull clayme vnto the Copy[3] gave leave that he should make an end of this impression allowing to the house for the same according to the order in that behalfe made vnto wch. he willingly submitted & promised to pforme the same Provided that if in Case a lawfull Right should be found. Then the said Harp is to give such satisfaction as this Co^rt^. shall thinke fitt.

Moses Bell to have the Loane of xij^li^. — Moses Bell is to have the next xij^li^. that [comes] in putting in good security.

Bernard Alsop xij^li^. — Bernard Alsop likewise to have xij^li^. putting in good security.

FOL. 121^b^

3°. Decembris 1632.

Present — M^r^. Cole M^r^. Weaver M^r^. Aspley M^r^. Waterson M^r^. Swinhow M^r^. Kingston M^r^. Ockold M^r^. Purfoot M^r^. Harrison M^r^. Smethwicke & M^r^. Rothwell.

Joseph Hunscotts revertion of the Beadles place. — At a full Co^rt^. holden this day Joseph Hunscott a brother of this Company preferred a peticõn vnto the Table for the Revertion of the Beadles place of the said Company. Where vpon they entring into Consideracõn thereof & finding the said Joseph to be a fitt pson for the place & for some other Reasons then and there given vpon debate of the Matter wth. a generall Consent graunted vnto him the Revertion of the said Beadleship when it shall fall void by death Resignacõn or otherwise.

[1] Forty marks would amount to £26. 13*s*. 4*d*., but from the account in the *Book of Fines*, 24^b^–25^a^, they paid only £8 apiece. Although the volumes are not of equal size, the work appears to have been divided roughly among the printers by volumes.

[2] STC 15196.

[3] Harper had some difficulty on this point, for it was originally entered to Bishop, Newbery, and Barker, 6 June 1597 (Arber iii. 85). Bishop's part was transferred to T. Adams, 14 Mar. 1611 (Arber iii. 454), but apparently was thought to be of little worth and was not included in the titles which A. Hebb had of Bishop's widow, 6 May 1625 (Arber iv. 139–40); Newberry's rights evidently lapsed; but Barker transferred his rights to Francis Constable, 14 Jan. 1633 (Arber iv. 290), and Harper was forced to obtain Constable's acquiescence, which he did 5 July 1633 (Arber iv. 298).

14°. Januarij 1632.

Present — Mr. Cole Mr. Weaver Mr Aspley Mr. Waterson Mr. Swinhow Mr Kingston Mr Ockold Mr. Purfoot Mr Harrison Mr. Smethwicke & Mr Rothwell.

Those that are behind for Plate are to bring it in. — This day it was ordered that those that are behind hand for plate[1] are to bring it in by the first of March & the wardens are to take a view wth workemen for the remedy of keeping of the plate better for there being a vault vnder neath the said roome causeth the said plate to loose the Couler as is conceived & they are to take what order they shall find fittest for the same.

Rich: Badger to have xxs. euery poores day — This day it was ordered that Richard Badger (by generall consent of the Table) shall have xxs euery quarter on the poores day for his paines to warne the Pencõners as the Clarke hath for keeping the Account & entring the names in the Register booke.[2]

Mr. Purfoot. — This day Mr. Purfoot had Leave to engage halfe his Assistants part in the English Stocke vnto Mrs. Joyce Norton for Cviijli. for one yeare, the former engagement to Mr Locke[3] being discharged.

19°. Januarij 1632.

Present — Mr. Cole Mr. Weaver Mr. Aspley Mr. Waterson Mr. Islip Mr Ockold Mr Harrison Mr Smethwicke Mr. Rothwell.

Mr. Butler & Mr. Harrison. — Whereas vpon Complaint made vnto my Lord of London by one Mr. Butler against Mr. Harrison one of this Company concerning a Copy called Butler of Bees[4] the said booke being writt by the said Mr. Butler. In Consideracon of (*blank*) paid vnto Mr. Harrison this day in the prsence of the Master wardens and Assistants he the said Mr Harrison did resigne all his interest in the said Booke vnto him.

eodem die predict'

FOL. 122a

Mr Bourne Bills of Lading. — This day it was ordered That Mr. Bourne should have all the Bills of Lading taken from Mr Mathews the printer wch. was about 3. Rheams & he received them accordingly.[5]

[1] Cf. *C–B.C*, 105a, 2 Nov. 1629.

[2] As a matter of fact he had been receiving a pound each quarter since Mar. 1631, according to the accounts in *Liber pro pauperibus*. Cf. *C-B.C*, 103b, 4 July 1629.

[3] Cf. *C–B.C*, 117a, 14 Jan. 1632.

[4] STC 4193. This book was originally published by J. Barnes in Oxford, 1609. His son assigned it to Roger Jackson, 26 Feb. 1619 (Arber iii. 642). Just how Harrison obtained any control of it is not clear, but the next edition, STC 4194, was published at Oxford by W. Turner 'for de Author', 1634.

[5] Cf. *C–B.C*, 104b, 5 Oct. 1629.

30°. Januarij 1632.

Present vt ante

Precept for D^r. Lambes death. This day all the Company was warned to the hall to contribute their shares according to the assessment imposed vpon the Company by vertue of a Precept from the Lord Mayo^r & Co^rt. of Aldrẽn for the Murther of Doc^r Lamb the sum̃e imposed being xiiij^li was gathered & paid accordingly.[1]

4°. ffebruarij 1632.

Present M^r. Waterson loco Magr̃i. M^r. Weaver M^r. Aspley M^r. Swinhow M^r. Islip M^r. Kingston M^r. Ockold M^r. Harrison M^r. Smethwicke & M^r. Rothwell.

Order for a Veiw The wardens are to veiw the Councell Roome to morrow & the Carpenter & Bricklayer are to be there & some Course is to be forthwith taken for the safety of it to be propt or otherwise for the p^rsent vntill further order be taken for repayre & then to veiw the house in Woodstreet.

1°. Martij 1632.

Present. M^r. Cole M^r. Weaver M^r. Aspley M^r. Waterson M^r. Swinhow M^r. Islip M^r. Kingston M^r. Ockold, M^r. Purfoot M^r. Harrison Mr Bateman Mr Smethwicke & M^r. Rothwell.

Stockeepers for the English Stocke	M^r. Islip M^r. ffetherston	M^r. Downes M^r. Parker	M^r. Stevene M^r. Lee

M^r. Weaver Threasurer et Jurat'.

Auditors	M^r. Purfoot M^r. Smethwicke	M^r. Moore M^r. Sam: Man	M^r. Seile M^r. Milborne

4°. Martij 1632.

M^r. Jennings Legacy of 80^li to m^r. Harrigate children. This day M^r. Harrigate came vnto the Co^rt. about a Legacy of 80^li given vnto his children by their late [*Grandfather*] [unckle] Tho: Jennings [directed in the will] [*&*] to be paid into the Stacõners hall. The Co^rt. hath [*considered*] [giuen Consent] that the said John Harrigate may vse the meanes (as by good Counsell shall be advised) for the getting in of the money & to vse the Companies name if occasion be, provided the Company be sufficiently saved harmeles before any suite comensed

[1] The precept is not transcribed in the *Letter Book*, but the exaction was for the failure of the City authorities to protect 'Dr.' John Lambe, the Duke of Buckingham's astrologer, against a London mob. According to the *Book of Fines*, 24^b, £16. 9*s*. was raised, and the Bill of Assessment is given in the *Letter Book*, 140^a–142^b. The Assistants were fined 3*s*., the Livery 2*s*., the Yeomanry 1*s*.

in their names & when the 80li. is paid then this Cort. will advise what couse (*sic*) to take therein.

Mr Whittaker. This day Mr Whittaker had leaue to engage his yeomandry part in the English stocke vnto Mrs. Joyce Norton for 80li. to be paid the 10th of March 1635.

27°. Martij. 1633. FOL. 122b

Present Mr. Cole Mr. Weaver Mr. Aspley Mr. Waterson Mr. Swinhow Mr. Islip Mr Ockold Mr. Purfoot Mr. Harrison Mr. Smethwick Mr Rothwell Mr ffetherston.

Mr. Withers The now Stockeeps mr Islip and the rest are requested by the Table to treat wth Mr. Withers about his proporcõns concerning his himnes & to Certify the Table of their doeings.[1]

Rentors This day Mr. Higgenbotham haveing served Rentor for a yeare & being called desired he might be excused from further service & referred himselfe to the Table & they considering of the matter passed it ouer for this tyme. Then Mr. Man was called who earnestly desired to be admitted to fyne, wch. vpon his importunity & some reasons alleadged by him was graunted & was then fined at xxiiijli. vnto wch. he willingly submitted & promised to pay the same vnto Mr Warden Aspley by Monday next. Then Mr. ffran. Constable & Mr. White being next the Table tooke them into Consideracõn & for that they appeared not (being warned) & for other Causes were both passed ouer & to keep as they are. Then Mr. Hoth was chosen though absent & Mr Parker to ioyne wth him for the next yeare following.

3°. Aprilis 1633.

Present vt supra.

Mr. Jo: Waterson This day ffifty pounds formerly lent vnto Mr John Waterson for three yeares & now expired, vpon his Request was continued to him againe for 3. yeares more.[2] And it is ordered by & wth. his Consent that ye residue of his pte in the English stocke wch besides the Cli. engaged to Mrs. Joyce Norton is sixty pounds shall be & remaine in the hall & not taken out nor any more lent vpon it, but to be kept & reserued for Mr Mattocke & Mr Dawbeny (who stand bound for the said money) for their security. Prouided that if the said Mr Waterson doe pay the Cli to Mrs. Joyce Norton & the ffifty pounds to the Company at the dayes & tymes appointed, then the said pte shall be free & not otherwise.[3]

[1] A year later Wither petitioned the Privy Council for aid against the Stationers in this matter, cf. *State Papers Dom. 1633–1634*, p. 533. When he published his *Psalms* (STC 2735) in 1632 he sent them to Holland to be printed.

[2] Cf. *C–B.C*, 105b, 18 Jan. 1630. His bonds were registered 8 Apr. 1633, *Liber C2*, 117a.

[3] Cf. *C–B.C*, 119b, 26 Mar. 1632.

3°. Junij. 1633.

Present | Mr. Waterson loco Magři Mr. Weaver Mr. Aspley Mr. Islip Mr. Ockold Mr Purfoot Mr. Harrison Mr. Smethwicke & Mr Rothwell. or Mr came late.

Mr Leakes fourth part of his stocke conferred vpon his sonn William Leake

Fol. 123a 113.

Whereas by an Order made the 16th. day of May 1631.[1] at the request of Mr. Leake (an ancient Master of this Company) one fourth part of his [*stocke*] English stocke was conferred vpon William Leake his sonne who was therevpon admitted a Partner for a yeomandry part in the said Stocke & tooke his oath as is vsuall in like Cases. Now the said Mr. || Leake the ffather being lately dead, the said William Leake the sonne came this day vnto the Table & humbly prayed a Confirmacōn of the former order touching the said fourth part. Wherevpon the Cort. taking the matter into Consideracōn have thought fitt & so ordered that the said fourth part & all the profitts thereof shall be & remayne vnto the said William according to the guift & meaning of the said ffather expressed in his life tyme. Provided when it shall happen the now Widdow of the said Mr. Leake the ffather to marry agayne or to depart this mortall life Then the whole part to be disposed of at the discretion of the Master Wardens & assistants for the tyme being according to the Ordinance and one fourth part of the whole Stocke appertaining to the said Mr. Leake deceased is to [be payd &] come to the said William Leake [his] sonne & the other three parts to the Widdow. And it is further ordered that from the tyme that the whole entier stocke is to be taken out as aforesaid the said William Leake the sonne shall stand as haveing no part at all in the said stocke vnles he shall be a new elected to a yeomandry part according to course. And it is further thought fitt & by Mutuall Consent ordered that the first order made for conferring the said fourth part shall not hereafter at any tyme be brought into Example or become a president to any in the like Case.

7° Martij. 1632. — this should haue byn entred in the foregoing page.

Present. | Mr Cole Mr Weaver Mr Aspley Mr Swinhow Mr Ockold Mr Harrison Mr Purfoot Mr Smethwicke.

Order for new building part of the Hall. by mr Williams Bricklayer

This day Mr. Williams the Brickelayer (being sent for) was agreed wthall to take downe the Chimney in the Councell Chamber & all the west side of that Roome wth. the stairecase & the Chimney in the Kitchin & rebuild the same wth bricke & make a new Chimney in the same Chamber to goe vp wth. the [kitchin] Chimney & he is to haue 90li to doe the same substantially.

[1] Cf. *C–B.C*, 113a.

FOL. 123b

Mr: Islip} Master
Mr: Weauer} wardens.
Mr. Aspley}

Present — Mr. Islip Mr Weauer Mr. Aspley Mr. Waterson mr. Swinhow mr Cole mr Kingston mr Ockold mr Purfoot mr. Harrison mr Smethwicke & mr Rothwell.

9°. Julij 1633. Nono Car' Regis.

Mr Kingston. fyne.

After the new Election & they being sett in the Parlor, Mr. Weaver being elected vpperwarden agayne to hold for the next yeare spake vnto them, that mr. Kingston being before him in tyme might be first admitted to fyne for his not holding second tyme vpperwarden before he were sworne agayne for that respect was to be had, that Mr Kingston should hold his ancientry, wch. the Table held fitt & being putt to voyces he was fyned at Twenty Nobles and soe to take his place according to his antiquity.

Money borrowed by the Company of St. ffaithes parish.

147.

This day (the Company wanting money by reason of their late building) sealed wth. their Comon Seale a Bond of 400li. for the payment of 221li. & interest for six monthes vnto the Parson and Churchwardens of St. ffaithes pish, they are to pay 6li. p Cent' for it, & haue promise from them to Continue it Longer if they will. The Bond is due the 11th. of January next

1°. Augusti 1633.

Present. — Mr. Islip Mr. Weauer. Mr Aspley Mr Waterson Mr Cole Mr Purfoot Mr Harrison.

ffifty Pounds & a peece of Plate. Mr Lockes legacies giuen to the Company.

This day the Executors. of Mr Locke[1] came to the table & paid downe the ffifty pownds bequeathed by [*the said*] him towards the buildinge of or hall as alsoe a peece of plate of the valew of Ten pounds bequeathed as aforesaid by him to the Company. And then the Company sealed a Release vnder their Comon seale for the receipt thereof.

5°. Augusti.

Present. — Mr Islip Mr. Mr Weaver Mr Aspley Wardens Mr Waterson Mr Ockold Mr Purfoot Mr Harrison.

The third warehouse in the garden Lett vnto or Master. Mr Islip

The warehouse wch was Lett vnto Mr Bill being the third in the garden was this day vpon request of Mr Islip our now Master granted vnto him, and he is to haue a Lease paying the fyne & Rent as others doe & vpon like Condicōn.[2]

[1] Presumably John Locke the lessee of some of the Abergavenny property, cf. *C–B.C*, 69b, 25 Sept. 1621, 125a, 20 Dec. 1633.

[2] Cf. *C–B.C*, 106a, 10 Mar. 1630, and 146a, 27 Mar. 1637.

2°. Sept: 1633.

Present — Mr. Islip Mr. Weaver Mr Aspley mr waterson Mr. Kingston mr Purfoot &c.

Two Presses & Letters to be restored to Mr Roger Norton.

This day Mr Roger Norton brought a note vnder mr Robte Barkers hand for the Deliuery of Two presses & Letters formerly taken in Dukes place, and it is granted he shall haue them agayne, Prouided the Company be in all points sufficiently saued & kept harmeles & the messenger that went to seize them contented for his paynes.[1]

18. Septembris 1633. pn'tibus vt [*vt*] supra

Mrs. Pauiers Part assigned for security for Clxxli. to her Children.

The Master and wardens haueing notice giuen them of an order lately made by the right honble: the Lord Maior & Court of Aldrēn concerning the Orphans of Thomas Pauier late one of the Assistants of this Company, caused this day a Meeting to be had, & there appeared before them Mary Pauier widdow late wife of the said Thomas Pauier Wch. order was now openly read & she the said Mary Pauier prayed that according to the Contents of the said order she might haue leaue granted vnto her to assigne ouer her pte of Money being the sume of CCCxxli. or thereabouts. wch. she hath in the priuiledge called the English stocke for the security and payment of Clxxli. in manner as in the said order is directed, Wch vpon Consideracōn had was granted vnto her. And then & there in the prsence of the Master wardens & [some of the] Assistants she the said Mary Pauier by a deed vnder her hand & seale did assigne & sett ouer her said pte for security as aforesaid. And it is this prsent day ordered by the Mr. wardens & Assistants now prsent that the said stocke of money shall not be taken out by the said Mary Pauier nor any other pson whatsoeuer vntill the said sume of Clxxli. be fully satisfied & paid according to the true meaning of the said order.

The deed of assignement & the order are in the Drawer in the study

2°. Octobris 1633. pn'tibus vt antea.

Mr Symson Minister giuen him iijli for dedicating his booke to the mr & war.

Whereas Mr. Andrew Simpson hath heretofore dedicated a Booke[2] vnto the Master and Wardens of this Company & gaue divers of his said Books vnto pticular psons of this society as by his Letter is Intimated. The Table haue thought fitt to send him Three pounds (as a gratuity) by Mr. Haviland the bearer of his Letter wch was accordingly done.

[1] This is probably connected with the disputes concerning the King's Printing Office.
[2] STC 22563.

Mr. Shelton & Mr Cartwright — The difference between Mr Shelton Mr Cartwright about the new Booke called Techigraphia[1] was by both their Consente referred to Mr. Seile & he is requested by the Table to take some paines therein & Certifie this Cort. his opinion therein by the next weeke.

eodem die

Fol. 124b

Chosen into the Assistants — This day mr. Butter mr Downes mr Moore & mr Bourne were Chosen into the Assistants of this Company.

7o. octobris. 1633.

Abraham Ripley. — It is ordered that Abraham Ripley[2] shall haue fifty pounds of mr John Nortons bequest putting in good security.

Tho: Weaver chosen into the Liuery — This day Thomas Weaver was called into the Liuery of this Company & he paid downe xxli. according to the Custome in that behalfe.

Mr Shelton & Mr Cartwright — This day mr Seile certified ye Table touching the difference betweene Mr Shelton & Mr Cartwright to him referred[3] that he had dilligently perused & Compared Mr Sheltons new booke called Techigraphia wth. his other booke of Short writing wch he sold to Mr Cartwright & did find that ye said Techigraphia was most pte of it taken out of Mr Cartwrights booke & transposed meerely to defraud the said Cartwright & spoile ye sale of his booke. wch the Table taking into Consideracōn haue ordered that the said Cartwright shall be at Liberty likewise to print the said Techigraphia.

28o. Octobris 1633.

Present. — Mr Islip mr Weaver mr Aspley mr Waterson mr Kingston mr Ockold mr Harrison mr Purfoot mr Smethwicke mr Rothwell Mr Butter Mr Downes mr More & Mr Bourne.

Chosen into the Liuery — This day William Crawley[4] John Marriott, John Morrett,[5] Mathew walbancke Richard Coates Samuell Cartwright Humphrey Mozeley & Henry Overton came into the Liuery of this Company

[1] Cartwright entered Shelton's *Short-writing*, 17 Apr. 1626 (Arber iv. 159). No copy of the first edition is known, but three copies of the second edition, 1630, are recorded, STC 22404; and a 'third edition', f. S. Cartwright, 1633, is in Bodley. His *Tachygraphy* was apparently not printed by Cartwright at this time, although he later published it, cf. *C–B.C*, 175a, 1 Mar. 1640.

[2] Made free 5 Sept. 1614 (Arber iii. 684).

[3] Cf. *C–B.C*, 124a, 2 Oct. 1633.

[4] Made free 16 Jan. 1610 (Arber iii. 683).

[5] Made free 1 Mar. 1617 (Arber iii. 684).

4°. Nouembrie 1633. pn'tibus vt antea

Billingsgate. This day m[r] Dickins came to the Co[rt]. and desired the renueing of his Lease.[1] The table haue appointed M[r] Kingston M[r] Ockold M[r] Harrison M[r] ffetherson & M[r] Downes or any four of them to informe themselues aswell by veiwing the Writings as the house and to Consider what Course is best to take either for Letting or setting of the Companies estate, and to treate wth. M[r] Hamond who dwells in some pte of the Tennem[t]. and what may be the most Comodious Course for the Companie to take herein & to Certifie of their doeings & opinions by the next montly Co[rt].

John Benson. It is ordered that John Benson shall haue ffifty pounds of m[r] John Nortons bequeast.[2]

2°. Dec. 1633. pn'tibus vt antea

Bryan Greenhill This day vpon the humble peticõn of Bryan Greenhill[3] who lately casually broke his Leg the Table thought fitt to giue him three pounds for his releefe.

FOL. 125[a] eodem die

M[r]. Purfoots part mortgaged. This day m[r] Purfoot had leaue to engage his Assistant pte in the English stocke vnto M[rs]. Joyce Norton for a yeare (the former engagement[4] is to be deliuered vp) for the payment of 216[li]. from the expiracõn of the said engagement for one yeare more.

Mr Kingston and Mr Harrison to peruse ye Joyners Bill } It is ordered that Mr Kingston & Mr Harrison doe puse the Joyne[rs]. Bill for the worke he hath done for the Company & what they shall see fitting, to allow him.

20°. December 1633. pn'tibus vt antea

Widdow Hurlocke part in y[e] Eng: stocke assigned ouer to Geo: Hurlocke .... } This day Joseph Hurlocks widdow assigned ouer her part in the English stocke vnto George Hurlocke & he tooke his oath accordingly. Alsoe she then assigned vnto him all her Copies & pts of Copies belonging vnto her.[5]

M[r]. Badgers security to the Executors of m[r] Locke for his Childrens Legacies by him red[d]. beforehand ...... } At a Co[rt]. holden this day Richard Badger had License granted him. That Eight pounds pt of his yomãry share wch. he hath in the priuiledge comonly called the English stocke should be deposited & kept there to this end & purpose. That whereas John Locke Late of London Taylor deceased by his Last will & Testament did giue & bequeath (amongst diuers other Legacies) the sume of Ten pounds amongst the Children of the said Richard Badger he haueing then at the decease of the said John Locke fiue Children (viz[t].) Thomas, John, Christopher, George, & Richard Badger,

[1] Cf. *C–B.C*, 85[b], 4 Apr. 1625.

[2] His bonds were registered 2 Apr. 1634, *Liber C2*, 117[b].

[3] Made free 4 Apr. 1608 (Arber iii. 683).

[4] Cf. *C–B.C*, 121[b], 14 Jan. 1633.

[5] Entered 16 Jan. 1634 (Arber iv. 312).

wch. four last mencõned Children are vnder age & not Capable to giue discharge for the said Legacy to them bequeathed. And forasmuch as mr Clement Mosse & Mr Geo: Britten the Executors. of the Last will & Testamt. of the said John Locke haue paid the sum̃e of forty shillings vnto the said Thomas Badger who then gaue a discharge for the same. And likewise haue paid vnto the said Richard Badger the ffather the sum̃e of Eight pounds in full of the said Legacie for the vse of his said other four Children who haue not as yet attayned [*un*]to the age of xxjty. yeares & are not Capable to giue discharge for the same. It is therevpon ordered by & wth the Consent of the said Richard Badger (for the Indempnity & saueing harmeles of the said Mr Clement Mosse & Mr Geo: Britten their Executors. & Assignes. That the said sum̃e of Eight pounds ꝑt of his stocke aforemencõned shall not be taken out or ꝑted wthall vntill the said four Children doe seuerally discharge the said Mr Clement Mosse & Mr George Britten for the said Eight pounds by them paid as aforesaid. Provided that if the said Richard Badger or his Executors. shall take out his said yeomandry ꝑte before the said Children shall all haue attayned the age of xxjty. yeares & seuerally discharged the said Exers. That then soe much of the said Eight pounds as shall be vndischarged by the said Children shall be & remayne there vntill discharge be seuerally giuen by the said Children as aforesaid.

16°. Jan: 1633. — Fol. 125b

Present. Mr. Islip Mr Weaver Mr Aspley Mr Waterson Mr. Ockold, Mr Purfoot Mr Harrison Mr Smethwicke Mr Rothwell Mr. ffetherston Mr Butter Mr Downes Mr Moore Mr Bourne. Mr Kingston came late.

Tho: Haughton admitted Tennant to the Company for the ffeather Taverne in pauls church yard.

This day Thomas Haughton Vintner came to the Table, & humbly requested (shewing his Assignemt. of the ffeathers Taverne[1] in Pauls Church yard) that he might be admitted Tennant to the Company & to pay his Rent to the Rentor as it growes due. wch the table [haue] thought fitt & soe ordered.

12°. Jan: pn'tibus vt ante

To provide Corne.

The Table haue requested both the wardens Mr Kingston Mr Harrison [&] Mr ffetherston or any four of them to take some paynes for the provision of Corne for this yeare for the Company & to take some prsent Course for serveing the Marketts & for a Granary wch. the Company ought to haue from the Citty.[2]

Cooke to the hall mr Hunlocke

Christopher Hunlocke haueing the Revertion of the Cookes place formerly granted vnto him[3] vpon his peticõn was admitted

[1] Cf. *C–B.C*, 105a, 2 Nov. 1629, where it was leased to Mr. John Locke.

[2] This is in accordance with a precept of 7 Dec. 1623, cf. *Letter Book*, 120b, in which the Company is directed not to use an agent such as a Chandler or Baker but to provide their own warehouse. The granary which is mentioned is one which the City built and toward which the Company contributed £40, but which they could not obtain leave to use, cf. *Letter Book*, 106b, 22 Nov. 1627.

[3] Cf. *C–B.C*, 61b, 27 June 1620.

Cooke to the Company in the roome & stead of mr Pinfould who is lately dead, & he is to haue the same fee formerly giuen to the said Pinfould discharging the place honestly as he ought to doe.

Three Pounds giuen to Dr. Holland gratis — This day Henry Holland haueing prferred a peticõn to the Table in the behalfe of his ffather Dr. Holland[1] for some Releife. the board taking the same into their Consideracõn Haue ordered that three pounds shall be giuen him out of the house stocke wch was then accordingly paid.

28th of January 1633.

Present. — Mr. Islip Mr Weauer Mr Aspley Mr Waterson Mr Kingston Mr Purfoot Mr Harrison Mr Smethwicke Mr. Rothwell ffetherston Mr Butter Mr Downes Mr. Moore Mr Bourne.

Order from the Councell table what to be ioyned wth the Bible. — This day by order all the Company in generall of Bookesellers and Bindesrs. were warned to appeare at the hall & then the order from the Lords of his Mats. most honble privy Counsell was openly read, the effect whereof was, that nothing should be ioyned wth the Bible but onely the booke of Comon prayer & the Psalmes in Meeter vpon payne of forfeyture & punishment.[2]

Fol. 126a

3o. die ffebruarij 1633.

Present — Mr. Islip. Mr. Weauer Mr. Aspley. Mr Swinhow, Mr Kingston Mr Ockold. Mr Purfoot Mr Smethwicke, Mr Downes Mr. Moore Mr Bourne.

Leaue to print Mr Latimers sermons. — This day Richard Coates vpon his Request vnto the Table had leaue giuen him to Imprint one Imprssion of Latymers Sermons[3] paying to the house for the [*house of the*] vse of the Poore (according as vsually hath byn at the discretion of the Table vnto wch. he hath willingly submitted. And he hath promised vpon the finishing of the Booke to pay the same accordingly.

Genealogies — This day mr. Trumball one of the Clarkes of the Councell Came from the Lords of his Mats most honble: priuy Councell and deliuered from them. That whereas lately an order was made that nothing should be bound wth Bibles but the Comon prayer & Psalmes in Meeter allowed. And sithence vpon the humble peticõn of Dr. Speed to the Councell Table The Lordę haue taken into their Consideracõn his humble suite. And haue Comaunded the said Mr Trumball to declare vnto the Mr. wardens & Assistants of the Company of Stacõners That they are pleased that the said Company may & doe proceed in the venting & selling of [the] [*Dr. Speds*] Genealogies[4] as by Pattent is granted & hath

[1] Dr. Philemon Holland, the translator general.
[2] Cf. *C–B.C*, 126a, 3 Feb. 1634.
[3] STC 15283. Cf. also *C–B.C*, 142b, 28 Sept. 1636.
[4] STC 23039. Cf. *C–B.C*, 130b, 19 Dec. 1634.

byn formerly vsed vntill some further order be taken for the firme setling thereof; vnto wch message the M^r^. Wardens & Assistants humbly for their p^ts^ submitted [*vnto themselues*]

1°. Martij 1633.

Present. M^r^. Islip Mr Weaver M^r^. Aspley Mr Waterson Mr Swinhow Mr Kingston M^r^. Ockold. Mr Purfoot, Mr Harrison Mr Smethwicke M^r^. Rothwell Mr Butter Mr Downes.

Stockeepers for the English Stocke.	Mr Butter, Mr Moore	Mr Mead, Mr Latham	Mr Legatt, Mr Partridge.

M^r^. Weauer Treasurer et Jurat^r^.

Auditors chosen.	M^r^. Kingston, Mr Harrison	Mr Bruister, Mr Grismond	John Wright, Raph Mabb

1°. Martij predict' 1633. FOL. 126^b^

Gerards Herball This day a Letter was brought from the Kings Ma^ty^: directed to the M^r^. wardens & Assistants of this Company, & openly read in Co^rt^. on the behalfe of Mr Islip, M^rs^. Joyce Norton & Richard Whittaker That none p^r^sume to imprint any Abridgment or Abstract of their Copie called Gerards Herball.[1] as in the Letter at Large appeareth.

26°. Martij 1634.

Rentors chosen. M^r^. Parker & Mr Constable are Chosen Rento^rs^. for the yeare ensewing.

vltimo Martij 1634.

Present. Mr Islip Mr Weaver Mr Aspley Mr Waterson M^r^. Swinhow Mr Cole Mr Kingston Mr Ockold M^r^. Purfoot Mr Harrison Mr Smethwicke Mr Rothwell Mr Butter & Mr Bourne.

Revertion of the Clarkes place vnto Mr James Gresham. vpon my Lord of Canterburies Letter/ This day a Letter was read from my Lords grace of Canterbury to the Company for the Reuertion of the Clerkeship of this Company to Mr James Gresham.[2] and it was granted vnto him. Prouided that when it shall fall vnto him That he be in all points according to the Custome of the Company fitt for it, and doe take vpon him the execution of the said place, and discharge it in his owne pson and not otherwise, which he promised (in the p^r^sence of the whole Co^rt^. this day p^r^sent). to performe.

[1] STC 11751.

[2] Apparently unconnected with the Company.

A revertion of the said Clarkes place vnto William Wethered vpon the free Consent of the Cort.

This day likewise the Revertion of the said Clarkeship was granted vnto William Wethered (vpon the humble suite of his Master) after the said Mr. Gresham. Provided that when the same shall fall void, he execute the same in his owne ꝑson & not otherwise/

FOL. 127a

5°. Maij 1634.

Present Mr Islip Mr Weaver Mr Aspley Mr. waterson Mr Swinhow Mr Ockold Mr Purfoot Mr Harrison Mr Smethwicke Mr Rothwell Mr ffetherstone Mr Butter Mr Downes and Mr Bourne.

Revertion of ye Beadles place to John Badger.

This day vpon the Letter of the right honoble. Sr Thomas Coventry Lord Keeper of the great Seale of England for the Revercõn of the Beadleship of this Company vnto John Badger[1] when it shall fall void by the Death of Richard Badger & Joseph Hunscott[2] or by their Resigneing or otherwise The Table hath thought fitt to grant the said place vnto him Provided that when it shall fall void as aforesaid hee shalbe found Capable of it & take vpon him ye Execucõn of ye said place in his owne ꝑson and not to alienate it to any other.

Auditors. chosen for ye Rentors Accompt.

Mr Harrison & Mr Bourne are this day appointed to Auditt the Accompt of the Rentor warden.

Order from ye Councell Table touching the Genealogies

This day Dr Speed brought an Order of ye Councell Tab[le] dated ye 25 of Aprill last purporting that ye said Dr Spe[ed] shall enjoy his present Pattent for ye Genealogies accord[ing] to ye full Extent of ye sd Pattent for Seaven yeares on[ly] no longer which was read openly in Court.[3]

10 May 1634

Present Mr Islip Mr Weaver Mr Aspley Mr Waterson Mr Swinhow Mr Kingston Mr Purfoot Mr Harri[son] Mr Smethwick Mr Rothwell Mr ffetherstone Mr Butter Mr Downes and Mr Bourne.

Mr Sparkes suspended for ever being of the Livery.

At a Court holden this day the Table tooke into Conside[racõn] the matter concerning Michaell Sparkes hee standing Con-[victed] by a Censure in the Starr Chamber.[4] And that hee was to [stand] by Mr. Pryn vpon the Pillory with a Paper on his Hat. Censure was this present day executed accordingly. Now

FOL. 127b f[or yt] no scandall may come or accrue to the Society here[by] || And for other his

[1] Possibly the J. Badger made free 1 Aug. 1636 (Arber iii. 687).

[2] Cf. *C–B.C*, 121b, 3 Dec. 1632.

[3] Speed's petition to the Council is recorded *State Papers Dom. 1633–1634*, p. 576. The Council's order to the Stationers is recorded in the Register P.C. 2/43 (605–6).

[4] Cf. *Documents relating to the proceedings against William Prynne*, edit. S. R. Gardner, Camden Soc., N.S. xviii (1877), 16–28.

great offences The Court thought fitt and soe Ordered That the said Michaell Sparkes shall from henceforth bee Suspended from the Livery & not to bee warn'd to attend or bee present with ye rest of the Livery at any tyme. And in Case hee shall contemptuously offer to come without warning Then ye Table haue thought fitt not only to remoue him pn'tely but to take such further Course as shalbe thought fitt.

Jonah Mans Yeo: ꝑte fell on Mr Robinson.

This day Jonah Man being lately deceased The Table went to Election of another Partner in his stead There stood in Eleccõn Mr Robinson Mr Walbanke & John Webb[1] and it fell on Mr Robinson & hee tooke his Oath accordingly.

3° Junij 1634.

Present. Mr Islip Mr Weaver Mr Aspley Mr Waterson Mr Ockold Mr Purfoot Mr Harrison Mr Bateman Mr Rothwell Mr Butter Mr Downes & Mr Bourne.

Widdow Man & Benja: Fisher

Whereas a Controversie is now depending concerning the Copies lately belonging vnto Mr Thomas Man & Conveyed by him vnto his Sonnes Paul & Jonah Man[2] & now belonging vnto ye Widdow of ye sđ Paul Man[3] & Benjam: ffisher It is thought fitt & by their Consents Ordered That Mr Harrison & Mr Bourne chosen by the Widdow & Mr ffetherston & Mr Downes chosen by ye sđ ffisher That they shall haue ye hearing of ye Matter & end it if they can otherwise to Certifie their opinions & doings by the next Court. Provided that none of the Copies bee in the meane tyme Printed.

[Th]o Paines ꝑte [mo]rtgaged to mr Walley.

This day Tho: Paine had leaue of ye Co^rt^. to Mortgage his Yeom: ꝑte in ye English Stocke vnto Mr Walley for 40^l^ for 6 months.

12°. Junij 1634.

Present. Mr Islip Mr Weaver Mr Aspley Mr Waterson Mr Ockold Mr Purfoot M^r^ ffetherston Mr Smethwick Mr Rothwell Mr Downes and Mr Bourne.

[Wi]ddow Man & [Ben]: Fisher

The matter in difference between ye Widdow of Paul Man & Ben: ffisher being referred as by the Order of ye Third of this month appeareth.[4] Now for that ye Refferees haue acquainted the Table wth their ꝑceedings & haue not as yet ended ye Difference. Jone Man widdow & Ben: ffisher here present this day in Court haue || entred into Assumsit of Two hundred Pounds a peece to stand to submitt & abide the Award & order by them to be made & reported vnto the Table. And in Case they end it not quite, Then the Master Wardens and Assistants will determine & end the same. FOL. 128^a^

[1] Made free 16 May 1621 (Arber iii. 685).

[2] Cf. *C–B.C*, 81^a^, 5 Apr. 1624, and Arber iv. 117, 3 May 1624.

[3] Paul Man died before 7 June 1630, cf. *C–B.C*, 107^a^.

[4] See above.

Provided that the said Refferrees doe Certifie their opinions & doeing by the Twelueth of the next Month & in the meane tyme none of the Copies are to be printed by either pty.

Joane Man
Beniamyn ffisher.

Mr. Young & Mr Stansby

This day Mr Young came vnto the Cort. & Complay[ned] that Mr Stansby had begun to imprint his part of Mr. Hieron on the 51. Psalme.[1] They being both prsent in Cort., wth. their Consents the difference was referred to Mr Harrison & Mr Downe & they to Compose it if they can, otherwise to Certifie the Table of their proceedings herein by the next Cort.

vltimo die Junij 1634. pn'tibus vt ante

John Sharpes halfe yeomandry Part fell vpon Mr. Walbancke.

John Sharpe being lately dead haveing a halfe yeomandry pte in the English stocke. The Cort. went to election of another Partner & it fell vpon Mr Walbancke, their stood in election wth him Mr Mozeley & John Webb.

3° Julij 1634.

Present

Mr. Islip Mr Weaver Mr. Aspley Mr. Waterson Mr Kingston Mr Harrison Mr Smethwicke Mr Rothwell Mr Butter & Mr Bourne.

Widdow Man & Ben: ffisher

This day a Cort. was Called for the hearing & ending of the difference betweene the Widdow of Paul Man and Beniamyn ffisher concerning the Copies lately belonging vnto Paul & Jonah Man,[2] and diuers orders & Assignemts. being produced & read Concerning those Copies, the Refferrees deliuered their opinions desireing the resolution of the Table, And vpon long debate of the Matter & hearing both parties being prsent. It is ordered that the interest of the said Copies shall be & remayne
Fol. 128b vnto them both equally (vizt.) || the one Moyety to the Widdow and the other to Beniamyn ffisher as they stand now entred (& reserveing all other mens Right) And whereas it was alleadged that a Beaver hatt of the valew of iiijl. was heretofore proffered vnto the widdow for her Consent for the passing ouer of the [*Consent*] said Copies (wch. Consent she affirmes she never gaue). The Table haue thought fitt & soe ordered that the said Beniamyn ffisher shall pay vnto her forthwith the sume of

[1] Young owned a third part of this title, STC 13394a, which had been entered to W. Welby, C. Legge, and W. Butler, 9 Feb. 1617 (Arber iii. 602). Stansby had acquired Welby's part from T. Snodham's widow, 23 Feb. 1626 (Arber iv. 152), Snodham having obtained it from Welby, 2 Mar. 1618 (Arber iii. 622). Stansby had also acquired Butter's part from his widow, 4 July 1626 (Arber iv. 162); while Legge's part had been transferred to J. Boler by his widow, 1 June 1629 (Arber iv. 212), and from Boler to Young, 19 Dec. 1633 (Arber iv. 310). This was evidently a nuisance move on Young's part, for Stansby needed the copy for his editions of Hieron's *Works*, STC 13384.

[2] Cf. *C–B.C*, 128a, 12 June 1634.

Three pounds. And further whereas the said Widdow exhibited a Noate of Certaine Copies by her alleadged to be printed vnderhand & w^th^out her Consent & soe had noe allowance for them.[1] Mr Downes & Mr Bourne are requested by the Table to Examine ye Matter & what they find soe printed to giue allowance as they shall iudge fitt & soe all quarrells & differences to be ended betwixt them. Provided none of these Copies are to be assigned ouer or Confirmed vnto any of them vntill the order be in all points performed.

7°. Julij 1634 pn'tibus vt ante

Mr Islip} M^r^
Mr Purfoot } Wardens.
Mr Rothwell }

Election of M^r^. & Wardens — M^r^. Islip was this day Chosen M^r^. for the yeare ensewing & Mr Purfoot & Mr Rothwell wardens.

Auditors chosen for ye Wardens accompt — Mr Harrison and Mr Downes are Chosen Audito^rs^. for the Wardens Accompt the last yeare.

15°. Sept. 1634.

John Edwards yeomanry Part in ye Eng: Stocke fell on Godfrey Emerson & Jo: Webb. being devided — M^r^. Edwards[2] being Lately dead who haueing a yeomanry part in the English stocke, the Co^rt^. went to Election of another Partner. And forasmuch that there were diuers suito^rs^ for the same the Table thought fitt to devide the same. And it fell vpon Godfrey Emerson and John Webb[3] & they tooke their oathes accordingly there stood in election wth them Mr Thrale & Mr Mozeley.

3°. Octobris 1634.

Widdow Aldee Bern: Alsop — Whereas Bernard Alsop & Widdow Aldee Printe^rs^. were this [day] warned to appeare in Co^rt^. vpon a Complaint made for printing a Booke called. The soules preparacõn for Christ[4] the Copie of wch. Booke now stands entred vnto Robert Daulman[5] It was thought fitt & by generall Consent of the Table ordered That for their vndue printing of the said Booke contrary to the decree in Starchamber & the Ordinances of this Company, Their seuerall spindles & Barrs shall be forthwith taken away & brought to the Stacon^rs^. hall as in these Cases is accustomed.

[1] Among the books which might have been included on that list are STC 5289, 11898, 12822, 22122 (of which there is an issue with imprint 'T. Harper f. B. Fisher, 1633'), 25321, and 25700^a^ (of which there are four unrecorded issues).

[2] Made free 8 Mar. 1614 (Arber iii. 684).

[3] Made free 16 May 1621 (Arber iii. 685).

[4] STC 13736. Cf. *C–B.C*, 129^b^, 21 Nov. 1634.

[5] Arber iv. 263, 29 Oct. 1631.

Fol. 129a 6o. Octobris 1634. pn'tibus vt ante

Bern: Alsops Nutt & spindle deliuerd to him againe } Whereas by the Order of the Last Cort. the Nutt & spindle of Barnard Alsop (for printing another Mans Copie) was taken away. Now vpon the humble peticõn of the said Bernard read this day The Cort. Considering his pouerty & that he offended ignorantly haue fined him at fiue shillings & he is to haue his Nut & spindle againe vpon Condicõn he offend not in the like nature againe.

27o. Octobris 1634.

Present. Mr Islip Mr Purfoot Mr Rothwell Mr Waterson Mr Harrison Mr Smethwicke Mr Butter Mr Downes & Mr Bourne.

Almanacks. Whereas the Companies Almanacks which haue byn heretofore printed are now questioned in the high Comission Cort. for not being Licensed according to Order. The Table haue taken it into Consideracõn and ordered That noe Almanacks shall be hereafter printed wthout Lawfull License. And the same to be entred [in] the Register booke of Copies.[1] And the Printers that print the same are to deliuer backe the written Copy & License that the same may be safely kept from tyme to tyme.

Widdow Man Ben: ffisher } This day mr. Downes & mr. Bourne brought in a Certificate vnder their hands (according to an Order of the third of July last) touching the setling of all differences betweene the Widdow of Paul Man & Beniamyn ffisher, Their Certificate being read the Table approved of the same & accordingly haue ordered the said Copies to be entred Joyntly betweene them.[2]

4o. Nouembris 1634. pn'tibus vt ante

Mr. Young & Mr Stansby } The difference betweene Mr Stansby and Mr Young concerning the printing of Hieron vpon the 51. Psalme.[3] for that it appeared by the report of the former referrees Mr. Harrison and Mr Downes that the third part of the said Copie belonged vnto

Fol. 129b Mr Young || by Assignemt. from Mr. Boler, as appeareth in the hall Booke, Now forasmuch as the said Mr. Stansby hath lately Imprinted the said Third pte of Hieron wch. belonged vnto Mr Young. It is ordered [&] (by and wth. their Consents) That Mr Parker & Mr Allott brethren of this Company who are desired to take the Consideracõn of the Matter & to giue Mr Young for his said part printed by Mr Stansby And farther to propound vnto Mr Young what they thinke fitt Mr. Stansby shall haue for the parting wth his Right in the said pte & to sell it vnto him if he will,[4] And soe all difference are to be ended betweene them wherevnto the said ptīes haue sett their hands.

By me William Stansby
Robert Young.

[1] This order does not seem to have been obeyed. Presumably this question was raised when the High Commission looked into the renewal of the Patent which expired this year.

[2] Entered 12 Aug. 1635 (Arber iv. 344–5).

[3] *C–B.C*, 128a, 12 June 1634.

[4] Stansby evidently tired of the matter and sold his interest to J. Beale, 7 Dec. 1635 (Arber iv. 352).

21° Nouemb^r. 1634.

Present. M^r. Islip Mr Purfoot Mr Rothwell M^r. Waterson Mr Kingston Mr Weauer Mr Harison M^r. Smethwicke Mr Bateman M^r ffetherston.

Mr Daulman
Mr Clifton

Whereas a difference hath byn betweene Robert Dawlman and ffulke Clifton brethren of this Company about a booke called The soules preparacõn for Christ,[1] and that some of the sheets are in the Wardens Custody Now forasmuch as the difference is ended betwixt them It is ordered that those sheets that are in the hands of the Wardens shall be deliuered vnto Mr Allott and he is not to deliuer any of them out of his hands vntill such fine as shall be imposed vpon ffulke Clifton for his offence shall be paid to the Wardens.

M^r. Attorneye Letter on the behalfe of M^r. Walbancke

This day a Letter was brought to the Table from Mr Attorney S^ir John Bancks by one of his men in the behalfe of M^r. Walbancke to make vp his halfe yeomandry p̱t a whole one wch. vpon election afterwards was p̱formed.

eodem die predict'

Fol. 130^a

M^r. Ockolds Liuery Part disposed off

This day (Mr Ockold[2] being dead) his Liuery Part in the English stocke was to be disposed of and according to the Custome in that behalfe they went to election of another Partner,

Mr Edwards a Liuery Part.

There stood for the same Mr Edwards Mr Bowler & Mr Whittacres and it fell vpon Mr Edwards. Then they went to Election for Mr Edwards yeomandry p̱te & [*it fell vpon*] [by]

Mr Walbancke halfe a yeo: Part

reason of many suito^rs the Table thought fitt to devide the same & accordingly went to Election for one half of the same, there stood for the same Mr Walbancke Mr Mozeley & M^r

Mr Hunscott halfe a yeo: Part.

Overton & it fell vpon Mr Walbancke. Likewise for the other halfe there (*stood*) Mr Mozeley Mr Overton & Joseph Hunscott [& it fell vpon Joseph Hunscott] & they tooke their oathes accordingly.

1°. Decembris pn'tibus vt ante

John Day turned ouer to the Brewers Company.

John Day[3] vpon his humble peticõn, had Consent of the Co^rt. (for that he had lately married a Brewers Widdow) to be translated from this Company to the Brewers, And the said John Day of his owne Accord promised to giue the Company xx^s.

[1] Cf. *C–B.C*, 128^b, 3 Oct. 1634.

[2] Richard Ockould.

[3] This is presumably the grandson of J. Day, the printer. No record of his freedom appears to be recorded, but he published STC 24397–8 and transferred his rights in STC 25078, Arber iv. 231, 25 Mar. 1630. His shop was at the Guildhall Gate.

ffulke Cliftons fyne.

According to an Order of the Last Co[rt]. for a fyne to be Imposed vpon ffulke Clifton for printing another mans Copie.[1] The Table this day tooke Consideracõn of the Matter & haue fined him at xx[s]. And soe Mr Allott is to deliuer the sheets according to the said former order vpon the paym[t]. of his fyne to the warden.

M[r]. Prins Histrio Mastix to be crossed out of the Hall booke

By Comand this day from M[r]. Attorney Noy The Booke called Histrio Mastix [*by order of this Co[rt].*] is to be Crossed out of the Entrance booke of Copies. w[ch] this day accordingly was pformed.[2] But the same is to be entred to him againe in case it shall be allowed to be sold.

M[r] Purfoots Assist. Part Mortgaged to M[rs] Joyce Norton

This day M[r] Purfoot had leaue to engage his Assistant pt in the English stocke vnto M[rs]. Joyce Norton for 216[li]. for one yeare from the tenth day of December next/[3]

Fol. 130[b]

19°. Decembris 1634.

Present.

M[r]. Islip M[r]. Purfoot M[r] Rothwell, M[r] Kingston M[r] Weauer M[r] Harrison M[r]. Smethwicke M[r] Downes M[r] Bourne.

To renew the Couen[ts] wth D[r]. Speed

At a Co[rt]. holden this day a letter of Assistants brought by M[r] D[r]. Speed was read from the Lords of his Ma[ts]. most hon[ble]. priuie Councell directed to the M[r]. Wardens & Assistants of this Company for the putting in Execution his Pattent for the Genealogies according to a former Order of the Councell table bearing date the ffiue and Twentieth day of Aprill last.[4] And whereas about that tyme M[r] D[r]. Speed made a proffer to the Table that the Couenants [made] betweene him & the Company for his Genealogies might be renewed for a further tyme vpon the Like Couen[ts]. & Condicõns as the former were w[ch] proffer was well approved of by the Table of Assistants then p[r]sent. And now this day the M[r]. wardens & Assistants againe taking the same into their serious Consideracõn Haue w[th]. a generall Consent thought fitt & ordered that the said Couenants shall accordingly be new drawne vp forthwith betweene them for Three yeares more to Comense from the Expiracõn of the former Couen[ts]. (w[ch]. end at Midsomer next) w[th]out any Alteracõn at all in the same. And to be sealed w[th]. the Comon seale of the hall as formerly they were.

23° Decembris 1634. pn'tibus vt ante

The Couen[ts]. between D[r]. Speed & the Company sealed

This day according to the order of the 19[th]. of December last. The Couenants betweene the Company and M[r]. D[r]. Speed for his Genealogies were sealed wth the Comon seale of the Hall by the Wardens for Three yeares from Midsomer next.

1 Cf. *C–B.C*, 129[b], 21 Nov. 1634.

2 Cf. Arber iv. 241.

3 Cf. *C–B.C*, 125[a], 2 Dec. 1633.

4 Cf. *C–B.C*, 126[a], 3 Feb. 1634. Dr. Speed had petitioned the Council in April that the booksellers were not abiding by the order of January to append the *Genealogies*, see *State Papers Dom. 1633–1634*, p. 576.

Suspending Parts for printing the Psalmes in Scotland

The Matter Concerning the printing of the Companies Psalmes[1] in Scotland was taken into Consideracōn And for that Miles fflesher John Hauiland Robert Young & Richard Adams haue wth. others printed the same Contrary to the allowed Ordinances & their oathes taken in that behalfe. It is therefore thought fitt that their diuidents shall be suspended vntill further order be taken therein.

8°. Januarij Anno 1634. Fol. 131ª

Present. Mr. Islip, Mr. Purfoot Mr Rothwell Mr Harrison Mr Smethwicke Mr Aspley Mr ffetherstone Mr Butter Mr Downes & Mr Bourne.

Daltons Country Justice of Peace

Whereas a Booke called Daltons Country Justice,[2] belonging vnto the English stocke, and the same is now printed by Miles fflesher John Haviland and Robert Young, vnder pretence that the same is Comprehended in the Law Pattent. This day the Table hath taken the same into their serious Consideracōn And haue ordered that the said Bookes now printed by the said fflesher Haviland and Young shall be forthwith by them brought to the hall, And there to remaine vntill the Right of the said Booke be decided. And whereas the said Daltons Country Justice is now likewise imprinting for the said English stocke. It is ordered that the said Impression shall be alsoe brought to the hall and there remaine till the right thereof as aforesaid be decided. But if the said fflesher Haviland and Young shall refuse to bring in the said Impression. The table haue thought fitt & ordered that the Wardens wth. others whome they shall appoint to assist them shall p'sently seize the said Bookes wheresoeuer they find them & bring them into the hall and there to remayne & be sequestred as abouesaid And the Bookes soe printed for the English stocke shall be then at Liberty & be putt to sale at their pleasure.

14°. Januarij 1634. pn'tibus vt ante

Widdow Drapers part in the Eng: stocke disposed

This day (widdow Draper[3] being lately deceased) election was made for her halfe yeomandry p̱t in the English Stocke. There stood for the same Mr Thrall Mr Morrett[4] & Mr Overton, And it fell vpon mr Morrett & he tooke his oath accordingly.

[1] Cf. *C–B.C*, 139ª, 11 Apr. 1636. Robert Young was appointed King's Printer in Scotland in 1632 and, with the aid of his London partners, set about making a good thing of it. One of his first projects was to print the Authorized Version in Scotland, STC 2311, and with it an edition of the *Book of Common Prayer*, STC 16394. As these two were normally sold bound with an edition of Sternhold and Hopkins, instead of buying copies from the English Stock he set about providing them, viz. STC 2642 and 2650 (two editions). Copies of all three have been seen bound with his Bibles of 1633. Regarding the Bibles herewith imported, cf. *State Papers Dom. 1636–1637*, p. 267.

[2] On the expiration of Wight and Norton's patent for law books a new one was issued to John More, 19 Jan. 1618, cf. Plomer, *Dictionary*, p. 131. When, in 1629, More assigned his rights to Flesher and his partners, they proceeded to profit by it and issued an edition of the Dalton, STC 6209. What was the final decision in this matter is not clear, but the two editions were published, STC 6210–11. There is a complaint of the assigns of John More against Felix Kingston and others for printing Dalton's book in Privy Council Papers, P.C. 2/44 (353), 28 Jan. 1634–5.

[3] Widow of Thomas Draper, made free 1 Oct. 1604 (Arber ii. 738).

[4] Made free 1 Mar. 1617 (Arber iii. 684).

FOL. 131[b]

19° Januarij 1634.

Present. Mr. Islip Mr. Purfoot Mr Rothwell Mr Weaver Mr Smethwick Mr. ffetherston Mr Downes. mr Swinhow & mr Harison came late.

Robte Raworth. Whereas vpon the last day of December the Barr & Spindle of Robert Raworth were by the Wardens taken [*downe*] away for that he had erected lately a printing presse Contrary to order. This day vpon his humble peticõn & the Mediation of Mr Weckerlyn by his Letter to the Company, the Table haue thought fitt & Consented that his Barr & spindle shall be restored vnto him vpon Condicõn That if wthin six Monthes next, he shall not gett himselfe Lawfully a Mr Printer according as in his peticõn is by him desired That then he will quietly desist and putt himselfe downe wthout any further trouble and bring his Barr & Spindle to the Hall againe. This he humbly desireth and acknowledgeth as a great favour done vnto him and for the pformance hereof he hath subscribed his hand.[1]

p me Robert Raworth.

4°. ffebruarij. pn'tibus vt ante

Mr Mead & Mr Beale. Assistants. This day mr Mead & mr Beale were chosen Assistants into the Company.

The Parish of St. Martins. suitors for a part of the Garden. This day Dr. Jurman and the Churchwardens exhibited a peticõn desiring that they might haue part of the garden for a Buriall place. The table haue thought fitt to take the Matter into their Consideracõn and to giue them an Answere the next Cort.

FOL. 132[a]

17°. ffebruarij 1634

Present Mr. Islip mr. Purfoot Mr Rothwell Mr Swinhow mr Kingston Mr. Weaver Mr Harrison Mr Smethwicke mr Butter mr Downes mr Bourne mr Mead mr Beale.

Widdow Taylors part in the English stocke disposed of. This day Widdow Taylor[2] being dead her yeomandry part in the English stocke was to be disposed of, And by reason of many suitors the Table thought fitt to devide the same and accordingly went to election for one halfe thereof there stood Mr Bartlett Mr Thrale and Mr. Mozeley & it fell vpon Mr Thrale, And for the other halfe there stood Mr Bartlett Mr Mozeley and Mr. Overton, & it fell vpon Mr Bartlett and they tooke their oathes accordingly.

Rich: ffeilds Legacy of 30li. giuen him by Mr. (*sic*) Lucretia East paid him. This day Richard ffeild humbly desired the Table that the Thirty pounds giuen him by Mrs. Lucretia East (as a Legacy)[3] might be paid vnto him [he] being Capable to receiue the same wch. was accordingly ordered to be paid vnto him by the Wardens, the wch. sume he this day

[1] Cf. *C–B.C*, 136[a], 5 Oct. 1635.
[2] Judith Taylor, widow of Richard Taylor.
[3] Cf. *C–B.C*, 116[a], 6 Sept. 1631.

received and gaue a discharge w[ch]. is Written in the Booke of Precepts of the Company at the Latter end thereof[1]

2°. Martij 1634.

Present. Mr. Islip Mr Purfoot Mr Rothwell Mr Swinhow Mr Cole Mr Kingston Mr Weaver Mr Harison Mr Smethwicke Mr Aspley Mr ffetherston Mr Butter Mr Downes Mr Bourne Mr Mead Mr Beale.

Those that take vp [Bookes] of the English stocke to cleare their Reckonings twice a yeare/

Whereas diuers of the Company are behind hand in their payments for Bookes taken from the English stocke, soe that Marchants and Workemen cannott be paid as they should whereby the Companies Creditt is impaired, diuidents Lessened, and the making of them vnreasonably delaid It is therefore thought fitt and this day ordered by a full Co[rt]. That all money due by any pson vnto the stocke shall be paid [in] vnto the Threasorer and his Reckoning twice cleared euery yeare that is to say At or before Christmas and at or before o[r] Lady day. And whosoeuer shall be behind or leaue any part w[ch]. he or they are to pay after the said tymes shall not haue any more Bookes deliuered And the Thresorer is to Certifie the name or names of them w[ch] shall be soe behind hand vnto the Table vpon some Co[rt]. day convenient to the end that such Course may be taken for the recouering of the said debts as shall be thought fittest/

2°. Martij predict' FOL. 132[b]

Stockeepers for the English stocke.	Mr Harison Mr Downes	Mr Hawkins Mr Waterson	Mr Whitaker Mr Robinson

Mr Weaver Treasorer et Jurat.

Auditors chosen.	Mr Smethwicke Mr Bourne	Mr Seile Mr Milborne	ffran: ffalconer Godfrey Emerson

The Kings Letter for Mr Parkinsons Herball.

This day a Letter was brought & read directed to the Mr Wardens & [Assistants of this] Company from the Kings Ma[ty]. concerning one Mr Parkinson an Apothecary about printing his workes.[2]

6°. Martij 1634.

Present. Mr. Islip Mr Purfoot Mr Rothwell Mr Swinhow Mr Cole Mr Kingston mr Weaver Mr Harison Mr Smethwicke Mr Aspley Mr ffetherston Mr Butter Mr Downes Mr Bourne & mr Beale.

The difference about ye Threasorer Mr Weaver ended

This day a Co[rt]. was called to advice and setle some Differences Concerning the Threasorer mr Weaver for the giueing security for the discharge of all Matters Comitted to his Charge. And vpon full debate it was Ordered and agreed by all pties in the p[r]sence of the Mr. Wardens and Assistante aboue named, the old and new Stockeepers and diuers others of the Partne[rs], w[th] the Consent of m[r]

[1] *Letter Book*, 183[a], but dated 11 Feb. 1635.

[2] The letter has not been found, but it no doubt refers to STC 19302 which bears on its title the line 'And Published by the Kings Majestyes especiall privilege'.

Weaver then likewise p^r^sent. That the said m^r^ Weaver and Thomas Weaver his sonne shall assigne ouer all their pts and shares wch. they now haue in the English stocke vnto the now M^r^ and Wardens and their Successo^rs^. (wch amounts vnto the sum̃e of four hundred pounds or thereabouts) [*to and*] [for] [*the vse of*] [security of his place in making iust Accompt to] all the Partners in the said stocke And alsoe giue their Bond of 1000^li^. And likewise the said Mr Edmond Weaver [*is to*] [did] assigne ouer [*is to ass*] all his Copies & parts of Copies for security as aforesaid, wch. was this [day] accordingly pformed by the said Mr Weaver & his sonne And further the said Mr Weaver is not to print any of his Copies w^th^out leaue first had from this Co^rt^.

Mr Legatt had this Bond & Assignem^t^. (being a stockeep) to keepe the same in the warehouse.

Fol. 133^a^

9° Martij 1634 pn'tibus vt antea

Journimen Printers} This day a peticõn was deliuered on the behalfe of the Journimen Printers and Certaine greivances were read at the Table for wch. they prayed remedie, And vpon the hearing of what was read The Table haue thought fitt to referr the Consideracõn of the said greiuances vnto both the wardens Mr Kingston M^r^ ffetherston M^r^. Downes & Mr Bourne who are requested to take some paines in the busines and to haue Conference wth. some of the Journimen printe^rs^ & being satisfied what is fittest to be done, then to Certifie their doeings & opinions to the Table wth. all Convenient speed That therevpon such order may be taken Concerning the Redresse of the said greivances as vpon Mature deliberacõn shall be thought fitt.[1]

17°. Martij 1634.

Present. Mr Islip Mr Purfoot Mr Rothwell Mr Swinhow Mr Cole Mr Weaver Mr Harison Mr Smethwicke Mr Butter Mr Downes Mr Bourne Mr Mead Mr Beale

Mr Simon Watersons Part disposed of } This day Mr Waterson (being dead) his Assistant part in the English stocke was to be disposed of and according to the Custome in that behalfe they went to Election of another Partner [*in that behalfe*] there stood for the same Mr Rothwell M^r^ ffetherston & Mr Butter and it fell vpon m^r^ Rothwell Then they went to Election for m^r^ Rothwells Liuery pt, & there stood for the same Mr Boler Mr Whittaker & Mr Allott and it fell vpon Mr Boler. Then they went to Election for his yeomandry pte And by reason of many suito^rs^. the table thought fitt to devide the same and accordingly went to Election for one halfe thereof, there stood for the same Mr Thrale Mr Mozeley & Edmond Hussey[2] and it fell vpon Mr Mozeley. And for the other halfe there stood m^r^ Cartwright m^r^ Overton & Edmond Hussey and it fell vpon Edmond Hussey And they all tooke their oathes accordingly.

Mr Rothwell an Assistant Part.

Mr Boler a Liuery Part }

Mr Mozeley a halfe yeomandry Part }

Edm: Hussey a halfe yeomandry Part }

[1] Cf. *C–B.C*, 136^b^, 16 Nov. 1635.

[2] Made free 19 Jan. 1624 (Arber iii. 685).

26°. Martij 1635

Rentors chosen.
mr Constable, mr Edwardę, mr Boler, mr Stansby, mr Hawkinę } fined for Renter wardens 24li. a man

This day (Mr Parker haueing serued out his tyme of Rentor) Mr Constable being eldest Rentor for the next yeare ensewing Came this day vnto the Table and desired he might be admitted to fyne. The Table tooke it into Consideracõn and haue fined him at xxiiijli. and he is to pay it to the now Wardens before they goe out of their places to wch. he willingly submitted. Mr Edwards Mr Boler Mr Stansby & mr Hawkins fined at xxiiijli. a man for Rentors. [Then] Mr Whittaker and Mr Latham were chosen who accepted of the same to hold for the yeare ensewing.

Mr Whittaker & Mr Latham } Rentors.

4° Maij 1635

Present. Mr Islip Mr Purfoot Mr Rothwell Mr Swinhow Mr Weaver Mr Harrison Mr Smethwicke Mr Aspley Mr Downes & Mr Bourne.

John Turnor hath left him 40li. in the hall by mr Bateman vntill his Indenture be expired

This day Mr Bateman[1] one of the Assistants of this Company made his request to the Table that xlli. being the money of one John Turner[2] should be kept in the hall vntill the said Turners yeares of Apprentiship were expired not giueing any Consideracõn for the same. vnto wch. the Table haue Condiscended. And it is Ordered that the said Turner vpon the Expiracõn of his Indenture or wthin six monthes then next following (vpon his request made to the Company) shall haue the said fforty pounds paid him. And in Case the said Turner dye before the Expiracõn of his said Indenture, then the same to be paid to his Assignee or whomesoeuer he shall appoint wthin the tyme aforesaid And the Wardens to giue an Acquittance vnder their hands for their Receipt of the same and putt it vpon the house Accompt.

John Turnors 40li. paid him.

The 13th day of May 1639. Receiued then by me John Turner the sume of xlli. mencõned in the order aboue written of the wardens of the Company. I say receiued the said sum̃e of forty pounds

6 Maij 1635. The m'ke of John X Turner

6°. Maij 1635.

Rentors Accompt brought in } Mr Parker Rentor warden brought in his Accompt wch came to 60ti. 2s. 4d. wch. mr warden Rothwell received.

[1] Made free 18 Jan. 1580 (Arber ii. 681).

[2] J. Turner is not recorded as having been made free, although the entry below would indicate he had completed his apprenticeship.

25°. Maij 1635

Present — Mr Islip Mr Purfoot Mr Rothwell Mr Weaver Mr Aspley Mr Butter Mr Downes Mr Bourne & Mr Mead Mr ffetherstone came late.

Order about a Proclamation — Whereas diuers strangers doe dayly bring into this Kingdome great quantities of Bookes wch are printed as well against Religion & state [*os*] as alsoe against the Kings Letters Pattents granted to diuers ꝑsons and alsoe diuers Books ꝑticularly beloñging to diuers ꝑsons of this Company to the great disturbance in the State and losse to many Members of this Company. It is this day ordered That Dr. Reeue the Kings Advocate be prsently attended and he to advice wth mr. Attorney Generall & mr Sollicitor for speedy Order to be taken for redresse And mr ffetherston Mr Downes [&] George Tompson [wth] the Clarke are requested to follow the buisines And to doe what shall be advised therein for the obteyning of a Proclamacõn for that & other things now exceeding hurtfull to the Company in generall.[1]

John Cleaver to haue 8£. toward the marriage of his daughter. — This day John Cleauer[2] (haueing a daughter to be married) desired the Cort. (he being vnable) to doe something for him towards his Charge Wherevpon the table taking the same into their Consideracõn haue thought fitt that he shall haue giuen him Eight pounds vizt. ffour pounds from the warden vpon the house Accompt And four pounds from the Partners. of the English stocke & mr weaver is to giue it him.

Order John Phillipe Part of a Presse — Whereas John Phillips[3] hath voluntarily brought in part of a Presse & deliuered it into the hands of the Beadle. It is ordered that he may sell the same to such a Customer as the wardens shall thinke fitt & to none other.

1°. Julij 1635

Present. — Mr. Islip mr. Purfoot mr Rothwell mr Kingston mr Weaver mr Harison mr Smethwicke mr Aspley mr ffetherston mr Downes mr Bourne mr Beale & mr Mead.

None of the Assistants or Liuery to Come to the Hall vpon solemne days of Meeting in falling Bands — Whereas diuers of late tymes aswell Assistants as others of the Liuery haue vpon solemne dayes of Meeting repaired vnto the hall & other places wearing falling Bands, doubletts slacht & Cutt wth other vndecent apparell wch. at such tymes wee conceiue ought not to be done as not suiting wth the habitt of Cittizens. It is therefore thought meet & soe ordered that from henceforth the Assistants shall vpon euery Cort. day come to the hall in Ruffe Bands & not in falling Bands. And alsoe that none of the Liuery

[1] The proclamation was not very speedily obtained, for it was nearly a year later, 1 May 1636, that it was issued (STC 9064), and only after another visit to the Attorney General, cf. *C–B.C*, 138b, 11 Apr. 1636.

[2] Made free 5 Mar. 1604 (Arber ii. 736).

[3] This is probably not the press referred to in *C–B.C*, 93a, 5 Dec. 1626.

shall p'sume to Come to the hall to dynner vpon any feast day or goe to the buriall of a Brother of the Company in a falling Band or other vnseemely habitt vpon payne that euery one offending Contrary to this order shall forfeit & pay for his offence xij^d^.

7°. Julij 1635 Fol. 134^b^

Present. Mr Islip mr Purfoot mr Rothwell mr Cole mr. Weaver mr Harrison mr Smethwicke mr Aspley mr Butter mr Downes mr Bourne mr Beale & mr Mead.

Election of Mr & Wardens mr Kingston mr mr Smethwicke mr ffetherston war: — This day by Consent the box of Election was opened It fell vpon Mr Kingston to be Master & Mr Smethwicke & mr ffetherson wardens & they then tooke their oathes accordingly

Mr Harrison fyned for first tyme vpperwarden — After the Election mr Smethwicke (being Chosen vppwarden) spake vnto them that Mr Harrison being before him in tyme[1] might be first admitted to fyne for his not holding first tyme vppwarden, wch the Table held fitt & being putt to voices he was fyned at 5li. & soe to take his place according to ancientry.

Auditors chosen to audite the old wardens Accompt — Mr Aspley & mr Mead are Chosen Auditors to audite the wardens Accompt for the last yeare.

Gratuity giuen the Clarke for his Extraordinary Paines. — This day mr Islip Mr of the Company moued the Table [*moved the Table*] in the behalfe of the Clarke that Consideracõn was to be had of his many Imployments & extraordinary paynes taken about the Affaires of the Company wch being by them Considered, the Table thought fitt to giue him ffifteene pounds for his encouragemt. & the warden is to pay it him & bring it in his Accompt.

Mr Badger to haue 50li. for 3. yeares his part engaged to his suerties for their discharge. — Richard Badger vpon his humble request [*had*] is to haue the 50li. now due (of Mr Nortons bequeast) to be renued for three yeares more putting in good security.[2] And that his pte in the English stocke might be made ouer to his suerties Mr. Queeney & Mr Myn, for their security. wch the table likewise granted/

John Rothwell — John Rothwell to haue the next 50li. that comes in[3]

Rich: fferrers. — Richard fferrers to haue the next 50li. after him[4]

[1] The time referred to is admission to the livery.

[2] Cf. *C–B.C*, 119^b^, 9 Apr. 1632. His new bonds were registered 8 July 1635, *Liber C2*, 118^b^.

[3] His bonds were registered 31 July 1635, *Liber C2*, 119^a^.

[4] His bonds were registered 5 Oct. 1635, *Liber C2*, 119^a^.

FOL. 135ᵃ Mr. Kingston} Master
Mr. Smethwicke} Wardens.
Mr. ffetherston

16° Julij A°. 1635. xj°. Car. Regis.

Present — Mr. Kingston Mr Smethwicke Mr ffetherston Mr Islip Mr Weaver Mr Purfoot Mr Harison Mr Rothwell Mr Mead.

That none of the Assistants doe divulge any Busines done in Cort. — Whereas many of the businesses of this Court haue beene divulged abroad by some [*of the Assistants*] of this Company to the great scandall of the gouerment thereof. Now this Cort. weighing the prsent disgrace & iniury arising thereby, and intending the redresse thereof for the future if neither their oath and Comon discretion will not guide them It was this day ordered That if any of the Assistants of this Company shall henceforth divulge or giue intimation of any busines whatsoeuer of secrecy done in Cort. shall vpon probable testimony thereof be fyned or suspended from his place at the discretion of the Master wardens & Assistants or the more pte of them.

20° Julij 1635

Present — Mr Kingston Mr. Smethwicke mr ffetherston Mr Islip Mr Weaver mr Purfoot Mr. Aspley Mr Rothwell Mr Butter Mr Mead & Mr Beale.

Mrs. Pauiers Assistant part disposed of
Mr Aspley an Assistant part
Mr Whittaker a Liuery part
Joseph Hunscott halfe a yeomandry Part
Tho: Knight halfe a yeomandry part

This day Mrs. Pavier being dead the Table went to Election of another Partner for her part (being an Assistants pte). there stood in Election for the same Mr ffetherston Mr Aspley [&] Mr Butter and it fell vpon Mr Aspley and he tooke his oath accordingly. Then Election was made for mr Aspley Liuery pte, there stood in election Mr whittaker Mr Allott & Mr Harper And it fell vpon mr whittaker, Then Election was made for mr whitakers yeomandry pte And because there were diuers suitors. the table thought fitt to devide the same. there stood in Election for one halfe thereof Joseph Hunscott John Dallum[1] & Thomas Knight & it fell vpon Joseph Hunscott. And for the other halfe there stood John Dallum mr Overton & Thomas Knight & it fell vpon Thomas Knight and they tooke their oathes accordingly.

Robert Gurney 12li. — Robert Gurney[2] is to haue the next Twelue pound that comes in putting in good security.

[1] Made free 25 Jan. 1619 (Arber iii. 685).
[2] Made free 15 June 1626 (Arber iii. 686). The loan is not recorded in *Liber C2*.

7°. Septembris 1635. FOL. 135b

Present. Mr. Kingston Mr. Mr. Smethwicke & Mr ffetherston wardens Mr. Purfoote Mr Harrison Mr Aspley Mr Butter Mr Downes Mr Bourne & Mr Mead.

Mr Stansby
139
Whereas the Stockeepers hath putt the Psalter in 24. to Mr. Stansby to be printed,[1] And the same being very badly done insomuch that they are vnfitt for sale, they came this day and shewed to the Cort. the said Psalter wch. they tooke into Consideracõn and ordered that the said Stansby should beare the losse of his ill workemanship and the stocke to beare the losse of the pap And whereas the said Mr Stansby hath the Middleborough Psalmes[2] to print It is ordered he shall not goe forward wth them And that he shall forthwith deliuer backe to the Stockeeps such paper he hath of the [*Companie*] [said] Stocks. And that Mr. Weaver shall deteyne in his hands such moneys as is due vnto Mr Stansby for worke vntill further order be taken therein.[3]

26°. Septembris 1635 pn'tibus vt antea

Mr. Islips pte of Riders Dictionary assigned to Mr Grismond

This day Mr. Islip desired the Cort. to Assigne over to John Grismond his part of Riders Dictionary wch. the Cort. hath ordered accordingly to be Entred vnto Mr Grismond. Provided that the said Mr. Islip is alwaies to haue the printing thereof, doeing the same as [*the*] well & as reasonable as any other Printer will.[4]

5°. Octobris 1635

Present. Mr Kingston Mr. Smethwicke Mr. ffetherston Mr. Cole Mr. Islip Mr Weaver Mr Harrison Mr Purfoot Mr. Rothwell Mr Butter Mr Downes Mr Bourne & Mr Mead.

Order for the deliuery of Cottons Pattent for the Concordance int° the Wardens hands

This day Mr. Bourne and mr. Young made their request to the Table and desired that the Pattent of priviledge of the breife Concordance of the Bible (granted by his Maty. vnto Clement Cotton)[5] togeither wth. the Copies of two Assignemts [6] made by the said Clement Cotton vnto

[1] In the Morgan Library is a copy of an unrecorded 1635 edition of Sternhold and Hopkins Psalms, 24° in 12's. It is probably not the edition here referred to.

[2] The Middleborough Psalms were presumably the Psalms in metre used in the Church of Scotland, STC 2722 being an edition of this year.

[3] Cf. *C–B.C*, 139b, 28 Apr. 1636.

[4] Entered 5 Nov. 1635, Arber iv. 350.

[5] See T. Rymer, *Foedera*, xix (1730), 153. The patent is there dated 16 Apr. 1630, but in *State Papers Dom. 1629–1631*, p. 53, there is a grant of the same privilege dated 8 Sept. 1629.

[6] In his petition, 8 Mar. 1630 (*State Papers Dom. 1629–1631*, p. 208), Cotton states that he had assigned the privilege to Nicholas Bourne. Presumably the second assignment includes Young.

The bibliography of this book is somewhat confused. Cotton originally compiled *The christians concordance* [of the N.T.], 1622 (STC 5842). This was followed by *A concordance . . . of the Old Testament* (STC 5843). These were published by N. Newberry,

the said Nicholas Bourne and Robte Young Might be deposited and kept by the wardens of this Company for the tyme being, To this end and purpose that the said Pattent should there remaine for the ioynt vses of them the said Nich: and Robert their Executo^{rs}. and Assignes. And that when they the said Nicholas and Robert their Executo^{rs}. or Assignes shall togeither repaire vnto this Co^{rt}. and make their request for the Redeliuering of the said Pattent and Copies, That then they should accordingly be deliuered vnto them vnto them (*sic*) both and not otherwise. Wherevpon this Co^{rt}. hath thought fitt and soe ordered that according to their desire the Wardens shall (*keep*) the said Pattent and Copies of Assignem^{t}. (being putt in a little box wth 2. locks [*and*] to it by them the said Nich: and Robte) and reserue the same in a Chest in the Inner Roome for the end and purpose afore mencõned.

This box wth the Pattent was deliu'ed to Mr Bourne by order of Co^{rt}. of the 22th October 1649.

Fol. 136^{a}

5°. Octobris 1635 predict'

Robte Raworths presse to be taken downe.

Whereas Robert Raworth hath not (according to his promise vnder his hand)[1] brought in his printing presse and deliuered it vp to the Wardens or gotten sufficient Authority for the keeping of the same It is therevpon ordered that his presse shall be taken downe by the warden and brought to the hall and there to remaine vntill further order be taken therein.

who transferred his rights to T. Downes and R. Young, 3 Oct. 1629 (Arber iv. 219). In 1631 they published a combined folio edition under the title *A complete concordance* (STC 5845); and in 1635 they published 'The second edition', also in folio, under the title *A large concordance* (STC 5846). In the same year there was published in quarto an edition of *A complete concordance* 'againe reuiewed and corrected by H.T.', with imprint 'Printed Anno Dom. 1635' (copies of which are in Folger, Huntington, and Trinity College, Cambridge). None of the preceding was intended to be bound with Bibles.

In 1630, after Cotton received his patent for 'a certaine briefe *Concordance*', the Assignes of C. Cotton published a quarto edition entitled *A briefe concordance* (copies of which are at Folger, Union Theological, and Trinity College, Cambridge). This edition has a note 'To the Reader' signed by J. Downame, in which he states 'I have for thy vse collected this small Concordance', and the title states 'Allowed by Authoritie to be printed, and bound with the Bible in all Volumes'. An octavo edition (STC 7126) having the same features was published with the imprint 'Imprinted at London, 1630'; a 12mo edition was issued the following year (STC 7127); and a quarto the year after (STC 7128). This last has the imprint 'Printed by the assignes of C. Cotton, 1632', but, from the ornaments, all of them were printed by H. Lownes and R. Young. The same text was reprinted in an undated quarto bearing the title *A concordance* and with the imprint 'Printed by the Assignes of C. Cotton'. This likewise was printed by H. Lownes and R. Young, and from the only known copy, in the Huntington Library, has a text which places it between STC 7128 and STC 7129. Another unrecorded octavo edition dated 1633 is in T.C.D. and C[12].

Two undated octavo editions entitled *A briefe concordance*, but which state that they were 'enlarged by J. Downame' and which do have added material, are dated *c.* 1633 (STC 7129 and 7130). These also were printed by Lownes and Young for the Assignes of C. Cotton.

It is hard to state what relation the 'briefe concordance' has to the larger work issued under Cotton's name. Downame claimed the former as his work, but all editions of it were published under Cotton's patent and it appears to be merely a reediting of Cotton's text.

It may be that Young was not dealing fairly with his partner Downes, and that some of these editions were not shared with him, so that for his own protection Downes insisted on placing the documents in the hands of the Company.

[1] Cf. *C–B.C*, 131^{b}, 19 Jan. 1635. He obtained his press again by order of the Court of High Commission, cf. *State Papers Dom. 1635–1636*, p. 468, 23 Jan. 1636.

2°. Nouembris 1635:

Present. Mr Kingston Mr. ffetherston Mr. Smethwicke Mr Swinhow Mr. Islip Mr. Harison Mr Aspley Mr Rothwell & mr Downes.

Plate to be brought in by those that are behind hand.

It is this day ordered that all those that are behind hand for plate shall bring in their proportion betweene this and the Last day of this Month.[1]

Mrs. Busbies part mortgaged to mr Mead.

This day Mrs. Busbie had leaue to engage her Liuery pte in the English stocke vnto Mr Mead for payment of 104li at six Monthes end. to Comence from the date hereof.

10°. Nouembris 1635. pn'tibus vt antea

Mr Beale fyne of ffour pounds for binding an appr. at a Scrivenrs.

Whereas Mr. Beale was fyned at ffour pounds for binding one Robert Hughes[2] at a Scrivener Contrary to order and the said ffyne is not yet paid. It is this day ordered that the said ffyne shall be brought in and paid betweene this and the Last day of this month to the warden vnto wch. mr Beale hath submitted [*wherevpon Mr*] [And vpon payment] thereof Tho: Elie shall be bound vnto him who was putt by before.

A note of the Mr. Printers deliuered to Dr Reeue.

This day a note of all the Mr. Printers. allowed and not allowed was by Comand from my Lords grace of Cant. deliuered vnto Dr. Reeues.[3]

16°. Nouembris 1635

Present Mr Kingston Mr Smethwicke Mr ffetherston Mr Swinhow Mr Harrison Mr Purfoote Mr Aspley Mr Rothwell Mr [*Purfoote*] Downes Mr Bourne Mr Mead and Mr. Beale.

Bookebinders.

Vpon a peticõn deliuered of the Bookebinders touching diuers abuses in the binding of Bookes &c. The Table taking the same into Consideracõn haue referred the same vnto the hearing of [*the*] Mr. Warden ffetherston Mr Harrison Mr. Rothwell Mr Downes and Mr Bourne or any four of them And it is ordered that six of the Peticõners are to attend the Refferres. And the said Refferrees are requested by the Table to take paines herein and Certifie the Table of their opinions what may be done therein for the good of the peticõners as soone as they can conveniently.

[1] Cf. *C–B.C*, 105a, 2 Nov. 1629

[2] Probably the man made free 7 Aug. 1637 (Arber iii. 688).

[3] These may be the lists recorded in *State Papers Dom. 1634–1635*, p. 231, under 8 Oct. 1634.

Fol. 136[b]

16°. Nouembris predict'.

The Refferrees report touching the Journimen Printers ...... This day the Refferrees (appointed for Considering the [*abuses*] Complaints of the Journimen printers and the obiections of the M[r]. Printers against the said Jourimen (*sic*)) brought in a report digested into 19. Articles with a provisoe on the behalfe of either of them vnder the said Refferrees hands.[1] Which being openly read in Co[rt]. the Table approved of the same in euery perticuler And haue ordered that the same Articles be Entred in the Register Booke of Orders of this Company. And that the Clarke due giue a true Copie thereof aswell vnto the said M[r]. Printers as Journimen printers to the end the said Articles may be duely executed by either of them.

Thomas Weaver & The Irish Partners The Cause of the Controversie[2] betweene Thomas Weaver and the Partners in the Irish stocke was this [day] opened vnto the Table by Thomas Weaver on his pte. And forasmuch as the said Thomas Weaver hath subpena'd diuers of the said Partne[rs]. into the *Starchamber* and great Costs and trouble will be Comenced against each other. The table thought good to propose a way vnto the said Partno[rs]. and Thomas Weaver whereby to Compose the said difference vnto wch they both submitted. And it was ordered wth their Consents that either pties should be bound in a valuable sum̃e of Money by Bond to stand to the Arbitration and full determinacõn of the now wardens of this Company, soe that the said Wardens gaue up their Arbitration vnder their hands vnto this Table by the Nineteenth day of december next And in Case they could not agree. Then by their Consents it [*is*] was ordered That Mr Lightfoote should be the vmpire to end the Same soe that he gaue vp vnder his hand the determinacõn of the said Controversie by S[t]. Thomas day next. And it was further ordered by Consent on both sides that noe prosecution in Law should be had nor noe Advantage taken during the tyme aboue Lymited.

Fol. 137[a]

13°. Januarij 1635.

Present. M[r]. Kingston M[r]. Smethwicke & m[r]. ffetherston M[r]. Swinhow M[r]. Weaver M[r]. Harrison M[r]. Aspley Mr Butter Mr Downes & M[r]. Mead.

Tennant of ye ffeathers Taverne This day the Tennant of the ffeathers Taverne[3] came to the Table about taking a new Lease of his house, Divers proposicõns being made to him he refused the same. Notwithstanding it was offered vnto him that if he should provide himselfe elswhere and leaue his house before the expiracõn of his Lease and deliuer it vp vpon any quarter day before, the Company would take it into their owne hands and acquitt him of further Rent.

[1] This report and accompanying documents are recorded in *State Papers Dom. 1635*, pp. 483–4, and are reprinted in full in Arber iv. 21–23. Nevertheless, the articles here agreed on appear not to have been kept, see petition of Journeymen, 2 Mar. 1637, *State Papers Dom. 1636–1637*, p. 482.

[2] What the controversy was about is not clear. The Stock was not doing well and was sold out to Bladen in 1639.

[3] Cf. *C–B.C*, 125[b], 16 Jan. 1634.

Mr Beales fyne of iiijli. paid — This day mr. Beale paid his fyne of ffour pounds formerly imposed vpon him for binding his Apprentice at a scrivenors. Contrary to order.[1]

14° Januarij 1635

Present. — Mr. Kingston Mr. Mr. Smethwicke & Mr. ffetherston War: Mr Swinhow [Mr Cole] Mr. Weaver Mr. Harrison Mr. Aspley Mr. Rothwell Mr Butter Mr Downes Mr. Bourne Mr Mead & Mr Beale.

Mr. Purfoote Assistant part transferred vpon Mr Mead. — At a full Court this day Mr. Mead produced a deed vnder ye hand and seale of Mr. Purfoote for transferring his Assistant part in the English stocke to the said Mr. Mead (reserving to the said Mr. Purfoote his Liuery pte onely.) The Cort. taking the same into Consideracõn did therevpon elect ye said Mr. Mead to the said Assistants pte & he tooke his oath accordingly. And it was then ordered that the said Mr Purfoote should not for euer hereafter be eligeable for an Assistants pte. And whereas his said Assistants pte is Mortgaged to Mrs. Joyce Norton for 216li.[2] It is ordered that 108li. thereof shall be disengaged. And his said Liuery pte vpon his request is to be mortgaged to the said Mrs. Norton for security of 108li. the residue of his debt for one yeare to Comence from the date hereof.

Mr Gunters workes assigned to Mrs. Bowler. — This day Wm. Jones by a Warrant vnder his hand & seale assigned ouer vnto Mrs. Bowler all his Right & Interest to Mr. Gunters workes reserving the workemanship thereof to his house doeing ye same as reasonable as any other[3]

24°. Januarij 1635 pn'tibus vt ante — Fol. 137b

Grant of a Lease of ye ffeathers Taverne to Mr Nicholls — This day Mr. Nicholls had a grant [*of the Cort for*] of a Lease of the ffeathers Taverne in Pauls yard for the Terme of 51. yeares paying for a fyne the sum̃e of 200li. at the sealing of the Lease and 40li. p ann' Rent to Comence from the Expiracõn of the former Lease. And it was ordered that the Lease should be forthwith made & sealed to Mr Nicholls.[4]

Lease of the Roomes at Somers Key, lett to Mr ffran: Lenthall — This day the Company sealed wth the Comon seale a Lease of their Roomes at Som̃ers key[5] vnto Mr. ffrancis Lenthall for 31. yeares to Comence from Michaelmus Last in Consideracõn of a fyne of [*60li.*] Threescore and Ten pounds, & of one hundred pounds (to be bestowed wthin seauen yeares after the date of his Lease,) in new building & bettering of those Roomes. Rent 14li. p Ann' quarterly.

[1] Cf. *C–B.C*, 136a, 10 Nov. 1635.
[2] Cf. *C–B.C*, 130a, 1 Dec. 1634.
[3] This was entered 4 Mar. 1636 (Arber iv. 356). The only work published by Mrs. Anne Boler under this agreement has her husband's name in the imprint, viz. STC 12523.
[4] Cf. *C–B.C*, 125b, 16 Jan. 1634, and 137a, 13 Jan. 1636. The rent and fine had risen greatly, cf. *C–B.C*, 137a, 13 Jan. 1636.
[5] On the south side of Thames Street, next to Billingsgate west. Possibly this is part of Mr. Dickens's house, cf. *C–B.C*, 85b, 4 Apr. 1625, and 170a, 19 Feb. 1640.

Memorandu' Mr Lenthall paid downe 30^li. of his fyne and gaue his Bond for 40^li. the residue of his fyne, to be paid at Midsomer next.

15°. ffebruarij 1635

Present. Mr Kingston M^r. Smethwicke M^r. ffetherston Mr Islip Mr Purfoote Mr Rothwell Mr Butter Mr Downes [Mr Bourne] M^r. Mead Mr Beale.

A Lease of the ffethers Taverne lett to Mr Nicoll. According to a former order,[1] this day the Company sealed a Lease of the ffeathers Taverne in Pauls Church yard to Mr Basil Nicoll for 51. yeares to Comence from Christmas 1637. Rent 40^li. p Annu' quarterly. And the said Mr Nicoll paid downe his fyne of 200^li. to M^r warden ffetherston.

FOL. 137*a

17°. ffebruarij 1635

Present. M^r. Kingston M^r. M^r. Smethwicke M^r. ffetherston war: M^r. Swinhow M^r. Islip M^r. Weaver Mr Purfoote M^r. Harrison M^r. Aspley M^r. Rothwell M^r. Butter Mr Downes Mr Bourne & Mr Mead.

Mr Badger. Whereas there hath byn paid vnto Richard Badger by the Wardens of this Company the sum̃e of ffour Pounds p Ann', W^ch money is Entred in the Register Booke of the Wardens Accompts for the tyme being in these Words (vizt.) Giuen to Richard Badger the Beadle for his extraordinary paines this yeare ffour pounds. Now forasmuch as some question hath byn moued whether the same should be paid as wages and soe demaunded as belonging to the office of ye Beadle as pte of his ffee or whether the same hath byn giuen him as a gratuity. The Co^rt. hath this day vpon debate thought fitt and declared That the said ffour pounds shall be giuen him as a Gratuity during pleasure and not otherwise And whereas alsoe four nobles is allowed for making Cleane the Hall. It is ordered that fiftie three shillings four pence shall be added to make it vp four pounds wch. is in leiw of other benifitt heretofore receiued and by him voluntarily forgone, And this alsoe to Continue during pleasure and noe longer.[2]

1°. Martij 1635

Present. Mr Kingston M^r. Smethwick M^r. ffetherston Mr Swinhow M^r. Islip Mr Weaver M^r. Purfoote M^r. Harrison M^r. Aspley Mr Rothwell Mr Butter Mr Bourne Mr Mead & Mr Beale.

Mr Weaver. Vpon an accusacõn of M^r. Butter against M^r. Weaver touching his Accompts of the English Stocke. The Co^rt. thought fitt to desire M^r. Warden ffetherston wth such others whome he should thinke fitt (wth all Convenient speed) to examine M^r. weavers Accompts & satisfie the Co^rt. therein.

[1] See above.

[2] Cf. *C–B.C*, 121^b, 14 Jan. 1633.

Stockeepers for the English stocke — Mr. Bourne, Mr. Mead; Mr Man, Mr Dawson; Mr Bruister, Mr Trale . .

Mr. Weaver Treasurer et Juratr.

Auditorꝭ chosen — Mr. Aspley, Mr Beale; Mr Hoth, Mr Parker; Mr Bloome, Raph Mabb

Tho: Knights Copies assigned to Mr. Alchorne

This day by order of Cort. vpon a note vnder the hand & seale of Thomas Knight. All the Copies & ꝑts of Copies of the said Thomas (vpon his request) were assigned vnto Thomas Alchorne.[1]

5°. Martij 1635 Fol. 137*b

Present. Mr Kingston Mr Smethwicke Mr. ffetherston Mr. Swinhow Mr Islip Mr Weaver Mr Purfoote Mr Harrison Mr Aspley Mr Rothwell Butter Mr Downes Mr Bourne Mr. Mead Mr Beale.

Mrs. Aldees Liuery part disposed of.

Mr Bruister ye Liuery ꝑt.

Mr. Thrale halfe a yeo: ꝑte

Jo: Dallum the other halfe

Mrs. Aldee[2] being lately deceased her Liuery part in the English stocke fell to be disposed of by the Company. There stood in Election for the same Mr. Legatt Mr. Bruister Mr Seile And it fell vpon Mr Bruister Then the Cort. went to Election for Mr Brusters yeomandry ꝑte And because of many suitors. they thought fitt to devide the same. There stood for one halfe thereof Mr Thrale Mr Mozeley Mr. Overton & it fell vpon Mr Thrale There stood for the other halfe Thomas Brudnell John Dallum[3] & Henry Taunton & it fell vpon Jo: Dallum And they all tooke their oathes accordingly.

7°. Martij 1635 pn'tibus vt ante

Mr. Roche xs. for Attorning Tennt. in ye Roome of Mrs. Trussell

This day Mr. Roche haueing bought the Lease of the house wherein he now dwells called the Blacke Boy of Mrs. Trussell[4] desired the ffeoffees that according to the Couent. in that Lease he might become Tennt. to the said ffeoffees paying according to Couent. Ten shillings to ye vse of the said ffeoffees & ffiue shillings to the Clarke for an Endorsemt. wch. the Cort. taking into Consideracõn ordered that Mr Roche should be admitted Tennt. And the said Mr Roche paid the said sum̃e of xs. & vs. accordingly.

26°. Martij 1636.

Present. Mr Kingston Mr Smethwicke Mr ffetherston Mr. Purfoote Mr Aspley Mr Rothwell Mr Butter Mr Downes Mr Bourne Mr Mead Mr Beale.

Mr Wellins chosen Rentor.

According to Custome the Cort. went this day to Election of Rentors and Mr Wellins[5] being next by Antiquity the Table

1 Entered 8 Mar. 1636 (Arber iv. 357).

2 Mrs. Elizabeth Allde.

3 Made free 25 Jan. 1619 (Arber iii. 685).

4 Cf. *C–B.C*, 97b, 19 Nov. 1627, and 98a, 8 Dec. 1627. Presumably this is the same property, though it is there called The Hand and Dagger.

5 Made free 20 Mar. 1602 (Arber ii. 731).

Chose him to ioyne wth M[r] Latham for the yeare ensewing. But forasmuch as the said M[r]. Wellins did craue tyme to Consider of the same the Co[rt]. ordered he should haue tyme till Wensday next to Consider thereof And then to giue his Answere whether he will hold or fyne. w[ch] he promised in Co[rt]. to ꝑforme.

Fol. 138[a] 30°. Martij 1636

Present. M[r]. Kingston M[r]. M[r]. Smethwicke M[r]. ffetherston War: M[r]. Purfoote M[r] Aspley M[r]. Rothwell M[r] Butter M[r] Downes M[r]. Bourne M[r] Mead and M[r] Beale.

Order about the 600[li] borrowed by the Latyn stocke for w[ch]. the house seale is giuen. 156. 159.

Whereas the Master wardens and Assistants of this Company wth. diuers others of the Liuery and yeomandry were in the yeares 1619. and 1620. interressed in a ioynt stocke or ffactory of Copartnership comonly called by the name of the Latin Stocke. And the said Partne[rs]. haueing occasion for moneyes then tooke vp two seuerall sum̃es of 300[li]. a peece.[1] Which sum̃es soe taken vp were meerely for the vse and benifitt of the Partne[rs]. ioyned in the saide stocke and noe way Conducing to the proffitt or benifitt of this Corporacõn (and wch. said money was and is the portions of two Children of one Ellen Martin of London widdow deceased) And the then said M[r]. wardens and Assistants in the name of the Master and Keeꝑs or Wardens and Cominalty of this Company Entred into one Obligacõn or deed obligatory bearing date the Third day of July Anno 1620. in the sum̃e of 800[li]. for payment of 600[li]. and Interest at vj[li] ꝑ Cent' pro Anno vnto one Nicholas Reeue Cittizen and Scrivene[r] of London Executo[r]. of the Last will and Testament of the said Ellen Martin and for the vse and sole behoofe of the said Children wch. said sum̃e of Six hundred pounds was not to be repaid vntill the said Children should attaine their seuerall ages of 21. yeares according to the true meaning of the Last will and Testament of the said Ellen wth. sundry Couenants prouisoes Articles and Agreementę as by the Condicõn of the said recited Obligacõn more plainely and at large appeareth vnto wch. said obligacõn and Condicõn the said then M[r]. Wardens and Assistants Caused the Common seale of this Corporacõn to be affixed. And for more security of payment of the said 600[li] and Interest the then M[r]. and Wardens and three of the then Assistants entred into a Recognizance to the then Chamberlaine of the Guildhall of the City of London for and on the behalfe of all the rest of the said Partne[rs]. for true payment of the said sum̃e of 600[li]. vnto the said two Children as thereby appeareth. Of w[ch]. said sum̃e of 600[li]. the Partne[rs]. of the said Latyn stocke doe alleadge to haue paid 300[li]. Now forasmuch as the said debt is vnsatisfied And the said Latyn stocke long since failing and nothing being left to satisfie either the said Interest or principall.
Fol. 138[b] And for that most of the || said ꝑties that are entred into the said Recognizance are dead. And the said money now growing nigh due soe that if Speedy Care and provision be not forthwith taken the said debt will inevitably fall vpon the said Corporacõn to pay. Wherefore after sundry motions propounded at seuerall Co[rts]. touching the same The full Co[rt]. of Assistants this day seriously weighing the dainger thereof Haue by generall Consent authorised appointed and requested M[r]. Henry

[1] Cf. *C–B.C*, 62[a], 1 July 1620.

ffetherston now one of the Wardens of the said Company wth such others as he shall thinke fitt to [*advice*] aide & Assist him to repaire vnto Councell and to advise vpon and to prosecute & mainteyne such suite Course and proceedings in the name of the said Company for freeing the said Corporacōn from the said obligacōn and from their payment of the said money as shall be by him from tyme to tyme thought fitt. And what Charges he shall in that behalfe lay forth or expend shall vpon his request be allowed & repaid vnto him by the Wardens of the said Company for the tyme being.

M[r]. Latham } Rentors
M[r]. Wellins }

This day according to the order of the last Co[rt].[1] M[r] Wellins came to giue his Answeare touching his houlding the place of Rentor warden for the yeare ensewing w[ch] he now tooke vpon [him] to pforme & soe he is ioyned wth M[r] Latham.

11th. of Aprill 1636.

Present. M[r] Kingston M[r]. M[r]. Smethwicke M[r]. ffetherston War: M[r]. Purfoote M[r]. Harrison M[r] Aspley M[r]. Butter M[r] Bourne M[r] Mead & M[r] Beale.

To procure a Proclamation

The Co[rt]. this day hath requested M[r] Downes M[r]. Mead & M[r]. Beale M[r]. Whitaker M[r] Robinson M[r] Walbancke and M[r]. Thomasin to follow a buisines now in agitation w[ch] is for the obteyning of a Proclamation against sundry abuses in this Company. M[r]. Downes m[r] Beale & the Clarke are requested to attend M[r] Atturney generall for dispatch thereof.[2]

Cannons & Homilies

M[r] Aspley is requested to veiw the Entrance about the said Bookes and to take paines there[*of*] [in] to know whose right they are & Certifie the Co[rt]. his opinion therein.[3]

11°. Aprilis 1636 predict' Fol. 139[a]

M[r]. Stansby. part mortgaged to M[r] Islip. This is satisfied H: W:[4]

This day M[r]. Stansby had leaue to engage his Liuery pte in the English stocke vnto M[r]. Islip for 100[li]. and Interest for six Monthes.

[1] Cf. *C–B.C*, 137[b], 26 Mar. 1636.

[2] Cf. *C–B.C*, 134[a], 25 May 1635. This visit was evidently successful, for the proclamation, STC 9064, was issued 1 May 1636.

[3] The books disputed were STC 10075–9 and 13661 (another edition, not 'anr. issue', to judge by the Huntington copies, but see McKerrow and Ferguson No. 223) and 13676[a]. These books were originally the property of the Royal Printing Office, but on 26 Aug. 1632 Bonham Norton transferred his rights to Mrs. Joyce Norton and Richard Whitaker (Arber iv. 285). Robert Young as, with his partners, the assign of John Bill was here claiming at least part of the rights in these works. The final decision in this dispute is not recorded (cf. *C–B.C*, 142[a], 1 Aug. 1636), but apparently Young was content to take the *Canons* (STC 10080) and left the *Homilies* (STC 13662 and 13677) to Whitaker. More than one of the editions of the Canons (STC 10075–9) may have false imprints.

[4] Henry Walley, the Clerk.

Hum: Woodalls parte Mortgaged to Will: ffaired als ffox This is satisfied. H:W:

Humphrey Woodall[1] had leaue likewise to engage his yeomandry pte vnto William ffaired als ffox for 50^{li}. and Interest for 6. monthes. the former engagem^{t}. to Mr Downes being first satisfied.[2]

Nich: Vavasor to haue Leonard Becketts Copies Entred vnto him.

This day Nicholas Vavasor Came to this Co^{rt}. and desired that the Copies lately appertayning vnto Leonard Beckett deceased (whose widd he hath married) might be Entred vnto him in the Hall Booke of the Entrance of Copies, wch. the Table granted And haue ordered the same Copies to be Entred vnto him reserving euery mans Right.[3]

M^{r}. fflesher Mr Haviland Mr Young
115

Whereas by an Order of the 23th. of December 1634. The severall parts and Dividents of Miles fflesher John Hauiland and Robert Young were suspended for [*importing hither*] great quantities of Psalmes (wch they had [soe] imprinted in Scotland) vntill further order were taken therein as thereby appeareth.[4] [And the said Psalmes being since imported hither & seized] Now forasmuch as the said Miles fflesher John Haviland & Robte Young haue acknowledged their offence and become humble suitors to this Co^{rt}. and haue freely and willingly submitted themselues to abide such order as the Master Wardens and Assistants or the more pte of them shall herein thinke fitt. The Co^{rt}. this day taking seriously into their Consideracõn that this Enterprize of theirs was of very evill Consequence and tended in a great pte to the ruine & destruction of the Companyes Grant for the said Psalmes.[5] And that their offence was much aggravated by their being themselues Partne^{rs}. therein and therefore ought and were bound to haue vsed their Endeavo^{rs}. for the good of the same and not any way haue practized the Contrary. And whereas by the expresse words of the said Grant to the Company and the Ordinance thereupon made euery pson soe doeing and offending the same being duely proved shall be punished therefore by Imprisonment penalty or forfeiture of his stocke Portion and Interest that he shall then haue in the premises or any pte thereof according to the qualitie of his or their offence. At the discretion of the M^{r}. Wardens and Assistants for the tyme being or the more pte of them. Soe that all their said stocks are by this their offence absolutely forfeited. Yet notwithstanding this Co^{rt}. well weighing alsoe that some favour is to be shewed them by reason of some passages
Fol. 139^{b} since the Cōmitting of their offence. Haue thus ordered that they shall pay for a fyne amon'gst them forty markes (vizt.) euery yeomandry share xx. Nobles a peece to the vse of the Poore of this Company. W^{ch}. money it is ordered shall be deducted out of the Dividents of their said stocks. And after such payment made by either of them then their said shares and proffitts to retorne to the said pties as formerly they were And ye Co^{rt}. further ordered that y^{t} (*sic*) they should be allowed forty pounds towards their Charges.[6]

1 Made free 20 May 1617 (Arber iii. 684).
2 Cf. *C–B.C*, 165^{a}, 20 June 1639.
3 Entered 18 May 1636 (Arber iv. 363).
4 Cf. *C–B.C*, 130^{b}, 23 Dec. 1634.
5 Cf. *C–B.C*, 115^{b}, 5 Sept. 1631.

6 Evidently Richard Adams's name was here omitted by accident. Forty marks and four times twenty nobles both equal £26. 13*s*. 4*d*. It is not known what the 'passages' were which caused them to be treated with such clemency, but presumably

28°. Aprilis 1636.

Present Mr Kingston M^{r}. Smethwicke M^{r}. ffetherston War: Mr Weaver Mr Purfoote Mr Rothwell Mr Butter Mr Downes & Mr Mead.

M^{r}. Stansby.
135

Whereas by an Order of the seauenth of September last.[1] It was ordered that the money oweing by the English stocke vnto m^{r} Stansby for worke, should be detayned by m^{r}. Weaver vntill further order were taken therein as thereby appeareth. And the said Mr Stansby being this day p^{r}sent in Co^{rt}. submitted himselfe to such order as this Co^{rt}. should thinke fitt wch. being taken into serious Consideracõn And for that it appeared M^{r}. Stansby had wilfully persisted in the Imprinting and finishing of the Midleborough Psalmes [in 16] after expresse warning giuen him to desist by the Stockeeps and Treasurer (he then haueing done but two sheets) The Co^{rt}. hath this day ordered that he shall loose the workemanship of the ffiue sheets he printed after notice giuen him to the Contrary. And that the stocke shall pay him for his workemanship of the said two sheets. And for the Paper made wast of the said Midleborough Psalmes and Almanacks by his default in Imprinting. The Co^{rt}. hath taken him into their favorable Consideracõn & haue ordered that he shall pay but the sum̃e of x^{li} towards the said Losse And the Stocke to beare the residue. And soe all things are to remitted (*sic*). And that vpon such Abatement Mr Weaver shall satisfie vnto Mr Stansby the residue of the money soe due vnto him by the said stocke.

2°. Maij. 1636.

Fol. 140^{a}

Present. M^{r}. Kingston M^{r}., M^{r}. Smethwicke M^{r}. ffetherston War: Mr Islip Mr Weaver Mr Purfoote Mr Harrison Mr Aspley Mr Rothwell Mr Downes Mr Bourne Mr Mead & Mr Beale.

M^{r}. Bourne
M^{r} ffussell
Mr Moseley.

The matter of Difference betweene M^{r}. Bourne M^{r} ffussell and Mr Mosley[2] is referred to four Brothers of this Company. M^{r}. Bourne hath Chosen M^{r}. Whitaker & Mr Stevens. And m^{r} ffussell and Mr Moseley haue Chosen Mr Robinson and Mr Marriott. And they are to examine the difference between them And Certifie the Table their doeings and opinions therein.[3]

M^{rs}. Griffin fyne at xx. nobles.

This day the Stockeeps made their Complaint against M^{rs}. Griffin for that she hath printed the Psalmes in [ ] for the English stocke wth soe large a Margent that they cannott [be Joyned] to any other booke. The Co^{rt}. taking the same into Consideracõn thought fitt to fyne her [*Nobles*] at Twenty Nobles towards the losse of the said Psalmes.[4]

the £40 were allowed for the costs of printing and transporting the Scottish printed *Psalms*. Cf. *C–B.C*, 157^{a}, 28 June 1638.

[1] Cf. *C–B.C*, 135^{b}.

[2] Fussell and Moseley were at this time in partnership and had bought books of Bourne.

[3] Cf. *C–B.C*, 140^{b}, 13 June 1636, and 141^{a}, 17 June 1636.

[4] STC 2656 has large outer and lower margins, but there is no reason why it should not be bound with some Bibles.

Mr Waterson — Mr. Waterson vpon his request for forbearance of the 50li he borrowed of Mr. Nortons bequeast. due in Aprill last had tyme giuen him vntill October next for repayeing the same.[1]

6o. Maij 1636. pn'tibus vt antea

The Rentors Accompt. Mr Whittaker — This day Mr. Whitakers Accompt of Rentorship was audited and there appeared to be due 54li. 7d. wch. was paid accordingly by Mr. Whittaker to Mr Warden ffetherston.

30o. Maij 1636

Mr Bourne. — These seuerall thing (vizt.) Bills of Lading in English ffrench Italian & Dutch. Indentures for Virginia St. Christophers and the Somer Islands. Bills of Debt for Money. ffor Tobacco are by order of the Cort. to be Entred vnto Mr Bourne. saluo Jure cuiuscunqꝫ.[2]

Fol. 140b

1o Junij Anno 1636.

Present. — Mr. Kingston Mr. Smethwicke Mr. Aspley loco Gardian Mr Purfoot Harrison Mr Downes Mr Bourne Mr Mead.

Mr Sherres Mr Young — This day mr. Young who was bound wth. mr Sheeres to Mr. Weaver for 37li. 8s. 2d. Came to the table about the said money, ꝑte thereof haveing byn due aboue a twelue month since. the said Mr young paid downe 7li. 8s. wch. Mr Downes receiued for Mr Weaver. And desired the Cort. that he might pay the residue according to the tenor of his Bond by 5li. a quarter the first payment to begin at Midsomer next. the wch request was granted.

13o. Junij 1636

Present. — Mr Kingston Mr. Smethwicke Mr. ffetherston Mr. weaver Mr Harrison Mr Downes Mr Bourne Mr Mead Mr Beale.

Mr. Bourne Mr. ffussell Mr. Mosley — This day mr. Bourne mr. ffussell and mr. Moseley wth some of ye refferrees chosen by them, Came & Certified the Table that they could make noe end of the difference[3] by reason they were not bound to stand to such order as the said Refferrees should thinke fitt to sett downe. Now it is agreed by and wth the Consent aswell of Mr. Bourne on the one ꝑte as Mr ffussell & Mr. Mozeley. on the other ꝑte. That the said fformer Refferrees or any three of them shall heare & examine the said difference and Certifie their doeings & opinions therein And therevpon the table will putt such

[1] This money was originally borrowed 2 Feb. 1630 (*Liber C2*, 114a) and renewed 8 Apr. 1633 (*Liber C2*, 117a).

[2] Entered 8 June 1636 (Arber iv. 364).

[3] Cf. *C–B.C*, 140a, 2 May 1636, and 141a, 17 June 1636.

end as to right shall appertaine, vnto w[ch] end M[r]. Bourne M[r]. ffussell & m[r] Mosley haue willingly submitted themselues.

17°. Junij 1636. FOL. 141[a]

Present. M[r] Kingston M[r]. Smethwicke M[r]. Weaver M[r]. Purfoote M[r]. Harrison M[r]. Aspley M[r] Butter m[r] Downes and M[r]. Mead.

M[r]. Bourne
M[r] ffussell
M[r]. Mosley.

Whereas by an order of the 13th day of this Month of June[1] It appeareth that y[e] difference depending between M[r]. Bourne [on y[e] one pte] M[r] ffussell & m[r]. Mosley on the other pte could not be Composed by the Refferrees (elected by them the second day of May last). And whereas by the said order of the 13[th]. of this Month It was mutually Consented and agreed betweene the said M[r] Bourne M[r]. ffussell & M[r]. Mosley p[r]sent in Co[rt]. That the said Refferrees by them elected the said second day of May, or any three of them should againe haue the hearing & examinacõn of the said difference & Certifie this Co[rt]. of their doeings & opinions therein. And the Table therevpon to putt such end as in their Judgments should be thought fitt. And whereas the said Refferrees haue now taken a great deale of paynes to Compose the said difference. And to that end haue brought a Certificate vnder their hands (bearing date the 16th. day of this month of June) of their proceeding therein, w[ch] being read this day in Co[rt]. was well approved of. And forasmuch as it appeareth by the said Certificate that m[r]. ffussell & m[r]. Mozely doe acknowledge themselues indebted to M[r]. Bourne in the sume of 76[li]. 16[s]. 7[d]. for Bookes already by them receiued [*of*] from him according to the tenor of Certaine Articles of Agreem[t]. betweene them made bearing date the 19[th] day of december 1633. And it alsoe appeareth that M[r] Bourne hath not fully pformed to them his pte of the said Articles, the Co[rt]. taking the same into their serious Consideracõn haue thought fitt & soe ordered in the p[r]sence of both pties That in full Recompence to M[r]. ffussell & M[r]. Mosley for all damage as might arise to them by the non pformance of M[r]. Bournes pte of the said Articles That the said M[r]. Bourne shall abate them 8[li]. out of the said 76[li]. 16[s]. 7[d]. And that m[r]. ffussell & M[r]. Mosley shall pay vnto M[r] Bourne betweene this & Teusday next 68[li]. 16[s]. 7[d]. being the residue of the said debt of 76[li]. 16[s]. 7[d]. And therevpon the said Articles & Bonds for pformance of them to be Cancelled and all differencę touching the same to be ended.

2°. Julij 1636 FOL. 141[b]

Present. M[r]. Kingston M[r]. M[r] Smethwicke M[r]. ffetherston war: M[r] Cole M[r] Islip M[r] Weaver M[r] Purfoot M[r] Harison M[r] Aspley M[r] Butter M[r] Downes M[r] Bourne M[r]. M[r] (*sic*) Mead & M[r] Beale.

Election of new M[r]. and Wardens. This day Election was made for new M[r]. and wardens for this yeare ensewing. M[r]. Kingston was Chosen Master againe M[r] Harrison vppwarden & m[r] Downeę second warden.

[1] Cf. *C–B.C*, 140[a], 2 May 1636, and 140[b], 13 June 1636.

Auditors for the auditing ye old war: Accompts — Mr. Purfoote and Mr Butter were Chosen Auditors. to audite Mr. Smethwick & Mr ffetherstons Accompt. for this yeare past.

Mr. Alchorne part mort: to Tho: Bourne — Mr. Alchorne had leaue to engage his pte in the English stocke for 80li. vnto Thomas Bourne for a yeare.

mr Pullen & mr Wright Liuery men — This day Mr. Pullen & Mr. Tho: Wright were admitted into the Liuery of this Company.

Mr. Purfoote — Mr Purfoot was admitted to fyne for his second tyme vpp warden. The table fyned him at 5li. & he is to take his place according to his Antiquity.

Mr Butter. — Likewise mr. Butter was fined at 5li. for his first tyme warden and he is likewise to take his place according to his antiquity.

Mr: Roche a suitor for a new Lease of the blacke Boy........... — This day Mr. Roach became an humble suitor to his (*sic*) Cort. for the renewing of ye Lease of his now dwelling house[1] wherevpon [this] Cort. referred the Consideracõn thereof vnto or Mr. Mr. warden ffetherston Mr Harrison Mr Aspley and Mr Downes or any three of them And ye Cort. hath requested them to veiw the house & Consider of the valew of the same & all other thinge that may tend to the profitt & good of this Company. And to Certifie their opinions therein wth all Convenient speed.

Fol. 142a Mr. Kingston} Master.

Mr. Harrison
Mr. Downes} Wardens.

1o. Augusti 1636. xiio. Car. Regis.

Present. — Mr Kingston Mr. Mr. Harrison Mr. Downes war: Mr. Islip Mr. Weaver Mr. Purfoote mr. Aspley Mr Butter mr Bourne mr. Mead and Mr Beale.

Mr. Smethwicke & Mr. ffetherston fyned for not making their Election dynner — Whereas by a Precept from my Lord Mayor.[2] It is Commanded that noe ffeasts be made by any of the Companies of this Citty; but that Charge soe to be expended to be Converted for releife of the Poore. And whereas the wardens of this Company were to make a dynner at their Charge on the Election day & towards the same [Charge] to haue twenty markes from the house according to Custome. Now forasmuch as ye said wardens haue allowed themselues in their Accompt to the house the said Twenty Markes & yet

[1] Cf. *C–B.C*, 137*b, 5 Mar. 1636.
[2] Transcribed in *Letter Book*, 123a, 9 May 1636, and 123b, 28 July 1636.

not w[th]standing made noe Dynner. The Co[rt]. this day taking the same into Consideracõn hath ordered that the said wardens M[r]. Smethwicke & M[r]. ffetherston shall retorne to the now warden of this Company the said Twenty markes they allowed themselues from the house And moreouer shall pay for a fyne betweene them the sum̃e of Twenty Markes.

M[r]. Young about ye Cannonę & Homilies — This day m[r]. Young came againe to the Hall and desired some end might be made touching M[r] Whittaker and him for the Cannons & Homilies of the Church. It was formerly referred to M[r]. Aspley:[1] But the Co[rt]. thought fitt this day to ioyne vnto him Mr Butter, And they are requested to take paines therein And Certifie their doeings therein wth all Convenient speed.

Mr Benson to print 1500. of the Golden Meane. giueing Consideracõn to ye vse of the Poore. — John Benson Came this day vnto ye Co[rt]. and Craved leaue to Imprint one Impression [*one Impression of Latimers sermons*] [of a] [*the*] [Booke Called the Goulden Meane[2]] he giueing such Consideracõn vpon the finishing of the said Impression as this Co[rt]. should thinke fitt or vsuall in this kind, wch. the Co[rt]. taking into Consideracõn hath ordered that he shall (*have*) Liberty to Imprint 1500. of the said bookes paying therefore vpon the finishing of the Impression such fyne as this Co[rt]. shall thinke fitt.

Mr Sankey fyne of xx[s]. for attorning tennant for the Pyne Aple in Avie Mary Lane ...... — This day William Sankey haveing bought ye Estate of Ambrose Martin of the Lease of the Pyne Apple in Avie Mary lane, came and desired to Attorne tenn[t]. to the ffeoffees of those Rents, paying xx[s]. vnto the said ffeoffes & v[s]. vnto the Clarke according to the tenner of the Lease, wch. the Table taking into Consideracõn did accept of the said wm. Sankey for their tennant, And the table ordered the said xx[s]. to be paid vnto the English stocke.[3]

28[o]. Septembris Anno 1636. — Fol. 142[b]

Present. — M[r]. Kingston M[r]. Harrison M[r] Downes war: M[r] Weaver M[r] Smethwicke M[r]. Purfoote M[r]. Butter M[r]. Bourne & M[r]. Mead.

M[r]. Coates fine of three pounds & six shillings for leaue to print Latimers sermons paid to the warden — M[r]. Coates being warned to the table this day about the payment of some money for leaue to Imprint an Impression of Latimers sermons as appeareth by a former order,[4] Came and paid the Court the sum̃e of Three pounds and six shillings, it being in full according to the Rate of Twelue pence in the pound for the said Impression.

[1] Cf. *C–B.C*, 138[b], 11 Apr. 1636, and 147[b], 5 June 1637.

[2] STC 17759. There is at the Folger another issue, undated, without Haviland's initials.

[3] Cf. *C–B.C*, 48[b], 1 Sept. 1617, and 142[b], 7 Nov. 1636.

[4] Cf. *C–B.C*, 126[a], 3 Feb. 1633. According to the *Book of Fines*, 26[b], Cotes actually paid on this date £3. 6*s*. 6*d*.

Mr. Harper to pay his fyne of xxty. Nobles.

This day Mr Harper being likewise warned to the Cort. to bring in his fyne of xx. Nobles imposed vpon him for printing the Psalmes as appeareth by a former Order. Desired the Cort. that in respect of the deadnes of trading he might be forborne [for] a short tyme & he would pay the same wch. the Cort. granted.[1]

7o. Nouembris 1636.

Present. Mr. Kingston Mr. Mr Harrison Mr Downes wardens Mr Smethwicke Mr Aspley Mr Butter Mr Bourne & Mr. Mead.

A Lease of the blacke boy in Avie Mary Lane lett vnto mr Roach for xxxjty. yeares.

This day the Cort. hath graunted a Lease of the Blacke Boy in Avie Mary lane vnto Mr Roach for the Terme of one and Thirty yeares to Comence from or Lady day next vpon surrender of a former Lease Lett vnto Mrs. Trussell and the said Mr Roach is to giue Two hundred Markes for a ffyne for the same. of wch he this day paid Twenty Markes & is to pay the rest at the sealing of his Lease. The Couents. to agree wth the former at the Rent of Eight pounds ꝑ Annu' quarterly.[2]

Mr. Bradley new Liuery.

This day Mr Bradley[3] was admitted into the Liuery of this Company.

Mrs. Moores Liuery Part conferred vpon mr Chappell

This day Mrs. Moores[4] Letter was read in Cort. wherein she desired that her Liuery part in the English stocke may be Conferred vpon Mr. Chappell[5] wch. the Cort. taking into Consideracõn did accordingly Conferr the said Part vpon him & he tooke his oath accordingly.

Mr Chappell yeo: ꝑte vpon mr Thomasin

Then the Cort. went to election of a Partner for mr Chappells yeomandry ꝑte, there stood for the same Mr Dainty Mr Tompson & william Hope & it fell vpon Mr Thomasin & he tooke his oath accordingly.

Fol. 143a

7o. Nouembri predict'

Mrs. Allotts yeo: part Conferred vpon mr. Roger Norton.

This day a Letter was likewise read from Mrs. Allott wherein she desireth the Cort. to transfferr her yeomandry ꝑte in the English stocke vpon mr. Roger Norton wch. the Cort. taking into Consideracõn haue accordingly Conferred the same vpon him and he tooke his oath accordingly.

[1] Cf. *C–B.C*, 119b, 26 Mar. 1632. At that time he was fined 20 marks or £13. 6*s*. 8*d*., whereas 20 nobles equals only £6. 13*s*. 4*d*. Under the date 29 Mar. 1638, *Book of Fines*, 27b, Harper finally paid £10.

[2] Cf. *C–B.C*, 142a, 1 Aug. 1636.

[3] Either John B. or George B.; the first was made free 1 Dec. 1628 and the second 15 Sept. 1631 (Arber iii. 686).

[4] Mrs. Anne Moore, widow of Richard Moore.

[5] John Chappell, made free 12 Jan. 1624 (Arber iii. 685).

Mrs. Allotts Copies assigned to Mr Legatt & Andrew Crooke.

This day a deed of Bargaine & Sale vnder the hand of Mrs. Allott (wherein she hath bargained and sold all her Copies & part of Copies vnto Mr. Legatt & Andrew Crooke) was read in Cort., the wch. (according to the Custome of the Company) she humbly desired [*according to*] this Cort. to assigne the same Copies & parts of Copies vnto the said Mr. Legatt & Andrew Crooke reserveing euery mans right. Wch. the Crt. hath accordingly granted and haue ordered that the said Copies be entred vnto them.[1]

Mr. Allotts guift of xxli. paid to the Company

Mr. Chetwyn[2] who is to marry the widdow of mr Robert Allott deceased, Came this day vnto the Cort. and paid downe Ten pounds being the guift of mr. Robert Allott for a dynner for the Company. And alsoe Ten pounds more being likewise the guift of the said Mr Allott to be disposed by the Company for the good of poore Members of the same.

Paid 6li. for three Impressions of the Mirror of Martyrs

The said Mr. Chetwin paid downe six pounds for three Impressions of the Mirror of Martyrs[3] according to the Entry of the said Booke to Mr Budge who sold the same to mr Allott. And the Cort. ordered that the said Booke shall be Entred to Mr Legatt & Andrew Crooke as it was to Mr Budge that vpon euery Impression thereof he shall pay xls. to the vse of the Company.

All Copies entred and belonging to John Kingston George Robinson & Tho: Orwyn to be Entred to or Mr. Mr Kingston.

Vpon the requeast of or Master Mr. Kingston that the Copies Entred vnto John Kingston George Robinson and Thomas Orwyn wch are not passed away [to] other men might be entred to him The Cort. taking the same into Consideracõn hath ordered that all such Copies shall be entred vnto him wth. this proviso reserveing euery mans right.[4]

21°. Nouembri 1636. Fol. 143b

Present. Mr Kingston Mr. Mr. Harrison Mr. Downes wardens Mr. Weaver Mr Smethwicke Mr. Aspley Mr Rothwell Mr. Butter Mr. Bourne Mr Mead Mr Beale.

Mr. Roach his fyne of two hundred Markes paid & his Lease sealed.

This day mr. Roche paid downe the residew of his fyne for his Lease of the blacke boy in Avie Mary lane being in all Two hundred Markes and vpon payment thereof the lease of his house being openly read in Cort. was sealed by the ffeoffees then present. Wch. said Two hundred Markes was received by mr Bourne & Mr Mead now Stockeepers for the vse of the English Stocke.[5]

[1] Entered 1 July 1637 (Arber iv. 387–8). Cf. *C–B.C*, 146b, 3 Apr. 1637.

[2] Philip Chetwind, who was apparently not then a member of the Company. He was a Clothworker.

[3] STC 5851. Cf. *C–B.C*, 39a, 9 May 1615. The three editions which Chetwind paid for were presumably an edition, 'G.P. f. J. Budge, 1625' (of which a copy is in the Folger); STC 5850; and 'The fourth edition enlarged', 'E.A. f. R. Allot, 1633' (of which copies are in the B.M., O., and Folger). See entry 1 July 1637 (Arber iv. 387).

[4] These were not entered. F. Kingston's mother married successively G. Robinson and T. Orwin.

[5] Cf. *C–B.C*, 142b, 7 Nov. 1636.

Mr. Purfoots Liuery part Conferred on Mr Thrale & Mr Thrales yeomandry part on mr Bradley

Mr. Purfoot haveing sent a Note vnder his hand vnto the Cort. this day wherein he desired to Assigne ouer all his Liuery part in the English stocke vnto Mr Bradley[1] wth whome he had Contracted which being taken into Consideracõn It was mutually agreed That forasmuch as Mr. Purfoot had [entred] [*agreed*] into Bond to the said Mr Bradley to performe his said Bargaine although the Cort. vtterly disliked his Contract wth soe young a man for his Liuery part. Notwithstanding the Cort. in much favour to Mr. Purfoot thought good that Mr Thrale should haue his Livery part & Mr Bradley mr Thrales yeomandry part, they equally paying what mr Purfoot had Contracted for wth mr Bradley wch. was 180li. Of wch said sume 108li. is to be deducted for Mrs. Joyce Norton according to an Order in that behalfe made.[2] And the said Mr. Thrale and Mr Bradley tooke their oathes accordingly.

5o. die Decembris 1636.

Present Mr. Kingston Mr. Mr. Harrison & Mr Downes wardens Mr Weaver Mr Smethwicke Mr Aspley Mr Rothwell Mr ffetherston Mr Butter Mr Bourne.

Rentor warden fyned for not making his dynner on my Lord Mayors. day

fforasmuch as by reason of the sicknes, all publique Dynners were putt by, [by] a precept from my Lord Mayor[3] & for that Mr. Latham now Renter warden should haue made a Dynner for the Company on my Lord Mayors day the wch Charge for the reason aforesaid was spared. The Cort. this day taking the same into Consideracõn haue thought fitt to fyne the said Rentor warden, for not making his said ffeast. And the same being putt to voices, he was fyned by the Maior pte at vijli. 6s. 8d.

Fol. 144a

5o. Die Decembris 1636. predict'.

Mrs. Adams yeomandry Part disposed of

Mr Meighen one halfe

Wm. Hope the other halfe

This day Mrs. Adams[4] being lately married her yeomandry part in the English Stocke fell to be disposed of by Election. And because of many suitors the Cort. thought fitt to devide the same. There stood in Election for one halfe thereof Mr Meighen Mr Morrett[5] and William Hope, and it fell vpon William Hope. And for the other halfe thereof there stood Mr Meighen Mr Morrett & Edward Medlicott,[6] and it fell vpon Mr Meighen. And the said Mr Meighen and wm. Hope tooke their oathes accordingly.

[1] Cf. *C–B.C*, 137a, 14 Jan. 1636, and 142b, 7 Nov. 1636.

[2] Cf. *C–B.C*, 130a, 1 Dec. 1634. Presumably George or John Bradley was the 'soe young a man'.

[3] Cf. *C–B.C*, 142a, 1 Aug. 1636, and *Letter Book*, 123b, 28 July 1636.

[4] Mrs. Thomas Adams.

[5] John Morrett, made free 1 Mar. 1617 (Arber iii. 684).

[6] Made free 14 Jan. 1622 (Arber iii. 685).

20°. Decembris 1636.

Present. Mr. Kingston Mr. Mr. Smethwicke loco gardiani Mr. Downes Mr Weaver Mr. Purfoote Mr Aspley Mr Rothwell Mr ffetherston Mr Bourne Mr Butter Mr Mead.

Barth: Downes his yeomandry part in ye English stocke Conferred vpon his sonne Tho: Downes

A Letter was read this day from Bartholomew Downes an ancient Brother of this Company wherein he humbly desired this Cort. to Conferr his yeomandry part wch. he hath in the English Stocke vpon his sonne Thomas Downes. Wch. the Court vpon Consideracõn thought fitt to grant his request & accordingly Conferred the same vpon him And he tooke his oath according to the Custome.

28° Decembris 1636. pn'tibus [vt] antea

Mr. Marriott a yeomandry Part in the English Stocke

Mrs. Burr[1] being lately deceased, her yeomandry part in the English Stocke fell to be disposed of by the Cort. There Stood in Election mr Marriott mr Dainty and John Rothwell and it fell vpon mr: Marriott and he tooke his oath accordingly.

11°. January 1636.

Mrs. Griffin leaue to print some of Beacons workes

Vpon the humble request of Mrs. Griffin vnto this Court for leaue to reprint certaine Tracts taken out of Mr Thomas Beacons workes (vizt.) Newes from heauen. Christmas Bankett. Jewell of Joy. Davids Harpe. Gouermt. of vertue. A Comfortable Epistle. A Supplication to God. The display of Popish Masse.[2] & the Relicts of Rome. The Cort. thought fitt (in Case the said tracts were perused and vnquestionable) to grant her request. And it is ordered that vpon the finishing of an Impression of either of the said Bookes she shall pay to the vse of the poore at the discretion of this Cort. And the said Mrs. Griffin promised to performe the same.

21°. Januarij 1636. Fol. 144b

Present. Mr Kingston Mr. Mr Smethwick loco Gardian Mr Swinhow Mr Weaver Mr ffetherston Mr. Butter and Mr Mead.

Mr. Hollands part Conferred vpon Dan: Pakeman

This day mr. Holland came and desired the Table to giue leaue vnto him to transferr his yeomandry part which he hath in the English Stock vpon Daniell Pakeman, which the Cort. taking into Consideracõn granted his request and the said Daniell Pakeman tooke his oath accordingly.

[1] Mrs. Walter Burre.

[2] According to W. Prynne, *Canterburies doome*, 1646, pp. 183–4, 513–14, 516, Prynne caused Michael Sparke Sen. to set Mrs. Griffin on the printing of this (STC 1719) and Becon's *Reliques of Rome*. As soon as the first was printed Laud caused it to be seized, and Mrs. Griffin was frightened from continuing the printing of the second book. Evidently this was done in anticipation of the Decree of Star Chamber regarding printing.

Mr Lenthall — Whereas in the Lease lett vnto mr Lenthall of the Roomes at Billingsgate these words are inserted (ouer and aboue the Ordinary repaires) This day vpon his request for the leaueing the same quite out, the Cort. Condiscended therevnto. The repaires being done betweene this and the yeare 1640.[1]

13° ffebruarij 1636.

Present. — Mr Kingston Mr Harrison Mr Downes Mr Swinhow Mr Aspley Mr Butter Mr ffetherston Mr Bourne and Mr Mead.

Mr Grismonds part Conferred vpon Edw: Medlicott and Moses Bell. — This day vpon Mr Grismonds request his pte in the English Stock was Conferred vpon Edward Medlicott[2] and Moses Bell. and they tooke their oathes accordingly.

Oxford. — Mr. warden Harrison Mr Mead Mr Young the Clarke and Beadle are by Consent & order of this Cort. to goe to the vniuersity of Oxford to Conclude the agreement of the former offer of CCli. p Annu' wth. other pticular instructions in that buisines.[3]

Mrs. Higgenbothams Liuery part Conferred vpon Mr Dawlman. — This day Mrs. Higgenbotham[4] desired the favour of the Cort. that she might Conferr her Liuery share in the English Stock vnto Mr Dawlman reserveing her yeomandry pte vnto her selfe. wch being taken into Consideracõn was granted and the said mr Dawlman tooke his oath accordingly.

Fol. 145a

20°. ffebruarij 1636.

Present — Mr Kingston Mr Harrison Mr Downes. Mr Swinhow Mr Weaver &c.

Moses Bells Part Mortgaged. This is Satisfied. — This day Moses Bell had had leaue to engage his halfe yeomandry part in the English Stock for 40li. for 6. monthes at 7li. p Cent'. vnto Mr Roger Norton.

Mr Bourne to haue a Lease of the fourth warehouse in the Garden. — Mr Bourne this day hath a grant of the Cort. for a Lease of the fourth warehouse[5] in the Garden for 21ty. yeares at the Rent of 4li. p Annu' fyne xls. & such Couenants as are vsed in the leases of the rest of the warehouses.

[1] Cf. *C–B.C*, 137b, 24 Jan. 1636.

[2] Made free 14 Jan. 1622 (Arber iv. 685).

[3] In January 1636, Laud had obtained a new grant of liberties for the University, which extended the right to print books even to those formerly granted to the Stationers' Company, and named the number of printers and presses that might be there employed (cf. *State Papers Dom. 1635–1636*, pp. 168–9). The Company was forced to conclude an agreement with the University printers whereby they paid an annual fee of £200 for the promise of the University printers not to print certain books. Cf. F. Madan, *Oxford books*, i. 285–7; ii. 526–30; iii. 406–8; and J. Johnson and S. Gibson, *Print and privilege*, pp. 18–19.

[4] Mrs. Richard Higgenbotham.

[5] Cf. *C–B.C*, 106a, 10 Mar. 1630. This warehouse was then allotted to the partners in the music patent.

Mrs. Pauier. The Cort. hath ordered that mr Warden Downes shall pay vnto Mr Kendrick Administrator of mrs. Pauier deceased the sum̃e of 150li. (being pte of her Stock) according to a Report from the Cort of Aldermen wch was this day produced and read in Cort.[1]

27o. ffebruarij 1636.

Present. Mr Kingston Mr Harrison Mr Downes Mr Swinhow mr Weaver Mr Purfoot Mr Aspley Mr Rothwell Mr Butter Mr Bourne Mr Mead.

Tho: Halle part disposed of.

Mr Morrett his halfe pte made vp.

Mr. Cartwright a halfe part.

This day Thomas Hall[2] being lately deceased the Cort. thought fitt to elect another Partner in his Roome. There stood in Election for the same Mr Bartlett Mr. Morrett[3] & Mr Cartwright And it fell vpon mr Morrett. Then Mr Morrett haveing a halfe part the Cort. went to Election for the same. There stood Mr Bartlett Mr Cartwright & John Rothwell and it fell vpon Mr Cartwright. And the said Mr. Morrett & Mr Cartwright tooke their oathes accordingly.

Mr Purfoot to haue no voyce in the Election of a Partner nor any other in the future in like Case

Whereas Mr Thomas Purfoot one of the Assistants of this Company vpon his request hath obteyned Leaue to putt of all his Shares which he had in the English Stock, and hath recd. full Consideracõn for them, soe that now he is become noe Partner therein.[4] It is thought fitt and soe ordered That Mr Purfoot shall not henceforth be Called vnto any Meetings about the mannageing of that Stock, nor haue any voyce in the Election of a Partner or in any other thing whatsoeuer concerning the same. And [that] this order shall be obserued generally for all psons in the like kind hereafter.

1o. Martij 1636. Fol. 145b

Present. Mr Kingston Mr. Harrison Mr. Downes Mr. Swinhow Mr Cole Mr. Weaver Mr Smethwick Mr Aspley Mr Butter Mr Bourne Mr Mead

Stockeepers chosen for the English Stock.	Mr Smethwick	Mr Latham	Mr. Bellamy
	Mr Aspley	Mr Dawlman	Mr Stevens

Mr. Weaver Treasurer et Jurator

Auditors.	Mr ffetherston	Mr Harper	Godfrey Emerson
	Mr. Butter	Mr Legatt	Edward Blackmore

[1] Mrs. Pavier's assistant's part was disposed of 20 July 1635, *C–B.C*, 135a.

[2] Made free 4 Sept. 1626 (Arber iii. 686).

[3] John Morrett, made free 1 Mar. 1617 (Arber iii. 684).

[4] Cf. *C–B.C*, 137a, 14 Jan. 1636, and 143b, 21 Nov. 1636.

24°. Martij 1636.

Present. Mr. Kingston Mr. Mr Harrison & Mr Downes war: Mr Swinhow Mr Cole. Mr Weaver Mr Smethwick Mr Aspley Mr Rothwell Mr Butter Mr Bourne and Mr Mead.

Mrs Higgenbothams yeo: part Conferred vpon Tho: Badger — Mrs. Higgenbotham came this day vnto the Cort. and desired that her yeomandry part in the English stocke might be conferred vpon Thomas Badger. Which the Cort. taking into Consideracõn admitted the said Thomas Badger to her pte And he tooke his oath accordingly.

Mr Mead & the Clarke to goe to Oxford .... — The table haue requested Mr. Mead to goe wth the Clarke vnto Oxford to Carry or pte of the Agreement and to take the vniuersities pte for the Company. on Tewsday next[1]

Carmina Prouerbialia to be entred to mr Constable .... — Mr Constable by order of the Cort. is to haue the booke called Carmina Proverbialia Entred vnto him wth this provisoe Saluo Jure cuiuscunq;.[2]

Edw: Wood to haue the loane of 50li. for 3. yeares — The Cort. hath granted Edward Wood[3] the loane of 50li. when it comes in putting in good security.

Mr Young to haue all mr ffishers Copies Entred vnto him. — This day mr. young came vnto the Table a deed of Mortgage vnder the hand and Seale of Beniamin ffisher vnto the said mr Young of all the Copies and ptes of Copies belonging vnto the said Ben: ffisher. And desired the Cort. to giue order that they might be entred vnto him according to the tenor of the said deed wch. the Cort. taking into Consideracõn ordered That if the said Mr Young
Fol. 146a would vndertake || to pay the said ffishers debt wch. he oweth vnto the English Stock they should be entred vnto him accordingly. Provided that if the said Ben: ffisher doe pay vnto the said Mr Young, the sume by him borrowed mencõned in the deed on the day limited as alsoe the debt wch the said Mr Young shall pay downe for him to the English stock wth. the forbearance for the same And the Charge of the Entry of the said Copies. That then the Entrance of all the said Copies vnto the said Mr. Young shall be void.[4]

[1] Cf. *C–B.C*, 144b, 13 Feb. 1637, and *Letter Book*, 122b, 9 Mar. 1635.

[2] Entered 24 Mar. 1637, Arber iv. 376. This book, originally entered to Christopher Barker, had been printed at least eight times by 1609, always by Barker or his assign, T. Dawson. Constable published one edition, STC 14065, which has the imprint 'Londini, in off. I. Haviland, impensis F. Constable, prost apud N. Butter, 1637'.

[3] Made free 5 May 1628 (Arber iii. 686). His bonds were registered 18 May 1637, *Liber C2*, 120a.

[4] Entered 27 Mar. 1637 (Arber iv. 377–80).

27°. Martij 1637.

Present. Mr. Kingston Mr Harrison Mr Downes Mr Swinhow Mr weaver Mr Smethwick Mr Aspley Mr Rothwell Mr Butter Mr Bourne & Mr Mead.

Mr. Thrale & Andrew Crooke to haue a Lease of the third warehouse in the Garden............

Whereas on the 5th. day of August 1633. This Cort. then granted vnto Mr Islip their Consent for a Lease of the third warehouse in the Garden And to this tyme hath enioyed the same wthout payment of any Rent.[1] The Cort. this day hath ordered (that in regard the said Mr Islip hath neglected the sealeing of the said Lease & non paymt. of the Rent.) That a Lease of the said warehouse shall be lett vnto Richard Thrale and Andrew Crooke for 21ty. yeares to Comence from or Lady day last at ye Rent of 4li p Ann' & a fyne of xls. and such Covenants as are vsed in the Leases of the other warehouses there.

Mr Wellins & Mr Dawson Rentors

This day Choice was made for Rentors. And mr Wellins[2] being Junior Rentor was this day required to giue his Answere whether he would hould or not And he then accepted of the same Then choise was made for another to ioyne wth him. Mr Ephraim Dawson being next was required to giue his Answere whether he would hould And [he] then likewise accepted of the same/

Mr Rice Williams Fyned for Rentor xxiiijli.

This day mr Rice Williams[3] being called to be Rentor desired to be putt to his fyne. wch the Cort. taking into Consideracõn fyned him at xxiiijli. wch he paid accordingly in the Cort.

Rich: Rogers to haue 12li.

The Cort. hath granted vnto Richard Rogers[4] the loane of 12li for 3. yeares putting in good security.

3°. Aprilis 1637 Fol. 146b

Present. Mr Kingston Mr. Harrison Mr Downes wardens. Mr Swinhow Mr Weaver Mr. Smethwick Mr Rothwell Mr Bourne Mr Mead, Mr. Cole & mr Butter came late

Bernard Alsop.

This day vpon the humble peticõn of Bernard Alsop the Implements of his presse formerly taken from him for printing pte of Bookers Almanack were by order of this Cort. restored vnto him wth strict

[1] Cf. *C–B.C*, 123b.

[2] Cf. *C–B.C*, 137b, 26 Mar. 1636.

[3] Apprenticed 16 Jan. 1604 (Arber ii. 274).

[4] Made free 1 Apr. 1622 (Arber iii. 685). His bonds were recorded 5 Apr. 1637, *Liber C2*, 23a.

Admonicõn giuen vnto him of noe favour at all to be shewed if in Case he euer offend againe.[1]

Mr Thrale to. haue Vincents Copies Entred to him.......

This day vpon request of Mr Thrale to haue the Copies and parts of Copies belonging vnto George Vincent and his father decd. to be entred vnto him. He haueing giuen satisfaction to the widdow of the said George Vincent The Cort. taking the same into Consideracõn haue granted his request. And haue ordered that all the Copies belonging vnto the said Vincent be entred vnto the said Mr Thrale Saluo Jure cuiuscunq̧.[2]

Tho: Gillett to haue a Lease of his house in ffrier alley in woodstreet. for 21ty yeares Rent vjli. p Annu' quarterly

Thomas Gillett one of the Tennants in woodstreet came this day vnto the Cort. and desired a Lease of his now dwelling house in ffrier alley for ye Terme of 21ty. yeares at the Rent of 6li. p Annu' wch. being taken into Consideracõn, And for that the said Gillett hath laid out moneyes in the repayring of the said house The Cort. ordered that he shall haue a Lease sealed vnto him for 21ty. yeares from or Lady day last at ye Rent of 6li. p Annu' wthout paymt. of any fyne and such Couents as the other houses are lett wth.

Mr Allotts Copie if not Entred by the next Court to be printed for the Company

Whereas the Copies of Mr. Allott deceased by order of this Cort. the 7th. of November last were Conferred vpon Mr. Legatt and Andrew Crooke and soe to be entred vnto them according to the Custome of this Company in the Register booke of the Entry of Copies.[3] Now forasmuch as notice hath byn giuen them to Enter their Copies but they hitherto haue neglected the same, But since the said grant to them doe print diuers of the said Copies. It is this day ordered. That if the said Legatt and Crooke doe not Enter their Copies betweene this and the next Cort. leaue shall be giuen for the printing of them for the Companies vse.

The writings of or agreemt. wth Oxford in the Wardens Custody

This day Mr Mead and the Clarke deliuered vp to the warden a Box wherein are the Articles of or Agreement wth. Oxford.[4]

Will: Cooke to haue 50li.

William Cooke is to haue the next 50li. putting in good security for 3. yeares.[5]

[1] Alsop had offended in this way 3 Oct. 1634 (cf. *C–B.C*, 128b). There is in the Balliol Library an unrecorded *Almanack: sive prognosticon astrologicum* (*for London*) 8°, Oxford, W. Turner, and sold at London by W. Harris, 1637, by John Booker, which may be the offending item.

[2] Entered 28 Apr. 1637 (Arber iv. 383).

[3] Cf. *C–B.C*, 143a. They were finally entered 1 July 1637 (Arber iv. 387–8).

[4] Cf. *C–B.C*, 145b, 24 Mar. 1637. The text is printed in F. Madan, *Oxford books*, i. 285–7.

[5] The loan was made 25 Sept. 1637, *Liber C2*, 120a.

27°. Aprilis 1637 FOL. 147[a]

Present. Mr Kingston Mr Smethwick loco Gardiani Mr Downes Mr Swinhow Mr Weauer Mr Rothwell Mr Butter mr Bourne Mr Mead.

The 221li. borrowed of St. ffaiths. paid & the Bond Cancelled 123. — This day mr warden Downes produced the Bond vnto wch. was the house Seale for 221li. by the Company borrowed of the pish of St. ffaithes wch. money the warden paid the 17th day of this instant month and the said Bond was this day Cancelled.[1]

Oxford Priuiledge — Whereas the Company haue agreed wth. the vniuersity of Oxford for their late Priviledge And for the same doe giue a valuable Consideracõn. Now forasmuch as the said Priviledge is to Comprint aswell wth. the kings Printers And the Printer of the Gramer As the Company. And for that mr young and the rest of that side of the Kings Printing house will not stand to their owne proposicõns.[2] The Cort. this day weighing how the 200li. p Annu' wch they are to pay to Oxford should be raised (The Assignes of the kings Printers refusing to pay their proporcõns) Haue thought fitt and ordered That the mr. and wardens & Stockeepers shall take prsent Course for the casting of new Letter to print the Quarto Bible English And to take such order for the printing of the same and all things therevnto belonging as they shall thinke fitt and Convenient.

Genealogie — This day Docter Speed came vnto the Cort. and propounded the renewing of the Couenants betweene himselfe & the Company for the Genealogies,[3] for the Terme of Three yeares, vpon the like Condicõns as the Couenants now in force betweene them. for that the terme thereof is nigh expired. And he not knowing by reason of the prsent Visitation when he should come to Towne againe desired the resolution of the Cort. therein. Or that he might be free vpon the expiration of the Couenants to dispose thereof; Which the Cort. taking into Consideracõn, vpon debate thereof, It was by a generall Consent thought fitt & ordered That new Couents shall be forthwith drawne vp for the terme of Three yeares to Comence from the Expiration of the said Couenants now in force wch. ends at Midsomer 1638. without any alteration of the same.

29°. Aprilis 1637. FOL. 147[b]

Present. Mr Kingston Mr Harrison Mr Downes Mr Weauer Mr Smethwick mr Butter Mr Bourne & mr Mead.

The Couenants with Dr: Speed sealed — This day according to an Order of the last Cort. the Couenants betweene Dr. Speed and the Company were sealed wth. the Comon Seale of the Corporacõn for three yeares to Comence from Midsomer 1638. wthout any alteracõn from the former Couenants.

[1] Cf. *C–B.C*, 123[b], 9 July 1633.

[2] The articles of agreement between the Company, the King's Printer, and the 'Printer for the Gramer', *Letter Book*, 181[a], provide that the King's Printer will pay £85 per annum. Cf. J. Johnson and S. Gibson, *Print and privilege*, p. 20.

[3] STC 23039. Cf. *C–B.C*, 130[b], 19 Dec. 1634.

5°. Junij 1637.

Present. Mr Kingston Mr Harrison Mr Downes mr Weaver mr Smethwick mr Aspley mr Rothwell mr Bourne mr Mead & mr Beale.

New ffeoffees chosen for the houses in Woodstreet. This day the Cort. thought fitt to nominate new ffeoffees for the houses in Woodstreet for that all the old ffeoffees (saue onely Mr Swinhow & Mr. Cole) are dead[1] There were nominated Mr Kingston Mr Harrison Mr Downes Mr. Weaver Mr. Smethwick Mr Aspley Mr Rothwell Mr. ffetherston Mr Bourne & Mr Mead And it is ordered that the old ffeoffees doe assigne ouer all the deeds & Estate to them in trust to the new ffeoffees.

Mrs. Hawkins Liuery Part assigned to Mr Meredith. & Mr Merediths yeomandry Part to John Rothwell.......... This day Mrs. Hawkins[2] came vnto the Cort. & there resigned vp her Liuery part in the English Stock and prayed that the same might be Conferred vpon mr Meredith wch. the Cort. in much favour granted. And the Cort. then conferred Mr Merediths yeomandry Part vpon John Rothwell And they both tooke their oathes accordingly.

Mrs Hawkins Copies The Copies belonging to Mrs. Hawkins by order of this Cort. are to be Entred vnto mr Mead & Mr Meredith in trust for her Children.[3]

Cannons and Homilies A Certificate touching the right of the Homilies & Cannons of the Church now in Controuersie between Mr Whitaker and mr Young was this day read in Cort. & It is ordered that the same shall be deliuered to my Lo. [grace] of Cantebury.[4]

6°. Maij 1637. prn'tibus vt antea

Mr. Latham his Rentors Accompt Mr. Latham this day brought in his Accompt for his Rentership wch. being audited came to 55li. 9s. 8d. The wch was paid to Mr warden Downes.

Fol. 148a

6°. Maij 1637. predict'

Present. Mr. Kingston Mr. Harrison & Mr. Downes war: Mr. Weaver Mr Rothwell Mr Bourne & Mr Mead.

Election Dynner. It is ordered that if the wardens make noe Election dynner by reason of sicknes or otherwise. That then the Twenty markes allowed them towards the Charge of the said Dynner shall be spared and noe other fyne imposed vpon them.[5]

Raph Mabb to haue 50li. This day the Cort granted vnto Raph Mabb the loane of ffifty pounds for 3. yeares of Mr John Nortons bequeast putting in good security.[6]

[1] Cf. *C–B.C*, 56b, 31 Aug. 1619, and 65a, 7 Aug. 1620.

[2] Mrs. Ursula Hawkins, widow of Richard Hawkins.

[3] Entered 29 May 1638 (Arber iv. 420).

[4] Cf. *C–B.C*, 138b, 11 Apr. 1636; 142a, 1 Aug. 1636.

[5] Cf. *C–B.C*, 142a, 1 Aug. 1636.

[6] His bonds were registered 31 Jan. 1638, *Liber C2*, 120b.

Lo: Sterlins Psalms printed by mr Harper.......... This day a note was read signed by my Lord Sterlin about his Psalmes printed by mr Harper wch. said note is entred in the Booke of Letters.[1]

23°. die Junij 1637

Present — Mr Kingston [*loco*] Mr. Smethwick Mr Downes mr Weaver mr Rothwell mr ffetherston mr Butter mr Bourne & mr Mead.

Mr. Tooley 27li. paid him for interest of 300li. [*paid*] oweing by the Latyn Stock — This day Mr Tooley came vnto the Cort. and demanded Twenty seauen pounds being three six monthes Interest now due for 300li. taken vp by the Latyn Stock for which the Seale of the house is giuen.[2] And forasmuch as the said mr Tooley threatned to arreast the Company for the said Interest. This Court seriously taking it into their Consideracõn and weighing the Charge trouble & disgrace the house should be putt vnto in Case they should be sued, & that the said Mr Tooley would by noe meanes be pswaded to forbeare any longer It was ordered that mr warden Downes should lay out the said money for the prsent and the Partners of the [said] Latyn Stock being prsent promised to repay the same vnto the house by any debts that should come in owing vnto that stock or otherwise to pay their parts & to gett the residue of the partners to pay their shares alsoe. The said 27li. was paid & an acquittance receiued for the same.

Mrs. Day widdow 6li. giuen. — Doctor Dayes widdow came this day vnto the Cort. and declared that one of her sonns[3] was to be putt to Cambridge but wanted some necessaries for him & therefore humbly desired the Cort. to Contribute towards her charge therein wch being taken into Consideracõn the Cort. gaue her Six pounds.

26°. Junij 1637. — Fol. 148b

Present: — Mr Kingston Mr. Mr. Harrison & Mr Downes war: Mr Weaver Mr. Smethwick Mr Aspley Mr Rothwell Mr Butter Mr. Bourne & Mr Mead

New Assistants chosen — This day the ancient Assistants being decayed and vnable to service it was thought fitt to call in three new assistants being the ancientest of the Liuery (vizt.) Mr Man[4] mr Hoth[5] & Mr Parker.

[1] This was not transcribed in the *Letter Book*, but refers to STC 2736 which was printed by Harper both in folio, to be bound with STC 16606, and in octavo, STC 2736a and b. These are a much revised form of the first edition, STC 2732 (STC 2733 is a ghost, the three copies listed being examples of STC 2736b). The Earl of Sterling received a privilege for the printing of this translation, which he had largely revised, 21 Jan. 1628, for twenty-one years (cf. *State Papers Dom. 1627–1628*, p. 524). According to Laing, *R. Baillie Letters*, iii (1842), 530, the patent was for thirty-one years and was dated 28 Dec. 1627. Cf. *C–B.C*, 152a, 4 Dec. 1637.

[2] Cf. *C–B.C*, 138a, 30 Mar. 1636.

[3] Probably the Thomas Day, B.A. 1640–1.

[4] Probably Samuel Man, whose first book was entered in 1613.

[5] Made free 24 Apr. 1598 (Arber ii. 720).

Mr Walley for a gratuity xvli. in respect of extraordinary Paines	The Court this day tooke into their Consideracōn the many businesses of late the Company are ingaged in, And forasmuch as the Clarks Care and Travell hath byn extraordinary for executing of the same The Co^{rt}. thought fitt to giue him xv^{li}. for a gratuity And m^{r} Warden Downes then paid the same accordingly.

1°. Julij 1637.

Present: M^{r}. Kingston Mr Harrison M^{r}. Downes Mr Weaver Mr Smethwick Mr Purfoot Mr Aspley, M^{r}. Rothwell Mr Butter Mr Bourne m^{r} Mead M^{r}: Beale, Mr Man, Mr Hoth, Mr Parker. Mr Wellins & m^{r} Dawson Rentors.

Priuate Election

Mr Smethwick fyned for vpper warden xx^{ty}. nobles M^{r}. Aspley xx^{ty}. Nobl for vpper warden.	M^{r}. Smethwicke this day being desired to hold vppwarden Craved the favour of the Co^{rt}. that he might be putt to his fyne, and the Co^{rt}. then fyned him at Twenty Nobles. Then m^{r} Aspley being next, he desired the like favour to fyne wch was granted & he was fyned at Twenty Nobles for his first tyme vpperwarden.
Mr Rothwell, M^{r} ffetherston, Mr Butter Mr Downes fyned at v^{li}. a peece for second tyme vnder wardens	Mr Rothwell being now in choice for Second tyme vnderwarden desired he might be putt to his fyne, wch for some reasons was thought fitting & he was then fyned at v^{li}. Likewise M^{r} ffetherston Mr Butter & Mr Downes desired the like favour to fyne for their second tyme vnderwarden wch was granted & they were fyned at v^{li}. a peece.

FOL. 149^{a}

3°. Julij 1637.

Present. Mr Kingston M^{r}. Harrison Mr Downes m^{r} Weaver Mr Smethwick m^{r} Aspley Mr Rothwell, M^{r}. Bourne Mr Man Mr Hoth & Mr Parker

Election day.

M^{rs}. Dawsons yeomandry Part. Conferred on her sonne John Dawson

This day M^{rs}. Dawson came vnto the Co^{rt}. and humbly desired that her yeomandry part in the English Stock might be Conferred vpon her sonne John Dawson, wch the Co^{rt}. taking into Consideracōn (the said John Dawson being Capable thereof) [*hath granted*] had the same [granted vnto him]. And the said John Dawson tooke his oath accordingly. And whereas the said part was engaged by m^{r} John Dawson the father the 4th of ffebruary 1623 vnto Mr Ephraim Dawson by Consent of this Co^{rt}. for security of 100^{li}. wch. said 100^{li}. is not satisfied but the said John Dawson the sonne hath Entred into Bond for the payment thereof.[1] The said John Dawson humbly desired that his said Part now Conferred vpon him might

[1] Cf. *C–B.C*, 80^{a}.

in like manner as before be engaged for security of the said 100li. to mr Ephraim Dawson wch the Cort. accordingly granted.

Mrs. Dawson Copies to be entred to her sonne John Dawson

The same day vpon the request of Mrs. Dawson That all her Copies might be Entred vnto her Sonne The Cort. then gaue Consent that the same should be entred vnto him accordingly.[1]

Mr Bourne fined at 5li. for printing my Lord of Lincolnes booke. Mrs. Purslow & Rich: Oulton fined at 3li a peece.

This day the Cort. tooke into Consideracõn the vndue printing of my Lord of Lincolnes Booke called the holy Table name & thing, by mr Bourne wthout the wardens hands & orderly Entrance, & fyned him at 5li. for his offence. And whereas mrs. Purslow & Richard Oulton printed the said Booke the Cort. fyned them at 3li. a peece[2]

Mr Weaver} Mr.
Mr Aspley & Mr Bourne} War:

In the Afternoone the box being opened it appeared Mr Weaver to be Master Mr. Aspley & mr Bourne wardens and they tooke their oathes accordingly.

Auditors chosen to peruse the old wardens Accompts

Mr Smethwick and mr Mead are Chosen Auditors. to examine the old wardens Accompts.

Mr. Weaver} Master.
Mr Aspley Mr Bourne} Wardens.

Fol. 149b

7o. die Augusti 1637. Ao. 13o. Car: Re.

Mr. Weaver Mr Asley (*sic*) mr Bourne mr Harrison mr Smethwick mr Rothwell mr Downes, Mr Beale Mr Man Mr Hoth & mr Parker.

mr Hebb & mr Islip

This day mr. Hebbs Refferrence from Sr. John Lamb to the Company about the Turkish history was read in Cort. And the Table hath appointed mr Butter mr Downes mr Man & mr Parker who are intreated to examine the Bookes of Orders & Entries touching the right of the said Booke & to report to this table their opinions therein wthall Convenient Speed.[3]

[1] Apparently no entry made.

[2] STC 25724–6. There are at least four editions at Harvard. The book bears a licence from Bishop Williams for the Diocese of Lincoln but apparently was not otherwise licensed or entered. It was evidently a fast selling book and it is probable that not all the editions were printed for Bourne, since Sir John Lambe records that Alsop and Fawcett, A. Mathewes, and Mrs. Griffin all reprinted the book (cf. Arber iv. 528). In October 1641, Bourne seized copies of an edition of this book from Charles and Thomas Greene, and became involved in a lawsuit concerning it (cf. *C–B.C*, 179a).

[3] STC 15055. Cf. *C–B.C*, 155b, 30 Apr. 1638. According to the report of the referees, preserved in *State Papers Dom. 1637–1638*, p. 379, Islip claimed that the original entry of 5 Dec. 1602 (Arber iii. 223), which has annexed a note that a half share belonged to G. Bishop and J. Norton, should have been limited to one impression. Bishop's fourth part was transferred to T. Adams, 14 Mar. 1611 (Arber iii. 454), and later to A. Hebb (cf. *C–B.C*, 95b, 4 June 1627).

John Benson. 50^{li}.

Vpon the request of John Benson this day for the loane of 50^{li}. of the guift of m^{r}. John Norton The Co^{rt}. ordered that putting in good security he shall haue the next 50^{li} that comes in.[1]

Rich: Oulton to haue all m^{rs}: Aldees Copies Entred to him.

The Co^{rt}. hath ordered that all m^{rs}. Aldees Copies shall be entred to Richard Oulton her sonne wth this clause reserueing euery mans Right.[2]

John Cowper 50^{li}.

John Cowper[3] by order of Co^{rt}. is to haue the loane of 50^{li}. putting in good Securyty.

Fol. 150^{a}

4°. die Septembris 163[*8*][7]

Present.

M^{r}. Weaver M^{r}. Aspley & m^{r} Bourne war: M^{r}. Harrison m^{r} Purfoot m^{r}. Smethwick m^{r} Rothwell m^{r} Butter m^{r} Downes

m^{r}. Mead m^{r} Beale Mr Hoth m^{r} Man & m^{r} Parker.

A Gratuity of xx^{li}. giuen to the Kings Attorney touching the new Decree in Starchamber.

This day the Co^{rt}. tooke into their Consideracõn what should be giuen to m^{r} Attorney for his Loue & kindnes to the Company about the new decree.[4] Wherevpon it was ordered that xx^{li}. should be sent him, W^{ch} the warden accordingly p^{r}sented him wth.

28°. Septembris 1637. pn'tibus vt antea.

John Stafford fyne for his admittance into this Company. xl^{s}.

John Stafford this day produced an order of [the] Co^{rt}. of Aldrẽn for to come into this Company by Redemption his fyne being putt to voices the Mayor p̱te consented that he should pay xl^{s}. wch. he [then] accordingly paid

Those of the Assistants that Come late to the Co^{rt}. to pay xij^{d} and to sitt as they come.

Whereas the M^{r}. wardens and diuers of the Ancient Assistants of the Company, come to keepe their Co^{rt}. at Nine of the Clock, and by reason that many of the Assistants come soe late they are forced to procrastinate necessary busines. The Co^{rt}. this day ordered (according to ancient order) That if any of the Assistants come after Nine of the clock or when the M^{r}. & wardens are sett in Co^{rt}. They shall pay xij^{d}. for a fyne for the same & to sitt as they come.[5]

74.

[1] His bonds were registered 7 Aug. 1637, *Liber C2*, 120^{a}.

[2] Not entered until 22 Apr. 1640 (Arber iv. 507).

[3] J. Cowper, made free 13 Apr. 1629 (Arber iii. 686), was a bookseller 'at the Holy Lambe, at the East end of Saint Paules Church'. His bonds were registered 11 Nov. 1637, *Liber C2*, 120^{a}.

[4] STC 7757 (2 editions), reprinted Arber iv. 528–36.

[5] Cf. *C–B.C*, 74^{a}, 7 Oct. 1622.

2°. Octobris 1637. FOL. 150b

Present. Mr Weaver Mr Aspley Mr Bourne mr Purfoot Mr Smethwick mr Rothwell Mr Butter mr Downes mr. Mead mr Beale mr Man mr Hoth & mr Parker.

Widd Smiths halfe yeomandry Part in the English stock Conferred on John Badger:

This day Widdow Smith[1] came vnto the Cort. and desired that her halfe pte in the English stock might be Conferred vpon John Badger[2] wch. the Cort. taking into Consideracõn gaue Consent, and the said John Badger tooke his oath accordingly/

Latyn Bookes belonging to the English stocke to be disposed of to print by the wardens & Stockeepers.

Whereas diuers Latyn Bookes were Entred vnto the English stock,[3] and hitherto litle proffitt hath accrued to the said Stock by the same The Cort. hath this day ordered That the wardens wth the Stockeepers shall dispose of the printing of the said Bookes for the benifitt & good of the stock.

6°. Novembris 1637. pn'tibus vt antea

ffran: Groue fined xxs.

Whereas vpon a Search by mr Butter mr Waterson & mr Miller deputed by the wardens they came vnto the house of ffrancis Groue to Search for bookes vnlawfull & demanding his servant to show them his warehouse, he gaue them very vnfitting words insomuch that they told him he deserued to be whipt at the hall wch. his Master hearing told them that the wardens had as good kisse his breach. Wch. words being this day averred in Cort. before the said Groue. The Table fined him at xxs.

13°. die Novembris 1637 FOL. 151a

Present. Mr Kingston loco Magrĩ Mr Aspley mr Bourne war: Mr Purfoot Mr Harrison Mr Smethwick Mr Butter mr Downes Mr Mead Mr Beale Mr Man Mr Hoth & mr Parker.

The Book called The English Schoole. to be crossed out of the hall Booke.

The booke intituled the English Schoole entred to mr Bellamy about two yeares since[4] is by order of this Cort. and by mr Bellamies Consent to be crossed out of the Hall booke for that it is predudiciall to the Stocks booke called The English Schoolemaster[5] And what bookes he hath vnsold is to be brought into the hall, And moreouer to pay xxs. for a fine for the same and the said Booke to belong to the English stock. To all which he willingly submitted vnto And in testimony thereof the said Mr Bellamy hath sett his hand.

John Bellamie.

[1] Mrs. Francis Smith.

[2] Made free 1 Aug. 1636 (Arber iii. 687).

[3] Entered 22 June 1631 (Arber iv. 255 and v. 250).

[4] No copy can be traced. In the entry 23 Mar. 1635 (Arber iv. 335), it is said to be by 'J.P.'.

[5] STC 5715.

John Okes his booke called the English Accidence to be crossed out of the Hall Booke

This day John Okes being warned to the Co[rt]. for printing of a Booke called the English Accidence[1] wch booke conteyneth a part of the English Schoolemaster[2] belonging to the Stock The Co[rt]. taking the same into Consideracõn Ordered that the said Booke should be crossed out of the hall booke[3] & moreouer the said Okes to pay for a fine iij[li].

John Bodington to haue 12[li]. vpon good Security.

The Co[rt]. hath this day ordered that John Bodington[4] shall haue [*of*] the loane of 12[li]. for three yeares putting in good security.

4[to]. Decembris 1637.

Present. M[r] Weaver M[r] Aspley M[r] Bourne M[r] Harrison m[r] Smethwick [*m[r] Aspley*] mr Rothwell mr Butter m[r] Downes m[r] Mead m[r] Beale m[r] Man m[r] Hoth & m[r] Parker

Hen: Gossons yeomanry part in the English stock engaged to m[r] Haviland for 60[li]. for a yeare.

This day Henry Gosson came vnto the Co[rt]. and desired that his yeomanry part in the English stock might be engaged to m[r] Haviland for 60[li] for a Twelue month w[ch]. the Co[rt]. granted/

Fol. 151[b]

4[to]. Decembris predict' 1637

M[rs]. Bolers Liuery Part conferred vpon m[r] Stevens, & her yeo: Part vpon ffran: Egglesfeild

152.

This day a Letter of m[rs]. Bolers[5] was read in Court wherein she humbly desired that her Liuery part in the English stock might be Conferred vpon M[r] Stevens and her yeomandry part vpon ffrancis Egglesfeild her servant, wch the Co[rt]. tooke into Consideracõn. And for that m[rs]. Boler is indebted vnto the Stock aboue the sum̃e of the said Liuery part. It being putt to voices was then fully Concluded vpon & soe Ordered That for her Liuery part it should be Conferred vpon Mr Stevens And that the yeomandry p̱te (in regard of her Earnest request haveing seauen children most of w[ch]. being very young) besides many debts owing her the wch as she affirmed were best knowne to her said Servant (of whose faithfullnes & Care she hath good experience) And by this favour would be the more tyed to vse his best endeavors for the getting in of the said debts should be Conferred vpon ffrancis Egglesfeild. Vpon this Condicõn neuertheles That the said Mr Stevens & ffrancis Egglesfeild shall giue good Caution for paym[t]. of the said M[rs]. Bolers whole debt in such manner and times hereafter mencõned (vizt.) 100[li]. thereof forthwith, the next diuident of her said

[1] No copy has been traced.

[2] STC 5715.

[3] The entry has not been traced.

[4] Made free 1 July 1633 (Arber iii. 687).

[5] Mrs. Anne Boler. Francis Eglesfield was evidently conducting the business for her and may even have moved it for a short while to Cheapside, for the Union Theological Seminary in New York has a copy of STC 1224 with a variant imprint, 'Marigold, in Goldsmith-row, in Cheapside', though he was in the same year and again later at the 'Marigold in Paul's Church-yard'. Cf. *C–B.C*, 152[a], 11 Dec. 1637.

Part to be deducted, And the residue of her said debt the first day of March now next Comeing. And they performing this Act are to be sworne (according to the Custome) the next Co[rt]. And the Co[rt]. did then further declare That this shall not be drawne into President for any in this nature hereafter.

4[to]. Decembris predict'. Fol. 152[a]

Mr Harper fined at x[li]. for printing the Psalmes. — Mr Harper being this day warned to the Co[rt]. for printing the Psalmes in Octavo.[1] By which Act according to the Ordinances of the English stock his part in the said stock was to be Confiscated to the vse of the poore. Neuertheles the Co[rt]. in much favour to him thought good to fine him w[ch]. being putt to voices he was fined at x[li]. And soe all offences were to be remitted And the said M[r] Harper submitted therevnto in Co[rt]:

11°. Decembris 1637.

Present. — M[r] Weaver. M[r] Harrison loco gardiani, M[r] Bourne. M[r] Swinhow M[r] Kingston M[r]. Smethwick M[r] Rothwell M[r] ffetherston M[r] Butter M[r] Mead M[r] Beale M[r] Man M[r] Hoth & M[r] Parker.

Docter Speed. — Doctor Speed came this day vnto the Co[rt]. and shewed Two Orders of the Lords of the Councell touching the Genealogie[2] the w[ch]. w[th] a Letter of Assistance and the Lres' Pattents for the said Genealogie were openly read in Co[rt]. in the p[r]sence of diuers of the Company And o[r] Master wished those then p[r]sent to take notice of the said Orders accordingly.

M[r]. Stevens & ffran: Eggleffield 151. — This day according to an Order of the last Co[rt]. M[r] Stevens and ffrancis Egglesfeild haueing paid 100[li]. of the debt of M[rs]. Boler & promised payment of the rest, according to the intent of the said last recited Order.[3] The said M[r] Stevens was elected vnto the Liuery part of m[rs] Boler And the said ffrancis Egglesfeild vnto the [*her*] yeomandry p̱te. And they both tooke their oathes accordingly.

15°. January 1637. Fol. 152[b]

Present. — M[r] Weaver M[r] Aspley m[r] Bourne m[r] Kingston m[r] Purfoot m[r] Harrison m[r] Smethwick m[r] Rothwell m[r] Butter m[r] Downes m[r] Mead m[r] Man & m[r] Hoth.

M[r] Harper for printing Licosthenis — The Co[rt]. this day ordered that the Stockeepers should sett downe what rate either by the Reame or otherwise m[r] Harper should pay for printing a booke called Licosthenes[4] belonging to the stock.

[1] Unless it be the octavo edition of King James's *Psalms* (STC 2736[a] and [b], two issues), regarding which cf. *C–B.C*, 148[a], 6 May 1637, this edition has not been identified.

[2] STC 23039.

[3] Cf. *C–B.C*, 151[b], 4 Dec. 1637.

[4] STC 17004. The 1635 edition printed by Harper for the Company is fairly common, although the earlier editions are not. It is therefore unlikely that Harper printed an edition at this time.

To advise for the passing ouer of the houses in Wood street

Mr Downes mr Mead & the Clarke are required by the [*Clarke*] Table to advise concerning the passing ouer of the houses in Woodstreet from mr Swinhow to new ffeoffees wth all Convenient Speed.[1]

Andrew Crooke & Phillip Nevill to haue 4s. a Reame for Psalmes they had of Mr Grismon

Whereas mr Harper some yeares past printed a part of the Companies Psalmes & sold them to mr Grismond & Sparkes.[2] And the said mr Grismond haueing passed all his Estate to Andrew Crooke & Phillip Nevill who thereby haue the said Psalmes. Now the Cort. weighing the inconveniences of their haueing the said Psalmes & being willing to prvent any danger wch might accrue thereby, thought good & doe hold it requisite That the same should be bought in by the stock. Wch being moued at the table by warden Aspley who had conferred wth the said Crooke & Nevill & they submitting themselues to him, Two sum̃es being propounded [*by*] [to] the table. The Maior ꝑte gaue their voices that the said Crooke & Nevill should haue 4s. a Rheame for the said Psalmes.

Edward Ranse of Henley in whose house the 8o. Psalmes were printed by Tho: Winter & others

This day the Cort. tooke into Consideracõn the busines of Edward Ranse the Maultman of Henley in whose house Winter[3] & the rest printed the Octavo Psalmes And forasmuch as his Carriage & dealing in that buisines hath giuen the Company cause to Consider his [*great*] losse, he being led into that Error by the instigation of the said Winter. The Cort. thought fitt to referr the Consideracõn thereof vnto ye Mr & wardens Mr Downes & Mr Mead who are requested to doe therein as they shall thinke fitt.

FOL. 153a 5o. ffebruarij. 1637. pn'tibus vt antea.

Mr Robinsons Part Suspended for Counterfeit Psalmes he had of Woodward 157b.

Whereas certaine Psalmes were taken by mr Downes (when he was warden) from one William Tubbins at his Lodging in Lombard street wch. were printed beyond the Seas (being about the number of 600). And the said Tubbins being examined in the high Comission vpon Intergatories (*sic*) did therein declare mr Robinson[4] had Fifty of the said Psalmes in his hands and the residue Consigned vnto him by one Woodward beyond sea wch Act of mr Robinson being a Partner in the Stock hath not onely depriued him of his Stock (according to the orders made in that behalfe) but he hath thereby infringed his oath. Now the Cort. taking the same into Consideracõn thought fitt to Suspend the said Robinson from his ꝑte for the prsent & to Doe therein according to the Merritt of his offence.

Mr Hunscott admitted into the Liuery

This day Joseph Hunscott was admitted into the Liuery of this Company And touching his fyne of xxli. It was thought fitt (in regard he hath done the Company good service in many buisinesses) that the same should be remitted. And it was then

1 Cf. *C–B.C*, 147b, 5 June 1637.

2 Cf. *C–B.C*, 119b, 9 Apr. 1632.

3 Thomas Winter, made free 3 July 1626 (Arber iii. 686). Cf. *C–B.C*, 156a, 7 May 1638.

4 Humphrey Robinson? There appears to be no record of this interrogation. Cf. *C–B.C*, 157b, 2 July 1638.

ordered that if it shall happen the said Mr Hunscott to enioy the Beadles place of this Company (he haueing a Revertion thereof)[1] That then he shall Constantly take his place last in the Liuery. But in the meantime to take his place according to his prsent Election & antiquity.

1°. Martij 1637.

Present. Mr Weaver Mr Aspley Mr Bourne Mr Kingston Mr Harrison Mr Smethwick Mr Rothwell Mr Butter mr Downes Mr Mead mr Man & mr Parker

Stockeepers chosen for the Eng: Stock } Mr Hoth, Mr Parker } mr Haviland, mr Meredith } mr. Marriott, mr Moseley }

Mr Weaver Threasorer et Juratr.

Auditors. Mr Butter, Mr Downes } mr Whitaker, Mr ffiesher } mr Lee, mr ffussell }

John Greensmith[2] 12li. The Cort. hath ordered that he shall haue the loane of 12li. for three yeares putting in good security.

1°. Martij 1637. predict9. Fol. 153b

Tho: Paines yeo: Part in the Eng: Stock ingaged to mr Walley for 60li. for 6 months } This is satisfied & the same is engaged againe to Will: ffained als ffox the .20th of June 1639.[3]

Whereas Thomas Paines yeomandry part in the English stock by Consent of this Cort. was engaged vnto mr Walley the 5th. day of June 1634 for Security of 40li. Wch said 40li. [not] being paid And the said Thomas Paine haueing further occasion for 20li. more. He humbly desired the Cort. That his said part might be now engaged for 60li. vnto the said Mr Walley for 6. monthes. wch. the Cort. granted.

5°. Martij 1637.

Present. Mr Weaver mr Aspley mr Bourne mr Harison mr Rothwell mr Smethwick mr Butter mr. Downes mr Beale mr Man mr Hoth & mr Parker

mr Crooke admitted into the Liuery. } This day Andrew Crooke was called to be on the Liuery who being prsent in Cort. consented and paid downe xxli. for his fine & he was sworne accordingly.

Bernard Alsop & Thomas ffawcett. The difference touching Bernard Alsop & Thomas ffawcett concerning the Apprentice lately bound vnto the said Bernard was this day heard. both parties being prsent, And the Cort. weighing the equity of the Complaint made by the said Thomas ffawcett That the said Alsop haueing the title of Mr Printer had an Apprentice lately

[1] Cf. *C–B.C*, 121b, 3 Dec. 1632.

[2] Made free 19 Jan. 1635 (Arber iii. 687). His bonds were registered 23 July 1639, *Liber C2*, 24a.

[3] Cf. *C–B.C*, 165b.

bound vnto him the benifitt whereof he wholly assumed to himselfe notwithstanding his Couenants to the Contrary. W^ch^. the Co^rt^. taking into Consideration haue thought fitt & ordered That according as the said Alsop & ffawcett in all things appertayning to their trade are Copartne^rs^. Soe likewise the benifitt of the said Apprentice shall be equall betweene them. And for the Charge of keeping the said Apprentice by Consent of both ꝑties It was ordered That the said ffawcett shall weekely allow 2^s^. 6^d^. vnto the said Alsop for his proportion in the Charge in mainteyning the said Apprentice in dyet Apparell lodging & all other Necessaries during the terme of his App^r^ntiship.

FOL. 154^a^

5to. Martij 1637. predict'.

m^r^ John Nortons Liuery Part mortgaged to M^rs^. Joyce Norton for 60^li^. for a twelue month

This day m^r^ John Norton haueing occasion for 60^li^. desired the Co^rt^. he might haue leaue to engage his Liuery part in the English stocke to M^rs^. Joyce Norton who is willing to lend him the same wch the Co^rt^. granted.

29°. Martij 1638.

Present. m^r^ Weaver m^r^ Aspley m^r^ Bourne m^r^ Harrison m^r^ Smethwick mr Rothwell mr Butter mr Downes mr Mead mr Man mr Hoth & mr Parker.

Election of Rentors.

Mr Dawson, Mr Harper, M^r^ fflesher, M^r^. Haviland, Mr Meighen, M^r^. Waterson, M^r^. Tho: Cotes, Mr Young, Mr Walley, Mr Legatt — fined for Rentors

Mr Miller, Mr Bruister — Rentors

This day m^r^. Ephraim Dawson being now Elder Rentor was demanded whether he would hould for this year ensewing, who therevpon desired to be putt to his fine wch. the Co^rt^. granted And he then paid downe xxiiij^li^. Then m^r^ Harper m^r^ fflesher m^r^ Haviland Mr Meighen m^r^ waterson m^r^ Thomas Coates M^r^. Young M^r^ walley & Mr Legatt being in Election for Rento^rs^. desired all to fine wch the Co^rt^. taking into Consideracõn granted they should fyne. And they all paid downe xxiiij^li^. a peece Then the Co^rt^. Elected M^r^. Miller & Mr Bruister Rentors for the yeare ensewing.

Mr Constable. This day m^r^. Constable came and demanded to haue his place according to his antiquity when as this Court conceiued he had great favour in the forbearance of his fine when his turne came to be Rentor in respect of his great Charge of Children and to take his place next the Rentorwardens for the time being. wherefore the Co^rt^. wished him to desist therein and to Continue as he now is wch. he refused But the Co^rt^. neuertheles ordered that he should as before sitt in place next the Rentor wardens of this Company for the time being.[1]

[1] On 26 Mar. 1635, Constable was fined £24 for second time rentor warden (cf. *C–B.C*, 133^b^). However, although the four others fined at the same time with him are recorded as having paid their fines (cf. *Book of Fines*, 25^b^), Constable apparently asked, and was granted, forbearance, although there is no record of it (cf. *C–B.C*, 159^a^, 27 Aug. 1638).

Admitted into the Liuery — This day M[r]. Hodgkinson M[r] Leake M[r]. Rothwell. M[r] Thomas Badger M[r] Dawson M[r] Griffin m[r]. Clarke M[r] Vavasor m[r] Harford m[r] Pakeman M[r] ffawne M[r] Slater. m[r] Hope m[r] Oulton m[r] Gould mr Bishop & m[r] Nicholls were admitted into the Liuery of this Company.

Edw: Blackmore 50[li]. — The Co[rt]. hath ordered that he shall haue the next 50[li]. that comes in putting in good security.[1]

Law: Chapman 50[li]. — He is likewise to haue 50[li]. when it comes in putting in good security.[2]

M[rs]. Bolers Copies. fine xx[s]. — The Executors and Overseers of M[rs]. Bolers will, came this day vnto the Co[rt]. and desired that all the Copies and parts of Copies apperteyning to her, might be entred in trust, (according to her request in her life tyme desired) vnto the Master and wardens, for her two sonns, vntill they come of age. W[ch]. this Co[rt]. taking into Consideracõn, and finding that by the antient Custome of this Company, all the said Copies of her late husband and hers being vndisposed of at her death, doe fall of right vnto this Company. Nevertheles the Co[rt]. againe weighing her weake Estate and great charge of Children, in much favour to the said Children, haue thought fitt & so ordered, that the said Executo[rs]. paying vnto the vse of this Company the sum̃e of xx[s]. for a fine & acknowledgm[t]. of their Right therein shall haue all the Copies of her late husband and hers accordingly entred vnto the said Master & wardens for the time being, for the vse of the said Children. Which said sum̃e of xx[s]. the said Executo[rs]. promised to pay vpon the Entry of the said Copies [the] w[ch]. [*xx*[s].] was paid accordingly.[3]

The Wardens to make vp the 190[li] they haue rec[d]. towards the 300[li]. due by the Latyn Stock to the Orphan of M[rs]. Martin. — Divers Conferences haueing been had wth M[r]. [Tooley] the Executor of M[rs]. Martin and the Orphan touching the 300[li]. lately due vnto the said Orphan taken vp long since for the Latyn Stock for wch the Seale of this || Corporacõn was giuen,[4] Fol. 155[a]
And for that the said mr Tooley and the Orphan cannott be persuaded to grant time vntill the Partno[rs]. in that stock can make vp the said money, But threaten if the money be not forthwith paid they will sue the Corporacõn vpon their Bond. It was thought fitt by the Master wardens & some of the Assistants (in respect 190[li]. of the said money was now in the wardens hands paid by m[r]. Swinhow Mr Islip & others of that stock and the residue in a forwardnes to be brought in,) That the wardens shall make vp the 300[li]. [& interest] out of the house money. The said Partne[rs] haueing promised to make good all such moneys as shall be disbursed in this buisnes either out of the debts belonging to the said stock or otherwise to beare & pay their proportionable parts thereof.

[1] His bonds were registered 14 Apr. 1638, *Liber C2*, 120[b].
[2] His bonds were registered 9 May 1638, *Liber C2*, 120[b].
[3] Entered 7 Sept. 1638 (Arber iv. 435–7).
[4] Cf. *C–B.C*, 62[a], 1 July 1620, and 138[a], 30 Mar. 1636.

9°. Aprilis 1638

Present. Mr Weaver Mr Aspley Mr Bourne Mr Kingston mr Harrison mr Smethwick mr Rothwell, mr ffetherston, mr Butter mr Downes mr Mead mr Beale mr Man mr Hoth & mr Parker.

ffran: Archers yeo: Part in the Eng: Stock disposed of to mr Moseley & mr Overton.

This day ffrancis Archer (being lately dead) his yeomandry part in the English stock was disposed of And because of many suitors. It was thought fit to devide the same. There stood for one halfe Mr Mozeley Mr Overton & mr Dainty & it fell vpon mr Mozeley. There stood for the other halfe Mr Overton mr Cartwright & Edward Wright[1] and it fell vpon Mr Overton. And they tooke their oathes accordingly.

Fol. 155b

30°. Aprilis 1638.

Present. Mr Weaver Mr Aspley Mr Bourne Mr. Kingston Mr Harrison Mr Smethwick Mr Downes Mr Mead Mr Man Mr Hoth & Mr Parker

Mr Hobson. & Mr Whatman.

This day vpon Complaint of Mr. Hobson dwelling in one of the Companies Tenemts. in Avie Mary lane against one Mr whatman his next neighbor about a Shed intended (by the said Mr whatman) to be erected [in his yard] the wch will much priudice the said Mr Hobson The Cort. therevpon requested mr Kingston Mr Harrison Mr Downes mr Mead & mr Parker to veiw whether the same would be Convenient, or noe & to report to this table their opinions therein.[2]

Mr Islip & Mr Hebb.

Whereas the difference betweene Mr Islip & Mr Hebb about the Turkish history by a Refference obteyned by the said Hebb from Sr. John Lamb & Dr. Duck was referred vnto this Cort. the seaventh day of August last.[3] And the same was then referred by this Cort. to Mr Butter Mr Downes Mr Man & Mr Parker. This day the said Mr Downes Mr Man & mr Parker gaue vp vnto this Cort. vnder their hands their opinion touching the Right of the said Booke wch. being openly read was generally approved of And it was then ordered that their said Report should be transcribed verbatim & putt in the name of the Master wardens & Assistants & deliuered to Sr. John Lamb & Dr Duck wch. was this day accordingly pformed.

7° Maij 1638. pn'tibus vt antea.

Mr Wellin his Rentors Accompt

This day mr wellins brought in his Rentors Accompt being 48li. 16s. 8d. & mr warden Bourne receiued the same.

[1] Made free 12 Aug. 1611 (Arber iii. 683); a bookseller at Christ Church Gate.

[2] Hobson evidently occupied one of Mr. Petty's tenements (cf. *C–B.C*, 106b, 19 Apr. 1630), and may be the William Hobson who leased from the Company (*C–B.C*, 49a, 9 Oct. 1617). Mr. Whatman was a subtenant of Lot Sivedale, who not only appears to have leased property in Milkstreet from the Company (cf. *C–B.C*, 60a, 7 Feb. 1619), but may have also taken over Mrs. Fairbrother's tenement in Ave Maria Lane (cf. *C–B.C*, 93b, 15 Dec. 1626). Cf. *C–B.C*, 156a, 7 May 1638.

[3] Cf. *C–B.C*, 149b, 7 Aug. 1637.

Mr Roch about adding of yeares to his Lease. 156.

Mr Roch came this day vnto the Cort. & shewed ye great charge he hath susteyned by building pte of his now dwelling house belonging vnto ye Company occasioned by the weakenes and Rottennes thereof & desired he might be considered therein by adding more yeares to his Lease or otherwise which should be thought fitting wherevpon the Cort. desired mr warden Bourne Mr Harrison Mr ffetherston mr Butter Mr Downes & mr Mead or any four of them to Consider of his demand & report vnto this Cort. wth all Conveniency therein.[1]

7°. Maij 1638. predict'. FOL. 156a

mr Hobson mr Whatman mr Sivedale mr Pettie

Vpon a Complaint last Cort. day made by mr Hobson tennant to mr Pettie against mr Whatman tennt to Mr Siuedale touching a Shed or warehouse intended to be erected in mr whatmans yard, the wch as mr Hobson alleadged tended greatly to his priudice in respect of his Lights wch there by would be greatly hindred & impaired, And that the said mr Hobson haueing a sinck or water course through the said mr whatmans yard wch. for these dozen yeares & vpwards hath byn permitted & not excepted against, the said Mr whatman threatned to stop vp the same, wherevpon the Cort. taking the same into Consideracõn thought fitt to haue mr Siuedale & mr Pettie the imediate Tennants to the Company to be Warned in that soe the difference betweene their Tennts. might be composed This day the said Mr Pettie Mr Siuedale Mr Hobson & Mr whatman being prsent in Cort. the said Mr Sivedale mr whatmans lanlord promised that noe shed or warehouse should be erected by him or his Tennts. in his said yard to priudice the said mr Hobson mr Petties Tennt. And that the Sinck or watercourse should haue free passage through his Tennts. yard for that mr Petty as he then acknowledged had accomodated him touching his houses in matters of as great moment.

A gratuity of xxvli. giuen the Clarke for his Extraordinary Paines this yeare

The Cort. this day taking into their Serious Consideracõn the great paines which the Clarke hath lately taken about the generall affaires of this Company and especially in the prosecuting & bringing Winter Ashfeild & Barrett (who printed the Psalmes at Henley) to be sentenced in Starchamber.[2] Haue thought fitt & freely giuen him xxvli. for his further encouragemt. in the like endeavors. vpon all occasions.

4°. Junij 1638. FOL. 156b

Present. Mr Kingston loco Magistri mr Aspley mr Bourne mr Harrison mr Smethwick mr ffetherston Mr Butter mr Downes Mr Mead Mr Man Mr Hoth & mr Parker.

Mr Roch about his request to renew his Lease....... 155.

The Refferrees appointed last Cort. day to veiw mr. Roach his house and to Consider of his demands touching adding more yeares to his now Lease.[3] This day they reported vnto the Table that they haueing veiwed his house & his disbursemts.

[1] Cf. *C–B.C*, 142b, 28 Sept. 1636, and 156b, 4 June 1638.

[2] Cf. *C–B.C*, 152b, 15 Jan. 1638.

[3] Cf. *C–B.C*, 155b, 7 May 1638.

for the same the wch. was somewhat extraordinary. Yet for that his Lease was lately renewed for xxxj[ty]. yeares they Conceiued that that Accomodation would Countervaile his disbursm[ts]. & soe noe Addicõn of yeares to be added. Wherevpon the Co[rt]. generally assenting to the said Refferrees opinion called the said Mr Roch into the Co[rt]. & Signified their Resolution therein That they held it not fitt to add any more yeares to his said Lease being soe lately renued & for soe long a terme. And the Co[rt]. then tould him that touching his Jetty made out of his kitchin that if the said Jettie was found inconvenient that then the same should be taken downe.

M[r] Chillingworths booke to be entred to M[r] Clarke

M[r] Clarke brought m[r] Chillingworths booke called the Religion of Protestants a Safe way to Saluation (w[ch] booke was printed at Oxford) & desired the same might be entred to him haueing the Authors & the printe[rs]. Consent. w[ch] being Shewed in Co[rt]. It was ordered that the said booke should be entred vnto him accordingly.[1]

M[r] Waterson & mr Hebb.

The difference betweene Andrew Hebb & m[r] John Waterson touching their interest in the Copie of Josephus,[2] was this day by & wth their Consents referred to m[r] Butter m[r] Mead m[r] Man & m[r] Parker who are desired to examine the Bookes of Entries & orders & what writinge the said M[r] Hebb & m[r] Waterson can produce for the clearing of their said Rights. And if they can to Compose the said difference or otherwise to Certifie this Co[rt]. their Opinions therein soe soone as Conveniently they can.[3]

Fol. 157[a]

12°. Junij 1638.

Present. M[r] Islip loco M[ri]. Weaver defunct', M[r] Aspley M[r] Bourne. M[r] Kingston M[r] Smethwick M[r] Rothwell M[r] ffetherston m[r] Butter m[r] Mead m[r] Beale m[r] Man m[r] Hoth and m[r] Parker.

M[r] Weaver his Assistant Part in the Engl: Stocke disposed of.

M[r] ffetherston y[e] Assistant Part

M.[r] Seile y[e] Liuery Part

M[r] Hodgkinson & Edw: Wright y[e] Yeomandry Part

This day M[r] Weaver our late Master (being lately deceased) his Assistant part in the English stock fell to be disposed of. There stood in Election for the same M[r] warden Bourne M[r] ffetherston & M[r] Butter & it fell vpon M[r] ffetherston. Then the Co[rt]. went to election for m[r] ffetherstons Liuery part there stood for the same M[r] Harper M[r] fflesher & M[r]. Seile, and it fell vpon m Seile Then M[r]. Seiles yeomandry pte (in respect of many Suitors) was ordered to be devided. There stood for one halfe M[r]Rich: Coates Edward Wright and Thomas Brudnell & it fell vpon Edward Wright. There stood for the other halfe M[r] Rich: Cotes M[r] Hodgkinson & Thomas Brudnell And it fell vpon m[r] Hodgkinson. And the said M[r] ffetherston M[r] seile m[r] Hodgkinson & Edward Wright tooke their oathes accordingly.

[1] STC 5139. Entered 4 June 1638 (Arber iv. 421).

[2] STC 14813.

[3] Cf. *C–B.C*, 157[b], 28 June 1638; 158[a], 19 July 1638; 158[b], 13 Aug. 1638; and 159[b], 27 Aug. 1638.

28°. Junij 1638.

Present. Mr. Islip Mr. Aspley Mr. Bourne mr Harison mr Smethwick mr Rothwell mr Butter mr Downes mr Mead mr Beale mr Man mr Hoth and mr Parker

Mr ffflesher...... Mr Haviland.... Mr Young, the .. residue of their fyne to be remitted

Whereas Mr ffflesher Mr Haviland & Mr Young by an Order of the 11th. of Aprill 1636. were fined forty Markes for the vse of the poore of this Company for printing the Psalmes in 8°. in Scotland and importing them into this Realme, wch. said sume was to be deducted out of their diuidents as by the said Order appeareth.[1] And whereas Twenty pounds thereof was lately distributed amongst the said Poore. This day vpon the humble suite of the said Mr. ffflesher Mr Haviland & mr Young the Cort. ordered that the residue of their fyne should be remitted And that their pts formerly suspended should be free vnto them againe/

28°. Junij predict' Fol. 157b

Mr Waterson & Mr Hebb.

This day the Refferrees appointed to heare the difference betweene Mr Waterson & Andrew Hebb touching Josephus came vnto Cort. and deliuered their opinions thereof That they haueing examined the Booke of Entrances, found, That the said booke was onely Entred wth. this provisoe of getting more sufficient License, but could not find that the same was euer after Entred wth. Licence[2] And therefore the said Copie in strictnes belonged vnto the Company And soe left the same to their further Consideracõn.

2°. Julij 1638.

Mr. Kingston loco Mri. defunct' mr Aspley mr Bourne mr Harison mr Smethwick mr Rothwell mr Butter mr Downes mr mr (*sic*) Mead mr Beale mr Man mr Hoth mr Parker.

mr Thrale fined at xxs. for vnfitting words.

Mr Thrale being warned this day to pay his fine of xijd. for being absent the 6th. day of May last & being demanded the same gave the Cort. vnfitting words to witt that they dealt vnreasonably and vniustly wth. him, wch being taken into Consideracõn he was fined at xxs.

Rich: Cartwright 50li.

The Cort. hath granted him the loane of 50li. for Three yeares putting in good security.[3]

[1] Cf. *C–B.C*, 139a, 11 Apr. 1636.

[2] Cf. *C–B.C*, 156b, 4 June 1638. Entered 26 June 1598 (Arber iii. 119) before it was translated. The owners of the copy then were Waterson, Short, and Adams. Before the book was published in 1602, Bishop became associated with the others, and his part was transferred, 14 Mar. 1611, to T. Adams, who then presumably owned a half share. His widow transferred her rights to Hebb, 6 May 1625 (Arber iv. 139). Short's rights may have also been acquired by Hebb, but of this there is no record. John Waterson registered his father's part 19 Aug. 1635 (Arber iv. 346).

[3] His bonds were registered 16 July 1638, *Liber C2*, 121a.

Mr Robinson fined at 5^{li}. for taking Counterfeit Psalmes from beyond Sea.

Whereas by an order of the 5th. of ffebruary last, Mr Robinsons pte in the English stock was Suspended for taking Counterfeit Psalmes from one Woodward beyond Sea as by the said Order appeareth.[1] This day the Co^{rt}. tooke the same into their Consideracõn and for that the same was his first offence It was thought fitt he should be putt to his fine. Wherevpon the same being putt to voices he was fined at 5^{li}. The wch. is to be deducted out of his next diuident, for the [vse of the] Poore. And the same was paid accordingly.

3°. Julij 1638 pn'tibus vt antea.

Election day
Mr Harison} m^{r}
m^{r} Rothwell} war:
mr Mead

This day the box being opened it appeared Mr Harrison to be master. Mr Rothwell & Mr Mead wardens.

Auditors.

m^{r} Smethwick & m^{r} Parker are chosen Audito^{rs}. to audite the old wardens Accompt.

Fol. 158^{a} Mr John Harison} Master.
Mr John Rothwell} Wardens
Mr Robert Mead.

19° Julij 1638.

Present:

Mr Harison Mr Rothwell Mr Mead [m^{r} Kingston] Mr Smethwick, m^{r} Aspley m^{r} Butter mr [Downes] M^{r}. Bourne Mr Beale Mr Man Mr Hoth & m^{r} Parker.

Mr Waterson & Andrew Hebb.

Mr Waterson and Andrew Hebb came this day and desired the resolution of the Co^{rt}. touching Josephus.[2] Wherevpon it was shewed by the Refferrees appointed in that buisines, that the said Booke doth belong vnto the Company for that the Originall Entry is wth a provisoe of getting sufficient Licence which was neuer after entred wth Licence. Nevertheles the Co^{rt}. in favour to them held it fitt That if the said Mr Waterson & Andrew Hebb would submitt vnto this Co^{rt}. for such fine as should be thought fitting The said booke should be entred vnto them according to their Right therein. Vnto all wch. the said Mr Waterson & Andrew Hebb willingly assented and submitted themselues.

6°. Augusti 1638. pn'tibus vt antea.

The warden and others to agree wth Mr Martin that ye Bond of 800^{li} may be taken in for wch ye Seale of the hall was giuen for the Latyn Stock

Vpon the motion of warden Mead that he vnderstands that the Bond of 800^{li}. concerning Mr Toley for the Orphan of M^{rs}. Ellen Martin is already to be putt in Suite whereby Charges will come (if not prevented)[3] It is this day referred vnto m^{r} warden Mead Mr Downes m^{r} Parker wth the Clarke, who are by the Co^{rt}. desired to take some paines in the busines And to be advised either to defend the suite or make the best Composicõn they can that the Seale of the house may be brought in, and the Company noe further troubled in this busines And the warden is to pay what sum̃e shall be agreed vpon out of the house

138.

[1] Cf. *C–B.C*, 153^{a}. [2] Cf. *C–B.C*, 157^{b}, 28 June 1638, and 158^{b}, 13 Aug. 1638. [3] Cf. *C–B.C*, 148^{a}, 23 June 1637.

vntill money comes in. And then both this and all the former money disbursed must be paid in againe.

Will: Wethered 50li.

The Cort. hath granted the loane of 50li. for Three yeares. putting in good sucurity.[1]

6o. Augusti predict'. Fol. 158b

Mr Badger to avoid all the Roomes in the hall by or Lady day next.

Mr Badger was this day called into the Cort., and had warning giuen him to avoid all the Roomes which he hath in the Hall, and to provide himselfe otherwise betweene this and or Lady day next, for that they intend otherwise to dispose of the same. He had likewise warning to remoue all such things as he had in the Companies buttery And to lett the same be ready against Monday next for their vse which he promised to doe.[2]

13o. Augustj 1638.

Present.

Mr Harison mr Rothwell mr Mead mr Kingston mr Smethwick mr Aspley mr Butter mr. Beale mr Hoth and mr Parker.

Mr Waterson & Andr: Hebb.

Whereas by an Order made the 19th. day of July last Mr Waterson and Andrew Hebb referred themselues vnto the Table concerning all differences about the Copie of Josephus. This day the Cort. tooke the same into Consideracōn. And haue ordered that three parts of the Copie shall be entred vnto Andrew Hebb and the fourth part vnto Mr Waterson. And that they shall pay to the house for the vse of the Poore Three pounds share and share like according to their proporcōns of right in the Copy. And to print Twelue hundred and ffiftie this Impression. And in Case they shall refuse to performe this order That then the said ꝑties shall haue noe benefitt hereby & the said Copie to belong vnto the Company.[3]

18o Augusti. 1638. Fol. 159a

Present.

Mr Harrison mr Rothwell mr Mead mr Kingston Mr. Smethwick mr. Aspley mr Butter mr Downes, mr Bourne mr Beale mr Mr. (*sic*) Man mr. Hoth & mr. Parker.

Mrs Adams her Assistant Part in the English stock disposed of.

This day (Mrs. Adams[4] being dead) her Assistant part in the English stock fell to be disposed of, and according to Custome the Cort. went to Election there stood for the same Mr Butter, Mr Downes and mr Bourne & it fell vpon Mr Butter. Then mr Butters Liuery part fell to be disposed of, there stood in Election Mr Harper mr fflesher & mr Meighen & it fell vpon mr Harper. Then Mr

[1] His bonds were registered 1 Sept. 1638, *Liber C2*, 121a.

[2] He had had the room over the 'Inward Councell Chamber' since 12 Nov. 1621 (cf. *C–B.C*, 70a), and the warehouses over the 'Buttrye' and the 'Old Irish warehouse' since 10 Mar. 1629 (cf. *C–B.C*, 106a).

[3] Cf. *C–B.C*, 159b, 5 Oct. 1638. Evidently they did not bother to make any other entry.

[4] Mrs. Thomas Adams.

Harpers yeomandry part fell to be disposed of, And because of multitude of Suito[rs]. the Co[rt]. thought fitt to devide the same. There stood for one halfe M[r]. Cotes M[r] Dainty & m[r] Cartwright & it fell vpon M[r] Cartwright. There stood for the other halfe m[r] Brudnell mr Emerson & Charles Greene & it fell vpon m[r] Emerson. And the said m[r] Butter m[r] Harper m[r] Cartwright & m[r] Emerson tooke their oathes accordingly.

27°. Augusti 1638. pn'tibus vt antea

The Bond of 800[li] to Mr Reeue wth the Comon Seale for the Latyn Stock Cancelled 138. 158

This day M[r] warden Mead brought into the Co[rt]. the Bond of 800[li]. w[th] the Comon seale of the Corporacõn w[ch]. Bond by agreem[t]. w[th] M[r] Martin was surrendred into his hands. The said M[r] Martin had in full satisfaction 40[li]. paid by m[r] warden Mead m[r] Downes M[r] Parker & the Clarke being p[r]sent at the agreem[t]. All w[ch]. being declared vnto the Co[rt]. the same was well approved of, & the Bond then Cancelled.[1]

M[r] Constable.

Whereas m[r] Constable did lately peticõn my Lord Mayor about taking his place in the Liuery and therevpon the Master & wardens & diuers of the Assistants of this Company were warned in before my Lord Mayor to show cause why the said m[r] Constable should not take his place according to his antiquity.[2] And the difference being heard my Lord desired the m[r] wardens
Fol. 159[b] and Assistants to call before them those that had fined || and served the place of Rentor since he served the same and to perswade them that the said M[r] Constable might assume his place againe. This day the Co[rt]. caused to be warned in the said ptíes viz[t]. M[r] Edwards m[r] Stansby m[r] whitaker and m[r] Latham. And according to the direction from my Lord Mayor the Co[rt]. moued the said Mr Edwards & the rest in the behalfe of the said Mr Constable. But the said parties would by noe meanes assent vnto it.[3]

Mr Badger to haue the warehouse vnder the hall for fifty shillings vntill o[r] Lady day next.

Vpon the request of M[r] Badger to haue the warehouse vnder Hall w[ch] was M[r] Weavers.[4] The Co[rt]. hath granted he shall haue it vntill o[r] Lady day, (he paying l[s]. for the same) & noe longer.

M[r] Milborne for printing the Welsh Psalmes was fined at 5[li].

M[r] Milborne haveing lately printed the Welsh Psalmes[5] w[th]out leaue of the Co[rt]. It was ordered [he] [*she*] should pay for a fine for the vse of the poore fiue pounds.

[1] Cf. *C–B.C*, 158[a], 6 Aug. 1638. They would doubtless have saved at least the £40 costs if they had paid the debt without attempting to avoid it.

[2] Cf. *C–B.C*, 154[a], 29 Mar. 1638.

[3] Cf. *C–B.C*, 160[a], 5 Oct. 1638.

[4] There appears to be no record of Weaver's renting this. It was probably used by him as an office granted without rent.

[5] STC 2747. It is not certain who printed this for Milbourne but it is not improbable that Stansby did. As he was on his deathbed at this time, the fact that no printer was fined may be confirmatory evidence.

5°. Octobris 1638.

Present. Mr. Kingston loco Mag'ri Mr. Rothwell, Mr Mead, Mr Smethwick Mr Aspley Mr ffetherston Mr Downes Mr Bourne Mr Man Mr Hoth and Mr Parker.

Mr. Waterson & Andrew Hebb. This day mr Waterson and Andrew Hebb according to an Order of the 13th. of August last came and paid their fyne of 3li. for the vse of the poore for printing Josephus.[1] And the Copie is to be entred vnto them according as is sett downe in the order of the 13th of August last.

Mrs. Stansby 5li. for the Liueries attendance at her husbands buriall. This day Mrs. Stansby sent 5li. by mr Smethwick vnto the Company for the Liueries attendance at her husbands buriall The wch warden Mead receiued.

5°. Octobris predict'. Fol. 160a

Mr. Constable to take his place in the Liuery next Mr Ephraim Dawson. This day the Table tooke into Consideracōn the Complaint of mr. Constable Concerning his taking place in the Liuery And it was thought fitt and soe ordered That in regard of his weake Estate & great charge of Children and haueing serued one yeare Rentor, That his fyne of 24li. should be remitted And that he should take his place next Mr Ephraim Dawson. wch favour the said Mr Constable thanckfully accepted of.[2]

23°. Octobris 1638.

Present. Mr Harrison Mr Rothwell Mr Mead Mr Kingston Mr Smethwick Mr Aspley Mr Bourne Mr Beale Mr Man Mr Hoth & Mr Parker.

Mr Badger fyned at xs. for absence from the Cort. fforasmuch as Mr Badger absented himselfe from the Cort. there being speciall occasion for him It was thought fitt to putt him to a fyne for his neglect herein And the same being putt to voices, by generall vote of the table he was fyned at xs.

A Precept for 80li. for renewing the Citties Charter. This day a Precept from my Lord Mayor[3] was read touching 80li. to be levyed in or. Company towards the Charge of 8000li. alotted to be paid by all the Companies in London for renewing the Citties Charter, wherevpon they Consider how the same should be raised And by generall Consent it was thought fitt that the Assistants should pay 16s. a man The Liuery xs. a man. And the yeomandry 5s. a man.

[1] Cf. *C–B.C*, 158b, 13 Aug. 1638. STC 14813 and 14813a. It is interesting to note that almost three times as many copies with Hebb's imprint are recorded as with Waterson's.

[2] Cf. *C–B.C*, 159a, 27 Aug. 1638.

[3] Transcribed in *Letter Book*, 124b, 20 Oct. 1638. The 'Bill of assessment' is given in *Letter Book*, 144a–146b.

Will: Lambert to be Carver to the Company as M[r] Harvest was.

M[r]. Harvest the Companies Carver haueing lately surrendred vp his place whereby the Company are destitute of one to execute the said place. This day William Lambert[1] a brother of this Company being one of the Sheriffs Carvers desired to be admitted to the place of the said M[r] Harvest w[ch]. the Co[rt]. taking into Consideracōn ordered that the said M[r] Lambert should be Carver to the Company as M[r] Harvest was & to haue the yearely sallary as he had.

Fol. 160[b]

7°. Nouembris 1638.

Present. M[r] Kingston loco Mag'ri. M[r] Rothwell M[r]. Mead M[r]. Smethwick M[r] Butter M[r]. Downes m[r] Bourne M[r] Man M[r] Hoth & M[r]. Parker.

D[r]. Speed. 127. 147

Whereas some differences concerning the Accompt betweene the Company & D[r]. Speed hath lately fallen out & diuers meetings haue byn concerning the same this day each party being desirous to putt a quiet end therevnto. It is agreed betweene them that D[r]. Speed shall be paid the sum̃e of 200[li]. in full of all Accompt℮ & reckonings due by reason of Genealogies[2] vntill the first day of September last. And whereas there is a demand made to D[r]. Speed for allowance of searches w[ch] he is behind in & haue not byn demanded. D[r]. Speed hath promised to pay or allow for all such searches as shall appeare to be iustly due according to the Couenants.

19°. Nouembris 1638.

Present. M[r] Harrison M[r]. Rothwell M[r]. Mead, M[r]. Kingston M[r] Smethwick M[r] Aspley, M[r] Butter M[r] Downes M[r]. Bourne M[r]. Man M[r] Hoth & M[r] Parker.

M[r] Havilands Liuery Part disposed of.

This day (M[r] Haviland being lately dead) the Co[rt]. thought fitt to goe to Election for his Liuery part, there stood for the same M[r] fflesher M[r] Meighen & M[r] Young & it fell vpon M[r] fflesher. Then m[r] fflleshers yeomandry part fell to be disposed of & because of Many suito[rs]. the Co[rt]. thought fitt to devide the same there stood for one halfe M[r] Cotes M[r] Clarke & m[r] Slater & it fell vpon m[r]. Clarke There stood for the other halfe Thomas Brudnell Robert Howes & Charles Greene: & it fell vpon Thomas Brudnell. And the said M[r]. fflesher M[r] Clarke & Thomas Brudnell tooke their oathes accordingly.

Will: Lamberts halfe yeoman: part in the English stock engaged to M[r] fflesher. for 40[li].

William Lambert[3] the printer vpon request vnto the Co[rt]. had leaue granted to engage his halfe yeomandry part in the English stock vnto M[r]. fflesher for 40[li]. for a Twelue month

[1] Made free 14 Jan. 1622 (Arber iii. 685). [2] STC 23039. [3] Made free 14 Jan. 1622 (Arber iii. 685).

19°. Nouembri predict. FOL. 161[a]

Dr. Speeds proffer for the sale of his Pattent | Doctor Speed came this day vnto the Cort. & offered to sell the remainder of his Terme in his Pattent for the Genealogies[1] wch being taken into Consideracõn The Cort. desired Mr warden Mead Mr Butter Mr Downes Mr Bourne Mr Parker wth the Clarke to treat wth the doctor about the same & doe therein as they should thinke good & report to this table their proceedings therein by the next Cort.

23°. Nouembris 1638.

Present. Mr Harrison Mr Rothwell Mr Mead Mr Kingston Mr Smethwick Mr Aspley Mr Butter Mr Downes Mr Bourne Mr Man Mr Hoth & Mr Parker.

Mr. Tho: Weaver. whereas diuers meetings & debates haue byn had concerning the debt oweing by mr Thomas Weaver vnto the English stock.[2] It is this day fully concluded That if mr Thomas Weaver doe pay the sume of 180li. betweene this & the next Cort. He shall haue his part in the English stock and his Copies that are engaged free vnto him. And in Case he shall refuse this favour & not pay the said sume. Then the Table are resolued forthwith to dispose of them for the best advantage, And for the remainder of his debt they will take him into their Consideracõn wth much favour & pitty.[3]

Dr Speeds Sale of his Pattent of the Genealogies to the Company. | This day according to an order of the last Cort. Mr warden Mead and the rest declared vnto the Cort. of their treaty wth Dr. Speed for his Pattent.[4] That they had agreed to giue the Doctor 700li. for his pattent & his now stock of Genealogies[5] in the Companies & Mr Kingstons hands & the Materialls for printing of the Genealogies.[6] In wch. Sume of 700li. is included 50li. wch. the Doctor was to receive of the 200li. ordered him the Seaventh of this instant month.[7] And the said 700li. to be paid in this manner (vizt.) 100li. downe 100li. at or Lady day next And soe 100li. euery six monthes vntill the said Sume be paid ffor security whereof he should haue the Companies Bond wth the Comon Seale And whereas the doctor by his Consent to the [*the*] Order of the 7th. of this month was to allow so || much as should be iustly due to the Company for searches about the Genealogies, the same [is] to be remitted. All wch agreement the Cor. generally approved of. And ordered that the said 100li. should be paid the doctor at his sealing And that a Bond should be giuen the doctor for payment of the 600li. wth the Comon Seale. And the Bargaine & sale being ready engrossed the Doctor this day in open Cort. Sealed the same. And the Master & wardens then likewise in the name of the whole Corporacõn sealed FOL. 161[b]

1 STC 23039. Cf. *C–B.C*, 40[a], 21 Nov. 1615.

2 It is not clear what had happened, cf. *C–B.C*, 137*[a], 1 Mar. 1636.

3 Cf. *C–B.C*, 161[b], 3 Dec. 1638.

4 Cf. *C–B.C*, 161[a], 19 Nov. 1638.

5 STC 23039.

6 Cf. *C–B.C*, 78[b], 20 Aug. 1623.

7 Cf. *C–B.C*, 160[b].

the said Bond to the Doctor wth the Comon seale. And the Cort. then thought fitt to giue the Doctors. wife xli. for his loveing Conclusion.

3°. Decembris 1638.

Present. Mr Harison Mr Rothwell Mr Mead, Mr. Smethwich Mr Aspley Mr Butter Mr Downes mr Bourne mr Man mr Hoth.

To goe to my Lo: Mayors. to Dynner

It was thought fitt That Twelue of the Assistants shall goe to my Lord Mayors to dynner.

New ffeoffees chosen for Abergavenny houses.

A Rent to be paid for the Hall

27. 83.

fforasmuch as the ffeoffees for Abergavenny houses are all dead but Mr Islip & mr Kingston.[1] The Cort. thought fitt that new ffeoffees be appointed in trust for the English stock. And that the said Mr Islip & Mr Kingston doe make ouer their Right vnto these hereafter named vizt. Mr. Harrison Mr Rothwell Mr Mead Mr Smethwick Mr Aspley Mr ffetherston Mr Butter & Mr Downes. And because advice is to be taken of Councell therein. The Cort. hath desired Mr warden Mead Mr Parker & the Clarke to take some paines in the buisnes for the Speedy effecting thereof. And it was further thought fitt that a Rent be paid vnto the English Stock from the Corporacōn for the vse of the hall for an acknowledgmt. that the same belongeth vnto the said Stock.

Mr Tho: Weaver.

Whereas by an Order of the 23th. of Nouember last.[2] It was ordered. That if Mr Thomas Weauer did not pay 180li. to redeeme his part & all the Copies (heretofore made ouer) by the next Cort. That
Fol. 162a then his said part & the Copies should be sould to the best advantage || towards the payment of the said debt. This day the said Thomas Weaver brought into the Cort. 130li. And desired that 50li. wch he alleadged was oweing vnto him by the Irish Stock [*wch*] might be accepted of wch in all amounts to 180li. according to the said order. Wch said sum̃e of 180li. togeither wth his fathers stock[3] of 320li. comes to 500li. But the Cort. held it not fitt to accept of the 50li. oweing by the Irish partnors. for that they denyed the same to be due vnto him. Nevertheles the Cort. in favour to the said Thomas Weaver were content that Mr warden Mead should for the prsent lay downe the said 50li. for him vpon Condicōn that he should pay the same by the next poores day, wch he thanckfully accepted of & promised to doe & performe accordingly. Wherevpon the Cort. ordered Mr warden Mead to receiue the said sum̃e of 130li. And it was ordered by the full Consent of the Cort. That the said Thomas Weaver vpon payment of the said 50li. should haue his said part & Copies from thenceforth free & to receiue the diuidents of his stock from tyme to tyme And that for the Remainder of his debt he should be favorably dealt wthall.

[1] Cf. *C–B.C*, 84a (bis), 7 Feb. 1625.
[2] Cf. *C–B.C*, 161a.
[3] Disposed of 12 June 1638, *C–B.C*, 157a.

20th. of December 1638.

Present. Mr Harison Mr Rothwell Mr Mead Mr Smethwick Mr Downes Mr Man & Mr Hoth.

Mr. Weauers Copies engaged to Mr Miller for Security of 100li. for .6. monthes

This day according to an Order of the last Cort. Thomas Weaver brought in the 50li. Mr warden Mead laid out for him. And the said Thomas Weaver then desired leaue of the Cort. to Engage his Copies vnto Mr Miller for 100li. for 6. monthes wch was granted. And the said mr weaver made a Bill of Sale of his said Copies to the said Mr Miller for Security of the said 100li. & sealed the same in the Cort.[1]

Mr Vavasor to haue 50li.

The Cort. hath granted him the loane of 50li for 3. yeares putting in good Security.[2]

25°. Januarij 1638.

Fol. 162b

Present. Mr Harrison Mr Rothwell Mr Mead Mr Aspley Mr Butter Mr Downes Mr Bourne Mr Man Mr Parker.

Mr Leake to haue the Copies wch. were Mrs. Hawkins Entred to him.

This day mr Leake came and shewed to the Cort. a warrant vnder the hands & seales of mr warden Mead & Mr Meredith directed to this Cort. for the turning ouer vnto the said william Leake certaine Copies & parts of Copies entred vnto them In the Register booke of the Entry of Copies the 29th of May 1638.[3] wch said Copies were assigned vnto them by Consent of Mrs. Hawkins widdow & order of this Cort.[4] Wch. being taken into Consideracõn It was ordered that the said Copies should be accordingly entred vnto the said Mr Leake.[5]

Mr. Milborne fyned xxs. for printing the welsh Psalmes

Mr Milborne being warned to the Cort. for payment of 5li. wch he was fined at ye first of October last for printing the Welsh Psalmes wthout leaue of the Cort.[6] This day he came & brought ye said 5li. & humbly desired that in regard he did not the same wilfully that some abatemt. might be made thereof. Wch being taken into Consideracõn It was thought fitt to putt the same to voices, wch by the mayor ꝑte there was remitted 4li. Soe that he paid onely xxs. for the said offence.

[1] Weaver was unable to pay his debt, for these copies were transferred to Miller, 28 June 1639 (Arber iv. 471), cf. *C–B.C*, 166a, 1 July 1639.

[2] His bonds were registered 2 Mar. 1639, *Liber C2*, 121b.

[3] Arber iv. 420.

[4] Cf. *C–B.C*, 147b, 5 June 1637.

[5] Entered 25 Jan. 1639 (Arber iv. 452–3).

[6] Cf. *C–B.C*, 159b. Note that date of order would appear from the Court Book to be 27 Aug.

4°. ffebruarij 1638. pn'tibus vt antea.

Mr Sivedale to haue the Lease lett to Mr Ayres made in his owne name for the remainder of the terme therein xxs. for Alyenacõn [*paid*] to [*the*] be paid at the Sealing

This day mr. Sivedale (haueing bought the terme of yeares in the Lease lett vnto Mr Ayres of his late dwelling house in Woodstreet)[1] Came this day vnto the Cort. & desired to Attorne Tennant vnto the Company paying xxs. lymited in the Lease for that purpose And that ye said Lease might be made in his owne name for the remainder of the yeares vnexpired therein Wch. the Cort. taking into Consideracõn hath thought fitt to grant his request & order that the same shall be forthwith dispatched.

ffran: Leech 50li.

ffrancis Leech by order of this Cort. is to haue the next 50li. that comes in putting in good security.[2]

Fol. 163a

1°. Martij 1638.

Present. Mr Harrison Mr Rothwell Mr Mead Mr Smethwick Mr Aspley Mr Butter Mr Downes Mr Bourne mr Man Mr Hoth and Mr Parker.

Stockeepers chosen.	Mr Downes Mr Mann	mr Seile mr whitaker	mr ffussell mr. Cartwright

Mr Brewster Threasurer et Juratr.

Auditors	Mr Smethwick Mr Aspley	mr Edwards mr Dawson	mr Bartlett mr Clarke

5°. Martij 1638.

Present. Mr Harison Mr Rothwell Mr Mead Mr Smethwick Mr Aspley Mr Butter Mr Downes Mr Bourne mr Man & mr Hoth.

Mr Dell to haue the Lease of the ffeathers Taverne wch. he bought of Mr Nicholls in his owne name. And to haue Ten yeares more gratis.

This day Mr Dell my Lord of Canterburies Secretary came vnto the Cort. and shewed that he had contracted wth Mr Nicholls for the lease of the ffeathers Taverne in St. Pauls Church yard wch. the said Mr. Nicholls lately tooke of the Company.[3] And therevpon desired the Co. to admitt him to be their Tennant and to grant him a further time in the said Lease. Which request being taken into Consideracõn. It was thought fitt by and wth the full Consent of this Cort. & soe ordered (in respect the said Mr Dell hath alwaies byn ready to doe the Company many friendly offices & for the future may [the more] be enduced to Continue his Loue & furtherance of the Companies busines) That he shall haue the said Lease

[1] Cf. *C–B.C*, 83a, 9 Sept. 1624.
[2] His bonds were registered 29 Apr. 1639, *Liber C2*, 121.
[3] Cf. *C–B.C*, 137b, 15 Feb. 1636.

made in his owne name and Tenn yeares more added to the Terme in the said Lease gratis. At the same yearely Rent & vnder the same Covenants of the said Lease lett to Mr Nicholls. verte.

20°. Martij 1638. FOL. 163b

Present. Mr Harrison Mr Rothwell Mr Mead, Mr Kingston Mr Smethwick mr Downes mr Bourne mr Beale Mr Man Mr Hoth & mr Parker.

A new Lease of the ffeathers taverne Sealed to Mr. Dell.

This day according to an order of the last Cort. A new lease of the ffeathers Taverne was sealed wth. the Comon Seale vnto Mr Dell for Threecore yeares to Comence from Christmas last at the yearely Rent of xlli. p Annum[1] And the said Mr Dell deliuered vp the late new Lease Lett vnto Mr Nicholls for 51ty. yeares of the said Taverne to be Cancelled wch accordingly was done.

26°. Martij 1639.

Mr Harrison mr Rothwell Mr Mead Mr Smethwick Mr Aspley Mr Downes Mr Bourne Mr Man Mr Hoth & Mr Parker

Election of Rentors

Mr Brewster, mr Milborne fyned for Rentors

Mr Seile, Mr Bloome Rentors.

Mr. Miller haueing served Rentor was wished this day according to order to bring his Accompt the sixt day of May next. Then mr Brewster being vnderwarden was chosen in his place. And the said Mr Brewster then desired to be admitted to his fyne in regard of his place of Treasurership[2] wch. the Cort. granted And ye said Mr Brewster was fyned at 24li.[3] Then Mr Milborne being next was called, but he desired to fyne, Wch was granted & he promised to pay the same on Saterday next. Then Mr Seile being next was called to hold Rentor wch. he accepted of & Mr Bloome was chosen to ioyne wth him for the yeare ensewing/

29°. Aprilis 1639. FOL. 164a

Present. Mr. Harrison Mr Rothwell Mr Mead Mr Kingston Mr Smethwick Mr Aspley Mr Downes Mr Man Mr Hoth Mr Parker.

The Couenants for the Treasurer to be Sealed wth ye Comon Seale

This day was read a draught of the Covenants betweene the Master and wardens, & Mr Brewster the Treasurer wch. were well liked of. And the Cort. hath ordered that the same shall be forthwith engrossed & sealed wth the Comon seale.

[1] This lease is still preserved in the archive of the Stationers' Company, No. 503.

[2] Apparently appointed Treasurer on the death of Edmund Weaver.

[3] Cf. *C–B.C*, 166a, 1 July 1639.

Mr Harpers Liuery Part mortgaged to Mr Parker

A note vnder the hand & seale of mr Harper was this day read in Cort. wherein he desired leaue to engage his Liuery part in the English stock vnto Mr Parker for a certaine sume of money wch he oweth him. Wch the Cort. taking into Consideracon held it fitt & soe ordered That if the said Mr Parker will vndertake to Satisfie his debt to the English stock at the next diuident. That then his said part shall be engaged to him. The wch mr Parker promised in Cort. that the same should be pformed accordingly. And therevpon the Cort. gaue Consent.

9°. Maij 1639. pn'tibus vt antea

The Couenants with the Treasurer sealed with the Comon Seale.

This day according to an order of the 29th. of Aprill last, the Covenants betweene the Company and the Treasurer were sealed wth the Comon seale. And Mr Bruister & Mr Miller entred into one Bond of 500li. for performance thereof. alsoe Mr Stevens & Mr Meredith entred into one other Bond of 500li. for the Treasurers pformance of the Couenants.

11°. Maij A°. 1639.

Present.

Mr. Kingston loco Magistri, Mr Rothwell & Mr Mead wardens, Mr Smethwick Mr Aspley Mr Downes Mr Bourne Mr Man Mr Beale Mr Hoth & Mr Parker.

Mr Butters Assistant Part & Copies Mortgaged to Mr fflesher for 600li.

Fol. 164b

This day a note vnder the hand & seale of Mr Butter was read in Cort. wherein he desired leaue to engage his Assistant part in the English stock to Mr fflesher for security of three hundred pounds for one yeare at || six pounds p Centum wch. the Cort. taking into Consideracon thought fitt. That if mr fflesher will vndertake for mr Butters debt to the Stock to be paid at Midsomer next, That then his said part shall accordingly be made over vnto him; To wch the said Mr fflesher willingly assented. And the Cort. further held it fitt, that Mr Butter should haue noe Creditt at the Stock wthout security or prsent money.

Likewise vpon the request of mr Butter by another note vnder his hand & seale That he might haue leaue to mortgage all his Copies & pts Copies vnto Mr fflesher for another sume of 300li. at six pounds p Cent' for three yeares according to the tenor of certaine Articles to be drawne vp betweene them to that purpose. The Cort. taking the same into Consideracon haue ordered the said Copies & parts to be accordingly entred vnto the said Mr fflesher for security as aforesaid.[1]

10°. Junij 1639.

Present.

Mr Harrison Mr Rothwell Mr Mead, Mr Smethwick Mr Aspley Mr Downes, Mr Bourne mr Beale Mr Man and Mr Parker.

Mr. Sivedales Lease of Mr. Ayres house in Woodstreet Sealed.

This day according to an Order of the fourth day of ffebruary last[2] the Lease formerly lett to mr Ayres of one of the Companies houses in Wood street was new sealed vnto Mr Siuedale for the remainder of the yeares vnexpired in Mr Ayres Lease,

[1] Entered 21 May 1639 (Arber iv. 466). There are twenty-five copies or parts of copies, including *Lear*, in this mortgage.

[2] Cf. *C–B.C*, 162b.

(the said Mr Sivedale haueing bought the same of the Executors. of the said Mr Ayre) And the said Mr Siuedale then paid xxs. for the Alyenacõn of Mr Ayres Right to him.

Tho: Bates to haue the 12li. he borrowed for 3. yeares more

Vpon the humble peticõn of Thomas Bates for renewing his Bond of 12li. wch is now due the Cort. hath ordered that the same shall be Continued for three yeares more putting in good security.[1]

10°. Junij 1639: prdict'. Fol. 165a

Mr. Morretts yeomandry Part mortgaged to Mr Meredith.

Whereas Mr Morrett is indebted vnto Mr Meredith in the sume of Threescore pounds, and vnto the English Stock the sume of Eighteene pounds od money. This day the said Mr. Morretts wife came vnto the Cort. and testified her husbands humble request, That his yeomandry part in the English Stock should be made over according to the Custome of the Company for Security of the said Sumes. Wch. ye Cort. taking into Consideracõn held it fitt and hath soe ordered (That forasmuch as the said Mr Meredith is willing to pay the said 18li. od money vnto the Stock for the said Mr Morrett betweene this and mid-somer day next) That the said Mr Morretts full yeomandry part shall be engaged vnto the said Mr Meredith for paymt. of both the said Sumes.

20°. Junij 1639.

Present.

Mr. Harrison Mr. Rothwell Mr Mead, Mr Kingston Mr Smethwick Mr Aspley Mr Downes Mr Man Mr Hoth & Mr Parker.

Humph: Woodalls yeo: Part mortgaged to mr Walley for 50li. for 6. months

Whereas Humphrey Woodall the 11th. day of Aprill 1636. had leaue of this Cort. to engage his yeomandry part in the English Stock vnto William ffayred als ffox for Security of 50li. for six monthes.[2] Wch. said sume being satisfied. The said Humphrey came this day vnto the Cort. and desired the like leaue to engage his said yeomandry part vnto Henry Walley for security of 50li. borrowed of him for six monthes. Wch. the Cort. taking into Consideracõn have giuen Consent therevnto.

20°. Junij 1639. predict'. Fol. 165b

Tho: Paines Yeomandry Part mortgaged to Wm. ffayred als ffox for 110li & Interest at 8li. p Cent for a Twelue month.

Whereas Thomas Paine the first day of March 1637. had leaue of this Cort. to engage his yeomandry part in the English stock vnto Henry Walley for security of 60li. for six monthes.[3] Wch said sume the said Henry Walley being satisfied. The said Thomas Paine this day Sent a Note vnder his hand & seale, wherein he desired leaue of this Cort. that his said pte might be made over vnto Wm. ffox als ffayred towards the security of 110li. for a Twelue month wth Interest at 8li. p Cent', wch the Cort. taking into Consideracõn haue giuen Liberty & way vnto the said Paine to engage his said part vnto the said Wm. ffayred als ffox.

[1] The original registry of 12 May 1636, *Liber C2*, 23a, is docketed 'paid in & lent to him againe'.

[2] Cf. *C–B.C*, 139a.

[3] Cf. *C–B.C*, 153b.

27°. Junij 1639. pn'tibus vt antea

Mr. Beale to pay for Paper & loose his workmanship for his ill printing Puerilis.

Mr Beale haueing printed Puerilis[1] in such ill manner that they are not fitt to be sould. The Cort. taking the same into Consideracõn haue thought fitt & soe ordered that Mr Beale shall pay for all the paper imployed in the printing of the said Booke & shall not be allowed anything for his workemanship thereof.

Mr Waterson & Charles Greene Debts to be putt in Suite.

The Cort hath ordered that the Clarke shall take course against Mr Waterson & Charles Greene for their debts to the Stock.

1°. Julij 1639.

Present.

Mr. Harison, Mr Rothwell, Mr Mead, Mr Smethwick, Mr Aspley, Mr Downes, Mr Bourne & Mr Man.

Mr. Young fyned at xls. for binding Evan Tyler contrary to Order.

Mr Young haueing bound Evan Tyler[2] at a Scrivenors. Contrary to Order was fyned at xls., but vpon some reasons alleadged by him, his fyne was remitted to xxs. wch. he paid accordingly.

Fol. 166a

1°. Julij 1639. predict'.

Mr Brewsters fyne of xxiiijli. for Rentor warden remitted to xli.

This day Mr Brewster brought in his fyne of xxiiijli. for Rentorwarden,[3] but the Table taking into Consideracõn his great Care in his place of Treasurership haue thought fitt & so ordered that xiiijli. thereof shall be remitted & so the warden recd. Ten pounds for his said fyne.

Mr. Tho: Weavers Part in the English Stocke, his Parts in the Irish Stock & all his Copies mortgaged to Mr Miller for 250li. payable the 25th. Dec'. 1642.

Mr Thomas Weauer came this day vnto the Cort. (& according to the Custome of the Company) humbly desired leaue that his yeomanry part in the English stock, his parts in the Irish stock & all the Copies by him formerly made ouer vnto Mr Miller[4] for Security of 100li. wch. should haue byn paid on Midsomer day last, may now be engaged vnto the said Mr. Miller for the said 100li. & 150li more to be paid the 25th. of December 1642. And that the dividents & proffitts arising from tyme to tyme by his said Seuerall parts may be paid vnto the said George Miller in Consideracõn of the forbearance of the said money wch the Cort. taking into Consideracõn haue thought fitt & so ordered. That his said pte in the English & parts in the Irish stockes & the said Copies shall accordingly be made ouer & paid vnto the said Mr miller for security & forbearance of the said Sum̃e of 250li.

Mr. Griffin to haue 50li.

The Cort. hath granted him the loane of 50li. for 3. yeares putting in good security.[5]

[1] *Pueriles confabulatiunculae*, cf. Hazlitt i. 84.

[2] Made free 1 July 1639 (Arber iii. 688).

[3] Cf. *C–B.C*, 163b, 26 Mar. 1639.

[4] Cf. *C–B.C*, 162a, 20 Dec. 1638.

[5] His bonds were registered 20 July 1639, *Liber C2*, 122a.

Geo: Hurlock & Mr Oulton about the printing of Witte private Wealth.

The matter Complayned of by George Hurlock against Mr Oulton for printing witts private wealth[1] being (as he alleadgeth) his Copie, is referred vnto Mr Bourne & Mr Man, who are desired by the table to heare the said difference & putt such end to it as shall be iust, or if they cannott, then to Certifie their opinione by the next Cort. And in the meane tyme the said parties are to attend the said Refferrees.

Edw: Husbands 50li.

The Cort. hath granted him the loane of 50li for 3. yeares putting in good security.

6o. Julij 1639. Fol. 166b

Present. Mr Harrison Mr Rothwell Mr Mead, Mr. Kingston Mr Smethwick Mr Aspley, Mr Downes, Mr Bourne, Mr Beale, Mr Man Mr Hoth & Mr Parker; Mr Seale & mr Bloome Rentors.

Election of Mr & Wardens

This day the box being opened, it appeared. Mr Smethwick to be Master, Mr ffetherston & Mr Bourne Wardens.

Auditors Chosen to audite the old Wardens Accompts.

This day likewise mr Downes & mr Hoth were chosen Auditors to audite the old wardens Accompts.

27o. Julij 1639. pn'tibus vt antea.

John Benson to print 1500. of the Tragedies of Albovine paying xls. to the Poore.

Mr Benson desired leaue of the Cort. to print an Imprssion of the play called The Tragedy of Albouine made by Mr Davenant wch was printed in Anno 1629.[2] & neuer entred & therefore in the disposall of this Cort. Vpon Consideracõn thereof It was ordered that the said mr Benson should haue leaue to print an Imprssion of 1500. paying to the Poore of this Company xls.

To treat with mr Buck & mr Daniell for a Composicõn as wth. Oxford.

The Cort. hath desired the wardens, Mr Aspley, Mr Downes mr. Parker & the Clarke, to treat wth Mr Buck & Mr Daniell about a Composicõn for their priuiledge of printing as wth Oxford.[3]

Sam: Enderby 50li.

The Cort. hath granted him the loane of 50li for 3. yeares putting in good security.[4]

1 STC 3712. No trace of Oulton's edition has been found. Hurlock could show a well documented right to the book (Arber iii. 309, and iv. 259, 312), and Oulton's edition may have been destroyed, although as only two copies of Hurlock's can be traced it is hazardous to speculate.

2 STC 6307. This proposed edition was not published.

3 They were the printers to the University of Cambridge.

4 His bonds were registered 3 Sept. 1639, *Liber C2*, 122a.

Fol. 167[a]

12°. Augusti 1639.

Present. Mr Smethwick, Mr. Mr ffetherston Mr Bourne War: Mr Kingston, Mr Harison, Mr Aspley, Mr Downes Mr Beale Mr Hoth & Mr Parker.

Bacons Essaies. Whereas mr Beale hath gone forward wth the printing of my Lord Bacõns Essaies,[1] wch he affirmes is his Copie by an ancient Entrance. This day it was alleadged vnto the Cort., that the said Copie belongs to Mr Haviland[2] wherevpon the Cort. admonished him not to goe forward wth the printing of the same vntill the right thereof did appeare.

ffrancis Smiths Copies. The Bills of Sales touching ffrancis Smithes Copies are to be brought in by mr Beale John Wright Junr. & John Thomas & produced in Cort. whereby Consideracõn may be had of the proceedings of mr Beale & order taken for setling the Right of them.[3]

The Couenants wth. Oxford to be renewed for 3. yeares more. It was thought fitt this day by generall Consent of the Cort., that the Couenants wth. Oxford should be renued for 3. yeares more from the Expiracõn of the Agreement now in force.[4] And that the seale of the house should be giuen for pformance thereof as before, And the Cort. then entreated mr warden Bourne Mr Mead mr. Parker, wth the Clarke to goe to oxford to see the same dispatched.

The Companies part of the said Couenants Sealed. In the afternoone the same day the same Covenants being ready engrossed was sealed wth. the Comon seale of the Corporacõn by the Master & Wardens & diuers of the Assistants then prsent.

Fol. 167[b]

2°. Septembris 1639.

Present. Mr Smethwick Mr, mr Aspley loco Mag'ri ffetherston mr. Bourne War: Mr Kingston, Mr Harison Mr Rothwell, Mr Downes, Mr Mead, Mr Man mr Hoth & mr Parker.

Mr Beale. Bacons Essaies. Whereas mr Beale by an order of the last Cort.[5] was admonished not to goe forwards in the printing of the Lord Bacõns Essaies vntill the right thereof did appeare Now forasmuch as he still proceeds in the printing of the same in Contempt of the said Order. This day the Cort. taking his disobedience into Consideracõn haue thought fitt That Mr Warden Bourne taking wth him the Beadle & such others as he shall thinke fitt doe prsently repair vnto Mr Beales house & take downe the Barr & Spindle of his presse & the same bring vnto the hall vntill further order be taken therein.

[1] STC 1151.

[2] Hannah Barrett's rights were transferred to Parker, who transferred them to Haviland and Wright, 4 Sept. 1638 (Arber iv. 433). Several others, including Beale, certainly had rights at this time. The controversy was not settled until after 7 Sept. 1640 (cf. *C–B.C*, 172[b]).

[3] No further record of this dispute has been found. Smith's copies were of a very popular type and may have been of value.

[4] Cf. *C–B.C*, 144[b], 13 Feb. 1637.

[5] Cf. *C–B.C*, 167[a], 12 Aug. 1639.

Mr Bladen admitted into the Liuery & 18^{li}. of his 20^{li}. fyne remitted.

This day m^{r} Bladon was admitted into the Livery of this Company & touching his fyne of 20^{li}. the Co^{rt}. Considering his good service for the Company[1] haue thought fitt to remitt 18^{li}. thereof & the residue being xl^{s}; he then paid.

John Raworth 50^{li}.

The Co^{rt}. hath granted him the loane of 50^{li} for 3. yeares gratis putting in good security.[2]

W^{m}: Clarke[3] 6^{li}.

The Co^{rt}. hath granted him the loane of 6^{li}. for 3. yeares gratis putting in good security.[4]

26°. Sept' 1639. pn'tibus vt antea.

The vniuersitis part of the Agreem^{t}. wth. the Company brought to the Co^{rt}. by m^{r} Langton.

This day the Counterpte of o^{r} Agreem^{t}. wth Oxford[5] sealed wth the Comon seale of the Vniuersity was deliuered from the vice chancello^{r} by one m^{r} Langton to the m^{r} & wardenę.

3°. Octobris 1639. Fol. 168^{a}

Quarter day.

Present. Mr Smethwick, m^{r} ffetherston, m^{r} Bourne Mr Kingston, Mr Harison, Mr Aspley, Mr Rothwell m^{r} Downes Mr Mead, Mr Man Mr Hoth & m^{r} Parker.

Mr Beale.

Whereas by two seuerall orders of this Co^{rt}., one of the 12th. of August & the other of the 2^{d}. of September last[6] m^{r}. Beale was ordered not to goe forwards in the printing of my Lord Bacõns Essaies wch he was then at worke vpon vntill the right of the said Booke were made to appeare in respect the same was alleadged to belong vnto others, & the said Mr Beale being this day warned vnto the Co^{rt}. & appeared not, & m^{r} whitaker & m^{r} Hodgkinson[7] attending the Co^{rt}. to shew their Right in the said Booke. It was therefore ordered by full Consent of the Co^{rt}. that forasmuch as the said Mr Beale Contrary to the fore writed orders & his promise to the Co^{rt}. not to goe forward in the printing of the said [*print*] Booke, hath since finished the impression of the said booke,[8] And (as the Co^{rt}. is informed) exposeth the same to sale: And for that such actions of one in his Ranck ought to be exemplary to the Conformity of the good orders of this Company & not to open such a gapp to the disrespect of this Co^{rt}. That for his Contempt he shall pay Twenty nobles for a fyne for the vse of the poore of this Company & moreouer to be suspended from the Co^{rt}. as an Assistant vntill further order be taken therein.[9]

1 Probably as Dublin agent.

2 His bonds were registered 1 Dec. 1640, *Liber C2*, 122^{b}.

3 There were two William Clarkes, one made free 23 Nov. 1623 (Arber iii. 685), the other, 20 Mar. 1639 (Arber iii. 688).

4 There is no record of this loan in *Liber C2*.

5 Cf. *C–B.C*, 167^{a}, 12 Aug. 1639.

6 Cf. *C–B.C*, 167^{a} and ^{b}.

7 Whitaker was a partner with Hannah Barrett, 13 Mar. 1625 (Arber iv. 137), but what rights Hodgkinson may have had is not clear.

8 STC 1151.

9 Cf. *C–B.C*, 172^{a}, 4 July 1640.

FOL. 168[b] 7°. Octobris 1639. pn'tibus vt antea

Bacons Essaie — This day the difference in question touching the right of my Lord Bacons Essaies is referred by the Co[rt]. vnto the Wardens M[r] Downes & M[r] Parker, who are desired to heare & examine the same, & report to the table their opinions therein. And the Co[rt]. haue thought fitt & doe order that M[r] Beale doe bring in the Impression of the said Booke by him printed vnto the hall forthwith, there to be kept vntill the Right thereof be determined.[1]

Hen: Ockold to haue the Copies belonging to his father entred to him, paying 5[s]. to the Poore. — The Co[rt]. hath ordered that the Copies duely belonging vnto m[r] Ockold deceased, shall be entred vnto his sonne Henry Ockold vpon paym[t]. of 5[s]. to the vse of the poore, w[ch] he now paid to the Warden in Co[rt]. accordingly.[2]

4°. Novembris. 1639. pn'tibus vt antea

M[r] Bartlett 100[li]. — The Co[rt]. hath granted him the loane of 100[li] (it being the first by them to be disposed of) for 3. yeares putting in good security.[3]

2°. Decembris 1639.

Present. — M[r] Smethwick M[r] M[r] Aspley loco Mag'ri ffetherston m[r] Bourne, M[r] Kingston, M[r] Harison, M[r] Rothwell M[r] Downes M[r] Mead M[r] Man & m[r] Parker.

The Ordinances of y[e] Company to be renued — This day the Co[rt]. thought fitt & hath desired That both the Wardens M[r] Kingston M[r] Downes M[r] Mead w[th] the Clarke or any four of them doe forthwith take advice for the renueing of the ordinances of this Company.

FOL. 169[a] 2°. Decembris 1639. p[r]dict'

D[r]. Speed. — This day d[r]. Speed came vnto the Co[rt]. & Shewed that whereas vpon the sale of his Pattent to the Company.[4] This Co[rt] did then seale a Bond vnto him w[th] the Comon seale for 600[li]. payable at seuerall tymes as thereby appeareth. Of w[ch] said sum̃e of 600[li]. he hath rec[d]. 200[li]. Now the said D[r]. Speed haueing speciall occasion for the remainder being 400[li]. desired that vpon deliuery in of the said Bond of 600[li]., this Co[rt]. would be pleased to seale a new Bond for the remainder, wch being taken into Consideracõn It was thought fitt & so ordered by full Consent of this Co[rt]. That accordingly the same should be done.

[1] STC 1151. The decision of the arbiters is not recorded, cf. *C–B.C*, 172[a], 4 July 1640; 172[b], 7 Sept. 1640.

[2] The payment is recorded in the *Book of Fines*, 29[a], 3 Oct. 1639, but no entry was made in the Registers.

[3] This money was from John Norton's bequest and the bonds were registered 14 Nov. 1639, *Liber C2*, 158[a].

[4] Cf. *C–B.C*, 161[a], 23 Nov. 1638.

Rich: Bishop & Mr Butter.

Vpon the Complaint of Richard Bishop this day against mr Butter for printing one of his Copies called The differences of the Ages of mans Life by mr Cuffe.[1] wthout the knowledge & Consent of the (*said*) Rich: Bishop. It was ordered that the warden taking wth him the Beadle & such as he should thinke fitt should goe & prsently seize vpon the said Booke so disorderly printed & bring them vnto the hall there to remaine vntill further order were taken therein.

4°. Decembris 1639.

Present.

Mr. Smethwick Mr ffetherston Mr Bourne Mr Kingston Mr Harison Mr Rothwell, Mr Downes, Mr Mead, Mr Man, Mr Hoth & Mr Parker.

Dr. Speed.

This day according to an order of the last Cort.[2] Dr Speed deliuered in his Bond of 600li. to be Concelled, & the Mr & wardens in the prsence of the Assistants sealed a Bond wth the Comon seale for 400li. being the remainder vnpaid of the said 600li. vnto Thomas Swinhow to be paid in such manner & forme as the same was to be paid to dr Speed.

7°. Decembris 1639. Fol. 169b

Present:

Mr Smethwick Mr ffetherston, Mr Bourne, Mr Kingston Mr Harison Mr Aspley. Mr Rothwell, Mr Downes, Mr Mead, Mr Man, Mr Hoth & Mr Parker.

Mr Alcornes yeomanry Part. mortgaged to mr Tho: Bourne disposed off to Rapha Harford

Mr Alchorne haueing formerly mortgaged his yeomanry pte in the English stock vnto Thomas Bourne for 80li.[3] wch. hath byn long due & often called for [in] to be disposed of according to mr Alchorne deed by this Cort. The same being taken into Consideracõn It was thought fitt to dispose of the said pte to such pson as should vpon his election into the said pte pay vnto the said Thomas Bourne the said 80li. There stood for the same Mr Harford Mr Emery & Wm. Rothwell.[4] & it fell vpon Mr Harford & the said Mr Harford paid vnto the said Tho: Bourne the said 80li. & tooke vp mr Alchorne Bond & Assignemt. of the said pte to the said Thomas Bourne & Cancelled the same, & was sworne into the said pte according to the vsuall forme.

18°. Decembris 1639. pn'tibus vt antea

Mrs Parsons printing [*Pres*] Stuffe to be devided among the Printers.

This day according to the Direction of Sr. John Lamb all the Mr. Printers were warned vnto the Cort. touching the taking of the Printing Letters. Presses & Implemts. of Mrs. Parsons,[5] & the Cort. wished them to Consider of a Speedy Course for the effecting the same.

[1] STC 6105. Bishop would seem to have a sound case, for his rights may be traced back through five registrations to the original entry of Martin Clarke (cf. Arber. iii. 338, 341, 421, 621; iv. 153 and 459). Butter, on the other hand, could show an assignment to him by John Barnes of 10 Oct. 1620 (Arber iv. 41), but what documentation of Barnes's right he could show is not known, nor the disposition of the dispute.

[2] Cf. *C–B.C*, 169a, 2 Dec. 1639.

[3] Cf. *C–B.C*, 141b, 2 July 1636.

[4] Made free 4 July 1631 (Arber iii. 686).

[5] Regarding Marmaduke Parsons and his relation to A. Mathewes, cf. *Trans.* xvi (1936), 425–32.

19°. Decembris 1639.

Riders Dictionary to be Entred to mr Kingston mr Whitaker mr Waterson mr Crooks mr Nevill and the Pattent to be kept by the Wardens.

This day the Partners. in Riders Dictionary[1] desired the Cort that the said Booke might be entred to them in the Register booke of the Entry of Copies according to their seuerall interests therein, And that the Pattent might be deposited in the Custody of the wardens for the tyme being for the ioynt vse of all the said ꝑties And that the same should not be deliuered to any one of the ꝑties, but vnto the Maior ꝑte of them. Wch the Cort. taking into Consideracõn haue thought fitt & so ordered that the said Copie called Riders dictionary should be entred vnto them according to their request. And that the Pattent shall be kept by the wardens for the tyme being for their vse.

Fol. 170a

3°. ffebruary 1639.

Present

Mr Smethwick, mr ffetherston, Mr Bourne Mr. Kingston Mr Harison mr Aspley Mr Downes, Mead Mr Man mr Hoth & mr Parker.

Mr Harison Mr Badger

Concerning the Warehouse Mr Harison[2] hath & the Roomes Mr. Badger hath,[3] it is to be Considered of next Cort.

Mr Harrigates yeomanry part mortgaged to Mr Partridge

This day mr Harrigate vpon his request by a note vnder his hand & seale, had leaue to mortgage his yeomanry ꝑte in the English stock vnto Mr Partridge for 80li. for a Twelue month at 8li. ꝑ Cent'. The said note beareth date the 3d. of July 1639.

19°. ffebruarij 1639

Present

Mr. Smethwicke Mr. ffetherston Mr Bourne Mr. Kingston Mr. Harrison. Mr. Downes Mr Mead Mr. Man Mr. Parker.

Mr Dickens

This day by consent of a Court an Indenture of agreement betweene Mr Dickens and the Company touching the howse of Office and Stairecase belonging to the howse at Somers Key,[4] were sealed & with the Comon Seale.

2do. Marcij 1639.

Present

Mr. Smethwick Mr. ffetherston Mr. Bourne Mr Kingston Mr. Harrison Mr Aspley Mr Downes. Mr. Mead Mr. Man Mr Hoth. Mr Parker.

Stockeepers.

Mr. Harrison, Mr. Mead	Mr Dawson, Mr. Thrale	Mr. Partridge, Mr. Thomason

Mr. Brewster. Threr' et Juratr.

[1] STC 13621 and 13621a. There are also variant imprints: 'F. Kingston f. A. Crooke, 1640' (copy in Bodleian), and 'F. Kingston, 1639' (copy Harvard), so that all of the partners had copies with their names except Nevill.

[2] This is probably the cellar next the garden, cf. *C–B.C*, 30b, 22 Dec. 1612.

[3] Cf. *C–B.C*, 159b, 27 Aug. 1638.

[4] Cf. *C–B.C*, 85b, 4 Apr. 1625, and 124b, 4 Nov. 1633.

Auditors.	Mr. Hoth Mr. Parker }	Mr. Meredith }	Mr. Marriott Mr. Mozeley.

26°. Martij 1640 Fol. 170b

Present Mr. Kingston loco Mag'ri Mr. ffetherston Mr. Bourne Mr. Harrison Mr Rothwell Mr. Downes Mr. Mead. Mr Man Mr Hoth.

Elleccōn of Rentor wardens. Mr. Seale having served his Rentorshipp was this day wished by the Court (according to the custome) to bring in his Accompt the Sixt of May next which hee promised to doe accordingly, Then Mr Bloome beinge younger Rentor. was chosen in his place for this yeare ensueinge, and the Court elected Mr Bellamy younger Rentor to ioyne with him which they both accepted of

Rentor wardens to bee fyned for not attendance on Court dayes fforasmuch as the Court hath often taken notice of the neglect of the Rentor Wardens in absenting themselues from their attendance at the hall on Court dayes whereby many delinquentę for arrere of quarteridge haue passed without payment which ought to have bin demaunded by the Rentor. It is therefore ordered This day by full consent of the Court That the Rentors for the time to come shall attend at the hall on every monthly Court day, And in case they faile of appearance without iuste excuse That for every such default they shall pay such fyne as the Mr wardens and Assistantę for the tyme beinge shall thinke fitt to impose vpon them.

30°. Martij 1640

Present Mr. Kingston loco Mag'ri Mr Smethwicke Mr. ffetherston Mr. Bourne Mr. Harrison, Mr. Aspley Mr. Downes Mr Mead Mr Man, Mr Hoth Mr Parker.

William Lamberts halfe yeomanry part assigned over to John Lambert. This day William Lambert[1] came to the Court and desired That his halfe yeomanry parte in the English stocke might bee conferred vpon John Lambert[2] his brother a Jornyman Printer, which the Court taking into their Consideracōn gave their consent And the said John Lambert [*gave their consent*] was admitted in the roome of the said William and tooke his oath accordingly.

John Philips 12li. The Court hath graunted to John Philipps the loane of 12li. for 3 yeares putting in good security.[3]

[1] Made free 14 Jan. 1622 (Arber iii. 685).
[2] Made free 31 Mar. 1634 (Arber iii. 687).
[3] On 23 Dec. 1642, bonds were registered in the name of Richard Morgan 'for Jo: Phillips', for the loan of £12, *Liber C2*, 25b.

Mr. Purfoots copies that are not already assigned to bee entred to Richard Lewty.

This day Richard Lewty shewed vnto the Cort. a deed vnder the hand and Seale of Mr Purfoot his father in lawe lately deceased (bearing date the ffourth day of August 1630) and desired that accordinge to the tenor of the said deed the Coppies therein mencõned might bee entred vnto him which deed being read in Court It appeared that the seaven wise masters of Rome and divers other Coppies [*therein mencõned might bee entred vnto him, wch deed beinge read in Cort it appeared the Register booke of this Compie:*] were lately assigned by the
Fol. 171a said Mr. Purfoote to Mr. Blackmore[1] || and others[2] and entred vnto them in the Register booke of this Company Wherevpon the Court ordered (with the consent of the said Richard Lewty) That the seaven wise masters of Roome and the rest of the [*Companies*] Copies that are already made over shall bee crossed out of the said deed and for all other Copies that did of right belong vnto the said Mr. Purfoot at the tyme of his decease (except the breifes)[3] The Court hath ordered shall bee entred to the said Richard Lewty.[4] And concerning the Clayme of [*Richard*] Mr Badger to the said breifes the Cort. hath referred the same vnto Mr. Mead Mr. Man and Mr. Parker whoe are desired to heare and examine the same and report to this Cort. their opinions therein.

The difference concerning the breifes referred to Mr. Man and Mr. Parker

4o. Maij 1640.

Present.

Mr. Smethwick, Mr Aspley loco Gardiani, Mr Bourne, Mr Kingston, Mr Rothwell Mr Downes mr Mead Mr. Man Mr Hoth & Mr Parker.

Rich: Ockold [to] haue his Generall veiwe of Holy Scripture wch. were seized vpon by Mr Hodgkinson.

This day Richard Ockold shewed vnto ye Cort. a peticõn wth a referrence therevnto directed to the Mr. & wardens of this Company about a booke entituled a generall veiw of holy Scripture,[5] the wch were seized & brought to the Comon hall of this Company by mr Hodgkinson & others from Mr Beales house, the Cort. taking the same into Consideracõn haue thought fitt (according to the power to them giuen by the said Refference) and do order that ye said Richard Ockold shall have all the said Bookes deliuered vnto him forthwith.

Mr Clarke to haue 50li. for 3 yeares gratis

The Cort. vpon ye request of Mr Clarke haue granted him the loane of 50li. for 3. yeares gratis putting in good security.[6]

[1] Entered 21 Aug. 1638 (Arber iv. 429).

[2] Other transfers were registered 16 Nov. 1638 (Arber iv. 444) and 1 Feb. 1639 (Arber iv. 454).

[3] Regarding Purfoot's patent for printing briefs, cf. *C–B.C*, 46a, 16 Jan. 1617.

[4] Entered 8 May 1640 (Arber iv. 510).

[5] STC 12983. Cf. Arber iii. 329, 523, and iv. 482. R.O. was dead and this refers to his son, Henry.

[6] His bonds were registered 21 May 1640, *Liber C2*, 122a.

1°. Junij 1640 pn'tibus vt antea.

Mr Okes
Mr Browne
Mr Downes Junr admitted into the Liuery. This day John Okes Samuell Browne & Thomas Downes were admitted into the Liuery of this Company & they paid their fynes of 20li. a peece accordingly.

4°. Junij 1640. Fol. 171b

Present. Mr Smethwick, Mr, Mr Aspley loco Gardiani Mr Bourne mr Kingston Mr Rothwell Mr Downes Mr Mead mr Man Mr Hoth & mr Parker.

Mr Bloome fined for Rentor

Mr Bellamy & Mr Lee Junr Rentors.

This day mr Bloome came vnto the Cort. & shewed that in regard of his often being in [the] Country, he could not doe that service in his place of Rentor warden[1] as he ought & therefore desired he might be admitted to his fyne, wch being taken into Consideracõn it was thought fitt to giue way therevnto & promised to pay his fyne of 24li forthwith. And the Cort. therevpon chose Mr Bellamy & mr Lee Junr. to ioyne wth him to be Rentorwardens for the yeare ensewing.

10°. Junij 1640. pn'tibus vt antea

[*pn't*] Present. Mr Smethwick Mr, Mr Aspley loco Gardiani mr Bourne Mr Kingston, Mr Rothwell Mr Downes mr Mead Mr Hoth Mr Man & Mr Parker

Mrs Jane Nortons pte disposed of.

This day Mrs Jane Norton[2] being dead, election was made for her assistant pte in the English stock, There stood for the same mr Downes mr Bourne & mr Man & it fell vpon mr downes. Then Election was maide for mr downes Liuery pte, there stood for the same mr Meighen & Robte Young & [mr] Roger Norton & it fell vpon mr Norton, Then Election was maide for mr Nortons yeomanry pte & because of many Suitors, they thought fitt to devide the same, one halfe thereof fell vpon mr. Rich: Cotes & the other halfe vpon ffrancis Smethwick & they all tooke their oathes accordingly.

1°. Julij 1640

Arthur Nicholls xxxs. to release him out of prison

Arthur Nicholls[3] prferred a peticõn to ye Cort. this day & shewed that haueing layne many monthes in prison was now to be released onely he wanted a matter of 30. or 40ty shillings to pay his Charges & therefore desired the Company to grant him so much, wch being taken into Consideracõn, was accordingly done & the Clarke is to Carry the xxxs & see him discharged

[1] Cf. *C–B.C*, 170b, 26 Mar. 1640.

[2] Mrs. Bonham Norton.

[3] Made free 3 Dec. 1632 (Arber iii. 687). He was a typefounder and worked for the King's Printers who were setting up a Greek Press at Laud's instigation, cf. his petitions, *State Papers Dom. 1637–1638*, pp. 71–72.

Fol. 172[a]

4°. Julij 1640.

Present. Mr. Smethwick Mr. mr Rothwell loco Mri. ffetherston gar', Mr Bourne Mr. Harison mr Aspley, Mr Downes, Mr Mead, Mr Man, Mr Hoth & Mr Parker.

Priuate Election of Mr & Wardens.}

Mr. Rothwell fyned xxty Nobles for second tyme vpper-warden

Mr Rothwell being by his antiquity to be second tyme vpper warden desired the Cort. in regard of his weakenes & age that he might be putt to his fyne, Wch being taken into Consideracõn was granted & the said Mr Rothwell promised to pay the [accustomed] fyne of xxty. nobles forthwith.

The ffeast day to be on Tewsday Come sennight }

In regard the ffast day is on Wensday next[1] It is by Consent ordered that the Election feast day shall be putt of till Tewsday come sennight.

Mr. Beale readmitted to the Assistants & his fyne of 20ty. Nobles remitted to 3li. }

Whereas Mr Beale by an order of the third of October last[2] for the Causes therein expressed was fyned at xxty. nobles for the vse of the Poore & also suspended from this Cort. as an Assistant vntill further order were taken therein, This day the said Mr Beale came & humbly submitted himselfe vnto ye Cort. & promised paymt. of the said fyne of 20ty. nobles & entreated the Cort. that he might be admitted to his place as formerly he was wherevpon ye Cort. taking this his submission & tender of his fyne into Consideracõn, haue thought fitt to accept of Three pound & to remitt the rest of his fyne & that he shall take his place as formerly. wch said 3li. was accordingly paid to mr Warden Bourne.

14°. Julij 1640. pn'tibus vt antea

Election of Mr & Warden.

This afternoone the balletting box by Consent being opened it appeared Mr Aspley to be Mr., mr Downes & mr Man wardens.

mr Wm. Aspley} Mr. } mr. Downes, mr Man } wardens

Auditors for the old wardens Accompt} mr Mead, mr Hoth.

Accompt day to be on the 11th. of August. }

In regard there was a weeke lost[3] of ye accustomed tyme to make vp the wardens Accompt It is ordered that he shall haue till the 11th of August to finish his Accompt.

[1] Wednesday, 8 July 1640, was appointed a general fast, cf. proclamation, STC 9159, and prayers, STC 16557.

[2] Cf. *C–B.C*, 168[a].

[3] Cf. *C–B.C*, 172[a], 4 July 1640.

7°. Septembris 1640.

Mr. Will: Aspley} Mr.
Mr. Tho: Downes} War:
Mr Sam: Man.

Present. Mr. Aspley Mr., Mr Downes Mr Man war. Mr Kingston Mr Smethwicke Mr Mead Mr Hoth & Mr Beale.

Mr. Edwards Mr Whitaker Mr Latham chosen Assistants. This day the Cort. thought fitt in regard diuers of the old Assistants are dead to Call in Mr Edwards, Mr Whitaker & Mr Latham to be assistants wch were accordingly admitted & they tooke their places.

Bacons Essaies Mr Beale brought a Refference this day from my Lord privy Seale[1] to the Mr. & wardens touching a booke called Bacõns Essaies[2] wch the Cort. taking into Consideracõn haue thought fitt to desire Mr Meighen & Mr Bellamy to Consider of the Matter in the said Refference & report to this Cort. their opinions therein wthall Conveniency. And the Cort. hath ordered that ye parties mencõned in the said Refference doe attend the said Mr Meighen & Mr Bellamy that this Cort. may Compose the said difference or report to the Lord privy Seale their opinions therein.

5°. Octobris 1640

Mr. Beale to pay for the ill printing of Puerilis. 6li. 18s. by the next Cort. The Cort. hath ordred that Mr Beale shall pay for the paper Spoiled [in printing] [*about*] Puerilis between this & the next Cort. wch comes to 6li. 18s. at 3s. 6d. p Rheame. & the paper by him printed to be burnt in regard it is vtterly vnserviceable.[3]

Mr Harisons warehouse Concerning the Rent of mr Harisons warehouse,[4] it being putt to voices it was fully agreed he should pay ls. p Ann'.

7°. Octobris 1640.

A letter from the King & diuers Lords & ye Lo: Mayors letters for borrowing of 500li. This day a Letter from my Lord Mayor wth. a Copie of the Kings & the Lords letters inclosed for the Loane of 500li. was read in Cort.[5] And it was thought fitt that enquiry should be made for the taking vp of the said sume at Interest for the supply of the said Loane.

1 Sir John Finch.

2 STC 1151. The decision of the arbiters is not recorded, but at least three copies are known of a reissue of this book with a cancel title having imprint, 'Printed by Jo: Beale for Richard Royston, and are to be sould at his Shop at the Signe of the Angell in Ivie-Lane, 1642'. This may indicate that the matter dragged on for some time.

3 Cf. *C–B.C*, 165b, 27 June 1639.

4 Cf. *C–B.C*, 170a, 3 Feb. 1640.

5 The letters were not transcribed.

Fol. 173a

10. Octobris 1640.

Present. Mr Aspley Mr Downes Mr Man Mr Smethwick Mr. Harison Mr Bourne Mr Mead Mr Beale Mr Hoth Mr Edwards & mr Whitaker.

About the Loane of 500li. to the King — This day a Second Letter was read from my Lord Mayor to this Company for the aforesaid loane of 500li. for his Mats. vse to be lent in Munday next at the furthest wch being taken into Consideracõn It was thought fitt by the generall Consent of this Cort. That for taking vp of the said 500li. wth Interest the ffeathers Taverne shall be mortgaged for the security thereof. And the Court being informed by Mr Parker that Mr fflesher is willing to Lend the said sum̃e vpon the said security for 7li. ꝑ Cent for a yeare. It was thought fitt this day by full Consent of this Cort. That ye said Miles fflesher shall haue a Lease made vnto him of the ffeathers Taverne for fourscore yeares wth an Assignement of the Rent of the said Taverne due vpon mr Dells Lease,[1] wth a proviso that if ffiue hundred Thirty fiue pounds be paid on the day of October 1641. Then ye said Lease to be void, wth such other Couenants as is vsuall in the like nature, and that ye same be engrossed forthwith & sealed wth the Comon seale of this Corporacõn.

Henry Euersden 50li for 3. yeares. — The Cort. hath granted him the Loane of ffifty pounds for 3. yeares gratis putting in good security.[2]

14th. of October 1640.

A Mortgage of the ffeathers Taverne to Mr. fflesher for 535li. for a Twelue month. — This day according to an order of the last Cort. the Mr. wardens & diuers of the Assistants being prsent, The Mortgage of the ffeathers Taverne was sealed wth the Comon seale to mr fflesher for 535li. for a Twelue month.[3]

2o. Novembris 1640. pn'tibus vt antea

Mr. Roger Norton about ye 22li. ꝑ Ann' — Mr Roger Norton came this day in the behalfe of this (*sic*) brother Executor of Mrs Jane Norton deceased & desired payment of his Mothers stock,[4] wherevpon ye Cort. demanded how the Company should be secured the payment of ye 22li. ꝑ Ann' for Newton during Mrs Joyce Norton Life,[5] to wch he made answeare he could say nothing to it, [*for*] but for the Rent due at Michaelmas he agreed should be deducted out of the [first] payment now due.

Luke Norton 12li. — The Cort. hath granted him the Loane of 12li. for the three yeares gratis putting in good security.[6]

[1] Cf. *C–B.C*, 163b, 20 Mar. 1639.
[2] His bonds were registered 27 Oct. 1640, *Liber C2*, 122b.
[3] This does not appear to have been repaid.
[4] Cf. *C–B.C*, 171b, 10 June 1640.
[5] Cf. *C–B.C*, 36b, 22 Nov. 1614.
[6] His bonds were registered 16 Nov. 1640, *Liber C2*, 24b.

Wm. Sheeres xls. for printing of a booke called Edw. ye 5th & Rich ye third

The Cort. hath ordered that Wm. Sheeres shall pay forty shillings to the Poore for the Impression of the Booke called the History of Rich: ye 3d and Edw: 5th in 12°.[1] Wch was printed by Thomas Paine And that the title of the booke shall be altered & said to be printed for the Company & to be sould by Wm. Sheeres or whoome he shall appoint.

Mr ffussell for Psal. & Geneal:

The Cort. hath ordered that Mr ffussell shall haue 8000. Psal. in 8° Minion & 8000. geneal' in 8°. at xd. a peece & one odd hundred Psal: at vjd a peece. The tyme for payment is left to the Stockeepers to appoint, provided it be to the likeing of the Table.

Mr Oulton to haue the printing of the Primer leafe againe wch. was taken from him

whereas the Primer leafe[2] printed by Mr Oulton was taken away from him, for his ill printing thereof by the Stockeepers. This day vpon his humble request & promise not to Comitt the like error againe. It was ordered he should haue ye printing of the said primer Leafe againe.

mr Milborne vli. for the Liueries attendance at his wifes funerall

This day Mr Milborne came vnto ye Cort. & gaue 5li. for the Liueries attendance at his wifes funerall.

Tho: Paines yeomanry Part & the Proffitts thereof mortgaged to Hen: Euersden in part of security of 148li. 16s. 4d for 3. yeares at 8li p Cent'.

Whereas Thomas Paine ye 20th. of June 1639. had leaue of this Cort. to engage his yeomandry pte in the English Stock vnto Wm. ffox als ffaired in pte of security for 110li. wth Consideracõn for the same at 8li. p Cent' for one yeare,[3] Wch sume being fully satisfied vnto the said Wm. ffox als ffaired. The said Thomas Paine this day sent a note vnder his hand & seale & therein humbly desires this Cort. to grant him leaue to mortgage his said pte & the proffitts thereof vnto the said Henry Euersden in in (*sic*) pte of security of 148li. 16s. 4d. wth Consideracõn for the same at 8li. p Cent' for 3. yeares. Wch. the Cort. taking into Consideracõn It was ordered that the said Thomas Paine should haue leaue & liberty to engage his said pte & the proffitts thereof vnto ye said Henry Euersden according to his request as aforesaid.

1 By Sir Thomas More, Wing M 2688. There are two states of the title, the first having the imprint, 'Printed by Thomas Payne for William Sheares, and are to be sold by Michael Young, . . . 1641' (cf. Hazlitt i. 295), and the other with a cancel title with imprint, 'Printed by Thomas Payne for the Company of Stationers, and are to be sold by Mich: Young, at his shop in Bedford-street in Covent-Garden, neere the new Exchange, 1641'. The claim of the Company to this book was that it was reprinted from More's *Workes*, 1557.

2 Presumably the single sheet 12°, *The ABC: with the catechisme*, of which there are several editions (unrecorded in the STC) printed for the Company.

3 Cf. *C–B.C*, 165b.

Thomas Paine & Henry Euersden. | Whereas Henry Euersden hath lately borrowed vpon Bond[1] of the Company the sume of 50li of mr John Nortons bequest for 3. yeares vpon the security of himselfe, his brother George Euersden Cittizen & Skinner of London & Wm. White Cittizen & Haberdasher of London. And whereas Thomas Paine this day mortgaged his
Fol. 174a yeomandry pte in the English stock vnto the || said Henry Euersden for 3. yeares for security of a certaine sume oweing by the said Thomas vnto the said Henry as by the Order therevpon appeare. This day the said Henry made his request to the Cort., that for the security & saueing harmeles of his said suerties from ye payment of ye said 50li. the said Paines yeomanry pte mortgaged to him should be lyable for their security. Wch the Cort. taking into Consideracōn haue thought fitt & so ordered That the said Mortgage to the said Henry shall be for the Counter security of his said suerties.

7o. Decembris 1640

Present. Mr Aspley Mr., Mr Downes Mr Man, wardens mr Harison mr Smethwick mr Rothwell mr Bourne, mr Mead, mr Parker, mr Edwards mr whitaker mr Latham.

Mr Rouses Psalmes entred to mr Nevill to be crossed out of the hall booke. | fforasmuch as Mr Nevill hath lately procured mr Rouses Psalmes printed beyond sea to be licensed here & entred in the Register booke to him.[2] The Cort. this day being enformed that diuers of the Psalmes in the said Booke are Verbatim wth the Companies & litle variacōn in the most pte thereof. It was ordered by full Consent of the Cort. that ye said Entry shall be crossed out of the hall booke & the printing thereof staied.

Wm. Lugger to print The Marriners Mate &c paying xijd vpon a Reame to the Poore | Wm. Lugger had this day leaue of ye Cort. to print an Imprssion of a booke called The Marriners Mate[3] &c paying for the vse of the Poore xijd vpon ye Reame.

To dyne at ye Lord Mayors. | The wardens & Eight others of the Assistants are to goe to my Lord Mayors. to dynner.

Mr. Badger. Vpon the Request of mr Badger to haue [the] Warehouse vnder the hall vntill Winchesters workes[4] be printed wch will be betweene this & the first of March next the Cort. hath granted his request.

[1] Cf. *C–B.C*, 173a, 10 Oct. 1640.

[2] Entered 25 Nov. 1640, Eyre and Rivington i. 3. The book had been printed at Rotterdam in 1638, STC 2737.

[3] Lugger published the second edition of STC 3432 in 1641 under the title *A mate for mariners*, printed for him by B. Alsop and T. Fawcet. A copy of this book, unrecorded by Wing, is in the library of Harrison D. Horblit. T. Woodcock's widow transferred her rights in it to Paul Linley, 9 Feb. 1596 (Arber iii. 58), and Linley's rights were transferred to J. Flasket, 26 June 1600 (Arber iii. 165). On Flasket's death they evidently became derelict.

[4] The fourth edition of Launcelot Andrewes *XCVI sermons* was printed by Badger in 1641. Cf. *C–B.C*, 159a, 27 Aug. 1638.

19°. Decembris 1640. Fol. 174[b]

Present. Mr Kingston loco Mag'ri Aspley defunct', Mr Downes, Mr Man, Mr Harison, mr Smethwick mr Rothwell Mr Bourne Mr Mead Mr Beale mr Hoth Mr Parker Mr Edwards, Mr Whitaker Mr Latham.

Mr Aspleys Assistant Part disposed of. Mr Aspley or late Mr. being dead, ye Cort. went to Election for his Assistant pte, there stood for the same Mr Man mr Bourne & mr Hoth[1] & it fell vpon mr Bourne. There stood for mr Bournes Liuery pte, mr Meighen Mr young & mr Legatt & it fell vpon Mr Meighen. Then in respect of many suitors the Cort. thought fitt to devide Mr Meighens yeomanry pte, one halfe thereof fell to Mr Bartlett & the other to mr Nevill. And they all tooke their oathes accordingly.

[1] Made free 24 Apr. 1598 (Arber ii. 720).

FOL. 79ᵃ

xixᵗʰ June 1604

Receiued by me John pollard Treasurer of the Hospitall of Bridewell, of the mʳ and wardens of Stationers of the citie of London the Sum̃e of fiftene pounds for the vse of the poore harbored in the sayd Hospitall being the fourth parte of a stocke that Raffe Nubery late Stationer of London deceased, bequeued to the vse of the sayde poore by his last will and testament[2] I say R̸ [and is in full payment] } xvˡᵇ—0ˢ.—0ᵈ.

by me *John Pollard* Threasorer/

xxixᵗʰ June 1604.

Receiued by vs Robert paramoure and Edward Matthew churchwardens of the parish of Sᵗ. Brides aƚƚ Sᵗ Bridgettę in the Suburbs of the Citie of London the Sum̃e of fisteene (*sic*) pounds to the vse of the poore of the sayd parish being the fourth parte of a stocke that Raffe Nubery late Stationer of London deceased bequeued to the vse of the sayd poore by his last will and testament we say Rec. in full.... } xvˡⁱ—0—0

Robert paramor
Edward mathewe } Churchwardens

xixᵗʰ Maij 1605

Receiued by me Robert Cogan Treasurer of christs his hospitall, of the master and wardens of Stationers of the Citie of London the Sum̃e of fifteene poun̄ds, to the vse of the poore Children harbored in the foresayd Hospitall being the fourth part of a stocke that Raffe Nubery late Citizen and Stationer of London deceased, bequeued to the vse of the sayd poore children by his last will and testament and is in full payment of his sayd bequest I say R̸.............. } xvˡⁱ—0—0

Robart Cogan thʳ

1604 2° R R J [*in another hand*]

FOL. 79ᵇ To the Mʳ & Wardens of
the Companie of Stacon's

By the Mayor

Where at the Coẽn Councell Holden in the Guildhall of this Cytie the xxiijᵗʰ of this instante Auguste yt was amongeste other thingę enacted graunted and Agreed that the som̃e of ffyftene Thowsand poundę should be p̲n'telie lente vnto the Kingę moste excellent Maᵗⁱᵉ: by all the seu'all Companies of this Cytie,[3] The same to be

[1] There is no title but the early eighteenth century binding is labelled 'ORDERS OF | PARLIAMᵀ· & | Lᴰ· MAYOR | LIBER | A | '.

[2] Newbery's will is calendared in Plomer, *Wills*, pp. 39–40.

[3] Cf. F. C. Dietz, *English Public Finance* (1932), p. 115.

repayed by his highnes at or before the xxiiijth of Marche 1605, And to be taxed accordinge to the rates agreed vppon the xxvjth of Auguste in the time of the Maieraltie of Sr Richard Saltonstall Knight deceased/ At w^{che} time the Citizens of London lente to o^{r} late sou'eigne Ladye quene Elizabeth the som̃e of Twentie Thowsand poundꝭ In ꝑformance whereof theis shalbe in his Ma^{te}: name streightlie to Charge and Comaund you that ꝑn'tlie vppon the receipte hereof wthout any maner of delaye you call before you the Assistantꝭ and Suche others of yor said Companie as you shall thinke good and indeferentlie taxe vppon such ꝑsons of yor Companie as free of the Citie the som̃e of Cxij^{li} x^{s}, Allotted and proportioned vnto yor said Companie to lend/ And the same to levy ꝑn'tlie And to paye ou' to Sr Thomas Lowe Knight appointed Thr̃er in that behalf before the ffyveth daye of September next insuinge Whereof see you fayle not as you tender his heighnes service and will Answere the contrarie at yor ꝑill yf through yor defaulte the same shall not be dulie & spedilie effected./ Guildhall this xxiij of Auguste 1604

Sebright./

Mr Man: M^{r}
Mr John Norton } W^{r}dens
Mr Leake }

Accordinge to the w^{che} precepte the said M^{r} and Wardens on the xxvijth of Auguste 1604 did holde A Courte of Assistenteꝭ, And wth thassent [of the] same Courte of Assistenteꝭ did indiferentlie taxe & Assese the foresaid Cxij^{li} x^{s} to be levyed and Receaved vppon theis ꝑsons and in theis rates followinge/ viz

Assistenteꝭ Mr Man . . . . vj^{li}
Mr Norton . . . . vj^{li}
Mr Leake . . . . iiij^{li}
Mr Byshoppe . . . . vj^{li}
Mr Harryson thelder . . . . iiij^{li}
Mr Dawson . . . . iij^{li}
Mr Barker . . . . x^{li}
Mr Windet . . . . ij^{li}
Mr Whyte . . . . iiij^{li}
Mr Seaton . . . . iij^{li} Fol. 80a
Mr Waterson . . . . iij^{li}
Mr Hoop . . . . ij^{li}
Mr Easte . . . . j^{li}
M^{r} ffeild . . . . iij^{li}

57^{li}

Liu'ye Mr Grene . . . . ij^{li}
Mr Seres . . . . ij^{li}
Mr Askewe . . . . iiij^{li}
Mr Keyle . . . . [*ij^{li} iiij^{li}*] ij^{li}
Mr Linge . . . . ij^{li}
Mr Standishe . . . . ij^{li}
Mr Lownes . . . . iij^{li}
Mr Rogers . . . . ij^{li}
Mr Adames . . . . iij^{li}

Mr Burbye	iijli
Mr Occold	iijli
Mr Newton	[iijli] ijli
Mr Cole Procter	iijli
Mr Banckworth	iijli
Mr Swenoe	iijli
Mr Mathewe Lownes	[iijli] ijli
Mr Jagger	ijli
Mr Orien	ijli
Mr Guiltman	ijli
Mr Cooley	ijli
Mr Smithe	ijli
Mr Jones	jli
Mr Holmes	ijli
Mr Dight	jli
Mr Knight	jli
Mr Pavier	jli
	57li
	Sm̃ to is—114li—0s—0d

Fol. 80b And yt is ordered by the same Courte That yf his Matie: repay not the foresaid some of Cxijli xs at or before the xxiiijth of Marche 1605/ That then the said ꝑsons vppon whome the same is Assessed as aforesaid shall make payment thereof to the Companie after the rates sett downe againste their names as before appeareth.

Fol. 81a 1609. 7mo Regis/

Mr Bysshopp mr
Mr H. Hooper }
Mr H. Lownes } wardē

The Copy of the receipte vnder Sr Thomas Smithes hand for the Compnies: adventure into Virginia/[1]

viz

Sr Tho: Smithe for the receipte of the 125li for Virginia/.

Virginia [18° hand]

Receiued this 28th of Aprill 1609. of mr Humfrey Hooper & Humfrey Lownes wardens of ye Stacon's of the City of London the sum̃e of one Hundrethe Twenty & ffyve poundē, And is for the sayd Compnies adventure in the voyage to Virginia I say Rd..... } 125li: 0s: 0d:/.

Thus subscribed *Tho: Smythe/.*

Here followeth the Copye of the bill of Adventure vnder seale for the same matter/.

viz̃.

The bill of adventure vnder seale for Virginia/

Whereas the mr & keepers or wardens & Com̃unaltye of the mysterye or Arte of Stacõners of the City of London haue payd in ready money to Sr. Thomas Smythe knight Thr'earer

[1] The Company is recorded in STC 24835 as having ventured £125. For further information cf. Alexander Brown's *Genesis of the United States*, i (1890), pp. 292–3.

for Virginia the sum̃e of one Hundreth Twenty & ffyve pounde for their adventure towarde the sayd voyage It is agreed that for the same they the sayd mr & keepers or wardens & their Successors. (for the tyme beinge) shall haue ratably accordinge to their adventures their full pte of all suche lande, Ten'te, and hereditamte as shall from tyme to tyme be there recou'ed, planted, & inhabited; And of all suche mynes & mynerals of gold, silver, & other mettalls or treasure, Pearles, pretious stones, or any other kind of wares or m'chandizes, com̃odityes, or profitte whatsoeu' wche shalbe obtayned or gotten in the sayd voyage, Accordinge to the porcõn of money by them ymployed to that vse in as ample manner as any other adventurer therein shall receiue for the like sum̃e, Written this 10th of Maye/ 1609.

Thus subscribed/ *Richard Atkinson*/

The wche sum̃e of Cxxvli: was levyed & disbursed in the Compnie: in sorte as followeth viz/.

The disbursers of the 125li: for Virginia/.	mr Byshopp mr of the Compnie	10li:—0s:—0d.
	mr Bonham Norton	5li:—0s:—0d.
	mr Hooper elder warden	3:—0:—0:
	mr H: Lownes yonger warden	6:—5:- -0
	mr Harrison thelder	5:—0—0:
	mr Barker	5:—0—0:
	mr Mann thelder	5:—0—0:
	mr John Norton	10:—0—0:

1609. 7mo. Regis. (*in another hand*) Fol. 81b

[signatures in this column only]		
Edw. Bishop	mr Dawson	3li:— 0s:—0d:
Humfry Hooper/	mr Seton	3:— 0:—0:
Humfrey Lownes	mr Leake	6:— 5:—0:
John haryson	mr Standishe	5:— 0:—0:
Robt Barker	Richard Collins	2:— 0 —0
John Norton	mr Keyle	2:— 0 —0
Thomas Dawson	mr Adames	10:— 0 —0
Simon Waterson	mr Ockold	2:—10 —0
Edward whit	mr Bankworth	3:— 0 —0
Gre: Seton	mr Swinhowe	2:— 0 —0
William Leake	mr John Jaggard	2:— 0 —0
Richard Field	mr Gylman	2:— 0 —0
John Standishe	mr Cole	3:— 0 —0
John Harison	mr Smithe	2:— 0 —0
Ri: Collins	mr Dighte	2:— 0 —0
	mr Knighte	2:— 0 —0
	mr Pavyer	2:— 0 —0
	mr Edw: Bysshopp	2:— 0 —0
	mr Byll	3:— 0 —0

m^{r} Cooke	2:— 0 —0
m^{r} Islipp	2:— 0 —0
m^{r} Kingstone	2:— 0 —0
m^{r} Weaver	2:— 0 —0
m^{r} Lawe	2:— 0 —0
m^{r} Cotton	2:— 0 —0
Richard Boyle	5:— 0 —0
	Sum̃a—125^{li}:—0^{s}—0^{d}.

Thorder for the profitt that shall com̃e of ye aduenture into Virginia/.

Wherevpon it is concluded & ordered this 26th day of June 1609. 7mo. Regis Jacobi/ That eu'y of the same seu'all ꝑtyes that haue seu'ally disbursed the same seu'all sum̃es of money to the sayd adventure, in suche seu'all porcõns as before appeareth, & the seu'all heyres, executo^{rs}. admi'strato^{rs}. & assignes of eu'y of them, shall haue seu'all righte in the sayd adventure & all thingę to proceede thereof, accordinge to the seu'all ꝑporcons of the sayd seu'all sum̃es of money by them seu'ally disbursed & layd downe to the sayd adventure/. And that from tyme to tyme & att all tymes for eu' hereafter, all & eu'y the profittę, com̃odityes, landę, Ten'tę, mynes, myn'alls, estatę, advantages, goods, chattells, wares, m'chandizes, & whatsoeu' els shall resulte & com̃e from tyme to tyme of their sayd adventure, shalbe equally hadd, enioyed, & deuyded betweene the sayd ꝑtyes their heyres executo^{rs} admi'strato^{rs}. & assignes, accordinge to the proporcoñ's afore expressed, wthout any advantage to be hadd or taken to the contrary by survivo^{r}shipp or otherwyse/.

FOL. 82^{a}

1611. 9mo. Regis Jacobi. [*in another hand*]
26to. Octobris.

Mr John Norton m^{r}
m^{r} Rich: Feilde }
m^{r} Hum: Lownes } wardens/.

At Staconers hall in Ave Mary lane/.

Nathanael Butter.

English Stock
[18° hand]

fforasmuche as Nathanaell Butter beinge interessed to a yeomans ꝑte in the graunte & Privilege graunted by the Kinges most excellent Matie. to the Company, by his Highnes ɫres Patentę vnder the greate seale of England Dated the 29th. day of October in the ffirst yeare of his graces raigne of England ffraunce and Ireland, and of Scotland the 37th for the printinge of the booke called Prym̃ers & diuese (*sic*) other bookę, Hathe most vniustly, vndutifully, and deceiptfully and deliberatly, wittingly, and willingly, offended agaynst the sayd grañte & Privilege, & agaynst the good & lawfull ordonñauncę & constitucõns of the Comp^{nie}. made, established, & confyrmed, in due forme of lawe, for the good gouernement & direccoñ of the mayster, wardens & Com̃unalty, concerninge the due execucõn of the sayd grañte & ɫres Patentę/ In that of late he caused & ꝑcured diuerse greate quantityes & numbers of the sayd Prym̃ers, to be printed, at his chargę, & for himself, & to his owne vse, at Dorte in the ꝑties (*sic*) of beyond the

Seas, by George waters a printer there,[1] to whom̃e he wrote letters vnder his owne hand, for the printinge of the same, & sente him a Copy or example ⟨to⟩ printe them by, And besides vsed & hadd, in the ꝑcuringe & accomplishinge thereof, the meanes & furtherañce of Jacob Neuell a Taylo^r. who vpon the ymprintinge of the same bookę, receiued them from him, & brought them ou' to London, for the vse of the sayd Butter, & there delyuered them vnto him, who ꝑcured the sayd Neuell to sell them, in the behalf of him the sayd Butter & for his vse, to one m^r Greene of London bridge, Of whome the sayd Neuell receiued satisfaccõn in money for the same & delyuered it to the sayd Butter/. All w^che offences & matters are done & ꝑcured by the sayd Butter directly & purposedly agaynst the sayd ł̃res Patentę & ordonñances, and are duely & lawfully prooued agaynst him, by the seu'all examinacõns & deposicõns of the sayd Neuell & waters, taken vpon their oathes, at Dorte, before the Burroughmasters, Aldermen, & Councell there, & certifyed vnder their seale, as by the same may appeare/. ffor the whiche offences, The mayster, wardens, & Assistantę beinge this day assembled in full Courte holden in their Com̃on hall, hauinge deliberately consulted & considered of the same, & of the sayd proofes & certificates thereof, & findinge the same offences thereby duely prooued, & purposeinge to proceed agaynst him, for the same, accordinge to the qualitye of his offence, Doo order and Judge, That the stocke, porcoñ, & Interest, that the sayd Nathanaell Butter nowe hath in the premisses or any ꝑte thereof, is & shalbe forfeyted, by force of the sayd ordonñances, to the vse in the same ordonñances expressed, And that his ꝑte & place in the premisses is voyde/ And doo further order, That w^thin one moneth nexte,[2] there shalbe an eleccoñ, accordinge to the sayd ordonñancę, made, of a fitt ꝑson in the Comp^nie. to haue & supply the same ꝑte & place so voyde.

(*Blank page*) Fol. 82 b

Mr Bonham Norton Mr Fol. 83a
Mr Richard ffield } wardens
m^r Rich Ockolde }

The Coppie of a ł̃re written by the lord Maior about the Lotterye/[3]

To my verie lovinge freinds the M^r and wardens of the Companie of Staconers/

After my hartie Comendacõns, Theis are to lett yo^u vnderstand, the I am required by the lordę of his Ma^tę most ho^ble privie Councell to recomend vnto yor Care the effecting of there Lo. desires for the furtherance of the Virginia plantacõn as by there Lo. ł̃res herew^thall sent may appeare/ Wherefore I pray and require yo^u forthw^th to Call a Court and to vse yor best endevo^rs to accomplish there Lo. pleasures in regard it is for so Charitable and Christian worke and by wch meanes we may be disburdened of many Idle and vagrant ꝑsons wch otherwise are and wilbe more and more chardgable dangerous and troublesome vnto the State and so I bid yo^u hartely farewell 20 Aprilis 1614.

Signed./ yor Loving ffreind
Thomas Middleton Maio^r

[1] No copies of these Dort printed primers are known.
[2] Cf. *C–B.C*, 28a, 18 Nov. 1611.
[3] A copy of this letter addressed to the Grocers' Company is printed in Alexander Brown, *Genesis*, ii (1890), p. 688.

The Coppie of the Counsells ler to the same purpose[1]

To or. verye loving freinds the master wardens and assistants of the companie of Stationers.

After or hartie Comendacons wee send you herewth a true declara⟨con⟩ of the estate of the english Colonye planted in Virginia together wth a proiect by help of a Lotterye to bring at length that worke to the succese desired. We shall not need to comend vnto you that worthy and Christian [*exercise*] enterprise full of honor and profitt to his Matie the whole realme if the ende in the said Declaracon expressed may in proces of time be attayn'd vnto, whereof the hopes (as you may perceiue) nowe are great, for the advaunceing and bringing whereof to some good pfection wee hartely pray you to imploye yor good endevors amongst the brethren of yor Company to adventure in the said Lotterye destined to so good a purpose such reasonable somes of money as each of them may conveniently and can willing⟨ly⟩ spare, nothing doubting but that excited by yor good example and perswasion they will shewe them selues forward to adventure in so faire a Lotterye where in happiely they may be Gaynors, and whatsoeuer any one shall loose shalbe bestowed on so good a worke and so behouefull to the whole realme./

You shall alsoo receiue herewth from the Treasurer and Counsell of Verginia such Bookes as ar requisate for the registring of the said somes adventured wch wee pray you wth as much expedicon as may be in regard of there present wante to sett forth a shipp thether this Spring to returne wth the mony gathered to the said Threasurer from whom wee will take notice of yor proceedinge herein that we may accordingly giue you deserved thanke for the same. And so wee bid you hartely farewell, from the Court at Whitehall this first of Aprill 1614/.

Signed/ Yor Loving freinde

G: Cant: | T Suffolke | E Worcester | Lenox
Pembroke | Exeter | W. Knowlles
Jul: Caesar.
Tffuhoppe.[2]

Fol. 83b Junij 12° 1614/ A Coppie of a note from Sr Tho: Smith about ye Lotterie/ (*in another hand*)

Whereas the some intended to be raysed by the late Lotterye for the suppartacon o fthe Plantacon of Virginia proved fare short of the proposicon by reason the want of time prevented the procuring of a Competent some but yet gave the world good satisffaction of the iust and vpright Carriage thereof, The Counsell and Company therefore desireing to make better vse of his Mate most gratious graunt have re-solued of an other standing Lottery according to a Declaracon herewthall sent, And doe intreat you the Master wardens and assistante of the Company of Stacionrs to moue yor brethren and pticuler freinde to make such adventures vnto the same wch shalbe carryed wth as even a hand as the former desireing you to Returne the

[1] This is printed from the Grocers' Company records in Alexander Brown, *Genesis*, ii (1890), pp. 685–6.

[2] That is what the signature appears to be but it may stand for Sir Ralph Winwood who was sworn of the Council 29 March 1614, and was present this day.

booke it self vnto Sr Thomas Smith Knight or Threasurer wth the names of all such as shall aduenture together wth there somes of money to be entred into or Lottery bookes wth all expedicōn the better to enable vs to send supplyes into Virginia and prepare the busines in a readienes for the spedier drawing of it out and also to prevent the infinite trouble and confusion or officers are drawne into when the names and money are deferd and not brought in till the vtmost tyme. and vpon Receipt of the same or said Threasurer will giue an acquittance for every some ꝑtionlerly (*sic*) geoven vnder or seale the 14th Day of Aprill 1614

Signed Tho. Smith./

Mr Norton mr.
mr ffield }
mr Ockold } wardens

Upon the receipt of these lrēs the Mr and wardens at a Court of Assistantę holden the 17th day of May[1] wth the Assent of the same Court did agree and order that the [*the*] some of 45li should be put in to the Lotterye in the name of the Companye, and that if any prize or profitt come thereon it should be to the Stocke and devided among the ꝑteneres in the priveledg according to the rate that is venterd by them that is to say every assistant xxs. everye liverye man—xs and the [*liverye*] yeomandry vs a peece. Wch amounteth to the said some of 45li. wch was delivered to Sr. Thomas Smith 27° Junij 1614

Teste *Tho Mōntforte*

24th June 1614 A Coppie of a Precept to forbid all feasts in Halles for sixe Monethes (*in another hand*) Fol. 84a

By the Mayor[2]

To the Mr and Wardens of the Companye of Stacioners

Mr Norton Mr.
Mr ffeild }
Mr Ockold } Wardens.

Whereas my self and my Brethren the Alldermen haue entred into due Consideracōn of the excessiue prizes and Rates of all sortes of Grayne and other kind of victualles not onely wthin this Cittie, but also through the whole realme, And in regard thereof and for remedie therein as much as in vs lyeth have thought fitt to make a restraynt amongest the seu'all companyes of this Cittie from the excessiue spending of all kind of victuall by reason of there seu'all feastę and dinneres these are therefore to will and require you to forbeare the makeing of any feast or dinner at the election of yor Master and wardens this yeare as in former yeares you have accustomed or any other dinner or supper at all at yor hall for the space of sixe monethes nowe next ensuing But that you doe for the Cōmon good of yor Companye collect and receive of such persons as ought to be at the Chardge thereof so much as should haue ben expended [*thereby*] thereby And to be very Carefull to obserue this Cōmand as you will answer the Contrary Dated this 24th of June 1614

Weld

[1] Cf. *C–B.C*, 34a.

[2] Cf. *C–B.C*, 35b, 19 Oct. 1614

FOL. 84[b]

By the Maio[r]

To the M[r] and wardens of the Company of Stationers

supply must forthw[th] of

M[r] Man Mr.
M[r] Leake. } wardens
M[r] Adames}

for Ireland

Whereas the sōme of fortie thousand poundę hath heretofore ben taxed and gathered of the seu'all Companies of this Cittie for and towards the plantacōn in Ireland and forasmuch as the sōme is whollie expended, And further necessitie be made It was therefore at a Cōmon Counsell holden at Guildhall on the eleventh day of this instant moneth of January enacted and agreed that a pñte taxacōn of seaven thousand and fiue hundred pounds shalbe made to be taxed and leved of the seu'all Companyes of this Cittie according to the late allotment and proporcōn whereby the last fiue thousand poundes was taxed and assessed. And that fiue thousand pounds a part thereof shalbe spedily raised levied and paid on or before the last day of this pñte moneth of January vnto Mr Cornelius Fish Chamberleyne of this Cittie who is appointed Thrcasurcr for the receit and payment thereof and two thousand and fiue hundred pounds the residue thereof shalbe paid on or before the first day of the moneth of may nowe next coming And whereas according to the rate and proporcōn whereby the last fiue thousand pounds was levied and Gathered, and according to the true intent of the said act of Cōmon Counsell yor Company is to furnish and pay towards the said sōme of seauen thousand and fiue hundred pounds the some of one hundred and fiue poundes. These are therefore in his Ma[ties] name straightly to Chardg and Cōmand yo[u] pñtely to call a Court of Assistants and then to elect such of yo[r] Company as yo[u] shall thinke fitt to Joyne w[th] yo[u] the Master and wardens in taxeing and assessing of the some of one hundred and fiue pounds by the pole or otherwise w[th]in yo[r] Company and pñtely to Collect the same and that yo[u] pay two parts in three parts to be devided of the said sōme of one hundred and fiue pounds in m[r] Chamberleynes office in the Guildhall before the last day of this instant moneth of January, and that yo[u] pay the other third part of the said some of one hundred and fiue pounds in the said m[r] Chamberleines office before the said first day of May, and hereof faile yo[u] not at yo[r] perrill, Dated at Guildhall the xvi[th] day of January. Anno 1614[1]

Weelde.

FOL. 85[a]

By the Maior./[2]

To the M[r] and Wardens of the Company of Stacioners./

M[r] Man m[r].
M[r] Leake } Wardens
M[r] Adames}

Where I and my brethren Th'aldrēn haue Resolued and agreed that for and toward the provision of Corne for this Cittie especially for the poore in the same the quantitie of ten thousand quarters of wheat should be forthw[th] prouided and bought by all the seu'all Companyes of this Cittie according to the quantitie as every Company by Act of Common Counsell lately made in that behalfe haue ben rated att. In accomplishm[t] whereof These are to will and require yo[u] and in his Maties (*name*) straightly to Chardge and Cōmand yo[u] that yo[u]

[1] Cf. *C–B.C*, 26[b], 27[a].

[2] Cf. *C–B.C*, 38[a], 22 Mar. 1615.

provision of Wheate./

buy and prouide one hundred and fortie quart[rs] of wheat w[ch] rateably is appointed and proporcõned for yo[r] Company according to the same act and that the same be bought provided and layd vp in Granaryes w[th]in this Cittie for the service and prouision thereof before the last day of March next at the furthest as yo[u] tender the good of this Cittie and will answere the Contrary if thorough yo[r] default that servuice shall in any part be neglected, This xxxj[th] of January, 1614/

Weld.

M[r] Man m[r]
m[r] Leake. } wardens.
mr Adames }

Copia/ A lẽr written by the Lord Archbishop of Canterburie his Grace to the Lord Maior in the behalfe of the Stacioners/

After my hartie Comendacons I am enformed by the m[r] and wardens of the Companye of Stacionrs that one wm Nethersall and an other Called Richard Peirce haue made Complaint vnto yo[r] Lo[p] That by vertue of a warrant granted from his Ma[ties] Comission[r]s for Causes ecclicall certayne bookes of thers haue ben seized vpon and that o[r] messengers in the executing of the same haue enfringed the Liberties of the Cittie: ffor myne owne part I knowe what belongeth to such a worthie place as whereof yo[r]. Lo: is at this time his Ma[ties] Leifetenant and a principall officer. and I shall ever be carefull to preserue the rights belonging to the same. But I pray yo[r]. Lo: to consider whether it appertayneth vnto yo[u] to iudge of matters concerning bookes and whether it be any encrochment or no, that the B[p]. of London or the archbishop of Canterbury either as a high Comissione or otherwise should deale in Causes ecclicall w[th]in that Cittie, since his Ma[tie] accordinge to the Custome of [his] predecessors hath granted his Comission for Causes ecclicall to be executed throughout all England and Ireland in places exempt and not exempt and by name hath comitted vnto vs all questions and differences concerning printing and selling of bookes, and there be auncient orders of starchamber from time to time renewed concerning that matter And whether o[r] purseuante shall execute o[r] Mandate in these kindes I hope yo[r] Lo: will not nowe dispute in as much as that hath ben time out of minde w[th]out all Contradiction performed and we cannot order any thinge appertayneing to o[r] Jurisdiction vnles that o[r] messengers carryeing themselues Lawfully may w[th] free Libertie performe those thinge w[ch] [*as*] [are] given them in Chardg from vs; all w[ch] I recomending to yo[r] Lo: Care doe rest

Seizure of Books.

Yo[r] Lo: verye Loving freind
G: Cant:

Lambith febr 8.
1614.

To the right ho[ble] S[r] Thomas Hayes knight
Lord Maior of the Cittie of London. }

Fol. 85b By the Mayor

To the Master and wardens of the Company of Station[rs]

Mr Dawson. Master.
Mr Lounes sen' } wardens.
Mr Swinhowe }

Whereas at the Cōmon Counsell holden the first day of May nowe last past it was enacted that diuers aldreñ and Cōmon[rs] of this Cittie should take Consideracõn of all greavances hinderances and Inconveniences arisinge to this Cittie and the freemen theirof by aliens & strangers borne or other forreno[r]s as doe dwell or reside in this Cittie or the liberties thereof. And to consider of some meanes for redresse thereof And whereas it is desired by the said Cōmittees and thought fitt by my self and my brethren that their should be a certificat made by all the seu'all companies of this Cittie vnto the said Cōmittees of such greavances and other Inconveniences as they shall finde in their seu'all companies or can any way giue Informacõn of or concerning the same. Theis are therefore to require yo[u] forthw[th] vpon the Receite hereof to assemble a gen'all court of assistantę and call before yo[u] such other of the Company as yo[u] shall think fitt And amongst yo[r]selues to take deliberate Consideracõn of the said Cause and therevppon to make Certificate vnder yo[r] handę vnto the said Cōmittes of all such greavances as yo[u] shall finde concerninge the said aliens strangers and forreno[r]s and likewise of such Inconvenieñcę as yo[u] shall conceive fitting to be reformed, And that yo[u] deliuer the same yo[r] Certificate ou' to M[r] Towneclarke before the twentith day of this Instantę July to the Intent that vpon the Certficate (*sic*) made by all the said Companies that the said Comittees may grounde a reporte accordinge as is required by the said act of Coēn Counsell for the reformacõn of the same in such manner as they in their discretions shall thinke fitt, And herein I require yo[u] not to faile as yo[u] tender the good of this Cittie in gen'all and eu'y of yor owne goodes in perticuler dated at Guildhall this viij[th] of Julye 1615.

Weld./

Aliens (*in another hand*)

To the right ho[ble] S[r]. John Jolles Knight Lo. Maior of the Cittie of London and to the right wor[ll] the aldermen of the same.

The humble peticõn of the Company of Stationers in London, Humbly shewinge vnto yo[r] good Lo. and wor[ps] that thorough the multitude and exceeding great number of Aliens forreno[rs] and strangers dwellinge enhabiting and lodging w[th]in this Cittie and subvrbes thereof wee the freemen shopekeprs and others are dayly hindered and much Impou'ished ffor that the said strañgers contrary to the auncient lawes of this land and ffran[chizes of this] Cittye haue encroached into there handę the greatest part of the traffique & tradinge, and by there repaireing hether house rent and victualls are growne to so high arate that we are not able to maynetane o[r] selues o[r] wiues and families &c. Wee therefore pray yor lo. and wor[ps] to become peticõners to his ma[tie] to giue speedie remedie to theis grevances &c. and we shall euer pray &c.

Fol. 86a To my wor[ll] frendes the Master and wardens of the Company of Printers

After my very hartie Cōmondacõns. Whereas Mr Adams one of yor Company doth challendge a booke called the table of yeares[1] &c. as rightfully belonging vnto him

[1] STC 13779.

& you haue caused an other booke wch you name the Concordancie of yeares[1] &c. likewise to be published; betwixt which two bookes sauing that in yors their are some little additions,[2] there is no materiall difference as by the pvsall thereof wch I haue caused carefully to be made doth appeare. theis are therefore to wish you (it coming vnto my notice by iust complaint and greavance) that you forbeare hereafter to depriue him of his due concerning that booke by Imprinting the other. Considering that it may be the [*Cause*] Case of eu'y perticuler man amongst you to suffer the like, & that vnkindnes and breach amongst your selues may giue occasion to others to offer vnto you those wronge wch you would lothlye endure, & wch for myne owne part I shall euer be readie wth my best assistance to keepe you from, So comending you all to the Grace of God I rest. ffrom ffulhm this 14th of Septemb 1615./

Literary property [18° hand]

Yor. very loving freind
John London.

To my worll freindes the Master and wardens of the Company of Printers be theise/

After my very hartie Comendacōns. I nothing doubted but that at yor last being wth me I had made an ende of the quarrell betwixt Mr Adams and you. I delt as equally and vnpartially as possibly I could on both sides. thinkeing it vnfitt on the one part, that Mr Adams should printe more then his owne Copie or you defraude him of that Copie by imprinting some few addicōnall notes and rules. vnder colour whereof his booke should become altogether fruitlesse. besides I grounded my self therein opon an order made by yor selues wch you ought not to infrindge. This order and Conclusion then made I held to be very iust and indifferent and Continue still of the same minde. Notwthstanding I am since enformed that you goe onward wth the imprinting of that other booke contrary to yor owne order and my resolution and to the manfest (*sic*) and willfull iniury of a brother of yor. owne societie wch once more I wish and require you to forbeare, otherwise it may fall out in the ende (whereof I shalbe loth) to proue some vnkindnes betwixt you and me, wherein first or last yor part may be the worse but I hope you will be wiser and frindlier, & so I comend you to the grace of god, and rest

yor very loving freind
Fulham septemb. 29 1615. John London.

To the Master and wardens of the Company of the Stationrs

Theis are to require you that you giue presente order to Okes the printer at holborne bridge that he proceede not wth the impression of the booke called the Concordancye of yeares[3] wch he is in hand wth at his and yor perilles London house in hast this 14th of Octob. 1615.

John London.

[*Blank*] Fol. 86b

[1] STC 12166. [2] This is not exactly true. [3] STC 13779. Cf. *C–B.C*, 42b, 6 Mar. 1616.

FOL. 87a Mr Carmarden his Petecõn

To the Kings most excellent Matie
The humble peticoñ of Richard Carmarden.

Mr Dawson Mr
Mr Lownes Sen } wardens
Mr Swinhowe

Fines [*another hand*]

Sheweth that whereas it pleased yor Matie to bestowe vpon yor humble Supliant, for recompence of service done to yor Matie two third partẹ of an ouer plus of money receiued by Peter Vanloue vpon the transportacoñ of 15000 broade wollen Clothes free of Custome and other duties which the right hoble the Lo: Chamberleine that nowe is would not suffer to [*pase*] passe the seales for some reasons wherewth his Lope acquainted yor maitie as he then alledged vnto the peticõnr Neuertheles it pleased yor highnes to promise any other thinge in yor Maties Guifte that I could find out.

Nowe forasmuch as there are diuers fines and forfeitures taken by the Company of statioñrs to the late queenes and yor maties vse by vertue of a Decree made (*by*) the Courte of Starchamber the 23th Day of June in the 28th yeare of the said late queene and afterwardes Confirmed by yor Maties Leřs pattentẹ made in the first yeare of yor Maties raigne alwaies reservinge the right of the said ffines and forfeitures vnto yor owne vse yor heires and successors. All which said fines and forfeitures the said Company haue Cõverted to there owne vse neuer payinge or makingẹ any account for the same. And haue also contrary to their owne ordinances doubled the prizes of Bookẹ vpon the subiectẹ of this Kingd⟨om⟩

May it therefore please yor most excellent Matie. to grant vnto yor humble suppliant all the arrerages of those fines and forfeitures paieinge one third parte of such moneyes as shalbe recou'ed into the receite. And also to grant a lease of fortye yeares of all such fines and forfeitures as shall hereafter growe due vnto yor Matie. yor heires and successors for which yor peticoñr will pay into the Receite a hundred Markẹ yearely, and euer pray for yor Maties longe life &c.

FOL. 87b The answere therevnto.

The most humble answere of the Master and wardens of the Company of Stationrs of the Cittie of London to the peticoñ of Richard Carmarden

ffirst as to the vniust Chardge by the peticõnr burthened vpon the Company of stationrs in receiuinge and Convertinge to their owne vse of diu's fines and forfeitures by vertue of the Decree of the Court of starchamber made in the 28th yeare of the raigne of the late quene Eliz. They say and doe mainetaine that nether they nor any of their predecessors to their knowledge did at any time receiue any fines or forfeitures to the vse of the late queene or of the kingẹ matie by vertue of the said Decree nether had they any power thereby so to doe. Onely they haue warrant by the said decree to seaze bookẹ printed Contrary to lawfull authoritie which warrant they haue soñe times vsed and thereby haue meet wth popish schismaticall and other vnlawfull bookẹ and from time to time brought them to the Lo. Arch. [of Canter] his Grace or the Lo. Bishoppe of London and so by one of their Comandemtẹ the said bookẹ haue ben burnte. And also some fewe other bookẹ printed Con-

trary to privelege they haue also seazed but neuer Converted them to any benefitt and they are laide vp in their hall extant at the pleasure of his Matie and the Chardge in seazinge and findinge out thereof doth far surmount the value of the said bookes. Secondly touchinge the doublinge of prizes vniustly supposed by the peticoñ[r] they affirme and are readie to averr that they haue not there in done any thinge against any lawe or statute of this Realme nor haue they exceeded in the prizes so farr as any haue Cause to Complaine thereof. And for the other part of the peticõnrs suite which is for a lease for 40 yeares of all such fines and forfeitures as shall hereafter growe to the Kinge Matie his heires and successo[rs] the said M[r] and wardens affirme there hath ben no fines or forfeitures incurred since the arte of printinge began which can incourage the peticõnr if he meane plainely to yeald to his ma[tie] such rent as he offereth in his peticoñ, [*and*] and therefore vnder that pretense aymeth at some other thinge which it seemeth he is ashamed to expresse, as all other doe that vnder pretence of faire showes vnduly endevo[r] to gett the benefitt of penall lawes into their owne handes by way of monopoly. And the purpose of the peticõnr must of necessitie be to haue power of himself for private vniust gaine to dispense wth all offendo[rs] that shall print or binde english bookes beyond the seas and transport them hether or otherwise print vnwarranted booke here in England and of himself Clerely to overthrowe the Care as well of the high Court of parlement as of the ho[ble] Court || of Starchamber for establishinge of good and wholesome Lawes and ordi- Fol. 88[a]
nances in the arte of printinge bookesellinge and booke bindinge, w[th]out which the peticõner can by this suite make any profitt att all, as the said master and wardens are readye to maintaine which Course the said master and wardens hope his Ma[tie] will Consider is agaiñst his highnes gratious purpose which alwaies hath ben to giue life to the lawes and not to Coñitt the dispensacõn thereof to any subiect of the peticõnrs place and quallitie.

The Copies of 2 acquittances by Captaine Dauis and m[r] Christian and m[r] Mottershed Fol. 88[b]
for the paymt of 40[li] paid by the partenors in the English stocke according to a sentence in the high Comission Court against Tho. Dawson[1]/

Tho: Dawson Memorand That where a fine of ffortie pounds was the twelth daie of October last past imposed and set by his Maties Comission[rs] for causes Ecclesiasticall, vpon Thomas Dawson of London Stacõner. And where the Kings Matie by his highnes letters patents vnder the great seale of England dated the 25th. daie of March last past hath giuen and granted vnto me Edward Dauies of March Baldwyn in the Countie of Oxford Esquire one of his Maties. gentlemen Vshers, quarten wayters, the said some of ffortie pounds excepting a fourth part heretofore granted by his hignes by letters Patents to Robert Christian Esquire, and Thomas Mottershed gentlemen, as by the said letters patents to me graunted inrolled in his highnes Court of Exchequer in the custodie of his Maties remembrancer more at large maie appeare. Nowe theis presents witnes that for consideracõns me moving,

[1] Dawson, who was Master at this time, apparently was fined in his official capacity. The English stock had evidently printed some Psalms infringing Barker's privilege, cf. grant of the 'mitigated fine of £40' (i.e. it had originally been much more) to Captain Edward Davis, *State Papers Dom. 1611–1618*, p. 356; *Sign Manual*, vol. v, n. 88, 20 Mar. 1616; and memorandum *C–B.C*, 43[b], 7 June 1616.

I the said Edward Dauies have remitted and released the said Thomas Dawson the said three parts, of the said fyne or some of ffortie pounds to me as aforesaid graunted, In witnesse I haue herevnto sett my hand and Seale this first daie of May, Anno Dñi 1616

Edw. Davys

Sealed and deliu'ed in the pc̃e
of Sam Neyland
N Browne

Memorandũ that whereas a fyne of ffortie pounds, was the twelfth daie of October last, ymposed and set by his Maties. Comission[rs] Ecclesiasticall vpon Thomas Dawson of London Stacõner, one fourth part whereof, is by his Maties. letters patents vnder the great seale of England given and granted vnto vs Robert Christian, and Thomas Mottershed his Maties. Collecto[rs] & Receiuo[rs] of all the fynes and forfeitures accrewing to his Matie. by vertue of his hignes Com̃ission or Com̃ission[rs] Eccłicall, and growne due vnto vs his highnes said Receiuers. Knowe all men by their ꝑn'tes That wee his Maties. Collecto[rs] and Receiuo[rs] aforesaid, for and in consideracõn of the some of Ten pounds of lawfull English money to vs paid, haue remitted and released and for euer by their ꝑn'tes, doe remitt release and acquite the said Thomas Dawson his heires Executo[rs] [*and*] Adm'strato[rs] and Assignes, and everie of them, of the said some of Ten pounds due to vs his highnes said Receiuo[rs], And by theis pn'tes doe clerelie discharge them for euer, In witnes whereof wee haue sett to our hands and seales this first daie of Maie. Anno dñi 1616

Rob. Christian
Tho. Motteshed (*sic*)

Sealed and Deliu'ed in the pc̃e
of Tho Jones.
Tho Montforte

Fol. 89[a]

The Copie of a writeinge vnder the Com̃on seale.
to his ma[tis] Printer m[r] Robert Barker/[1]

To all xxĩan people to whom this pñte writinge shall come we Thomas Dawson m[r] Humfrey Lownes and George Swinhowe keepers or wardens of the Art or mistery of Station[rs] [*and*] of the Cittye of London, and the Cominaltie of the said arte or mistery. Doe send greetinge in our Lord God eu'lastinge. Where as vpon a surrender made by vs of the lẽrs pattentɇ of o[r] sou'aigne Lord the Kingɇ Ma[tie]. vnto vs formerly graunted, amongst other thingɇ of the priveledge of printinge of Prim[rs] psalters and psalmes. It hath pleased his ma[tie] of his gratious pleasure in respect of some defectɇ which we doubted to be in the said pattent to renewe the same lrẽs pattentɇ vnto vs wth amendement of the defectɇ therein and hath signed a bill in that behalf which bill beinge so signed and readie to passe the privie seale amongst other thingɇ Contayneth an exception in theis wordes, vizt. The bookɇ of Com̃on praier vsually reade or to be reade in the Churches of Englande together wth all bookɇ Contayned in the lrẽs pattentɇ of the office of o[r] printer granted to Robert

[1] Cf. *C–B.C*, 42[a], 5 Mar. 1616.

Barker, and Christofer his sonne (other then the said booke or booke͡ɛ or prim^rs psalters and psalmes in meeter or in prose alwayes excepted and foreprised, And whereas the said Robert Barker and Christopher Barker haue taken exception at theise words (other then the said booke or booke͡ɛ of prim^rs psalters and psalmes in meeter or in prose) and are vnwillinge that theis wordes should be inserted and passed in the lrẽs pattente͡ɛ to be newly granted vnto vs in respect they were not expressed or mencõned in the lrẽs pattente͡ɛ by vs surrendred as aforesaid, and feareinge and suspectinge that theis wordes may heareafter be expounded or Constreued to the Damage or hinderance of them and their assignes exerciseinge the office of printer to o^r sou'aigne Lorde the Kinge͡ɛ Matie his heires and successo^rs for the time beinge. Therefore nowe knowe [*wee*] yee That wee the said Master and keeps or wardens and Cōmunaltye of the said Art or mistery of Station^rs of the Cittye of London, to the ende that all scruple or doubt concerninge the Interpretacõn of the wordes aboue mencõned might at all times hereafter be cleared remoued and vtterly taken away doe for o^r selues and o^r successo^rs, Master keepers or wardens and Comuñaltie of the said art or misterye for the time beinge Couenant promise grant and agree to and wth the said Robert Barker and Christopher Barker their executo^rs administrato^rs deputies and assignes by their pñtes that nether wee the said master keepers or wardens and Comuñaltie of the said arte or mistery of Station^rs no^r o^r successo^rs or assignes for the time beinge shall at any time or times hereafter take any benefitt or advantage against the said Robert and Christofer Barker or against their deputies or assignes by reason of the said exception and words incerted vizt (other then the said booke or bookes of || prim^rs psalters or psalmes in meeter or proes) in the said newe Lers pattente͡ɛ granted vnto vs but will wholly relye vpon the wordes of the said Grant and the true entent and meaneinge of the same. In witnes whereof we haue herevnto sett o^r Comon seale this fiveth day of march 1615 and in the yeares of the reigne of o^r sou'aigne Lorde James by the Grace of God Kinge of England Scotland, ffrance and Irelande͡ɛ Defendo^r of the faith &c; that is to say of England ffrance and Ireland the thirteenth and of Scotland the nyne and fortith./ FOL. 89^b

primers Psalters Psalms [18° hand]

A ler̃ from my Lo. Grace of Cant about s^r Walter Rawleys Cronicles/[1]

To my very louing freinds the Master and wardens of the Company of Statiōnrs giue theis/

After my hartye Cōmendacōns I haue receiued expresse direction from his Matie that the booke Lately published by Sr Walter Rawleigh[2] nowe prisoner in the Tower should be suppressed and not suffered. heareafter to be sould, This is therefore to require yo^u in his Ma^tyes name that pñtely yo^u repaire vnto the printer of the said booke͡ɛ as also vnto all other stationers, and bookesell^rs which haue any of them in their Custodie, and that yo^u doe take them in and wth all Conuenient Speed that may

[1] Reprinted Arber v. lxxvii.

[2] STC 20637. In a letter from Chamberlain to Carleton, *State Papers Dom. 1611–1618*, p. 269, 5 Jan. 1615, it is explained 'Sir Walter Raleigh's book, which he hoped would please the King, is called in, for too free censuring of Princes'.

bee Cause them to be brought to me, or to the Lo B. of London And this shalbe yo[r] sufficient warrant in that behalf. ffrom Lambeth the 22[th] of Decemb. 1614:

Yo[r] very louing ffreinde
G. Cant.

M[r] Dawson master
M[r] Lownes sen' } wardens
Mr Swinhowe }

Lithgowes trauellę printed by Nicho: Okes

I require the master and wardens of the Company of Station[r]s to take in to their Custodie all those bookę which they shall finde of this Title imprinted vizt the Trauelles of Lythgoe[1] June 7[th] 1616.

John London/

FOL. 90[a]

The Copie of a lẽr from his Ma[tie] to the Companye
James Rex.

Trustie and wellbeloued wee greet yo[u] well. Whereas wee are Credibly [*informed*] geiuen to vnderstande, that Diuers persons free of yo[r] Company haue heretofore presumed w[th]out o[r] Licence to imprint diuers of o[r] workę which we haue ben pleased to write, in the ymprintinge whereof they haue also escaped such grose erro[r]s as o[r] royall meaneinge may be misinterpreted and thereby we may Consequentlye be abused. ffor reformacõn thereof we haue thought it Conuenient not onely to ꝑuse all such o[r] writeingę and workę which haue ben formerly published to the ende that all former erro[r]s may be corrected and amended. But also wee haue Caused them, together w[th] such other o[r] workę as haue not heretofore ben published, to be reduced into one volume[2] and haue authorised, licensed and Cõmanded o[r] trustie and welbeloued Seruant John Bill and his assignes onely, from henceforth as his and their proper Copie to imprint all such o[r] workę as heretofore wee haue written or hereafter shall be pleased to writte. Wherefore wee doe hereby require and straightly Comand yo[u] that yo[u], and yo[r] Successo[r]s shall from time to time, from and after the sight of theis o[r] lr̃es, (and a true Copie thereof Deliu'ed vnto yo[u] for yo[r] Instructions) doe and vse yo[r] vttermost Diligence and endeuo[r] that no person or persons free of yo[r] Societye (other then the said John Bill and his assignes) doe or shall directly, or indirectly imprint or Cause to be imprinted any of o[r] said workę or writeingę, either in the Lattin or english tongue vpon paine of o[r] heauy Displeasure, any former vse, order, vsurpacõn, or pretence, whatsoeuer, to the Contrary not w[th]standinge. And to the ende that none may pleade ignorance for excuse of their Contempt of this o[r] Cõmandement Our will and pleasure is, that at yo[r] next gen'all Court or assembly by yo[u] to be holden, yo[u] cause theis o[r] lers̃ to be openly reade and shall signifie o[r] pleasure herein at lardge: And after the publicacõn thereof to deliu' theis o[r] lers̃ to the said John Bill, retayninge a Copie thereof wth yo[u], And here of faile yo[u] not as yo[u] will answere the Contrary

Mr Dawson mr
Mr Lownes sen' } wards̃
Mr Swinhow }

King James s works [18° hand]

[1] STC 15711. Why this 'Second Impression Corrected and enlarged' should have been called in is not apparent, except that the enlargement is imperceptible.

[2] STC 14344.

at yor perills: Giuen vnder o^r^ signett at o^r^ manno^r^ of Greenewich the 25th day of June in the fouretenth yeare of [*the*] o^r^ raigne of England ffrance and Ireland and of Scotland the nyne and for'th.

To o^r^ trustie and welbeloued the
Master and wardens of the Company
of Statiōers in o^r^ Cittye of London

This lẽr was openly reade vpon the
first of Julye 1616 being quarter
Day. per *Tho. Mōtforte* No ^arij^.

A Copie of a lẽr from his ma^tie^ about Sr Walter Rawleyes booke[1]

James Rex/ Fol. 90^b^

Trustye and welbeloued wee greete yo^u^ well Whereas heretofore at o^r^ Comandem^t^ yo^u^ made seizure of Certaine bookes entituled The Historye of the world written by Sr Walter Rawleigh knight o^r^ will pleasure and Comandem^t^ is that forthw^th^ vpon the receite hereof yo^u^ doe deliu' vnto John Ramsay the bearer here of all the said bookẹ so seized to be by him disposed of at o^r^ pleasure. And this shalbe yor sufficient warrant and discharge in that behalf. And hereof see yo^u^ faile not as yo^u^ will answere the Contrary at yor vttermost perills From the Courte at Theobalds the eighteenth day of September 1616. In the fouretenth yeare of o^r^ Raigne of great Brittaine France & Irelande.

To o^r^ trustye and wellbeloued the
Master wardens and assistantẹ of the
Company of Station^r^s in o^r^ Cittye
of London

m^r^ Man m^r^
m^r^ Adams }
m^r^ Lownes } wardens

A Copie of an order made by the reverende father in God the lo. B. of London about printinge the Psalter./[2] Fol. 91^a^

Tertio Septemb. 1616.

Mr Man ^mr^
Mr Adames }
Mr Lownes } wardens

Whereas it was referred, by the Lo: Archbishoppe of Canterbury his Grace to the reverende father in God, the Lo. Bishoppe of London, to heare and determine a variance which had longe Continued, betwixt the m^r^ wardens and Company of Station^r^s in London on the one side, and the office of the Kingẹ printer on the other, touching the ymprintinge of the psalter or psalmes of Davide, which beinge printed alone w^th^out sōme other helpe would proue not greatly beneficāll vnto

[1] STC 20637. Ramsay must have sold the books, for copies are now not at all uncommon.

[2] Cf. *C–B.C*, 43^b^, 7 June 1616. The Stationers had published editions of the Great Bible *Psalter* in quarto and duodecimo in 1615 (STC 2408–9), to which Barker had objected because it infringed upon his privilege for the *Book of Common Prayer*. By this decision the Stationers printed editions in quarto in 1618, in octavo in 1624, 1634, and 1635, and in 16° in 1635. Regarding the last named cf. *C–B.C*, 135^b^, 7 Sept. 1635; and 139^b^, 28 Apr. 1636. Barker printed a separate folio edition in 1617.

the said Company and wth lardger allowance, then were fitt would become preiudicall to the office aboue named.

The said reverende ffather being the more willinge, to deale in this perticuler that he might putt an absolute [*and reall*] ende to all quarrells and Jarres, betweene them to which purpose he had vsed often and serious admonicōn and havinge taken a promise on either [*side*] parte that they would from henceforth desist from suitꝭ in Lawe and would moue no future questions about rightꝭ and titles but liue in amitye and loue as good Christians and men linked [*together*] nerely together by the bande of the same societye ought to doe. Did at the length in the pñce and wth the Consent of both partyes (the mr wardens and Company of Stacionrs cravinge no more then the said Reverende ffather in his Discretion should thinke fitt to allowe), And the deputies or Assignes for the said office yealding their full accord therevnto order in manner and forme as followeth vizt/

That it should be lawfull for the said mr wardens and Company to imprinte the psalter wth this Title ensueing.

Psalter [18° hand] The psalter or psalmes of David after the translacōn of the great bible pointed as it shalbe saide or songe in Churches wth the addicōn of morninge and eveninge prayer

After which title the vsuall Kallender from the beginning of Januarye vntill the ende of December being next placed shall followe the morning prayer according to the vsuall manner as namely

ffirst sentences of the scripture

At what time soeuer a Synner &c.

2 the exhortacōn

Dearely beloved brethren &c.

3 Ageñ all Confession.

Almightie and most mercifull father &c.

4 The absolucōn or remission of Sinnes.

Almightye god the father of or Lord Jesus Christ &c.

Together wth the Lordꝭ prayer and the versicles and answeres that followe therevpon, as also, Venite exvltemus, Te deum laudamus Benedicite orā opera Benedictus,
FOL. 91b Jubilate Deo (wthout any other Rubric || or Titles to the aforesaid psalmes or hymes. The Creede wth the Versicles and answeres and the Collects for peace and praire annexed therevnto./

In like manner shall it be lawfull for them to ymprint the euening prayer wth Magnificat, Cantate Domino, Canticū novum Nunc Demittis, and Deus misereatur nostis (*sic*), together wth the two Collectꝭ accustomably ioyned to euening prayer as also the Creede Qui cunqꝫ vult, The Lateny wth all the Suffrags and prayers and Titles of thos prayers to the ende of the Lateny. And finally the Catechisme sett downe in the booke of Coñon praier. wth theis and no other addicoñs did his Lop. thinke it fitt to authorishe them to ymprint the psalter in all volumes at their libertye and Discretion saue onely in folio.

Concordat. cum originali } Rob Christian Deputat regrarij regij

Ex^tur per Reg. Edwards notariũ publicũ.

To the m^r and wardens of the Company of Stationers[1] Fol. 92^a

By the Maio^r.

Theis are in his Ma^tyes name straightly to Chardge & Comande yo^u that yo^u take p̃nte order for the buyinge providinge and furnishinge of yor proporcõn of wheate beinge—140 quarters, And that yo^u haue the same in readienes laide vp in Granaryes in or nere this Citty before the last day of february next Cominge. And further that yo^u then doe Certifie me in writinge vnder yor Hande of the same yor proporcõn and where yo^u lay the same. To the intent that my self or such others as I shall appoint may take a viewe thereof whereby wee may be prepared to serue the markette therew^th as occasion shall require. And as yo^u shalbe therevnto appointed. And that yo^u [*app*] ymploy neither Chandlo^r. nor Baker in the furnishinge thereof or seruinge the markette when yo^u are appointed so to doe, and hereof I require yo^u not to faile as yo^u tender the goode of this Citty and will answere the Contrary when an account shall be required of yo^u in the execucõn of this my precept. This 29th of Nouemb. 1616.

Welde

At the Court at white hall the 9th of March 1617[2]

Present

Lo: Archb: of Canterbury	Lo: Carew
Lo: Treasurer	Mr Treasurer
Lo: Steward	Mr Comptroller
Lo: chamberlaine	Mr Secr: Lake
E. of Arondell	Mr Secr: Nauton
Lo: vi: Wallingford	Mr Chanc: of the Exch:
Lo: B^p. of Ely	M^r of the Rolles./

It is this day ordered by there Lo^pps. that whereas John ffrancton his Ma^tes printer in Ireland is become Insufficient to dischardge that office, in respect of his poore abilitie and many Infirmities; His Maiestie therefore is to be humblie moued to grant the like lr̃es Patente of the same office vnto ffelix Kingston Mathew Lownes & Bartholomew Downes Citizens and Stationers of London being nominated and recommended vnto there Lordshipps by the Companie of Stationers of London on the behalfe of the said Companie to hold the said office vnto the said kingston [*and*] Lownes and Downes there executors administrators and assignes During the Terme of 21 yeares from and after the expiracõn surrender, forfeiture or other Determinacõn of the Patent of

Ireland [18° hand]

[1] Cf. *C–B.C*, 46^b, 3 Feb. 1617. [2] Cf. *C–B.C*, 50^a, 2 Mar. 1618. The foundation of the Irish Stock.

the said ffrancton nowe his Mate printer in Ireland. Prouided that the same graunt be not in anie wise repugnant or Contrarie to anie other grant heretofore made by his Matie. vnto Robert Barker his Mate Printer in England or to Bonham Norton./

FOL. 92b By the Maior

To the Mr & wardens of the
companie of Stacōners

Whereas I and my Brethren the Aldermen haue resolued and agreed that the full quantitie of Ten thousand Quarters of wheate shalbe bought and prouided by all the seu'all Companies of this Citie betweene this and the fower & twentith Day of June next Coming according to such rates and proporcōns as the same Companies haue heretofore ben seuerallie assessed and taxed at towardes the furnishing of the like proporcōns. In accomplishment whereof theis are to will and require you that you buy and provide one hundred and fortie quarters of wheate which is rateablie appointed and proporcōned for your Companie according to the said former provisions of Ten Thousand quarters, and that the same be bought and provided and laid vp in garners within this Citie and for the seruice & provision thereof before the said fower and twentith day of June at the furthest, And that you depend not vpon the Chandlers Bakers or anie others to make the same provision as you tender the good of this Citie and will answer the Contrarie if through yor default this seruice shall in anie pte be neglected. Guildhall the last of Aprill 1618

Weld

FOL. 93a To the right honorable Sr Hen: Mountague Knight
Lord Cheife Justice of England/
The humble peticōn of John Jaggard[1]
Bookseller and Stationer of London

Sheweth That his matie in the first yeare of his raigne for the Advancmt of the Companie of Stacon's by his Highnes Lr̃es patente granted vnto them, the sole printing of diuers bookes. And afterwarde ordayned, that the mr. warden and Assistante of the said Corporacōn should haue power to make ordinances for the due execucōn of the said lr̃es patente. Soe as the said ordinances were approoued by the Lord Chancellor. of England, and the Chiefe Justice of either Bench. Theis ordinances were grounded vpon the humble peticōn of Booksellers and Booke printers the principall entent and meaning being to exclude strangers and reduce the benifitt thereof to such (who according to his maties: first intencōn) had not meanes to liue and maintaine their charge vpon [*but*] but by printing binding and Selling of Booke and not to such, who being (onlie accordinge [to] custome) made free of the Companie; were yet strangers to the Trade, as Grocers; Goldsmiths, and such like. Accordinglie in the Sixt yeare of his Maties: raigne the said Mr. wardens and Assistante made diuers ordinances, and (amongst the rest) ordered that when anie place should fall void, either by the death; Resignacōn or forfeiture of anie partie interested in the benifit of the said Lr̃es Patente that then the said Mr. wardens &c should elect another fitt pson in his roome, wherin speciall regard is to be had to the Antientie (*sic*), honestie and good

English Stock
[18° hand]

[1] Jaggard was not elected to the next part for which he is recorded as standing, cf. *C–B.C*, 62a, 27 June 1620.

behauio[r] of the ꝑtie, *And that alsoe he should bee a Bookseller, a Printer, a Bookebinder or one that dealeth in Bookes,* The which lawes were shortlie after approoued and signed by the then Lo: Chancello[r]. and the Cheife Justice of either Bench. But nowe contrarilie, and to the manifest breach of the said ordinance, the said master wardens &c. in their late eleccõns haue supplied and doe maintaine to Supplie the foresaid vacant roomes (according to their owne partialities) wth such freemen of the said Companie (who according to the true intent of the said decree) haue neuer ben brought vp, neither nowe haue or euer had anie Reall dealing in Printinge, Bindinge, or Sellinge of Bookes.

His humble peticoñ therefore is, to your good Lopp[s], That in this soe vndue & dangerous a course, yor hono[r] would be pleased by yor Subsciption herevnto, to signifie yor Honorable advise vnto the said Maister and wardens for the Continuing and restoring of the said ordinances to their former integritie, intent, and vsage; ffor the which yor peticõner with the rest of the poore companie shall haue cause allwaies to pray for yor Lopp[s]: health and Hono[r] longe to continue./

Let the M[r] and wardens of the Stationers see this for I hold it fit they due obserue their owne orders and in their elections prefer Booksellers before others.

H Mountague./

To the right ho[bl]: S[r]: Francis Bacon Knight
Lo: Chancello[r]: of England.
The humble peticõn of John Jaggard

10 Maij 1618

Sheweth vnto yor Lo[p]: That whereas diuerse lawes and ordinances haue ben signed and sealed by the handes and seales of the late Lord Chancello[r] and the Cheife Just: of either Bench, to the Companie of Stationers, for the better releiuing of such poore men of the Companie who are trulie bookesellers Bookprinters and Bookebinde[rs], and haue ben and nowe are wholie brought vp in that profession;

Soe it is may it please yo[r] good Lo[p]. That some Certaine prime men of the said Companie, to whome the Gouerment (*sic*) of the said orders are instrusted (*sic*); nowe of late (neglecting and ꝑverting the said orders) haue admitted, and doe maintaine to admitt into the benifitt of the said ordinances, diuerse welthy persons of different professions, to great p[r]iudice and future vndoeing of the said Bookselle[r]s and Bookprinte[r]s: Wherevpon yo[r] peticoner exhibited A peticõn to the nowe Lo: Cheife Justice; with A copie of the order; which his Lo[p]. vpon Consideracõn was pleased to subsigne; as may appeare vnto yo[r] Lo[p]. being here vnto annexed.

Yo[r] peticon' therfore humbly desireth yo[r] Lo: for the better ratificacõn and confirmacõn of the same to signifie your Lo[ps]. like pleasure herein. And yor peticon' shalbe for euer bound to pray for yor Lo[ps]. health and prosperitie.

Take lr̃es to the Stationers signifying that my opinion Concurreth with that of my Lo: Cheife Justice.

Fr: B: Ca:

FOL. 93b To my loving freindes the Mr. wardens and Assistantę of the Companie of Stationers London./

After my heartie comendacons Whereas I am informed by a peticõn lately exted vnto me; That you the Master, wardens and Assistantę of the Companie of Stationers haue preferred vnto the benifitt of yor lr̃es patentę, certaine psons not being *Booksellers, Bookprinters, or Bookbinders,* contrarie to yor owne Orders heretofore established, ayminge rather (as it is conceiued) at yor owne private gaines, then due regularitie and pformance of your owne Ordinances, prouided for the good and benifitt of the poorer sorte of Bookbinders &c. especially those of honest conversacõn, and not for the behoofe of men of different trades and contrary professions, as latelie (it is prtended) you haue giuen way vnto./ I haue therefore thought good to signifie vnto you, that I concurr, and agree in opinion with my Lord Cheife Justice, whom I find hath ben formerlie acquainted with this matter: And doe therfore wish and advise you to rectifye these thingę, and that hencforth you see the said orders more dulie executed, and obserued for avoyding further trouble or Complaint. Soe not doubting but you will shewe such Conformitie herevnto as is meete I bid you farewell.

Your loving freind
Fr: Bacon Canc:

At Yorkhouse 15o Maij 1618.

To my loving freindę the Mr. wardens
and assistantę of the Companie of
Stationers &c.

After my hartie comendacõns. Whereas I am giuen to vnderstand by John Jaggard one of your society, of some wronges offered vnto him by you the Master, wardens and assistantę of the Companie of Stationers; And because I my selfe am vnwilling that your discontentę should be Controuerted in publique, and the partie at my mocõn is easily intreated to compromise his greiuance vnto me: I haue thought goode for the pacyfying of differences amongst brethren of one societie to request you Mr Leake, Mr Adames, mr Gylman, Mr Waterson and Mr Humphrey Lownes, or anie others to whome it may appertaine, to be at my house on Monday the thirteenth of this moneth; where I will be readie to heare all obiections, and accordinglie indeauor to conclude a peace and a freindlie reconcilemt betweene yu Soe fare yu well.

Your loving freind
Anth: Benn./

10th of July 1618

James Rex
FOL. 94a To our trustie and Welbeloued the Master and wardens
of the Companie of Stationers of the Citie of London./

Trustie and Welbeloued wee greete you well whereas our trustie and welbeloued seruant *John Bill,* hath heretofore by our direction, at his great costę and charges, printed in faire good paper, and in a seemelie letter; *verbatim* according to the originall Copies, diuers workes or bookes published in the Latine tongue, Aswell by the Reuerend ffather in God *Marcus Antonius de Dominis* Archbishop of Spalato,[1] and *Isaack Casaubon* deceased[2] as others by our com̃and and permission. In the vndertaking of which busines, but Cheiflie by sending ouer into fforraine Contries by our appointment some great quantities of the said Archbps. workes, ymediatelie vpon the first ympression thereof,[3] Our said seruant hath receiued great losse and hindrance, being lyable to the seueritie of an Edict published by the Princes and States of those Contries, who are enemies to the true profession of godę word and by force of the said Edict, all the bookę soe sent ouer, or the greatest part of them were seised and confiscated. And forasmuch as wee are informed that since the first edition of the said Archbishops and Casaubons late workes, the same haue of late bin ymprinted beyond the Seas,[4] in naughtie paper, and in a bad letter; and lesser volumes with manie Errataes in them, which neuerthelesse are imported into this our Kingdome, by some of your trade or Societie and manie of them heere sold, whereby our prerogatiue and Royall Intention, that our said seruant John Bill should during his life, haue the sole ymprinting of all and euerie the said bookes, is infringed, and our Subiectes the buyers of them much wronged and deceaued; Wherefore wee doe hereby require and straightlie Charge and Com̃and you and euerie of you, That neither you nor yor successors nor any ꝑticular member of your Societie either by your selues or anie other (except the said John Bill) and his assignes, doe from henceforth during the naturall life of the said John Bill presume to printe or cause to be ymprinted the said Archbishop of Spalatoę and Casauboneę workes, either within this our kingdome, or in the Contries of anie fforaine prince or State; nor anie of our writingę or workę, nor anie other bookę which heretofor haue ben or hereafter shalbe sett forth in the Latine tongue or anie other fforaine language by our Royall Comand or ꝑmission, nor to import into this our Kingdome or put to sale anie of the said bookę. vpon paine of Confiscacõn and forfeiture of them. And our will and pleasure is that the said bookę soe Confiscated & forfeited shalbe seised and answeared to the vse of vs our heires and Successors. And for the due execucõn of this our will and pleasure wee doe hereby com̃and you the Master & wardens of the Companie of Stationers of London for the time beinge by vertue of theis our letters from time to time in the Companie of the said John Bill, and when soeuer you sha⟨ll⟩ be therevnto requested [*by the said John Bill*] on his behalfe, to enter and make search in anie houses, shops, warehouses, Sellers, and other places whatsoeuer belonging to your said Companie or anie other ꝑson suspected for all and euery or anie of the said bookes, and if anie such shalbe founde to seize and deliuer them ouer from time to time to the Keeper of our librarie: And in case of need wee doe hereby Com̃and all & euery our Sheriffes, Constables, and other our officers vpon all occasions to be ayding & assisting in the ꝑformance of this our will and pleasure in theis our letters mencõned and expressed, And because none of your Societie shall plead Ignorance in excuse of their Contempt against this our Com̃ande-

1 e.g. STC 6994, 6996, and 7002.

2 e.g. STC 4744.

3 Cf. letter of James I to Dominis, *State Papers Dom. 1611–1618*, p. 474, stating that the dedication to himself is to be inserted in copies to be sold in England, but omitted in those for export.

4 There is, for example, an edition of STC 4744, in 127 pages instead of 129, which was printed in the Netherlands, though with the same imprint as Bill's edition. STC 6994 was reprinted in Heidelberg, 1618; editions of STC 6996 were printed *s.l.*, 1616, Hague, 1616, Leyden, 1617, and Campidoni, 1617; while there is a Frankfurt, 1617, edition of STC 7002.

ment wee doe hereby reque⟨st⟩ you to Cause theis our lr̃es to be openlie read foure times euerie yeare at your generall Courtę or Assemblies[1] And that after the first reading thereof you enter the Tenor of them in your Registrie or hall booke, deliuering to our said seruant John Bill theis our lr̃es signed with our signe Manuall, And hereof faile you not as you will answer the Contrarie at yor p̣lls. Giuen vnder our signet at our mannor of *Greenwich* the 27th day of May in the 16th yeare of our Raigne of England ffrance and Ireland and of Scotland the one and ffifteeth./

FOL. 94b By the Maior/.

To the Mr and wardens of the Companie of Stationers./

fforasmuch as vpon deliberate advise and consideracõn had with my Brethren the Aldermen; It is for sundrie respectę thought meet and ordered that for the better provision and forniture of this Cittie with Corne for the releefe of the poore of the same; That the nomber of Ten Thousand Quarters of Wheate shall be provided by the Companies of this Citie respectivelie according to former proporcõns allotted to euerie Companie: Theis are therfore in his Matę. name to Charge and Com̃and you for your part to buy and provide One hundred and ffortie Quarters of good and sweete wheate; soe that you haue the same laid vp in your Granaries before the first day of May nowe next Cominge; readie to supplie the M'kettę of this Citie when you shall be therevnto appointed In the making of which yor prouision you are to vse such Care and discretion that you giue no Cause to inhaunce the price of Corne; And that you by noe meanes compound with anie baker, Chandler or other person to furnish the Markett with meale for you which is a manifest defrauding of that seruice. And hereof faile [*you*] not at yor p̣ill, Dated the xxvith Day of Januarie 1618.

Weld./

To the Mr and wardens of the Companie of Stationers./ By the Maior Powder (*in 18° hand*)

Theis are to will and require you and in his Maties: name straightlie to charge and Com̃and you, that ymediatelie vpon receipt hereof you make Survey of all the Match and Poulder of your Companies store and prouision. And on or before Monday next to Certifie to me in writing vnder your handę the true & precise quantitie and Waight of the Match and poulder that you haue, And hereof not to faile as you will answer the Contrarie at your perill ffrom Guildhall this xijth of ffebruarie 1618

Weld./

To the right hoble: Sr Sebastian Harvey knight
Lo: Maior of the Citie of London and to the
right worth. the Aldermen his brethren./

Stationers. According to a precept of the xijth of this instant ffebruarie wee haue made survey for match and poulder in our Companies store And doe most humblie Certify vnto yor lo: and worps: That wee haue at this time not anie

[1] Cf. *C–B.C*, 52a, 4 Oct. 1618.

prouision at all either of match or poulder in our said Companie. This 15th day of ffebruarie 1618.

Wm. Leake. M^{r}.
Tho: Adames } wardens./
Anth: Gilmyn }

To the M^{r} and wardens of the Company of Stationers[1] FOL. 95^{a}

By the Maio^{r}

There hath bin a petition latelie presented to the kings Matie. by the Lord Maio^{r} and Courte of Aldermen on the behalf of the whole Citie that his Matie. would bee gratiouslie pleased by his highenes lr̃s patentȩ to confirm and secure to the Citie. And all the companies thereof and all the ꝑishes therein the landȩ and possessions which they hold for the maintaynance of the poore or other publick vses. Soe to free them from feares and dange^{r}s his Matie. hath returned herevnto a most gratious answere and hath granted the petition to the full Mr Recorder and some othe^{r}s of the councell with the (*sic*) Cittie haue consulted allreadie aboute drawing vp of the Patentȩ. yee amongst othe^{r}s may if yee please be ꝑtakers of this grace and favo^{r} yf yee find yee may haue either cause or suspition of feare touching any of your landȩ. If you be willing not to be left out I pray repaire as speedilie as you may on Tewsday next at the furthest to Mr Recorder, Mr Coen' Serieant or Mr Stone to giue instructions for soe much as concerneth your selues & by the subscription of your names sugnifie yor consent to beare a part of the Charge (which will not be much) in such proporcõn as Mr Recorder, Mr Coen' serieant and Mr Stone shall indifferently thinke fitt and sett downe vnder their handȩ, ffrom my house this first of May 1619

Weld.

To the Master and wardens
of Stationers

By the Maio^{r}.

Whereas his Matie: is gratiouslie pleased to ratifie and confirme vnto the seuerall companies of this Citie all the landȩ and the rentȩ and arrerages of the same, which they nowe enioy or possesse. And whereas for the passing of this assurance it hath ben latelie ordered by me and my brethren that the Clarkes of the seuerall companies of Grocers, Drapers, Goldsmiths & Haber-Dashers should take vpon them the paines and trauell in passing the said assurance: Therefore theis are to will and require you, on or before the 5th Day of June next at the furthest to giue notice in writing vnto anie one of the said foure Clarkes (if you purpose and resolue to take benifitt by his Ma^{tȩ}. said graunt) of the true name of yor incorporacon', together with the ꝑticuler of the landȩ and rentȩ, which you Desire to haue passed and secured from his Matie:, wherein faile you not, as you tender yor owne future safetie. This last Day of May 1619

Weld./

[1] A composition of £6,000 was exacted from the London livery companies for the confirmation of defective titles at this time, cf. F. C. Dietz, *English public finance*, 1932, p. 179.

FOL. 95[b] To the M[r] and wardens of the Company of Station[rs]/.

By the Mayo[r].

Whereas for the better defence of this kingdome and safetye of this Cittye direction is given from the Lordę of his Ma[tyes]. most ho[ble] privy Counsell among other provisions that 50 Last of pouder shall be forthwith prouided and kept w[th]in this Cittye to be in readyenes when occasion shall require, Towardę which store m[r] Chamƀlen by order of the Courte of Lord Mayo[r] & Aldrẽn hath bought to the Cittyes vse 53636[li] of powder at the price of xj[d] ꝑ pound which amounteth to the sõme of 2400[li] and od money,[1] and is readie to be distributed among the Companyes of this Cittye according to the proprocõn of 10000 quartrs of Corne whereof is allotted to yo[r] Companye, 751 pounds of powder which after the rate aforesđ amounteth to 34[li]—8[s]—5[d] Theis are therefore in his Ma[tyes] name to Chardge and Cõmande yo[u] that forthw[th] vpon the receite hereof yo[u] take in yo[r] Custodye the said quantitye of powder and vpon receite thereof forthw[th] to pay vnto the said m[r] Chamƀlen the said some of 34[li]—8[s] 5[d], And that yo[u] keepe it for the store of this Cittye having a Care for the placeing thereof from Danger of fire whereof see yo[u] faile not as yo[u] tender his Ma[tyes] service & the wellfare of this Cittye and will answere the Contrary at yo[r] vttmost perrillę Guildhall this xij[th] of July 1619

34[li]—8[s]—5[d] Weld.

M[r] Towreson dwelling by ffanchurch will direct yo[u] where yo[u] may receue yo[r] powder.

By the Mayo[r].

To the Master & ward: of the Company of Statione[r]s

Whereas for the better defense of this kingdome and safetye of this Cittye Direction is given by the Lordę of his Ma[tyes]. most ho[ble] priuye Counsell among other prouisions that a good quantitye of Match shalbe forthw[th] provided and kept w[th]in the Cittye to be in readyenes when occasion shall require towardę which store CCLxxj bundles of mach are lately bought and doe remaine at Guildhall and are to be equally distributed among the Companyes of this Cittye according to the rates for provision of pouther whereof yo[r] Company is to take sixe bundles for the which yo[u] are to pay to Mr Cornelius ffish Chamberlein after the rate of ixs vid ꝑñte money at the receit of the match Theis are therefore in his Ma[tyes] name to Chardge and Comand yo[u] that vpon receit hereof yo[u] take into yor Custodye the said match and pay for the same at the price aforesđ And that yo[u] keepe the same for the store of the Cittye And hereof faile not at yo[r] perriles Guild hall this [*xxiiij[th]*] 24th of Aprill 1619

2—17—0 Weld.

Receiued the xix[th] daie of October 1619 of the M[r] and wardens of the Companie of Stationers London for their proporcon' of Gunpowder allotted to the said Companie the some of Thirtie fower poundę eight shillingę & five pence lawfull money, I say rec' } xxxiiij[li] viij[s] v[d]

ꝑ me Arthuru' Panther Clerk
Cornelij ffish Camerarij Civitatis London.

[1] Actually £2,458. 6*s*. 4*d*.

Fol. 96^{a}

By the Mayo^{r}

To the Master and wardens of the Company of the Statioñers

Whereas vpon the Com̃andem^{t} of the Lordę of the Counsell for the provision of powder for the store of this Cittye I haue directed my precept vnto yo^{u} and the rest of the Companyes for receivinge of the quantitye of powder and payeinge for the same as in the said precept was expressed. Notwthstandinge as I am enformed yo^{u} haue hitherto all together neglected the execucõn of my said precept, And to the end yo^{u} may not be ignorant if vpon this yor Contempt some other Course be taken against yo^{u} I doe hereby eftsoones require yo^{u} and in his Ma^{tyes} name Chardg and Com̃and yo^{u} forthwth vpon receit hereof to receive the said quantitye of powder and pay for the same to mr Chamberleyne as by the said precept yo^{u} were required whereof faile yo^{u} not as yo^{u} will answere the Contrary Guyldhall this 12 of Septemb 1619

Weld./

By the Mayo^{r}.

To the M^{r} and wardens of the Companie of Stacõners

Livery Gowns [18° hand]

fforasmuch as of late yeares a great disorder is growne in the seuerall companies of this Citie, in not being decentlie and orderlie attired or arrayed in their gownes to be faced with furr accordinglie as in antient time hath ben accustomed vpon the daies of solempnitie in the winter season, when the Lord Mayo^{r} is by them attended, Of which neglect a speciall veiue and obseruance hath of late beene taken ffor reformacõn of which disorder it hath ben thought fitt by me and my brethren the Aldermen to addresse preceptę to the M^{r} and wardens of euery Companie within this Cittie. And herefore (*sic*) theis are to will and require you forthwith to Call a Court of Assistantę, and with them to sett downe & establish such an order in your Companie that yearelie hereafter in the winter season, and cheiflie vpon those daies of solempnitie at which are ꝑn'te manie noble and worthie spectato^{r}s aswell strangers as Natiues borne the M^{r} wardens and Assistantę and those of the liverie for the time beinge doe in decent and graue manner were their gownes faced with furre euerie man respectiuelie according[*lie*] to his precedence & degree in his Companie, and not to haue their gownes faced with stuffes in much disorderlie manner, as of late hath ben vsed whereby that antient estate and grauitie of this Cittie hath receiued much disgrace. And that the rates of the seu'all sortę of furres for facing of liverie gownes maie the better be knowne you shall receiue herewith annexed a note of the same. And that, that order be obserued and Continued yearlie from before the feast of Saint Michaell the Archangell vntill the feast of Easter be past and be put in due execucõn before Christmas next. That thereby the grace and honor which of late yeares hath beene greatlie impaired for & in respect of the Cause afore mencõned maie nowe and at all times hereafter be reped & amended, And hereof not to faile in your best indevo^{r}s as you tender and respect the the (*sic*) hono^{r} of this Cittie, This Thirtieth daie of Nouember 1619.

Weld./

A note of the rates of seuerall sorte of ffurres for facinge of Liuerie gownes./

ffaces of Budge[1] are of seuerall prises according to their goodnes vizt. from xxv^s to iij^li some xxvi^s viij^d some xxx^s or xxxiij^s iiij^d some xxxv^s vj or vij & xxx^tie, some xl^s some l^s, some more some lesse.

ffaces of foyne powles[2] likewise accordinge to their goodnes, some xlv^s, some xl^s, so⟨me⟩ l^s, some lv^s some iij^li some more some lesse according to their goodnes.

Fol. 96^b ffaces of Martens of the which the Cheife Conpanies doe weare likewise according to their goodnes some [*xlv^s*] x^li some ix^li some viij^li x^s or viij^li some vij^li x^s or vij^li &c.

Martens powles some 6^li some iiij^li x^s some v^li x^s or vj^l according to their goodnes of euerie seuerall face of all theis kinde and according to theis seu'all prises they haue been sold time out of minde.

To the M^r and wardens
of the Company of Stationers./

By the Mayo^r.

Whereas by lr̃es lately receiued from the right ho^ble the lorde & others of his Ma^te. most ho^ble privie Councell,[3] My selfe and my brethren are advertized of the Complainte that haue ben made to their lo^ps. from seu'all ꝑtes of the Kingdome of the great inconveniences lying vpon the ffarmers and Husbandmen by the extraordinarie lowe rates that [*nowe*] corne nowe beareth To the intent therefore that farmo^rs maie in some sorte be accomodated and releived, And that some good quantitie of Corne maie be taken from them, manie of them havinge great quantities lying by them on their handes and Cannot vent the same, And withall that the Citie maie be fullie furnished & provided of Corne for the store & provision thereof according to the wonted & accustomed proporcõn of Ten Thousand quarters in this time of plentie, Theis are to will & require y^u and in his Ma^te name streightlie to Charge and Comand yow that you take order that y^r Companie betweene this & Easter next be fullie furnished with 140 quarters of good sound and sweet (*wheat*) which is the rateable proportion allotted to your said Company towarde the Complem^t of Ten Thousand quarters And that you not (as many of the Companies of this Citie heretofore haue accustomed to doe) rest and relye to haue it serued in vpon occasion, by Chandlers, Bakers, or such like persons, But that the said quantitie be reallie ꝓvided & laid vp in yor Companies granaries for the store & seruice of this Citie, but all upon all occasion within the time aforesaid, ffor that it is intended by my selfe and my brethren that all the Companies about the said time p'fixed shalbe visited whether they haue made ꝓvision of Corne accordinge to this Direction, And those that shall faile therein shalbe Called to a strict accompte for their neglect & Contempt on this behalfe, And further whereas their lo^ps. by the said lr̃s seeme to take notice of the great scarcitie of gunpowder and Match within this Citie notwithstanding their lo^ps. former sugnificacõn for providing of Certaine quantities of the same Theis are likewise to require you in his Ma^te name that vpon or before monday next you faile not, trewlie to Certifie & retorne vnto me vnder your hande what quantitie of seruiceable powder and Match your Companie is at this present stored

[1] Sets of lambskin furs.

[2] Beech-marten neck pieces.

[3] This letter, dated 25 Jan. 1620, is calendared in *Analytical index of remembrancia*, pp. 384–5.

and provided of, And that you do not sell or depte away with the same or anie parte thereof, but keepe that by you for the store & provision of this Citie vpon all occasions, ffor that the present veiwe must be taken of this alsoe to the intent y[t] true Certificate may be made and retorned to the lordꝭ accordinglie as by their hono[r]s lr̃es is required, ffaile you not in the performance of the premisses as you tender his Ma[tꝭ] seruice and will answer the Contrarie at your pills Guildhall this xxvj[th] of January 1619.

Weld.

Stacõners

To the right ho[ble]. S[r]. Willm Cockaine knight
Lord Mayo[r] of the Citie of London./

According to a precept of the xxvj[th] of January last past wee doe most humblie Certifie yor Lo[p]: That wee haue at this pn'te 751 poundꝭ of Powder, & six bundles of Match which quantitie accordinge to a former precept hertofore directed vnto vs we bought & pr'uided our selues of for the store of this citie. This first day of ffebruary 1619

By the Mayo[r] Fol. 97[a]

To the M[r] and wardens
of the company of stacõners

Where the kingꝭ most excellent Matie. intendeth to Come in his Ma[tꝭ]. most Royall person, on the xxvj[th] day of this pn'te moneth, from whitehall to Paules to heare a sermon,[1] Theis therefore shalbe to require and charge you in his Ma[tꝭ]. name, that you take speciall Care that all persons of the liuery of y[r] said Company may be in a readines against that time with their livery hoodes attired in their best apparrell, To waite and attend his Ma[tꝭ] Coming, and that yee and the liuery of y[r] said Company receiue Direccõns from Mr Leake, M[r] ffox, Mr Moulson, and Mr Williams or anie one of them appointed by me and my brethren the Aldermen for the ordering and disposing of all thingꝭ needfull for that seruice requiring you not to faile hereof as you will answer the Contrarie at y[r] perill At the Guildhall of the Citie of London the xx[th] of March 1619.

Weld.

The whole number of y[r] Liuery./

Whifflers with coatꝭ of veluett, & Chaines of gold, ten at the least./ Yo[r] standinges to be stronge and well rayled, the foreraile to be Couered with a fair blew Cloth, and to Certifie me tomorrowe next by eight of the Clocke in the morninge the length of your railes and standingꝭ.
Yo[r] standerdꝭ and stream[rs] to be sett vp as shall best beseeme the place./

To the right ho[ble] S[r] william Cockaine
Knight Lord Mayo[r] of the Citie of London
& to the right wor[ll]. the Aldermen his brethr⟨en⟩

May it please y[r] Lo: and wor: The master and wardens of the Stacone[r]s with the residue of the Liuery of the said Company doe entend (god willing) to be in readines

[1] The purpose of this visit was to view the ruinous condition of St. Paul's. As a result a Royal Commission was appointed to consider what should be done.

to waite his Ma^te Coming to Paules on the xxvj^th day of this p̄n'te moneth according to a p^r cept of the xx^th of the same./

The number of their liuery is xl persons
Whiflers the number of Ten.
The length of the rayles and standinge is to be lxxx foot long at the least.

Dated this xxi^th of March 1619

FOL. 97^b

By the Mayo^r.

To the M^r and wardens
of the Companie of
Stationers[1]

Whereas my selfe and my Brethren haue receiued lr̃es from the Lorde of his Ma^te. most honorable privie Councell on his Ma^te. behalfe, desiring present Contribution from this Citie of some reasonable some of money towarde the recouery of the Pallatinate allready invaded by the Enemy, being the antient inheritance of his Ma^te sonne in lawe, and which is to descend to his Maties. posteritie, and a matter of that importance which euery good subiect is sensible of And howe much it doth and may concerrne his Matie. himselfe, his Children and posteritie, and the welfare of this Kingdome and the State of Religion. Theis are therefore to entreat you, that forthwith you collect amongst your selues, by some way or meanes, as in your owne Judgment shall thinke fittest the some of One hundred pounde towarde the Contribution expected at the hande of this Cittie, which is the like some which ye haue paid vpon the like occasion heretofore, And which the greatest p̄te of the other companies haue alreadie conformed themselues vnto. And that ye send the money before Saterdaie the xxiij^th daie of this present December to Mr Chamberlaine, who is directed to receive the som̃e at his office in the Guildhall London Dated the xiiij^th Daie of December 1620

Weld./

To the m^r & wardens
of the Company of
Station^rs.

Where as I and my brethren the aldrẽn haue resolued and agreed that the full quantitye of 10,000 quarters of wheate shalbe bought and prouided by all the seu'all Companyes of this Citty between this and the last day of September next coming according to such rates and proporcõns as the same Companyes haue heretofore ben seu'ally assessed and taxed att toward the furnishing of the like proporcõn In accomplishm^t whereof Theis are to will & require yo^u and in his Ma^tyes name straightly to Chardg & Comande yo^u that yo^u buy and prouide Cxl^ty quarters of wheate which is Rateably appointed and proporcõned for yor Company according to the said former provisions of ten thousand quarters and that the same be bought provided and laid vp in granaryes w^thin this Cittye for the service and provision thereof before the said last day of Septemb. at the furthest. And that yo^u depend

[1] Regarding this gift see F. C. Dietz, *English public finance*, p. 187.

not vpon Chandlers Bakers or any others to make the same provision as yo^{u} tender the good of this Cittye and will answer the Contrary if through yor default this service shall in any parte be neglected, Guildhall this 17th of July 1621

Weelde.

Mr Nortons peticoñ against Cantrell Legg printer of Cambridge for printing the Gram̃er[1] Fol 98^{a}

To the right Ho^{ble}: the Lordę and others of his Maties most honourable Priuie Counsell.

The humble petition of Bonham Norton Printer to the Kingę most excellent Matie in Latine, Greeke, & Hebreue &c.

Grammers (*18° hand*) Most humblie shewing: That whereas the Kingę Matie. that nowe is by his hignes letters patentę vnder the great seale of England, dated the sixt daie of January in the Tenth yeare of his Maties raigne of England &c. hath giuen and granted vnto this peticõner the office of Printer, Typographe and Bookseller of his Matie his heires and Successo^{r}s (amongst other thingę) of all and singuler Gram̃ers and Gramer bookes, Greeke, or Latine, or in the Greeke or latine Tongues, and either of them, being before that time made Compiled or set forth, and after that time to be made Compiled or set forth, either intermingled or not intermingled with the English Tongue, And also full power lycense preuiledge & authority to imprint the same. To haue hold, enioy and exercise the said office, previlidge, power license and authoritie to this peticõner his Executo^{r}s Administrato^{r}s and Assignes from the date of the said letters Patentę vnto the end and terme of Thirtie yeares then next enseuing, prohibiting all others for the imprinting thereof, during the said Tearme.

Which preuiledge hath been quietlie inioyed by the peticõner and other Patentees and their Assignes from the first yeare of the Raigne of King Edward the sixt vntill this time without anie Claime or disturbance of anie person or persons whatsoeuer./

Yet maie it please your lo^{ps}. that nowe of late one Cantrell Legg Printer to the vniu'sitie of Cambridge by Colour of some license from the vice Chancello^{r} and others of that vniu'sitie, hath imprinted a great nomber of the said Gram̃ers and doth intend to disperse and sell the same at his pleasure in Contempt and derogacoñ of his Maties prerogatiue Royall and to the great hurt and hinderance of this peticõner and his Assignes.

The peticõner doth most humblie beseech your lo^{ps}. to referre the Consideracoñ of the said letters patentę and the pretẽnce of right of the said Cantrell Legg to some of the Kingę Maties. learned Councell who maie Call both p^{ties} before them, and heare what Can be said on either parte and Certifie your Lo^{ps}. there opinions therein. And that in the meane time your Lo^{ps}. wilbe pleased to write your honourable letters to the vice Chancello^{r} of Cambridge requiring him to take a note of the nomber of gram̃ers that the said Legg hath imprinted and to take order that none of the same

[1] Bonham Norton had assigned the Grammar Patent to the partners of the Grammar Stock (cf. *C–B.C*, 58^{b}, 21 Dec. 1619). He presumably was here acting for his assignees (cf. *C–B.C*, 69^{a}, 26 June 1621). Legge had printed, probably among others, an edition of Lily and Colet's *A shorte introduction of grammar*, 8°, Cambridge, C. Legge, 1621, a copy of which is in the Folger.

Gram̃⟨ers⟩ be sold or dispersed vntill your Lo^ps^. vpon the Certificate of his Maties. learned Counc⟨ell⟩ shall take further order therein.

And he shall praie &c.

24 Julie 1621

The Lordę thinke fitt that his Maties Councell learned shall take this petition into their consideration calling both parties, and certifie their opinion to the Board.

Geo: Caluert.

Mr Atturney and m^r^ Sollicitorę [*first*] Reporte.
May it please your Lo^ps^:

According to your[Lo^ps^] direccoñ, wee haue called before vs aswell the peticõner as Cantrell Legg printer to the vniu'sitie of Cambridge with whome also came some on behalfe of the vniu'sitie and insisted vpon the preuiledges of the vniu'sitie grounded vpon seuerall Chr̃es and an Act of parliament of the 13th yeare of Queene Eliz: by which they suppose the printing of the bookes Complayned of to be well warranted. But because none of the Councell of the vniu'sitie could be had in this time of vacacõn to defend their right they pressed to haue time vntill the terme which wee held not just to denie, yet because the Peticoñer conceiveth he shall sustaine much preiudice by that Delaie, wee at his instance haue thought fitt to Certifie your lo^ps^. thereof, that you maie take such further Course in the meane time, as to your hono^rs^ shalbe thought expedient

30. Julij 1621 Thomas Coventry.
Ro: Heath.

FOL. 98^b^ Against the printer of Cambridge

To the Kingę most excellent Matie.

The humble petition of Bonham Norton your Maties. Printer in the Latine, Greeke and Hebrue &c.

Most humbly sheweth

Grammars [18° hand] That whereas your Matie by your highnes lr̃es patentę vnder the great seale of England Dated the sixth daie of January in the Tenth yeare of your Maties. Raigne of England &c did giue and graunt vnto your peticõner the office of printer to your highnes (amongst other thingę) of all Gram̃ers in greeke and latine for the Terme of Thirty yeares from the Date of the said letters patentę, ꝓhibiting therby all others for the imprinting thereof during the said Terme. Which previledge hath beene enioyed quietlie by the peticõner and other former patentees euer since the raigne of King Henry the eight, without anie Claime or Disturbance of anie ꝑson or persons whatsoeuer.
Yet maie it please your ma^tie^. that nowe of late one Cantrell Legg printer to the vniu'sitie of Cambridge by Colour of some license from the vice Chancellor and others of that vniu'sitie hath imprinted a great nomber of the said Gram̃ers, in contempt of your Maties. said Grant and to the great hinderance of this peticõner and his assignes./

The peticõner therefore conceiuing himselfe to be wronged by the said Legg, exhibited a peticoñ, sythence the beginning of your Ma^{te}. progresse to the Lordę of your Ma^{te}. privie Councell who referred the Consideracoñ thereof to you Maties. learned Councell wherevpon your Maties Atturney and Solliciter called both parties before them, and then the said Legg claymed the printing thereof by a Chr̃e made to the vniu'sitie by King Henry the viijth, but neuer inioyed as to the point in question, but because the learned Councell of the vniu'sitie could not be had this time of vacacoñ your Maties. said learned Councell gaue them time till the next terme, as by their Certificate annexed appeareth./

In the meane time maie it please your Matie. the said Legg Disperseth the said bookes, which as this peticõner conceiveth are forfeited to your Matie. and xij^{d} for euery booke that he hath [im] printed.

Nowe for that the Lordę doe not sit this time of vacacoñ the peticõner is forced to Complaine to your Matie. and humbly praie that your Matie. wilbe pleased to require the vice Chancello^{r} of the saide vniu'sitie to take a note of the nomber of Gram̃ers that haue ben printed there, and to take order that none be dispersed or sold vntill your Ma^{bies}. said learned Councell haue Certified either to your Matie. or to that ho^{ble} boorde their opinions concerning the same, And that therevpon it be decided whether the right therof be in your Matie or in the vniu'sitie.

And he shall pray &c.

At the Court at Aldershot. 2. September, 1621

His Matie holding the humble suit of this petitioner to be reasonable Is gratiously pleased to require the Vicechancellor of the said vniu'sitie to take a note in writing of the nombre of Gram̃ers which haue been of late printed their and to take order that none of them be dispersed or sold vntill this difference to whome the printing of them doth of right belong be ended and decided as is humbly desired.

Jo: Suckling

Mr Atturney and
m^{r} Solliciter their
Certificate[1]

May it please your lo^{pps}:

Wee haue considered of the peticoñ of Bonham Norton his Maties. Printer, and haue heard the Counsell of the peticoñer, and of the vniu'sitie of Cambridge, on the behalfe of Cantrell Legg their printer, and haue advised of a Chr̃e granted by King Henry the eight to that vniu'sitie in the six and twentith yeare of his Raigne, wherevpon it was insisted before vs that the Printer of the vniu'sitie might by allowance of the vice Chancello^{r} & three Docto^{r}s print Gram̃^{r}s or anie other bookes, but vpon due consideracoñ of the scope and true intent of that Charter togither with the Continuall practise and vsage euer since, wee are of opinion that the vice Chancello^{r} & docto^{r}s cannot authorish their printer to imprint such bookes, wch his Matie. hath by his patent of p^{r}viledge appropriated to anie others, Neu'thelesse in respect there was some colourable ground for the said Legg to imprint, & as it is Credibly informed vs the not venting of the bookes already printed might be the [*vtter*] ou'throw of the

[1] Cf. *State Papers Dom. 1619–1623*, p. 313, no. 124.

poore man, wee wish that the peticoñer should take of from him the bookꝭ already printed at some reasonable rate that maie make the poor man a fauer, which wee are also enformed maie be done, & the peticõnrs haue some moderate gaine, & for the future the printing agt. his Mate. prviledge granted to his owne printer to be forborne.

25. Nouember 1621: — Thomas Coventry, Ro: Heath.

FOL. (98a *repeated*)

By the Mayor

To the Master & wardens of the Companie of Stationers

fforasmuch as I haue of late receiued letters from the Lordꝭ of his Maties. most honourable privie Councell requiring me to take especiall care for the prouision of Corne within this Citie. And forasmuch as I conceiue you haue not as yet made your full prouision of Corne [*of Corne*] according to the precept to you Directed in that behalfe in Julie last past. Theis are therefore to will and require you, and in his Maties. name streightlie to charge and Coṁand you to buy and make vp youre full prouision of Cxl. quarters of wheate, which is rateablie appointed and proporcõned for your Companie according to the former prouision of Ten Thousand quarters to be bought and prouided by all the seuerall Companies of this Citie. And that the same be bought prouided and laid vp in granaries within this Citie, for the seruice and prouision thereof before our ladie daie next coming at the furthest. And that you depend not vpon Chandlers, Bakers, or anie others to make the same prouision, as you tender the good of this Citie, and will answer the Contrarie if through yor Defaulte this seruice shall in anie parte be neglected and for the better accomplishment of their Lops. Coṁand, my selfe purposeth (god willing) before that time to take a streight accompt of your performan⟨ce⟩ hereof and to veiwe whether you haue made your said prouision, accordinglie or not, Guildhall this Tenth of Januarie 1621.

Wheate [18° hand]

Weld.

By the Mayor

To the master and wardens of the Company of Stationers.

Corne (*18° hand*)

These are to will and require you that vpon Wednesday next and so from thenceforth weekely vpon the wednesday in euery weeke vntill you receive order from mee to the contrary you bringe or cause to be brought to the meale markett at Newgate markett wthin this Cittye Three quarters of wheate meale of yor Companies store and provision which you haue or ought to haue and that you there sell the same to the poore people by the half pecke, pecke or half bushell and not aboue to any one ꝑson at one time at the rate of sixe pence the bushell vnder the price that the like meale shalbe sold for in the same markett yt same day and not at any higher or greater Rates. And hereof faile you not as you will answere yor default in yt behalf This xxvijth day of August 1622.

Weld.

Present

Mr Waterson master	mr Norton	mr Jaggard
m^r^ Swinhowe } wardenę	m^r^ Feild.	mr Cooke
m^r^ Knight }	mr Lownes sen'	mr Islip

Fol. (98^b^ *repeated*)

3° Decemb. 1621

Geo. Wood[1] Almanacks primmers (*18° hand*)

Whereas Geo. Wood hath erected and sett vp a printing presse at Stepney in the Countye of Mđđ and therew^th^all hath printed diuers Almanackes and prim^rs^ Contrary to the Decrees in Starchamber. This day it was ordered that the said presse lr̃es and instrum^tę^ of printing should be seized vpon and brought to the station^rs^ hall to be disposed of as by the said Decree is ordayned & appointed.

Mđ this presse was p̃ntely after seized and brought to stationr̃s hall and there the said presse lẽrs and all other instruments of printing were battered [*mouten*] moulten and defaced according to the Decree.

A Copie of the Order of the high Com̃ission Court for the defacinge of Geo: Woodę presse and lẽrs.

Fol. 99^a^

Die Jovis vizt decimo quarto Die mensis ffebr. Anno Đm 1621 Coram Com̃issionarijs Regijs apud Lambehith Judicialiter seden' p̃nte Thoma Mottershed No^rio^. pub^co^.

Officiu' Dnorũm Coñ Georgiũ wood.
Joħen Hanson, ffrancisũ Boate
Thomũ Hales et Roƀm Raworth.[2]

The cause is to be enformed in and finally sentenced vnles some matter of Defence was giuen in on the behalf of the defendantę, and admitted by munday at eight Last past, There is no Defense admitted. This day vpon motion of m^r^ Do^r^ Rives his Maties aduocate being of Counsell for the office who moued the Court & desired that the Cause might goe to report vpon the Defendantę answeres. It was then by him made Knowne to the Court out of there p̱sonall answeres and Confessions that the presse nowe lately by authoritye of this Court seyzed and by the Defend^tę^ imployed for printing of bookę was at the first erected for printing of Linnen Cloth and ymployed to that vse onely but of late it hath ben ymployed in printing of bookę, by the sđ Defd^t^ George Wood who hath erected and kept the same in a secrett Corner vizt at Stepney in the Countye of Miđđ where it was taken and that the rest of the Defend^tę^ haue ben of late by him sett on worke to printe bookę in and vpon the same presse, nether the said Wood himself nor any other of the Defend^tę^ being Master printers or lawfully appointed or authorished to haue the gou'm^t^ of a presse or printing house Contrary to the Decree in Starchamber sett downe in the 28th yeare of her late Maties. raigne Wherevpon the Court ordered and decreed the said printing presse and lẽrs wth all other instrum^tę^ for printing forth wth to be defaced and molten and made

unlicensed press [18° hand]

[1] Cf. *C–B.C*, 71^a^, 15 Feb. 1622.

[2] Hales took up his freedom 5 June 1626 (Arber iii. 686). Raworth was made free 31 March 1606 (Arber iii. 683); got into trouble for printing *Venus and Adonis* (Arber iii. 701); and in 1635 again had his press taken down (supra, pp. 264 and 272) and only returned to him by order of the High Commission (*State Papers Dom. 1635–6*, p. 468).

vnseruiceable for printing any more bookę hereafter as by the said Decree in Starchamber is ordayned and appointed, and for the further sensuring of the defendtę, the Court assigned the Cause to be informed in and finally sentenced the next Court Day and the said Defendtę were ordered & monished to be here p̃nte the same day to heare and receive the further finall order and iudgmt of the Court

Concordaę cum Originali
Rober' Christian Deput.
Registrarij regij.

FOL. 99b A Copie of the Order of the highe Comission Courte for the Imprisoning of George Wood.

Die Jovis vizt. Nono die Mensis Maij 1622 Coram Comissionarijs Regijs apud Lambehith Judicialiter seden' pn'te Robto Christian deputat Regrarij Regij.

Officiũ dnorũ Con' Georgiũ Wood, Johem. Hanson, ffranciscũ Boate Thomam Hales, et Robtũ Raworth do: Ryues

The Counsell for the office insist on the parties defendantę answeres, and they are to appeare by bond to receiue the finall order and Judgment of the Courte out of that which is by them Confessed in their personall Answeres, made to the Articles obiected against them. At which daie and place, the said George Wood, and the rest of the said parties defendantę, appeared personally, and then the Articles obiected against the said Defts with their answeres made therevnto together with the Decree of Starchamber made and sett downe in the 28th yeare of the late Queene Eliz: of famous memorie, for the better ordering and Reforming abuses in Printers, were there publiquely read, by which it appeared plainly to the Courte, that the said George Wood, without the privitie, direccõn or appointment of the Lord Archbishop of Canterbury, and the Lord Bishop of London, As alsoe of the wardens and Assistantę of the Companie of Stacõnrs London or the more parte of them, and without anie allowance or admittance of his Maties. Comissionrs Ecclicall (whose Consentę and approbacõns are by the said decree for that end and purpose necessarily required) sett vp a printing presse in private places out of the Citie of London, and with the help of the rest of the Defts therewith printed seuerall sortę of bookes, contrary to the said Decree in Starchamber. The Courte finding by daylie experience the manifold mischiefę, and Inconveniences which arise by meanes of such ill disposed persons, as haue taken vpon them in such places to erect and sett vp printing presses for the printing and publishing of bookes, without sufficient warrant and Authority, did hold the said George Wood for his offence in this kinde well worthy to be punished, and soe pronounced and adiudged him to be and according to the said Decree in Starchamber comitted him to prison for a twelue moneth and Condempned him in Charges or costę of suite, which are to be taxed the next Court daie. But for the said Hanson, Boate, Hales and Raworth inasmuch as they were
FOL. 100a only imployed by the said || Wood as his seruantę or workmen, and that it did not appeare to the Courte, that they were partnors or had anie stocke or proffitt with the said wood in that worke, as was obiected. Therefore they were by opinion of the

Court Discharged without allowance of anie Charges to either parte. And whereas the said Wood by himselfe and his Counsell alleadged in his excuse, that he had warr[t] vnder the great Seale of England, for the setting vp of a printing presse and that he might print prim[rs] and Almanackȩ, he being free of the Companie of Stacõn[r]s. The Courte were of opinion that this Allegacõn did noe wayes extenuate, but aggrauate his offence, for that therein, he had much abused his Ma[ties]. grante which allowed him to sett vp a printing presse for the Imprinting of lynnen Cloth, and had for sometime imploy'd it to that vse: But nowe he had contrary to the expresse wordes & meaning of his highnes graunte misimployed the said Presse, and therwith printed Bookes without Authoritie as aforesaid. And therevpon the Lo: Archb[p]. of Canterbury in the name of the whole Courte, Juditially admonished the said printers and euerie of them to obserue the said Decree of Starchamber, & not hereafter to Intermeddle in the erecting of anie printing presse, or with imprinting or publishing anie bookes contrary to the said Decree./

Exãitur per Mottershed./

To the m[r] and wardens
of the Company of Statiõers By the Maior/

Whereas yo[u] haue fayled to bring meale to the Markett wherevnto yo[u] were Directed by former preceptȩ Theise are to require yo[u], that yo[u] continue to serue those markettȩ wth the like quantities and at those Dayes and prizes and in such manner as yo[u] were formerly appointed vntill yo[u] shall receiue order from me to the contrary. The which service I entend to ympose vpon you no Longer then the Necessitye of the tymes shall Compell and hereof faile yo[u] not at yo[r] ꝑill from my house the first of Nouember 1622/

Weld.

M[r] Feild master
mr Gilmyn } wardenȩ
mr Pavier. }

23°. Septemb. 1622 ℞ Jac. 20°. FOL. 101[b]

Whereas Geo. wood hath erected and sett vp one other presse at his house in Grubstreet London[1] This day the Wardens seized vpon the said presse and brought the same to the Stationrs hall to be disposed of as by the said Decree in starchamber is ordayned, and the said presse was afterwards broken and the lr̃e melted and deliu'rd againe vnto him/

An order from my lordȩ grace concerninge Geo. woode

I vnderstand that Geo. Wood prisoner in yo[r] custody hath libertye often times to goe abroad which there is good reason to presume is to euill purpose I doe therefore hereby require yo[u] to take such order wth him as that he be no more ꝑmitted to goe forth out of the prison which if it shall be found that he doe I must be forced to cōmitt yo[u] to the ffleet for yo[r] neglect & want of Care in this behalf, ffrom Croydon August 23. 1622. Geo. Cant.

To the warden of the new prison in Mayden lane./

[1] Cf. *C–B.C*, 71[a], 15 Feb. 1621.

Vnder an other peticon of Geo. woods
it pleased my lordes grace to
vnder write as followeth.

I would haue Geo. Wood to submitt himself and putt in bandes into the Company not to offend againe, this being done I giue my consent that he should be released out of prison and after that other thingę may be discussed as reason doth require
Octo. 30. 1622 Geo: Cant

FOL. 101[a] Geo Woode To the most reu'end ffather in god George Lo. Archb. of Canterburye his grace

The humble peticon of Geo. Wood.

humblye sheweth

That he hath ꝑformed yo[r] graces order and is nowe discharged out of prison for which vndeserved favor he is and eu' will be humbly thankefull vnto yo[r] grace in regard he hath referred himself vnto the Company. hee most humbly beseecheth yo[r] grace to be his ho[ble]. good freinde to order or otherwise as yo[r] grace shall thinke fitt that he may haue those goodes againe that were last taken from him and such recompence for other goodę formerly taken as in yor graces wisdome yo[u] shall thinke fitt, And he and his shall eu' pray for yor graces eternall hapienes &c.

This person being penitent and havinge obeyed my order I pray the m[r] and wardens of the statiońrs to take into their Consideracońs and favor.

G. Cant

Peticõn against Geo. Woode

To the most reverend father in god the lord Archb. of Canterbury his grace.

The humble peticõn of the m[r] & wardens of the Statiońrs

Sheweth that the peticońrs about Mechaelmas last past goeing by authoritye of the high Cōmission Court to seaze a presse (erected by Geo. Wood Contrary to the decrees in Starchamber) were violently opposed by foure workemen ymployed by the said Wood wth swordę and othe[r] weapons in y[e] manner as the like heretofore hath not ben knowne contemning both yo[r] graces warrant and all other authoritye then present for which their disobedience and willfull Contempt ther stand all bound to answere the same in the said high Commission Court before yo[r] grace.

Nowe perceiving yo[r] grace gratiously inclyninge rather by mercye to win them then by a due Course of lawe to punish them, for our ꝑtę (notw[th]standing their iniurious dealeingę w[th] vs both in wordę & deedę) we desire not their punishment but amendmt and therefore humbly submitt them and their Contemptuous dealeingę to yo[r] graces censure. Desiring that they may as Wood hath enter into bondę w[th] suerties not to attempt the like againe or to stand Cōmitted or otherwise as yor grace shall thinke it fitt.

And as concerning the said Wood (who in his peticõns and otherwise vseth vs at his pleasure alledging that wee vndoe him by keeping his goodes and him out of ymploymt and that by o[r] delaies he and all his shall perrish except yo[r] grace be pleased to sett downe some order for him. Of w[ch] Imputatōns wee doubt not but yo[r] grace is well ꝑsuaded otherwise of vs, And notw[th]standing all the wrongę and hinderances done by him and his, against vs & o^r Company yet he knoweth that when wee had iust Cause to prosecute against him and [to] haue him kept in prison we did aduise w^t him how to gett him out of prison and also to further him in any good or lawfull Course he would deuise. And are likewise willing if it may seem good to yor grace that the goodꝭ last taken being yet vndefaced, may be valued and the vtmost worth thereof to be giuen him that so nether he nor wee by occasion may be further troublesome to yor grace as wee haue ben.

The answer to this
peticon followeth
in the next page
vert. foł.

The Copie of my lord of Canterb. order vnder the former peticõn FOL. 101b

If those foure men doe enter bond to carry themselues orderly hereafter they may be dismist out of trouble otherwise order will be giuen for their Cōmittment. And for wood if the presse be sold lett him haue the money but I hold it most fitt that he should worke at Jorney worke for a convenient time and if [in] the meane while he doe carry himselfe soberly so that he giue contentm^t to the Company vpon their suit hereafter I should not be against it that vpon sufficient bondꝭ for his good behavior he be admitted a master printer if any such place should fall void And wth this order I wish him to hold himselfe contented./ Decemb. 2 1622.

G. Cant./

Geo: Woodꝭ release vnder his hand and seale.

Whereas I Geo: wood lately erected and sett vp a presse at Stepney in the Countye of Midđ and therew^th all printed prim^rs and almanackꝭ contrary to the decrees in Starchamber which presse together wth all instrum^tꝭ of printing and certaine bookes now seazed vpon and taken by the m^r & wardens of the stationr̃s in December 1621 and brought to the stationrs hall & there battered moulten & defaced according to the decrees. And whereas afterwardꝭ I the said Geo. wood erected and sett vp one other presse at my house in Grubstreet which likewise was seazed vpon & taken by the said m^r & wardens and brought to the stationr̃s hall to be defaced and moulten according to the said decrees but vpon my humble peticõn to my lord Archb. of Canterbury his grace It pleased his grace to desire the m^r & wardens I being penitent to take me into their Consideracoñ and afterwardꝭ vnder an other peticoñ to order, that if the presse be sold I should haue the mony which presse lers̃ and other thingꝭ being valued by indifferent men amounteth to the some of foureteene poundꝭ sixetene shillingꝭ. Nowe knowe all men by theise p̃ntꝭ That I the said Geo. Wood doe acknowledg to haue receiued and had before the ensealing hereof of the said m^r & wardens of the stationr̃s the some of fifteene poundꝭ of lawfull money of England And I doe hereby for me my ex^rs adm^rs and assignes remise release and quiet claime vnto the mr & wardens of the said Company and their successo^rs, all and all manner of accõns suitꝭ pleas quarrells some and somes of money trespasses & demandꝭ whatsoeu' which against the said m^r & wardens or any of them I the said George Wood heretofore haue had nowe haue or hereafter shall [or may] haue for vpon or by reason of their seazing or taking of my presses letters bookes & instrum^tꝭ of printing or of for vpon or by reason of any other matter Cause [or] thing whatsoeu' from the beginning of the world to the day of the date of theise p̃ñtę In witnes whereof I the said Geo. wood haue herevnto sett my hand & seale the 14th day of decemb. in the twentith yeare of the raigne of or sou'aigne lord King James &c.

George Wood

Sealed and deliu'ed in the p̃ñce of Tho. Montforth
Norye. John Barrett.

Fol. 102a To the Mr. & wardens of the Companie of Stationers.

By the Mayor.

Whereas I and my brethren the Aldermen for the prouision of this Citie haue bought 2100 quarters of forraine wheate after the rate of xlvjs the quarter to be Distributed and deuided amongst the seuerall Companies of this City to be by them laid vp for the Cityes store to furnish the Markettę from time to time as occasion shall require of which 2100 quarters there is allotted to your Compny ffifty quarters which is nowe remayning at the Bridghouse. Theis are therefore to require you that presently upon sight hereof you take order to receiue the same ffifty quarters of wheate at the Bridghouse which is allotted to your Companie to receiue as aforsaid and laie vp the same in your granary for the purpose aforesaid And that you doe alsoe make present payment vnto the Chamberlayne of this Citie at his office at the Guildhall after the rate of xlvjs the quarter for the same wheate which you shall soe receiue And besides you are to pay for the meatage and other Duties for the taking vp and bestowing the same there according to the vse and Custome of this City in that kinde, vnto the said Chamberlayne after the rate of fower pence vpon euery quarter of wheat which you shall soe receiue And hereof faile you not at your perill, This first day of ffebruary. 1622

Weld./

To the Master & wardens
of the Company of Stationrs By the Mayor.

Theise are to will & Comand you on Wednesday next and so from thenceforth weekely vpon [the] wednesday eu'ye weeke vntill you receive order from me to the Contrary you bring or Cause to be brought to the meale markett at Newgate Markett wthin this Cittye three quarters of wheate meale of yor Companies store and provision and that you there sell the same to the poore people by the half pecke, pecke half bushell and not aboue to any p̱son at one time after the rate of vjs the bushell and not at any higher or greater rate and hereof faile you not as you will answere yor default in yt behalf this xiiijth day of ffebr. 1622

Weld./

Die Jovis vizt sexto die Mensis ffebr Anno Dni inxer [?] 1622 Coram Comissionarijs Regijs apud lambehith Judicate seden' p̃ñte Tho. Mottershed./[1]

Officũ Duorũ p̱not p̱ valentinũ Symmes con mruñ et Gardianos siue Custod' et Comunitat' misterij siue Artis Stationarę Ciuitatis london

This day vpon report of sr Henry Martin who together wth sr Wm Bird had herd this Cause according to a refference made vnto them by a former [order] of this

[1] Cf. *C–B.C*, 75a, 13 Dec. 1622.

Court, y[t] was thought meet and so ordered That the said Valentine Symes shall not henceforth worke as a master printer And whereas the Company of Stationr̃s did heretofore allowe him towardꝭ his mayntenance after the rate of foure poundꝭ a yeare they shall giue him ten poundꝭ ouer and besidꝭ his said pencõn to be payd in five yeares next ensueing (that is to say) fortye shillingꝭ a yeare ouer and besides his said yearely pencõn of ffoure poundꝭ yf he the said Symmes shall liue so long and so the said Symes is to rest satisfied/[1]

To the m[r] and wardens of the Companie of Stationrs./ By the Mayo[r]. Fol. 102[b]

Theis are in his Ma[ties]. name straightlie to chardg and Comande yo[u] that for the better store of this Cittie w[th] corne and the better furnishing of the m'kettꝭ w[th]in the same yo[u] buy and make vp yo[r] ffull provision of one hundred and fortie quarters of wheate which is Rateablie appointed and proporconed for yo[r] Company according to the former provision of Ten thousand quarters to be bought and provided by all the seu'all Companies of this Cittie. And that the same be bought provided and laid vp in Granaries w[th]in this Cittie for the service and provision theirof before o[r] ladie day next Coming at the furthest. And yt yo[u] depend not vpon Chandlers Bakers or any others to make the same provision as yo[u] tender the good of this Cittie and will answer the Contrarie if thorough yo[r] default this service shall in any part be neglected, And for the better performance of the p'misses myself purposeth (god willing) before that time to take a strict accompt of the performance hereof and to see whether yo[u] have made yor provision accordinglie or not. Guildhall this xxiij[th] day of febr: 1623

Weld./

Cambridge — To the right ho[ble]. the Lordꝭ and others of his ma[ties] most ho[ble]. privie Counsell. Fol. 103[a]

The humble peticõn of the m[r] and wardens of the Company of Stationẽrs[2]

Psalms: (*18° hand*) Sheweth That in the first yeare of his Maties Raigne the priveledg for the sole printing of Psalters, Psalmes, Primers and Almanackes was in the handꝭ and possession of Divers perticuler persons and had ben quietlie enioyed for many yeares.

The peticõnrs having Compounded wth the former Patentees (which Composicõn cost them wth astocke raised great somes of money) It then pleased his Ma[tie] by his lr̃es patentꝭ vnder the great seale to grant y[e] same vnto them for the gen'all good of the whole companie w[th] an expresse prohibicon that no person whatsoeu' should print any bookes tending to the same or the like purpose any Act, ordinance or othe[r] matter to the Contrarye not w[th]standing

The peticonr̃s have eu' since the granting of the said lẽrs patentꝭ yearelie distributed and by an ordinance in that behalf made are to distribute 200[li] p annu' for eu' among the poore of the said Companie in respect of the said grant/

[1] Simmes had been a printer of recusant books and it may be that it was thought to be easier to pension him than to keep a watch on his work.

[2] This petition is recorded *State Papers Dom. 1623–1625*, p. 98, under date 17 Oct. 1623.

And whereas also in a Decree made in the high court of Starchamber Concerning printing and selling of bookes it was ordayned that none should ymprint anie bookes or copies against any lr̃es patentȩ or prohibytions vnder the great seale vpon payne of Confiscation of the said bookes and sixe monethes ymprisonment/

Neu'theles Cantrell Legg printer to the vniu'sitie of Cambridg about two yeares since ymprinted great numbers of gram^{rs} and accedencȩ wch were in priveledg to an other, and being complained of for the same before this ho^{ble}. Boord, The said Legg endeuored to Justifie the doeing thereof by gen'all wordȩ in a grant made to the said Vniu'sitie by K: Henry the eight and the matter being referred by yor lops̃. to his Maties learned Counsell They after they had heard what the vniu'sitie could alledge did certifie yor lo^{ps}. That the said grant of Hen: 8 did not extend to the printing any such bookes which his Matie had appropriated to any others and yet his Matie was gratiouslie pleased at the instance of the Vice Chancellor and Do^{rs} of the said vniu'sitie and in regard of the povertie of the said Legg as was pretended That the ympression of bookes then printed might be sold but wth an expresse com̃and to printe no more bookes which his ma^{tie} by his lẽrs patentȩ had appropriated to any others/

Nowe the said Cantrell Legg notwthstanding his Maties said gratious favor and permission towardȩ him hath since Contrarie to his highnes said prohibitioñ and in derogacõn of his Royall Progatiue, and contrarie to the entent of the priveledg granted to the peticoñrs and the Decree in the high Court of Starchamber not onelie againe ymprinted greater nombers of the said gram^{rs} and accedencȩ, but also of late hath printed the psalmes in divers volumes, and if he shall be suffered to goe on in this sort, he will not onelie vndoe the poorer sort but Ruyn the whole companye and make his Maties prerogatiue in this kind of no validitie.

The peticoñrs doe most humblie pray the assistance of this ho^{ble}. boord for the better execucõn of his Maties said lẽrs patentȩ and seazing of the said bookes. And that the said Legg may be dealt wthall [for his contempt] as to Justice shall appertaine, And thei shall pray &c.[1]

Fol. 103^{b} *(Blank)*

Fol. 104^{a} Cambridge Printer/ At Whitehall the 10th of December 1623/[2]

Lo: Archb. of Canterburye	Lo. vis: Grandison
Lo. Thresurer	Lo. Carewe
Lo. President	m^{r} Threasurer
Lo. Privye seale	mr Controller
Lo. Steward	mr Chan: of ye Excheq
E. of Carleile	mr of the Rolles/

The matter in Controuersie betwen the vniu'sitie of Cambridge on the behalf of their printer and the Statioñrs and printers of london, touching their priveledges of printing of bookes being brought to heareing in a full Counsell before the boord

[1] The Privy Council wrote to the Vice-Chancellor of Cambridge regarding this petition, 17 Oct. 1623 (cf. *Acts of P.C. June 1623–March 1625*, p. 102), and the same day sent for Legg to appear before them (*op. cit.*, p. 102), and again 25 Oct. 1623 (*op. cit.*, p. 108). He appeared 1 Nov. 1623 (*op. cit.*, p. 109), and on 21 Nov. 1625 (*op. cit.*, p. 119) a discussion of the matter was held.

[2] This decision is recorded in *State Papers Dom. Addenda. 1580–1625*, pp. 658–9, and also in *Acts of P.C. June 1623–March 1625*, pp. 141–2.

There was produced on the behalf of the vniu'sitie a Charter granted them 26 Hen. 8 authorishing them to Choose three Stationr̃s and to giue them power to printe all manner of bookes allowed or to be allowed by the Vicechancello^{r} and three Docto^{r}s The printers and Stationr̃s of london on the other part shewed forth seu'all lẽrs patentę beareing dates since the said Charter to the vniu'sitie wherein was granted to the said Companie and to some pe^{r}ticuler members of the same the priveledg of sole printing of divers p̱ticule^{r} bookes in the said lẽrs patentę specified, The validitie of which said Charter and lr̃es patentę being stronglie insisted vpon on both sides and the matter heard at lardg: Their lo^{ps}: thought fitt to acquaint his Matie wth the debates and to receive his Royall direction therein whose pleasure was that all lawfull fauo^{r}s should be extended to the vniu'sitie yet so as that neither partie should have cause to Complaine, And to that ende [directed] that some fitt accomodacõn should be made in ye busine⟨s⟩.

Their lo^{ps}. therevpon calling all parties before them propounded such p̱ticulers as [*they*] thought reasonable and equall for both sides to yeld vnto wherevnto the vicechancellor whose Discretion and moderacõn in the Carriage of the busines their lo^{ps}. did well approue & Comeñd/ submitted and gaue assent in the name of the vniu'sitie And the Stationr̃s and printers / though they much pressed howe Chardgable theise priveledged bookes had ben vnto them yet in Conclusion [they] applied themselues to that Course which the lordę did then thinke fitt to pronounce, as indifferent betwen the vniu'sitie and them as followeth vizt/

ffirst that all bookes printed and to be printed should be sold at reasonable and fitt prizes otherwise the forme of the Statutes to be put in execucõn which is for the setting a rate at what price eu'ye booke should be sold for. That the prizes of bookes in respect of the many priveledges are extreamelie raysed/

Bibles
common prayer books
Grammars
Psalmes
Psalters
primmers
Common Law books
(*18° hand*)

That the Vniu'sitie should comprinte wth the Stationr̃s & printers of london in all bookes whatsoeu' as well priveledged as others, saue onelie the Bible, Bookes of Com̃on prayer, Gramers, Psalmes Psalters, primers, and bookes of the Com̃on lawe, or any parte of them wth this limitacõn neu'theles that the vniu'sitie shall sett on worke, but one presse onelie for the printing of all or any of the said || Fol. 104^{b}
priveledged bookes allowed by vertue of this Article, And the bookes whereof the first Copies shall be brought either to the vniu'sitie printer or to the printers of london to goe according to the gen'all vse which is to such partie to whom the Copie shall be first brought and no other/

Almanacks
&
prognostications
(*18° hand*)

That the vniu'sitie shall not printe any Almanackes whereof the Copies are nowe belonging to the Stationr̃s nor any other Almanackes to be hereafter published whereof the first Copies shall be brought to the Stationr̃s but the vniu'sitie shall print such prognosticacsõn hereafter to be made whereof the first Copie shall be brought to their Printer/

That the Companie of Stationrs of london shall not by any ordinancę made or to be made wthin their Companie hinder or impeach the printer of the vniu'sitie in the sale of [*his*] [such] bookes as are allowed to be there printed but that it shall be free for any of their Companie or others to buy of the vniu'sitie printer any of the said bookes/

Lastlie it is thought ffitt that the Printer of the vniu'sitie shall have libertie notwthstanding the order of this boord of the 17th of october last freelie to vtter and sell all those Gramers and Psalmes[1] which he hath already printed, and y^{t} such of the said bookes as have ben seized by the Stationrs and printers shalbe forthwith restored wherein their lo^{ps}. wish that according to the offer of Bonham Norton printer and some other of the Stationrs made to the Boord/ they will take of from the vniu'sitie printer all the said Gramers and Psalmes at such reasonable prizes as shall be agreed vpon betwen them/

W: Beecher/

To the m^{r} and wardens
of the Company of Stationrs By the Mayo^{r}/

Whereas I and my brethren the aldermen have resolued and agreed that the fful quantitie of 10000 quarters of wheate shalbe brought and provided by all the seu'all Companies of this Cittie betwen this and Candlemas Day next according to such rates and proporcōns as the same Companies have heretofore ben seu'ally assessed and taxed at towarde the furnishing of the like proporcōn, In accomplishm^{t} whereof theis are to will and require yo^{u} in his Maties name straightly to chardg and Cōmand yo^{u} that yo^{u} buy and provide *Clx*^{tie}[2] quarters of wheat which is rateably appointed and proporcōned for yor Company according to the said former provisions of 10000 quarters, and that the same be bought and provided and layed vpon granaries wthin this Cittye for the seruice and provision thereof before the said Candlemas Day at the furthest: And that yo^{u} depend not vpon Chandlers Bakers or any others to make the same provision as yo^{u} tender the good of the Citty and will answere the Contrarie if thorough yor default this service shall in any pte be neglected. Guildhall the last day of Novemb. 1624

Weld.

FOL. (*105^{a}*) To the m^{r} and wardens of
the Company of Stationrs By the mayo^{r}/

Theise are to require yo^{u} to repaire forthwith vnto the Bridghouse wharfe and there to receive out of the Shippes of m^{r} John Webber marchant ffiftye quarters of ffrench wheate which is allotted to yor Company out of the quantitye which is bought for the Cittyes provision, and lay the same by in granaryes vntill yo^{u} shall receive Directions from mee to serve the m'kette therewth. And further that yo^{u} vpon receipt thereof doe paie into the Chamber of London after the rate of xl^{s} the quarter for the same according as the Cittye is to paie vnto the m'chant This 7th of Aprill 1625.

Weld./

To the m^{r} and wardens
of ye Company of Stationrs By the Mayor

Whereas there is a vaine and riotous Custome of late taken vp of meeting of Countrye men of seu'all shires and Countries of this Realme at halles and Tavernes wthin this

[1] Legg seems not to have printed by this date very much that has survived. An edition of Sternhold and Hopkins, STC 2584, and one of Lily's *Shorte introduction*, 1621, a copy of which is in the Folger, are all that have been traced. After 1626, however, he printed much more.

[2] This is probably an error.

Cittye which meetingę doe occasion much vaine expence of money and many times by men that can hardly spare the same/ ffor prevention of which said meetingę Theis are to require you[u] that you[u] forbeare heareafter especially in theis times of godę visitacõn wth the Contagious sickenes of the Plague to permitt and suffer yor Companyes hall to be lett out or vsed for any such meetingę. whereof I require yo[u] not to faile This x[th] day of June 1625.

Ex[r]/ Weld.

To the m[r] and wardens of the Company of Stacõners — By the Mayor.

Theise are to will and require you that vppon ffriday next and so from thenceforth weekelie vppon the ffridaye in every weeke vntill you receive order from me to the Contrary you bringe or Cause to be brought to the Meale markett at Queenehith within this Cittie three quarters of Wheate meale of yo[r] Companies Store and provision w[ch] you have or ought to have And that you sell the same to the poore people by the halfe pecke, halfe Bushell and not above to any person at one time after the Rate of vj[d] the Bushell vnder the price that like meale shalbe sould for in the same Markett the same daye. And hereof fayle not as you will Answere yo[r] defalt in that behalfe This 23th of November. 1625.

Weld.

To the m[r] and wardens of the Company of Stacõners — By the Mayor

Theise are in his Ma[te] name to will & require you that before Tuesday next you Certifie me in writeinge vnder the handes of all or some of you what quantitie of Powder there is in Store remaineinge in yo[r] Companies Hall or at yo[r] Cõmaunde for the vse service or defence of this Cittye & yo[r] Company, if occasion shall require, And that you fayle not hereof at yo[r] perill this xxx[th] daye of december. 1625

Weld

To the M[r] & wardens of the Company of Statiońrs — By the Mayo[r]. Fol. (*105*[b])

Whereas I and my brethren the Aldermen duely Considering the great want and miseries which a number of poore people in and about this Cittye doe endure by reason of godę heavy visitacõn vpon the same, And considering the ꝑn'te Calamitie of this time have thought good in pittye and Compassion towardę them: That all publique feastingę and dinn[rs] at all and eu'ye the seu'all halles and Cõmon meeteingę of Corporacõns & Companies w[th]in this Cittie shall for this yeare ensueing be wholly forborne and left of. And that the whole Chardgę and expences entended to be bestowed and spent vpon the said feastingę & dinners shalbe bestowed and given amongst the poore distressed people of the seu'all Companies of this Cittye at the discretion of the master and wardens and greater ꝑte of the Assistantę, Theis therefore shalbe in all Christian Charitye to pray and desire yo[u] to take ꝑn'te order that for and during this ꝑn'te yeare, yo[u] wholly forbeare to keepe any Cõmon feasting at yor hall or elsewhere/ And that the monyes that shalbe contributed towardę the chardg of any of yor Cõmon feastę or dinners be collected by some honest discreet ꝑson or ꝑsons of yor Company to be by yo[u] appointed for that purpose, And the said money be wholly given and distributed amongst the poore of [*the*] [yor] Company according to yor good Discretion and the greater sort of yor assistantę, And that w^th^in one moneth after yor entended feastę or comon dinners yo^u^ certifie me & the Court of Aldren what somes of money have ben collected and distributed as aforesd and to whom in leiu of the said ffeastę and Dynners, And theis are therefore further to desire yo^u^ not to ꝑmitt any Shire feast to be kept at y^r^ hall, But to signifie that it is the desire of me and my brethren the Aldren that thes feastę be forborne & left of this ꝑn'te yeare, Hereof not to faile as yo^u^ will answere the Contrarye for yor backwardnes & negligence herein, This sixt of June. 1626

Weld.

To the m^r^ and wardens of the Company of Stationrs — By the Mayo^r^

Theise are in his Maties name straightly to chardg and Comand yo^u^ that forthwith yo^u^ receive of m^r^ Evelin his Ma^te^ gunpouder-maker five barrellę of poulder at his poulder house in Southworke for which yo^u^ are to pay after the rate of fower poundę three shillingę and fower pence the barrell and to take care that the same be laid up in some Convenient place in or nere vnto yor hall there to be kept and be in a readinesse for the service of this Cittye as occasion shall require, And hereof faile yo^u^ not. This xix^th^ of July 1626. yo^u^ are to repaire to mr Aldren ffreeman from whom yo^u^ shall receive further direction for the receipte of the powlder/

Fol. (*106^a^*) To the m^r^ & wardens of the Compañy of Stationers — By the Mayor.

Whereas my selfe and my brethren the Aldermen are informed that the Companies of this Cittye are not stored & provided wth graine for the service of this Cittye according to former presidentę and provisions of 10000 q^r^ters of Corne. Theise are therefore to will & require you, and in his Maties. name streightlye to chardge & Comaunde you that you buy & provide 140 q^r^ters of wheate wch is rateablye appointed & proporcoñed for your Companie according to former provisiones of 10000 q^r^ters of Cornc to bc bought provided & layd vp in granaries w^th^in this Cittye for the service and provision thereof before the ffirst day of May next at the furthest. And that you depend not vpon Chaundlo^r^s Bakers or anie others to make yor provisions herein as you tender the good of this Cittye, and will answeare the Contrarye, yf through yor default this service be neglected. And hereof fayle you not at yor perill This 16th of ffebruary 1626.

To the M^r^ & wardens of the Company of Stacõners — By the Mayor.[1]

Theise are in his Maties. name streightlye to Charge & Comaund you that forthw^th^ you receive of Mr Evelin[2] his Maties. Gunpowder maker ffive barrells of powder at his powder house in Southwarke for wch you are to paye after the Rate of ffower poundę three shillingę & ffowe⟨r⟩ pence the barrell, and to take Care that the same bee layd vp in some Convenient place in or neere vnto yor hall there to be kept, & bee in a

[1] This precept was already transcribed on 105^b^.

[2] Richard Evelyn, father of the diarist.

readynes for the service of this Cittye as occasion shall require, And hereof ffayle you not this xix[th] of Julye 1626.

you are to repayre to Mr Aldrañ ffreeman from whom you shall receive further direccõns for receipt of the powder./

To the m[r] & wardens of the Company of Stationers

By the Mayor

Theis are in his Maties. name to will and require you, that forthw[th] vpon receipte hereof you Cause Certificate to be made to me and my brethren the Aldren' vpon Thirsday next at the guildhall by Nyne of the Clocke in the fforenoone at the furthest subscribed by one of the wardens of yo[r] Companye. what quantitye of wheate you nowe haue in areadines in yo[r] Granary or else where, for the store and provision of yo[r] Company whereof I require you not to fayle this xix[th] of Novemƀ: 1627.

Weld.

To the right ho[ble]: the Lo[d]. Mayor of the ho[ble]. Citty of London

The Answear to the former precept./ Fol. (*106[b]*)

According to a precept of the Nineteenth of this Instant Novemƀ: wee the wardens of the Companie of Stacõners doe humblye Certifie yo[r] Lo[p]. That (in respect wee have noe Roome or granary wherein Convenientlye we can keepe our provision of Corne) wee haue ben forced to deliu' forth all our store and soe at this time wee haue none at all left. And wee humbly pray yor good Lo[p]. That (if there be cause that wee be comaunded to provide anie more) that yo[r] Lo[p]. will take order that wee may haue our Granary in Bridewell for w[ch] heretofore wee haue paid towardꝭ the building thereof. 40[li] and could neu' gett the possession thereof. And we shall pray for yo[r] Lo[pps] happines. This xxij[th] of Novemƀ: .1627.

Clement Knight./
Ed: Weaver./

The Copie of lrs written by the ffarm[r]s of the Customehouse to the Port townes vnder written.

After o[r] Heartye Com'endacõns. Whereas complaint is made that of late daies there are a great sortt of English bookes printed beyond the Seas especially in the lowe Countryes as Bybles[1] Primers psalters psalmebookes & others of that kinde, and are brought ou', and secretlye Conveyed into this kingdome in & by divers of the out portꝭ, by such meanes great abuse is done to the Comon wealth by dispsing abroad theise bookes w[ch] (as is alleadged) are very ill & falslye printed, and alsoe great wronge done to his Maties. printer and the Companye of Stacõners, vnto whom by vertu of their Charters and lres patentꝭ the Care of the printinge of all theise bookes are Comitted. Wee therefore pray you to take especiall Care that both you and all the Rest of o[r] Deputies in yor port be very watchfull vpon all occasions to prevent the secrett & private wayes of bringing anye such bookes into yo[r] portꝭ and Members thereof, and to seize all such bookes as you shall soe finde & Certifie vs thereof

[1] Probably some editions of the 4° Geneva Bibles, STC 2174–2180[a].

Wherevpon order shalbe given you how to dispose of the same, and Care wilbee taken to recompence you for yor paines therein. And so desyring you herein to be very Carefull

we rest yor Loving ffreinds
Pa: Pinelar
John. Worsnam
Jacob (*blank*)[1]

Lynne, Jarmouth, Ipswich, Colchester, Maldon, Mylton, Feuersham, Sandwich, Douer

Fol. 107ª To the M[r] & wardens of the Company of Stacõners[2] — By the Mayor.

840[li] to be lent to his Matie./ Whereas by Acte of Cōmon Councell holden in the Chamber of the guildhall of this Cittye the xvij[th] day of this instant December it was for especiall causes that Court movinge enacted & agreed that this Cittye shall furnish his Matie. wth the sōme of one hundred and Twentye thousand pounde̜ viz[t] threescore thousand pounde̜ thereof wthin Ten dayes next after his Ma[tie]. and the Lorde̜ wth others of his highnes most ho[ble]. privye Councell shall signe the articles of agreem[t] betweene his highnes and this Cittye touching the assurance of his Maties. lande̜ to be absolutely Conveyed in fee farme to this Cittye after the rate of xxviij[tie] yeares purchase for and in satisfaccõn aswell of the said Cxx[m].[li]. as of the Cittyes former debte wth interest for the same. And the other threescore thousand pounde̜ to be paid at Sixe monethes after the signeinge of the said articles. Soe as in the meanetime the bookes and assurance from his Matie. be fully passed and perfected. And whereas it was alsoe agreed that the said ffirst Threescore Thousand pounde̜ shalbe forth wth raysed and levyed by and vpon all the seu'all Companies and Corporacõns of this Cittye according to their seu'all rates and proportions as they are rated at towarde̜ their provision of Ten thousand quarters of Corne. And that all the moneyes to be disbursed by the said Companies or Corporacõns for and touchinge the said busines together wth an allowance for their forbearance thereof after the rate of Sixe pounde̜ p̱ Cent. p̱ Añn' for the time they shalbe out of their said moneyes shalbe paid vnto them by the ffirst moneyes to be made and received by this Cittye by their sale thereafter to be made by or out of the said lande̜, and that before anie parte of the Citties former debte̜ shalbe in anie wise satisfied or paid As by the said Act of Cōmon Councell amongst other things appeareth. And in asmuch ⟨as⟩ the said Contracte wilbe soe spedelye p̱fected as that the ffirst threescore thousand pounde̜ will very sodenlye become payable to his Ma[tie]. Theis are therefore for the better furnishing his Ma[tie]. wth the said moneyes by the tyme appointed straightlye to Chardge and Cōmaunde you that vpon sight hereof you leavye and provyde wthin yor Company the sōme of

840[li]. Eight hundred and fortye poundes being yor ratable parte of the said threescore thousand pounde̜ according to yor Companies proporcõn of one hundred and ffortye quarters of Corne at wch you are rated for

[1] Evidently the clerk could not read this signature.
[2] Regarding this sale of grants of land, see F. C. Dietz, *English public finance*, 1932, p. 235.

provision towardꝭ the said ten thousand quarters of Corne and that forthwth you take Course touchinge the raysing and provydeing of the said Eight hundred and ffortye poundꝭ soe that you may haue the same in areadynes at the time limitted forthwth to pay the same to the Chamƀlen of this Cittye at the guildhall London whereby the same wth other moneyes to be raysed for that purpose may be readye for his Ma[tie] in satisfacōn of the said lx[m li] according to the said Act of Cōmon Councell. And hereof fayle you not as you tender his Ma[te] service and will answeare the Contrary at yo[r] perrill Guildhall this xviijth of December 1627.

Weld.

To the M[r] and wardens of the Company of Stationers — By the Mayo[r] — Fol. 107[b]

Whereas I have lately directed my precept vnto yo[u] to provide and paie to M[r] Chamƀlen of this Citty the some of Eight hundred and fortie pounds for yo[r] Companies proporcōn toward the raysing of lx[m].[li] granted by act of Cōmon Counsell to be forthwith levied vpon the seu'all Companies of this Cittye As by the said Act is appointed Theis are straightly to chardg and Comande yo[u] that yo[u] paie the said some of viij[c] xl[li] vnto mr Robert Bateman Chamƀlen of this Cittye on thursday next w[th]out further delay And hereof faile yo[u] not at yo[r] perills This xxix[th] of decemb 1627.

Weld./

Copie of the Acquitance

Received the xi[th] day of January 1627 of the M[r] and wardens of the Company of Statiōnrs London the some of Eight hundred & fortie poundꝭ of lawfull money of England according to the preceptꝭ before written I say Received } 840[li]

ꝑ me Arthur Panther Clir Roberti
Bateman Camerarij Civitatis London.

9[o]. Januarij 1627.

Present M[r] Cole M[r] Knight M[r] Waterson M[r] Swinhowe M[r] Bill M[r]. Islip, M[r] Kingston M[r] Blount M[r] Harrison M[r] Bateman and the Maior parte of the parteners in the English stocke./

After divers meetings and Consultacōns had by the Companye in gen'all about the raysinge of 840[li] where wth this Companye are forth wth to furnish his Ma[tie]: according to a precept of the 19th. of december last, Nowe the Companye at their meetinge this daye finding it very difficult to raise such a sōme speedelye by the pole, Have Concluded and agreed that because they are much prest to have it paid in presentlye, aspedye Course be taken for the borrowing of the foresaid sōme. wherevpon the M[r] of the Companye and some others procured some freindꝭ of theirs to lend the Companye 390[li] vpon certaine ꝑcells of plate belonging to the house of wch the ꝑties soe lending the money are to have seu'all billes of sale vnder the seale of the house wth provisoes for the redemption thereof at 6 monethes, 100[li]. more is taken vpon the account of the house from M[r] Weaver as warden of the Companye, and 50[li]. more wch M[r] Trussell paies || for a fine for alease of a house belonging to the Fol. 108[a]

Hall wch belongs to the English stocke, And Mr Cole Mr Knight Mr Weaver and Mr Swinhowe are intreated to take vp 300li more vpon their owne Creditte and to stand Bounde for the same. And for their Endempnitye they are by generall Consent of those present to keepe the seale of the house and the remaynder of the plate and all other the vtensells of the house, till such time as they are disengaged by the Companye in generall, or by the Mr and wardens that shalbe Chosen for the next yeare, the interest to be paid in the meane time for the money to be taken vp vntill it be paid in, is by waye of assessmt. to be Collected and paid by the Liverye of the Companie in generall by their owne Consente and agreemt. It is both hoped and expected that the lande wch the Companye are to have in ffee farme from his Matie: in leiue of their money will hereafter dischardge the debte, or be worth soe much as is to be disbursed when the assurance is past to the Cittye, but in case it shall happen to be otherwaies that theise debte cannott be paid nor plate redeemed that way in convenient time vizt wthin the space of 2 yeares. Then it is ordered and agreed, That all the whole sum̃e shall be borne by the English stocke as the plantacõn in Ireland and other like paymente and Chardges have ben borne heretofore. Provided notwthstanding that the Master and wardens may assesse and Collect from those of the Companye that are not in the stocke such som̃es of money as they shall thinke fitt towarde the raysinge of the said som̃e of 840li above mencõned.

Parte of the plate belonging to the Hall sould and đđ to Mr Cole for 100li. 10. January 1627.

		ounzes
	Imprimis Mr Hulette Cupp wth a Cover waighing	61—0—0
	Item Mr Jaggarde Cupp wth a Cover	21—0—1
	Item Mrs Lownes Cupp wth a Cover	31—1—0
	Item Humphrey Lownes Mathew Lownes and George Cole	25—1—0
	Item Colledge pott of George Bishopps	18—0—1
	Item a Salt wth a Cover of Humphrey Hoopers	27—0—0
	Item a Salt wth a Cover	33—1—0
	Item one other Salt wth a Cover	22—0—0
	Item Mr Thomas Adams Salt	27—0—0
	Item one glasse fashion boule H H W.	9—0—0
Parcell gilt	Item one Collet boule of Thomas Man	14—0—⟨1⟩
	Item 2 Collett boules more	24—1—1
	Item one Can H F.	19—0—0
	Item one Beaker Thomas Man	7—0—0
White plate	Item a standing Cupp of Wiłłm Stansbye	18—1—0
	Item a Colledge pott of Gabriell Cawoode	17—1—⟨ ⟩
		377—0—⟨ ⟩

(*All the above list crossed out in ink used in following note in margin*)

10 Julij 1629 Paid to mr Cole this day 112li for the said plate & received it backe to the hall./

More sould and đđ to Mr Swinhowe
the same day for 100li more./

	Imprimis one Bason and Ewer given by Mr Barker	84—0—0
	Item one standing Cupp wth a Cover	33—1—0
	Item one standing Cupp R: Newbery	37—1—0
	Item Coll: pott Rob̄: Barker	20—1—0
	Item Coll: pott Ch: Barker	16—0—0
	Item Round Salt wth a Cou' T. D. H. A.	10—1—1
	Item Sacke boule R. Barker G: Seaton	11—0—0
	Item a hooped Cupp wth a Cou'	11—1—0
	Item Ale Cupp Willm Seres	9—0—0
	Item pinke Cupp Willm Leake	6—0—0
white plate	Item Bason and Ewer Rob̄: Barker	80—0—0
	Item Beere boule George Swinhowe	13—0—0
	Item Beere boule George Swinhowe	12—1—0
	Item Beere boule George Swinhowe	6—1—0
	Item Nest of boules Tho: Man and others	23—1—0
	Item Suger Boxe and a spoone	17—0—0
		392—1—0

(*The above list crossed out in ink which wrote the following in margin*)

10 July 1629, paid mr Swinhow this day 112li: and rec this plate into the hall.

More sold and đđ to Mr Bill the
same day for 100li more./

	Imprimis one Salt wth a Cou' Sr Tho: Bodley	60—0—0
	Item one salt wth a Cou' Mr Newton	42—0—1
	Item one standing Cupp wth a Cou' Thomas Man John Norton and others	54—1—0
	Item one barrell Can John Norton	23—1—0
	Item one other Barrell Can John Norton	21—1—0
pcell guilt	Item one Bason & Ewer Bonham Norton	85—0—0
white plate	Item one Colledge pott Rich: Watkins	14—1—0
	Item Coll: pott Rich: Watkins	15—1—0
	Item Coll: Pott ffr: Coldocke	15—1—0
	Item Coll: pott Willm Norton	14—0—0
	Item Coll: pott John Gonell	14—1—1
	Item Coll. pott John Harrison	14—0—1
	Item Colledge pott John Daye	15—1—0
		390—1—0

(*The above list crossed out in ink which wrote the following note in margin.*)

10 July 1629 paid mr Bill 112li and received this plate back to the hall.

More to Mr Knight for 10li.

Imprimis one sixe square salt .... 13—1—0
Item a trencher salt wth a Cou' .... 3—0—1

white Plate } Item one beere boule Anthonye Gilmyn and John Jaggard } .... 15—0—0
Item beere boule Willm Leake .... 12—0—1

44—0—0

(*The above list crossed out in ink which wrote the following note in margin*)

4° Augusti 1628/ This plate was brought in to the house by mr knight & and (*sic* his money [*left*] lent vpon it allowed him out of the wardens account/

Fol. 109a

More to Mr Lownes for 20li

Imprimis one Rac'd boule Peter Short .... 12—0—1
Item 2 Rac'd boules H: Lownes .... 23—1—1

white plate } Item Beere boule Hum: Lownes .... 12—1—1
It: fflatt wine boule H. Lownes .... 8—1—0
Item fflatt wine boule Thomas Man .... 8—1—0
It: fflat wine boule Tho: Adams .... 8—1—0

74—0—1

(*Crossed out as above*)

10 July 1629 paid to him 22li 8s and received his plate into the hall.

More to Mr Weaver for 20li.

Imprimis foure square Salt wth a Cou' .... 19—1—0
Item a Cupp wth G. C. .... 6—0—1
Item Egg boule Edw: White .... 7—0—1

white plate } Item Coll: pott. Ascanius .... 17—1—0
Item Nest of boules Rich: ffield .... 26—0—0

76—1—0

(*Crossed out as above*)

4° Augusti 1628. This plate was brought in by mr weaver and the money lent vpon it allowed vnto him out of the wardens account:

More to Tho: Montfort for 40li.

Imprimis foure dozen and Nyne spoones } .... 144—1—0

(*Crossed out as before*) 11 July 1629. paid 44li 16s & the spoones dd in to the hall.

Plate left in the Hall

gilt	Imprimis one square salt	9—1—0
white	Item one barrell Can Tho: Dawson	26—1—0
	one beere boule Isaack Bing	10—1—0
one fflatt boule John Standish S: Waterson		12—0—0
one beere boule Rich: Ockold		8—1—1
one wine boule Ch: Barker		4—1—1
fflatt boule Isaack Bing		7—1—1
fflatt boule Tho: Dawson		7—1—1
Bough [wine] boule Tho: Stirropp		11—1—1
fflatt boule John Wingate		7—0—1
Bough boule S: waterson		9—1—1
one beaker Tho Man: Sym: waterson		6—0—0
old wyne boule Dockway kevell & Lambe		6—0—0
old wyne boule Ponsonby		7—0—0
wyne boule Jaques, Walley, Turke, Mayler		6—0—0
wyne boule wolfe and Lobley		6—0—0
wyne boule Mr Judson		5—0—0
old wyne boule M^{r} Ch: Barker		5—0—0
		166—0—1

To the M^{r} and wardens of the Companye of Stationers./[1] By the Maior./ Fol. 109^{b}

Whereas the Court of coen' Councell holden in the chamber of the Guildhall of this instant moneth of June taking notice of the landę already passed by his Matie: to this Cittye to above the valew of vij^{m} vij C^{li} ꝑ annu' and the forwardnes of the rest now in passing whereby the som̃e of xx$^{m\ li}$ a remaynder of the sõme of Cxx$^{m\ li}$ formerly agreed by Coẽn Councell to be advanced to his Matie: for and in respect of the said landes wilbe very shortlye dewe to be paid to his highnes according to the Cittyes Contract in that behalfe. And whereas that Court vpon long debatinge of the matter conceived the fittest way for levyinge and raysinge of the said xx$^{m\ li}$ would be by and vpon the seu'all Companies and incorporacõns of this Cittye and the rather in regard that since the paym^{t} of the Lx$^{m\ li}$ lately made by the seu'all Companyes of this Cittye the som̃e of xl$^{m\ li}$ ꝑcell of the other remayning of the some of Lx$^{m\ li}$ together wth v$^{m\ li}$ more agreed to be paid to his Ma^{tye}: for the alteracõn of the Tenure from a Capite to a socage of a great parte of the said Landę hath ben paid by the Lord Maior and Aldr̃en of this Cittye and nowe onely but xx$^{m\ li}$ of the whole Cxx$^{m\ li}$ remaineth vnpaid to his highnes vpon the said Contract, did therefore at the said Coen' Councell of xxjth of this Instant June enact grant and agree that the said xx$^{m\ li}$ should be forthwth raysed and levyed by and vpon the seu'all Companies and incorporacõns of this Cittye according as they are seu'ally rated towardę the provicõn of x^{m} quarters of Corne, where by the same may be readye to be paid to his Ma^{tye}: by this Cittye, as by the Articles of agreement betweene his Matie: and the Lordę on the one parte and the Cittye on th'other parte is mencõned and

[1] Cf. *C–B.C*, 100^{a}, 17 July 1628.

expressed. And the said Court did further enact and agree that all the said xx^m li nowe to be disbursed by the said Companies or incorporacōns touchinge the said busines together wth an allowance for the forbearance thereof after the rate of viij li p C. p annū for the same, for the time the said Companies shalbe out of their moneyes shalbe paid vnto them as pte of the ffirst Cxx^m li to be raysed by the sale of the said Lande in such sort as by former actes of coēn Councell in that behalfe is Lymitted or intended. Theis are therefore in his Maties: [name] streightlye to Chardge [*to*] and require you that forthwth vpon sight hereof

280li you levye and provide wthin yor Companye the some of 280li being yor rateable parte of the said xx^m li according to yor Companies proporcōn of x^m quarters of Corne, at wch you were rated for provicōn thereof, And y^t forthwth you take Course touching the raysinge of the said moneyes soe y^t you haue the same in areadynes at or before the second day of July next to paye the same to the Chamberlaine of the Cittye aforesaid, whereby the same may be readye for his Ma^tye: in satisfaccōn of the said xx^m li according as by the said act of Coen' Councell is ment and intended, And hereof fayle you not this xxvj^th of June 1628./

Weld.

[*R 27mo Junij 1628*]

Fol. 110a To the m^r and wardens of the Company of Stationrs

By the Mayo^r/

2d precept for the 280li

Whereas by my precept of the xxvj^th of June last past yo^u were required vpon sight thereof to levye and provide wth in yor Company the some of 280li being yor Companies rateable parte of xx^m li wch they were rated at for provision thereof, for such purpose As in the said precept is mencōned and to have it in a readienes at or before this instant second day of Julye to paie the same to the Chamḃeleine of this Cittye to be readie for his ma^tie. in satisfaction of the said xx^m li according as by the Act of Comōn Counsell in that behalf made is ment and entended, And forasmuch as I have latelie received a speciall order and direction as well from his Maties owne mouth as otherwaies by lrēs for the speedie and pñte [levyinge] of the said xx^m li his ma^ties pn'te extraordinary and pressinge occasions requiring the same, Theis are therefore in his Maties name, straightly to chardge and require yo^u, yor monies being not as yet paid in as aforesaid, vpon sight hereof to take such speedie Course in the due execucōn of my former precept for the providing and raysinge of yor said moneies as that yo^u haue and paie the same into the Chamber of london to the Chamberleine of the said Cittie before the ffift day of this instant Julie at the furthest as yo^u will Answere the Contrary, And hereof faile not this second of July 1628

Weld

To the m^r and wardens of the Company of Stationrs

3d precept for the 280li

By the Mayor/

Whereas by my former precepte yo^u were required to paie vnto the Chamḃlene of the Cittye of London the some of 280li which according to an Act of Coeñ Counsell lately made was assessed to be paid by yor Company toward the furnishing of the 20,000^li^ which was remaineing to to (*sic*) be paide vnto his Matie, and albeit, the necessitie of the busines for many respecte hath required the same yet for that yo^u^ have made default in the performance thereof, And forasmuch as I have rec speciall Comandes from his ma^tie^. for the speedie and pn'te paiem^t^ of the money yet vnpaid vnto his Matie vpon the Contract, Theis are therefore once more to require yo^u^ according to the said act of Comon Counsell that yo^u^ make pn'te paiem^t^ vnto the said Chambleine of the said Cittye of london of yor proporcon of the 20000^li^ which was assessed vpon yo^u^ to be paid as aforesaid and so much thereof as is vnpaid if any parte thereof be by yo^u^ alreadie paide So that the busines may not suffer by yor default, And herein I require yo^u^ not to faile as yo^u^ tender his Maties service and will answere the Contrarie at yor perrills the 23 of July 1628/

Weld.

Copie of the Acquittance — Received the first day of August 1628 of the m^r^ and wardens of the Companie of Station^r^s london according to the precept w^h^in written the some of 280^li^ of lawfull money of England I say received.................................... } 280^li^ — Fol. 110^b^

p me Arthuru' Panther Clric
Robu Bateman Camerarij Cn^te^ london/

9° Julij 1629
The precept was carryed to Guild hall
and 300^li^ 10^s^ 8^d^ received this day
from the Chamber of London:

primo Augusti 1628

m^r^ Cole m^r^
mr Islip } wardens/
mr Weaver }

Mdd the said some of 280^li^ was taken up in this manner 200^li^ thereof borrowed of one Anthony Smith vpon m^r^ Islip m^r^ waterson and m^r^ Kingston & m^r^ Harisons bond for 6 monethes the other 80^li^ was paid by m^r^ warden Weaver and allowed vnto him in his wardens account/[1]

12° Junij 1629[2]

present
mr Cole: M^r^
mr Islip } wards
Mr weaver }
mr Norton
m^r^ waterson
mr Swinhow
mr knight
mr Kingston
mr Bill
mr Blount
mr Purfoote
mr Harison
mr Bateman

This day the bonde wherein Mr Cole m^r^ Knight m^r^ Weaver and m^r^ Swinhow were bound to m^r^ Locke for 300^li^ and the bond wherein m^r^ Islip mr waterson mr Kingston & m^r^ Harison were bound to one Anthony Smith for 200^li^ were both brought in and Cancelled, and the whole 500^li^ was borrowed of m^r^ locke and a lease of the ffeathers in Paules Churchyard made to mr locke for securitye, and sealed this day wth the Comon seale and a bond for the pformance of Couentes was likewise sealed wth the said Comon seale

[1] Cf. *C–B.C*, 100^a^, 17 July 1628.   [2] Cf. *C–B.C*, 125^b^, 16 Jan 1634.

10 Julij 1629

This day m^r weaver warden received from the Chamber of london, 300^li 10^s 8^d as appeare before[1] and the plate that was at pawne was forthwith redeemed, [*vizt*?] vt ante, debts paid, Billes of sale and Bondes taken vp and Cancelled

Printers of Cambridge

At the Starr Chamber on wednesday the 25th of January 1625[2] present

Lo. Archb. of Canterbury	m^r Pres:
Lo. Keeper	mr of the wards
Lo. President	mr Chanc. of the Exchequer
Ear. Marshall	mr of the Rolles

prognostications (*18° hand*)

Vpon a difference betwen the Vniu'sitie of Cambridge in the behalfe of their printers and of the Staconrs and printers of london touching the Vse [*of*] and sence of the word prognosticacõns which is menconed in an order of the Boord of the Tenth of December 1623 by which order the Controu'sie betwixt both ꝑties was determined in such sort as was Conceiued to be most indifferent in regard of both, Their lo^ps. to preuent the like mistaken hereafter and thereby to Cutt of all further Contencõn doe hereby declare and explane the entencõn of the Boord in that behalf vizt that [the] aforesaid word Prognosticacõns, is no other wise to be vnderstood, then according to the ordinarie vse of speakeing in which, Almanackes and Prognosticaconẹ [are] [*is*] meant & taken for the same thing, whereof both ꝑties are required to take notice that the Boord be no more troubled wth this matter./[3]

Ex^t. J Dickenson

Fol. 111^a Printers of Cambridge
Printers of London

At whitehall the 16th of Aprill 1629

Present/

Lo: Keeper	Lo: Visc. Dorchester
Lo: President	Lo: Bp: of Winchester
Lo: Privie Seale	Lo: Bp of London
Ea: of Holland	mr Sec: Cooke/

This day the lordẹ and otherẹ Comittees did heare the Controversies betwen the Vniuersitie of Cambridge on the one part, and the printers to his Matie. and the Companie of Staconers on the other part referred to them from his Matie by three generall Refferenceẹ. the one of the first of Nouember 1628 the other the 4th of Decemb. 1628 and the third the 15 of May 1628 and after long Debate of Counsell learned on both sides in the ꝑn'ce of all the parties. It was finallie ordered by their lo^pps wth consent of all the parties for an absolute ende of all Controuersies betwen them, notwithstanding any pretences or allegacõns on either side by reason of any

[1] Cf. *Letter Book*, 108^a–109^a.

[2] Recorded *Acts of P.C. March 1625–May 1626*, p. 328.

[3] A copy of this order is in *State Papers Dom. 1628–1629*, p. 520, no. 62; and of the report of the Lords Chief Justices, 18 Mar. 1629, on which it is based, *op. cit.*, p. 496, no. 4.

Charters lr̃s patentẹ decrees orders Reportẹ or provisions whatsoeuer That the Vniversitie of Cambridge (besides the benifitt allowed vnto them by the order of this Board of the 10th of Decemb: 1623[1] for the printing and selling such Bookes as are therein Conteyned, which benifitt is by this order entirely reserved vnto them) shall likewise have libertie to Comprint wth the Kingẹ printers and the Staconer̃s of london by their printers from henceforth for euer English Bibles in such volumes as are now in hand in the said vniversitie, vizt in quarto and the Median folio without restraint of any number or sort of letter together wth the Letourgie of the same Volume in the beginning of the bookes conteyning the booke of Comoñ praier and the Psalmes vsuallie reade in the Church and the Collectẹ for the daie and a Titularie Refference to the new Testamt of the Epistles and Gospells appointed for the day and in the end of the said Bibles the singing Psalmes,[2] Prouided that the said Printers of the vniu'sitie shall not print any more of the said Letourgies || and singing Psalmes then will serve to be ioyned wth the Bibles allowed to be printed by them, and provided that though the said printers shall sell any of the said Bibles wthout the said Letourgies or singing Psalmes ioyned wth them yet it shall not be lawfull for the said printers to sell any of the said Letourgies or singing Psalmes apart, And it is further ordered by the Board and agreed by the said parties that the said printers of the Vniv'sitie of Cambridg may printe euery yeare henceforward for euer Three thousand Lillies Gram̃ers and no more in one yeare[3] And it is further ordered and agreed, that the said Printers shall not printe the said Bibles in any other volume nor any other Booke conteyned wthin the Patentẹ of priveledg granted to the Kingẹ printers or to the Corporacõn of Staconer̃s other then such as are expressed in this order or in the order of the Board of the 10th of December 1623 Notwthstanding any Charters lr̃s patentẹ Decree order Report or prouision whatsoeu' And for the avoyding of all [*further*] Controu'sie it is ordered that this order shalbe entred in the Register Booke of the Actẹ of the Counsell, and that as well the Vicechancellor and printers of the said Vniu'sitie and other members thereof present at the debate as also the said printers to his Matie. and the mr wardens and other members of the Corporacoñ of Stacoñrs present hereatt shall sett their handes to this order entered in the Counsell booke. It is also ordered and agreed that it shalbe lawfull for the Printers of the said Vniu'sitie to fiñish those Gramer̃s Accedencẹ and primrs which were in their presses, and alreadie begun before this day of heareing and aswell those bookes as all other Bookes which they have allreadie finished freelie to sell and vtter, so as the said Vicechancellor and printer of Cambridg doe give in a note to be entred with this order both of the sortẹ and of the number of the said Bookes allreadie printed now remayning in their

Bibles (*18° hand*)

Liturgy (*18° hand*)

Singing Psalms (*18° hand*)

Fol. 111b

Lillies Grammar (*18° hand*)

Accedence primmers (*18° hand*)

[1] Cf. *Letter Book*, 104a.

[2] In accordance with this order the Bucks printed within the year a Bible in folio (STC 2285) and two editions in quarto (STC 2292 and 2293); an edition of the Book of Common Prayer in folio (STC 16374) and one in quarto (STC 16380); and an edition of Sternhold and Hopkins in folio (STC 2613) and one in quarto (STC 2624).

[3] There is at King's College, Cambridge, an edition of Lily in 8° printed by the 'Printers to the Universitie of Cambridge', 1629.

handes or which are now in printing, and it is lastly ordered that both his Maties Printers and the Company of Staconers shall euer hereafter vtterlie forbeare to seize [*and*] any of the said Bookes or any other booke or bookes or any part thereof which shalbe printed by the printers of the said Uniu'sitie according to this order or other-
FOL. 112ᵃ wise to || molest or hinder them in the sale thereof, And that as well his Maties printers as the Company of Staconrs shall make present Restiticōn (*sic*) to the said Vniu'sitie printers of whatsoeu' of their Bookes they have seized since the afore-named order of the 10th of December 1623, Prouided that if either of the said parties or those that hereafter shall enioye their Rights shall breake this p̄nte Order or the Order of the 10th of December 1623 the partie so breakeing the said orders or any parte of them shall vtterly loose all benifitt which they might receive by the said orders but the said orders shall stand good to all other intents and purposes./

Psalmes in 8	150[1]
Psalmes in 12	380[2]
Psalmes in 24	303
Psalmes in 32	121
Gramers	304
Accedences	900
Testamte in 24	250[3]
Gram̄ers vnfinished	7000[4]
Primers vnfinished	11000

Extr. Wiłł: Becher/

Math. Wren: Vicecan:

Tho. Bucke printer to
the Vniu'sity of Cambridge

Bonham Norton
John Bill

Geo: Cole magr
Adam Islip } wardens
Edm: Weaver }
Clement Knight
Felix Kingston
Tho. Downes
Tho. Mōntfort./

FOL. 112ᵇ To the Mr and wardens of the Company of Staconers/

By the Mayor/

Whereas of late yeares it hath pleased his Matie, the queene and sundrie Embassaders Nobles and multitudes of Strangers to be spectators of the solempnities p̲formed the day of the lord Mayors takeing his oath at westmr who observing the Disorderlie goeing of the barges to and from Westmr have Censured the directors of that busines, His lop: having received so notice thereof hath thought fitt for reformacōn of the same disorder to appoint some of the Mrs of the watermen wth their boats to attende and to marshall the Companies barges both at the the (*sic*) setting forth and at the returne home according to such Directions as have ben given heretofore in that behalf Theis are therefore to require you to giue order to thos that are of the

[1] Two editions of Sternhold and Hopkins printed in octavo at Cambridge, 1628, are known (STC 2608 and 2609).

[2] An edition in 12° dated 1628 is recorded (STC 2610).

[3] Two editions in 24° dated 1628 are recorded (STC 2932 and 2933).

[4] See note above.

Clothing of yo[r] Company that are to have ymploym[t] in yo[r] bardge vpon the water by eight of the Clocke tomorrow morning at the furthest./ And w[th]all to give yo[u] notice that yo[u] are to Row along w[th] the Bardge of the ffruterers[1] to keepe 60 foote distance betwen yo[r] bardge and the bardg and the bardg (*sic*) that goe before yo[u] and follow after yo[u] for the more grace of the show whereof I require yo[u] not to faile the 28[th] of October 1629

Weld:

Md The Statonrs neu' attended
wth any Bardge.

To the Master and wardens
of the Company of Staconers   By the Maio[r].   Fol. 113[a]

Whereas at a Comon Counsell holden in the Chamber of Guildhall of the Cittye of London the thirteenth day of October last past in the time of the Maioraltye of S[r] Hugh Hamerslie Knight & Alderman It was enacted granted and agreed by that Court that the some of 4300[li] which the Chamber of London have disbursed and paid for and touching the makeing of the pageant*e* and other solemnities and shewes and work*e* for y[e] bewtifieing of this Cittie against the late entended time of his ma[ties] passage through the same for his highnes Coronacōn and for other the necessarie and publiq*ue* service of this Cittie shalbee raysed and levied of and amongst the seu'all Companies of [this] sd Cittie according to the proporcōn of ten thousand quarters of Corne as each Companie is rated at to provide, And that the said 4300[li] shalbe so levied and paid into the Chamber at foure sixe monethes then next ensueing by equall pcells viz[t] 1075[li] one pcell thereof on the 13th day of Aprill then next following, And so the like pcell of 1075[li] at the ende of every sixe monethes vntill the said 4300[li] be Collected and paid as aforesaid, as by the said Act of Comon Counsell (among other thing*e*) appeareth: fforasmuch as not any parte of the said 4300[li] is as yet paid into the Chamber and y[t] 2150[li] wilbe due to be paid on the xxiiij[th] day of this instant October by the seu'all Companies; Theis are therfore to require yo[u] that vpon sight hereof yo[u] levie and prouide w[th]in yo[r] Companie the som of 30[li]. 2[s] being yo[r] ratehable parte of the said 2150[li] according to yo[r] Companies proporcōn of 140 partes of Corne at which yo[u] are rated for provision toward*e* the said 10,000 quarters of Corne/ And that yo[u] paie the same into the Chamber of London at the time limited as aforesaid, And hereof not to faile as yo[u] tender the good and welfare of this Citie and will answere the Contrarie at yo[r] pill Guildhall this 6. of Octob. 1629.

Weld.

To the master and wardens
of the Company of Staconrs   By the Mayo[r].   Fol. 113[b]

Whereas by a late precept to yo[u] directed dated the Sixt daie of this pn'te moneth yo[u] were required to levie and provide w[th]in yo[r] Company yo[r] rateable parte of 2150[li] and paie the same into the Chamber on the xiiij[th] of this pn'te October being pcell of 4300[li] which that precept doth mencōn should be raysed of and among the seu'all Companies of this Cittie according to the proporcōn of Ten thousand quarters

[1] According to an order of the Council, 28 Oct. 1561, the Stationers were to follow next to the Poulterers, cf. Arber i. 496.

of Corne by Act of Comon Counsell holden the xiij^th of October in the time of the Maioraltye of Sr Hugh Hamerslie Knight and Alderman and should be paid into the Chamber of London at 4.6 monethes then next ensueing by equall pcells as by the same precept is more at larg expressed vpon further pusall of the said Act of Comon Counsell it was found that the same was made in the Maioraltie of Sr Cutberd Hackett knight and Aldren in the xiij^th day of October and so recorded which is now full two yeares past and that it was merely an error and mistake of the writer of the former precept to mencon the said Act to be made in the time of Sr Hugh Hamerslie, whereas inded it was made in the time of Sr Cutbert Hackett as aforesaid fforasmuch as it appeareth y^t the said 4300^li should have ben all paid into the Chamber by the xiiij^th of this enstant October, Theise therefore are further to require yo^u that vpon sight hereof to levye and provide wth in yor Company the some of lx^li 4^s being yor rateable proporcõn of the said 4300^li according to the Companies proporcoñ of Corne mencõned in yor former precept and to take speciall Care that the same wth all Convenient speed bee paid into the Chamber and hereof not to faile as yo^u tender the good of the Cittie and will answere the Contrary at yor perill/ Guildhall the xxviij^th day of October 1629.

60^li. 4^s to be paid towards the makeing of pageant℮.

Weld/

Fol. 114^a

Deane Maior — Jovis xxx die Julij 1629 Annoq
Re℮ Caroli Ang^o A^o Quinto/

fforasmuch as this Court was informed that many Appn'tices have their Indentures made at Scrivenors shoppes and elswhere in private places by meanes whereof divers abuses and wronges are Comitted as well to the Appn'tices as to the Companies which afterward℮ come to be enrolled before the Chamblen of London and obtayne the Freedome of this Cittie It is therefore thought fitt and so ordered by this Court that from henceforth no Appn'tice shall be enrolled in the Chamber of London but such as shall have and present his Indenture made at the Companies hall whereof in right he ought to be free and to be firmed by the Clarke of the same Company/ And the seu'all Companies of this Cittie are to take knowledge of this order.

That all Indentures for appr'ces are to be made by the Clarkes of Companies

Weld.

Mr Bonham Norton: Master
Mr John: Bill } wardens/
Mr Tho Purfoote }

Present/ — 14° dec: 1629 Re℮ Car' quinto/

Mr Waterson loco m^ri/ m^r Bill m^r purfoote m^r Lownes m^r Swinhow m^r Cole m^r Knight m^r Islip m^r King℮ton m^r Weaver m^r Blownt m^r Harison m^r Bateman m^r Tombes m^r Smithick/

840^li paid to the Company by m^r Basell Nicoll

Whereas vpon the xi^th day of January 1627: vpon a precept from the lord Maior This Company lent the Cittie (to his Maties. vse) 840^li for which the Company are by that precept to have

Intrest at 6 p Cent, This day it was propounded at the Table/ whether the Company would accept of the said 840li wthout Intrest if any man would pn'tely pay it in/: The Company beinge (desirous to have in the money) ordered [by] full Consent that if the principall were brought in it should be accepted of, And all the Asurance the Company have to be deliu'ed vp to the partie that should [*layd*] [laie] downe the said principall some of 840li:

The said 840li was brought in by Mr Basell Nicoll, and the precept deliu'ed vnto him and a deed vnder the Comon seale of the Company: the Copie whereof is as followeth on the next page/

The Interest came to 100li, mr Nicolls (*sic*) put it to the table what he shold have, and they allowed him 50li and the Company had the other 50li so the Company had in all 890li

The Copie of the Assignemt of the said 840li made to mr Basell Nicoll/[1] Fol. 114b

To all people to whom theis pn'te shall come, Wee the Master and keeps or wardens and Cominaltie of the misterie or Art of Stacōners of the Cittie of London send greeting in or lord god eu'lastinge/ Whereas by Act of Comon Counsell in the Chamber of the Guildhall of the Cittie of London the xvijth day of December 1627 It was enacted that (for his Maties vse) the some of 60000li should be forthwith levied and raysed by and vpon the seu'all Companies and Corporacōns of the said Cittie according to there seu'all Rates & proporcons as they were rated towardes the provision of 10000 quarters of Corne/ According to which proporcōn wee the said mr and Keeps or wardens and Cominaltie by precept from the right hoble the Lo. Mayor of the said Cittie dated the xviijth day of the said moneth of December were Comanded forthwith to levie and provide wthin our Companie the some of 840li and to paie the same vnto Mr: Rob: Bateman Chamblen of the same Cittie which was paid to the said Mr Ro. Bateman Chamberlen aforesaid according to the said precept/ Now Knowe yee that wee the said Master and Keeps or wardens and Cominaltie [*did agree to and wth Basill Nicoll his executo'rs and assignes That he the said Basell Nicoll his executo'rs and assignes shall and may in the name of or said Company but*] in Consideracōn of 840li to vs before the ensealeing hereof well and trulie paid by Basill Nicoll Citizen and haberdasher of London by the direction and appointment of Daniell Britten gent: doe for vs and our successo'rs hereby agree to and wth the said Basell Nicoll his executo'rs and assignes That he the said Basill Nicoll his ex'rs and assignes shall and may in the name of or said Companie but to the onely vse and behoofe of the said Daniell Britten his ex'rs and assignes aske demande receive take and enioy the said some of 840li and all such part and porcōn of landes tenemte and hereditamte out of his Maties lande in fee farme or otherwise as shall or ought to belong or fall to be due vpon divident to or said Company for or in respect of the said some of 840li, together wth all Benifitt advantage and profitt which shall or may by any waies or meanes arise growe or become due or become paieable for or by reason of the same wthout any lett trouble or interuption of vs the said mr and Keeps

[1] Cf. *Letter Book*, 107a et seq.

or wardens and Cominaltie or o[r] successo[r]s In Witnes whereof the said Master and keeps or wardens and Cominaltie of the said mistery or Art of Staconrs the Comon seale of the said Company vnto theise pn'te have Caused to be putt this pn't xvij[th] day of December in the fiveth yeare of the raigne of o[r] sou'aigne lord Charles king of England Scotland ffraunce & Ireland Defender of the ffaith 8° 1629

md m[r] lockes debt was paid, the old hall redeemed the morgage Cancelled vt patet in Compoto m[r] purfoote nunc Guardian'

Fol. 115[a]

By the Mayor/

Whereas I and my brethren the Aldren have resolved and agreed that the full quantitie of 10000 quarters of wheate shalbe bought and provided by the seu'all Companyes of this Cittie betwen this and May day next according to the rates and proporcons as the same Companies have heretofore ben seu'allie assessed & taxed at towarde the furnishing of the proportions In accomplishm[t] whereof Theis are to will and require yo[u] in his Ma[ties] name strictlye to chardg and Comande yo[u]. that yo[u] buy and provide 140 quarters of wheate which is rateably appointed and proporconed for yo[r] Company according to the said former provisions of 10000 quarters and that the same be bought and provided and layed vp in Granaries w[th]in this Cittie for the service and provision thereof before the first day of May next at the furthest And that yo[u] Depend not vpon Chandlers Bakers or others to make the same provision as yo[u] tender the good of this Cittie and will answere the Contrary if through yo[r] Default this service shall in any parte be neglected. Guildhall the vi[th] of ffebr. 1629.

Weld.

To the m[r] and wardens
of the Company of Staconrs.

To the m[r] & wardens
of the Comp. of Staconrs

By the Mayo[r]./

Theise are in his Ma[ties] name to will and require yo[u] that forthwith vpon the receite hereof yo[u] Cause Certificate to be made to me and my brethren the Aldren vpon Teusday next at the Guildhall by ten of the Clocke in the forenoone at the furthest subscribed by one of the wardens of yo[r] Company what quantities of wheat yo[u] have provided by vertue of my former precept to yo[u] directed, and now have in readines in yo[r] granarie or else where for the store and provision of yo[r] Company where of I require yo[u] not to faile the fift day of may 1630.

Weld

Fol. 115[b] To my very loving ffreinde the m[r] and wardens
of the Company Staconrs[1]

Dyners/ After my very hartie Comendacons &c fforasmuch as the visitacon of the plague is much feared to encrease, within this Cittye by reason whereof it is not now a time of ffeasting but of fasting and prayer to almightie god to avert his Judgm[te] from [vs]/ I have therefore thought fitt by and w[th] the advise of my brethren the Aldren hereby to intreat yo[u] to forbeare all manner of feasting or makeing of any publique Dynn[r]s at yo[r] Coen hall or else where or there to suffer

[1] Cf. *Analytical index of remembrancia*, p. 341.

any publique meetingℯ for burialls Marriagℯ or like occasions to be had during the time of this visitacõn. And that yo^u take Course that the moneyes to be spared by the forbeareing of the said feastℯ which otherwise would be spent vpon the same be kept in safetie in the handes of some one of the wardens of yor said Companye to be expended from time to time if occasion shall require toward the releife of such poore people whose houses shalbe visited and are not able to helpe & releife themselues in their great need and necessities the same being an Act of Charitie and exceeding acceptable to god, And this desireing yor Care and futherance in so pieous a worke hereby entended I Comitt yo^u to god, And rest

yor loving ffriend

xvij° maij 1630 James Cambell Maio^r/

You are further to take knowledg that I am expresly required to make true Certificate of the quantities of Corne layd vp in the granaries by the seuerall Companies for the provision of the Cittie vpon former order given vnto yo^u by Direction of the lords, and forasmuch as yo^u have not made Certificate to me what proporcõn of Corne yo^u have in a redienes according to my late Precept which maketh me to Conceive that yo^u are wholly vnprovided Theise are therefore in his Maties name to pray and require yo^u to take order that I be forthwith Certified what proporcon yo^u have, and that what is wanting of yor proporcõn of 140 quarters be spedily provided in forreine partℯ, and not out of that small quantitie which Cometh to the Cittye for prouision of the Bakers, nether to relye vpon the service of Chandlers as heretofore many have done, whereby his Maties Care for prevencõn of a Dea^rth and scarcitie much to be feared may not be frustrate, as yo^u will answere the Contrary at yor perills/

To the M^r and wardens of the Company of Stacon̄rs./ Fol. 116a

By the Maior/

Theise are to will and require yo^u, that vpon Wednesday being the Eighteenth day of this instant August and so from thence forth weekely vpon the Wednesday in euery weeke vntill yo^u receive order from me to the Contrarie yo^u bring or Cause to be brought to the markett at queenehith w^thin this Cittye fower quarters of Red wheate meale of yor Companies store and provision which yo^u have or ought to have in a readienes And that yo^u there sell the same to the poore people by the halfe pecke pecke and half bushell and not aboue to any ꝑson at one time after the Rate of sixe shillingℯ the Bushell and not at any higher or greater Rate. And this yo^u are to doe by yor officer or other ꝑson who shall not be a Chandler or Baker or servant vnto either of them And hereof see yo^u ffaile not as yo^u will answer the Contrary at y^r perills This 10th of August 1630.

Weld/

To the master and wardens of the Company of Staconres[1]

By the Mayo^r.

fforasmuch as long since I appointed yor Company and all other the seu'all Companyes of this Cittye to Cause to be bought and provided such seu'all quantities of

[1] Cf. *Analytical index of remembrancia*, p. 387, 6 Sept. 1630.

Corne for the furnishing of 10000 quarters of wheate for the store and prouision of this Cittye as were heretofore seu'ally taxed and assessed vpon the said Companies in that behalf, which provision being for the most part neglected and the Cittie thereof vnfurnished, his Matie hath taken speciall notice of the ꝑmisses [and] of the said se'all Companies neglect or Contempt, and being much displeased therewith hath expreslie chardged and Comanded myself and my brethren the Aldren to take speedie Course that the said proporcōn of 10000 quarters of wheate be spedilie furnished by the seu'all Companies of this Cittye for the store and provision of the same as they will answere their neglect and Contempt hereafter in that behalf Theise are therefore in his highnes name straightlie to Chardge & Comande that forthwith yo^u take Course for the buying and providing of Cxl quarters of wheate which is yor Companies rateable proporcōn allotted them for and towardꝭ the said provision of 10000 quarters. In which yor said Companies provision yor speciall Care shalbe that the same be made in forreine partꝭ or in such remote places from this Citty as that the providing thereof may be no hinderance to the Cittyes prouision otherwise or a meanes for the enhanceing of the price of Corne in this Cittye or in the markettꝭ in or nere about the same, And wth all that yo^u neith⟨er⟩ deale Contract with nor depend vpon any Chandle^rs, bakers, or like persons for or touch-
Fol. [116^b] ing the said provisiōn or yor serving of the || merkettꝭ but that the same provision be made by your Company and layd vp in yor granaries in or nere this Cittie before the first day of Januarie next ensueing whereby the same may be then there veiwed by such as shalbe appointed and afterwardꝭ sold and disposed of for the service of this Cittye and furnishing the Merkatꝭ thereof as yo^u shalbe appointed in y^t behalfe

And hereof faile yo^u not as yo^u will answere the Contrary and vndergoe such punishm^t for yor default as wilbe therefore ymposed vpon yo^u This first of October 1630/

Weld

To the master and wardens
of the Company of Staconers̃

By the Mayo^r

Whereas my self by and with the advice of my brethren the Aldren did heretofore by my lẽrs intreate yo^u to forbeare all manner of feasting or makeing of any publiqꝫ dynners at yor Comōn hall or else where during the time of this visitacōn for the reasons in thos my lẽrs expressed and y^t the moneyes to be spared by the forbearance of the saide feastꝭ should be kept in safetie in the handꝭ of some one of the wardens of yor said Company to be expended from time to time if occasion should require towardꝭ the releife of such poore people whose houses should have ben visited and they not able to help or to releife themselues in thier neede and necessities: Theise are therefore nowe further to entreat yo^u that yo^u forthwith for the ꝑn̄te doe bring or Cause to be brought into the Chamber of London and there paie ouer to m^r Robt̄ Bateman Chamberleine of the same Cittye, the moytie or one half of all such moneyes as have in that Kinde ben spared as aforesaid to the intent that the same may be distributed in sort before declared, This first of October 1630.

Weld:

To the m^{r} and wardens
of the Company of Staconr̃s By the Mayo^{r}/ Fol. 117^{a}

fforasmuch as I am Credibly Informed that notwithstanding the Precept sent vnto yo^{u} by my predecesso^{r} for the bringing in to the merkett of newgate merkett vpon the wednesday in euery weeke weekely ffower quarters of Redd wheate of yor Companies store, yor Companie hath ben verie remisse and negligent in due observance of the direction of y^{t} precept whereby the markett hath not ben furnished in that sort as was appointed, Theis are therefore to will and require yo^{u} that from henceforth weekely vpon the said wednesday in euerie weeke vntill yo^{u} receive order to the Contrarie yo^{u} bring or Cause to be brought to the said m'kett of Newgate m'kett wthin this Cittye foure quarters of Redd wheate meale of yor Companies store and provision wch yo^{u} have or ought to have in a Readynes, And that yo^{u} there sell the same to the poore people by the halfe pecke pecke and halfe Bushell and not aboue to any one ꝑson at one time Vizt Redd wheat meale after the Rate of vj^{s} vj^{d} the bushell and Rye after the Rate of v^{s} the bushell and not at any higher or greater rate And that yo^{u} doe the same by yor Officer or any other ꝑson (*not*) being a Chandlo^{r} or Baker or servant to any of them And hereof faile yo^{u} not as yo^{u} will answere the Contrarie at yor ꝑill This 2^{d} day of november 1630

Weld./

To the m^{r} and wardens of the Company of Stationers

Theis are to will and require yo^{u} in his Maties name, That vpon monday next and soe euye m'kett day thenceforth yo^{u} send into the m'kettꝭ heretofore assigned yo^{u} a double proporcoñ of meale for the better supply & furnishing of ye same m'ketꝭ and the better to keepe downe the high rates which meale men and others formerly sold at and to Cause them to sell at the rates and prizes by me lately sett downe and to sell out the same there to poore people by the half pecke pecke and halfe bushell and not aboue to any one person at one time, & to continue this Course vntill yo^{u} shall receive order from me to the Contrarie And theis are further to require yo^{u} forth wth to paie into the Chamber of London all such moneyes as yo^{u} have spared by not makeing and keeping of yor wonted feastꝭ and Dynn^{rs} or at the least the Moytie thereof to the end the same may be disposed according to his Maties proclamacoñ and the teno^{r} of a former precept heretofore sent vnto yo^{u} in that behalf Of all wch p'misies I require yo^{u} not to faile, This 19th of December 1630

Weld

To the M^{r}. and Wardenꝭ of
the Company of Stacōn^{er}s By the Maio^{r}, Fol. 117^{b}

Whereas by my former p^{r}ceptꝭ vnto you lately directed you were required to send vnto the Meale markett assigned you a double proporcōn of Meale for the better furnishing of the same markett & supply of the Poore the rather thereby to pull downe the high rates wch Meale men & others did there sell at, And there to sell & vent the same to poore people by the halfe pecke, peck, & half bushell, & not aboue to any one parson at one tyme & to Continue the same Course vntill you receiued order from me to the Contrary And by the same p^{r}cept were alsoe required forth with to bring into the Chamber of London the moiety at least of all such moneye as yor Company spared by not making & keeping yor wonted feaste & dynners to th'end the same might be disposed of according to his Ma^te. order & direction giuen in that behalfe both wch. haue byn by you too too (*sic*) much neglected wch hath byn the Cause that I haue byn & dayly am pressed by the King & Lorde & haue byn taxed [*by*] [of] Remisnes in not seeing the same effected, Whereas it meerely ariseth by the neglect of you & other the wardene of Companies of this City who should have byn more carefull to execute the Comaunde of the Magistrate in these thinge for Redresse therefore of former neglecte These are in his Ma^te. name once agayne to will & require you in respect of the misery of the [*misery of the*] tymes and extreame want of the Poore as alsoe of his Ma^te. speciall Comaund that lyeth vpon me to see the same performed that you make some amende for yor former neglecte in yor speedy & Carefull pformance of the p^rmises in both the particulars before remembered & the rather for that his Maty at my intercession hath byn gratiously pleased to giue order that some of the porte shall be open for the bringing of Corne from all parte of his Kingdomes where by great quantities are dayly expected for the full furnishing of this Citty & Supply of those Companies that want. Whereof I require you not to faile this 9th. of ffebruary 1630/

Weld

FOL. 118a To the Master and Wardens of the Company of Staconers — By the Major.

Theis are to require you that the next weeke & so euery weeke following vntill you haue order from mee to the Contrarie yo^u send the full quantitie of 4 quarters of Meale to Mr Deputie Edwards Deputy of the ward of Cripplegate there to bee by him distributed amongst the poore inhabitante within that ward whereof I require you not to faile at your pill This Sixt day of May 1631.

Ro: Ducie Major./

To the Master & Wardens of the Company of Staconers — By the Maio^r.

Whereas by late Precepte to you directed you were required to levy and provide wth in yor Company & pay into the Chamber of London the some of lx^li iiij^s being yor rateable pte of 4300^li wch that precept did mention should be raised of & amongst the seuerall Companyes of this Citty according to the proporcõn of Tenn Thousand quarters of Corne by an act of Coen̄ Councell holden the Thirteenth day of October in the tyme of the Maioralty of S^r. Cuthbert Hackett Kn^t. & Alderman and to be paid into the Chamber of London as by the said precepte was more largely expressed And notwithstanding all the Twelue principall Companyes of [*of*] this Citty & sundry other Companyes haue paid their seuerall Rates allotted vpo⟨n⟩ each of them respectiuely into the Chamber of London towarde the payment of the said some of 4300^li. And yet neuertheles yor said Company hath not paid in their said parte as by the said precepte you were required These are therefore to Charge & require you That wth in fourteen daies next at the furthest you take expeciall Care to pay in the said some of lx^li. iiij^s. into the Chamber of London or that in the meane tyme you make your appearance before me & my brethren the Aldren of this City in the

Chamber of the Guildhall of the said Citty to answere yo[r] neglect in the premises where of I require you not to faile This Eighth of June 1630/

Weld

The Coppy of the Lord Maio[rs]. order for the Brewers[1]

Duodecimo die Julij. 1631/ Fol. 118[b]

Ducy Maior Whereas in obedience to the Lr̃es of the Lordę of his Ma[tę] most hon[ble] priuy Councell signifieing his Ma[tę]. pleasure for the Translacõn of such as vse the mistery of brewinge free of other Companies vnto the Company of Brewers of this Citty & vpon the humble peticõn of Robte Triplett, Andrew Bilton, Edward Morrante & Hugh Bowyer[2] made to the Company of Stacoñers whereof they are members but vse the mistery of brewing, the said Company of Stationers are Contented & haue promised before his Lor[p]. to translate the said Robte Triplett, Andrew Bilton Edward Morrante & Hugh Bowyer vpon Thursday next vnto the said Company of Brewers, And whereas there is one Edward Prentice[3] alsoe free of the said Company of Stationers, who now vseth the mistery of brewing and by reason of some infirmity w[ch] is vpon the said Edward Prentice he cannot now be soe conveniently translated as the rest, Wherevpon the m[r] & wardens of the Brewers promised before his Lor[p]. that hereafter wth all Conveniency they shall & [will] doe their best & vttermost endeavor to cause the said Prentice to be translated from the said Company of Stationers vnto the said Company of Brewers or otherwise cause him leaue of brewing./

Clement Mosse

To the mr & Wardens of the Company of Stacoñrs

By the Maior.

Whereas divers Merchantę trading into the East Countries have of late brought into the Kingdome great quantity of Corne (being Rye) & for quality as good or better then vsually that of the grouth of this Kingdome, Yet notwithstanding the said Merchantę cannot vent the same. And whereas the said Merchantę (vpon the motion of the right hon[ble]: the Lordę of his Ma[tę]. most hon[ble]. privy Councell are contented & have offered to sell the same Corne at the price of vj[s]. vi[d]. the bushell being lesse by xviij[d]. the bushell then the same Corne hath stood them in And whereas their Lo[pę]: have therevpon thought fitt ordered & required that aswell for their p[r]sent releefe in venting their said Corne & for their future Encouragement vpon the like occasion & for supply of the Citty that my selfe & my brethren the Aldren should presse the seuerall Companies of this Citty to take of the same Corne at the price aforesaid & have much blamed me & my brethren of former remisnes in not compelling the several Companies to take the same In Conformity & Accomplishment of wch their Lor[pę] said order. Theis are to require you forthwith to repayre vnto m[r] Alrãn Clitherow, Governor of the Eastland Company & to buy & take of him &

[1] The Brewers had been agitating to have those who were brewing but not free of their Company translated, cf. petition of Tryamore Sparkes, a Clothworker (*State Papers Dom. 1629–1631*, p. 420); the letter of the Common Council to the Privy Council (*Analytical index of remembrancia*, p. 108, Feb. 1630); and the petition of the various Companies, including the Stationers (*State Papers Dom. 1629–1631*, p. 440).

[2] Triplet is the only one known to have exercised the mystery of a Stationer. He was made free 17 Jan. 1603 (Arber ii. 734). Bilton was made free 6 May 1606 (Arber iii. 683); Morrant, 27 June 1608 (Arber iii. 683); and Bowyer, 3 May 1620 (Arber iii. 685).

[3] Made free 9 Apr. 1621 (Arber iii. 685). What his infirmity was is not apparent.

other the Marchantꝭ of that Company the quantity of Seaventy quarters of the said Rye at the said price of vj^s^. viij^d^. the bushell being one halfe of yor Companyes proportion & being after the rate of 1000 (*sic*) quarters of Corne wch you are to have in a Readines for the [*supply*] store & [*furnishing*] provision of this Citty according to the ancient Vsage & Custome & that you lay vp the same in yor Companies Granery to be in a Readines for the supply & furnishing the markettꝭ of this Citty as tyme & occasion shall require. And hereof faile you not as you tender their Lor^pe^. said order & expresse Comaund This xv^th^. of June 1631/

Weld

FOL. 119^a^

Die Mittigacõnis finium die Sabbati (vizt.) 9° die Mensis Julij Anno Dni' 1631. Coram Comissiõrijs Regijs apud Lambhith Judiciatr sedentẽ presen' Thomam Mottershed Regrarij Regij Deputato./[1]

Officium Dnorũ coñ Guil: Slatyr sacrae Theologia professor — This day M^r^ D^r^. Slatyr was ordered to be enlarged vpon Bond entred to appeare here agayne primo Michis & he was ordered to bring all his bookes lately printed wth the scandalous Table annexed & they were all ordered to be burned in the Registers house privately, notwithstanding the former order for the burning of them in Paulꝭ Churchyard & the m^r^ & Wardens of the Company of Stacoñers are desired by the Co^rt^. to take care to see all D^r^. Slatyrs bookꝭ wch they have in their Custody to be fortwith (*sic*) sent to the Registers office of this Co^rt^. by some of their officerꝭ who may see them burned accordingly And the register was required to draw a forme of submission to be performed by the said Dr Slatyr wch is to be perused & allowed by some of the Comissione^r^s Judges of this Co^rt^.
Tho: Mottershed Deputatus
Geo: Paull Militis Regrarij Regij/

To the m^r^ & Wardens of the Company of Stacoñers — By the Maior

Whereas divers Merchantꝭ trading into the East Countries have of late brought into this Kingdome great quantities of Corne (being Rye) & for quality as good or better then is vsuall that of the growth of this Kingdome yet notwithstanding the said Merchantꝭ cannot vent ye same And whereas the said Merchantꝭ vpon the motion & treaty of my selfe & my brethren the Aldren are contented & have offered to sell the same Corne at the price of iiij^s^ ix^d^ the bushell being lesse by farr then the same Corne ha⟨th⟩ stood them in. And whereas the right hon^ble^. the Lordꝭ & others of his Ma^te^: most hon^ble^. privy Councell have thought fitt ordered & required that aswell for their p^r^sent releife in venting their said Corne & for their future encouragem^t^ vpon the like occasion & for the supply of the Citty that myselfe & my brethren the Aldrẽn should presse the severall Companies of this Citty to take of the same Corne at the price aforesaid & have much blamed me & my brethren of remissnes in not Compelling the severall Companies to take of the same. In Conformity & accomplish-

[1] The book was STC 22635, concerning which Slatyr was reprimanded by the High Commission, 30 Oct. 1630. The B.M. copy does not have the table annexed, but collates A–B^12^.

ment of wch their Lo^pe^ said order Theis are to require you forthwith to repayre vnto m^r^ Mathew Cradocke & to buy & take of him the quantity of 14 quarters of the said Rye at the said price of iiij^s^. ix^d^ the bushell being in part of yor Companies proporcõn wch you are to have in a Readines for the store & provision of this Citty according to the ancient vsage & Custome & that you lay the same vp in the Companies Granary & serve forth the same to the Markettę of this Citty for the supply & furnishing of the same as tyme & occasion shall require & hereof faile you not as you tender their Lo^p^ę said order & expresse Comaund This xxij^th^ of July 1631.

Weld.

To the M^r^ & Wardens of the Company of Staco͞ners — By the Maior — Fol. 119^b^

Whereas I have received a Comaund from the kingę most [*ho^ble^ privie Councell*] excellent Ma^ty^. & direction from the right hon^ble^ the Lordę [*of the*] and others of his Ma^te^. most hon^ble^. privy Counsell. That the full quantity & proporco͞n of Ten thousand quarters of wheat taxed & assessed on all the seu'all Companies of this Citty be forthwith furnished and provided w^th^out procrastinaco͞n or further delay. his Ma^ty^. & the Lordę takeing notice of the remissnes & neglect in former tymes In accomplishment of wch his Maties. said pleasure & direction of their Lo^pe^: Theis are in his Ma^te^. name streightly to Charge [*and comand*] you that at the most fitting & Convient (*sic*) tymes betweene this & Candlemas next you doe buy & provide 140. quarters of wheat wch is yor rateable alottment towardę the said proporco͞n of 1000 (*sic*) quarters & that the same be layed vp in Granaries w^th^in this Citty for the service & provision thereof as occasion shall require. And that herein you depend not vpon Chandlers Bakers or any others to make the same ꝑvision for you as you tender the good of this Citty & will answere the Contrary if through yor default this service shall in any part be neglected. Wherein you are to take notice that it is thought fitt by my selfe & my brethren: That at Candlemas next a survey shall be made of the Granaries of this Citty to see whether you & other Companies have duely ꝑformed what you & they have byn hereby required. Guildhall this xx^th^. of September 1631/

Weld

To the m^r^ & Wardens of the Company of Stacone^r^s./ — By the Maior

Whereas by speciall direction & order from his Ma^ty^. & the Lordę of his highnes most hon^ble^. privy Councell you were charged & Comaunded by precept of my Predecessor the late Lord Maio^r^. dated the xx^th^ day of September last to buy & provide Cxl^ty^: quarters of wheat being yor Companies rateable proportion & allottment towards the furnishing of the full quantity of 1000. (*sic*) quarters of wheat taxed & assessed on all the seuerall Companies of this Citty & to have the same layed vp w^th^in [the] Granaries of this Citty for the service & provision of the same before Candlemas next, the same p^r^cept being wth such further Directions as therein is mencõned Theis are in his Ma^te^. name straightly to charge & Comaund you carefully to see that all & euery the Contentę of the said precept be in all pointę duely ꝑformed hereby giveing you further to vnderstand that it is thought fitt by my selfe & my brethren that at Candlemas next a survey shall be made of all the Corne in the Granaries of this Citty to see whether you & other Companies have duely ꝑformed what you & they have byn by the said Precept as alsoe by theis p[r]sentę required & hereof faile you not this xxviij[th]. of Nouember 1631./

Weld

FOL. 120[a] To the M[r]. & wardens of the Company of Stacōne[r]s[1] By the Maior/

fforasmuch as yo[r] Company (as I am informed) have not yo[r] proporcōn of Wheat as part of 1000. (*sic*) quarte[r]s for the store of this Citty ꝑvided & layed vp in Granaries as by my former precept they were required whereby they have not onely hazarded the Displeasure of his Ma[ty]. & the Lordę (they straightly requiring the provision both of the said 1000. (*sic*) quarters & of a great quantity) But yo[r] said Company have much neglected my precept & hazarded as much as in them is by the like extremity to fall vpon this Citty as happened the Last yeare by the Companies want of provision of their seuerall want of ꝑporcōns. Theis are therefore once more straightly to Charge & Comand you in his Ma[tę]. name. That w[th]out further delay you make vp & provide yo[r] said proporcōns of Corne according to my precept formerly sent in that behalfe whereby the same may be made ready when I shall Cause a veiw to be made thereof, for the better informacōn of his Ma[ty]: & the Lordę as occasion shall require And that you take Care that there be not a proporcōn of Corne layd vp in yo[r] Granaries by Bakers & others as heretofore by some Companies hath byn vsed to Colour the buisines & defraud the Citty for the saveing of the Companies expence & laying out of their moneyes but that yo[r] Companies proporcōn be made & layd vp bona fide w[th]out fraud or Colour as you will Answere the Contrary at yo[r] ꝑill Guildhall this xvj[th] day of Aprill 1632/

Michell

To the M[r] & Wardens of the Company of Stacōne[r]s/ By the Maior/

Theis are to will & require yo[u] that henceforth weekely vpon the Wednesday in euery weeke vntill you recieve order from me to the Contrary you bring or Cause to be brought to the meale markett at Newgate Markett w[th]in this Citty Three quarte[r]s of wheat meale of yo[r] Companies store & provision & that you there sell the same out to the poore people by the halfe pecke, pecke halfe bushell & bushell & not aboue to any ꝑson, at one tyme after the rate of v[s]. iiij[d]. the bushell & not at any higher or greater rate And hereof faile you not as you will answere the Contrary This 22th. of August 1632/

Michell/

FOL. 120[b] To the M[r] & Wardens of the Company of Stacoñers. By the Maior

fforasmuch as I & my brethren the Aldrēn are informed that the Companies of this Citty are not stored & provided w[th] Graine for the service of this Citty according to the proporcōn of Ten thousand quarte[r]s of Corne. Theis are therefore to will & require you & in his Ma[tę]: name straightly to charge & Comaund you that you buy & provide Cxl[ty]. quarte[r]s of wheat w[ch] rateably appointed & proporcōned for yo[r] Company according to the former provisions of 1000. (*sic*) quarte[r]s of Corne to be bought & provided by all the seuerall Companies of this Citty. And that the same be bought provided & layd vp in Granaries w[th]in this Citty for the service & provisicōn thereof

[1] Cf. *C–B.C*, 120[a], 28 June 1632.

before Candlemas day next at the furthest. And that you depend not vpon Chandlers Bakers or any others to make yo[r] provisions herein as you tender the good of this Citty & will answere the Contrary (if through yo[r] default this service shall be neglected And hereof faile you not at yo[r] pill This 5[th] day of October 1632/

Michell

To the Master & Wardens of
the Company of Stacone[r]s[1] By the Mayor

fforasmuch as I & my brethren the Aldrẽn are informed that the Companies of this Citty are not stored & provided w[th] graine for the service of this Citty according to the proporcõn of Ten thousand quarters of Corne. These are therefore to will & require you & in his Ma[te] name streightly to charge & Comand you. That you buy and provide Cxl. quarters of wheat w[ch] is rateably appointed & proportioned for yo[r] Company according to the former provisions of 10000 quarters of Corne to be bought & provided & Laid vp in Granaries w[th]in this Citty for the service & provision thereof before the last day of ffebruary next at the furthest. And that you depend not vpon any Chandlere Bakere or any others to make yo[r] provisione therein as you tender the good of this Citty And will answere the Contrary if through yo[r] default this service shall be Neglected. And hereof faile you not at your pill. This vij[th]. day of December 1633/

Michell/

To the M[r] & Wardens of the
Company of Stacõne[r]s By the Mayor. Fol. 121[a]

fforasmuch as a Precept was sent from me in December Last and directed to you for yo[r] Companies provision of their rateable proportion of wheat allotted vpon them towarde the quantity of the Ten thousand quarters [*of wheat*] to be provided by all the Companies for the store & service of this Citty & furnishing of the Markette of the same as in former tymes have byn accustomed. And although by the same Precept you were appointed to have yo[r] said proportion of wheat bought & provided & Laid vp in Granaries in this Citty for the service & provision aforesaid before the Last day of this instant ffebruary at the furthest, it is Conceived yo[r] Company is now short & wanting of that provision, w[ch] want may prove to the offence of his Ma[ty] & to the preiudice of this Citty. Theis are therefore to require you & Charge you That before the sixt day of March next you Certifie vnto me vnder [some of] yo[r] hande what quantities of wheat your Company have bought & provided & now is Laid vp & remayneth as yo[r] Companies owne Corne in Granaries [as] aforesaid & where the same Corne Lyeth whereby the same may be now & from tyme to tyme vewed by such as shall be appointed in that behalfe And that you faile not to make yo[r] Companyes full provision if any be wanting according as you have been appointed as aforesaid as you will answere the Contrary at yo[r] pill this xxvj[th]. of ffebruary 1633/

Weld/

To the Master & Wardens of the
Company of Staconers./ By the Mayor/

I and my brethren the Aldrẽn haueing taken into [a] Consideracõn the high prizes

[1] Cf. *C–B.C*, 125[b], 12 Jan. 1634.

of all manner of victualle wch haue suddenly of late growne wthin this Citty & finding that the same haue been Cheifely occasioned & raised by the vnnecessary feasting or makeing of publique Dynnere & suppere at the Comon halle & elsewhere wthin this Citty for the great & vsuall Meetinge of those that call themselues Countrimen to the great preiudice of his Maties subiecte & especially the poorer sort, there being procured by the said feaste a scarcity & dearnes of victualle in the frequent Consumption thereof in an excessive manner, haue thought it [*fitt &*] needfull & very fitt that the said feaste should be spared & wholly laid downe, for remedie of the aforesaid inconveniensies & better effecting of what I & my brethren the Aldrẽn ha⟨ve⟩ intended. These are to intreat & require you that after Monday next you pmitt not any of the said feaste to be made wthin the Comon hall of yor Company but that you giue espetiall order that no such Company or meeting be for the said purpose received therevnto. And hereof not to fayle as you tender the good of this Citty & will answere the Contrary at ⟨your⟩ pille. from the Guildhall the 21th of Nouember 1633./

Michell.

FOL. 121b To the Master & Wardens of the Company of Staconers/ — By the Mayor./

Whereas you haue byn required by former Precepte to make provision of yor ratable part of Ten thousand quarters of Corne for the service of this Citty. And whereas I & my brethren the Aldrẽn are informed that many of the Companies of this Citty are not stored & provided wth their full proporcõn as by the said precepte are required. These are therefore to will & require & in his Mate: name streightly to Charge & Comand you that you by the last of this instant [*month*] May doe buy & provide soe much Corne & graine as will make vp yor full proportion of Corne allotted vnto yor Company to provide wth that wch you haue already sent into the Markette for the service of this Citty. And hereof faile you not as you will answere the Contrary if through yor defalt this service shall be neglected. This xxth of May 1634./

Michell./

To the Mr and Wardens of the Company of Stacõners — By the Mayor.

fforasmuch as my selfe & my Brethren the Aldrẽn are informed that there is a great quantity of fforraine Corne allready brought in & more dayly expected wch. may be had at reasonable rates & prizes. And in that respect wee conceiue it a fitt tyme now to make yor new provision for the yeare ensewing. These are therefore to will & require you in his Mate. name streightly to Charge & Comand you, that you buy & provide Cxlty: quarters of wheat wch. is Rateably allotted & assessed vpon yor Company for the next yeares provision according to the former proporcõn of 10000 [*of*] quarters of Corne to be bought & provided by all the seuerall Companies of this Citty, & that the same be bought provided & laid vp in Granaries wthin this Citty for the service & provision thereof before ye second day of ffebruary next at the furthest. And you therein depend not vpon Chandlers Bakere or any othere to make yor provision thereof. And lastly that you doe Continue yor serveing the Markette wth. meale out of yor old store as by former precepte you were required. And hereof faile you not at yor perill. This ixth. of october 1634./

Michell

To the Master and wardens
of the Company of Stacoñe[rs]. By the Maior. Fol. 122a

In regard of the scarcity & [extreame] dearnes of Victualls at this p[r]sent tyme & for the p[r]venting of many Inconveniences w[ch] may happen aswell thereby as otherwise, if the feastinges at Halls & in Companies within this Citty & libties thereof shall be Continued as in former tymes hath beene vsed & to the intent that poore within this Citty may in some sort bee the better releived, by the saving expences of the said feastes then otherwise they should be These are therefore with advise of my brethren the Aldren' of this Citty to will & require you that you take speedy course that there be noe quarter diners Stewards dynner, [election dynner] or any other dynner or feasting made within yor Comoñ Hall, or else where, for yor said Company wherevnto either the gen'allity or the livery shall come or repayre, vntill you shall have from me order to Contrary, But that for yor quarter day Eleccõn day & other dayes & tymes of meeting for yor said Company, you cause your dynner (if you have any at all) to be made very moderate & sparing, & onely for the assistantę of yor said Company & none others, & that you likewise take such Charitable care & ꝑvision that the poore of your Company may be the better releived & comforted by all or some good ꝑte of the Charge, as by forbearing the said feasts dynners & expences shall be saved, & hereof not to faile this Eleventh day of June 1635.

Michell.

To the M[r] & wardens of
the Company of Stacõners } By the Maior.

These are to will & [These are to will and] require you that by the xx[th] day of this Instant June you Certifie vnto mee in Writing what quantity of Powther & match you have for yor Companyes store in readines to be vsed as any occasion shall require, And that if you have not such fitting quantity as yo[r] Company Ought to ꝑvide, & shall be necessary, that then you cause a speedy provision & supply of the same to be made Whereby his Matę service & this Cittyes safety if cause should be, may not be in Hazard of daunger & hereof faile not at yo[r] perill. This xvth of June 1635./

Michell.

At Whitehall the 9th: of March 1635. Present Fol. 122b

Present.

The kingę most excellent Ma[ty].
The Lo: Archb[p]. of Cant

Lo: Keeper	Ea: of Mooreton
Lo: Thrẽr	Lo: Newburgh
Lo: Priuie Seale	Lo: Cottington
Lo: high Chamberlaine	M[r] Thrẽr
Lo: Chamberlain	m[r] Comptroller
Ea: of Salisbury	m[r] Vicechamblaine
	m[r] Secretary Coke

M[r] Sec' Windebancke

Whereas theren haue rise diuers Debates & Controuersies heretofore [*beene*] [betweene] the Vniuersity of Cambridge & the Printe[r]s there and the Kingę Printer &

the Company of Stacõners in London for the printing of diuers Bookes in regard of a Charter for printing granted to the vniuersity of Cambridg 26. Hen: 8th: Wch: Controuersies & Contentions vpon seuerall referencȩ from his Maty: haue byn setled by two Orders of this Board wth. Consent of all the ꝑties, the one of the 10th of December 1623.[1] The other of the 16th. of Aprill 1629.[2] In regard his Maty: of his equall Indulgence and grace to the Vniuersity of Oxford. Hath granted the like Charter for printing to the said Vniuersity of Oxford as was formerly granted to the [*said*] Vniuersity of Cambridge.[3] It was this day Ordered by the Board according to the Kingȩ espresse pleasure declared That the Vniuersity of Oxford and their Printers shall for the tyme to Come enioy the benifitt of all the Articles & Clauses in the said Orders of the 10th of December 1623. And of the 16th. of Aprill 1629. As if the said Orders were here incerted.

Oxford (*18° hand*)

Extr: Will: Becher

Fol. 123a To the mr & Wardens of the Company of Stacõners

By the Mayor.

Whereas my selfe & my Brethren the Aldrẽn are informed that the Companies of this Citty are not stored & provided wth Grayne for the service of this Citty according to former precedentȩ & prouision of Ten thousand quarters of Corne. These are therefore to will & require you & in his Mate. name streightly to Charge & Comand you that you buy one hundred forty quarters of wheate wch is rateably appointed & proportioned for yor Company according to the said proportion, and that the same be laid vp in Granaries wthin this Citty for the service thereof before the first day of March next at the furthest, And that you depend not vpon Chandlers Bakers or any others to make yor provision herein nor Compound wth them to serue the markettȩ in yor stead as you will Answere the Contrary if through yor defalt yor Company shall not be prouided of yor said full proportion vpon a veiw thereof intended to be taken. And hereof I require you not to faile this xxiijth day of Nouember 1635./

Michell/

To the mr and Wardens of the Company of Stacõners[4]

After my harty Comendacõns &c. for asmuch as the visitacõn of the plague is much feared to increase wthin this Citty by reason whereof it is not a tyme of feasting but of fasting & prayer to almighty god to direct his Judgmentȩ from vs, I haue therefore thought fitt by and wth the advice of my Brethren the Aldrẽn hereby to intreat you to forbeare all manner of feasting & making of any publique Dynners at yor Comon hall or elswhere Or there to suffer any publique meeting for Buriallȩ Marriages or like occasions to be had during the tyme of this visitacõn And that you take Course that the moneyȩ to be spared by forbearance of the said feastȩ wch otherwise should be spent vpon the same be kept in safety in the handȩ of some of yor wardenȩ vntill further Course shall be taken touching it. To be expended from

1 Cf. *Letter Book*, 104a.
2 Cf. *Letter Book*, 111a.
3 Cf. *State Papers Dom. 1635–1636*, pp. 168–9, 19 Jan. 1636.
4 Cf. *C–B.C*, 142a, 1 Aug. 1636.

tyme to tyme by my appointm^{t}. if occasion shall require towardꝭ the releefe of such poore people whose houses shall be visited & are not able to helpe & releeue themselues in their great need & necessities. The same being an Act of Charity & exceeding acceptable to god And that you certifie me in writing what so͞me of money shall be from tyme to tyme raised & Collected in yor Company for that purpose Thus desiring yor Care & furtherance in soe pious a worke hereby intended I Comitt you to godꝭ protection & rest

Yo^{r} Loveing ffriend

May 9th 1636/ Christopher Clitherow Maio⟨r⟩

To the m^{r} & Wardens of the Fol. 123^{b}

Company of Staco͞ne^{r}s By the Mayo^{r}.

fforasmuch as yor Companies proporco͞n of wheat for the Citties store & furnishing of the Markettꝭ wch by my p^{r}sent (*sic*) you were appointed to provide and haue in a Readines in yor Granaries long before this tyme is not as I vnderstand by yor Company furnished & provided accordingly. And to the Intent I may the better satisfie his Ma^{ty}: & the Lordꝭ as Cause may require of the p^{r}sent store of Corne wthin this Citty & of the defaultꝭ of those wch are short in their provisions & prevent an extremity wch may hereafter happen if tymely provision be not made by euery Company of their seuerall proportionꝭ these are therefore in his Ma^{te}. name straightly to Charge & Comand you, That on or before the sixt of August next you Certifie me in writing vnder some of yor handꝭ, how many quarte^{r}s of wheat yor Company haue bought & is now lyeing in yor Granaries for the publique service & furnishing of the Markettꝭ, And that you take speedy Course to supply yor defect in the said provision if the p^{r}sent store amounteth not to yor Companies full proportion as yo^{u} will Answere the Contrary at yor ꝑill ffrom Guildhall this xxvijth day of July 1636/

Michell

To the M^{r} & Wardens of the

Company of Staco͞ne^{r}s By the Maior.

Whereas my selfe wth the advice of My brethren the Aldermen did heretofore by my Lr͞es intreate you to forbeare all manner of feasting or making any publique Dynners at yor Co͞mon hall or else where during the tyme of this Visitation for the said Reasons in the same Lr͞es expressed And that the moneys to be spared by the forbearance of the said feastꝭ should be kept in safety in the handꝭ of some one of yor wardenꝭ of yor said Company to be expended from tyme to tyme (if occasion should require) towardꝭ the Releife of such poore people whose howses should haue been visited & they not able to helpe & releeue themselues in their needꝭ & necessities. These are now therefore further to intreat you that forthwith for the p^{r}sent you bring or Cause to be brought into the Chamber & there pay ouer to m^{r} Ro͞bte Bateman Chamb͞lyn of the said Citty the Moyety or one halfe of all such moneyes as have or shall in that kind byn spared as aforesaid as aforesaid (*sic*) to the Intent that the same be distributed in sort before declared And the rather for that I haue receiued p^{r}sent Directions from the Lordꝭ of his Ma^{te}. most hob^{ble}. priuie Councell for the distribution of moneyꝭ for the p^{r}sent Releife of some visited ꝑishes now in pouerty & extreame necessity. And hereof I pray you not to faile this xxviijth of July 1636/

Michell./

Fol. 124a To the master & wardens of the Company of Stacõners[1] } By the Maior

fforasmuch as the Inhabitantes of the Towne of Berry St. Edmondę in the County of Suffolke by their Peticõn exhibited to ye Cort: of Lord Maior and Aldrẽn of the Citty of London doe sett forth that the said Towne now is and soe since May last hath byn greiusly (*sic*) infected wth the Plague, inasmuch as now the Infection is dispersed into 19 seuerall Streetę And 143 seuerall ffamilies. And that aboue 500 seuerall Inhabitantę are now visited therewth. And that all the better sort of the Inhabitantę are fledd out of the Towne And that very small Releife Comes to that Towne out of the said County (a great number of the prsent Inhabitantę of the said Towne for want of worke and by extremity of sicknes haveing already spent their meanes and Estates are now like to perish if prsent Charity be not Supplied vnto them. And for that the said Inhabitantę by the said peticõn haue earsnestly (*sic*) desired this Citties Charity to be entended to the said Towne soe miserably afflicted as aforesaid. These are therefore by and wth the Consent of my said Brethren the Aldrẽn And for the better Comfor⟨t⟩ & releefe of the said Towne to pray & desire you to Call yor Company togeither & acquaint them wth the prmises. And that in yor Christian Charity you giue & allow (towardę the said Townes releefe) such som̃e of money as god shall move yor hartę to giue in that behalfe And the same money to pay & deliver into the handę of Captaine Langham Merchantaylor who is intreated to receive & send & Convey it for the said Townes Releife as aforesaid. And hereof I pray you not to faile from the Guildhall this 19th day of September 1637.

Michell.

To the mr & wardens of the Company of Stacoñers By the Maior.

Whereas you were heretofore required by seuerall precepts to make provision of yor Corne for the supplie of soe much of yor proportion as yor Company is rated at for the service of this Citty by supplie of the Markettę when you shall be required to serue the same. And the Cort of Aldrẽn being desirous to vnderstand how you haue pformed ye Comand in that behalfe. Theis are in his Matę: name streightly (*to*) charge & Comaund you. That wthin seauen dayes next ensewing you make Certificate vnto me in writing vnder yor handę what provision of Corne you haue in a readines laid vp in yor Granary for the purpose aforesaid. And if you be wanting in yor proportion that you make a prsent supply thereof. And that you be very Carefull therein in regard it is resolued That some shall be appointed to take a survey what Corne you haue. And hereof faile you not As you tender his Matę. service and will answere the Contrary at yor perill. This xxvjth day of January 1637.

Michell/

Fol. 124b To the Master & wardens. of the Company of Stacõners By the Mayor.

Whereas you were heretofore required by seuerall prceptę to make yor provision of yor full proporcõn of Corne as yor Company is Rated is (*sic*) for the Service of this Citty & my selfe & my brethren the Aldrẽn doe take notice of yor neglects therein, & that wee may be much blamed in the same. Theis are therefore in his Matę: name

[1] For letter of thanks for contributions see *Analytical index of remembrancia*, p. 348.

streightly to Charge & Comand you that before ye last day of this instant month of June you doe provide & furnish yor full proporcõn of Corne for this last yeares provision: And that you doe by a p^{r}sent Supply make vp y^{r} Corne wch you now haue ye full quantity of one hundred & forty quarte^{r}s being yor full proporcõn & wthin that tyme you lay vp the same in yor Granaries for ye Service of ye Citty. And that you be very Carefull therein. In Regard that it is resolued that some shall be appointed to take a Survey what Corne you haue. And hereof faile you not as you tender his Ma^{te}: Service and will answere ye Contrary at yor perill This xijth day of June 1638.

Michell.

To ye Master & Wardens
of ye Company of Stacõne^{r}s[1] By the Mayor.

Whereas by Comon Councell holden at ye Chamber of the Guildhall of ye Citty of London the sixteenth day of this instant month of October. It was enacted granted and agreed. That aswell ye sum̃e of Twelue thousand poundꝭ to be paid to his Ma^{ty}: as ye moneyes to be expended in & about ye passing of ye bookes & Pattentꝭ vnder the great Seale of England & other Charges incident there vnto for passing of ye said Bookes to this Citty & the seuerall Company (*sic*) thereof, should be raised & Levyed in this manner (vizt.) Eight thousand poundꝭ parcell thereof vpon all the Seuerall Companies of this Society And the residue of ye said Twelue thousand poundꝭ & the Charges for passing of ye said bookes & Pattents & other Charges incident therevnto to be paid [*und*] out of the Chamber of London As by the said Act of Com̃on Councell appeareth fforasmuch as ye said bookes are now vnder his Ma^{te} Signature & wthall (Fol. 125^{a}) expedicoñ are to passe vnder the great seale of England. Theis are therefore in his Ma^{te}. name To Charge & Comand you that forthwith vpon Sight hereof you levy & provide wthin yor Company the sum̃e of Eighty pounꝭ being yor rate- (80L) able part of ye said Eight thousand quarte^{r}s of Corne at wch by Com̃on ([18° hand]) Councell you are rated for provision thereof. And that forthwith you take such Course as that ye said money soe to be levyed be paid & deliuered ouer vnto Mr Rob̄te Bateman Chamb̄len of this Citty into ye Chamber of London. on or before the xxvijth day of this month. To the end that ye said money may be in a readines to be paid to his Ma^{ty}: for ye purpose aforesaid According as by ye said Act of Com̃on Councell is intended And hereof faile you not as you tender his Ma^{te} service & will answere the Contrary at yor perillꝭ. Guildhall this xxth of October 1638/

Michell.

To the Master & wardens of
the Company of Stacone^{r}s

fforasmuch as my selfe & my brethren the Aldrẽn haue byn informed y^{t} ye King & queenes most excellent Ma^{ty}: & her Ma^{te}. most royall mother the Queene mother of ffrance togeither wth diuers of ye Nobillity & great p̱sonages doe intend on wensday next to take their royall passage through ye Citty from Aldgate to Templebarr. And forasmuch as myselfe & my brethren ye Aldrẽn wth the Liueryes of ye seuerall Companies of this Citty are required to giue attendance on their Royall p̱sons. Theis are in his Ma^{te} name streightly to charge & Comand you that you take speciall Care

[1] Cf. *C–B.C*, 160^{a}, 23 Oct. 1638.

that ye Railes or standing of yor Company be forthwith made in a Readines & sent into yor Stacõn between Aldgate & Templebar & sett vp, on Tewsday next as you shalbe further directed for the Convenient & decent standing of yor Liuery in the place to be appointed for that purpose. And you are likewise required togeither wth all & euery of yor Liuery or Clothing of yor Company Except such as be of ye trayned band to repaire vnto & be at yor standinge in comely & decent apparell &
Fol. [125b] in yor Liuery gownes & hoode on || Wensday next by ten of ye Clock in the forenoone at the farthest, where you shall stay till their Ma^te. are past & you are likewise to take especiall Care that you haue yor Banne^rs Streamers & blew cloth ready at yor standinge And such as are in the Liuery of yor Company & of the trayned Band are to attend their Captaine in their Armes & to be discharged of their Attendance wth the Liuery And hereof faile you not. This 28th of October 1638.

Michell.

To the Master & wardens of the Company of Stacone^rs — By the Mayo^r.

You are hereby to take notice that vpon the service to be performed on wensday next. The Lord Maye^rs Company is to stand next Aldgate on the South side of the way, And from thence euery Company is to take their standing according to their precedency, wherein they are to enlarge themselues in their number & distance That the Companies may fill that side of the way from Aldgate to Templebar if it maybe. This xxixth of October 1638.

Michell.

To the Master & wardens of the Company of Stacõne^rs

Whereas my selfe & my Brethren the Aldrẽn are informed That ye Companies of this Citty are not stored & prouided wth graine for ye service of this Citty according to former p^rcedents & provisions of ten thousand quarte^rs of Corne These are therefore to will & require you & in his Ma^te: name straightly to charge & Comand you that you buy & provide one hundred quarte^rs of wheat wch is rateably appointed & proportioned for yor Company according to former provisions of Ten thousand quarters of Corne to be bought & provided by all the seuerall Companies of this Citty, & that ye same be bought & provided & Laid vp in Granaries w^thin this Citty for the service and provision of ye same before the first day of March next at the furthest And that you depend not vpon Bakers Chandlers or any others to make
Fol. 126a yor provision herein || nor Compound wth any of them to furnish the Marketts in yor stead, as you tender the good of this Citty & will answeare the Contrary if through yor default this service or provision shalbe neglected or if yor Company shall be vnfurnished of their full proporcõn vpon a veiw against the tyme intended to be made And hereof faile you not at yor perill this 7th of ffebruarij 1638/

Michell.

To the Master & wardens of the Company of Station^rs — By the Mayor.

Whereas my selfe & my brethren the Aldrẽn are informed that the Companies of the Citty are not stored & provided wth graine for the service of this Citty according to former Precepts & provisions of Ten thousand quarte^rs of Corne These are therefore to will & require you & in his Ma^ts. name streightly to charge & Comand you to buy & provide one hundred quarte^rs of wheat wch is ratably proportioned and appointed for yor Company according to former provisions of Ten thousand quarte^rs Corne (*sic*) to be bought & provided by the seuerall Companies of this Citty. And that the same be bought & provided & laid vp in Granaries wth in this Citty for the service & provision of the same before Candlemas day next at the farthest. And that you depend not vpon Chandlers Bakers or any others to make your provision herein nor Compound wth any of them to furnish the Marketts in yor steed As you tender the good of this Citty & will answere the Contrary if through yor defalt the service or provision shall be neglected. Or if yor Company, shall be vnfurnished of their full proporcõn vpon a [*tyme*] veiw against the time intended to be made. And hereof faile you not at yor perill. This fifth of december 1639/

Michell.

To the M^r & Wardens of the Company of Stationers } By the Mayor FOL. 126^b

These are to will & require you in his Ma^te: name to retorne vnto mee to morrow a true Certificate in writing vnder yor hande of what quantity of powder and Match you haue in Store. And of what condicõn the same is. And hereof not to faile as you will answere the Contrary at yor pill. This xij^th day of may 1640.

Michell.

To the right ho^ble: the Lord Mayor the City of London

Stationers (*18° hand*) According to a precept of the xij^th of this instant May Wee the Master & Wardens of the Company of Stacone^rs doe humbly certifie yor honor that wee haue not at this tyme any provision at all either of powder or Match in o^r said Company. This xiiij^th of May 1640./

John Smethwick} M^r
Hen: ffetherston } wardens.
Nich: Bourne }

By the Mayor

To the M^r & wardens of the Company of Staconers }

ffor the better defence of this kingdome & safety of this Citty it is thought fitt by me & my brethren the Aldrēn That two hundred & ffifty Barrells of [*Gun*] powder shall be forthwith prouided & kept wth in this Citty to be in a Readines [*shall*] when occasion shall require. And therefore these are in his Ma^te. name to Charge & comand you that forthwith vpon receipt hereof you provide three Barrells of powder good & well condicõned, and that you keepe it for the store of this Citty, haveing especiall care for the placing thereof in some fitt & remote roome from the danger of fire. And hereof see you faile not as you tender his Ma^te. service, the welfare & safety of this Citty And will answere the Contrary at yor pill this xxj^th day of August 1640.

Michell.

FOL. 127a To the Mr & Wardens of the
Company of Stationers By the Mayor

Whereas for the better defense of this Kingdome & safety of this Citty you were required by a late precept from me to provide forthwith vpon receipt there of three Barrellę of Powder good & well condicõned for the store & vse of this Citty. Now for especiall reasons herevnto moueing these are in his Matę. names to Charge & comaund you forthwith to double that yor proporcõn of powder, & to provide so much Match well Condicõned, & such quantity of Bulletts as may be answearable to that proporcõn of Powder, & that you haue an especiall care & regard for the placing of the said powder in some convenient & remote roome from the danger of fire, & by Tewsday next to certifie me in Writing vnder yor hands of yor doeing herein As also what number of compleat Armes yor said company hath in a Readines in store for the Cittyes vse & hereof not to faile as you tender his Matę. service the wellfare of this Citty. And will answere the Contrary at yor pillę This 4th day of September 1640.

Michell.

Stationers (*18° hand*) According to a precept of the fourth of this instant September wee the Mr. & wardens of the Company of Staconers London doe humbly certifie yor honor. That wee haue contracted for or proporcõn of six Barrell of powder warranted to be good & well condiconed, to be deliuered vnto vs on or before ffriday next. And that wee shall also forthwith provide or selues wth Bulletts & Match Armes [*accore*] answerable to that proporcõn. And wee further Certifie yor Lopp: that for wee haue now in a readines thirteene Corsletts & Pikes & four Musketts compleat. This 8th of September 1640

Will: Aspley} Mr
Tho: Downes}
Sam: Man} war.

FOL. 127b To the Mr & wardens of the
Company of Staconers By the Mayor

Whereas by a late precept from mee of the fourth of this month you were required forthwith vpon receipt thereof to provide six Barrellę of Powder good & well Condicõned, & so much match well Condicõned & such quantity of Bulletts as may be answearable to that proporcõn of powder for the store and vse of this Citty. And that you should haue an especiall Care & regard for the placeing of the said powder in some Convenient & remote roome from the danger of fier. And by Tewsday then next following wch was the 8th day of this month to certifie me in writing vnder yor hande of yor doeing herein, as also what number of compleat armes yor said Company hath in a readines in store for the Cittyes vse. Notwithstanding wch my precept you haue hitherto neglected to make that Certificate And therefore these are once more to will & require you & in his Matę: name straightly to charge & Comand you imediatly vpon sight hereof to make yor proporcõn of Powder Match & Bulletts required by my former precept as aforesaid. And in all thingę to pursue the same. And that you returne vnto mee by Thursday next at the furthest an Exact Accompt of yor doeing herein. And hereof not to faile as you tender his Matę. service and safety of this Citty. And will answeare the Contrary at yor perills. This 25th day of September A° dni' 1640.

Michell.

To the right ho^ble^: the Lord Mayor of the
City of London.

According to a p^r^cept of the 25th of September last Wee the M^r^ & wardenę of the Company of Stacōne^rs^ London doe humbly certifie yor honor. That wee haue bought six barrellę of well Condicōned powder wth Match & Bulletts answearable to that proporcoñ & taken especiall Care in the placeing of it to avoid the danger of fire. And that for Armes [wee] haue in a Readines, 8 Muskettę & 15 Corslettę wth Compleat furniture therevnto. This first of October 1642 (*sic*)

Will: Aspley} Mr
Tho: Downes} war.
Sam: Man

To the M^r^ & wardens of the Company of Stacōne^rs^/ By the Mayor. FOL. 128^a^

These are to will & require you in his Ma^te^ name streightly to Charge & Comand you. That you make a true Certificate vnto me vnder yor handę on or before Saturday next of all & singular the names & Surnames of all such ꝑsons as are of the Liuery of yor Company. And hereof not to faile as you tender the service of this, (*sic*) & will answere the Contrary at yor ꝑills. This first day of October 1640.

Michell/

To the right ho^ble^: the Lord Mayor of the
City of London.

According to a Precept of the first day of this instant October. Wee the M^r^ & wardens of the Company of Stacōne^rs^ doe humbly certifie yor honor. That these hereafter named are the names & surnames of such ꝑsons as are of the Liuery of o^r^ Company (vizt.)

Allen Orian alias Currant
ffelix Kingston
&c

This 3^d^ of October 1640

(*rest of 128a, 128b, 129a, most of 129b blank; the item on 129b at foot is dated 9 February 1640, i.e. 1641.*)

1632
Stacōners
Mr Cole} Master
mr Weaver} Wardens
Mr Aspley}

A Bill of Assesment[1] rated and assessed by the Master Wardens & Assistantę by vertue of a Precept from the Lord Mayor & by authority of an Act of Cōmon Councell whereon the said Precept was grounded towardę the payment of 1000^li^ (for the death of Doctor Lamb) whereof 14^li^ is this Companies proporcōn. FOL. 140^a^

Assistantę	M^r^. Cole	iij^s^.
	M^r^. Weaver	iij^s^.
	M^r^. Aspley	iij^s^.
	M^r^. Barker	iij^s^.

[1] Cf. *C–B.C*, 122^a^, 30 Jan. 1633.

M^{r}. Waterson .... iij^{s}.
M^{r}. Swinhow .... iij^{s}.
M^{r}. Islip .... iij^{s}
M^{r}. Ockold .... iij^{s}
M^{r}. Kingston .... iij^{s}
M^{r}. Purfoot .... iij^{s}
M^{r}. Bateman .... iij^{s}
M^{r}. Harrison .... iij^{s}
M^{r}. Smethwicke .... iij^{s}
M^{r}. Rothwell .... iij^{s}
M^{r}. ffetherston .... iij^{s}

Livery

M^{r}. Butter .... ij^{s}
M^{r}. Downes .... ij^{s}.
M^{r}. Moore .... ij^{s}.
M^{r}. Bourne .... ij^{s}.
M^{r}. Mead .... ij^{s}.
Mr Beale .... ij^{s}
M^{r}. Higgenbotham .... ij^{s}
Mr Man .... ij^{s}
M^{r}. ffran: Constable .... ij^{s}
Mr White .... ij^{s}.
Mr Hoth[1] .... ij^{s}
Mr Parker .... ij^{s}.
Mr Edwardę .... ij^{s}
M^{r}. Boler .... ij^{s}
M^{r}. Stansby .... ij^{s}.
M^{r}. Hawkins .... ij^{s}
M^{r}. Dawson sen' .... ij^{s}
Mr Whittacker .... ij^{s}
Mr Latham .... ij^{s}
Mr Wellinę[2] .... ij^{s}
Mr Dawson Jun .... ij^{s}.
M^{r}. Williamę sen' .... ij^{s}.

Fol. 140^{b}

M^{r}. Harper .... ij^{s}
M^{r} Jo: Norton .... ij^{s}
M^{r} fflesher .... ij^{s}
Mr Haviland .... ij^{s}
Mr Meighen .... ij^{s}
Mr Allott .... ij^{s}
Mr Sparkę .... ij^{s}
Mr Waterson Jn' .... ij^{s}
Mr Cotes .... ij^{s}
Mr Young .... ij^{s}

[1] John Hoth, made free 24 Apr. 1598 (Arber ii. 720).

[2] Jonas Wellings, made free 20 Mar. 1602 (Arber ii. 731).

Mr Adamę .... ijs
Mr Legatt .... ijs
Mr. Miller............................ ijs
Mr Brewster .... ijs
Mr Grismond .... ijs
Mr Milborne .... ijs
Mr Seale .... ijs
Mr Bloome............................ ijs
Mr Bellamy .... ijs
Mr Lee Jn .... ijs
Mr Bird .... ijs
Mr Chappell[1] .... ijs
Mr Sherriffe[2] .... ijs
Mr Mathewę .... ijs
Mr Robte Constable[3] .... ijs
Mr Bartlett .... ijs
Mr Stevenę .... ijs
Mr Harrigate .... ijs
Mr Partridge .... ijs
Mr Robinson .... ijs
Mr Thrall .... ijs
Mr ffussell .... ijs
Mr Meredith .... ijs
Mr Alchorne .... ijs
Mr Dolman .... ijs.

Yeomanry

Wm. Jones .... js
Wm. Cox[4]. .... js
Wm. Lugger .... js
ffran: Arther[5] .... js
Richard Brookebancke[6] .... js
Robte Rider .... js
Henry Gosson .... js
John Wright .... js

Fol. 141a

Walter Hayward[7] .... js
Bartholomew Downes .... js
Nich: Okes .... js
Nich: Sheffeild[8] .... js
James Randall .... js
Arthur Collinę .... js
John Browne .... js
ffran: ffalconer .... js

[1] John Chappell, made free 12 Jan. 1624 (Arber iii. 685).
[2] William Sherife, made free 15 Mar. 1624 (Arber iii. 685).
[3] Made free 12 Dec. 1614 (Arber iii. 684).
[4] Made free 9 Sept. 1597 (Arber ii. 719).
[5] Query Archer.
[6] Made free 3 June 1600 (Arber ii. 725.)
[7] Made free 2 May 1603 (Arber ii. 734).
[8] Made free 16 Jan. 1604 (Arber ii. 735).

Edw: Banbury[1] .... j^s^
Tho: Bailey .... j^s^
Tho: Smith[2] .... j^s^
Geo: Gibbe .... j^s^
Jo: Bennitt[3] .... j^s^
Hen: Holland .... j^s^
Raph Mabb .... j^s^
W^m^. Crawley[4] .... j^s^
John Thompson .... j^s^
Bernard Alsop .... j^s^
Tho: ffinch[5] .... j^s^
Mathew Tagell[6] .... j^s^
Cutbert Wright .... j^s^
Sam: Albyn .... j^s^
Edward Wright .... j^s^
Robte Lownes .... j^s^
Hen: Gibbone[7] .... j^s^
Joseph Hunscott .... j^s^.
Tho: Peirchey[8] .... j^s^
John Branch[9] .... j^s^
Godfry Emondson .... j^s^
Edw: Blackmore .... j^s^
Sam: Nealand .... j^s^
Edw: Napper[10] .... j^s^
Jo: Odell[11] .... j^s^
Abra: Ripley[12] .... j^s^
Lawrance Hayes .... j^s^
John Norgate[13] .... j^s^
Rich: Cartwright .... j^s^
John Marriott .... j^s^
Tho: Ellis .... j^s^
ffrancis Vinson[14] .... j^s^
Nath: Newbery .... j^s^

FOL. 141^b^ Rich: Hodgkinson .... j^s^
W^m^. Titon[15] .... j^s^
Richard Hackett[16] .... j^s^
Jo: Morrell[17] .... j^s^

[1] The only one of this name recorded was not made free until 3 Dec. 1638 (Arber iii. 688).

[2] Probably T. Smythe, made free 7 Dec. 1607 (Arber iii. 683).

[3] Apprenticed 2 Mar. 1601 (Arber ii. 252).

[4] Made free 16 Jan. 1610 (Arber iii. 683).

[5] Apprenticed 5 Oct. 1601 (Arber ii. 257).

[6] Made free 16 Apr. 1610 (Arber iii. 683).

[7] Made free 28 Jan. 1612 (Arber iii. 683).

[8] T. Piercey, made free 6 May 1612 (Arber iii. 683).

[9] Made free 2 Aug. 1612 (Arber iii. 683).

[10] E. Napier, made free 6 Dec. 1613 (Arber iii. 684).

[11] Unrecorded.

[12] Made free 5 Sept. 1614 (Arber iii. 684).

[13] Made free 12 Dec. 1614 (Arber iii. 684).

[14] Unrecorded.

[15] Unrecorded.

[16] Made free 17 Sept. 1616 (Arber iii. 684).

[17] Possibly J. Morret, made free 1 Mar. 1617 (Arber iii. 684).

Math: Walbancke ... j^s
Nath: Browne ... j^s
John Neave[1] ... j^s
Ben: Wilson[2] ... j^s
Roger Turner ... j^s
Rich: Leech[3] ... j^s
Rich: Albon[4] ... j^s
Jo: Dallum ... j^s
Jo: Clarke sen' ... j^s
ffulke Clifton ... j^s
Henry Eversden ... j^s
John Hinson ... j^s
Rich: Sharlacker ... j^s
Edm: Bollifont ... j^s
Tho: Kemb[5] ... j^s
Rich: Satterthwait[6] ... j^s
Geo: Greene ... j^s
Tho. ffawcett ... j^s
Jo: Web[7] ... j^s
And: Hebb ... j^s
Robte Ward[8] ... j^s
Ben: ffisher ... j^s
W^m. Sheeres ... j^s
Dan: Coop[9] ... j^s
Sam: Cartwright ... j^s
Tho: Bourne ... j^s
W^m. Parratt[10] ... j^s
Rich: Myn ... j^s
ffran: Grove ... j^s
Edw: Piggott[11] ... j^s
Anth: Turke[12] ... j^s
Timothy Gray[13] ... j^s
Ro: Goodridge[14] ... j^s
ffran: Masey[15] ... j^s
Geo: Cooke[16] ... j^s
Anth: Vincent ... j^s
Rich Colline ... j^s
Humphrey Mozeley ... j^s
Rich: Rogers ... j^s

[1] Made free 20 Apr. 1618 (Arber iii. 684).
[2] Made free 1 June 1618 (Arber iii. 684).
[3] Unrecorded.
[4] Made free 4 Jan. 1619 (Arber iii. 685).
[5] Possibly T. Ken, made free 15 Jan. 1621 (Arber iii. 685).
[6] Made free 6 Feb. 1621 (Arber iii. 685).
[7] Made free 16 May 1621 (Arber iii. 685).
[8] Made free 6 May 1622 (Arber iii. 685).
[9] D. Cowper, made free 7 Oct. 1622 (Arber iii. 685).
[10] Possibly W. Barret, made free 9 Apr. 1632 (Arber iii. 687).
[11] Made free 6 July 1623 (Arber iii. 685).
[12] Probably A. Tucke, made free 4 June 1627 (Arber iii. 686).
[13] Made free 2 Aug. 1630 (Arber iii. 686).
[14] Unrecorded.
[15] Made free 2 May 1631 (Arber iii. 686).
[16] Not made free until 7 July 1634 (Arber iii. 687).

Fol. 142ª

Rich: Salsbury[1] .... j^s
Geo: Brunt[2] .... j^s
Tho: Brisco .... j^s
Steven Pemell.......................... j^s
Wm. Hille .... j^s
Dan: Pakeman.......................... j^s
Tho: Jones .... j^s
Geo: Okeland[3] .... j^s
Hen: Isam[4].......................... j^s
Jo: Rothwell .... j^s
Rich: Hammond[5].......................... j^s
Am: Ritherdon .... j^s
Rob: Bostocke.......................... j^s
Nich: Vavasor.......................... j^s
Hen: Cottrell[6].......................... j^s
Luke ffawne.......................... j^s
Nich: Greenhill[7].......................... j^s
Walter Oke[8].......................... j^s
Wm. Kenwicke[9] .... j^s
Robte Wilson.......................... j^s
Wm. Law[10] .... j^s
Hen: Taunton .... j^s
Jasp Emery .... j^s
Octavian Pullen .... j^s
Nich: Alsop[11] .... j^s
Geo: ffeversam[12] .... j^s
Rich: fferrers[13]. .... j^s
Edm: Hussey[14].......................... j^s
Raph Harford.......................... j^s
Tho: Bates .... j^s
Hen: Overton.......................... j^s
James Crumpe.......................... j^s
Tho. Wright.......................... j^s
Tho: Johnson.......................... j^s
Rich: Dew[15] .... j^s
Rich: Batten[16] .... j^s
Am: Laite[17] .... j^s
Sam: Petty[18] .... j^s
Hen: Beech[19] .... j^s

1 Unrecorded.
2 Made free 3 May 1624 (Arber iii. 685).
3 Made free 25 Sept. 1620 (Arber iii. 685).
4 Unrecorded.
5 Made free 16 Jan. 1626 (Arber iii. 686).
6 Made free 5 Dec. 1625 (Arber iii. 686).
7 Made free 7 Feb. 1631 (Arber iii. 686).
8 Made free 6 Feb. 1626 (Arber iii. 686).
9 W. Kendrick, made free 7 July 1628 (Arber iii. 686).
10 Made free 8 Apr. 1616 (Arber iii. 684).
11 Made free 28 Sept. 1631 (Arber iii. 686).
12 Unrecorded.
13 Unrecorded.
14 Made free 19 Jan. 1624 (Arber iii. 685).
15 Made free 3 Oct. 1631 (Arber iii. 687).
16 Made free 18 Jan. 1619 (Arber iii. 685).
17 Made free 11 Jan. 1632 (Arber iii. 687).
18 Made free 18 June 1627 (Arber iii. 686).
19 Made free 28 June 1632 (Arber iii. 687).

Phil: Jones[1] .... js
Wm. Hope .... js

Wm. Adderton .... js FOL. 142b
Rich: Oates[2] .... js
Robte Howes .... js
Hugh Beeston .... js
Rich: Wright[3] .... js
Tho: Slaughter .... js
Ben: Allen .... js
Sam: Dawson[4] .... js
Geo: Bradley .... js
Wm. Atley[5] .... js
Wm. Stempe[6] .... js
Rich: Williame .... js
Geo: Phippes[7] .... js
Geo: Hurlocke .... js
Rich: Roiston .... js
Jo: Ellis[8] .... js
Jo: Horne[9] .... js
Nath: Deane[10] .... js
Rich: Gough[11] .... js
Rich Oulton .... js
John Treagle .... js
Tho: Hall[12] .... js
Hugh Perry .... js
Tho: Sare[13] .... js
Wm. Stevene[14] .... js
Hen: Bird .... js
Jo: Spenser .... js
Tho: Dainty .... js
ffran: Coles .... js
Hen: Atkinson .... js
Anth: Vphill .... js
Tho: Knight .... js
John Sutton[15] .... js

[FOL 143 *blank*]

1 Made free 5 May 1628 (Arber iii. 686).
2 Unrecorded.
3 Unrecorded.
4 Made free 3 Dec. 1627 (Arber iii. 686).
5 Made free 6 Dec. 1630 (Arber iii. 686).
6 Made free 20 Dec. 1623 (Arber iii. 685).
7 Made free 13 Jan. 1630 (Arber iii. 686).
8 Made free 9 Nov. 1630 (Arber iii. 686).
9 Made free 7 June 1624 (Arber iii. 685).
10 Possibly Nicholas D., made free 3 July 1626 (Arber iii. 686).
11 Made free 20 Jan. 1612 (Arber iii. 683).
12 Made free 4 Dec. 1626 (Arber iii. 686).
13 Made free 20 Mar. 1589 (Arber ii. 705).
14 Made free 3 Oct. 1627 (Arber iii. 686).
15 Made free 9 Nov. 1630 (Arber iii. 686).

FOL. 144a

Stationers

Mr. Harrison} Master
Mr. Rothwell} Wardens.
Mr. Mead}

A Bill of assessment[1] rated & assessed by the Master wardens & Assistants by vertue of a Precept from the Lord Mayor & by authority of an Act of Comõn Councell dated the xxth of October 1638. [*the Sume of towardꝭ the paymt of*] the sum̃e of ffourscore poundꝭ allotted to this Company [*towardꝭ*] for renewing the Citties Charter./

Assistants	Mr Harrison	xvjs
	Mr Rothwell	xvjs
	Mr Mead	xvjs.
	Mr Swinhow	xvjs.
	Mr Islip	xvjs.
	Mr Kingston	xvjs.
	Mr Smethwick	xvjs
	Mr Aspley	xvjs
	Mr ffetherston	xvjs
	Mr Butter	xvjs.
	Mr Downes	xvjs.
	Mr Bourne	xvjs.
	Mr Beale	xvjs
	Mr Man	xvjs
	Mr Hoth	xvjs
	Mr Parker	xvjs
	Mr Bateman	xs
Assistantꝭ widdows.	Mrs. Joyce Norton	xvjs
	Mrs. Jane Norton	xvjs
	Mrs. Leake	xvjs
Liuerie	Mr Exoll	xs
	Mr Edwardꝭ	xs
	Mr Whitaker	xs
	Mr Latham	xs
	Mr Rice Williams	xs
	Mr Wellins	xs
	Mr Ephr: Dawson	xs.
	Mr Constable	xs.
FOL. 144b	Mr Harper	xs
	Mr fflesher	xs
	Mr Haviland	xs
	Mr Meighen	xs
	Mr waterson	xs
	Mr Tho: Coates	xs
	Mr Young	xs

[1] Cf. *C–B.C*, 160a, 23 Oct. 1638, and *Letter Book*, 124b, 20 Oct. 1638. As a good many of the names in the preceding list are here repeated, only those not in the dictionaries of printers or previously identified are here footnoted. This list evidently includes freemen who followed other trades.

Mr Legatt	x^{s}	
Mr Miller	x^{s}	
Mr Bruister	x^{s}	
Mr Grismond	x^{s}	
Mr Milborne	x^{s}	
Mr Seile	x^{s}	
Mr Bloome	x^{s}	
Mr Bellamy	x^{s}	
Mr Lee Junr	x^{s}	
Mr Bird	x^{s}	
Mr Chappell	x^{s}	
Mr Bartlett	x^{s}	
Mr Stevens	x^{s}	
Mr Harrigate	x^{s}	
Mr Partridge	x^{s}	
Mr Robinson	x^{s}	
Mr Thrale	x^{s}	
M^{r} ffussell	x^{s}	
Mr Meredith	x^{s}	
Mr Alchorne	x^{s}	
Mr Dolman	x^{s}	
Mr Crawley	x^{s}	
Mr Marriott	x^{s}	
Mr Morrett	[*x^{s}*]	
Mr Walbanck	x^{s}	
Mr Rich: Cotes	x^{s}	
Mr Cartwright	x^{s}	
Mr Mozeley	x^{s}	
Mr Overton	x^{s}	
Mr Dainty	x^{s}	
Mr Roger Norton	x^{s}	
Mr Thomason	x^{s}	
Mr Triplett	x^{s}	
Mr Petty	x^{s}	
Mr Tho: Wright	x^{s}	
M^{r}. Pullen	x^{s}	
Mr Bradley	x^{s}	
Mr Emery	x^{s}	
Mr Hunscott	(*nothing*)	FOL. 145^{a}
Mr Crooke	x^{s}	
Mr Hodgkinson	x^{s}	
Mr Leake	x^{s}	
Mr Rothwell	x^{s}	
M^{r} [Tho:] Badger	x^{s}	
M^{r} [John] Dawson	x^{s}	
Mr Griffin	x^{s}	

	Mr Clarke	xs
	Mr Vavasour	xs
	Mr Harford	xs
	Mr Pakeman	xs
	Mr ffawne	xs
	Mr Slater	xs
	Mr Hope	xs
	Mr Oulton	xs
	Mr Gold	xs
	Mr Bishop	xs
	Mr Nicholls	xs
Widdowes of the Liuery	Mrs Busbie	xs
	Mr (*sic*) Smith	xs.
Yeomandry	John Wright sen'	vs.
	william Lugger	vs.
	Hen: Gosson	vs.
	Tho: Baley	vs.
	John Thompson	vs.
	Nath: Browne	vs.
	Edw: Blackmore	vs.
	Godfrey Emerson	vs.
	ffulke Clifton	vs.
	James Randall	vs.
	Hen: Bird	vs.
	ffran ffalconer	vs.
	Hen: Eversden	vs.
	Tho: Kemb	vs.
	Mich: Sparkes	vs.
	John Bennett	vs.
	Hen: Bennett[1]	vs.
FOL. 145b	Dan: Cowper	vs.
	Hen: Holland	vs.
	Rich: Gough	vs
	Simon ffarwell[2]	vs
	Math: Costerdyne	vs
	Hen: Gibbons	vs
	Edw: Banbury	vs
	William Tyton	vs
	Law: Chapman	vs
	Rich: Cartwright	vs.
	Edw: Wright	vs.
	Hum: Woodall	vs.
	Raph Mabb	vs.

[1] Made free 14 Dec. 1629 (Arber iii. 686).

[2] Made free 7 Mar. 1608 (Arber iii. 683).

Gabriell Baskervile[1] .... vs.
Rich: Hackett......................... vs.
Andrew Hebb .... vs.
John Oakes hotprsser[2] .... vs.
Tho: Bourne........................... vs.
ffran: Coles.......................... vs.
George Greene Claspemaker-[3] .... vs.
Robert Bostock........................ vs.
John Dallum........................... vs.
Anth: Tooke........................... vs.
Rich: fferrens........................ vs.
George Hurlock........................ vs.
John Smith paules alley .... vs.
Tho: Smith Scrivener................ vs
Jeremy Arnold[4]...................... vs
Edmond Hussey......................... vs
William Garrett....................... vs
Robert Dunscomb....................... vs
Edw: Hancock[5] .... vs
ffran: Grove.......................... vs.
Tho: Andrews .... vs.
Sam: Dawson........................... vs.
John Okes .... vs.
Jeremy Huson[6] .... vs.
William Adderton...................... vs.
George Okeland........................ vs
Roger Turner.......................... vs.
Robte Howes........................... vs
Robte Swaine .... vs.
Wm. Stempe .... vs
Rich: Myn .... vs.

John Webb .... vs FOL. 146a
James Crumpe.......................... vs
Tho: Bristoe[7] .... vs
Nich: Alsop .... vs
Robte Wilson.......................... vs
John Clarke Hot prsser .... vs
Ambrose Lait.......................... vs.
Ambrose ffenwick[8] .... vs
Tho: ffletcher[9] .... vs
[*ffran: Powithman*[10]................ *vs*]

[1] Made free 28 Jan. 1623 (Arber iii. 685).
[2] Presumably not the printer.
[3] This is presumably to differentiate him from his namesake listed below as living in Fleetstreet.
[4] Made free 6 Aug. 1623 (Arber iii. 685).
[5] Made free 17 Jan. 1625 (Arber iii. 686).
[6] J. Hewson, made free 6 July 1622 (Arber iii. 685).
[7] T. Briscoe.
[8] Made free 7 Dec. 1629 (Arber iii. 686).
[9] Made free 2 Oct. 1633 (Arber iii. 687).
[10] Unidentified.

Tho: whall[1] . . . . Vs.
william Atley . . . . Vs.
william Rothwell . . . . Vs
Andrew Kemb . . . . Vs.
Rich: Harper . . . . Vs.
Hen: Atkinson . . . . Vs.
Jo: Wright Jun' old baley . . . . Vs.
Dan: ffrere . . . . Vs.
John Cowper . . . . Vs.
Geo: Tomlyn[2] . . . . Vs.
John: Benson . . . . Vs.
Hen: Ockold . . . . Vs.
John Crooke . . . . Vs.
Thomas Lambert . . . . Vs.
John Williams . . . . Vs.
Thomas Maud[3] . . . . Vs.
Josias Cooke[4] . . . . Vs.
wm. Wells . . . . Vs.
Rich: Stevenson . . . . Vs.
william Hill . . . . Vs.
John Greensmith . . . . Vs.
Sam: Gillibrand . . . . Vs.
Rich: Serger . . . . Vs.
John Raworth . . . . Vs
Thomas Paine . . . . Vs
Timothy Gray . . . . Vs.
Hen: Isam . . . . Vs
Peter Cole . . . . Vs
George Hutton . . . . Vs.
John Maynard . . . . Vs.
Alexander ffifeild . . . . Vs
Geo: Greene in fleetstreet . . . . Vs.
Abel Roper . . . . Vs
Humphrey Blundon . . . . Vs

Fol. 146b

ffran: Egglesfeild . . . . Vs.
Charles Dunkan . . . . Vs
Barnard Langford . . . . Vs
John Aston . . . . Vs
Edw: Paxton . . . . Vs
John Coleby . . . . Vs.
fford: Pennithorne[5] . . . . Vs.
ffran: Church . . . . Vs.
Wm Law . . . . Vs.
wm. Colwell[6] . . . . Vs.

1 Made free 5 Oct. 1635 (Arber iii. 687).
2 Made free 20 Dec. 1633 (Arber iii. 687).
3 Made free 30 June 1634 (Arber iii. 687).
4 Made free 2 Apr. 1627 (Arber iii. 686).
5 Made free 3 Oct. 1636 (Arber iii. 688).
6 Made free 31 May 1634 (Arber iii. 687).

wm. Ley........................... vs.
John Carter[1]........................ vs.
Phillip Newill....................... vs.
Tho: Downes......................... vs.
Walter Edmondę.................... vs.
Hen: Hood .... vs.
Hen Sheapard....................... vs
Law: Blaicklock .... vs.
Edw: Husbandę..................... vs.
Joseph Surbutt[2]..................... vs.

Whereas on the Sixteenth day of ffebruary Anno Dni' 1636. An agree⟨mt⟩ was made between the Vniuersity of Oxford of th'one pte. The Company of Stationers London. The Assignes of his Mate Printers. And the Assigne⟨s⟩ for the Gram̃er on the other pte. ffor and Concerning the printing of Certaine Bookes belonging to the said Company his Mate Printer and the Printer for the Gram̃er as by the Articles of Agreemt. betwee⟨n⟩ them before named is Specified[3] *And* whereas the said Company the Assignes of his Mats Printers And the Assignes for the printing of the Gramer were to pay vnto the said Vniuersity Two hundred poundę p Annum for a Certaine terme. At two vsuall feastę (vizt.) Th'annuncio⟨n⟩ of the blessed virgin Mary and St. Michaell Tharchangell by even an⟨d⟩ equall porcõns. The first payment to be made on the fiue and Twent⟨ieth⟩ day of March next ensewing the date thereof w'th a Couent. for ⟨the⟩ Assurance of the said 200li. p Annum during the Terme therein agree⟨d⟩ as thereby appeareth. *Now* forasmuch as the Company stand soly en⟨gaged⟩ for the said 200li. p Ann' aforesaid, The said pties to the end the sa⟨id⟩ sum̃e may be paid betweene them according to their seuerall Interests by the said Agreemt. Doe hereby mutually agree a⟨nd⟩ declare. That the said 200li. p Ann' shall be paid by and between the said pties according to the proportions hereafter named (That is to say) The said Company to pay ffourscore and Ten poundę p Annu' The Assignes of his Mate Printers ffourscore and ffiue pou⟨nde⟩ p Annu'. And the Assignes for the Gramer Pattent Twenty and ffi⟨ue⟩ poundę p Annu'. Halfe yearely by each partie respectively accordin⟨g⟩ to the agreemt. made with the said vniuersity. *That* the Charge⟨s⟩ disbursed by the Company about the said Agreement with Oxford. The Assignes of his Mate. Printers and the Assignes for the printing of the Gram̃⟨er⟩ according to their proporcõns aforesaid shall on or before the (*blank*) day of Aprill now next ensewing the date hereof pay their equall shares thereof vnto the said Company. And ffurther that what moneyes shall be hereafter expended about that buisines (during the said Agreemt. wth. Oxford) by the Company. The Assignes of his Mate Printers and the printer for the Gram̃er shall pay their equa⟨ll⟩ and proportionable shares thereof. *Moreover* that if any Agreem⟨t.⟩ be made wth Cambridge tending to this effect wth Oxford. That aswe⟨ll⟩ the same proporcõnę of paymentę as alsoe all Charges about the sam⟨e⟩ shall be paid by each parties as aforesaid. *In Testimony* of the mu⟨tuall⟩ Consent of each partie to euery pticular Article or agreemt. aforesa⟨id⟩ the pties vndernamed for & on the behalfe of the Company. The Assignes of eith⟨er⟩ of his Mate. Printerę & the assignes for the printing of the FOL. 181a

[1] Made free 3 Oct. 1636 (Arber iii. 688).
[2] Made free 15 Mar. 1631 (Arber iii. 686).
[3] Cf. *C–B.C*, 147a, 27 Apr. 1637.

Gramer haue seuerally ⟨&⟩ respectiuely subscribed their names this (*blank*) day of (*blank*) Anno 163 (*blank*) Anno decimo (*blank*) Caroli Regis.

Subscribed & acknowledged by
the ꝑties interessed in the
p^r^sence of vs. (*blank*) } }

FOL. 181^b^ (*blank*) (*blank*)

FOL. 182^a^ The seaven & Twentieth day of Aprill A^o^. Dni' 1632.

Articles[1] agreed vpon to be observed & Kept by vs herevnder Written (vizt)

Edmond Weaver	Richard Moore	James Boler	John Grismond
John Harrison	Nicholas Bourne	Ephriam Dawson	William Lee
John Rothwell	Robert Mead	Robert Allott	Philemon Stevens
Thomas Downes	Samuel Mann	Edward Bruister	Robert Dawlman

Being Partners for the whole impression of the Booke of Martyrs.

Imprimis that the whole impression of the Booke of *Martyrs* being in number Sixteene hundred, shall remayne in one Roome or Warehouse in o^r^ Comon Hall, & there to be & remayne in ioynt stocke for & to the vse of all the aforesaid Partners vntill the end & Terme of Three yeares.

Item that three of the said Partners be chosen Stockeepers euery yeare, on the five & Twentieth day of March (if it be not the Sabboth day, then the day after) vnto whose Charge & Custody all the said book⟨es⟩ shall be Comitted during one whole yeare then ensewinge, & then to deliver out the said Bookę vnto those that shall have occasion to vse them at such a price & Vpon such Condicõns as hereafter followeth. Namely ⟨the⟩ Price of the said Booke agreed vpon by all the said Partno^rs^. to be fort⟨y⟩ six shillingę & eight pence every Booke at wch. price they shall deliver ⟨them⟩ at. delivering five & Twenty bookę to every quarterne of a hundred accord⟨ing⟩ to the Custome of the Company. And that for all such of the said bo⟨okę⟩ as any Copartnor or other shall take vp, shall be by him his executo^r^s or ⟨assignes⟩ paid for in manner & forme following (that is to say) ffor all such of the said bookę as shall be delivered after o^r^ Lady day & before the first of September, at Michaelmas day next following or w^th^in one month at the furthest. And for all such as shall be delivered after Michaelmas & before the first of March to be paid for at o^r^ Lady day then next following or w^th^in one month after at the furthest. and the like tyme to be allowed from Midsomer & from Christmas, and soe from six mon⟨thę⟩ to six monthes during the tyme they are to be stocked./

Item it is alsoe agreed that if any shall take vp but Twelue of the said Bookę at one tyme, that notwithstanding he shall have the next tyme delivered vnto him Thirteene of the said Bookę to the dozen. Provided that he shall take them vp w^th^in the same six monthes or the next six monthes after at the furthest he haveing paid for the said Twelue boo⟨kę⟩ before according to the Tenor of his Bill./

Item it is alsoe agreed that every Partnor or any other that shall take vp of the said Bookę shall give his Bill for the payment of them accord⟨ing⟩ as aforesaid vnto those Three that are chosen Stockeepers for the Year⟨e⟩ to deliver them./ And that

[1] Cf. *C–B.C*, 118^a^, 5 Mar. 1632.

those Three Stockeepers chosen for that yeare shall at every of the said dayes above mencõned or wthin fourteen dayes after (being thereto required by the rest of the Partnors or the mo⟨re⟩ part of them) deliver vp a iust accompt of all such bookę as are then remaininge as alsoe of how many hath byn delivered that halfe yeare, of what money they have received for them as alsoe what is due by b⟨ill⟩ for the said Bookę. And that the said three Stockeepers shall at the sai⟨d⟩ tyme & tymes make an equall devision of all such moneyę as they shall have received [*for them and also what is due by them*] vnto every one of the said Partnors as shall appeare to be due vnto them. And if any Partne⟨r⟩ or other shall refuse or delay to pay for all such Bookę as shall be by ⟨them⟩ oweing for at any of the six monthes end (being demanded) That ⟨then⟩ the said Three Stockeeps in whose names the Billę are taken sha⟨ll⟩ be therevnto required by the rest of the Partners or the more ⟨part of⟩ ‖ them Fol. 182^{b}
(*to*) put their Bill or Billę in suite and doe their best for the speedy recovery of the said money, and then to devide all such money vnto every of the said Partners as shall be due vnto them And that neither the said Three Stockeeps nor any one of them in whose name or names any Bill or Billę is taken shall doe any act or actę by giveing any Release or otherwise wch. may be any Barr in Law whereby the rest to whome the said money is due shall be disabled to recover the same and that at the request of the rest of the Partnors or the more part of them they shall assigne over all such Billę vnto whome soever they shall appoint (if it be required).

Item it is alsoe further agreed that when it shall please god to take out of this world any of the aforesaid Partno^{rs} that then his said stocke shall be vnto his Executo^{rs}. or assignes and that a true & iust accompt shall be made vnto the said Executo^{rs}. or assignes of all such moneyę as shall be due vnto the said Deceased at the tyme of his death & of all such bookę then belonging vnto him & shall from tyme to tyme make vnto him or them a iust & true Accompt of all such moneyę as shall growe due & of the Bookę belonging to him or them as is aforesaid to be donn to the rest of the Partno^{r}s./

Item it is alsoe agreed that the Rent of the said Roome where the said Bookę be & all other Chargę concerning that busines shall be equally borne by all the Partno^{rs}. interessed in the said stocke of Bookę. Lastly if any other difference shall arise amongst vs who are Partners in this Booke concerning it or that these Articles or Covenantę heremencõned vnto wch. wee have all subscribed; be not observed & kept by every one of vs, & that any Partner or Partno^{rs} be agreeved hereat That then wee are all well Contented that the party or parties agreeved shall make his Complaint vnto o^{r} Master & Wardens and assistantę for the tyme being & are all wth one generall Consent willing & agreed to stand to such end & Award as the more part of them shall in their iudgmentę thinke fitt to make in the buisines then in question

[*signed*] *Edmund weave^{r}.* *John Rothwell* *Tho. Downes*

Richard Moore *Robert Meade./*

James Boler *Ephram Dawson* *Robert Allott* *Edward Brewster* *John Grismond* *William Lee* *Philemon Stephens./* *Robert Dawlman.*

Memoran' that Christopher Meredith the now partner with Philemon Stephens hath a right in the ffull halfe of whatsoeuer belongeth vnto him the sđ Philemon in the booke of martirs mencõned in the Couenantę aboue written./

Witness my hand heerevnto subscribed

[*signed*] *Philemon Stephens.*

Subscribed in the p^r^sence
of *Henry Walley*
John Rothwell
Edward. Brewster

Fol. 183[a] Know all men by these pn'tes. That I Richard ffeild [*sonn*] Cittizen and Grocer of London the sonne of Richard ffeild late Cittizen & Mercer of London deceased Haue receiued & had the day of the date of these pn'tę of the Master & Keeps or Wardens & Cominalty of the Mistery or Art of Stacõners of the City of London the sum̃e of Thirty poundę of lawfu⟨ll⟩ money of England a Legacy[1] giuen & bequeathed to me by the last will and Testam^t^. of my said fatherę Aunt M^rs^. Lucretia Est late of Curdworth in the County of Warwicke widdow deceased. Of wch said sum̃e of Thirty poundę soe by me receiued [being my full Legacy] I doe hereby acquitt exonerate & for euer discharge said M^r^. & Keeps or Wardens & Cominalty their Successo^r^s & ass⟨ignes⟩ & euery of them by these pn'tes. In Witnes whereof I the said Ri⟨chard⟩ ffeild haue herevnto sett my hand & seale this Eleauenth day of ffebruarij A^o^. Dni' 1634. And in the Tenth yeare of the Raig⟨ne⟩ of o^r^ soueraigne Lord King Charles of England &c.

Sealed & Deliuered in the p^r^sence of *Richard fielld*
Henry Walley
John Cleauer
& of me *William Wethered.* [*seal*]

⟨Liber computi pro pauperibus⟩
[*last two leaves*]

The copie of the Journemens
petition[2]

To ye Right Ho^ble^ the Lord Elsmere Lord Chauncellor of England

16 Maij 1613

Most Humbly beseechinge your honor to Consider the miserable estate of a [*greate*] greate nomber of poore men who by reason of manifold disorders bred in our corporacoñ contrary to those orders made in the high court of [*chauncery*] Starchamber the 28th yeere of the raigne of the late queene Elezabeth & likewise confirmed since the happie entrañce of o^r^ Dread Sou'aigne are vtterly impou'ished together w^th^all those [*as*] [that] shall succeed vs in the same corporacõn, besides the damage, it will bringe in to the church & com̃on welth, Wee haue Laid open o^r^ intollerable greifies by way of Peticõn to the gou'n's of o^r^ companie but they will not herken to o^r^ complaintę/.

[1] Cf. *C–B.C*, 132[a], 17 Feb. 1635. [2] Cf. *C–B.C*, 31[b], 18 Mar. 1613.

Therefore in all submission wee humbly entreate your honors favour & furtherance in o^{r} ꝑceedingꝭ who onely seeke succour & releife for our distress[ed] cause And so wee humbly Referre yt to your honorable consideracoñ hoping that your honor will take veiwe of o^{r} grevancꝭ hereto annexed & so giue vs reference by strict com̃aund to the Superiors of o^{r} companie for better confirmacõn

Yo^{r} Honors most humble supplianteꝭ
the poore oppressed Journeymen Printerꝭ./[1]

William Smyth
John Pape
James Bentley
Georg Snowdon
George Bostocke
Marmaduke Parsons
Rob̄t Wodnet
John Boultor
John Orphane Strange
Richard Pytham
John ffryer
Henry Bell
Edward Gosson
ffrancis Henry

Peeter Rosewill
Henry Damport
John Wilkinson
Thomas Bedle
Richard Stratton
Edward Griffen
Edwin Bush
Georg Purslow
Hugh Brewer
Robt Cotton
Anthony Higgins
Thomas Streete

Richard Wilde
Bernard Alsop
Rob̄t Sogburne
John Bodley
Leonard Maskell
John Rixon
George Millar
ffrancis Langley
William Clowes
Myles fflesher
Thomas Morley
Rob̄t Younge
Rob̄t Chambers
Richard Jackson

Edward Morrant
Rob̄t Raworth
John Wright
Paris Vandew
Gyles Symson
Luke Norton
Thomas Cawforth
ffrancis Henden
John Monger
Richard Badger
Richard Roberteꝭ
Henry Jõhson
John Dowsing
John Hanson

ffirst that whereas by ye vertue of the decree [*had*] hee that should ⟨ ⟩ appn'tices keepeth foure & six & hee that should keepe but one keepeth ⟨ ⟩

Secondly that Whereas in Oxford & Cambridge there should be brought ⟨ ⟩ appn'tice a peece at one tyme they are suffered to take as many as they can ⟨ ⟩ by the article of the decree they should entertaine Journeymen/

Thirdly, that Whereas there should belong to one Printing howse, but one appn'tice at one tyme, by entring into ꝑtnershipp, And giving ouer againe at their pleasures there depends tenne appn'tices to one howse, Soe that by this vnconsionable liberty, the totall nomber of appn'ticꝭ is amounted to as many moe, as ought to bee, by the decree whereby diuers Journeymen are beggered for want of ymploym^{t} & som̃e constrayned to printe privately Sedicõus bookes, & all in generall would be vtterly impou'ished were yt not for the p^{r}sent ymploym^{t} they haue at the Kingꝭ ma^{ties} Printers./

Lett this bee Remembred at the Starrchamber
on Tuesday next/

T: E.

[1] All of those whose names occur below are recorded in Arber as free of the Company at this date, except James Bentley, Henry Damport, and Anthony Higgons, all of whom were registered apprentices; and Gyles Symson, Thomas Cawforth, Francis Henry, Francis Henden, and John Monger, none of whose names are recorded but that of Monger who was made free later.

[1a]

[FINE BOOK]

1605 A°. 3. R. R'is Jacobi

.6. Augusti

Mr. Barker. Mr
Mr. Norton } Wardens
Mr. feild

Mr. Linge	Receaued of him by thande of Jo chest:[1] for byndinge the said Jo prentise to him Contrary to order..................................	ili./

9. Sept'

Geo. Snodon	Red of him for kepinge a prntise vnpresented contrary to order..........................	vs.

14 oct'

Math Selman	Red of him for kepinge a prent' vnprsented contr' to ordr............................	ijs vjd

2 Jan'

mr hoop	Receaued of mr hoop for the rest of his fine for the Second vnderwardenship................	vli

20 Jañ

Jo Trundel	Red of hym̃ for a fine wche he oweth for a fine for kepinge a prentise much longer tyme then the Constitutions appoint.......................	ijs vjd

14 aprl

Jo porter	Red of him for kepinge a prentise vnpresented contrary to order..........................	vijs. viijd
	Rcd of him the duties of the prsentmt of the same appr'..................................	ijs. vid
		7li. 2d

[1] John Chest was made free 2 July 1605 (Arber iii. 683), so that this fine was evidently exacted upon his presentation.

3 oct'

Mr Barker. Mr
Mr. white } wardeñs
mr Leak

Mr pavyer Remitted by a Court	Yt is ordered that whereas, contrary to the ordenãce of the Company he hath bought (as he confesseth) 800 bookę of the grayne of mustard seede prynted by mr legat to the wrong of mr Burbye whose copie yt is./ He shall presently pay xls for a fine. and delyuer all the bookę as forsayed into the hall or satisfaccoñ for them to their Value. And his ymprisonmt is respited[1]	[*xx*s] xls Remitted by a Court 22 May 1609.

3 ffebr'

Noñe appancę	Receaued for noñe appearance on the Last quarter day	vs

2mrcij

George Eld Jo. wright	Rę d of them for printing a ballad of the ffloodę[2] disorderly. iijs iiijd A pece.	vis viijd

26 mrcij

Mr. Lawe	Rę d of hym for a fyne for vsinge vndecent speeches agt Clemt Knight his neighbor and a brother and freman of this Company wthin. . . .	[*x*s] vs
Mr Burby	Rę d of him for his dispensation and Discharge from the rentership this yere	xli
Mr Ockold	Rę d of hym for his dispensation from servinge the rentership for eu'	xxli

13 apr

Mr fosbook	Rę d of him for a fine for bynding of bookę contrary to thordonancę[3].	vijs

31li. 3s. 8

[1] William Perkins's *A graine of musterd-seede* was first printed in 8°, T. Creed f. R. Jackson and H. Burwell, 1597. Copies of that edition are in the Folger and Union Theological Libraries. It was entered to Jackson 7 Feb. 1597 (Arber iii. 80), and transferred to Burby 27 Apr. 1602 (Arber iii. 205). Legat printed editions of a collection of Perkins's works in 1600, 1603, and 1605. The first was in 4°, the others all in folio and all with continuous signatures. No separate edition of *A graine of musterd-seede* printed by Legat is known before 1611 (STC 19725).

[2] The Troyte-Bullock copy of *Miracle vpon miracle Or a true relation of the great floods . . . in Couentry . . .*, 4°, [G. Eld] f. N. Fosbrook & J. Wright, 1607, is in the Huntington. They probably published a ballad with it, as Blore evidently did at the same time, cf. Arber iii. 341, 23 Feb. 1607.

[3] This ordinance is given in *Letter Book*, 5a, 25 Mar.

15 Junij

M^{res} Linge extra	Jo Helme sworne & admitted a free man of this Companye........................	insil: Entred in the Book of fremen[1]

12 Octobr

Na fosbrook sequit' in prop pagina/ [this entry deleted]	Yt is ordered that he shall pay x^{s} for a fine for offending against thordoñances in vsinge vndecent language & speache of Mr Man one of thassistentę. The said fine to be paid the Second of ffebr' next	x^{s}

[2^{a}]

1607 5 Ris'.

M^{r}. Norton M^{r}
M^{r}. Seton
M^{r}. Standish } Wardens

12 Octobr'

M^{r}. ffeild	Receaued by order of Court of m^{r}. ffeild for his dispensation from beinge Chosen the second tyme yonger Warden[2]	xx^{h}
Na fosbrook	Yt is ordered that he shall pay x^{s}. for a fine for offendinge against thordonnancę in vsinge vndecent Language toward Mr Man one of thassistentę. The said ffine to be payd the Second of ffebr' next......................	x^{s}

2 Nov.

Edward Alde	Rę^{d} of hym for a fine sett vpon hym the last Court day as appeareth in the booke of orders[3]	x^{s}

7 decembr'

M^{r}. Edward White sen^{r}	Rę^{d} of him for a fine sett vppon hym as appeareth in the book of orders[4]	xx^{s}
Ma. Lawe	Rę^{d} of him for a fine sett vppoñ him as appeareth in the booke of orders[5]..............	xiij^{s}. iiij^{d}

1587, but evidently was in force much earlier. No book in folio above 40 sheets, in octavo above 12 sheets, in decimo-sexto above 5 or 6 sheets, might be stitched with an awl or bodkin but must be sewed on a press. There were earlier ordinances against binding books of similar sizes in vellum or skiver.

[1] Cf. Arber iii. 683.
[2] Cf. *C–B.C*, 14^{b}.
[3] Cf. *C–B.C*, 15^{b}, 26 Oct. 1607. For printing an edition of the *A.B.C. for children* for E. White.
[4] See above.
[5] Cf. *C–B.C*, 15^{b}, 16 Nov. 1607.

21 m^r^cij

Na ffosbrook	Vppon the hearinge & proofe of diu'se iniurious & reprochefull woordę & speaches by Na. ffosbrook against Mr Norton nowe M^r of the companye in ye p^r^nce of Sr Stephen Soame K^t & others yt is ordered y^t he shall p^r^sently pay xl^s for a fine. Whiche yf he refuse to pay. Then it is ordered y^t for his Disobedieñce he shalbe presently comitted to Ward	ij^li
	Uppon notice gyven to him of this order he doth refuse to pay this fine. And therefore is comitted accordingly/.	
		22^li. 3^s–4^d

1607. 5 Ris' [2^b]

22 m'cij p'd

Ri. Braddock	Yt is ordered that he shall pay xx^s for a fine for transgressinge thordonances in printing the Clerkę billę disorderly from m^r. Windett[1]	xx^s.
Jo. Browne	Yt is ordered that he shall paie xiij^s iiij^d for A fine for transgressinge thordonnancę in receavinge the said billę from Mr Braddock	xiij^s iiij^d paid to m^r Standish in his accompt

26 Marcij

M^r. Bankw^r^th	Receaued of him for his discharge from servinge the rentership	xx^li
M^r. Swynhowe	Receaued of him for his discharge from servinge the rentership	xxiij^li vj^s viij^d

29 Junij

Barth'ue Fowler	Of him for his abseñce on mydsom^r quarterday}	xij^d
Na Butter	Of Na. Butter for the lik cause..............	xij^d
Joseph Harison	Of Joseph harrison for the lyke cause........	xij^d
M^r. Chard	Of m^r. Chard for the like cause..............	xij^d
Ed yate	Of Edm. Yate for the lyke	xij^d
Mr Gilman	Of m^r Gilman for the lyke..................	xij^d
Rafe Kyrkham	Of Rafe Kyrkeham for ye lyke	xij^d
J. Everest	Of Everest for the lyke	xij^d

[1] Unless the entries of 1 Aug. 1603 covered the weekly bills, they belonged to Windet as printer to the city of London. The nearest bill to this date known is that for 12 Nov. 1607, printed by Windet, a copy of which is in the Public Record Office.

Ri. Yardeley	Of Ri. Yardeley for the lyke................	xijd
Rog. Style	Of Roger Style for the lyke................	xijd
Tho Yardeley	Of Tho. Yardeley for the lyk	xijd
mr Adams / mr Lawe	Of them xijd a pece for coming to the hall wthout their gownes on the quarter day	ijs
		43. 19. 8.

[3a]

1608. 6. Ris

Mr Bysshop mr.
Mr. Hooper / Mr. Lownes Wrdens

2 Augusti

Henr. Gosson.	Receaued of hym and the printer iijs iiijd a pece for pryntinge (wthout licence) of the complaint of Tobye Potter beinge a ballad[1]	vjs viijd

27. Sept

Mr. pavier payd	yt is ordered that he shall pay xxs for a fine for printinge an ymprssion of 1000. of the book called the Sweord agt swearinge:[2] wthout aucthoritie or entrance. beinge directly agt thorders of the Companye.....................	xxs. paid

7 Octob: Die Lunae

Nath: Butter	It is ordered that Nath. Butter shall bringe into the hall, so many of the bookę of Dentę sermons[3] wche he had from Oakes to the wronge of mr Harrison thelder as he hath nowe lefte in his handę. And for the rest that are wantinge or sold away by him, he shall pay to mr Harrison after the rate of 10s the Hundred/.	
	Also that he shall pay 40s for a fine for transgressinge thordinance in buyinge these bookę of Oakes/.	5 decẽbr. Rę d. by order of Court for this fine—xxs.
	And that he shall pforme all this att or before Munday nexte after this day vpon payne that yf he fayle therein, Then his pte in the stocke	

[1] Gosson did enter this between 22 July and 4 Aug. 1608 (Arber iii. 386). Cf. H. E. Rollins, *Anal. index to the ballad-entries*, No. 2093.

[2] STC 3048. No copy of an edition published by Pavier is known. The book was entered to R. Watkins 13 Feb. 1579 (Arber ii. 347), and assigned to G. Eld three days after the entry above (Arber iii. 391). Eld published editions in 1611 and 1618 (wrongly entered in the STC under A. Nowell, STC 18743 and 18743a).

[3] There is in the Bagford collection a title-page of an edition of A. Dent's *A sermon of repentaunce*, 8o, f. I. Harrison, 1607 (Harl. 5987(33)), which may be the edition here referred to. Presumably Okes printed extra copies which he sold to Butter. It is possible that the entry in the Fine Book under date 23 Mar. 1609 refers to this transaction.

& p^r^vileg~e~ shalbe sequestred accordinge to thorders in that behalf/.

5to. decembr

M^r^ ma Lownes Renter.	Receaued of him by order of Court in Lieu of his renters dynn^r^	xi^li^
		13^li^: 6^s^: 8^d^:

1608. 6 Ris [3^b^]

Primo Marcij

	Receaued of certen of the Lyu'ie for cōminge in clokes to thelection of Stockkeps &c. this day.	viij^s^
	Of others for Late cōming thereto	iiij^s^
	Of m^r^ Lawe for not cōming vntill thelection was made	xij^d^

23. m'cij

m^r^. harrison Senr.	Ow^th^ for a fine for arrestinge na. Butter for debt contrary to order..........................	x^s^
	To be paid wheñ he receaueth this debt	remitted 27mo. Sept 1613.

27 m'cij 1609. 7mo. Regis/.

M^r^. Orrian Solut'./	Ow^th^ for his dispensation for not servinge the rentership .xx^li^ to be paid the Sixt of maie next[1]	xx^li^. paid

2do. Maij 1609.

Mr Havilond Mr Hall	It is ordered that they shall pay 20^s^ for affyne for bindinge a prentice to the sayd m^r^ Havilond w^th^out p^r^sentment & contrary to order	xx^s^/ paid 17^s^ 6^d^ the rest remitted

30. Maij

Mr Knight Sa Macham Na. Butter Jo. Budge Bar. Sutton	Receaued of m^r^ Knight. Sa macham Na Butter, Jo Budge and Barth'ue Sutton for makinge open showe of wares to sell vppon thascention daye beinge holyday xij^d^ a pece /............	v^s^
Jo Budge/	Receaued of Jo. Budge for printinge Sr Rob. Sherleys travailes w^t^out entrance[2]	ij^s^. v^d^
Ni. Oak~e~ Tho. Archer	Receiued of theñ ij^s^ vj^d^ a pece for prynting the book of the ij maid~e~ of Moortlake[3] without entrance	ij^s^ vi^d^ a pece viz. v^s^.
		[*22^li^: 3^s^: 0^d^*]

[1] Cf. *C–B.C*, 20^b^, 27 Mar. 1609. [2] STC 17894. Budge entered it this day (Arber iii. 411). [3] STC 773.

26to: Junij

John Smythicke John Busby Jun'	Received of them for makeinge open shewe of wares to sell on the feast day of Ste. John Baptist beinge holydaye contrary to thorders xjjd a peece	ijs
Richard Moore	Receiued of him for a fyne for makeinge open shewe to sell wares on the sayd feaste day of Ste. John Baptist beinge holyeday contrary to thorders	iijs iiijd
		22li: 8s: 4d

[4a] 1609. .7. Ris

10 July

Item Receaued of mr wardens themseues. viz mr Hoop. and Mr Humfrey Lownes for a dispensation	xijli
	34li—8s—4 13 —6 —8
	47. 15 0

[4b] 1609. 7mo Regis/.

Mr Dawson Mr
Mr Waterson } Wardens/.
Mr Standish

21mo. Augusti/.

Nathanaell Butter	Red of Nathanaell Butter for a fyne for vseinge vnfittinge speeches agaynst Thomas Purfoote Jun	vjs/.

16 Octobr

Nic Oake	Yt is ordered that Nich'as Oake shall pay ffortie shillinge presently for a fine for Offendinge in pryntinge other mens copies Disorderly contrary to thordonnances	xls pd 10s. 4 July 1612. the rest beinge Remitted.

7mo. Februarij

Thomas Snodham/	Rd of Thomas Snodham for a fyne for retayninge a prentise contrary to the ordinañces	xs /.

22do. Februarij.

Niccholas Oakes	Rd of Niccholas Oake for a fyne for retayninge a prentise contrary to the ordiñance	iijs

26to Martij 1610. 8uo Regis.

Thomas Cotes/.	Rd of Thomas Cotes for a fyne for keepinge a prentise vnpresented contrary to order.......	vijd

2do. Aprilis Courte 1610

Mr Mann/.	Rd of mr Man for a fyne for not cominge to the Courte till it was ready to rise	vijd

16to. Aprilis 1610

Thomas Baylye[1]	Rd of Thomas Bayly for a fyne for keepinge a prentise a yeare & an half vnpresented contrary to order..................................	iijs

eodem 16to. Aprilis 1610

	Rd in fynes for noñe appearances & disorders in appearinge this day beinge qter day.......	xxiijs vjd/

18mo. Junij 1610

Bartholomewe Downes/.	It is ordered that Bartholomewe Downes shall pay vs. for keepinge a prentise vnpresented contrary to order..........................	vs paid 25. Junij being quarter day.

3o. Julij 1610

John Alshon:[2]	Receiued of him for causes appearinge reasonable to this Courte	vjs vjd

1610. 8uo Regis. [5a]

Mr Mann Mr.
Mr Leake } Wardens/
Mr Adames }

10mo. Augusti /

Raffe Turnor	Receiued of him for a fyne for keepinge a prentise vnpresented contrary to order	ijs vjd/.

5to. Nouemb.

Mr Pavier/.	Mr Pavyer is fined for printinge a ballad wthout license wherein william white was his printer[3].	xs/ pd ijs vid 4 July 1612. the rest being remitted

[1] Probably T. Bailey who was made free 5 Oct. 1607 (Arber iii. 683).

[2] Unidentified.

[3] None of these ballads has been identified.

William White/	And William White is fined for printinge the sayd ballad for m^{r} Pavyer..................	ij^{s} vj^{d} payd ij^{s} 20mo Januarij 1611/
Mr Pavier	And m^{r} Pavyer is ordered to bringe into the hall the rest of these balladȩ that are not sold/. And there vpon he brought certayne w^{che} were burnte/.	
George Elde	George Elde is fined for printinge ij balladȩ wthout license for Jo: Wright .... xx^{s}	p^{d} v^{d} a pece 4 July 1612. the rest beinge remitted
John Wrighte.	And John Wright is fyned for causinge the sayd balladȩ to be printed wthout license xx^{s} The ballads beinge very undecente/.	
Mr Aldee/.	Edward Aldee is fyned for printinge a booke concerninge Matters of Virginia, wthout license[1]	v^{s}/. p^{d}. ij^{s}. vj^{d} 4 July 1612. The rest beinge remitted
William Stansby.	R^{d} of William Stansby for a fyne for vsinge vndecent language to John Hardy thofficer of the Companie	iij^{s}
Nath: Butter/.	R^{d} of Nath: Butter for a fyne...............	x^{s}

15to Januarij

Mr Cooley Mr Derbysheire Joseph Harrison John Warde John Deane Robt Triplett Nath: Butter Laurence Lisle Roger Symons John Collins	R^{d} of eu'y of them xij^{d} a peece for none appearance on the ꝗter day	x^{s}.

[5^{b}] 1610. 8^{uo}. Regis.

15to. Januarij

Mr Lawe/.	Receiued of m^{r} Lawe for a fyne for offendinge in takeinge & sellinge the kingȩ last ꝓclamacoñ before it was ꝓclamed[2]	xx^{s} not paid payd x^{s} 20mo Januarij 1611.

[1] STC 21005.

[2] Query STC 8461.

4to. Marcij

Mr Orryan/.	Rd of him for a fyne for faylinge in attendance at appoynted meetinge....................	ijs/

.22. Martij

Wm. Ham̃ond.	Receaued of hym̃ for a fine Layd vppon him for iust cause by the discretion of the mr. wrdens & assistantę	xxs

1611. 9no. Regis

Primo Aprilis

John Combes	Receiued of him for a fyne for keepinge a prentise vnpresented contrary to the ordinan̄ces...	ijs vjd/.
John Ellis	Item of him for the like cause...............	ijs vjd
Brian Greenhill	Item of him for the like cause...............	xijd/.
Walter Haward	Item of him for the like cause...............	xijd/.

8uo. Aprilis

Mr Welbye.	Rd of him for a fyne for printinge a thinge of Virginia wthout license[1].....................	xijd/
Thomas Snodham alias Easte	Rd of him for a fyne for offendinge in byndinge a prentise att a Scriuenners contrary to order, beinge sett vpon him by a full court of Assistantę holden the first of this instant Aprill....	iijli: 0s: 0d

[10mo. Maij]

Mr Selman he hath accepted the Lyury & so is hereof discharged/.	*[M Selman refuseth to accepte the Lyuery accordinge to his election, And therefore itt is ordered that he shall pay for a fyne*	*vli: 0s: 0d*]

17mo Junij

William Stanesby	Rd of him for a fyne for offendinge agte th'ordin̄ance[2]	vs.

25to. Junij

	Rd in ffynes this day	ixs/.

[1] STC 25266. Welby entered this 6 July 1611 (Arber iii. 461).

[2] From the size of the fine the offence was probably printing an unlicensed book. Of the 17 books recorded as printed by Stansby in 1611, STC 1845 is the only one unregistered.

[6a] 1611. 9no. Regis.

ffrauncis Archer/.	Receiued of him for a fyne for refusinge to co͂me into the Lyuery beinge orderly elected there-vnto....................................	v^{li}. o^{s}. o^{d}.
		Sum͂a patet

[6b] 1611. 9no. Regis

Mr John Norton M^{r}
M^{r}. Richard ffeild } wardens/.
M^{r}. Humfry Lownes }

6to. Augusti/.

Mr John Browne/	Rd of John Browne for a fyne for keepinge a prentice vnpresented contrary to order.......	ij^{s} vj^{d}/.
Rich: Bonyon	R^{d} of Ri: Bonyon for a fyne.................	ij^{s} vj^{d}
Tho: Downes	R^{d} of Tho: Downes for a fyne...............	ij^{s} vj^{d}
William Stanesby	It is ordered that w^{m} Stanesby shall pay xl^{s}. for a fyne for printinge another mans Copy[1] contrary to order The w^{che} fyne he promiseth to pay betweene this & Michãs nexte...........	xl^{s}/ remitted 4 July 1612.
Rich: Taylor/.	It is ordered that Ri: Taylo^{r} shall pay xx^{s} for a fyne, before Symon & Judes day nexte for byndinge a prentice to him contrary to order. Whiche fyne he ꝑmiseth to pay accordingly...	xx^{s} p^{d}. v^{s} 4 July 1612 the rest beinge Remitted

12mo. Augusti

Rich: Taylor/.	It is ordered that Rich: Taylo^{r} shall pay vj^{li} for a fyne for contemptuously and wittingly offendinge ag^{te}. thordinañce in Couenously takinge an appr'tice, contrary to thordinance	vi^{li} Remitted 4 July 1612.
	Also his ꝑte in the stocke of the ꝑteners is sequestred vntill he satisfy this fyne of vj^{li}/.	
John West	R^{d} of him for a fyne for takinge the sayd appr'tice & enrollinge him & puttinge him ou' to Rich: Taylo^{r}. contrary to the orders of the Comp^{nie}....................................	iij^{s} iiij^{d}

8^{uo}. Octobris

Fynes	R^{d} in fynes for noñe appearancȩ on the last qrter day..	vij^{s}

[1] Unidentified.

Cantrell Legge	Rd of Cantrell Legge for a fyne for keepinge a Prentice vnpresented contrary to order	vjs viijd

20mo. Januarij

Robert Raworthe	Rd of him for a fyne for keepinge a prentise vnpresented contrary to order................	xs.
William White	Rd of him for his fyne sett vpon him 5to. die Nouembr. 1610[1]..........................	ijs.
Mr Lawe	Rd of him for his fyne sett downe 15to Jan: 1610[2]................................	xs.

18uo. Februaryij.

Ambr: Garbrand	rd̄ of him for a fyne for printinge the booke of Moll Cutpurse wthout entringe it[3]	vijd

Sum̃a ijli xijs vjd rd̄

1612 10mo Regis [7a]

26to. Marcij/.

Smithe	mr Smithe[4] is discharged of this nexte yeares service of the Rentershippe. And it is ordered that he shall presently pay for the same discharge xxli wche he is contented to doo........	xxli paid
mr Jones	mr Jones is discharged from seruinge the rentershippe And it is ordered that he shall pay xxli. for this discharge wche he is content to doo....	xxli. pd vli the rest remitted 27 Sept: 1613:
mr Dighte	mr Dighte is chosen renter And doth request to be dispensed wth And it is ordered that he shall pay xxli for dispensacõn wche he is contente to doo....................................	xxli. paid
mr Cooley.	mr Cooley[5] is chosen Renter, but doth request to be dispensed wth. And it is ordered that he shall paye xxli for his dispensacoñ wche he is contente to doo	xxli pd 7 Septe 1612. in the next yeres acompt

[1] Cf. *Book of Fines*, 5a.
[2] Cf. *Book of Fines*, 5a.
[3] This book is not extant but concerned the pranks of Mary Frith and was doubtless similar to the 'foule' book of her 'base tricks' referred to in STC 17908.
[4] Presumably Richard Smith, cf. *C–B.C*, 26b, 8 Apr. 1611.
[5] Thomas Cooley, made free 30 June 1604.

m^r^ Knighte	m^r^ Knighte is chosen Renter, but requesteth to bee dispensed wth And it is ordered that he shall pay xx^li^ for this dispensacoñ w^che^ he is content to doo	xx^li^ paid
m^r^ Pavyer	m^r^ Pavyer is chosen Renter but requesteth to bee dispensed wth And it is ordered that he shall pay xx^li^ for this dispensacõn w^che^ he is content to doo	xx^li^ payd
m^r^ Ed: Byshop	m^r^. Bysshopp is chosen Renter but requesteth to bee dispensed wth And it is ordered that he shall pay xx^li^ for this dispensacoñ w^che^ he is content to doo	xx^li^ paid

27mo. Aprilis

	R^d^ in fynes for noñe appearances on the last quarter day	vj^s^

29no. Aprilis

John Legat	R^d^ of him for a fyne for keepinge ij appr'tices vnp^r^sented contrary to order viz Edmond Whitinge and Danyell Graunge	xx^s^.

4to. Maij

	R^d^ in fynes for noñe appearanc on the laste q̃ter day	iij^s^
m^r^ Derbyshere[1]	R^d^ of him for keepinge a prentise vnpresented contrary to order..........................	vj^s^

4 July

Ni. oake.	Re^d^ of him for a fine[2]	x^s^
Edw. Alde	Re^d^ of him for a fine[3]	ij^s^ vj^d^
Ri. Tailor	Re^d^ of him for a fine[4] Vt antea notatur	v^s^
Jo. Wright	Re^d^ of hym for a fine[5]	v^s^
Geo. Elde	Re^d^ of hym for a fine[5]	v^s^
m^r^ pavier	Re^d^ of him for a fine[5]	ij^s^ vj^d^
	Suma	

[7^b^= blank]

[1] Thomas Derbyshire, made free 18 Jan. 1602 (Arber ii. 731).

[2] Cf. *Book of Fines*, 4^b^, 16 Oct. 1609.

[3] Cf. *Book of Fines*, 5^a^, 5 Nov. 1610.

[4] Cf. *Book of Fines*, 6^b^, 6 Aug. 1611.

[5] Cf. *Book of Fines*, 5^a^, 5 Nov. 1610.

Mr John Norton mr
mr Humfrye Hooper
mr John Harryson Junr } Wardē.

.7. Sept.

Mr. Aldee	Recd of him for a fine for byndinge Tho mylles[1] prentise to him, at a Scriveners contrary to order	vijs. vjd
Tho. Creede	Recd of him for a fine for bindinge Ri: Reade[2] prentise to him at a Scriuenrs contrary to order	7s vjd
Geo. Norton	Recd of him for a fine for Keping Willm petty[2] vnpresented contrary to order	7s vjd
Mr Cooley.	Receaued of mr Cooley for his fine sett vppon him in the last wardens tyme,[3] beinge for his dispensation from servinge the rentership	xxli

5. oct.

mr. Dawson	Recd of him for a fine for coming Late on the quarter day	xijd

29 oct'

Mr wardens. mr Hoop and mr Harison Jun'.	Yt is ordered that they shall pay xvjli in stede of michãs quarter dynner Last whereof they haue pd aforehand .xxxs—so resteth to be paid 14li—10s	14li. 10s

9. nov.

Wm. Stanesby.	Receaued of him for a fine for printing of Tho. purfootē brieues contrary to order[4] .... And besides he pd. xs. to purfoot for his damagē/	vs.
Tho. purfoot.	Recd of him for a fine for printinge a little thing of Wm Stanesbyes contrary to order .... And besidē he paid to Stanesby for his Damagē—3s—4d	xijd

28 Jan'

Mr Bonham Norton mr Willm Haughton/[5]	Receaued of him for a fine for strykinge his prentise in the presence of or mr. wardens & Assistantē here assembled	ijs. vjd

[1] Made free 3 June 1616 (Arber iii. 684).
[2] Evidently never made free.
[3] Cf. *Book of Fines*, 7a, 26 Mar. 1612.
[4] Cf. *C–B.C*, 46a, 16 Jan. 1617, note.
[5] He was free of the Company but there is no record of when.

1612: 10 Ris

28 Jan'

Wm Stanesby	Yt is ordered that he shall pay xls. for a fine presently for transgressinge in pryntinge m^r Adams his pte of m^r Brighte book of melancholy[1] and m^r Lownes his prentises Indentures[2] contrary to the constitutions	xls
	And m^r Adams to have thone half of thimpression for pap & pryntinge. and thother half as he can agree w^t w. Stanesby. And yf they cannot agree then the difference to be ordered by the table/	
Wm Jaggard 18 Jan'	he was ordered to pay m^r lownes x^s for damage and iij^s iiij^d to the house for a fine as is entred in the book of orders[2]	iij^s iiij^d

primo Martij

Noñe appearance	Receaued in fines for none appearance this day at the tally of the pten^rs in the stocke	xvj^s
Chr pursett[3] vide infera^r/	yt was ordered 25 ffebr that xx'ofer pursett shall pay xx^s for disobeyinge to pforme his m^te service, according to the lo. mayres p^rcept & the wardens direction And to be cōmitted to ward yf he be disobedient to this order	xx^s
Tho. Snodam	Re^d of Tho. Snodam for the like contempt....	xx^s
Na Butter	Na. Butter is ordered to pay for the lik contempt xx^s and to be cōmitted to ward yf he obey not this order	xx^s paid Vt inferi^9 patet

18 m^rcij

m^r. Bankw^rth	Receaued of him in discharge of all fines to this day[4]..................................	xxij^s ij^d
Chr. purfet	Receaued of him in pte of paym^t of his fine abouesaid	v^s
	And thother xv^s is to be p^d by v^s a q^rter And the first q^rter to be midsom^r next	

[1] Stansby acquired Windet's part in Bright's *Treatise* 11 Sept. 1611 (Arber iii. 466), and published an edition, STC 3749. Bishop's share was acquired with his other copies by Adams but not registered by him.

[2] Cf. *C–B.C*, 30b, 2 Jan. 1613.

[3] Made free 5 Sept. 1597 (Arber ii. 719). For service in the train bands at the Artillery Yard.

[4] These fines are not recorded.

28 Junij 1613

Ric. Brookbank[1]	Rc̶d of him for none appearance at our Lady day quarter	xijd
Na. Butter	Rc̶d of him for his fine for not servinge at thartilary yard as others of the compnie did........	xxs
ffr. Burton	Rc̶d of him for a fine......................	xs

40: 4: 6

1613. 11 Rc̶. (*no date*) July [9a]

Mr Bonham Norton Mr
Mr ffeild } Wardens
Mr Ockold }

27mo. Septembr:

Christopher Pursett	Rd of him in pte of his fyne for not servinge at the Artillery .vs. wch should haue bene pd at middsomer last	vs.
Mr Jones	Rd of mr Jones in pte of his fyne for not se'uinge the Renter shippe beinge xxli. the sume of vli the rest beinge remitted & forgyuen him	vli.
mr Haryson the youngest	Rd of him for a fyne for keepinge a pr'tice vnpresented contrary to order..................	ijs vjd.
Thomas ffynche[2]	Rd of him for a fyne for keepinge willm ffynche pr'tice to Christofer Payne deceased wthout turninge him ou', contrary to order..........	ijs vjd.

4to Octob. 1613 quarter day

mr Bateman Ed. Aggas Jo: Royston	Receiued of mr Bateman, Jo Royston and Edward Aggas for not appearing at middsomer quarter last xiijd (*sic*) a peece	iijs

11o Octob. 1613.

willm Parnell	Receiued of willm Parnell[3] for a fyne for keeping a prentice vnpresented contrary to order..	ijs vjd/	paid

6to decemb. 1613

Sam Albyn	Rc̶d of Samuell Albin for keeping of a prentice vnpresented contrary to order	ijs vjd.	paid

1 Made free 3 June 1600 (Arber ii. 725).
2 Made free 16 Apr. 1610 (Arber iii. 683).
3 Made free 8 June 1601 (Arber ii. 729).

Raph Blower	Item of Raph Blower for keeping of a prentice vnpresented contrary to order	ijs vjd. paid
Wm Stansbye	Receiued of wm Stansbye for a fyne for pryntyng mr Brightꝭ booke of melancholy and prentices indentures and also for keeping of a prentice vnbound contrary to order[1]	xls. pđ./

25 Januarij 1613.

ffraunces Archer	Receiued of ffrances Archer for keeping a prentice vnpresented Contrary to order	ijs vjd paid
Tho. Smith	Tho. Smith[2] for the like....................	ijs vjd paid
Mr Bradwood	It is ordered that mr Bradwood shall pay for a fyne for refusing to be stockekeꝑ being therevnto Chosen[3]	iiijli.
	11o Maij 1615, this iiijli was paid by Mr Griffin when he receiued his divident, to mr Adames warden./	

pnte *Tho: Montforte*

[9b] 8o Martij 1613

John Edwardꝭ translationerij	Recd of John Edwardꝭ[4] for accepting and receiuing him from the Joyners to be a free man of this Companye..........................	xli paid

4to Aprilis 1614.

	Recd of Mr Paver, mr Kempe, mr Barrett, Mr Eld, John Beale (*space*) Sidney[5] xijd a peece for being absent the last quarter day.................	vijs paid/
Joh: White/	Recd of John White appr to John Edwardꝭ for accepting him to be made free of this Company	[*vjs*] xls/ paid

6to July 1614

Rich: Meighen	Recd of Richard Mayghen for a fyne to be made free by redemption	xxs paid

1 Cf. *Book of Fines*, 8b, 28 Jan. 1613.
2 Made free 7 Dec. 1607 (Arber iii. 683).
3 Cf. *C–B.C*, 34a, 1 Mar. 1614.
4 He was made a liveryman 21 June 1616, cf. *C–B.C*, 44b, and died before 15 Sept. 1634, cf. *C–B.C*, 128b.
5 Thomas Sidney, made free 17 Apr. 1613 (Arber iii. 684).

30to Junij

Edw. Wilson	Edward Wilson for a fyne to be made free of this Companye ꝑ redemption	xi^s vj^d paid/

1614 Rę Jac' 12°. [10^a]

Mr Tho: Man Master
Mr Wm Leake }
Mr Tho. Adams } wardenę

15° July

Wm Hall	Receiued of wm hall for vnfitting wordę vsed to or Master and wardens[1]	x^s
Jo. Hoth[2]	Rę^d of John hoth for keeping a prentice Contrary to order.	xij^d
Joh. Kidd	Item of John Kidd for the like matter	xij^d
Wm Stansby	Receiued of wm Stansby for printing a booke wthout entrance	x^s all paid

14° Octob: 1614

Mr Aldee Tho Snodam Jo. Trundle	Rę^d of Mr Aldee, Thomas Snodam John Trundle for printing a booke called the warres in Germany wthout license[3].	xv^s. paid

17° Octob.

Mr Barker	Rę^d of Mr Barker for keeping a prentice Contrary to order.	vij^s vj^d paid
Joh Bennett	Rę^d of John Bennett[4] for the like matter	ij^s vj^d paid
Wm Harper	More of wm harper for the like	v^s. paid

20 Januarij

Non appearance	Rę^d of 18 seu'all persons xij^d a peece for being absent the last quarter day.	xviij^s paid

20 ffebr'

Rob. Triplett	Rę^d of Robert Triplet for binding a prentice at a scrivenors.	x^s paid

[1] Cf. *C–B.C*, 32^a, 27 Sept. 1614, and 35^a, 15 July 1614.

[2] Made free 24 Apr. 1598 (Arber ii. 720).

[3] Cf. *C–B.C*, 35^b, 14 Oct. 1614.

[4] Apprenticed 2 Mar. 1601 (Arber ii. 252).

6° Martij

Raffe Mabb Wm Bladon Geo. Gibbes ff. Constable	Req^d of Raffe mabb, wm Bladon Geo: Gibbes and ffrances Constable for a fine for printing abuses stript & whipt that was ffrances Burtons Copie[1]	iijli	paid
Mr Dawson	Req^d of Mr Dawson for Coming late vpon a Court day	xijd	paid

[10b]

9° May 1615

Joh. Budge	Req^d of John Budge for printing a booke called the mirror of Matrs, taken out of the booke of Martirs wch belonge to the Company[2]	xls	paid
Mr Welbey	Req^d of Mr Welby for not turning over a prentice at the hall according to order	ijs vjd	
Mr Bradwood	Req^d of Mr Bradwood as appeareth in the ffines of the last yeare[3]	iiijli	paid

17° Junij 1615

Mr Feild Mr Ockold	Req^d of Mr ffeild and Mr Ockold as appeareth in the booke of orders[4]	xijli	paid
Richard Harison	Req^d of Richard Harrison made free at the request of Mr Chamberlaine of London by redemption	xxs	paid
Tho. Snodam	Req^d of Thomas Snodam for a license to print a booke called sacrid himmes by Joyce Taylor taken out of the psalmes which belong to the Company[5]	xxs	paid

[11a]

1615° Req Jac. 14°./

Mr Tho: Dawson mr.
Mr. Hum. Lownes
Mr Geo. Swynhowe } wardens

16° Octob. 1615.

Roger Simondę	Rę of Roger Symondę[6] for keepinge of appr' vnpresented Contrary to order	xijd

[1] Cf. *C–B.C*, 38a, 1 Mar. 1615.
[2] STC 5849. Cf. *C–B.C*, 39a, 9 May 1615.
[3] Cf. *Book of Fines*, 9a, 25 Jan. 1614.
[4] Cf. *C–B.C*, 36b, 22 Dec. 1614.
[5] STC 21723. He likewise paid six pence to have it regularly entered, 19 June 1615 (Arber iii. 568).
[6] Made free 31 Jan. 1602 (Arber ii. 731).

27° Octob.

Joh Beales	Re of John Beale for a fine for byndinge of apprentice at a screuero^r (*sic*) Contrary to order[1]	v^li

21 Nouemb.

Nath. Newberye.	Res of Nathaniell Newbery for accepting and and (*repeated*) receiuinge him from the haberdashers to the freedome of this Company[2]	xl^s.

15 Januarij 1615

Absente	Re of m^r Norton m^r Cooke. Tho. Care[3] Richard Brookebanke Christo. Wilson Nath. Butter Eph^ra. Dawson John Hamon ffrances Archer of each of them xij^d a pece for beinge absent the last quarter day.	ix^s.

5° ffebr.

Edw. Wright	Re of [*of*] Edward Wright for disorderly printinge a Copie of m^r Jacksons called m^r Dents sermon of repentance[4]	xl^s
Mr Jackson.	Of m^r Jackson for the said booke so disorderly printed	x^s

20° ffebr. 1615.

Micha. Sparke Tho. Archer	Re of michaell Sparke for arestinge Tho: Archer wth out license of the Companye	v^s
Absente.	Re of m^r Lawe, m^r Serger m^r Bradwood m^r Vincent m^r Aldee m^r Harrison m^r Welby Tho. Havilonde Nicho. Bourne Nath. Butter Geo Edwarde Edward Gosson [*xx^d*] xij^d a peece for cominge Late i^mo Martij 1615	xij^s

1615 Martij 26° [11^b]

Mr Weaver	Receiued of m^r Weaver for beinge dispensed wth all for not servinge the Rentershippe beinge thervnto elected[5].	6^li—12^s paid accordingly
Mr Serger	Re of m^r Serger for refusinge to serue the Rentershippe beinge therevnto elected[5]	xx^li paid accordingly

1 Cf. *C–B.C*, 40^a, 21 Nov. 1615.
2 Cf. *C–B.C*, 39^b, 7 Aug. 1615.
3 Presumably T. Carr, apprenticed 2 Nov. 1591 (Arber ii. 172).
4 Cf. *C–B.C*, 41^b, 3 Feb. 1616.
5 Cf. *C–B.C*, 42^b, 26 Mar. 1616.

8° April 1616

Absent	Rę of m[r] Cole m[r] Bill m[r] Dight m[r] Islippe m[r] Blount m[r] Asply m[r] Jaggard M[r] Tomes m[r] Rodwell m[r] Johnson fined at xij[d] a peece for not attendinge at the buriall of m[r] Smith[1] . . .	x[s] paid

1[mo] July 1616

Rich. Foster	Rę of Richard ffoster[2] for [*bynding*] keepinge an appr' vnpresented Contrary to order	ij[s] paid
W[m] Lee	Rę of wm Lee for the same matter	iiij[s] paid

6° July

W[m]. Stansby	Rę of wm Stansby for bynding apprenticę at a scriveno[r]s Contrarye to order[3]	vj[li] xiij[s] paid accordingly

[12[a]]

Anno Dñi 1616

Rę Jac. 14°.

M[r] Man M[r]
M[r] Adames
M[r] Ma. Lownes } wardens

22° Julij 1616.

Christo: Barker	Rę of Christofer Barker for keeping Thomas Pevice[4] an appr' Contrary to order	x[s] paid accordingly
M[r] Jackson	It is ordered that m[r] Jackeson shall haue all Hugh Jacksons Copies Entered vnto him paying to the Company the some of[5]	xl[s] paid accordingly

26 Julij

Joh. Legatt	Rę of John Legatt for keeping appr'tice Contrary to order	x[s] paid accordingly
Tho: Mordant/	Thomas mordant[6] for keeping of appr'tice disorderly	v[s] paid

1 Cf. *C–B.C*, 43[a], 8 Apr. 1616.
2 Made free 2 Oct. 1615 (Arber iii. 684).
3 Cf. *C–B.C*, 40[b], 4 Dec. 1615; and 44[b], 21 June 1616.
4 Unidentified.
5 Cf. *C–B.C*, 45[a], 12 July 1616.
6 Thomas Morden, made free 3 Oct. 1609 (Arber iii. 683).

8° August 1616

W. Best	It is ordered that wm. Best[1] shall pay to the Company for keeping an appr'ice Contrary to order	xx^s	
Geo. Edwardę	George Edwardę for the like matter	xx^s	paid

4° Nouemb. 1616

mr Bateman	It is ordered that mr Bateman for vsing vnfittinge speaches to wm Best shall pay to the vse of the Company..........................	iij^s iiij^d	
Wm. Best	Item wm Best for vnfittinge speaches vsed to mr Bateman..............................	x^s	paid

16° Januarij 1616

Tho: Boles	Item that Tho. Boles[2] for vnfitting speaches vsed to wm Stansby......................	x^s	paid
Joh. Armestone	John Armestone[3] for keeping an appr'tice Contrary to order............................	[*x^s*] ij^s vj^d	
Tho. Tarsay	Thomas Tarsey[4] for the same matter.........	ij^s vj^d	paid

28 January 1616 [12^b]

Mr Vincente	George Vincent for keeping of appn'tice Contrary to order............................	v^s	
Mr Welby	Robert Milborne for not being turned ou' according to order..........................	v^s	paid
Mr Butter	Nathaniell Butter for printing of a booke of my lo. Ros his entertainment in Spaine and not Entring the same first[5]....................	vj^s	paid

1mo Martij 1616.

Barnar. Alsop	Rę of Barnard Alsoppe for Imprintinge of 3 sermons of mr. Hernes and putting mr H. Lownes name therevnto being the Copie of mrs Macham[6]	x^s	paid
[*Ric. Woodrife*	*Rich. woodriffe for the same matter*	*x^s*] not receiued	

[1] Made free 14 Mar. 1611 (Arber iii. 683).
[2] On this day he was made free (Arber iii. 684).
[3] Made free 22 Jan. 1605 (Arber ii. 738).
[4] Made free 14 May 1612 (Arber iii. 683).
[5] STC 4909.
[6] Cf. *C–B.C*, 47^a, 3 Mar. 1617.

M[r] Islippe	Item of m[r] Islippe for vnfitting wordes vsed to mr Feilde	vj[s] viij[d] pd

26. Martij 1617 Re 15° /

m[r] Bradwood.	Re of m[r] Bradwood for his dispensacon from his service of the Rentorshippe[1]	xx[li]
W[m] Butler	w[m] Buttler for keeping appn'tice Contrary to order	v[s] paid
Tho. Bracken	Tho Brracken[2] for the like matter	ij[s] vj[d]
Joh. Wright	Joh. wright for the like matter...............	ij[s] vj[d]
m[r] Butter/	Nath. Butter for the like matter	x[s] pd

6 May 1617

m[r] Griffin	m[r] Griffin for not turning an appn'tice ou' accorder (*sic*) to order	v[s] pd
mr Pickeringe	W[m]. Pickering[3] for keeping an appr' Contrary to order..................................	xij[d]
M[r] Jo. Harrison.	Yt is ordered that m[r] Joh. Harison [shall pay] for his dispensacon for not seruing the second time vnderwarden.........................	vj[li] xiij[s] iiij[d] paid accordingly

[13[a]]

Anno Dñi. 1617

Re Jac. 16°

M[r] Waterson m[r]
M[r] Hum: Lownes
M[r] Swinhowe } wardens

16° Julij 1617

Richard Meighen	Receiued of him for a fine for enticinge a Chapman from m[r] Smithwicke shopp contrary to order	iij[s] iiij[d]

21° Julij

Robert Willis	Receiued of Robert Willis for a fine to the Companie to be translated from the Inholders to this Company............................	v[li]

[1] Cf. *C–B.C*, 47[a], 27 Mar. 1617.
[2] Made free 2 Sept. 1616 (Arber iii. 684).
[3] Made free 22 Jan. 1601 (Arber ii. 727).

1mo Sept: 1617

Mr Ockold	Receiued of m^{r}. Ockold for his dispensacõn for not seruing the second time vnderwarden[1]....	xx^{li}
Tardy	Receiued of m^{r} Ockold m^{r} Harrison m^{r} Lownes Jun' m^{r} ffeild m^{r} Dauson for coming late vpon a quarter day xij^{d} a peece	v^{s}
Barnard Alsope	Receiued of him for printing a booke called Andrewes humble peticon &tę without entrance thereof[2]	iij^{s} iiij^{d}

30 Sept. 1617.

none appearance	Receiued 31 seuerall persons of this Company for not appearinge at this Call (*sic*) this quarter day	xxxj^{s}

4° Maij 1618 Rę 16°.

Thomas Ensor	Receiued of him for not turning ouer his appr' Jenkin Thomas[3] according to order	ij^{s} vj^{d}
Thomas Norton	Receiued of him for keeping Luke Sherman[4] vnbound contrarie to order.................	v^{s}
None app$^{r'}$	Receiued of m^{r} Bourne Robert Triplett Thomas Lilley[5] Thomas Yates[6] Gyles Bassett[7] Thomas Norton for being absent last quarter day xij^{d} a peece.........................	vj^{s}
Cantrell Legg	It is ordered that Cantrell Legg shall pay for binding Anthonie Squire[8] his appr' at a screiueno^{rs} contrarie to order	xl^{s}
Thomas Jones	Receiued of Thomas Jones for keeping his appr' Thomas Scott[9] vnbound contrary to order....	ij^{s} vj^{d}

9° Julij 1618 Rę Jac. 16°. [13^{b}]

Mr Leake m^{r}
Mr Adamę } Wardenę
Mr Gilmyn }

Receiued of m^{r} Bishoppe[10] m^{r} Coke mr Johnson m^{r} ffetherstone wm Baron[11] Richer Stile[11] Ed Gosson Edward white for being absent the last quarter day wthout lawfull excuse xij^{d} a peece.	viij^{s}	pđ

[1] Cf. *C–B.C*, 47^{b}, 5 July 1617; and 48^{b}, 19 Aug. 1617.

[2] No copy of an edition of this work before 1623 (STC 589) has been traced. The 1623 edition was printed by [G. Eld] f. J. Wright, and the book was not entered until 1630.

[3] Made free 6 Oct. 1617 (Arber iii. 684).

[4] Made free 4 May 1618 (Arber iii. 684).

[5] Made free 26 Mar. 1613 (Arber iii. 684).

[6] Made free 15 Nov. 1613 (Arber iii. 684).

[7] Made free 2 Sept. 1616 (Arber iii. 684).

[8] Made free 16 June 1618 (Arber iii. 684).

[9] Not presented.

[10] Edward Bishop evidently flourished after the date given by McKerrow. His latest dated book (STC 6631) was 1617.

[11] Not recorded.

13 July 1618

m[r] Man mr Dawson m[r] Swinhowe m[r] Ockold	ffor Cominge late this Court day fyned at xij[d] a peece	iiij[s]	Rec
W[m] Cheney[1]	Receiued of wm Cheney for keeping peter Baddy[1] his appr' contrary to order	2[s]—6[d]	Rec

25 Septemb 1618

Cutbert Wrighte	It is ordered that Cutbert wright shall pay to the Company for bynding of hen. Chamberleyne[1] an appr' at a scriveno[rs] and keepinge him Contrary to order[2]........................	v[li]	

5° Octob. 1618 R℮ 16°

Nath. Newbury	R℮ of Nath: Newbury for keeping an appr' Contrary to order............................	x[s]	Rec
non appearance	R℮ of 15 ꝑsons for being absent the last quarter day xij[d] a peece...........................	xv[s]	Rec
John White	It is ordered that Joh white for keepinge an appr' Contrary to order	x[s]	
Holye Dayes	Received of diu's ꝑsons for keeping open their shoppes on St Symon & Jud℮ day Contrary to order, xij[d] a peece	xv[s]	Rec

4° Novemb 1618

Math Walbanke	Received of Math. walbanke for keeping Robert wallbanke[3] appr to Tho. Jones Contrary to order he is also warned forth wth to putt him away	xx[s]	Rec

[14[a]] 7° Decemb 1618 R℮ 16°/

M[r] Fetherstone	Received of m[r] ffetherstone for keeping Robert martin[1] being not free nor bound as an appr' Contrary to the orders of this house[4].........	xl[s]	Rec
Jonas Wellins	Receiued of Jonas wellins[5] for keeping an appr' Contrary to order	ij[s]	Rec

[1] Not recorded.

[2] Cf. *C–B.C*, 51[b], 25 Sept. 1618.

[3] This is hardly the R. W. made free 14 Jan. 1628 (Arber iii. 686). Cf. *C–B.C*, 52[a], 11 Nov. 1618.

[4] Cf. *C–B.C*, 53[b], 17 Dec. 1619; and 54[a], 17 Feb. 1619.

[5] Made free 20 Mar. 1602 (Arber ii. 731).

26 Martij 1619 Reℓ 17

Mr Kempe	Receiued of him for not serving the Rentor shippe being therevnto elected	xxijli	Rec.
Mr Blounte	Receiued of mr Blount for his dispensacoñ for not serving the Rentor shippe being like elected[1]	xxli	Rec.
mr Barnett	It is ordered that mr Barnett shalbe dispensed wthall for the Rentorshippe and likewise pay to the Company[1]	xxli	
Mr Alldee	It is also ordered that mr [*Adle*] Allde shall pay for his dispensacoñ for the rentorshippe[1]	xxli	

Rec. vli et pdonatr Residiu'./

Jeames Randall	Received of Jeames Randall[2] for not Coming on to the livery being elected and for his dispensacõn neu' to be Called againe to the Clothing of this Company	vjli xiijs iiijd	Rec
John Hoth	It is ordered that John Hoth[3] shall pay for Refusing to Come on to the Livery being Chosen he afterward came out to the liverye and it was pardoned	xl s.	

Mr Feilde mr
mr Swinhowe
mr Jaggard } wardens

[14b]

26 Julij 1619.

Nic Okes	It is ordered that Nicholas Okes shall pay for printing of a booke called A preparacõn to the Psalter wthout Consent of the wardens[4]	xxs	agreed for
Tho. Archer	It is ordered that Tho Archer shall pay for bynding ffrances Williamson at a scrivenors contrary to order[5]	xl s	

4° Octob. 1619.

Edw. Griffin	Rec of Edw. Griffin for keeping Tho. Stephens[6] contrary to order..........................	vs
Mr Lawe	Received of mr Lawe for vnfitting wordℓ vsed to mr Purslowe at a court of assistantℓ.......	xs

[1] Cf. *C–B.C*, 55a, 26 Mar. 1619.

[2] Made free 6 Feb. 1604 (Arber ii. 736). Cf. *C–B.C*, 56a, 3 July 1619.

[3] Made free 24 Apr. 1598 (Arber ii. 720). Cf. *C–B.C*, 56a, 14 June 1619; and 57b, 8 Oct. 1619.

[4] Cf. *C–B.C*, 56b, 2 July 1619.

[5] Cf. *C–B.C*, 56b, 31 Aug. 1619.

[6] Made free 6 Feb. 1627 (Arber iii. 686).

mr Alldee	Received of mr Allde for his dispensacoñ for not serving the Rentorshippe[1]	vli

vltimo Janu 1619.

Absente	Re of Sam. Rand Edw wright Joh. Trundle Miles ffleshcr wm Lee mr Budge & mr Jackson for being absent the last qr day 12d a peece...	vijs
Geo. Fenton.	Rec' of Geo. ffenton for his admission to the freedom of this Company by Redemption	xxs
Rob. Triplett	Rec' of Robert Triplett for keeping of a printice vnbound contrary to order	vs
John Budge.	Item of John Budge for the like matter	vs

6 Martij 1619.

Tho Archer.	It is ordered that Tho. Archer shall pay to the Company for a fine for bynding a prentize at a scrivenors Contrary to order................	iijli

[15a] 3° April' 1620 Re Jac 18°.

Mr Butter	Rec' of Nathaniell Butter for keeping a prentice vnbound	ijs vjd
mr Beale	Rec' of John Beale for the like matter	ijs vjd

22 Junij 1620

Mr Islippe	It is ordered that mr Islippe [shall pay] for bynding of math. williamson[2] his appr' at a screuenors Contrary to order................	iijli
mr Legate	It is ordered that John Legate for bynding of an appr' at a scrivenors Contrary to order vizt Tho. Jackson[3]	ls

27 Junij 1620

mr Pavier	Rec' of mr Pavier for keeping an apprentize Contrarye to order	vs
Absente	Rec' of mr Lawe mr ffetherston mr moore mr meade & Cutberd wright xijd a peece for being absent the last quarter day.................	vs

1 Cf. *C–B.C*, 58b, 20 Dec. 1619.

2 Made free 6 Oct. 1623 (Arber iii. 685). Cf. *C–B.C*, 61b, 15 June 1620.

3 Cf. *C–B.C*, 61b, 15 June 1620.

1mo Julij 1620

mr Lownes	mr Math Lownes for his dispensacoñ for not serving the 2d time vnder warden[1]	vli	
mr Gilmyn	mr Gilmyn for the like matter[1]	vli	
mr Norton	Rec' of mr Bonh'm norton for keeping an appr' contrary to order	vs	

Mr Humph. Lownes master [15b]
mr Math. Lownes } wardens/
mr Geo. Cole }

7° August 1620 Re 18°

Andrew Bilton[2]	Rec. of Andrewe Bilton for keeping appr' contrary to order	vs	Rec.
John Legate	Rec' of John Legate the yonger for a fine for keeping a prentice contrary to order	ls	Rec'
Wm Stansby	It is ordered that Wm Stansby for printing a booke of mr Lidiate wthout entrance & obstinately refusing to come to the wardens & for vsing vnfitting speaches shalbe comitted to prison & pay a fine of	xls	
6°: Sept 1624/	Re 3s 4d et pdoned[3]		
Rog. Jackson	Rec' of Roger Jackson for keeping appr' contrary to order	ijs vjd	Rec'

5° Feb. 1620

ffr. ffaulkner	ffrances ffaulknor for the like matter	ijs ijd	Rec
Sam Walpoole	Sam Wallpoole[4] for the like matter	ijs ijd	Re

5 Martij 1620

mr Lawes.	Mr Lawe for keeping wm Garrett Contrary to order	ijs vjd	R.
Tho. Dewe	Received of him for a fine for being bound at a scrivenors & not being turned ou' according to order	xxv s	R.

[1] Cf. *C–B.C*, 62a, 1 July 1620.
[2] Made free 6 May 1606 (Arber iii. 683).
[3] STC 17046. Cf. *C–B.C*, 66b, 4 Dec. 1620.
[4] Made free 22 Apr. 1616 (Arber iii. 684).

13 Martij 1620

Barnard Alsop	Rec' of Barnard Alsop for keeping Geo. Blackwall in his house being m^{r} kingstons appr'....	iijs
	Tho. Downes for keeping an appr' Contrary to order	ij^{s} vj^{d}

[16^{a}] 7° Maij 1621 R Jac. 19°

m^{r} Alddee	It is ordered that m^{r} Allde shall pay for a fine for binding an appr at a scriueno^{r}s contrary to order[1]	xl s

Mr Waterson M^{r}.
Mr Swinhowe } wardens.
Mr Knight

9° Julij 1621 Rẹ Jac 19°./

Barn. Alsop	Received of Barnard Alsop for entertayning m^{r} Kingstonẹ apprentize wthout his masters Consent	ij^{s}
August. Mathewes	Received of Augustine Mathewes for ꝑcell of his fine of 4^{li}[2]	xx^{s}
Mr Alldee	Md m^{r} Alddee at a Court holden the 6 of August 1621 did agree that his fine of 40^{s} for bynding a prentize Contrary to order shall be payd by the Thrẽs out of his worke	xls
Tho. Archer	It is ordered that Tho Archer for Causing to be printed certaine bookes vnlicensed and vnentered shall pay for a fine[3]	xls
Aug. Mathewes	Rec' of August Mathewes more of his fine.... } so there remayneth vnpaid ....ls This ls was afterwards ꝑdoned for some seruice don to the Company	x^{s}

[16^{b}] 23 August 1621

Paule Man	Paule Man. Received of him for his admission unto this Company by translacõn[4]	xxs
John Grismond	Received of John Grismond for a fine for printing Withers Motto[5]	xx^{s}

[1] Cf. *C–B.C*, 67^{b}, 7 May 1621.
[2] Cf. *C–B.C*, 68^{b}, 4 June 1621.
[3] Cf. *C–B.C*, 69^{b}, 13 Aug. 1621.
[4] Cf. *C–B.C*, 68^{b}, 30 June 1621.
[5] Cf. *C–B.C*, 68^{b}, 4 June 1621.

Wm Jones 6o Nov. 1624	It is ordered that Wm Jones shall pay for printing orders for the west India Company without entrance[1] .... Rę xs. pdonat'/	iijli
Wm Sheffard.	wm sheffard is likewise fined for the same booke at xls but xs was accepted and the residue remitted	xs pd.
Nicho. Okes	Rę of Nich: Okes for pte of his fine of 5li for printing Witherę Motto[2]	xxs

12 Novemb 1621

Mr Butter	It is ordered that Nath. Butter shall pay for printing certayne lers from the Pope to the ffrench King wthout entrance[3] Compounded for	xls

14 Januarij 1621

John Fleminge	Rec' of John Fleminge[4] for keeping a prentice contrary to order..........................	xijd
Edw. Harrison	Item of Edw Harrison[5] for the like matter....	xviijd

4o Martij 1621

Mr Butter	Rec' of mr Butter for printing a book Called Davidę strait wthout Entrance[6]...............	vjs viijd
John Clark	Received of John Clarke for keeping a prentice contrary to order..........................	ijs vjd
Ric Heggenbothm̃ Fra. Constable.	They are fined at xijd a peece for being at bowles[7] when they should be heareing the ordinances read	ijs

26 martij 1622 Rę Jac 20o./ [17a]

Tho. Dewe	Received of Thomas Dewe for printing the little Catechisme which belongeth to the Company[8].	vis viijd
mr Fetherston	Received of mr Fetherston to haue his man Robert Martin[9] translated into this Company.	vjli xiijs iiijd

1 STC 24840. Cf. *Book of Fines*, 19a, 1 Sept. 1624.
2 Cf. *C–B.C*, 68b, 4 June 1621.
3 Cf. *C–B.C*, 70a, 12 Nov. 1621.
4 Made free 18 Jan. 1619 (Arber iii. 685).
5 Made free 17 Jan. 1620 (Arber iii. 685).
6 STC 4022.
7 Soon after the alley was turned into warehouses. Cf. *C–B.C*, 71b, 1 Mar. 1622.
8 Presumably an unrecorded edition of STC 21.
9 Cf. *C–B.C*, 53b, 54a, and 66b, and *Fine Book*, 14a.

3° Junij 1622

Geo. Edwardes[1] — Geo. Edwardes is to be translated to this Company for a fine of .... xx[s] — pd

6° Julij 1622

Mr Jaggard, mr Cole — It is this Day ordered that mr Jaggard and mr Cole shall pay 5li a peece for ther dispensacon in not serving the second time vnderwardens[2] — x li

Wm. Turnor — It is ordered that Wm Turnor shall pay for a fine for his admission into this Company[3] — xls — pd

[17b] Mr ffeld Master
Mr Gilmyn, mr Pavier — wardens

15 July 1622

John Marriott — It is ordered that John Marriott shall pay for buying bookes of a iorneyman printer and a prentice that belong to the stocke vizt 5 Daltons[4] and 10 west presidentes[5] .... — xij[s]

The fine is to be paid to mr weaver to the vse of the stocke/

Ric Brokebancke[6] — Rec' of Rich. Brokebanke for keeping of a prentice contrary to order .... — v[s]

20 Septemb: 1622

Wm Cheney[7] — Received of him for the like matter.......... — xij[d]

23 Septemb. 1622.

John Marriott — It is ordered that John Marriott shall pay for a fine for printing Withers Motto wthout license and entrance[8] .... — 3li — pd

Mr Lownes Junr, Mr Islip, mr Edwardes — for being absent at Choosing lord maior being warned xij[d] a peece .... — 3[s]

1 Presumably George Edwards Jr.
2 Cf. *C–B.C*, 73b.
3 Cf. Arber iii. 685, 24 May 1622.
4 STC 6207.
5 STC 25275.
6 Translated from the Drapers 3 June 1600 (Arber ii. 725).
7 Unrecorded.
8 Cf. *C–B.C*, 68b, 4 July 1621.

19° Octob 1622.

Absence	John Dawson Hen. Seile Geo. ffaireberd Robert Howes[1] Christo. Willson Geo. Alsope[2] Geo. Hodges xij^d a peece for being absent the last quarter day..........................	7^s
Absence	m^r ffetherstone m^r Beale Joh. Haviland W^m lee Aug. Mathewes Bar Downes for the like matter..................................	6s
Absence	M^r lawe m^r Budge m^r Heggenbotham Rich. Brokebanke Jeules Man[3] Edw Taylo^r[4] John Bird Nath Browne wm Best[5] for the same xij^d a peece..............................	9^s

19 Dec. 1622 [18^a]

Peter Coley[6]	Rec' of Peter Cooley for keeping of a prentice vnbound Contrary to order.................	xij^d

3° feb. 1622

	Mr Meade m^r Butter absente the last quarter..	2s
m^r Butter	It is ordered that m^r Butter [*& mr newbury*] shall pay for a fine for printing the King of ffrance his Edict being the Copie of m^r newbery[7]	v^s
	And it is further ordered that he shall pay to m^r Newbery for the Iniury done to him xls	
Absence	m^r Smithwicke m^r Jackson m^r Budg m^r More[8] m^r Meade mr Beale m^r Edwardę m^r White Joh. Hodgettę Eph. Dawson Rich. Hawkins Symeon woodcocke,[9] xij^d a pece for absence and Coming late the first of March	12^s
	Mr Butter Mr Edwardę sen' John Sharpe Sam̃ Nealand wiłł Bacon[10] for the like matter	4^s

vltimo Julij 1623

Alice Smith	Alice Smith[11] for binding a prentice at a screueno^rs Contrary to order	ij^s vj^d

vert

[1] Free 20 Apr. 1618 (Arber iii. 684).
[2] Free 15 Jan. 1621 (Arber iii. 685).
[3] Presumably Jonas Man.
[4] Free 5 May 1619 (Arber iii. 685).
[5] Free 14 May 1611 (Arber iii. 683).
[6] Free 25 Sept. 1618 (Arber iii. 684).
[7] Cf. *C–B.C*, 75^b.
[8] Richard More.
[9] Simon Woodcock, free 7 Dec. 1607 (Arber iii. 683).
[10] Free 4 Oct. 1613 (Arber iii. 684).
[11] She has not been identified.

[18b] Mr Swinhowe master
Mr Cole } wardens/
Mr Bill }

6o Octob 1623 Re. Ja: 21

Ben: Fisher	Received of Beniamin Fisher for a fine to the Company for vsing vnfitting speeches of the whole boord of assistante[1]	xxs	pd
	Re of divers for being absent the last quarter day xijd a peece..........................	xijs	

xxiiijo No. 1623.

Walter Haward	Re of willm Clarke[2] for not turning ou' his appr'tice according to order	ijs vjd	pd
Wm Stempe	of wm Stempe[3] for his admission to the fredome of this Company by redemption.............	xxxs	pd
Tho. Jurden	Rec' of Tho. Jurden[4] for keeping a pr'tice vnpresented aboue sixe weekes Contrary to order	ijs vjd	
Tho. Johnson	Rec' of Tho. Johnson for not turning ou' his appr'tice	ijs	

17 Feb. 1624

mr Gilmyn mr Pavier	Re of mr Gilmyn and mr Pavier for a bankett yt they should haue made last Ashwednesday for mr John Norton bequest	ls	pd

15 Martij 1623

Wm Shreue	Re of wm Sherife[5] for his admission to the freedome of this Company....................	xl s	pd
John Havilond	John Havilond for printing Minshewes Dictionarye[6] being the Companies Copie and so he is to pay vjd in ye li	xl s	pd

1mo July 1624.

mr Norton mr Bill	Mr Bonham Norton for malitiouslie and often striking of mr John Bill warden of the Company[7] is fined at	xxli	

[1] Cf. *C–B.C*, 79a.

[2] Probably the W. C. free 23 Nov. 1623 (Arber iii. 685).

[3] Free 20 Dec. 1623 (Arber iii. 685).

[4] Free 23 June 1613 (Arber iii. 684).

[5] Free 15 Mar. 1624 (Arber iii. 685).

[6] STC 17948.

[7] Cf. *C–B.C*, 81b.

6° Julij

Jonas Welling Ephram Dawson	Jonas Welling[1] and Ephram Dawson for refusing to Come on to the livery being elected are to pay 40^s a peece and to be eligable eu'ye yere according to the order in this behalf	iiij^{li}
		paid to m^r Coke

[19^a]

Mr Lownes sen' Master/
m^r Lownes Jun' } wardens
m^r Cooke......

25° Julij 1624 Re Jac: 22°/.

Nic. Okes	It is ordered that nicholas Okes for printing The golden watch bell[2] wthout Entrance shall pay for a fine	v^s
Eph: Dawson	This day Ephram Dawson for refusing to come on to the livery paid........................	xl s pd
Rob. Wallet	Robert wallett[3] for keeping a prentice vnpresented Contrarye to order	ij^s vj^d pd
John Smith	John Smith[4] for the like matter	ij^s vj^d pd
John Havilond	Joh: Havilond for printing the Spanish Dictionary[5] paid	xls pd

1mo Septemb. 1624.

Wm Jones	willm Jones an old ffine[6] for printing order for the west India Company vnlycensed .7^s 6^d and it is accepted for all ffines	vij^s vj^d pd
Mr Stansby	Wm Stansby for an old fine due to the house[7]..	iij^s iiij^d pd
Tho: Braken	Thomas Braken[8] for bynding a prentize at a scriuenors	ij^s vj^d pd
	This should have ben more but he is a poore man	

11° Octob. 1624.

Jonas Wellins	Jonas welling[9] for refusing to Come on to the livery being Called	xl^s pd

1 Free 20 Mar. 1602 (Arber ii. 731).

2 This apparently has nothing to do with T. Tymme's *Silver watchbell*, of which a 'Fifteenth edition' is dated 1625.

3 Perhaps a mistake for Richard Wallet.

4 There are too many John Smiths free of the Company to hazard an identification.

5 STC 19621 and 17948.

6 Cf. *Fine Book*, 23 Aug. 1621.

7 Cf. *Fine Book*, 7 Aug. 1620.

8 Free 2 Sept. 1616 (Arber iii. 684).

9 Free 20 Mar. 1602 (Arber ii. 731).

m^{r} Butter	ffor an old fine[1] of xl^{s} this day on hope of amendment there is accepted	xx^{s}	pd
Aug: Mathewes	ffor a fine of 30^{s} there is for some good service done to the Company in discou'ing a presse[2] .	x^{s}	pd
Mr Butter geo. Alsop Joh. legat m^{r} lawe	ffor being absent last quarter day xij^{d} a peece.	iiij^{s}	pd

[19^{b}] 6° Novemb:

Mr Pavier	m^{r} Pavier for Entring Ballettę that were neu' Entred before[3]	xx^{s}	pd
	This is answered in the Register of Copies		
Mr Butter	It is ordered that m^{r} Butter for printing Currantę with(*out*) Entrance[4] shall pay	vj^{s} viij^{d}	
Nich. Okes	Nicholas okes for printing a booke Called good newes from Breda without Entrance[5]	xls	
Tho. Archer	Thomas Archer for the same matter having had often warninge is to pay	iij^{li}	
Mr Butter	m^{r} Butter for vsing vnfitting wordę to m^{rs} Barrett[6]	vj^{s} viij^{d} paid & is Clere of all ffines	
Tho: Bayley	Tho. Bayley for absenting himself divers times being warned	ij^{s}	pd

4° April 1625 Rę Car' primo

Mr Okes	Mr Okes for all ffines vpon his humble submission and promise to be Conformable hereafter[7]	xs	pd
Wm Garret	w^{m} Garrett for vnfitting wordę vsed to m^{r} Gilmyn[8]	xx^{s}	pd

12 Jan 1625

Jonas Wellins	Jonas welling to come on to the livery xx^{li} he hath payd xls before and now v^{li} he is to pay xiij^{li} more	v^{li}	pd

[1] Cf. *Fine Book*, 30 Feb. 1622–3.
[2] Cf. *Fine Book*, 9 July 1621.
[3] Cf. *C–B.C*, 83^{b}.
[4] Cf. *C–B.C*, 83^{b}.
[5] Cf. *C–B.C*, 83^{b}.
[6] Cf. *C–B.C*, 84^{a} (*bis*), 7 Feb. 1624–5.
[7] Cf. *C–B.C*, 85^{b}.
[8] Cf. *C–B.C*, 86^{a}, 6 May 1625.

Eph. Dawson	Eph. Dawson is to pay xxli for his admission to the livery he hath paid xls and nowe viijli he is to pay xli more[1]	viijli	pd
Ric Meyhen	Richard Meighen for disorderly keeping boyes vnpresented & bound at a scrivenors[2]	xxs	[*pd*]
Rice Williams	Rice williams[3] his admission to the liverye this yeare	xxli	pd
Isake Jaggard	Isaake Jaggard for the like	xxli	pd
Tho. Harper	Tho. Harper for the like	xxli	pd

Mr Swinhow Master [20a]

mr Gilmyn } wardens
mr Islip }

16. Januarij 1626 Reg Car' primo/

Andr. Bilton	Andrew Bilton[4] is ordered to pay 40s at Candlemas next for refusing to take the Clothing vpon him being elected		
Mr lownes mr Cooke	mr Cooke[5] is ordered to paie for his dinner that should haue ben on the election day which was omitted by reason of the sicknes, vili and vli more he hath of his partener mr lownes deceased	xjli	
		paid mr Islip	
	ffor absentꝭ the first of march of vij pticular psons	vijs	

3 April'

	More for absentꝭ the first of march.	vijs	
Mr Knight Mr Bill Mr Cooke	Mr Knight mr Bill mr Cooke for not serving the second time vnder wardens vli a peece	xvli	

2° May

mr Apsley	Rec' of mr Aspley for not making a dinner for the livery on the lord mayors day [which] by reason of this sicknes he could not doe[6]	vijli vjs viijd	

[1] Cf. *C–B.C*, 86b, 12 July 1625.
[2] Cf. *C–B.C*, 87a, 22 June 1625.
[3] Apprenticed 20 Jan. 1604 (Arber ii. 274).
[4] Free 6 May 1606 (Arber iii. 683).
[5] Henry Cooke, cf. *C–B.C*, 89b, 6 Mar. 1625–6.
[6] Cf. *C–B.C*, 89b, 6 Mar. 1625–6, where the fine is recorded as £13. 6*s*. 4*d*.

Hen. Holland	hen: holland respited for Coming on to the livery & is to paie....................................	xl^s^
	Of John Bull[1] for keeping an appr' in his house disorderly....................................	ij^s^ vj^d^

[20b] Mr Norton Master
Mr Knight } wardens
Mr Kingston }

4° Septemb 1626.

Mr Purfoote	Received of Mr Purfoote for keeping an appn'-tice contrary to order....................	ij^s^ vj^d^
Rob Constable	Received of Robert Constable[2] for refusing the Clothing being there vnto elected...........	xls

19 Oct. 1626

Rich. harwood	Rec' of Rich. Harrwood[3] for his admission into the freedome by redemption................	xx^s^
Rob. Dolman	Rec' of Rob. dolman[4] for his admission into the fredome by Translacon....................	iiij^li^
Hugh Perry	The like of Hugh Perrye[5]..................	iij^li^
Hum. Moseley	Item of hum: Mosley	iij^li^
Absentę	Item received of diuers ꝑticular ꝑsons that were absent vpon quarter dayes when they had ben warned, Contrary to the order of this Company	xxvij^s^
m^rs^ Jaggard	mrs Jaggard[6] for the liveryes attendance at her husband funerall..........................	xls
m^r^ Weaver	mr weaver for the like attendance at his wives funerall..................................	iij^li^
m^rs^ Cooke	m^rs^ Cooke[7] for the like attendance at her hus-bandę funerall..........................	v^li^

1 Free 7 July 1612 (Arber iii. 683).
2 Free 12 Dec. 1614 (Arber iii. 684).
3 Free 19 Oct. 1626 (Arber iii. 686).
4 Free 15 Dec. 1626 (Arber iii. 686).
5 Cf. *C–B.C*, 93^b^, 15 Dec. 1626.
6 Elizabeth Jaggard, widow of John Jaggard.
7 This must be Henry Cooke, the elder, cf. *C–B.C*, 94^b^, 14 Jan. 1626–7.

Mr Cole mr of the Company./ [21a]

Mr Knight, Mr weaver — wardens

Tertio Septemb. 1627

mr Hawkins mr Edwardę mr Sparkę mr Man mr Havilond	Rec' of five seu'all persons of the Company for being absent at mr Alldees funerall,[1] having ben warned	vs

3o Octo. 1627.

John Dauson	Rec' of John Dauson for keeping a prentice disorderly vnbound aboue 6. weekes	ijs vjd
Mr Stansby	Mr Stansby is by order to pay for vnfitting wordę to or Master[2]	xxs

he afterwardę paid xs and it was accepted of.

3o Dec. 1627.

Nic: Okes	It is ordered that Nic. Okes for printing the names of the Shreiffę wthout lycense & for a stranger[3]	xs

14 January 1627

Tho. Walbanke	Rec' of Tho walbanke for not turning ou' his appr' according to order	ijs vjd

1mo. Martij 1627.

Absentę	This day mr warden received for absentę the last quarter day	ixs /

3. Martij 1627.

Mr Beale	It is ordered that mr Beale for vnfitting wordes vsed to the mr sitting at the Table[4]	xls
Ro: Hoskins	Rec' of Robert Hoskins[5] for his admission into the freedome of this Com: by Redemption	iijli
	Rec' of Joh. marret[6] for keeping a prentice disorderly	ijs vjd

[1] This settles the approximate date of Edward Allde's death.

[2] Cf. *C–B.C*, 96b, 31 July 1627, and 97b, 3 Oct. and 19 Nov. 1627.

[3] No copy is known.

[4] Cf. *C–B.C*, 98b.

[5] Free 3 Mar. 1628 (Arber iii. 686).

[6] Query John Marriot.

9° Junij 1628

Absentę	Rę for absentę the last quarter..............	ix s

[21b]

21 Junij 1628

mr Islip mr Kingston	It is ordered that mr Islip & mr Kingston shall pay for a fine to be dispensed wthall for not serving the second time vnderwardens, 5li a peece	xli

30 Junij 1628

Absentę	Rec' more for absentę the last quarter	xijs

7° Julij 1628

Edw. Harryson	Rec' of Edw. Harrison[1] for keeping a prentice vnbound Contrary to order..................	v s

[22a] Mr Cole Master
Mr Islip
mr Weaver } wardens.

6 Octo. 1629

Mr Parker	Rec' of mr parker for not turning of Wm lash[2] his appn'tice according to order in the Company	ijs vjd

3° Nov. 1628

Fra: Coules	It is ordered that ffrancis Coules for printing a song taken out of the Crumes of Comfort[3] shall pay for a fine..............................	x s
Rub. Coxe	Ruben Coxe to be admitted to the freedom of this Company is to paie for a fine	xls

1mo decemb 1628

Mr White	Receiv. of John White for not turning a prentice over according to order	ijs vjd

2° Martij 1628

Mrs Legg Joh. Sampson[4]	Rec' of mrs Legg for bynding a pn'tice and not turning him ou' at hall.....................	ijs vjd

[1] Free 17 Jan. 1620 (Arber iii. 685).
[2] Free 6 Oct. 1628 (Arber iii. 686).
[3] STC 23016. The verses, probably printed as a broadside, are entitled 'Verses of mans mortalitie: with another of the Hope of his resurrection'.
[4] Free 2 Mar. 1629 (Arber iii. 686).

26 Martij 1629

Mr Allott	Rec' of mr Allot for not turning ou' appn'....	ijs vjd
Mr Allott	And it is ordered that mr Allott for keeping appn' vnpresented contrary to order.........	vjs viijd

1mo Junij 1629.

Hen. Overton	Rec' of mris Sheffard[1] for making her man Hen: Overton free before he had served his terme of nyne yeares	v s.

2. Julij 1629

Mr Milborne	Robert Milborne keeping a prentice vnbound contrary to order..........................	v s

Mr Bonham Norton Master [22b]
mr Bill
mr Purfoote } wardens

2 Novemb. 1629.

John Powell	Received of John powell[2] to be translated from the Company of ffishmongers to the freedome of this Company	xl s

1mo Martij 1629.

Absences	This day mr Purfoote Rec' for absences of divers psons on AshWednesday when they should have (*been*) at the Sermon for the Comemoracoñ of Mr Joh. Norton	xx s

Mr: Swinhow} Master [23a]
Mr: Kingston
Mr: Harrison } Wardens.

vo. Julij 1630/

Absence	Receiued of diuers psons for absence the last quarter day	xis vjd

2 Augusti

Absence	Receiued more for Absences then............	vs
William Cominge[3]	ffor keeping William Okham Contrary to order}	ijs vjd

[1] William Sheppard must therefore have died before this date.

[2] Free 2 Nov. 1629 (Arber iii. 686).

[3] Probably not W. Commin, free 13 Apr. 1629 (Arber iii. 686).

	6°. Septembris	
Absence	Rec[d]. for fynes for Absence	ij[s]
	4°. Octobris	
M[r] Jo: Norton	M[r] John Norton three tymes absent	iij[s]
	9°. Nouembris	
John Bloome	ffor translating of John Bloome[1]	xxx[s].
M[r] Bowler	M[r] Bouler for not turninge ouer Richard Beomont[2]	ij[s] vj[d]
	12°. Januarij.	
M[r] Adams	Richard Adams[3] for keeping an Apprentice contrary to order............................	ij[s] vj[d]
	7°. Februarij	
Absence	Rec[d]. of 7 seuerall persons for absences last quarter day	vij[s].
	9°. Februarij	
Austen Mathewe fyne	Rec[d]. of m[r]. Mathewe for a fine for printing a booke of S[r]. Henry Woottone w[th]out entrance[4].	v[s]
Geo: Baker fyne	Rec[d]. of him for putting the same booke to printing w[th]out entrance..................	ij[s]
Edw: Blackamore fine	ffor printing a booke called Looke back to London w[th]out entrance[5]......................	ii[s].
	1° Martij	
Absence	ffor two psons for absence	ij[s]
Rich: Edwarde	Rec[d] of him for his making free by Redemption	v[li]

verte fol.

[23[b]]

	30°. Marcij 1631	
ffynes	Receiued for absence	xxij[s]
m[r] Exoll fyne	Rec[d]. of him for not making his Rentere dynner[6]	v[li]

[1] Free 9 Nov. 1630 (Arber iii. 686).
[2] Free 9 Nov. 1630 (Arber iii. 686).
[3] Free 22 Oct. 1618 (Arber iii. 684).
[4] Cf. *C–B.C*, 110[b].
[5] Cf. *C–B.C*, 110[b].
[6] Cf. *C–B.C*, 113[b].

22°. Junij/

Mr Bateman[1] fyne	Recd. of him to be dispensed wthall from bearing all offices in the Company	vli

7°. Junij

Absence	Recd. of 3 seuerall persons for coming late....	iijs

4°. July

fyne	Recd. more for absence last quarter day......	iijs.

Mr Cole} Master
Mr Islip
mr Smethwicke} wardens

[24a]

5°. Decembris 1631

Mr Grismond fyne	Recd. of mr. Grismond for bynding his appr' at a Scriueners Contrary to order	xs.

6°. decembris 1631

Geo: Bradley fyne	Recd. of George Bradley[2] for vsing vnfitting words to his mr formerly imposed vpon him...	xxs.

11°. Januarij 1631

Edm: Porter fyne	Recd. of Edmond Porter for bynding ffrancis Green[3] Contrary to order..................	ijs vjd.

15°. ffebruarij 1631

Mrs. Aldee fyne	Recd. of Mrs Aldee for making her sonn Richard Older[4] free by Redemption	xli

4° Junij 1632

Mr. Harper fyne.	Recd of Mr Harper [*for*] in part of his fyne for printing the Psalmes 8. Com: Contrary to order.[5] More to pay 6li. 13s. 4d	vjli. xiijs. iiijd

eodem die

Rich: Coates fyne/	Recd. of Richard Coates for the same as appeareth by order	xxs.

[1] Cf. *C–B.C*, 113b.
[2] Free 15 Sept. 1631 (Arber iii. 686).
[3] Free 11 Jan. 1632 (Arber iii. 687).
[4] Regarding whether R. Oulton was Elizabeth Allde's son or son-in-law, cf. Bradford Swan, *Gregory Dexter*, Rochester, 1949, pp. 15–17.
[5] Cf. *C–B.C*, 119b, 9 Apr. 1632.

6°. decembris 1631

Tho: Sclater fyne	Rec[d]. of Thomas Sclater[1] for keeping his appr.' Contrary to order	ij[s]. vj[d].

23°. Junij 1632

M[rs]. Griffin fyne.	Rec[d]. of m[rs]. Griffyn for bynding her appr' at a Scriveners	xiij[s]. iiij[d].

26th of March 1632

M[r]. Moore. fyne	Received of m[r]. Moore[2] for his dispensacoñ for not serving second tyme his Rentorship......	xxiiij[li].
M[r] Bourne fyne.	Received of m[r] Bourne[2] for his dispensacoñ for not serving the Rentorship being therevnto elected.................................	xxiiij[li].
Idem.	Rec[d]. more of him for desiring to be freed from being Stockeeper [*the*] being therevnto Chosen.	vj[li].
M[r]. Mead	Rec[d]. of him for his dispensacoñ for not serving the Rentorship being therevnto elected.......	xxiiij[li].

[24[b]] M[r]: George Cole} Master
M[r]: Edmond Weaver} Wardens
M[r]: William Aspley

19°. Januarij 1632.

Absences.	Rec[d]. of 15 seuerall ꝑsons being absent the last quarter day	xv[s]
D[r]. Lambes death fyne.	Rec[d]. at a generall assessment of the Company for the death of D[r]. Lamb[3]	xvi[li]. ix[s].

1°. Martij

Absence	Rec[d]. of 4. seuerall ꝑsons that came late......	iiij[s].
Absences.	Rec[d] of 4. ꝑsons that were absent on Ashwensday	iiij[s].
M[r] Mann fyne.	Rec[d]. of M[r] Man his fyne for not serving Rentor[4]	xxiiij[li].
M[r] Purfoot fyne	Rec[d]. of M[r] Purfoot for not serving warden the second tyme[4]	v[li].

[1] T. Slater?, free 6 May 1629 (Arber iii. 686).
[2] Cf. *C–B.C*, 119[a].
[3] Cf. *C–B.C*, 122[a], 30 Jan. 1632–3.
[4] Cf. *C–B.C*, 122[b], 27 Mar. 1633.

M[r] Harrison fyne.	Rec[d]. of M[r] Harrison for the same[1]	v[li].
M[r]. Smethwicke fyne	Rec[d]. of M[r] Smethwicke for the same[1]........	v[li].
M[r]. Islip. fyne	Rec[d]. of m[r] Islip for a fyne for the vse of the Poore for leave of the Company to print the booke of Martyrs[2]	8[li]
M[r] Kingston fyne	Rec[d]. of m[r] Kingston for the same...........	8[li]
M[r]. Burby.	Rec[d]. of M[r] Burby (being a gift to the Poore)..}	iij[li]

M[r]: Adam Islip} Master [25[a]]
M[r]: Weauer
M[r]: Aspley } wardens./

7°. octobris 1633.

Bar: Alsop & Tho ffawcett Fyne	Rec[d]. of them for suffering their prentices to sell the Prog:...................................	v[s].

15° octobris

M[r] Sparkes Fyne	Rec[d]. of m[r] Sparke̱ for absence last q[ter] day...}	xij[d].
Raph Triplett Fyne.	Rec[d]. of Raph Triplett[3] for a fyne for absence.}	ii[s] vj[d]
Absence.	Rec[d]. of two ꝑsons for absence	ii[s].
Tho: Bourne Fyne.	Rec[d]. of Thomas Bourne for a fyne for not coming on the Liuery	xl[s].
John Smith Fyne.	Rec[d]. of John Smith for the same ....}	xl[s].
Tho: Haviland Fyne.	Rec[d]. of Thomas Hauiland for his making free by Redemption	iij[li]:
Geo: Tomlyn Fyne.	Rec[d]. of George Tomlyn[4] for the same in regard of his great pouerty	iij[s]. iiij[d].

[1] Cf. *C–B.C*, 122[b], 27 Mar. 1633.
[2] Cf. *C–B.C*, 121[a], 23 Oct. 1632.
[3] Free 6 Mar. 1627 (Arber iii. 686).
[4] Free 20 Dec. 1633 (Arber iii. 687).

Mr Young Fyne.	Recd. of mr yong for a fyne for the vse of the poore for leaue of ye Company to print the Booke of Martyrs[1]	viijli. for the poors Account
Absence.	Recd. for absences	ijs
Absence.	Recd. for absences	iijs
Mr Rothwell Fyne.	Recd of Mr. Rodway (*sic*) for an apr' turned ouer to him bound at a Scriueners	xs.
Wm. Minshall	Recd of Wm. Minshall[2] for his making free by Redemption	xls.

[25b] Mr. Adam Islip} Mr.
mr. Purfoot }
mr. Rothwell} wardens.

10°. Octobris 1634.

Absence	Imprimis for two absences on ye quarter day . . }	ijs.
Mr Titon	Recd. of mr Tyton[3] for binding his man at a Scriueners contrary to order	xs.

1°. Decembris

John Day fine	Recd. of John Day for his turning ouer to the Bruerȩ Company[4]	xxs. not received
ffulke Clifton	Recd of him for a fyne for printing a booke vn-lawfully[5]	xxs
Wm. Turner	Recd. of him for binding his man contrary to order	xls.
Absences	Recd. of 3. seuerall ꝑsons for absences	iijs.
Mr Edwardȩ	Recd. of Mr Edwardȩ for a fyne for not serveing Rentor[6]	xxiiijli.
Mr Boler.	Recd. of him for the same	xxiiijli.
Mr Stansby.	Recd. of him for the same	xxiiijli.
Mr Hawkins	Recd. of him for the same	xxiiijli
mr Beale	Recd. of him for comeing late to the Cort.	xijd.

1 Cf. *C–B.C*, 121a, 23 Oct. 1632.
2 Free 7 July 1634 (Arber iii. 687).
3 Untraced.
4 Cf. *C–B.C*, 130a, 1 Dec. 1634.
5 Cf. *C–B.C*, 130a, 1 Dec. 1634.
6 Cf. *C–B.C*, 136b, 26 Mar. 1635.

Roger Turner.[1]	Rec^d^. of him for not turning ouer his man at the hall according to order....................	ii^s^ vj^d^.
Walter Oake.[2]	Rec^d^. of him for a fyne for not comeing on the Liuery..............................	xl^s^.
m^r^ Kingston & m^r^ Butter	Rec^d^. of them for com̃eing late to the Co^rt^. ...	ij^s^.
[*Edw. Winslow*[3]	*Rec^d^. of him being made free of this Company* ..	*v^li^*.]
Rich: Roiston	Recd of him for keeping his appr' vnbound...	ij^s^ vj^d^
Bar: Alsop.	Rec^d^. of him for printing a booke vnlawfully[4] .	v^s^

[26^a^]

M^r^. ffelix Kingston} M^r^.
Mr Smethwicke
M^r^ ffetherston } wardens

4°. Aug: 1635

Mr Bourne	Imprimis rec^d^. of him for Comeing late to the Co^rt^..................................	xij^d^
And: Hebb.	Rec^d^. of Andrew Hebb for not turning his Appr' at the hall................................	ij^s^ vj^d^
m^r^ Dawson.	Rec^d^. of mr Dawson for goeing to the buriall of one of the Liuery in a falling Band	xij^d^.
m^r^ Beale	Rec^d^. of m^r^ Beale for comeing late to the Co^rt^...	xij^d^.
m^r^ Beale	Rec^d^. of mr Beale for binding his appr' at a Scrivene^r^s contrary to Order[5]	iiij^li^.
Absence	Rec^d^. of Ten seuerall ꝑsons for not being at Pauls on Twelfe day.......................	x^s^.
Geo: Gibbe	Rec^d^. of Geo: Gibbe for not turning ouer his Appr' at the hall.........................	ij^s^ vj^d^
m^r^ Roach:	Rec^d^. of Mr Roach for a fyne for alienation of his house by mrs. Trussell to him[6]...........	x^s^.
Absence	Rec^d^. of Nine seuerall ꝑsons for being absent on Ashwensday..............................	ix^s^.

[1] Free 30 June 1618 (Arber iii. 684).
[2] Free 6 Feb. 1626 (Arber iii. 686).
[3] This may be the Pilgrim Father who was in England at this time and whose trade was printing.
[4] Cf. *C–B.C*, 128^b^, 3 Oct. 1634.
[5] Cf. *C–B.C*, 136^a^, 1 Nov. 1635.
[6] Cf. *C–B.C*, 137^b^, 7 Mar. 1636.

Mr Harrison	Recd. of Mr Harrison for his fyne for vpper-warden formerly imposed vpon him[1]	vli.

[26b] Mr. ffelix Kingston} Master
Mr: John Harrison }
Mr Thomas Downes } Wardens

28. September 1636. xij Car Regis.

Mr. Coats.	Recd. of Mr Coates for leaue to print an Impression of Latymerę sermonę for ye vse of ye Poore[2]	03li—06s—6d

3o. October 1636

Mr Coates	Recd. of him for a fyne for not turning ouer his appr at ye hall according to order............	00—02—6

7o. Nouembris 1636

Geo: Ray.[3]	Recd. of him for not being turned ouer at ye hall according to order........................	00—02—6
Mrs. Allott	Recd. of Mrs. Allott for a fyne for leaue to print 3. Impressionę of ye Mirror of Martyrę according to an order in that behalfe[4]	06—00—0

5o. Decembris

Mr Latham	Recd. of Mr Latham for a fyne for not making his dynner on my Lord Mayors day[5]	07—06—8

28. Decembris.

Mr Milborne	Recd. of him for not turning ouer his appr' at ye hall according to order	00—02—6

6o. ffebruarij.

Mr Sparkes	Recd. of him for a fyne for binding his appr' before he was prsented.....................	00—05—0
Mr. Purfoot	Recd. of him for his fyne for second tyme vpper-warden..................................	05—00—0
Mr Butter	Recd. of him for his fyne for first tyme younger warden	05—00—0

1 Cf. *C–B.C*, 134b, 7 July 1635.
2 STC 15283. Cf. *C–B.C*, 126a, 3 Feb. 1634; and 142b, 28 Sept. 1636.
3 Free 7 Nov. 1636 (Arber iii. 688).
4 Cf. *C–B.C*, 143a.
5 Cf. *C–B.C*, 143b.

1°. Martij 1636

for wearing falling Bande & absence	Recd. of three seuerall ꝑsons for wearing falling Bande & one being absent on Ashwensday ...	00—04—0

27°. Martij 1637

Mr Rice Williams[1]	Recd of him for his fyne for not serueing Rentor this yeare	24—00—0

15°. May 1637

Rich: Williams[2]	Recd. of him for a fyne for [his] making free of this Company by Redemption	03—00—0

26°. Junij 1637 [27a]

Sam: Gillibrand	Recd. of him for a fyne for not being turned ouer at ye hall according to order	li s d 00—02—6
Mr. Smethwicke	Recd. of him for his fyne for not making the Election dynner[3]	06—13—4
Mr ffetherstone.	Recd. of him for the same	06—13—4
Absence.	Recd. of fiue seuerall persons being absent at Guildhall on Midsomer day	00—05—0

Mr Edmond Weauer} Master. [27b]
Mr William Aspley
mr Nicholas Bourne} wardens

28°. Decembris 1637.

John Stafford.	Receiued of him for a fyne for makeing him free of this Company by Redemption	xls.

2°. octobris 1637.

Mr. Young.	Receiued of him for his Apprentice Thomas Maxie[4] [bound] at a Scriueners Contrary to order	xls.

16°. octobris 1637.

George Wilne[5]	Receiued of him for a fyne for being bound at Scriueners contrary to order	xls.

[1] Cf. *C–B.C*, 146a.
[2] Cf. Arber iii. 688.
[3] But see order 6 May 1637, *C–B.C*, 148a.
[4] Free 2 Oct. 1637 (Arber iii. 688).
[5] Free 16 Oct. 1637 (Arber iii. 688).

5°. ffebr. 1637.

Geo: Sadler[1]	Receiued of him for a fyne for not turning ouer his Apprentice at the hall according to order. .	ij^{s} vj^{d}

29°. Martij 1638

Mr Dawson	Receiued of him for his fyne for Renter warden	xxiiij^{li}
Mr Harper.	Receiued of him for a fyne for the Poore for indirect printing[2].	x^{li}.
M^{r} fflesher	Receiued of him for his fyne for Rentor warden	xxiiij^{li}.
Mr Haviland	Receiued of him for his fyne for the same	xxiiij^{li}
m^{r} Meighen.	Receiued of him for his fyne for the same	xxiiij^{li}.
m^{r} Waterson.	Receiued of him for his fyne for the same	xxiiij^{li}.
m^{r} Tho: Coates	Rec^{d}. of him for his fyne for the same	xxiiij^{li}.
m^{r} young.	Rec^{d}. of him for his fyne for the same.	xxiiij^{li}
m^{r} Walley.	Rec^{d}. of him for his fyne for thc same.	xxiiij^{li}.
Mr Legatt.	Rec^{d}. of m^{r} Legatt for his fyne for the same . .	xxiiij^{li}.
M^{r}. Smethwick.	Rec^{d}. of him for his fyne for second tyme vpper warden[3].	vi^{li}. xiij^{s} iij^{d}.
Mr Aspley.	Rec^{d}. of him for his fyne for first tyme vpper warden[3].	vi^{li}. xiij^{s} iiij^{d}.
[28a] M^{r}. Rothwell.	Rec^{d}. of him for his fyne for second tyme vnder-warden[3].	v^{li}.
M^{r}. ffetherston.	Rec^{d}. of him for a fyne for second tyme vnder-warden[3].	v^{li}.
Mr Butter.	Rec^{d}. of him for a fyne for second tyme under-warden[3].	v^{li}.
Mr Downes	Rec^{d}. of him for his fyne second tyme vnder-warden[3].	v^{li}.
Executo^{r}s of Mrs Boler	Rec^{d}. of them for a fyne to assigne ouer all her Copies fallen to the Company by her decease vnto p̲sons in trust for her Children[4].	xx^{s}.

1 Free 5 Feb. 1638 (Arber iii. 688).

2 This evidently refers to Harper's printing of STC 2736, cf. *C–B.C*, 148^{a}, 6 May 1637.

3 Cf. *C–B.C*, 148^{b}, 1 July 1637.

4 Entered 7 Sept. 1638 (Arber iv. 435–7), cf. *C–B.C*, 154^{b}, 29 Mar. 1638.

John Neave[1]	Rec^{d}. of him for a fyne for not turning ouer his Appr' at the hall	ij^{s} vj^{d}.
Mrs White[2]	Rec^{d}. of her for a fyne for not being turned ouer at the hall...............................	ij^{s} vj^{d}.
Tho: Paine	Rec^{d}. of him for a fyne for not p^{r}senting his Appr' in due tyme..........................	v^{s}
Mr Sparkes	Rec^{d}. of m^{r} Sparkes for a fyne for binding his Apprentice ffran: Backle[3] at a Scriveners Contrary to Order	iij^{li}.
M^{r}. Robinson	Rec^{d}. of him for a fyne for [*buy*] buying Counterfeit Psalmes brought from beyond sea[4]	v^{li}.
Absences.	Rec^{d}. of Twenty seuerall ꝑsons this yeare for absences	xx^{s}

Mr John Harrison} M^{r}. [28^{b}]
Mr John Rothwell }
Mr Robert Mead } Wardens.

1°. Octobris 1638

Mr Waterson & Andr. Hebb.	Receiued of m^{r} Waterson & Andrew Hebb for a fyne for the poore for printing Josephus[5] ...	03—00—00

19° decembris 1638

John Benson.	Receiued of m^{r} Benson for a fyne for the poore for printing ye golden Meane[6]	01—4—0

19°. Januarij 1638

wearing falling Bandꝭ	Rec^{d}. of two seuerall persons for wearing falling Bandꝭ on Christmas day	00—2—0

25°. Januarij 1638

Mr Milborne	Rec^{d}. of Mr Milborne for a fyne for printing the welsh Psalmes[7]	01—00—0

29 Apr 1639

for not turning ouer at ye Hall	Rec^{d}. of two ꝑsonꝭ not being turned ouer at the hall according to the Custome	00—05—0

[1] Free 20 Apr. 1618 (Arber iii. 684).
[2] Unidentified.
[3] Untraced.
[4] Cf. *C–B.C*, 157^{b}, 2 July 1638.
[5] Cf. *C–B.C*, 158^{b}, 13 Aug. 1638.
[6] Cf. *C–B.C*, 142^{a}, 1 Aug. 1636.
[7] Cf. *C–B.C*, 159^{b}, 27 Aug. 1638, and 162^{b}.

6°. Maij 1639

Idem	Rec[d] of a nother for not being turned ouer at the hall	00—02—6
Coming late to the Cort	Rec[d]. of m[r] Beale & m[r] Butter comeing late to the Co[rt]. 3 seuerall tyme	00—03—0

25° Junij 1639

M[r] Young	Rec[d]. of M[r] young the 25th of June for his fyne for Renterwarden last yeare	24—00—0

18 July. 1639.

m[r] Young	Rec[d]. of him for binding an Appr' at a Scriue-ne[r]s Contrary to order	1—00—0
m[r] Bruister	Rec[d]. of m[r] Bruister for his fyne for Renter-warden 24[li]. whereof 14[li] remitted [*according*] by order[1]	10—00—0
M[r] Milborne	Rec[d]. of m[r] Milborne for his fyne for Renter-warden	24—00—0
M[r] Beale	Rec[d]. of M[r] Beale for a fyne for first tyme [younger] Warden	05—00—0
Absences.	Rec[d]. of fifteene seuerall persons for absences this yeare	00—15—0

[29[a]] M[r] John Smethwick} M[r].
M[r] Hen: ffetherston} wardens.
M[r]. Nich: Bourne

3°. Octobris 1639

Hen: Ockould.	Rec[d]. of him for a fyne to assigne ouer some Copies vnto him w[ch] were his fathers[2] *for the vse of the poore*	00—05—0

2°. Decembris

Peter Cole.	Rec[d]. of him for not bynding his Apprentice in due tyme	00—02—6

2°. Martij 1639

Giles Hicks.[3]	Rec[d]. of him for a fyne for [*not being turned ouer*] [leave] to be translated to the Barber Surgeons being a poore young man	00—10—0

[1] Cf. *C–B.C*, 166[a], 1 July 1639. [2] Cf. *C–B.C*, 168[b], 7 Oct. 1639. [3] Free 20 Jan. 1640 (Arber iii. 688).

9°. Aprilis 1640

Mrs Purslowe	Recd. of her for leaue to print an Impression of the Second pte of the gentle Craft[1] *for the use of the Poore*	1—0—0

14°. July 1640

Mr Milborne	Recd. of him for not turning ouer his Apprentice at the hall according to order	0—2—6

eodem die

Mr Beale.	Recd. of him for a fyne for breach of Orders *for the vse of the poore*[2]	3—00—0
Absences	Recd. of thirteene seuerall psons for being absent on Quarter dayes	00—13—0

Mr. William Aspley} Master
Mr. Thomas Downes} Wardens.
Mr Samuell Man

[29b]

1640

William Sheeres.	Recd. of Wm. Sheeres for a fyne for the poore for printing an Impression of Edw. the 5 & Rich: 3d.[3]	02—00—0
Mr ffleshe r.	Recd. of him for not entring his apprentice in due tyme	00—02—6
Mrs Parsons	Recd. of her for binding John ffeild[4] her apprentice at a Scriveners	00—10—0
Mr Lee Jur.	Recd. of him for his fyne for Rentor warden	24—00—0
Mr Chappell	Recd. of him for the same	24—00—0
Mr Robinson	Recd. of Mr Robinson for the same	24—00—0
Mr Stephens	Recd. of Mr Stephens for the same	24—00—0
Henry Bird.	Recd. of him for his fyne not to come on the Liuery	02—00—0
Wm. Lugger.	Recd. of him for his fyne for the poore for printing an Impression of the Marriners Mate[5]	02—00—0

[1] STC 6556.
[2] Cf. *C–B.C*, 172a, 4 July 1640.
[3] Cf. *C–B.C*, 173b, 2 Nov. 1640.
[4] Free 4 Feb. 1635 (Arber iii. 687).
[5] Cf. *C–B.C*, 174a, 7 Dec. 1640.

Mr young.	Recd. of him for not bynding his apprentice in due tyme	0—02—6
Mr Rothwell	Recd. of him for his fyne for his dispensacõn of serveing the place of Master	05—00—0
Mr. Hoth.	Recd. of him for his fyne for first tyme vnder-warden	05—0—0

[30a] Mr: ffetherston} Master./
Mr Nicholas Bourne} Wardens./
Mr John Parker}

INDEX OF NAMES AND SUBJECTS

INDEX OF NAMES AND SUBJECTS

INDEX OF NAMES AND SUBJECTS

INDEX OF NAMES AND SUBJECTS

INDEX OF NAMES AND SUBJECTS

[1] How he managed to recover his part to which J. Waterson was elected is not told.

[1] This clerk evidently confused the Harrisons, cf. 55, 60, 62.

[1] Something is wrong about these entries, for J. Waterson is recorded as having first one and a half yeomanry parts and later two livery parts.

INDEX OF BOOKS PRINTED BEFORE 1641 REFERRED TO IN TEXT OR NOTES[1]

[1] For classes of books, ABC's, Briefs, Indentures, Playbills, Psalters, &c., mostly unidentified, *see* Index of Names and Subjects.

INDEX OF BOOKS PRINTED BEFORE 1641

INDEX OF BOOKS PRINTED BEFORE 1641

BOOKS DATED 1641, REFERRED TO IN TEXT

INDEX OF UNIDENTIFIED BOOKS OR ONES PRESUMABLY UNPUBLISHED REFERRED TO IN TEXT

PRINTED IN
GREAT BRITAIN
AT THE
UNIVERSITY PRESS
OXFORD
BY
CHARLES BATEY
PRINTER
TO THE
UNIVERSITY